D0141717

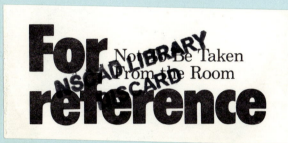
For
reference
NSCAD LIBRARY
DISCARD
Not To Be Taken
From the Room

THE PAINTINGS OF
EUGÈNE DELACROIX
I

Mephistopheles appears before Faust 46×38 cm (116)

THE PAINTINGS OF
EUGÈNE DELACROIX

A Critical Catalogue

1816-1831
Volume I · Text

LEE JOHNSON

NOVA SCOTIA COLLEGE OF ART
AND DESIGN LIBRARY
NSCAD LIBRARY
DISCARD

OXFORD · AT THE CLARENDON PRESS

1981

Ref.
ND
553
D33
A4
1981
V.1

Oxford University Press, Walton Street, Oxford OX2 6DP

OXFORD LONDON GLASGOW
NEW YORK TORONTO MELBOURNE WELLINGTON
KUALA LUMPUR SINGAPORE HONG KONG TOKYO
DELHI BOMBAY CALCUTTA MADRAS KARACHI
NAIROBI DAR ES SALAAM CAPE TOWN

Published in the United States by
Oxford University Press, New York

© *Lee Johnson 1981*

All rights reserved. No part of this publication may be reproduced,
stored in a retrieval system, or transmitted, in any form or by any means,
electronic, mechanical, photocopying, recording, or otherwise, without
the prior permission of Oxford University Press

British Library Cataloguing in Publication Data

Johnson, Lee
The paintings of Eugène Delacroix
Vols. 1 and 2
1. Delacroix, Eugène
I. Title   II. Delacroix, Eugène
759.4   ND553.D33   80-40988
ISBN 0-19-817314-8

Printed in Great Britain
at the University Press, Oxford
by Eric Buckley
Printer to the University

Preface

'La meilleure biographie d'un artiste c'est le catalogue de ses œuvres.'
Charles Yriarte (*Le Monde illustré*, 22 August 1863)

Excellent editions of Delacroix's prolific writings have been published in this century: the Elie Faure edition of the *Œuvres littéraires* in two volumes in 1923, André Joubin's three-volume edition of the *Journal* in 1932 and his edition of the *Correspondance*, issued in five volumes between 1935 and 1938. All of these publications, especially the last two, were a very marked improvement on nineteenth-century editions. Nothing comparable has been attempted for the paintings, and Delacroix was, after all, a painter. No *catalogue raisonné* of his work has been compiled since 1885, when Alfred Robaut's fundamental catalogue, which included the prints and drawings as well as paintings, appeared. It was reprinted without revision in 1969.

The present publication, which is planned to catalogue Delacroix's paintings in five volumes divided into the early years (2 vols.), movable pictures of the middle and late years (2 vols.), and the decorations for public buildings with their sketches in oils (1 vol.), rests on the belief that there can be no more urgent and vital a task in the present state of our knowledge than to determine Delacroix's visual *œuvre* more completely and accurately than has been done to date, and to define with precision what is known and what has been said about each picture that comprises that *œuvre*. But in an age when it is not uncommon to devote monographs to single paintings by major artists (separate books have been published on at least five paintings by Delacroix, three in this volume) the word 'definitive', applied to accounts of a productive artist's entire life and work, may be said to have become obsolete in the history of art. This catalogue does not, therefore, aim to be definitive. Its purpose is to supplement Robaut whose remarkable catalogue will never become wholly redundant but is nevertheless an inadequate tool for modern scholars for a number of reasons. It contains no photographic illustrations, and in the case of many paintings not even one of Robaut's small prints after the original. Scarcely any bibliography is given for single pictures. There is no argument in support of the dating of undated pictures, which frequently seems, and can sometimes be proved, to be arbitrary. Provenances, when listed, are usually very sketchy, there is virtually no record of exhibitions other than the Salons, and of course no history and no exhibitions after 1885 are recorded. As a substitute for this essential information, there are the commentaries in Robaut, most of which were contributed by his collaborator, Ernest Chesneau, a critic less profoundly committed to Delacroix studies, and tend to be of an evocative, literary character with little historical content.

I hope to have gone some way towards remedying these insufficiencies in our knowledge, and to remedy more as my work progresses. If it has not always been possible, in modifying Robaut's chronology, to advance definitive proof of the accuracy of a new date, it has at least been possible to bring attention to problems of dating that one would not be aware existed when consulting Robaut. Many pictures are reproduced that were not illustrated by Robaut. In portraiture, new biographical facts about some of Delacroix's sitters are presented. Though no attempt is made to catalogue the vast number of drawings Delacroix executed, or the dozens of sketch-books that he filled, a more complete account of how drawings are related to the individual pictures and where they are to be found than Robaut provides is attempted. More use is made of unpublished sketch-books, not to mention Delacroix's published writings, as an aid to dating paintings and to understanding their development.

A major problem bequeathed to his successors by Robaut, and it is particularly acute for the early work, is that of identifying the separate paintings that he listed in groups under single numbers, without illustrations or dimensions. In this he was often simply following the organizers of Delacroix's posthumous sale in the summary grouping into lots, and listing under single numbers, of whole categories of works—academy figures, copies, early composition sketches, landscapes, for example. Thus under Robaut No. 1470 will be found: 'Dix-sept études d'académies — 1820. Toiles. — De vingt à vingt-cinq. — No. 200 de la Vente post-hume.' Robaut's catalogue as published contained 839 paintings, including the murals, listed under only 768 numbers; about 180 numbers are assigned by Robaut to the paintings in the period covered by my first two volumes, up to the end of 1831, but the actual number of paintings catalogued, when sifted out of the group listings, is closer to 215, and the true number of pictures painted by Delacroix in that period, some of which were overlooked altogether by Robaut, more like 270. Much work remains to be done towards clarifying the contents of ill-defined lots, but, by reference to annotated sales catalogues, to Robaut's own notes and tracings (for he continued to pursue the problem after his catalogue was published), and to other sources, I can claim to have made some advance on Robaut's published work and to have laid the foundations for further progress. Often, alarmingly often, it has proved necessary, in spite of exhaustive researches, to catalogue works as lost, but, by recording everything that is known about their history and appearance, I hope that some may be brought to light. I am not of those who believe that only conclusive results should be published. Fragmentary evidence may lead others to useful discoveries that have eluded me. No useful purpose can be served by creating an illusory impression of completeness: a rich collection of fragments can be more valuable, if less superficially reassuring, than a spurious wholeness.

The extent of my debt to scholars since Robaut, and of my disagreement with them, which is also considerable, is made plain in the individual entries of the catalogue. I have chosen to work without research assistants, a choice that may have to be relinquished for subsequent volumes. While this decision has long delayed completion of the first part, my having checked everything personally will perhaps have made for greater reliability and a more critical scrutiny of the literature than would otherwise have been possible.

It has been my aim in the entries for major pictures, and for many lesser ones, to provide not only a full documentary history (a more creative task than might be granted by some art historians, leading as it has, for instance, to the rediscovery of lost pictures, of lost meanings, of lost knowledge of the placing of canvases painted by Delacroix in schemes which he did alone or to which other artists contributed), but some account of critical judgements since the works were painted, discussion of stylistic and literary influences, and, to a greater degree than is perhaps customary in *catalogues raisonnés* except in introductions, my personal interpretation—particularly with regard to such controversial questions as the retouching of the *Massacres of Chios* and the disjunctions of scale in the *Death of Sardanapalus*. The result is that I have come to write what are in effect small monographs for the most famous Salon paintings and forgone the traditional introduction. I have also compiled a chronology for the early years which contains more new material, in an easily accessible form, than is usual in this sort of table and might otherwise have had to be more summarily treated in an introductory essay. The consequent lack of generalities will, I hope, be vindicated by a gain in depth, in significant detail and in truth to the complexity of Delacroix's artistic personality. May the method prove to be a fruitful compromise between the general life-and-work type of monograph, with its inevitable over-simplifications and limited value as an instrument for further research, and the book that has a single painting as its subject.

London, June 1976   L. J.

Pre-Publication Note

No reference has been made to publications which have appeared after the date of the Preface, except to those I had seen in manuscript, or written myself, before that date. No additions have been made that are not based on my own independent findings and these are minor adjustments, save for the addition of the unpublished *Portrait of Fougerat* (Cat. 61a), for which I completed the entry in February 1978, and the *Seated Indian* (Cat. 23a), which was added in May of the same year and whose reappearance made some revision necessary to entries for related works. Also, the discovery of Jenny Le Guillou's birth and death certificates justified the addition of an important footnote to the entry for the portrait of her daughter (Cat. 84). A lucky, incidental find in a French private collection made it possible at a late stage to substitute an old photograph of the lost *Man in Greek Costume in a Landscape* for Robaut's thumbnail print (Cat. L39, pl. 146). A fine, rapid study in pencil for the boy with pistols in *Liberty leading the People* (22 × 22 cm), which passed through the hands of Richard Nathanson in London in July 1980 and into a private collection in New York, would have found a place on p. 150 had the page not already been in proof when it came to light. It shows the boy with a pistol in his left hand only, his upraised right hand empty. In addition to the stamp of his posthumous sale, it bears a note in Delacroix's hand of the name and address of a Jacques Brinté, possibly the model who posed for the boy in the painting.

The *Seated Indian*, since being added, has been cleaned and was sold at Sotheby's, London, on 2 April 1979, lot 21 (repr. in colour, after cleaning). The *Seated Figure in Turkish Costume (J.B. Pierret?)* (Cat. 33) had passed through Peter Nathan's hands and into a Swiss private collection by April 1978. It was shown in the exhibition *Alt und Neu* held at his gallery in Zurich from 20 April to 30 June 1978 (no. 7, repr. in colour). The early *Portrait of Charles de Verninac* (Cat. 62) has been bought by Messrs. Wildenstein, New York. *Tam o'Shanter* (Cat. 109) came up for sale at Sotheby's, London, on 18 June 1980 (lot 82, repr. in colour), and, it is a pleasure to record, was bought for the Castle Museum, Nottingham, the city where Delacroix's good friend Bonington was brought up. The *Apotheosis of the Duke of Buckingham* (Cat. R8), after Rubens, was sold at Sotheby Parke Bernet, New York, on 1 November 1978 (lot 5, repr. in colour), to Peter Nathan of Zurich in association with an American dealer.

With regret, I have to list a number of deaths that have occurred, or of which I have learnt, since writing the Preface: Count Doria and M. Claude Roger-Marx, distinguished French collectors; M. Raymond Escholier, an ardent champion of Delacroix, and M. Alfred Strolin (see Cat. 27). It is particularly sad that two colleagues mentioned in the Acknowledgements, both prematurely dead, have not lived to see the fruits of their encouragement: Mr. Benedict Nicolson, who, as editor of *The Burlington Magazine*, first published many of my findings with characteristic generosity, and Dr. John Maxon.

I am happy to report that the late Dr. Sara Lichtenstein's thesis, referred to in its unpublished form under Cat. 98 and 101, was issued by the Garland Publishing Company in 1979, under the title *Delacroix and Raphael*. It contains several suggestions of influences of Raphael on the early Delacroix, in addition to those I refer to, that I should like to have taken account of in this volume.

In conclusion, I gratefully acknowledge a handsome Publication Grant awarded by the British Academy in 1978.

London, December 1980   L. J.

Acknowledgements

Many institutions and individuals have given me valuable assistance over the years that have gone into the preparation of this catalogue. Of the busy museum officials who have found time to answer my many detailed inquiries and often to provide useful documentation, beyond the call of their routine duties, as well as special facilities to study the works in their care, I wish particularly to thank the successive heads of the indispensable Service d'étude et de documentation at the Louvre: Mme Hélène Adhémar, Mme Sylvie Béguin, who had an especially heavy burden of inquiries, answering them all with unfailing grace and efficiency, and M. Jacques Foucart; M. Jean Adhémar, Chief Curator of the Cabinet des Estampes at the Bibliothèque nationale, who, in addition to constant encouragement, has kindly given me permission to publish in this catalogue, as in earlier articles, notes from the annotated Robaut, drawings and tracings by Robaut and other documents in his charge; his staff, notably Mlles Barbin, Gardey and Villa; Dr. Haavard Rostrup, Curator of Modern Art at the Ny Carlsberg Glyptotek, Copenhagen, and Director of the Ordrupgaardsamlingen, who was extremely helpful with Danish literature and with problems generally of Delacroix in Scandinavian collections; Dr. Günter Busch, Director of the Kunsthalle, Bremen; Dr. John Maxon, Associate Director of the Art Institute of Chicago; Miss Sybille Pantazzi, Librarian of the Art Gallery of Ontario, from whose wide reading and vigilance in matters pertaining to Delacroix I have often benefited, most significantly perhaps in being provided with the clue that led to the identification of Count Demetrius de Palatiano as the subject of a famous portrait by Delacroix; Mr. J. G. W. Goodison and Mr. Malcolm Cormack, formerly Keepers of the Fitzwilliam Museum, Cambridge; Mr. Claude Blair, Keeper of the Department of Metalwork at the Victoria and Albert Museum, and Mr. A. V. B. Norman, Assistant to the Director of the Wallace Collection, who have been unstinting with expert advice on arms and armour.

I am also deeply indebted in numberless specific and general ways to individual scholars who are not employed in museums, but in universities or other institutions. Some of these debts are acknowledged in the relevant catalogue entries. Here I must express special thanks to Dr. R. W. Ratcliffe for his continuous encouragement, not only in conversation, but in many practical ways that have been of inestimable value, such as lending me for an unlimited period a large group of his matchless colour slides, indicating where rare books, fundamental for my researches, were to be found in out-of-the-way bookshops and, years ago, quietly drawing my attention to the comments by the perspectivist Thénot on the *Death of Sardanapalus*, a reference vital to the proper understanding of the spatial tensions in that painting. My thanks are also due to Dr. Hans Lüthy, Director of the Swiss Institute for Art Research, Zurich, for help in obtaining copies of Swiss exhibition catalogues and other documentation from Switzerland; to Mr. Giorgio Galansino of Chicago for telling me where the annotated catalogue of Delacroix's posthumous sale given by Philippe Burty to Maurice Tourneux was to be found; to Mrs. Stella Newton for advice on costume and hair styles; to Dr. Paul Joannides for some useful references to sales and exhibition catalogues; to Mr. Ronald Pickvance for providing me with particulars of Durand-Ruel's London exhibitions and with biographical details of James Duncan.

In a more general sense, I have benefited from and much appreciated the advice and encouragement of the following eminent scholars, not all of whom are specialists in nineteenth-century studies: Professor Sir Anthony Blunt, as whose student I first became seriously interested in Delacroix, Professor Francis Haskell, Professor Michael Jaffé and Professor Lorenz Eitner. The last named particularly has long sustained my faith in the value of compiling a *catalogue raisonné*, in face of the growing fashion for less exacting disciplines that are claimed to be more illuminating.

Private persons who have been exceptionally kind and helpful in special areas are Mme Boris Méra, proprietor, with her brother, of the Abbey of Valmont, where Delacroix often stayed with relatives, and owner of several paintings by him that are associated with his visits; Mr. Maurice Vila, who generously supplied me with much valuable information about the Pierret family, to which he is related; and Mlle Minet, who was formerly in charge of the collection of the late Mme D. David-Weill at Neuilly-sur-Seine. A place must also be found here for M. Pierre Angrand, independent spirit and 'grand chercheur', whose knowledge of the organization of the Archives nationales in Paris has saved me some futile searches.

Of the many dealers to whom I am indebted for photographs and information, my greatest debt is to the late M. Jean Dieterle, who was outstandingly generous in giving me access to his vast store of documentation and no less magnanimous in allowing me to profit from his wealth of first-hand knowledge of the Paris market in the late nineteenth and early twentieth centuries. It is a source of profound regret to me that he did not live to see his kindness fully acknowledged. I have also received assistance from M. Alfred Daber, M. Robert Schmit, the late M. Philippe Huisman, formerly manager of Messrs. Wildenstein's Paris branch, Mr. Roy Fisher, manager of their New York gallery, Dr. Peter Nathan and Frau Walter Feilchenfeldt, both of Zurich. I have further benefited from material supplied from the archives of Durand-Ruel and Bernheim-Jeune in Paris (M. Gilbert Gruet very kindly transcribed all the Delacroix entries from the latter's books for me) and of Knoedler in New York, where the late Dr. Helmut Ripperger was a most obliging and informative librarian, and in London, where Mr. Frank Simpson was librarian.

Mr. Benedict Nicolson, Editor of *The Burlington Magazine*, has kindly allowed me to reprint some passages which I originally wrote for that journal.

Acknowledgements are also due to the many collectors, museum curators and dealers who, though not named individually above, have nevertheless helped by supplying photographs, or enabling me to have photographs taken, of works in their possession or care, and given permission to reproduce them.

Without the generous support of the University of Toronto, which allowed me the time necessary to pursue my researches and, together with that enlightened government body, the Canada Council, granted me funds that enabled me to travel widely and to collect the documentation I needed, a publication of this scale could never have been contemplated.

If there are any names that I have unjustly omitted, I hope that I shall recall or be reminded of them in time to include them in my next volume.

Contents

VOLUME I

VOLUME II

List of Illustrations to Volume I

Fig. 1. *Eugène Delacroix c.* 1825. Lithograph after a lost portrait attributed to Thales Fielding.

A Brief Chronology of Delacroix's Early Years: 1798–1831

LIFE AND PRINCIPAL PAINTINGS, WITH SOME NOTES ON HIS READING

CHILDHOOD

1798

26 April. Born at Charenton-Saint-Maurice, on the south-eastern outskirts of Paris. His father, Charles Delacroix, was French Minister Plenipotentiary in the Low Countries at the time. His mother, Victoire, *née* Oeben, was the daughter of Jean-François Oeben, cabinet-maker to Louis XVI.[1]

1800

April. Father becomes Prefect of Marseille.

1803

April. Father becomes Prefect of Bordeaux.

1805

4 November. Father dies at Bordeaux.

1806

January. Mother moves in to live with her daughter, Henriette de Verninac, at 50 rue de Grenelle, Paris.

October. Delacroix enters the Lycée Impérial (now Louis-le-Grand) as a boarder. An able and receptive but unexceptional scholar, he learns to value the Ancients above all: 'the best result of a good education', as he was to put it (Piron, p. 40).

1807

Mother moves to 114 rue de l'Université, Paris.

Delacroix's second brother, Henry (b. 1784), killed in action at the Battle of Friedland.

1813

August. First visit to Valmont Abbey.

Before leaving Paris visits Guérin, regrets that he is unable to study with him this year, but hopes to do so upon quitting the Lycée, in order to acquire 'un petit talent d'amateur' (*Correspondance* I. 6).

Honourable mention (4th *accessit*) for drawing at the Lycée.

1814

3 September. Mother dies.

Honourable mention (1st *accessit*) for drawing at the Lycée.

TRAINING AND FIRST COMMISSIONS

1815

Leaves the Lycée at the end of the summer term.

On the recommendation of his uncle, the painter Henri Riesener, enters Guérin's atelier to study painting (see Léon Riesener in *Correspondance* (Burty 1878), p. xv)—'towards the end of 1815', according to Delacroix's own recollection (Piron, p. 50), on 1 October, according to Joubin (*Correspondance* v. 209). Guérin's studio was a place where new ideas circulated and was reputed to be less rowdy than Gros's. There Delacroix makes friends with Ary Scheffer, Champmartin and Champion, the last of whom, he is reported to have said, had an influence on Géricault and all the students in the atelier (L. Riesener, loc. cit., p. xvi). Delacroix later claimed that Guérin himself, however, 'ne m'a jamais encouragé' (Piron, p. 50).

1816

March. Enters the Ecole des Beaux-Arts (certificate of admission, dated 23 March 1816, exhibited Atelier Delacroix, Paris 1938).

13 July. Issued with a 'carte de travail' for the Cabinet des Estampes at the Bibliothèque royale (J. Lethève, 'Le Public au Cabinet des estampes au 19e siècle', in *Humanisme actif, mélanges d'art et de littérature offerts à Julien Cain*, Paris 1968, p. 105).

4 December. Guérin appointed Professor of Painting at the Ecole des Beaux-Arts (*Assemblées des professeurs et jugements*, MS. vol. III, Ecole des Beaux-Arts, hereafter *Assemblées*). In the course of this year meets Charles Soulier, an amateur water-colourist brought up in England, where he had recently learnt to paint in water-colour from Copley Fielding. Soulier instructs him in the technique, then rarely used in France (Soulier quoted in *Correspondance* I. 37 n. 2).

1817

March. Probably entered the competition at the Ecole des

---

[1] Charles was abroad at the time of the birth. On 13 September 1797, he had had a successful operation to remove a cancerous tumour weighing about 32 lb. from his left testicle. This fact has given rise to the belief that Charles could not have been the true father, and it has been suggested that Talleyrand, Foreign Minister at the time of Eugène's birth, was the father. But there is no firm evidence to substantiate this rumour. A full report of the operation was published in 1797 by the surgeon who performed it, A. B. Imbert Delonnes, and it is there stated that the right testicle was healthy. A note by Robaut on the copy of this publication that belonged to Delacroix (now in *BN Estampes*) records that professors at the Faculty of Medicine in Paris, studying the report in 1891, concluded that Charles could have fathered Eugène. Modern medical opinion that I have sought confirms this.

On a less clinical level, the researches of M. Loppin have recently shown that Charles's letters to his wife during her pregnancy reveal an affectionate concern for the safety of her unborn child, suggesting that, unless he was of a saintly tolerance, Charles thought he was, and knew he could be, the father (see P. Loppin, *Eugène Delacroix. L'Enigme est déchiffrée*, Paris 1965).

Beaux-Arts for an oil sketch representing the *Death of Orpheus*, judged 3 March and won by Albrier, pupil of Regnault (*Assemblées*, VI): there is a well developed composition for this subject in the Louvre sketch-book RF9146, fol. 6ʳ, which was certainly in use in 1817.

24 March. Placed 28th out of 56 in the competition for seats in the Salle du Modèle for the summer semester at the Ecole des Beaux-Arts (ibid.).

2 October. Placed 39th out of 51 for the winter semester (ibid. Not listed in any competitions for 1818 and 1819).

1818

Spends September, October and part of November at the Forest of Boixe, near Mansle, in Charente, a family property acquired by his mother in 1805. Dissects a fox while there (*Lettres intimes*, p. 58).

Evidently aiming to win the Prix de Rome one day, he writes in September of his sadness at the thought of spending years in Italy (ibid. 46).

1819

Paints his first commission, *The Virgin of the Harvest*, for the village church of Orcemont.

Receives commission for decorations in the house of Lottin de Saint-Germain on the Ile de la Cité—probably overdoors for the dining-room. Completes these before March 1820.

25 August. Salon opens, Géricault exhibits the *Raft of the Medusa*. Delacroix had posed for one of the figures.

Leaves Paris for the Forest of Boixe, where the Verninacs now settle.

Reading and translating passages from Dante and Shakespeare (*Lettres intimes*, pp. 70 f., 83 f.).

11 November. Returns to Paris with his nephew, Charles de Verninac.

1820

April. Moves from the rue de l'Université to 22 rue de la Planche.

25 April. Placed 11th (Alexandre Colin 1st) in the competition for seats in the Salle du Modèle for the summer semester at the Ecole des Beaux-Arts (*Assemblées*, IV).

1 May. Writes to his sister giving an account of how he spends his time (*Correspondance* V. 48): rises quite early and practises on his harpsichord or reads. After lunching frugally, he works either at the Louvre [copying] or at Guérin's studio. Attends the life class at the Ecole des Beaux-Arts three times a week, in the evenings.

July. Géricault passes on to him a State commission for a

Virgin of the Sacred Heart for the Cathedral of Nantes. (This was not finished before April 1821 and not delivered before May 1822. It was shipped to Corsica and installed in the Cathedral of Ajaccio in 1827.)

Advised by Henri Riesener to study under David in Brussels, says he has often considered doing so but remains undecided (*Correspondance* V. 61).

6 August. Placed 32nd out of 64 (Bonington 25th) in the competition for places in the Salle de la Bosse at the Ecole des Beaux-Arts (*Assemblées*, IV).[1]

End of August and first week of September. Stays with his brother, General Charles Delacroix, at Le Louroux, near Tours.

September to October. At the Forest of Boixe with the Verninacs. Ill with fever.

End of October. At Souillac, the native region of the family of his brother-in-law, Raymond de Verninac.

Beginning of November. Returns to Paris.

Continues to work with Guérin preparing for competitions (*Correspondance* I. 106).

1821

July. Renounces his ambition to win the Prix de Rome, 'comme je ne désire pas aller à Rome' (*Correspondance* I. 128).

Thinks of painting something for the Salon of 1822, subject undecided.

During the summer, paints the *Four Seasons*, overdoors for the dining-room of the famous tragedian Talma, rue de la Tour des Dames, Montmartre.

14 October. Arrives at Saint-Cyr for a short holiday.

3 November. Placed 30th out of 70 in the competition for places in the Salle de la Bosse at the Ecole des Beaux-Arts for the winter semester (*Assemblées*, IV).

(*continued*, p. xviii.)

DELACROIX'S READING LIST, *c*. 1816-21

Some titles of books noted down by Delacroix during the period of his training and not, to my recollection, mentioned by other writers on Delacroix are listed here, with some quotations of passages that may have had a formative influence on him. The editions given here are not necessarily those used by Delacroix.

Theory and Practice
Gérard Audran, probably *Les proportions du corps humain mesurées sur les plus belles figures de l'antiquité et gravées par Gérard Audran*, Paris, 1683 (*Journal* III. 338—March 1820: buys 'le livre de *Gérard Audran*.')

Charles Bell, *Essays on the Anatomy of Expression*, London,

---

[1] This was the first competition of its kind at the Ecole. Students who had already won a place in the Salle du Modèle were not required to compete for a place in the cast room, where they were allowed the same place awarded for the life class, but could compete if they wished to improve their place (*Assemblées*, IV, meeting of 8 July 1820).

1806. (Noted by Delacroix as the best book on anatomy for artists. *Bib AA*, MS. 250):

'Among the errors into which a young artist is most likely to be seduced, there are two against which the study of anatomy seems well calculated to guard him. The one of these is, the blind and indiscriminate imitation of the antique; the other, an opinion that in the academy figure he will find a sure guide in delineating the natural and true anatomy of the living body' (p. 3).

'The study of the action of the figure admits of a natural division; first, of motion and exertion simply; and secondly, of the effects of sentiment and passion. The knowledge of the former is necessary in order to paint the figure with correctness [. . .]. The second belongs more to the province of genius' (pp. 177 f.).

Albrecht Dürer, *Treatise on Proportion* (Louvre sketch-book RF9141, fol. 1. A copy of the 1557 French edition of Dürer's four Books of Human Proportion, translated by Meigret, passed in Delacroix's posthumous sale in 1864).

William Hogarth, *The Analysis of Beauty* (Louvre sketch-book RF9141, fol. 1).

Antoine Pernety, *Dictionnaire portatif de peinture, sculpture et gravure, avec un Traité pratique des différentes manières de peindre, dont la théorie est développée dans les articles qui en sont susceptibles*', Paris, 1757 (*Bib AA*, MS. 246*bis*, fol. 1: 'Dictionnaire d. Peinture par Dom Pernetti').

Quatremère de Quincy, *Considérations morales sur la destination des ouvrages de l'art . . .*, Paris, 1815 (*Bib AA*, MS. 246¹⁵, fol. 3ᵛ; 'De l'art etc. — par Mʳ Quatremere de Quincy' listed in the Louvre sketch-book RF 6736, fol. 60, probably also refers to this book):

'The imitation of bodies must be degenerate when it is no longer required that bodies should be the image of the soul' (English trans. by H. Thomson, London, 1821, p. 19).

'The knowledge acquired in schools is useful, but its errors should not be circulated out of them [. . .]: every one should walk with his own pace and soar with his own wings' (ibid. 28).

Jonathan Richardson, *The Theory of Painting*, London, 1715 (Louvre sketch-book RF9141, fol. 1: 'Traité de la peinture par Richar[d]son.' An edition in French was published in 3 vols. in Amsterdam in 1728). This contains many ideas which are clearly reflected in Delacroix's art and writings, and was probably a major influence throughout his career:

'Words paint to the imagination, but every man forms the thing to himself in his own way; language is very imperfect [. . .]: whereas the painter can convey his ideas [. . .] clearly, and without ambiguity.' (*The Works of Jonathan Richardson*, London, 1792, p. 6.)

'The pleasure that Painting, as a dumb art, gives us, is like what we have from music; its beautiful forms, colours and harmony, are to the eye what sounds, and the harmony of that kind are to the ear.' (Ibid. 7.)

'To paint a history, a man ought to have the main qualities of a good historian, and something more; he must yet go higher, and have the talents requisite to a good poet' (ibid. 12).

'So far should the painter be from inserting anything superfluous, that he ought to leave something to the imagination' (ibid. 31).

'Every picture should be so contrived, as that at a distance, when one cannot discern what figures there are, or what they are doing [. . .] the whole together should be sweet and delightful, lovely shapes and colours, without a name; of which there is infinite variety' (ibid. 52).

'There is often a spirit, and beauty in a quick, or perhaps an accidental management of the chalk, pen, pencil, or brush in a drawing, or painting, which it is impossible to preserve if it be more finished' (ibid. 70).

Art History
(All on a single sheet in *Bib AA*, MS. 250):
Carlo Amoretti, *Memorie storiche su la vita, gli studi, e le opere di Lionardo da Vinci*, Milan, 1804.

Anonymous, *Vita inedita di Raffaello da Urbino, illustrata con note da A. Comolli*, Rome, 1790.

G. Bellori, *Le Vite de' pittori, scultori ed architetti moderni . . .*, Rome, 1672.

G. G. Bottari (ed.), *Raccolta di lettere sulla pittura, scultura, ed architettura, scritte da' più celebri professori che in dette arti fiorirono dal secolo XV al XVII*, 6 vols., 1754-68.

Charles de Brosses, *Lettres historiques et critiques sur l' Italie . . . Avec des notes relatives à la situation actuelle de l'Italie, et la liste raisonnée des tableaux et autres monuments qui ont été apportés à Paris, de Milan, de Rome, de Venise, etc.*, 3 vols., Paris, 1799.

A. Condivi, *Vita di Michelagnolo Buonarotti*, Rome, 1553.

L. A. Lanzi, *Storia pittorica della Italia dal risorgimento delle belle arti fin presso al fine del XVIII. secolo*, 6 vols., Bassano, 1809 (3rd ed.).

C. Malvasia, *Felsina Pittrice. Vite de Pittori Bolognesi*, 2 vols., Bologna, 1678.

C. Ridolfi, *Le Maraviglie dell'arte, overo le vite degl'illustri Pittori Veneti*, Venice, 1648.

A. Zanetti, *Della pittura Veneziana . . .*, Venice, 1771.

INDEPENDENCE AND PUBLIC RECOGNITION

1822

March. Using unlet portion of his sister's house in the rue de l'Université as a studio (*Correspondance* I. 110). Painting the *Barque de Dante*.

6 April. Placed 59th out of 61 in the competition for places in the Salle du Modèle at the Ecole des Beaux-Arts for the summer semester (*Assemblées*, IV).

23 April. Death of his brother-in-law, Raymond de Verninac.

24 April. The Salon opens. Delacroix exhibits his first Salon painting, the *Barque de Dante*, which, being well received and acquired by the State, establishes his reputation. Though Guérin did not approve of its being exhibited, Gros compliments Delacroix so warmly as to make him insensible to flattery for the rest of his life (Delacroix quoted in Piron, p. 51), and apparently wishes to train him for the Prix de Rome. An ardent admirer of Gros's work, Delacroix is tempted to become his pupil.

11 May. Placed 31st out of 53 (Bonington 21st) in the competition for places in the Salle de la Bosse at the Ecole des Beaux-Arts for the summer semester (*Assemblées*, IV).

29 June. Guérin appointed Director of the French Academy in Rome (ibid.).

End of July. Leaves Paris to visit his brother at Le Louroux.

3 September. Begins his Journal at Le Louroux.

22 September. Returns to Paris.

October. On seeing the prize-winning torso and classical history painting by Debay, a pupil of Gros's, Delacroix is disenchanted with the school of Gros.[1] Decides to take his uncle Riesener's advice and follow an independent path (*Journal* I. 14).

1823[2]

Lives at 118 rue de Grenelle, Paris.

May. Decides to paint scenes from the Chios massacres for the Salon of 1824 (*Journal* I. 32).

Probably stays with the Rieseners in their country house at Frépillon for the first time and sketches there ('Vues de Frépillon la première année — 1823', Louvre sketch-book RF9150, fol. 1ᵛ).

23 November. After years of litigation, the Forest of Boixe is sold at auction to satisfy creditors, but does not fetch nearly enough to meet all debts and the Delacroix family is ruined. Eugène has to live from his art.

1824

January. Begins the *Massacres of Chios*, using a chapel near the Sorbonne, probably in the rue des Maçons-Sorbonne, as a studio. Also does preliminary work for *The Agony in the Garden*, a commission for the Prefect of the Seine for the church of Saint-Paul-Saint-Louis, Paris.

26 January. Death of Géricault. Delacroix is profoundly affected.

19 April. Byron dies at Missolonghi.

May. Intense interest in Byron. Reading *The Giaour*, *Childe Harold*. Writes of the description of the death of Selim at the end of *The Bride of Abydos*: 'Je sens ces choses-là comme la peinture les comporte.' Plans or begins to design subjects from Byron, including a *Mazeppa* and *Combat of Hassan and the Giaour* (*Journal* I. 98–100, 105).

10 May. Placed 14th out of 53 in the competition for places in the Salle de la Bosse at the Ecole des Beaux-Arts for the summer semester (*Assemblées*, V).

About this time, he also does studies three times a week from cadavers in the dissection amphitheatre at Clamart, according to Mirecourt (*Eugéne Delacroix*, Paris, 1870 ed., p. 36).

19 June. Sees works by Constable, no doubt the pictures that were to be shown at the Salon, including *The Hay Wain*. Says they do him a great deal of good.

25 August. Salon opens, exhibits *The Massacres of Chios*, which is interpreted as making a new departure and posing a threat to the accepted standards of the neo-classical school. It is nevertheless acquired by the State for the Musée du Luxembourg. Also shows *Tasso in the Hospital of St Anna* at the Salon.

October. Moves to Thales Fielding's Paris address, 20 rue Jacob, when the English artist returns to London. Discontinues his Journal, to be resumed in 1847.

1825

Takes a studio at 14 rue d'Assas.

19 May. Arrives at Dover on his way to London, where he stays till the end of August.

Visits Greenwich, Richmond, Hampstead, Westminster Hall, the Benjamin West gallery, the Marquess of Stafford's collection at Cleveland House, the Meyrick collection of arms and armour.

Received by Sir Thomas Lawrence, David Wilkie, C. R. Cockerell and probably Constable.

Meets up with Bonington, whom he knew from Paris, they sketch together and become close friends.

Sees Kean in *Richard III*, *Othello* and *The Merchant of Venice*; Young in *The Tempest*. A performance of an operatic version of Goethe's *Faust* with Wallack in the

---

[1] Both Debay's pictures are preserved at the Ecole des Beaux-Arts. The torso, though dull enough, is more fleshy and Rubensian in treatment than the other prize-winning entries since 1815. The title of the history painting is: *Egyste croyant découvrir le corps d'Oreste mort découvre celui de Clytemnestre*.

[2] Hardly any letters from this year have survived. Of the two assigned to 1823 in *Correspondance*, the date of the first is corrected to 1827 by Joubin, and the second should be dated to 1824. Of the four placed in 1823 in *Lettres intimes*, the two to Soulier should be re-dated 1824 (see J70, n. 1).

title role and Terry as Mephistopheles is to be a major inspiration for Delacroix's illustrations to *Faust*.

After his return to Paris, lives at 46 rue de l'Université with his friend Pierret, and Bonington works with him in his studio for a while. In January 1826 Delacroix recalls how greatly he profited from the collaboration.

29 December. David dies in Brussels.

1826

Beginning of his relationship with Victor Hugo and the Romantic *cénacle*.

25 April. Missolonghi falls to the Turks.

May. *The Execution of Marino Faliero* and *A Turkish Officer killed in the Mountains* shown at the exhibition for Greek relief at the Galerie Lebrun. Adds *The Combat of the Giaour and Hassan* in June and *Greece on the Ruins of Missolonghi* in August.

June. Stays with the Coëtlosquet family at Charité-sur-Loire. Probably begins the *Still Life with Lobsters* for the Count de Coëtlosquet at this time.

July. Receives a commission for a large painting for a room in the Conseil d'Etat in the Louvre; begins work on the final canvas, *Justinian drafting his Laws*, about August and completes it about a year later.

1827

6 April. Delacroix's sister, Henriette de Verninac, dies (b. 1780).

July. Exhibits five paintings, including *The Combat of the Giaour and Hassan*, at the Douai Salon; awarded a medal.

September. The English theatre company, with Kemble and Harriett Smithson, come to Paris and open a successful season of Shakespeare plays at the Odéon with *Hamlet*, followed in later months by *Romeo and Juliet*, *Othello*, *Macbeth*, *King Lear*, *Richard III* and *The Merchant of Venice*. This provides an important stimulus for the French Romantic movement. Delacroix writes excitedly of the event, without however specifying which plays he has seen (*Correspondance* I. 197, 198).

October. Stays with the Rivet family at Mantes. Returns to Paris on the nineteenth.

4 November. The Salon opens, the first since 1824. Delacroix exhibits nine pictures (four of the thirteen he submitted were rejected by the Salon jury). They include *The Agony in the Garden*, commissioned by 1824, and *The Execution of Marino Faliero*. *The Death of Sardanapalus*, which was to create a sensation, is not finished in time for the opening.

December. Victor Hugo publishes his preface to *Cromwell*.

1828

Moves to 15 rue de Choiseul, takes studio at 9 passage Saulnier.

January. The newly decorated rooms of the Conseil d'Etat, containing the *Justinian drafting his Laws*, are temporarily opened to the public.

February. The replenished Salon opens. Delacroix adds three pictures, notably *The Death of Sardanapalus*, his largest canvas to date, which provokes more general hostility from the critics and state officials than any major work he was ever to paint, and establishes—or brands—him as 'le chef patenté' of romanticism, a label he distrusted.[1] He is summoned by Sosthènes de La Rochefoucauld, *surintendant des beaux-arts*, and given to understand that if he wishes to receive any favours from the Government he must change his manner. From this moment, Delacroix finds the *Sardanapalus* far better than he had thought (quoted in Piron, p. 72).

13 February. Victor Hugo's *Amy Robsart*, adapted from Scott's *Kenilworth*, opens at the Odéon, with costumes designed by Delacroix. A fiasco. *The Execution of Marino Faliero*, withdrawn from the Salon, is exhibited at the British Institution in London, where it receives high critical acclaim.

June. *Mephistopheles appears before Faust* and possibly *Greece on the Ruins of Missolonghi* are shown at Hobday's Gallery in London.

July. Probably begins *Cardinal Richelieu saying Mass*, for the Duc d'Orléans's gallery in the Palais-Royal.

28 August. *The Battle of Nancy* is commissioned by the Government for the municipal museum of Nancy, in connection with a visit to the city by Charles X. This painting was not finished before 1831 and not exhibited till the Salon of 1834.

23 September. Bonington dies in London.

About the end of the month finishes *Cardinal Richelieu saying Mass*.

Late October to early November. Visits his brother, General Charles Delacroix, at Tours.

Towards the end of this year or the beginning of 1829 he receives further patronage from the Royal Family: paints *Quentin Durward* and *Le Balafré* for the Duchesse de Berry, to be followed by *The Battle of Poitiers* for the same patron, which is not finished till 1830.

[1] Two indications of how Delacroix understood the meaning of the term 'romanticism' as applied to French painting have come down to us. Théophile Silvestre quotes him as saying: 'Si l'on entend par mon romantisme la libre manifestation de mes impressions personnelles, mon éloignement pour les types calqués dans les écoles et ma répugnance pour les recettes académiques, je dois avouer que non-seulement je suis romantique, mais que je l'étais à quinze ans; je préférais déjà Prudhon et Gros à Guérin et à Girodet' (*Les Artistes français*, 1855, p. 28). And Paul Huet recalls that Delacroix defined romanticism thus: 'Le romantisme fut une réaction contre l'école, un appel à la liberté de l'art, un retour vers une tradition plus large: on voulut rendre justice à toutes les grandes époques, même à David!' (R. P. Huet, *Paul Huet*, Paris, 1911, p. 74.)

1829

End of January moves to 15 quai Voltaire, to combined living quarters and studio. Begins almost immediately to paint his masterpiece inspired by Scott, *The Murder of the Bishop of Liège*.

11 February. Alexandre Dumas's *Henri III et sa cour* opens at the Comédie-Française. The first major triumph of the French drama in France.

By the end of the month the oil sketch for *The Battle of Nancy* is ready to be submitted for approval.

27 April. The ballet, *La Belle au bois dormant*, opens at the Opéra; costume of the Majordomo, danced by François Simon, designed by Delacroix.

May. Publishes his essay, *Des Critiques en matière d'art*, in the *Revue de Paris*.

October to November. Stays with his cousins at Valmont Abbey. Returns to Paris via Rouen shortly after 19 November.

During the autumn and winter he probably works on *The Battle of Nancy* and *The Battle of Poitiers*.

1830

25 February. Victor Hugo's *Hernani* opens with much hullabaloo at the Théâtre Français, Mlle Mars playing the role of Doña Sol. The play brings Hugo personal fame and wealth, as well as marking a turning-point in the fortunes of the Romantic theatre. Deeply distrustful of his inflated reputation, Delacroix cools towards Hugo for good: 'H. [Hugo] fait oublier le Dante, qui se passe bien de vivre dans la réunion de ceux qui admirent H.' (*Correspondance* I. 257.)

May. *The Murder of the Bishop of Liège* is hung at the Royal Academy exhibition in London, where it is well received by the critics.

In the course of the spring and summer, Delacroix's essays on Raphael and Michelangelo are published in the *Revue de Paris*.

27-9 July. The July Revolution overthrows Charles X and his Ultra Government.

Attempts to create a Second Republic are soon frustrated and the Duc d'Orléans accedes to the throne as Louis-Philippe, King of the French.

The events inspire Delacroix to paint *Liberty leading the People*, which he probably begins in the autumn and completes around the end of the year.

30 September. The new Government announces a competition for three paintings to decorate the wall behind the rostrum in the new Chamber of Deputies in the Palais Bourbon. Delacroix will submit oil sketches for two of them: *Mirabeau confronts the Marquis de Dreux-Brézé* and *Boissy d'Anglas at the National Convention*, the closing dates being 1 February and 1 April 1831 respectively.

October. *A Young Tiger playing with its Mother*, Delacroix's largest animal painting to date, is shown at an exhibition in the Palais du Luxembourg for the benefit of citizens wounded in the July Revolution. (Gros also exhibited *The Plague at Jaffa*, *The Battle of Eylau* and *The Battle of Aboukir*, none of which had been shown publicly since the Empire.)

1831

1 March. The newly founded *l'Artiste* publishes a long letter from Delacroix, solicited by the editor, on the subject of public competitions for State commissions. He argues cogently against them, pointing out the difficulty of selecting disinterested judges, the dangers of inhibiting inspiration and promoting mediocrity. Artists of real talent ought not to be subjected to the indignity of competitions: 'Je me figure le grand Rubens étendu sur le lit de fer d'un concours.' And 'Quand Léon X eut envie de faire peindre son palais, il n'alla pas demander à son ministre de l'Intérieur de lui trouver le plus digne: il choisit tout simplement Raphaël.' (Though unsuccessful in the current competitions, he will be awarded two major commissions for decorations in the Palais Bourbon later in the decade, without competing.)

6 March. The *Mirabeau* sketches for the Chamber of Deputies are judged by a jury which includes Guérin, Gros and Ingres. Hesse wins.

14 April. The Salon opens, the first since 1827-8. Delacroix exhibits *Liberty leading the People*, which is purchased by the State but not left on public view for long. He shows seven more paintings, including *Cardinal Richelieu saying Mass*, *A Young Tiger playing with its Mother* and *The Murder of the Bishop of Liège*.

22 April. The *Boissy d'Anglas* sketches for the Chamber of Deputies are judged. Vinchon wins.

September to October. Stays at Valmont Abbey. Visits Rouen from there and finds inspiration in the Palais de Justice for the setting of *Interior of a Dominican Convent in Madrid*, which he paints later in the year.

December. Makes preparations for his departure for Morocco with Count de Mornay, on New Year's Day 1832 (*Lettres intimes*, p. 193).

A Summary Chronology of Delacroix's Later Years: 1832–1863

1832

January to July. The North African journey. Travels with a French government mission to the Sultan of Morocco at Meknes, led by Count Charles de Mornay. Visits Tangier, Meknes, Oran and Algiers. Also stops over briefly in Spain, visiting Cadiz and Seville.

1833

Guérin dies.

Through Adolphe Thiers, now Minister of Trade and Public Works, Delacroix receives the commission to decorate the Salon du Roi in the Palais Bourbon.

1834

Exhibits his first major painting inspired by the North African journey at the Salon, the *Femmes d'Alger*. Also has four other pictures accepted, including *Interior of a Dominican Convent in Madrid* and *The Battle of Nancy*, both dated 1831.

Greatly distressed by the death from yellow fever of his nephew, Charles de Verninac, in New York at the age of thirty.

Experiments with fresco technique by painting three small murals in the Abbey of Valmont: *Bacchus*, *Leda* and *Anacreon*.

1835

Gros dies.

Delacroix exhibits five paintings at the Salon, including *The Natchez* begun in 1823.

October. Moves to 17 rue des Marais Saint-Germain (now rue Visconti).

December. Ceiling and friezes of the Salon du Roi are finished in time for the opening of Parliament by the King. The eight monumental grisaille figures of rivers and seas on the piers remain to be done.

1836

St. Sebastian exhibited at the Salon, purchased by the State and installed in the church at Nantua.

The grisaille figures in the Salon du Roi are finished by the end of the year, but Delacroix continues to work on 'important modifications' to the scheme in the following year.

1837

First unsuccessful candidacy for the Institut.

The Battle of Taillebourg, commissioned in 1834 for the Galeries historiques at Versailles, is exhibited at the Salon.

December. All retouching of the decorations in the Salon du Roi is completed in time for the opening of Parliament by the King.

1838

Second candidacy for the Institut.

Exhibits five pictures at the Salon, including *Medea* and *The Fanatics of Tangier*.

Commissioned to paint *The Taking of Constantinople by the Crusaders* for the Galeries historiques at Versailles.

Receives commission for the decorations to the Library of the Chamber of Deputies in the Palais Bourbon, comprising two half-domes and five saucer-domes, and shortly sets up a studio in the rue Neuve-Guillemin to train assistants.

October. The public admitted into the Salon du Roi to see Delacroix's decorations.

1839

Third candidacy for the Institut.

Exhibits two paintings inspired by Shakespeare at the Salon: *Cleopatra and the Peasant*, *Hamlet and Horatio in the Graveyard*; two North African subjects and a *Tasso* rejected.

September. Travels to Belgium and the Netherlands with Elise Boulanger. Visits Antwerp, Amsterdam, The Hague, and studies Rubens closely.

1840

Exhibits *The Justice of Trajan*, his only entry, at the Salon.

June. The Prefect of the Seine commissions a mural painting for a chapel in the church of Saint-Denis du Saint-Sacrement.

September. Receives the commission to decorate the cupola and half-dome in the Library of the Senate, Palais du Luxembourg.

1841

Exhibits *Constantinople*, *Shipwreck of Don Juan* and *Jewish Wedding in Morocco* at the Salon.

1842

Seriously ill with laryngitis, which troubles him for the rest of his life and, apparently tuberculous, at length kills him. From about this time, he reduces his social commitments in order to preserve his strength for his work.

June. At Nohant with George Sand and Chopin.

From this year to 1844, engaged on the large schemes of decorations for the libraries of the Palais Bourbon and Luxembourg and, in the winter of 1843-4, painting the *Pietà* in Saint-Denis du Saint-Sacrement, Delacroix sends nothing to the Salons.

Takes a new studio and apartment at 54 rue Notre-Dame-de-Lorette in October 1844.

1845

Exhibits four paintings at the Salon, including *The Death of Marcus Aurelius* and *The Sultan of Morocco and his Entourage*; *The Education of the Virgin*, painted at Nohant in 1842, is rejected.

Spends a month in the Pyreness for his health during the summer.

December. The last member of his immediate family, General Charles Delacroix (b. 1779), dies at Bordeaux.

1846

Shows *Abduction of Rebecca, Farewell of Romeo and Juliet* and *Margaret in Church* at the Salon.

Made an officer of the Legion of Honour.

December. The decorations in the Library of the Palais du Luxembourg are completed and the critics admitted to view them.

1847

January. Resumes his Journal.

Shows six paintings at the Salon: three Moroccan subjects, a *Christ on the Cross* (Baltimore), an *Odalisque* and *Castaways in a Ship's Boat*.

December. The decorations in the Library of the Palais Bourbon are finished and the critics invited to see them.

1848

February. Revolution overthrows the July Monarchy. Delacroix's *Richelieu saying Mass* of 1828 is destroyed in the burning of the Palais-Royal.

Exhibits six paintings at the Salon, including a *Lamentation* (Boston), *Death of Valentine* and *Death of Lara*.

December. Louis-Napoleon is elected President of the Second Republic.

1849

Exhibits seven pictures at the Salon, including two of a series of four flower paintings and a small variant of the *Women of Algiers*.

Receives a commission to decorate a chapel in the church of Saint-Sulpice.

Death of Chopin, a close friend.

Fourth candidacy for the Institut; withdraws a fifth application.

1850

Exhibits five easel paintings at the Salon: two religious subjects, a nude, *The Giaour* and *Lady Macbeth*.

Receives the commission for the central painting on the ceiling of the newly restored Galerie d'Apollon in the Louvre.

July to August. Takes the waters at Ems. Visits Brussels, Antwerp, Cologne, Malines, studying Rubens and other artists.

1851

Sixth candidacy for the Institut.

Appointed a City Councillor.

October. Completes *The Triumph of Apollo* on the ceiling of the Galerie d'Apollon.

December. The *coup d'état*, which leads to the establishment of the Second Empire under Napoleon III in the following year.

About the end of this year, Delacroix is commissioned to decorate the Salon de la Paix in the Hôtel de Ville.

1852

Works on the decorations for the Salon de la Paix, assisted by Pierre Andrieu, and blocks in the four pendentives in the Chapel of the Holy Angels at Saint-Sulpice.

1853

Exhibits two religious paintings and *African Pirates abducting a Young Woman* at the Salon.

Seventh candidacy for the Institut.

Continues to work in the Salon de la Paix.

1854

February. Completes the decorations in the Salon de la Paix (destroyed by fire during the Commune in 1871).

In the course of the summer, begins work on the walls in the Chapel of the Holy Angels at Saint-Sulpice.

1855

Has a one-man show of thirty-six paintings from all periods of his life at the Exposition universelle. His own choice, they include some of his most famous early pictures, such as the *Barque de Dante* and *Murder of the Bishop of Liège*, as well as the large, recently completed *Lion Hunt* (Bordeaux).

Awarded the Grande Médaille d'Honneur and made Commander of the Legion of Honour.

1856

Continues to work in the Chapel of the Holy Angels at Saint-Sulpice, on the cartoon for the ceiling (*St. Michael defeats the Devil*) and on the walls (*Heliodorus driven from the Temple, Jacob wrestling with the Angel*). Also engaged on a variety of smaller easel paintings.

Work in Saint-Sulpice is interrupted by his illness at the end of the year.

1857

January. Finally elected to the Institut, following his eighth candidacy. Plans a Dictionary of the Fine Arts, which was never published and is known only from the copious notes for it in his Journal.

Unable to work at Saint-Sulpice owing to ill health.

At the end of December, moves to the apartment and studio in the place Furstenberg.

1858
Able to work briefly in Saint-Sulpice in July, more intensively during the autumn.

August. Buys the house at Champrosay that he has visited as a tenant almost every year since 1844.

1859
Exhibits eight paintings at the Salon, his last. They include three religious subjects, *Ovid among the Scythians* and *Banks of the River Sebou.*

Makes further progress with the decorations at Saint-Sulpice, which are reported to be three-quarters finished in December.

1860
Exhibits twenty-three paintings from various periods at the Galerie Martinet, Boulevard des Italiens.

Brings the decorations at Saint-Sulpice near to completion in spite of continuing ill health and difficulties with assistants.

1861
July. Completes the decorations in the Chapel of the Holy Angels at Saint-Sulpice and issues invitations for viewing. The paintings win high critical acclaim and excite the interest of his fellow artists, but Delacroix is disappointed at the lack of response from official dignitaries to his invitations.

December. *The Death of Sardanapalus* of 1827 is added to the exhibition at the Galerie Martinet.

1862
Health declines, yet he continues to work on a number of easel paintings, mostly variants of earlier subjects.

The Murder of the Bishop of Liège of 1829 is shown at the Universal Exhibition in London.

1863
Further deterioration in his health.

13 August. Dies in his apartment in the place Furstenberg, following a severe haemoptysis.

Notes to the Catalogue

ARRANGEMENT AND NUMBERING

Pictures are arranged according to subject and, as far as possible, chronologically within each category of subject. Copies, however, are not arranged in the sequence of execution but of the artists from whom they were done. An exception to the general chronological arrangement is also made for the Goubaux portraits, which are grouped together as a series in the order of their separate execution, uninterrupted by other portraits that were painted after the series was begun.

The separate sections for lost works and for doubtful works are arranged in essentially the same way as the section reserved for the extant *œuvre* which is judged to be secure. Untraced or destroyed paintings are included among the extant works when photographs of the originals exist; otherwise they are, with a few exceptions, catalogued in the special section for lost works. Exceptions are made for the lost Goubaux portraits that are known only from prints or drawings, because they were part of a series; for the lost oil sketches for the *Justinian drafting his Laws*, destroyed in 1871, so that they can be easily considered in relation to the extant studies; for the large and important *Richelieu saying Mass*, destroyed in 1848, and known only from a lithograph; and for *Charles V at the Monastery of Yuste*, which is unique among the lost works painted before 1832 in having been lithographed by Delacroix himself.

All references to numbers in this catalogue are preceded by the letter J, in order to avoid confusion with numbers in other catalogues and tedious repetition of such phrases as 'our number . . . ' J followed immediately by a number refers to a picture in the first section; the letter L in parentheses between J and the number refers to the section of lost works; the letter O, M, D or R in the same position, to the section of doubtful works (see the beginning of that section, p. 213, for the key to the meaning of each of these

four letters and an explanation of the sequence in which they are arranged).

DESCRIPTION AND DATING

Titles are given in English at the head of each entry, but French titles are often listed elsewhere in the entry and in the case of Salon paintings are always cited in full, together with any further explanation that went with them, from the official Salon catalogues.

Paintings are in oil on canvas unless otherwise stated.

Height precedes width. An asterisk after the dimensions indicates that the author has measured the picture. The absence of an asterisk does not mean that he has not seen the painting, but merely that he has not measured it. Where this is the case the dimensions are given from what seems the most reliable source. The measurements of a large painting in the Louvre, for example, will be taken from the Museum's latest catalogue of paintings.

The initials 'E.D.' following the dimensions indicate that the back of the picture bears, either on the stretcher or the canvas, the red wax monogram of Delacroix's posthumous sale, illustrated in Fig. 2.

If the author's dating differs from Robaut's, the latter's date is given in parentheses beside the Robaut number which is listed after the dimensions. If Robaut does not illustrate the painting, this is also indicated in parentheses in the same place by the abbreviation 'No repr.'

In order to avoid a too frequent use of '*circa*' or question marks in dating, an unqualified date is usually listed with the basic description of a picture at the head of an entry. In controversial cases, this is the date favoured here, which is supported by argument in the main text of the entry, and not necessarily an absolutely firm one. '*Circa*' and question marks are reserved for pictures for which an unqualified date cannot be proposed on the evidence available.

Cat. No. 26   Cat. No. 31

Fig. 2. Genuine (left) and false seals of Delacroix's posthumous sale.

xxv

Cat. No. 88

Cat. No. 113

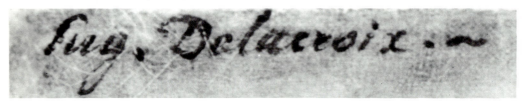

Cat. No. 91

Cat. No. 126

Cat. No. 104

Cat. No. 116

Fig. 3. Delacroix's signatures.

When dates are given covering more than a single year they are separated by a small dash if the picture was begun on the first and completed on the second date; by an oblique bar, if it was painted at some time within the period marked by the two dates. Thus '1824–8' would mean that a picture was begun in 1824 and finished in 1828; '1824/8', that it was painted at an undetermined time between 1824 and 1828.

PROVENANCE

Unless otherwise stated, sales were held in Paris and French owners are, as far as the author is aware, residents of Paris. For sales that lasted more than a day the date of the first day only is listed.

EXHIBITIONS

In addition to exhibitions proper, temporary loans and deposits of pictures at museums, with dates, are listed in brackets under this heading. *h.c.* = *hors catalogue*.

See pp. xxxi–xxxix for a full list of the abbreviations used for exhibitions.

LITERATURE

Moreau and Robaut references that are listed at the head of an entry are not repeated under *Literature*, nor are *Journal* and *Correspondance* references that appear in the main text of an entry.

Page references are not always given to the first edition of works by famous authors such as Baudelaire and Théophile Gautier; the title and date of the first edition are given, then in parentheses a page reference to a reliable and easily accessible later edition.

References are not given for every edition of museum catalogues by any one compiler, but only to one edition unless there are significant amendments between editions.

A more select bibliography is listed for the four major Salon paintings in the period covered by this volume, the *Barque of Dante*, the *Massacres of Chios*, the *Death of Sardanapalus* and the *Liberty leading the People*, than for the other authentic works. A complete list of reviews of the Salons in which these four pictures were noticed is attempted. After that, only critical or historical comments of some substance or special interest are included (a passing mention with no opinion expressed or an effusion without originality, for example, would not be noted); also references to basic museum catalogues, principal references in the major monographs, to picture books containing especially useful plates and to articles which contribute something new either from an interpretive or documentary point of view. Volume and page references to the *Journal* and to the Joubin edition of the *Correspondance* are given only when the text is quoted (the others can be found in the indexes to the Joubin editions of both publications).

See pp. xxix–xxxi for a full list of archival and bibliographical abbreviations and further explanation of the form of reference to individual works.

CONDITION

Detailed reports of condition have not been attempted, as these, to be of real value, would need to be based on a technical competence that the author does not possess and on scientific examination that it was not possible for him to have done by experts. An attempt has been made, however, to document restorations, particularly those done during the artist's lifetime, to indicate if a picture has been relined and to note the more obvious examples of damage and repainting, especially where these may create problems of attribution or dating.

An asterisk is placed after the names of owners of pictures that I have learned have changed hands between the date of the Preface, 1976, and the date of publication. Any information that I have about the changes of ownership or recent movements of these pictures is listed in the Pre-publication Note on p. viii, except for the following piece of information which arrived too late to be included in that Note. *Hamlet sees the Ghost of his Father* (Cat. L99) is in the Museum of the Jagiellonian University, Cracow. Signed and dated 1825, it is reproduced in *Folia Historiae Artium*, III (Cracow, 1966), fig. 1.

Abbreviations

ARCHIVAL AND BIBLIOGRAPHICAL

AB
The Art Bulletin

Arch A. Tripp
Books of Arnold, Tripp et Cie, Paris.

Arch B-J
Books of Bernheim-Jeune et Cie, Paris.

Arch D-R
Archives of Durand-Ruel et Cie, Paris.

Arch Goupil/Boussod
Books of Goupil et Cie, succeeded by Boussod, Valadon et Cie in May 1875, Paris.

[Baudelaire] *Œuvres* Pléiade ed., Paris 1932
Œuvres de Baudelaire. Texte établi et annoté par Y.-G. Le Dantec, vol. II (Bibliothèque de la Pléiade, Paris, 1932).

Bellier-Auvray
E. Bellier de la Chavignerie and L. Auvray, *Dictionnaire général des artistes de l'école française* (Renouard, Paris, 1882-7), 2 vols. + Supplement.

Berger
K. Berger, *Géricault et son œuvre*, translated from the German by Maurice Beerblock (Grasset, Paris, 1953. German ed., Schroll, Vienna, 1952).

Bib AA
Bibliothèque d'art et d'archéologie, University of Paris.

BN Estampes
Cabinet des Estampes, Bibliothèque nationale, Paris.

Bortolatto
L. Bortolatto, *L'Opera pittorica completa di Delacroix* (Rizzoli, Milan, 1972). Referred to in the Concordance only or for coloured reproductions not found elsewhere.

Brière 1924
G. Brière, *Musée national du Louvre. Catalogue des peintures exposées dans les galeries*, I, *Ecole française* (Paris, Musées nationaux, 1924).

BSHAF
Bulletin de la Société de l'Histoire de l'Art français.

Burl Mag
The Burlington Magazine.

Burty Ann ED
Annotated catalogue of Delacroix's posthumous sale, 17-29 February 1864, given by Philippe Burty, who catalogued the drawings for this sale, to Maurice Tourneux, 15 January 1871. The notes were evidently copied from a catalogue that was annotated at the sale (see Tourneux, p. 152 on the subject of annotated copies of the catalogue of this sale). Art Institute of Chicago.

Cassou 1947
J. Cassou, *Delacroix* (Editions du Dimanche, Paris, 1947). Especially valuable for plates, including full-page details 31 × 24 cm.

Christoffel 1951
U. Christoffel, *Eugène Delacroix* (Bruckmann, Munich, 1951). Text in German. Selective references only.

Clément
C. Clément, *Géricault. Etude biographique et critique avec le catalogue raisonné de l'œuvre du maître* (Didier, Paris, 1868 ed.).

Correspondance
A. Joubin (ed.), *Correspondance générale d'Eugène Delacroix* (Plon, Paris, 1935-8), 5 vols.

Correspondance (Burty 1878 [or 1880])
P. Burty (ed.), *Lettres de Eugène Delacroix* (Quantin, Paris, 1878); or revised and enlarged edition of the same (Charpentier, Paris, 1880), 2 vols. This abbreviation is used if one of these editions is cited alone; if one is cited immediately after a reference to the Joubin edition of the Correspondence, it is abbreviated simply as Burty ed. 1878 or Burty ed. 1880. References to Burty's editions of the Correspondence are given only if they contain a significant variation to Joubin's more complete edition, or supplementary information.

Delteil
L. Delteil, *Le Peintre-graveur illustré (XIXe et XXe siècles)*, vol. III, *Ingres et Delacroix* (Chez l'Auteur, Paris, 1908).

Dieterle R
Alfred Robaut's *catalogue raisonné* of Delacroix's work (see R for full title) annotated by Jean Dieterle. Contains valuable MS. notes on the history of pictures since 1885.

DNB
Dictionary of National Biography.

Escholier
R. Escholier, *Delacroix, peintre, graveur, écrivain* (Floury, Paris, 1926-9), 3 vols.

Escholier 1963
R. Escholier, *Eug. Delacroix* (Cercle d'Art, Paris, 1963). A drastically and inaccurately abridged version of Escholier, with colour plates of all paintings illustrated. Selective references only.

GBA
Gazette des Beaux-Arts.

Hourticq 1930
L. Hourticq, *Delacroix, l'Œuvre du maître* (Hachette, Paris, 1930).

Huyghe
R. Huyghe, *Delacroix*, translated from the French by Jonathan Griffin (Thames and Hudson, London, 1963. Published in France under the title *Delacroix ou le combat solitaire*, Paris, 1964).

Inv. Delacroix
H. Bessis, 'L'inventaire après décès d'Eugène Delacroix', *BSHAF* for 1969 (published 1971). A transcript, with notes, of the inventory of the contents of Delacroix's Paris apartment and studio and of his house at Champrosay, compiled in August and September 1863. As a rule, reference is made to this inventory, which is not an altogether reliable guide to either subject-matter or authorship, only when it adds significantly to the description of paintings listed in Delacroix's will and in the catalogue of his posthumous sale. Thus reference is made to the inventory in the case of a painting which is not specifically stated to be by Delacroix in his will but is attributed to him in the inventory.

Johnson 1963
L. Johnson, *Delacroix* (Weidenfeld and Nicolson, London, 1963).

Journal
A. Joubin (ed.), *Journal de Eugène Delacroix* (Plon, Paris, 1950 ed. [1st ed. 1932]), 3 vols.

Journal (1893-5 ed.)
P. Flat and R. Piot (eds.), *Journal de Eugène Delacroix* (Plon, Paris, 1893-5), 3 vols. References to this edition are cited only if they add something of historical significance to the Joubin edition.

JWCI
Journal of the Warburg and Courtauld Institutes.

Lettres intimes
A. Dupont (ed.), *Eugène Delacroix, Lettres intimes. Correspondance inédite* (Gallimard, Paris, 1954).

M see Mémorial

Maltese
C. Maltese, *Delacroix* (Club del Libro, Milan, 1965). Text in Italian.

Meier-Graefe 1922
J. Meier-Graefe, *Eugène Delacroix, Beiträge zu einer Analyse* (Piper, Munich, 1922 ed. [1st ed. 1913]).

Mémorial or *M*
M. Sérullaz, *Mémorial de l'Exposition Eugène Delacroix organisée au Musée du Louvre à l'occasion du centenaire de la mort de l'artiste* (Musées nationaux, Paris, 1963). See also abbreviations for exhibitions, under 'Louvre 1963'.

M-Nélaton Ann ED
Annotated catalogue of Delacroix's posthumous sale which belonged to Etienne Moreau-Nélaton. Cabinet des Estampes, Bibliothèque nationale, Paris.

M-Nélaton Doc.
Documents relating to Delacroix bequeathed by Etienne Moreau-Nélaton to the Louvre. Cabinet des Dessins, Louvre. See also 'Moreau N', which was part of this bequest.

M-Nélaton Port.
Etienne Moreau-Nélaton's portfolios of photographs and prints of works by Delacroix. Cabinet des Estampes, Bibliothèque nationale, Paris.

Moreau
A. Moreau, *E. Delacroix et son œuvre* (Librairie des Bibliophiles, Paris, 1873). Page references to Moreau are given alongside the Robaut number at the head of an entry only when they apply to the painting itself. References to prints of the painting are listed under Literature or Prints.

Moreau N
Adolphe Moreau, E. Delacroix et son œuvre — notes et correspondance. A bound volume of documents related to the preparation and publication of Moreau's book of 1873. Cabinet des Dessins, Louvre.

Moreau-Nélaton
E. Moreau-Nélaton, *Delacroix raconté par lui-même* (Laurens, Paris, 1916), 2 vols.

Œuvres litt
Eugène Delacroix, Œuvres littéraires (Crès, Paris, 1923), 2 vols.

Piron
[A. Piron], *Eugène Delacroix, sa vie et ses œuvres* (Claye, Paris, 1865). Published anonymously.

Planet *Souvenirs*
A. Joubin (ed.), *Louis de Planet, souvenirs de travaux de peinture avec M. Eugène Delacroix* (Colin, Paris, 1929).

R or Robaut
L'Œuvre complet de Eugène Delacroix, peintures, dessins, gravures, lithographies, catalogué et reproduit par Alfred Robaut, commenté par Ernest Chesneau (Charavay Frères, Paris, 1885).

R Ann
Robaut's personal copy of R, containing his annotations. Cabinet des Estampes, Bibliothèque nationale, Paris.

Robaut Tracings (Tracings alone when the context is clear)
Robaut's tracings and drawings of works by Delacroix, 5 vols. Cabinet des Estampes, Bibliothèque nationale, Paris.

Rudrauf

L. Rudrauf, *Eugène Delacroix et le problème du romantisme artistique* (Laurens, Paris, 1942). Occasional, selective references only. Contains an extensive bibliography.

Sérullaz *Dessins* 1952

M. Sérullaz, *Musée du Louvre, Les Dessins de Delacroix (1817–1827)* (Morancé, Paris, n.d. [1952]).

Sérullaz *Peintures murales*

M. Sérullaz, *Les Peintures murales de Delacroix* (Éditions du Temps, Paris, 1963).

Silvestre *Delacroix* (1855)

The list of works by Delacroix compiled by L. de Virmond and published in the first edition of Théophile Silvestre's *Histoire des artistes vivants, français et étrangers. Etudes d'après nature* (Blanchard, Paris, n.d. [1855]). Very incomplete, unreliable in chronology and not recording dimensions, this is nevertheless valuable in being the first catalogue of Delacroix's œuvre and the only one published during his lifetime.

T. Silvestre, *Les Artistes français*, 1855

The section on French artists from the *Histoire des artistes vivants*, reprinted in two volumes as *Les Artistes français* (Crès, Paris, 1926). Page references are to the 1926 edition only.

Silvestre *Documents nouveaux* (1864)

T. Silvestre, *Eugène Delacroix, Documents nouveaux* (Michel Lévy Frères, Paris, 1864). This is reprinted in vol. 1 of the 1926 edition of *Les Artistes français*. Page references are to the 1864 edition only.

Sterling-Adhémar

C. Sterling and H. Adhémar, *Musée national du Louvre, Peintures école française XIXe siècle* (Musées nationaux, Paris 1959), vol. II.

Thieme-Becker

U. Thieme and F. Becker, *Allgemeines Lexicon der Bildenden Künstler* (Engelmann—followed by Seemann, Leipzig, 1907–50), 37 vols.

Thoré Ann ED

Catalogue of Delacroix's posthumous sale, annotated by Théophile Thoré and with further annotations from Robaut's copy transcribed by L. Soulié. Library, Victoria and Albert Museum, London.

Tourneux

M. Tourneux, *Eugène Delacroix devant ses contemporains, ses écrits, ses biographes, ses critiques* (Rouam, Paris, 1886). A basic bibliographical study. Selective references only are given, since Tourneux often refers to works by Delacroix merely to list their appearance in exhibitions and sales or in books and articles which are here separately taken account of.

Trapp

F. Trapp, *The Attainment of Delacroix* (The Johns Hopkins Press, Baltimore and London, 1971).

EXHIBITIONS

The major posthumous exhibitions (over 100 paintings) are starred.

Agen–Grenoble–Nancy 1958
Romantiques et Réalistes au XIXe Siècle. May–December. (All works from the Louvre.)

Algérie, Paris 1930
Exposition du Centenaire de la Conquête de l'Algérie 1830–1930. Petit Palais, May–June.

Alsace-Lorraine, Paris 1874
Exposition au Profit des Alsaciens-Lorrain en Algérie. Palais Bourbon, 23 April.

Alsace-Lorraine, Paris 1885
Exposition au Profit de l'Œuvre des Orphelins d'Alsace-Lorraine. Salle des Etats, Louvre, June.

Amsterdam 1926
Exposition Rétrospective d'Art Français. 'Musée de l'Etat', 3 July–3 October. (Catalogue in French.)

Amsterdam 1938
Honderd Jaar Fransche Kunst. Stedelijk Museum, 2 July–25 September.

Amsterdam 1961
Polariteit. Stedelijk Museum, 22 July–18 September.

Arnhem 1936
Franse Schilderijen uit de 19e E. uit de Kröller-Müller Stichting. Gemeente Museum, April–June.

Art Musulman, Paris 1893
Exposition d'Art Musulman. Palais de l'Industrie.

Arts décoratifs, Paris 1930
Le Décor de la Vie à l'Epoque Romantique, 1820–1848. Musée des arts décoratifs, April–May.

Arts décoratifs, Paris 1934
Les artistes français en Italie de Poussin à Renoir. Musée des arts décoratifs, May–July.

Atelier Delacroix, Paris 1932
Eugène Delacroix et ses Amis. June–July. All the Atelier exhibitions listed here were held on the premises that Delacroix occupied at 6 place Furstenberg during his final years, either in his studio or, from 1937, in his adjoining apartment, or in both together. The newly restored studio and apartment were inaugurated as the Musée Delacroix in 1963.

Atelier Delacroix, Paris 1934
Exposition de Peintures et de Dessins d'Eugène Delacroix.

Atelier Delacroix, Paris 1935
I. Paysages de Delacroix et Lithographies . . . II. Exposition de la Collection Permanente . . .

Atelier Delacroix, Paris 1937A
Tableaux, Aquarelles, Dessins, Gravures, Lithographies . . .

Atelier Delacroix, Paris 1937B
Appartement de Delacroix. Exposition Temporaire.

Atelier Delacroix, Paris 1938
Appartement de Delacroix. Exposition Temporaire.

Atelier Delacroix, Paris 1939
Tableaux, Aquarelles, Dessins, Gravures, Lithographies . . .

Atelier Delacroix, Paris 1945
Chefs-d'œuvre de Delacroix. 31 July-1 October.

Atelier Delacroix, Paris 1946A
Chefs-d'œuvre de Delacroix. May-November.

Atelier Delacroix, Paris 1946B
Delacroix et son Temps (Gros-Géricault-Courbet). November.

Atelier Delacroix, Paris 1947
Delacroix et les Compagnons de sa Jeunesse. April . . .

Atelier Delacroix, Paris 1948
Delacroix et l'Angleterre.

Atelier Delacroix, Paris 1949
Delacroix et le Paysage romantique. May . . .

Atelier Delacroix, Paris 1950
Delacroix et le Portrait romantique. May . . .

Atelier Delacroix, Paris 1951
Delacroix et l'Orientalisme de son temps. 11 May.

Atelier Delacroix, Paris 1952
Delacroix et les Maîtres de la Couleur. 17 May.

Atelier Delacroix, Paris 1963
Delacroix, Citoyen de Paris. March-September.

Atelier Delacroix, Paris 1967
Eug. Delacroix, son Atelier et la Critique d'Art. June-August.

Atelier Delacroix, Paris 1968
Delacroix, René Piot (1866-1934) et la Couleur. 22 March-15 August. No Catalogue.

Atelier Delacroix, Paris 1969
Delacroix et son Temps (Costumes et Souvenirs). April-September. No catalogue.

Atelier Delacroix, Paris 1969-70
Delacroix et son Temps. Souvenirs. 19 December-April. No catalogue.

Atelier Delacroix, Paris 1970
Delacroix et l'Impressionnisme. April-September. No catalogue.

Atelier Delacroix, Paris 1971
Delacroix et le Fauvisme. 26 May-November. No catalogue.

Atelier Delacroix, Paris 1972
Delacroix et le Fantastique (De Goya à Redon). 10 May-November. No catalogue.

Atelier Delacroix, Paris 1973
Delacroix et la Peinture libérée. May-September. No catalogue.

Atelier Delacroix, Paris 1974
Delacroix et Paul Huet, précurreurs de l'Impressionnisme. 26 June-10 December. No catalogue.

Athens 1963
Exposition sur l'Insurrection Hellénique et le Philhellénisme français depuis le Directoire et jusqu'à 1830. Historical and Ethnological Museum, 10-30 May. No catalogue except article with this title in *Messager d'Athènes — Progrès,* 17 May.

Baltimore 1951
French Painting 1100-1900. Carnegie Institute, 18 October-2 December.

Baltimore 1954
Man and his Years. Baltimore Museum of Art, 19 October-21 November.

Baltimore 1968
From El Greco to Pollock. Baltimore Museum of Art.

Barye, New York 1889-90
Works of Antoine-Louis Barye [and paintings by other 19th-century French artists]. American Art Galleries, under the auspices of the Barye Monument Association, 15 November to 15 January.

Basle 1921
Exposition de Peinture française. Société des Beaux-Arts de Basle, 8-30 June.

Basle 1937
Kunstlerkopien. Kunsthalle, 18 September-17 October.

Basle 1939
Eugène Delacroix. Kunsthalle, 22 April-29 May.

Bd Italiens, Paris 1860
Tableaux de l'Ecole moderne tirés des Collections d'Amateurs et exposés au profit de la Caisse de Secours des Artistes . . . [catalogue entries by Philippe Burty]. 26, boulevard des Italiens, by early February, replenished May.

Bd Italiens, Paris 1861-2
Exposition de Peinture. 26 boulevard des Italiens. M. L. Martinet had provided a permanent exhibition gallery at this address in 1860; it became the official centre for the Société Nationale des Beaux-Arts when this was formally constituted on 7 May 1862. Catalogues were not usually issued, the periodical changes in the contents of the gallery being published in the *Courrier artistique.* This abbreviation denotes the period from the first number of the *Courrier,* 15 June 1861, to the last number to list additions of paintings

by Delacroix, 15 June 1862—under the heading *Société Nationale des Beaux-Arts. Première Exposition des Sociétaires Fondateurs.*

Bd Italiens, Paris 1864
*Œuvres d'Eugène Delacroix. Société Nationale des Beaux-Arts, 13 August.

Belgrade 1939
La Peinture Française au XIXᵉ Siècle. Muzej Kneza Paula. (The Catalogue is in French and Serbo-Croat. The second edition contains a supplement.)

Belgrade 1950
Izložba Radova Francuskih Slikara XIX. Veka. Umetnički Muzej, June.

Berne 1939–40
Sammlung Oskar Reinhart. Kunstmuseum.

Berne 1963–4
Eugène Delacroix. Kunstmuseum, 16 November–19 January.

Bernheim-Jeune, Paris 1936
100 Ans de Théâtre, Music-Hall et Cirque. Galerie Bernheim-Jeune, 25 May–13 July.

Bernheim-Jeune, Paris 1948
La Femme. Galerie Bernheim-Jeune, April–June.

Bernheim-Jeune, Paris 1952
Peintures de Portraits . . . au profit de la Société d'entr'aide des membres de la Légion d'Honneur. Galerie Bernheim-Jeune, 17 May–28 June.

Bib. nat., Paris 1951
Le Livre anglais, Trésors des Collections anglaises. Bibliothèque nationale.

Bib. nat., Paris 1957–8
Charles Baudelaire. 19 December–16 March.

Bordeaux 1960
L'Europe et la Découverte du Monde. Galerie des Beaux-Arts, May–September.

Bordeaux 1963
Delacroix, ses Maîtres, ses Amis, ses Elèves. Galerie des Beaux-Arts, 17 May–30 September.

Bordeaux 1964
La Femme et l'Artiste de Bellini à Picasso. Galerie des Beaux-Arts, 22 May–20 September.

Bourg-en-Bresse 1971
Le Style Troubadour, Musée de l'Ain, 26 June–4 October.

Bremen 1964
Eugène Delacroix. Kunsthalle, Bremen, 23 February–26 April. (The catalogue ran to two editions.)

Bristol 1950
Bristol–Bordeaux French Week. Exhibition of paintings from the Musée de Peinture and of life and work in Bordeaux. City Art Gallery, 13 February–11 March.

British Institution, Pall Mall, London 1828
A Catalogue of the Works of British Artists placed in the Gallery of The British Institution, Pall-Mall, for Exhibition and Sale. 1828.

Brooklyn 1921
Paintings by Modern French Masters, representing the Post Impressionists and their Predecessors. Brooklyn Museum, New York, April.

Brussels 1935
Exposition universelle internationale de 1889, à Paris. Beaux-Cinq Siècles d'Art. 24 May–13 October.

Brussels 1947–8
De David à Cézanne. Palais des Beaux-Arts, November–January.

Buenos Aires 1939
La Pintura francesa de David a nuestros dias. Museo nacional de Bellas Artes, July–August. (The catalogue ran to two editions. A separate album of illustrations.)

Cassirer, Berlin 1907
Eugène Delacroix. Gallery Paul Cassirer, 4 November–4 December.

Centennale, Paris 1889
Exposition universelle internationale de 1889, à Paris. Beaux-Arts, Exposition centennale de l'Art français (1789–1889).

Centennale, Paris 1900
Exposition internationale universelle de 1900. Exposition centennale de l'Art français 1800–1889.

Charpentier, Paris 1923
L'Art et la Vie romantique. Galerie Charpentier, February–March.

Charpentier, Paris 1926
L'Epoque Louis-Philippe. Galerie Charpentier.

Charpentier, Paris 1929
Cent Ans de Vie française. Galerie Charpentier.

Charpentier, Paris 1948
Chevaux et Cavaliers. Galerie Charpentier.

Charpentier, Paris 1950
Cent Portraits de Femmes. Galerie Charpentier.

Charpentier, Paris 1954
Plaisirs de la Campagne. Galerie Charpentier, 24 June–September.

Charpentier, Paris 1957
Cent Chefs-d'Œuvre de l'Art français 1750–1950. Galerie Charpentier, May.

Chicago 1930
Loan Exhibition of Paintings, Water Colours, Drawings and Prints by Eugène Delacroix. Art Institute, 20 March–20 April.

Chicago 1934
A Century of Progress. Exhibition of Paintings and Sculpture. Art Institute, 1 June–1 November.

Cleveland 1963
Style, Truth and the Portrait. Cleveland Museum of Art.

Copenhagen 1888
Illustreret katalog over udstillingen af franske kunstvaerker i Kjøbenhavn 1888.

Copenhagen 1914
Exposition d'Art Français du XIXᵉ Siècle. Royal Museum, 15 May–30 June.

Copenhagen 1928
Fransk Malerkunst fra den Første Halvdel af det 19. Aarhundrede. Ny Carlsberg Glyptotek, March–April. See also 'Copenhagen, Stockholm, Oslo 1928.' This shorter abbreviation is used to distinguish pictures that were shown in Copenhagen only, and did not proceed to the other cities.

Copenhagen 1945
Fransk Kunst. Maleri og Skulptur fra det 19. og 20. Aarhundrede. Ny Carlsberg Glyptotek, July–October.

Copenhagen 1957-8
Fransk Kunst. Statens Museum for Kunst.

Copenhagen, Stockholm, Oslo 1928
See 'Copenhagen 1928' for title and dates of Danish section. *Franskt Måleri från David till Courbet.* Nationalmuseum, Stockholm, May–June. *Fransk Malerkunst fra David til Courbet.* National Gallery, Oslo, July–August.

Daber, Paris 1956
Peinture et Impressionnisme de Géricault à Monet, Galerie Daber, 7 June–7 July.

Daber, Paris 1962
Peinture 1830-1940. Œuvres de Delacroix à Maillol. Galerie Daber, May.

Detroit 1950
French Painting from David to Courbet. Institute of Arts, 1 February–5 March.

Douai 1827
Salon de la Ville de Douai. 8 July–8 August.

Drouin, Paris 1943
Le Portrait français. Galerie René Drouin. June–July.

Durand-Ruel, New York 1887
National Academy of Design, 25 May. (No catalogue is known to me, but for the history and contents of the exhibition, see 'Mémoires de Paul Durand-Ruel' in L. Venturi, *Les Archives de l'Impressionnisme* (Durand-Ruel, Paris, New York, 1939), II, p. 218.)

Durand-Ruel, Paris 1878
Exposition rétrospective de Tableaux et Dessins des Maîtres modernes. Galeries Durand-Ruel.

Durand-Ruel, Paris 1938
Quelques Maîtres du 18ᵉ et du 19ᵉ Siècle. Galeries Durand-Ruel, May. For exhibitions by Durand-Ruel in London, see 'Society of French Artists'.

Düsseldorf 1928
Ausgewählte Kunstwerke aus der Sammlung der Frau H. Kröller-Müller, den Haag. Kunsthalle, August–September.

EBA, Paris 1883
Exposition de Portraits du Siècle (1783-1883) ouverte au Profit de l'Œuvre [Société Philanthropique]. Ecole nationale des Beaux-Arts, April–May.

EBA, Paris 1885
*Exposition Eugène Delacroix au profit de la souscription destinée à élever à Paris un monument à sa mémoire. Ecole nationale des Beaux-Arts, 6 March–15 April. (The catalogue ran to two editions. Two copies of the first edition annotated by Robaut are preserved in *Bib AA*, MS. 298 and 298ᵇⁱˢ, together with a copy of the second edition containing his notes and corrections, MS. 298ᵗᵉʳ.)

Edinburgh-London 1964
Delacroix. An Exhibition of Paintings, Drawings and Lithographs sponsored by the Edinburgh Festival Society and arranged by the Arts Council of Great Britain in Association with the Royal Scottish Academy. (Catalogue by Lee Johnson, Introduction by Lorenz Eitner.) Royal Scottish Academy, 15 August–13 September. Royal Academy of Arts, 1 October–8 November.

Essen 1954
Delacroix. Folkwang Museum.

Fogg 1955
Delacroix in New England Collections. Fogg Art Museum, Cambridge, Mass., 15 October–26 November.

Gal. Beaux-Arts, Paris 1844
Société des Artistes, Galerie des Beaux-Arts, bd Bonne-Nouvelle, January; refurbished in April. (I have not seen a catalogue of this exhibition. For the works by Delacroix shown, see *Bulletin de l'Ami des Arts*, official organ of the Gallery, II, pp. 42, 283.)

Gal. Beaux-Arts, Paris 1846A
Explication des Ouvrages de Peinture exposés dans la Galerie des Beaux-Arts, boulevard Bonne-Nouvelle, 22. Au profit de la caisse de secours et pensions de la Société des artistes . . . , 11 January. (Paintings by Delacroix appear only in the 'Suites du Supplément.')

Gal. Beaux-Arts, Paris 1846B
Ibid., 'Deuxième année', but now at 75 rue Saint-Lazare, 15 December.

Gal. Beaux-Arts, Paris 1848
Ibid., 'Troisième année', galeries Bonne-Nouvelle, January.

Gal. Beaux-Arts, Paris 1852
Ibid., 'Cinquième exposition'.

Gal. Lebrun, Paris 1826A
Explication des Ouvrages de Peinture exposés au profit des Grecs, Galerie Lebrun, rue du Gros-Chenet, n° 4, le 15 mai 1826.

Gal. Lebrun, Paris 1826B
The same exhibition, rearranged some weeks later and with a second catalogue dated 1826, without day and month.

Gal. Lebrun, Paris 1829
Explication des Ouvrages de Peinture et de Sculpture exposés au profit de la caisse ouverte pour l'extinction de la mendicité. Galerie Lebrun.

Geneva 1918
Exposition d'Art français. Musée d'art et d'histoire, 15 May-16 June.

Géricault, Paris 1924
Exposition d'Œuvres de Géricault au profit de la Société 'La Sauvegarde de l'Art français'. Galerie Charpentier, 24 April-16 May.

Ghent 1970
Chefs-d'œuvre du Musée des Beaux-Arts de Bordeaux. Musée des Beaux-Arts, 17 April-14 June.

Gobin, Paris 1937
Peintures, Aquarelles et Dessins par Eugène Delacroix. Maurice Gobin, 1 rue Laffitte, 26 November-18 December.

Hanover 1949
Französische Malerei im 19. Jahrhundert. Kestner-Gesellschaft, 31 August-23 October.

Hartford 1942
Night Scenes. Wadsworth Atheneum, 15 February-7 March.

Hartford 1952
The Romantic Circle. Wadsworth Atheneum, 15 October-30 November.

Hartford 110, 1952
110 Years. Wadsworth Atheneum, 17 April-1 June.

Hobday's Gallery, London 1928
Works of British and French Artists composing Mr. Hobday's Gallery of Modern Art, 53 Pall Mall. Tourneux (p. 105) records a catalogue of this title dated 1828, of which it has proved impossible to trace a copy. Open by 7 June. (Not to be confused, as Tourneux confuses it, with the British Gallery, which is where the British Institution held its exhibitions in Pall Mall.)

Knoedler, New York 1953
Paintings and Drawings from the Smith College Collection. Knoedler Galleries, 30 March-11 April.

Knoedler, New York and Chicago 1938-9
Gros, Géricault, Delacroix. Knoedler Galleries, New York, 21 November-10 December. Art Institute, Chicago, December-January.

Kyoto-Tokyo 1969
Eugène Delacroix. Municipal Museum, Kyoto, 10 May-8 June. National Museum, Tokyo, 14 June-3 August. Catalogue in Japanese with parallel French titles.

Lefevre, London 1954
French Paintings, XIX and XX Century. Lefevre Gallery, February.

Lefevre, London 1974
XIX and XX Century Paintings and Drawings. Lefevre Gallery, 21 November-20 December.

Liège 1955
Le Romantisme au Pays de Liège. Musée des Beaux-Arts, 10 September-31 October.

Liverpool 1968
Gifts to Galleries: an Exhibition of Works of Art acquired with the Aid of the National Art-Collections Fund for Galleries outside London. Walker Art Gallery.

London 1871
International Exhibition of 1871. (Official Catalogue, Fine Arts Department.)

London 1936
Masters of French 19th Century Painting. New Burlington Galleries, 1-31 October.

London 1942
Nineteenth Century French Paintings. National Gallery.

London 1959
The Romantic Movement. Fifth Exhibition to Celebrate the Tenth Anniversary of the Council of Europe. Tate Gallery, 10 July-27 September.

London 1974
Byron. An exhibition to commemorate the 150th anniversary of his death. Victoria and Albert Museum, 30 May-25 August.

London 1975
Treasures from the Burrell Collection. Hayward Gallery, 18 March-4 May.

Louvre 1930
*Eugène Delacroix. Centenaire du Romantisme. Musée du Louvre, June-July. (There was a provisional and a definitive catalogue, and a companion *Album* of illustrations.)

Louvre 1945A
Musées Nationaux, Nouvelles Acquisitions, 2 Septembre 1939-2 Septembre 1945. Musée du Louvre.

Louvre 1945B
Musée du Louvre. Chefs d'œuvre de la Peinture. Musée du Louvre. (A supplement to the catalogue was published in July.)

Louvre 1963
*Eugène Delacroix. Exposition du Centenaire. Musée du Louvre, May–September. (There was a summary 'Catalogue de visite' followed, after the closure, by a fully documented catalogue, compiled by Maurice Sérullaz and his associates, entitled *Mémorial de l'Exposition Eugène Delacroix organisée au Musée du Louvre à l'occasion du Centenaire de la Mort de l'Artiste.* When the number of a picture coincides in both catalogues, I list a single number; when it does not, I list the number from the 'Catalogue de visite' first, followed by *M* no. —, indicating the number of the same painting in the *Mémorial*. 'Repr.' means a picture is illustrated in the *Mémorial* only; '2 repr.', in both catalogues.)

Louvre, *Dessins* 1963
Delacroix Dessins. XXXe Exposition du Cabinet des Dessins. Musée du Louvre.

Lucerne 1940
Die Hauptwerke der Sammlung Hahnloser, Winterthur. Kunstmuseum.

Luxembourg, Paris 1830
Explication des ouvrages de peinture [. . .] exposés dans la galerie de la Chambre des Pairs au profit des blessés des 27, 28 et 29 juillet 1830. Palais du Luxembourg, 14 October. (There were no less than five supplements to the catalogue.)

Marseille 1975
L'Orient en Question 1825–1875. Musée Cantini.

Montauban 1967
Ingres et son temps. Musée Ingres, 24 June–15 September.

Montreal 1967
Man and his World. International Arts Exhibition Expo 67 Montreal Canada. 28 April–27 October.

Moscow 1969
Le Romantisme dans la Peinture française. Exposition des œuvres appartenant aux musées de France. (Catalogue in Russian, but this title also printed in French.)

Moscow-Leningrad 1956
Peinture française du XIX Siècle. Pushkin Museum, Moscow. The Hermitage, Leningrad. (Catalogue in Russian, but this title also printed in French.)

Moscow-Leningrad 1965
Chefs-d'œuvre des Musées de France. Pushkin Museum. The Hermitage.

Moulins 1836
Société centrale des Amis des Arts en Province. Exposition de 1836.

Munich 1964–5
Französische Malerei des 19. Jahrhunderts von David bis Cézanne. Haus der Kunst, 7 October–6 January.

Munich 1972
Weltkulturen und Moderne Kunst, Haus der Kunst, 15 June–20 September. (A shortened version of the German catalogue was published in English.)

Musée Colbert, Paris 1829A
Catalogue des Tableaux et Objets d'art exposés dans le Musée Colbert. November.

Musée Colbert, Paris 1829B
Ibid., 2nd Exhibition. December.

Musée Colbert, Paris 1830A
Ibid., 3rd Exhibition. February.

Musée Colbert, Paris 1830B
Ibid., 4th Exhibition. May.

Musée Colbert, Paris 1832
Explication des ouvrages de peinture [. . .] exposés à la galerie du Musée Colbert, le 6 mai 1832, par MM. les artistes, au profit des indigents [. . .] de Paris, atteints de la maladie épidémique.

Musée Galliera, Paris 1946
Peintures méconnues des Eglises de Paris. Retour d'évacuation. May–June.

New Orleans 1953–4
Masterpieces of Art: European and American Paintings, Delgado Museum of Art, 17 October–10 January.

New York 1893
Loan Exhibition. Building of the American Fine Arts Society, February.

New York 1939
Five Centuries of History Mirrored in Five Centuries of French Art. Pavillon de la France, World's Fair. (See also the next entry for a different exhibition at the World's Fair.)

New York 1940
Masterpieces of Art: European and American Paintings, 1500–1900. World's Fair, May–October.

New York 1941
French Painting from David to Toulouse-Lautrec. Metropolitan Museum of Art, 6 February–26 March.

Nice 1930
Eugène Delacroix [Collection Baron Joseph Vitta]. Palais des Arts, 20 March–20 April.

Orangerie, Paris 1933A
Voyage de Delacroix au Maroc, 1832, et Exposition Rétrospective du Peintre Orientaliste Mr Auguste. Musée de l'Orangerie. (Catalogue by Charles Sterling.)

Orangerie, Paris 1933B
Les Achats du Musée du Louvre et les Dons de la Société des Amis du Louvre, 1922-1932.

Orangerie, Paris 1941
Donation Paul Jamot. April-May.

Orangerie, Paris 1947
Cinquantenaire des 'Amis du Louvre.'

Orangerie, Paris 1951
Impressionnistes et Romantiques français dans les Musées allemands.

Orangerie, Paris 1952
La Nature morte de l'Antiquité à nos Jours. April-June. (Catalogue by Charles Sterling.)

Orangerie, Paris 1955
De David à Toulouse-Lautrec. Chefs-d'Œuvre des Collections américaines.

Orangerie, Paris 1956
Le Cabinet de l'Amateur. February-April.

Oslo 1928
See 'Copenhagen, Stockholm, Oslo 1928'. This shorter abbreviation is used to distinguish a picture that was shown in Oslo only, and not in the other two cities.

Oslo 1946
Fransk Utstilling. Kunstnernes Hus, 9 November-1 December.

Paris 1886
Maîtres du Siècle. Former studio of Gustave Doré, 3 rue Bayard, April-May.

Paris 1922
Cent Ans de Peinture française. Exposition au Profit du Musée des Beaux-Arts de Strasbourg. 18, rue de la Ville-l'Evêque.

Paris 1926
Exposition des Maîtres et des Petits Maîtres du 19ème Siècle. Galerie Siot-Decauville, 26 January-27 February.

Paris 1927
La Jeunesse des Romantiques. Maison de Victor Hugo, 18 May-30 June.

Paris 1937
Chefs-d'Œuvre de l'Art français. Palais National des Arts. (Catalogue with separate album of illustrations.)

Paris 1948
La Révolution de 1848. Bibliothèque nationale.

Paris 1961
Œuvres des Collections françaises. Musée Jacquemart-André, July-October. (No catalogue, but a special issue of *Arts* listed, with numbers, all the works shown.)

Paris 1966-7
Bonington, un Romantique anglais à Paris. Musée Jacquemart-André.

Paris 1972
Centaures, Chevaux et Cavaliers. Musée Bourdelle, June-September.

Paris and Berne 1939
Les Chefs-d'Œuvre du Musée de Montpellier. Musée de l'Orangerie, March-April. Kunsthalle, 15 June-15 August. (Separate catalogues.)

Paris, Detroit, New York 1974-5
De David à Delacroix. La Peinture française de 1774 à 1830. Grand Palais, 16 November-3 February. *French Painting 1774-1830: The Age of Revolution.* Detroit Institute of Arts, 5 March-4 May; Metropolitan Museum of Art, New York, 12 June-7 September 1975. (The numbering corresponds in the French and English language editions of the catalogue. The three paintings by Delacroix exhibited are illustrated in both editions.)

Petit, Paris 1884
Une Collection particulière [*Mme de Cassin*]. *Exposition de la Société Philanthropique.* Galerie Georges Petit, 1 October-10 December.

Petit, Paris 1892
Cent Chefs-d'Œuvre des Ecoles française et étrangères (*Deuxième Exposition*). Galerie Georges Petit, 8 June.

Petit, Paris 1910
Chefs-d'Œuvre de l'Ecole française. Galerie Georges Petit, 2-31 May.

Petit Palais, Paris 1925
Exposition du Paysage français de Poussin à Corot. May-June.

Petit Palais, Paris 1936
Gros, ses Amis, ses Elèves. May-July. (As well as two editions of the catalogue, one with a supplement, there is an album of plates with an introduction by Raymond Escholier.)

Petit Palais, Paris 1946
Chefs-d'Œuvre de la Peinture française du Louvre.

Petit Palais, Paris 1968-9
Baudelaire. 23 November-17 March.

Philadelphia 1893
Loan Exhibition by the Union League of Philadelphia of Paintings by Eminent Artists belonging to a few Citizens of Philadelphia. 11-27 May.

Philadelphia 1937
French Artists of the 18th and 19th Centuries. Pennsylvania Museum of Art, 20 March-18 April. (This exhibition, without catalogue, marked the opening at the Museum of ten rooms of French painting in its permanent collection and included some private loans.)

Philadelphia 1958
French Painting. An exhibition sponsored by the Alliance française of Philadelphia. Jane Harper Galleries. (No catalogue; cyclostyled handlist only.)

Philadelphia 1968
Summer Loan Exhibition, Philadelphia Museum of Art, ended 15 September. (No catalogue traced.)

Pittsburgh 1951
French Painting 1100–1900. Carnegie Institute, 18 October– 2 December.

Portraits, *EBA*, Paris 1885
Deuxième Exposition de Portraits du Siècle. Ecole Nationale des Beaux-Arts, 20 April. (For benefit of the Societé Philanthropique—see *EBA*, Paris 1883.)

Portraits, Philadelphia 1937
Problems of Portraiture. Pennsylvania Museum of Art, 16 October–28 November.

Providence 1975
Rubenism. An Exhibition by the Department of Art, Brown University and the Museum of Art, Rhode Island School of Design. Brown University, 30 January–23 February.

R.A. London 1896
Exhibition of Works by the Old Masters and by deceased Masters of the British School, with a Selection of Works by deceased French Artists. Royal Academy of Arts, 6 January– 14 March.

R.A. London 1932
Exhibition of French Art, 1200–1900. 4 January–5 March. (In addition to the catalogue, there was an illustrated 'Souvenir' with plates and introduction only.)

R.A. London 1949–50
Landscape in French Art, 1550–1900. 10 December– 5 March.

Richmond, Virginia 1947
Portrait Panorama. An Exhibition of Portraits by Artists of Six Centuries. Virginia Museum of Fine Arts, 10 September– 12 October.

Rome–Florence 1955
Mostra di Capolavori della Pittura francesa dell' Ottocento. Palazzo delle Esposizioni, Rome. Palazzo Strozzi, Florence.

Rome–Milan 1962
Il Ritratto francese da Clouet a Degas. Palazzo Venezia, Rome.

Rosenberg, Paris 1928
Delacroix. Galerie Paul Rosenberg, 16 January– 18 February.

Rotterdam 1935
Franse Schilderijen uit de 19e E. benevens Jongkind, Vincent van Gogh. Museum Boymans, December–January.

St. Petersburg 1912
Exposition centennale de l' Art français. French Institute.

Salle Ren., Paris 1929
Œuvres des 19ᵉ et 20ᵉ Siècles. Salle de la Renaissance, 11 rue Royale, 15–29 January.

San Francisco 1939
French Romantic Artists. An Exhibition of Paintings, Drawings and Watercolours by Gros, Géricault, Delacroix. Museum of Art, 19 April–14 May.

San Francisco 1940–2
The Painting of France since the French Revolution. M. H. de Young Memorial Museum, December 1940–January 1941 (1st showing); November 1941–January 1942 (2nd showing).

San Francisco 1962
The Henry P. McIlhenny Collection. California Palace of the Legion of Honour, 15 June–31 July.

Schaffhausen 1963
Die Welt des Impressionismus. Museum zu Allerheiligen.

Schmit, Paris 1972
Les Impressionnistes et leurs Précurseurs. Galerie Schmit, 17 May–17 June.

Soc. Amis des Arts, Bordeaux 1851
Explication des Ouvrages de Peinture . . . des artistes vivants, exposés dans la Galerie de la Société des Amis des Arts de Bordeaux. 15 November. (1st exhibition.)

Soc. Amis des Arts, Bordeaux 1855
The same, 6th exhibition, 30 December.

Soc. Amis des Arts, Bordeaux 1864
The same, 20 March.

Soc. Amis des Arts, Bordeaux 1869
The same, 18th exhibition, 20 March.

Soc. Amis des Arts, Paris 1825
Société des Amis des Arts [de Paris], Exposition de Tableaux, Dessins . . . acquis par la Société dans le cours de l'année, et devant former les lots destinés aux actionnaires de 1825. (Dated Paris, 1826.)

Society of French Artists 1, London 1870–1
1st of a series of exhibitions held by Durand-Ruel in his London gallery, 17 December; rearranged February 1871.

Society of French Artists 4, London 1872
4th exhibition, April–June.

Society of French Artists 6, London 1873
6th exhibition, April–June.

Springfield, Mass. 1939
The Romantic Revolution. Museum of Fine Arts, 7 February– 5 March.

Stockholm 1958
Fem Sekler Fransk Konst. Nationalmuseum, 15 August–9 November.

Tokyo, Fukuoka, Kyoto 1954–5
Catalogue de l'Exposition d'Art français au Japon. (Catalogue in French.)

Toledo-Toronto 1946–7
The Spirit of Modern France, 1745–1946. Museum of Art, Toledo, Ohio, November–December; Art Gallery of Toronto, January–February.

Tooth, London 1949
Anthology. French Pictures from Private Collections. Tooth Gallery, 8–28 June.

Toronto-Ottawa 1962–3
Delacroix. Art Gallery of Toronto, 1 December–7 January; National Gallery of Canada, 12 January–9 February. (Catalogue by Lee Johnson.)

Universelle, Paris 1855
Exposition universelle: Ouvrages de Peinture . . . des Artistes vivants, étrangers et français. Palais des Beaux-Arts, 15 May.

Universelle, Paris 1878
Exposition universelle: Notice historique et analytique des Peintures . . . exposé[e]s dans les Galeries des Portraits historiques au Palais du Trocadéro (by Henri Jouin, Paris 1879).

Venice 1956
XXVIII Biennale di Venezia. Ala Napoleonica, June–September. (In addition to the section devoted to Delacroix in the general catalogue of the Biennale, there is a booklet by Giuseppe Marchiori. Entitled *Delacroix alla Biennale,* it contains a list of the works shown and colour plates of six of the paintings.)

Warsaw 1956
Peinture française de David à Cézanne. National Museum, 15 June–31 July. (Catalogue in Polish, but this title also printed in French.)

Washington 1945
Eugène Delacroix. A Loan Exhibition. Phillips Memorial Gallery, Washington, D.C., 14 January–26 February.

Wildenstein, London 1952
Eugène Delacroix. Wildenstein Gallery, June–July.

Wildenstein, London 1960
Paintings and Drawings by Continental Masters, XVIth-XXth Centuries. 8 June–29 July.

Wildenstein, New York 1943
The French Revolution. A Loan Exhibition. Wildenstein Gallery, December.

Wildenstein, New York 1944
Eugène Delacroix. 18 October–18 November.

Wildenstein, New York 1945
The Child through the Centuries. 1–28 March.

Wildenstein, Paris 1936
La Collection Oscar Schmitz. Chefs-d'Œuvre de la Peinture française du XIXᵉ Siècle. Galerie Wildenstein.

Winnipeg 1954
Pre-Impressionist French Painters of the 19th Century. Winnipeg Art Gallery, 10 April–9 May.

Winterthur 1922
Meisterwerken aus Privatsammlungen. Kunstmuseum, 20 August–8 October.

Winterthur 1947
Grosse Maler des 19. Jahrhunderts aus den Münchner Museen. Kunstmuseum, 17 August–16 November.

Winterthur 1955
Europäische Meister 1790–1910. Kunstmuseum.

Zurich 1917
Französische Kunst des XIX und XX Jahrhunderts. Kunsthaus, 5–14 November.

Zurich 1939
Eugène Delacroix. Kunsthaus, 28 January–5 April.

Zurich 1943
Ausländische Kunst in Zürich. Kunsthaus, 25 July–26 September.

Zurich 1950
Ausstellung Europäische Kunst 13.–20. Jahrhundert aus Zürcher Sammlungen. Kunsthaus, 6 June–13 August.

Zurich 1958
Sammlung Emil G. Bührle. Festschrift zu Ehren von Emil G. Bührle zur Eröffnung des Kunsthaus-Neubaus und Katalog des Sammlung Emil G. Bührle. Kunsthaus (Inaugural Exhibition of the Bührle Foundation).

Zurich 1965
Auswahl von Werken aus dem Kunstbesitz der Vereinigung Zürcher Kunstfreunde. Kunsthaus, 16 October–12 November.

THE CATALOGUE

Academy Figures, Nudes

1 MALE ACADEMY FIGURE: Pl. 1
HALF-LENGTH, SIDE VIEW

Paper laid down on canvas: $15\frac{3}{4} \times 13\frac{3}{8}$ in. $(40 \times 34$ cm)* E.D.
Part of R1470 (1820. No repr.)
1818/20?
H. E. Lombardet, Lausanne

Provenance: Delacroix's posthumous sale, Feb. 1864, part of lot 200 ('Dix-sept études et académies', without dimensions); H. Vever?; with A. Vullier, Paris; bought from him by M. Mercier of Lausanne, Feb. 1897; by inheritance from him to the present owner, by 1963.[1]

Exhibition: Berne 1963–4, no. 1.

Literature: None, other than Robaut.

Although the history of this picture is obscure between 1864 and 1897, I can see no reason to doubt that it passed in the posthumous sale in the former year as part of lot 200: it bears the seal of the sale on the back of the canvas and it seems consistent in style and handling with J2, which has a clearer history. I am unable to determine who the buyer was at the posthumous sale (for a list of prices and buyers that cannot be attached to known works from lot 200, see J(L)10).

In the catalogue of the exhibition Berne 1963–4, this study is wrongly identified with R15, which passed in the Belly sale in 1878 where it was described as a 'Diable' (see J(M)1).

[1] The provenance from Vever down is given in a letter of 2 August 1963 from M. Lombardet to M. Maurice Sérullaz, who kindly showed it to me. According to this letter, the picture was claimed, when M. Mercier bought it, to have come from the sale of the Vever collection. That sale took place on 1 February 1897, but no work by Delacroix is listed in the catalogue. It is possible that the picture passed in the sale *hors catalogue* or was purchased privately before the public auction.

2 MALE ACADEMY FIGURE: Pl. 1
HALF-LENGTH, BACK VIEW

Paper laid down on canvas: $18\frac{1}{8} \times 14\frac{3}{4}$ in. $(46 \times 37.5$ cm)*
  E.D.
Part of R1470 (1820. No repr.)
1818/20?
The late Jean Dieterle, Paris

Provenance: Delacroix's posthumous sale, Feb. 1864, part of lot 200 ('Dix-sept études et académies', without dimensions), to Jules Dieterle, 200 fr. (Burty Ann ED);[1] Charles Dieterle, his son; sale his estate ('Succession de M. D . . .'), 10 Feb. 1936, lot 81 (repr.), to Jean Dieterle, d. Jan. 1972.

Exhibitions: None.

Literature: None, other than Robaut.

[1] Before finding this unpublished documentary evidence that an academy study from lot 200 was bought by Dieterle for 200 fr., I had been told by Jean Dieterle in 1966 that his grandfather bought this picture at the posthumous sale.

3 ACADEMY FIGURE: 'A BLIND   Pl. 2
MAN'

$35\frac{1}{16} \times 22\frac{5}{16}$ in. $(89 \times 56.7$ cm); enlarged from $31\frac{1}{4} \times 20\frac{11}{16}$ in.
  $(79.3$(maximum)$\times 52.5$ cm)*[1] Relined
Moreau p. 316. R171 (1826)
1819/20
The late Vicomtesse de Noailles, Paris

Provenance: Probably Delacroix's posthumous sale, Feb. 1864, part of lot 200 ('Dix-sept études et académies', without dimensions); Luquet, by 1864; Marquis du Lau; his sale, 5 May 1869, lot 10 ('Figure d'aveugle', 87×56 cm, and stated to be from Delacroix's posthumous sale), to F. Bischoffsheim, 2,085 fr.; by descent to Marie Laure, Vicomtesse de Noailles, d. 29 Jan. 1970, his granddaughter.

Exhibitions: *Bd Italiens*, Paris 1864, no. 110 ('L'Aveugle', 81×54 cm); *Centennale*, Paris 1889, no. 256 ('Aveugle mendiant;—étude', without dimensions); Atelier Delacroix, Paris 1938, no. 16 ('L'Aveugle de Jéricho'), repr. frontispiece; Louvre 1963, no. 41, *M* no. 24 ('L'Aveugle de Jéricho'), repr.

Literature: Inv. Delacroix, no. 50.

Moreau, followed by Robaut and the cataloguers of the two exhibitions in which it has been shown during this century, identified this picture as lot 111, 'L'Aveugle de Jéricho', from Delacroix's posthumous sale. The dimensions of that lot are, however, given in the sale catalogue as 45×38 cm and it is listed under 'Tableaux inachevés'. This picture can never have been that small, nor is there any reason to think that it was unfinished at the time of the sale. Lot 111, which was knocked down to Dauzats, appears, then, to have been another picture—possibly a narrative painting that passed under the title 'Aveugle de Jéricho', 48×40 cm, in a sale at the Galerie Charpentier on 16 June 1953 (lot 26, repr.). Inv. Delacroix confirms the existence of a study of a blind man, in addition to an unfinished picture of a Christ healing a blind man, in the artist's studio at the time of his death: no. 50, '1 étude: *L'aveugle*, par M. Delacroix, 10 fr.'; no. 253, '1 ébauche représentant *le Christ guérissant un aveugle* par Delacroix, 5 fr.'

Our picture, though intended perhaps, in view of the costume, to be associated with the blind man of Jericho of the New Testament, is essentially an academy study of a model posing as a blind man, and is most likely to have been one of the academy studies which comprised lot 200 at the posthumous sale. Luquet, who lent the picture to the exhibition in the boulevard des Italiens within six months of the sale, is not, however, recorded as the buyer of any of the items in lot 200, and I am unable to determine who the buyer was if it did form part of that lot (for a list of prices and buyers that cannot be attached to known works, see J(L)10).

Robaut places this study in 1826, but the date of 'peut être . . . vers 1820–1821' proposed without argument in *Mémorial* (1963) is clearly more acceptable on stylistic grounds. While not wishing to be too categorical, I favour a date of 1819/20, on the basis of analogies with drawings datable to that period, the closest being a study in black and white chalks, possibly of the same model, with a very similar treatment of the corded muscles and prominent ribs, contained in a sketch-book that was in use in 1819–20 (Louvre, RF23359, fol. 31ᵛ). That drawing appears a few pages before a study (fol. 37ʳ) for the *Virgin of the Sacred Heart* (J153), for which Delacroix received the commision in July 1820. The pose of the arms in this painting of a blind man also finds a close parallel in a preliminary drawing for the Infant Jesus (repr. *Mémorial*, no. 5) in the *Virgin of the Harvest* of 1819 (J151). Our study may also be contemporary with a drawing after Poussin's painting *Blind Men of Jericho* (Louvre), where Delacroix copies the upper half of the blind man in profile in the centre and the healing hand of Christ on his head, into a sketch-book that was at least partly in use in 1820 (Louvre, RF9153, fol. 48ᵛ).

Finally, there is a close analogy between this academy figure—in physical type, colouring, method of modelling flesh, even in head-dress—and the figure seated on the far left in one of the composition sketches in oils for Géricault's *Raft of the Medusa* (Louvre, Salon 1819). The sketch is also in the Louvre, RF1667; large colour repr. in. F. Haskell, *Géricault* ('The Masters' 47, 1966), pl. VI; black-and-white in L. Eitner, *Géricault's 'Raft of the Medusa'* (Phaidon, London, 1972), pl. 21.

¹ Strips of canvas 4.2 cm wide have been added along the bottom and right edges, and a strip varying from 5.5 cm on the left to 6.2 cm on the right has been joined to the top. These additions were evidently made between 1864, when the dimensions were listed as 81 × 54 cm in the Cat. Exh. *Bd Italiens*, and 1869, when they were given as 87 × 56 cm in the catalogue of the Marquis du Lau sale.

4 FEMALE ACADEMY FIGURE,   Pl. 4
PROBABLY Mlle ROSE: SEATED, FRONT VIEW

32 × 25⅝ in. (81.3 × 65.1 cm.)* Relined. Transferred E.D.¹
R83 (1823)

c. 1820
Bruno Pagliai, Mexico City

Provenance: Delacroix's posthumous sale, Feb. 1864, part of lot 200 ('Dix-sept études et académies', without dimensions), to Théophile Thoré (Robaut Tracings I), 420 fr. (Burty Ann ED); Paul Lacroix; Maurice Du Seigneur, d. Feb. 1892 (R Ann); F. Vieussa, by 1893 (R Ann); with Georges Bernheim, *c.* 1925; Dr. Georges Viau, Nov. 1926;² sale his estate, 11 Dec. 1942, lot 98 (repr. The picture was not auctioned, being in the U.S.A. at the time of the sale); 3rd sale estate Georges Viau, 22 June 1948, lot 4 (repr.), to Bader of New York, 1,750,000 fr.; Count Philippe de la Rochefoucauld, Château de Beaumont, nr. Montmirail; his sale, New York 19 May 1951, lot 56 (repr.), to Nicholas Acquavella for the present owner.

Exhibitions: Paris 1927, no. 266; Louvre 1930, no. 22; Petit Palais, Paris 1936, no. 231; Atelier Delacroix, Paris 1937B, no. 7; New York 1939, no. 347; Wildenstein, New York 1944, no. 2, repr.

Literature: W. Burger (pseudonym of Théophile Thoré), 'Eugène Delacroix. Exposition de ses œuvres à Paris', *L'Indépendance belge*, 28 Aug. 1864 (article reprinted by Maurice Du Seigneur in *Journal des Arts*, 19 and 30 Dec. 1890); Escholier I. 76, 287, repr. in colour opp. p. 76; Hourticq 1930, pl. 6; *Correspondance* I. 67 n. 2; W. Pach (trans.), *The Journal of Eugène Delacroix* (Covici, Friede, Inc., New York, 1937), bad colour repr., opp. p. 66 (same repr. in Jonathan Cape ed., London, 1938, opp. p. 66 & Crown ed., New York, 1948, opp. p. 64); W. Pach, 'Delacroix Speaks for Himself', *Art News*, XLIII (1944), repr. p. 10; J. Lassaigne, *Eugène Delacroix* (Longmans, Green & Co., London, New York, Toronto, 1950), pl. 9; G. Bazin, *Trésors de la peinture au Louvre* (Somogy, Paris, n.d. (1957)), p. 258; R. Huyghe, 'Delacroix and Baudelaire', *Romantic Art* (*Arts Yearbook* 2, New York, 1958), repr. p. 34; *Mémorial*, mentioned under no. 25; M. Gauthier, *Delacroix* (Oldbourne Press, London, 1964), pl. XIII; Maltese, p. 144, mentioned under no. 4.

This painting, called simply 'Académie de femme' by Robaut, was first stated to represent the model known as Mlle Rose in the catalogue of the exhibition Louvre 1930, and that identification has been widely accepted ever since. Dates ranging from *c.* 1820 (exh. Atelier Delacroix, Paris 1937B) to 1825 have been proposed. Escholier dated it to 1822 and Huyghe, to *c.* 1824; it was assigned to 1823/5 in the catalogue of the exhibition Petit Palais, Paris 1936, revised to *c.* 1821 in the *Errata and Addenda* in the second edition of the catalogue (p. 341). But no arguments have been advanced either in support of the model's identity or of the dates.

Comparison of the model with two drawings by other artists which certainly represent Rose makes it probable that this is indeed a painting of Rose. An academy drawing by Bonington, showing Rose in the nude from the back, seated, is inscribed lower right in the artist's hand: 'Rose April 30th 1820' (private collection; repr. Escholier I. 89). Though little can be seen of the face, the elaborate *coiffure* appears to be identical to that worn by the model in our picture, and the heavy proportions below the waist are also similar. An unpublished drawing of Rose standing in the nude, seen from the front, and inscribed 'rose' near her left foot is contained in a sketch-book filled by an unknown artist with drawings of Parisian models *c.* 1820 (private collection; Fig. 4). Here the head is in the same position as in our painting, and the hair-style, physiognomy and proportions of the body make it reasonable to suppose that it is the same woman.

Fig. 4. *Mlle Rose*, anonymous.

As for the date, the hair-style is as in the Bonington drawing which is dated 1820 and would in any case most likely not be found earlier than 1819 or later than 1821. A date of 1820 is also consistent with the presumed date of the only known reference in Delacroix's writings to Mlle Rose's posing for him: Delacroix wrote an undated note to Pierret inviting him to come and work with him the next day, adding: 'J'aurai modèle depuis 7 heures du matin rue de Sèvres, n° 11. Tu diras au portier que tu vas chez le jeune homme qui travaille à l'atelier de M. Monvoisin. [. . .] J'avais tâché de déterminer Félix [Guillemardet—law student] à venir nous tenir compagnie demain mais il m'a dit que le *régime dotal* l'emporterait sur le fessier de Mlle Rose pour cette fois.' (*Correspondance* I. 66 f.; Burty ed. 1878, p. 69; 1880, I. 94.) Although Burty had dated this note *c.* 1823 without argument (which may have been the reason why Robaut dated the painting to 1823), Joubin proposed a date of 1820 on the ground that in that year Monvoisin won a three-year scholarship in the competition for the Prix de Rome and Delacroix would not be working in his studio after he had left for Rome. Neither opinion is conclusive, but Joubin's date is more convincing: it seems very possible, for example, that Delacroix's attempt to bring Guillemardet and Pierret together for a session with Mlle Rose is the direct outcome of a desire he expressed in a letter to Guillemardet dated 20 October 1820: 'Ce que je désire beaucoup, c'est de le [Pierret] voir travailler et s'appliquer à la peinture.' (*Lettres intimes*, p. 119.)

The advanced colourism is, admittedly, hard to reconcile with a date as early as 1820; the legs, for instance, are rich in rainbow hues, recalling Delacroix's later remarks, as reported by George Sand, on a nude child by Rubens: 'C'est de l'arc en ciel fondu sur la chair.' On the other hand, parts of the figure, the upraised arm especially, are darker and tonally modelled, suggesting that the artist is still feeling his way experimentally, clinging to academic conventions in some parts, leaping forward precociously into the future in others, perhaps to revert to less daring exercises soon afterwards. Thoré's comments of 1864 on this picture, which have passed without comment by Delacroix scholars, are of the utmost interest in this connection:

Lorsqu'il était à l'atelier de Guérin, Delacroix a peint aussi des académies, dont un certain nombre s'est retrouvé à sa vente, l'année dernière. J'y ai acheté la plus belle, une étude de femme nue, assise, à laquelle se rattache une tradition d'atelier, que Riesener [Léon Riesener, Delacroix's cousin and a painter] m'a racontée. Jusque-là, Delacroix avait suivi la manière crayeuse de Champmartin,[3] qui passait alors pour le révolutionnaire de l'école. Un soir, oubliant Champmartin et songeant à Rubens et à Rembrandt qu'il pratiquait le jour au Louvre, Delacroix remarque, sur le modèle qui pose, des plans et des tons qu'il n'avait jamais vus: il brosse d'emblée sa figure, la termine en deux séances, l'emporte chez lui et déclare à ses amis qu'il sait peindre, — depuis la veille. On pourrait, en effet, mettre cette Femme nue, d'Eugène Delacroix, entre les Syrènes de Rubens, dans le *Débarquement de*

Marie de Médicis (no. 439 du Louvre) et la *Suzanne* de Rembrandt (collection de M. Lacaze, à Paris).

It is unfortunate that Thoré gives no clue as to when this revelation occurred, but from other evidence adduced in this entry it appears to have been as early as 1820. The academy figures that I have tentatively dated earlier are in any case relatively chalky.

According to R Ann, Delacroix 'avait peint cette étude à côté du peintre Auguste, de qui j'en ai vu un petit pastel (L. Charly).' This was presumably the pastel that was later in the Goetz collection (a reproduction is preserved in the Service de documentation at the Louvre, in the file for J(O)2); but it provides insufficient evidence, in my opinion, for believing that Auguste and Delacroix worked side by side when this study was painted, as the pastel seems more likely to have been done from Delacroix's painting than from the life.

Delacroix records Rose's address in an unpublished list of names and addresses of models contained in a sketch-book that was probably used in 1821 exclusively: 'Rose rue des noyers n° 22' (Louvre, RF9151, fol. 31ʳ). It has sometimes been claimed that Rose was one of Delacroix's favourite models, but there is no real evidence to support such a view.

---

¹ An old piece of wood, bearing the seal and presumably cut from the original stretcher, has been inlaid into the new stretcher.

² A label on the back of the picture, with a printed heading of the Viau collection, bears this inscription in ink: 'Nov^br 1926 Eug. Delacroix Académie de femme échangé contre un Daumier de femme tenant un enfant dans ses bras.' This evidently refers to the *Femme portant un enfant*, which is the latest known painting by Daumier and once belonged to Viau; it is now in the possession of the heirs of Emil Bührle, Zurich (see K. E. Maison, *Honoré Daumier. Catalogue Raisonné of the Paintings . . .* (Thames & Hudson, London, 1968), I, no. I-241, p. 182, pl. 35).

³ Charles Henri Callande de Champmartin, 1792-1883, pupil of Guérin, winner of the Prix de Torse at the Ecole des Beaux-Arts in 1820. His entry, for which Polonais apparently posed, is still preserved there.

---

5 MALE ACADEMY FIGURE,   Pl. 3
PROBABLY POLONAIS: STANDING

Paper laid down on canvas, 31⅞ × 21¼ in. (81 × 54)* E.D. Part of R1470 (1820. No repr.) and mentioned under R15
1821/2
Musée du Louvre

Provenance: Delacroix's posthumous sale, Feb. 1864, part of lot 200 ('Dix-sept études et académies', without dimensions), to Paul Huet, 165 fr.,¹ d. 1869; René Paul Huet, his son; by descent to M. Maurice Perret-Carnot, his son-in-law; gift of M. and Mme M. Perret-Carnot to the Société des Amis de Delacroix, *c.* 1935; acquired by the Louvre (RF1953-40), 1953.

Exhibitions: Atelier Delacroix, Paris 1935, no. 62; id. 1937, no. 66; id. 1939, no. 50; Zurich 1939, no. 302; Atelier Delacroix, Paris 1945, no. 37; id. 1946; id. 1946 A & B, no.

38; id. 1947, no. 3; id. 1948, no. 97; id. 1949, no. 121; id. 1950, no. 100; id. 1951, no. 118; id. 1952, no. 71; Bordeaux 1963, no. 1, repr.; Atelier Delacroix, Paris 1969 (no cat.); id. 1969-70 (no cat.)

Literature: R. P. Huet, *Paul Huet . . .* (H. Laurens, Paris, 1911), p. 381; Sterling-Adhémar no. 656, pl. 229.

An ink inscription on the stretcher, of uncertain date but probably written as late as 1928/35, identifies the model as 'Le Polonais'. This identification may well represent an oral tradition originating with Paul Huet, the first owner of the picture. The catalogues of the pre-war exhibitions at the Atelier Delacroix date the painting to *c.* 1820 and claim that the model was nicknamed 'le Polonais'; the same date has been retained in the post-war exhibition catalogues that list a date, and it is held in several of these that 'Le modèle était très connu dans l'atelier de Guérin, sous le nom du Polonais.' Polonais seems, however, to have been the true name of the model in question, for the minutes of meetings held at the Ecole des Beaux-Arts in 1818 show that on 28 February a letter was read from 'Julien et Polonais, qui demandent que l'assemblée veuille bien fixer leur sorts en les nommant l'un et l'autre modèles en titre aux deux places vacantes.' And on 28 March: 'Avant de se séparer l'assemblée a arrêté que Polonais seroit modèle en titre.'² It is no doubt to the same model that Géricault refers in a note *c.* 1814 contained in the back of the so-called Zoubaloff sketch-book in the Louvre (fol. 105): 'Polonais rue Dauphine n° 56'.

If the identification of Delacroix's model derives ultimately from Paul Huet, there can be no doubt that Huet was in a position to know what Polonais looked like, for both he and Victor Sollier, to whom he wrote about his purchases at Delacroix's posthumous sale (see note 1), competed at the Ecole des Beaux-Arts in 1821,³ where they could hardly have failed to see Polonais.

An assurance and, for this kind of study, freedom in the handling, a vigour and dynamism in the forms suggest that this is considerably later than the academy figure of a 'Blind Man'(J3), for example. A close stylistic analogy in an academy drawing is to be found in a nude figure which Delacroix drew, possibly from the same model, to compete for a seat in the life-class at the Ecole des Beaux-Arts in 1822; it is inscribed on the verso: '1822, 3ᵉ trimestre, 23 septembre. — M. Meynier, professeur. — E. Delacroix, élève de M. Guérin. — Place 72.' (R52. Repr. Moreau-Nélaton I, fig. 20.) The painting and the drawing may well have been done in the same year.

Another drawing of a nude which was apparently done from the same model as this painting is reproduced in Escholier I. 30.

The paper on which this study in oils was painted is slightly torn in several places. A piece (12.5 × 8.5 cm, at the outer edges) is missing from the lower left corner, which has been repaired. The canvas backing is stamped with the trademark of Haro, Delacroix's colour merchant.

For a mutilated painting which also appears to represent Polonais, see J(M)2.

[1] The sale slip for this picture, recording this price, was included in the exhibition Bordeaux 1963 (see under no. 1 in the catalogue), and the same price is also given in Burty Ann ED for one of the academy studies that Huet bought from this lot.

In a letter to Sollier dated 17 April 1864, Paul Huet states that, in addition to drawings, he bought the following works at the posthumous sale: 'une figure académique très belle [probably the present painting], deux chevaux (étude qu'on peut croire de Géricault) [J51], des costumes grecs [J30], et une toile sur laquelle sont divers fragments tels que des chevaux, une tête et une petite figure académique [J(L)4]' (R. P. Huet, ref. cited under *Literature*). But he is recorded in Burty Ann ED as the buyer of three academy studies from lot 200, for 165 fr., 170 fr. and 55 fr. The price of 170 fr. was no doubt paid for the last painting on Huet's list, and the study that he is recorded as buying for 55 fr. may have been so minor that he did not judge it worth mentioning; it was possibly J(O)1.

[2] *Assemblées des Professeurs et jugements*, Vol. IV, MS., Ecole des Beaux-Arts, Paris.

[3] Ibid., judgement of 5 May 1821, P. Huet placed 59th in the competition for the plaster-cast class; 3 November 1821, Victor Sollier 52nd.

6 STUDY OF A RECLINING   Pl. 5
FEMALE NUDE: BACK VIEW

$12\frac{5}{8} \times 18\frac{7}{8}$ in. (32×48 cm)
R106 (1824)
1824/6?
Whereabouts unknown

Provenance: Frédéric Leblond, d. 1872; presumably Mme Leblond, his widow; Dr. E. Gebauer, Mayor of Cléry (Loiret), his nephew, by 1 Sept. 1881 (Robaut Tracings 1); his sale, Cléry, 31 May 1904, lot 17; Jules Strauss, by 1926; his sale, 15 Dec. 1932, lot 38 (repr.), to Weisweller, 116,000 fr. (Dieterle R).

Exhibitions: EBA, Paris 1885, no. 85; Paris 1927, no. 271; Rosenberg, Paris 1928, no. 4; Louvre 1930, no. 23; R.A. London 1932, no. 358.

Literature: Escholier I. 88 n. 3, repr. opp. p. 86; R. Escholier, 'A propos d'une exposition Delacroix', *L'Art Vivant* IV (1928), p. 127, repr. p. 129; Hourticq 1930, pl. 7; *Correspondance* I. 67 n. 2; *Mémorial*, under no. 25; R. Huyghe *et al.*, *Delacroix* (Hachette, Coll. Génie et Réalitiés, Paris, 1963), repr. pp. 44-5.

The identity of this model, who reveals nothing of her face, has been accepted as Rose in all exhibition catalogues in this century and by most authors, yet the identification rests on nothing more solid than Robaut's assumption that the following lines in an undated letter from Delacroix to Pierret 'rapportent manifestement à notre étude' (R106): 'Je suis bien fâché de ne t'avoir pas vu, mon petit ami. [...] Mais du moins fais-moi le plaisir de m'en dédommager en venant

demain travailler avec moi. J'aurai modèle depuis 7 heures du matin rue de Sèvres, n° 11. [. . .] J'avais tâché de déterminer Félix [Guillemardet—law student] à venir nous tenir compagnie demain mais il m'a dit que le *régime dotal* l'emporterait sur le fessier de Mlle Rose pour cette fois.' (*Correspondance* I. 66 f. Burty ed. 1878, p. 69; 1880, I. 94.) It was also because Burty dated this letter *c.* 1823 (instead of 1820, which is a more probable date—see J4) that Robaut placed this study in 1824—a date which has not been questioned since.

While Joubin accepted that the model was Rose when he edited the *Correspondance* (I. 67 n. 2), he suggested later, in his notes to the *Journal*, that this was probably an early study which Delacroix described in 1850 as 'une étude couchée d'après *Caroline*' (*Journal* I. 383 and n. 3. For the full quotation in context, see J(O)8). Either identification could be correct, but they are both conjectural.

Though Robaut's date of 1824 was based on insecure evidence, it may well be correct and in any case is surely not far out. I have not seen the original, but it appears from photographs to belong in the 1820s, and it is suggestive that the four other pictures that had belonged to Leblond and passed in the Gebauer sale in 1904 can all be dated within the period 1824-7.

7 FEMALE NUDE RECLINING   Pl. 5
ON A DIVAN (Known as 'LA FEMME
AUX BAS BLANCS')

$10\frac{3}{16} \times 13\frac{1}{16}$ in. (25.9×33.2 cm)* Originally signed bottom to the left: *Eug. Delacroix*[1]
See R383, 384 (not catalogued or reproduced)
c. 1825/6
Musée du Louvre

Provenance: Frédéric Leblond, by 1832, d. 1872; presumably Mme Leblond, his widow; Dr. E. Gebauer, Mayor of Cléry (Loiret), his nephew, by 1885; his sale, Cléry, 31 May 1904, lot 16; Etienne Moreau-Nélaton; he donated it to the Louvre in 1906 (RF1657). At Musée des arts décoratifs 1907-34; transferred to Louvre 1934.

Exhibitions: Musée Colbert, Paris 1832, no. 142; Louvre 1930, no. 49; Atelier Delacroix, Paris 1963, no. 137; id., Paris 1968 (no cat.); id., Paris 1970 (no cat.); id., Paris 1974 (no cat.)

Literature: Anonymous notice of the exhibition at the Musée Colbert, in *Journal des Artistes et des Amateurs*, 6e année, I, no. XXI (20 May 1832), p. 370 (discussion of Delacroix's pictures reprinted in Tourneux, p. 108); anonymous [T. Gautier], 'Exposition du Musée Colbert', *Cabinet de lecture*, 29 May 1832 (reprinted in C. de Lovenjoul, *Histoire des œuvres de Théophile Gautier* (G. Charpentier, Paris, 1887), I, p. 30); *Journal* III. 371 and n. 3

(Supp.); *Catalogue de la collection Moreau* . . . (Frazier-Soye, Paris, 1907 and 1923), no. 54; Moreau-Nélaton I. 141, repr. fig. 104, II. 246; Brière 1924, p. 82; Escholier I. 214, II. 185 f., repr. opp. p. 100; Sterling-Adhémar, no. 675, pl. 238; Escholier 1963, p. 42, repr. in colour same p.; Trapp, p. 90 and n. 49; Bortolatto, repr. in colour, pl. XXXI.

Robaut was unable to identify the painting that was exhibited as 'Etude de femme couchée' at the Musée Colbert in 1832 under no. 142, and it was not until 1907 that this picture was connected with the exhibition, in the Catalogue of the Moreau Collection. Though the description in the exhibition catalogue is vague, specific details which confirm the identification are contained in two contemporary notices. Théophile Gautier (op. cit.), writing of Delacroix's pictures in the show, says: 'deux d'entre elles représentent une femme couchée et nue (dont l'une avec ses bas), qui sont un bijou de couleur.' And the anonymous reviewer for *Journal des Artistes* (op. cit.) writes: 'J'aime surtout la femme couchée qui a gardé ses bas; il y a là du moins de la décence.' It is also known from the catalogue of the exhibition that all the pictures by Delacroix were lent by Leblond, and from the catalogue of the sale of his nephew, Dr. Gebauer, that this particular picture once belonged to him. But I do not know of any evidence to support the statement in the Catalogue of the Moreau Collection that it was 'fait par Delacroix pour son ami F. Leblond, vers 1830'. That it was painted expressly for Leblond, who was a good friend of Delacroix's by the end of 1823 (*Journal* I. 39), seems likely, but probably not so late as 1830, which is the dating followed by the Louvre catalogues. It is in every respect a less assured exercise in painting a small-scale study of a single nude than the *Woman with Parrot* (J9), which is dated 1827 and was lent to the same exhibition by Leblond in 1832. The treatment of the nude also seems less accomplished than in the *Louis d'Orléans showing his Mistress* (J111), also lent to the same show by Leblond, or the *Lady and her Valet* (J8) and the Fitzwilliam *Odalisque reclining on a divan* (J10). It is perhaps the earliest in this group.

¹ As stated in Sterling-Adhémar, the signature mentioned in earlier catalogues is no longer visible, having apparently been covered in the course of restoration since 1930, but it can be seen on the Archives photographiques photograph MNADP97.

8 A LADY AND HER VALET   Pl. 6

$9\frac{5}{8} \times 12\frac{13}{16}$ in. (24.5 × 32.5 cm)* E.D.
R175 (1826)
1826/9
Dr. Peter Nathan, Zurich

Provenance: Delacroix's posthumous sale, Feb. 1864, lot 72 (Burty Ann ED: 'peint avant 1830 — fine, un peu mince,

mouvement de couleuvre — demi-teinte du fond excellente.'), to Haro, 410 fr.; Baron Joseph Vitta, by 1926;? Roger de la Palme (Dieterle R); with Jacques Dubourg (purchased at a sale in Feb. 1963?); acquired from him by the present owner, 1963.

Exhibitions: *Bd Italiens*, Paris 1864, no. 57 (MS. note in *BN Estampes* copy of cat., gift of B. Prost: 'ancienne période 1828'); Nice 1930, no. 3; Louvre 1930, no. 29, repr. *Album* p. 54; Berne 1963–4, no. 16, repr.; Munich 1972, no. 390, repr.

Literature: Escholier I. 214, repr. opp. p. 216; Escholier 1963, p. 43.

This picture has never been thought to be any more than a straightforward painting of a female nude on a bed; it was listed in the catalogue of Delacroix's posthumous sale simply as *Femme nue couchée* and has been known since 1885 by the incorrect title *Odalisque*, under which Robaut listed it. No one has ever commented on the presence in the left background of a figure of a man entering the bedroom. He is dressed in what is apparently a nineteenth-century stage version of European costume *c.* 1495–1530—a blue tunic and scarlet bonnet. The fact that he is included in the scene strongly suggests that the picture was intended to convey some narrative meaning which has been missed. The content could be of a most general nature and merely imagined by the artist: almost any woman in fact, contemporary with the costume, awaiting a husband or lover. But now that it has been shown beyond doubt that Delacroix painted one scene from Brantôme's *Les Vies des dames galantes* about the mid-1820s, namely *Louis d'Orléans showing his Mistress* (J111), a more precise interpretation can be advanced. In his Fifth Discourse, 'Sur ce que les belles et honnestes dames ayment les vaillants hommes, et les braves hommes ayment les dames courageuses', Brantôme recounts an erotic tale of a lady and her *valet-de-chambre*. For pictorial purposes, the essentials of the story are that a completely nude woman of some beauty is lying half-asleep close to the edge of her bed and with her back turned to the valet, who approaches from behind. Since all these details are to be found in Delacroix's painting, combined with a drowsy, sensual expectancy in the nude, the following text from Brantôme appears to have been his source:

J'ay donc ouy conter à un honneste gentilhomme mien amy, qu'une dame de son pays, ayant plusieurs fois monstré de grandes familiaritez et privautez à un sien vallet-de-chambre, qui ne tendoient toutes qu'à venir à ce point, ledit vallet, point fat et sot, un jour d'esté trouvant sa maistresse par un matin à demy endormye dans son lict toute nue, tournée de l'autre costé de la ruelle, tenté d'une si grande beauté, et d'une fort propre posture, et aisée pour l'investir et s'en accommoder, estant elle sur le bord du lit, vint doucement et investit la dame, qui, se tournant, vid que c'estoit son vallet qu'elle désiroit . . . [Further description and dialogue follow] . . . Et bien servit à elle de persister en sa prémière demande sans varier . . . et par ainsi continuèrent leurs coups . . .

long-temps après ensemble; car il n'y a que la prémière fournée ou la prémière pinte chere, ce dit-on.

Voilà un beau vallet et hardy! Et à tels hardis, comme dit l'Italien, il faut dire: *A bravo cazzo mai non manca favor*.[1]

In style and technique, this picture would seem to fit very conveniently between the Louvre's *Femme aux bas blancs* (J7) and the *Woman with Parrot* of 1827 (J9). Such a date also concords well with the possibility that the model for the nude is the same as for the *Young Woman in a Large Hat* of *c.* 1827 (J89). But a sheet of three brown-ink studies for the nude (Louvre, RF10279), one of which, though very free and schematic, establishes the final pose, are stylistically much closer to dated drawings in the same technique of 1829 and 1830 (e.g. Louvre, RF10368, dated 30 January 1830). A date around the close of the third decade cannot, therefore, be ruled out, and the anonymous visitor to the exhibition *Bd Italiens*, Paris 1864, who noted down a date of 1828 (see above, under Exhibitions) may have been nearer the truth (and better informed?) than Robaut, whose dating of 1826 is unsubstantiated.

[1] *Œuvres complètes du Seigneur de Brantôme, accompagnées de remarques historiques et critiques. Nouvelle édition . . .* , ed. L. J. N. Monmerqué (Foucault, Paris, 1822-3), 8 vols., VII (1822), pp. 477 f.

9 WOMAN WITH PARROT   Pl. 7

$9\frac{5}{8} \times 12\frac{13}{16}$ in. (24.5 × 32.5 cm.)* Signed and dated top to the left: *Eug. delacroix. 1827.*

R383 (1832. No repr.)

Musée des Beaux-Arts, Lyon

Provenance: Amable Paul Coutan; his sale (anon.), 9 March 1829, lot 50, 149 fr.; Frédéric Leblond, by 1832, d. 1872; Couturier de Royas, who gave it to the Musée des Beaux-Arts, Lyon (B-566), 1897.

Exhibitions: Musée Colbert, Paris 1832, no. 141; Paris 1927, no. 262 *quat.*; Louvre 1930, no. 44, repr. *Album*, p. 20; R.A. London 1932, no. 374; Petit Palais, Paris 1936, no. 829 (Supp.), repr. *Album*, pl. 54; Paris 1937, no. 315, repr. *Album*, pl. 90; Amsterdam 1938, no. 117, repr.; Basle 1939, no. 216; Zurich 1939, no. 312; Brussels 1947-8, no. 28, repr.; Balzac centenary exhibition, Bibliothèque nationale, Paris 1950, no. 312; Rome-Florence 1955, no. 36, repr.; Warsaw 1956, no. 37, repr.; Moscow-Leningrad 1956, p. 40, repr.; London 1959, no. 114; Louvre 1963, no. 106, *M* no. 109, 2 repr.

Literature: Anonymous notice of the exhibition at the Musée Colbert, in *Journal des Artistes et des Amateurs*, 6e année, I, no. XXI (20 May 1832), p. 369 (discussion of Delacroix's pictures reprinted in Tourneux, p. 108); anonymous [T. Gautier], 'Exposition du Musée Colbert', *Cabinet de lecture*, 29 May 1832 (reprinted in C. de Lovenjoul, *Histoire des œuvres de Théophile Gautier* (G.

Charpentier, Paris, 1887), I, p. 30); Tourneux, pp. 107, 140; *Catalogue sommaire des musées de la ville de Lyon* (Mugin-Rusand, Waltener & Cie, Lyon, n.d. [1899]), p. 56, no. 276; L. Rosenthal, *La Peinture romantique* (A. Fontemoing, Paris, n.d. [*c.* 1929]), pp. 113 f., repr. p. 115; Hourticq, repr. *peintures* (H. Laurens, Paris, 1912), p. 19, repr. pl. 104; Moreau-Nélaton I. 141, repr. fig. 105; Escholier I. 214, repr. opp. p. 218, II. 186; H. Focillon, *La peinture au XIXe siècle* (Laurens, Paris, 1927), pp. 225, 227, repr. p. 223; id., 'Chassériau ou les deux romantismes', in *Le Romantisme et l'art* (H. Laurens, Paris, 1928), p. 169; L. Rosenthal, *Florilège des musées du Palais des Arts de Lyon* (A. Morancé, Paris, n.d. [*c.* 1929]), pp. 113 f., repr. p. 115; Hourticq, repr. pl. 41; A. Joubin, 'Modèles de Delacroix', *GBA*, XV (1936), p. 355; M. Vincent, *Catalogue du Musée de Lyon*, VII, *La Peinture des XIXe et XXe siècles* (IAC les Éditions de Lyon, Lyon, 1956), pp. 36-42, repr. in colour pl. B; Escholier 1963, pp. 42, 64, repr. in colour p. 43; R. Escholier, *Delacroix et les femmes* (Fayard, Paris, 1963), p. 63; Huyghe, p. 204, full-page colour repr. pl. IX; Maltese, pp. 33, 151, 152, repr. pl. 22; Trapp, p. 90. (A less selective bibliography of secondary twentieth-century sources than is given here will be found in the entries for this picture in M. Vincent's catalogue of the Musée de Lyon, 1956, and the catalogue of the exhibition London 1959.)

The jewel-like colouring and delicate shadows which characterize this picture have been remarked on from the time when Gautier published (op. cit.) his anonymous notice of the exhibition at the Musée Colbert in 1832, writing of this 'bijou de couleur; le coloris en est admirable, et le ton de la femme dans l'ombre est d'une vérité et d'une finesse exquises, transparent sans faire jaspe, solide sans être noir.' The close affinities with the exquisite colouristic style Bonington developed after 1825, under Venetian influence and partly in conjunction with Delacroix, were first hinted at by Moreau-Nélaton and need to be stressed. Yet it has also to be noted that Bonington never attained the relaxed mastery of nude form that Delacroix displays here. A more abstruse influence than Bonington's, but a very likely one, is that of the *Venus and Cupid* in the Louvre by the Dutch Mannerist painter and pupil of Titian, Lambert Sustris. This influence first occurred to me when I saw a drawing by Ingres at Montauban in 1964 (Musée Ingres, Inv. 8673695), which I identified as a copy after Sustris' painting. Subsequently, when checking the bibliography for this entry, I found Rosenthal had suggested as early as *c.* 1929 (op. cit.) that the idea for this Delacroix had been inspired by the Sustris, but his pertinent suggestion had passed unremarked by later writers.

There has been much loose speculation, none of it convincing, about the identity of the model who posed for this painting, Rosenthal (*c.* 1929) seeing Rose in her; Joubin

(1936), often followed by others, Laure; and Escholier (1963, *Delacroix et les femmes*), Adeline.

The picture was known to Robaut only from the description in the catalogue of the 1832 exhibition. Its first owner, Coutan, was an early patron of Delacroix's and bought several of his smaller pictures during the 1820s. This collector's name crops up on several occasions in the *Journal* between December 1823 and April 1824.

A refined pencil study for this painting, bearing the stamp of Delacroix's posthumous sale, was acquired by the Musée des Beaux-Arts of Lyon at the Haviland sale, Paris, 7 December 1922 (lot 11, repr.); the final pose has been fully elaborated, but the setting and stuffs have not been worked out in detail. The drawing is reproduced in *Mémorial*, no. 110; better reproductions will be found in Rosenthal (op. cit., *c.* 1929, p. 115, and Huyghe, fig. 130).

10 ODALISQUE RECLINING ON A DIVAN

Pl. 7

$14\frac{7}{8} \times 18\frac{1}{4}$ in. (37.8 × 46.4 cm) Relined. Signed bottom right: *Eug. Delacroix*

Moreau p. 313. R140 (1825)

c. 1827/8

Fitzwilliam Museum, Cambridge

Provenance: Amable Paul Coutan; his sale, 19 Apr. 1830, lot 31 ('Odalisque sur un lit de repos', without dimensions[1]), to the artist?; Delacroix's posthumous sale, Feb. 1864, lot 69 ('Odalisque étendue sur un divan', 38 × 45 cm. Burty Ann ED: 'très-jolie ébauche'), Barroilhet, 705 fr.; his sale [M.B.], 12 Apr. 1866, lot 10 ('Odalisque couchée, demi-nue, un narguilé près d'elle', 37 × 45 cm), 860 fr. (apparently bought in); his posthumous sale, 15 March 1872, lot 118 ('Une Odalisque', 36 × 45 cm. 'Elle est étendue sur un lit de repos derrière lequel pend une draperie verte; sa tête est appuyée sur des coussins, le corps se détache sur une draperie de soie rouge. A terre, près d'elle, un narghilé.' M-Nélaton Ann ED: 'Signé Eug. Delacroix à droite.'[2]), 1,050 fr.; Dassonvalle; his sale, 3 March 1879, lot 51 ('Une Odalisque étendue sur un lit de repos', mention of signature but no dimensions); according to R Ann, passed in a number of sales over a period of several years before being acquired by P. A. Cheramy in 1891; his sale, 5 May 1908, lot 172, to T. Montaignac, 6,800 fr.;[3] sale estate of P. A. Cheramy, 15 Apr. 1913, lot 21, to Cassirer, Berlin, 7,000 fr.; A. Rothermundt, Dresden, by 1922; M. Silberberg, Breslau; his sale, Paris, 9 June 1932, lot 20 (repr.), 100,000 fr.; Percy Moore Turner, London, by 1937, d. 1950; by his bequest to the Fitzwilliam Museum with a life interest to his wife, who relinquished it to the Museum in 1957 (PD.3-1957).

Exhibitions: ? *Bd Italiens*, Paris 1864 (see J(L)5); Art Musulman, Paris 1893, no. 108; Paris 1937, no. 314, repr. *Album* pl. 73; Amsterdam 1938, no. 115; Belgrade 1939, no. 44; London 1942, no. 5a; Edinburgh–London 1964, no. 20, repr.; Providence 1975, no. 82, repr.

Literature: J. Meier-Graefe and E. Klossowski, *La Collection Cheramy . . .* (R. Piper, Munich, 1908), p. 88, no. 149 (repr.); Meier-Graefe, repr. p. 98; Escholier I. 214, repr. p. 215; *Journal* I. 383 n. 2; *Fitzwilliam Museum Cambridge Annual Report 1957* (University Press, Cambridge, 1958), p. 2, repr. pl. III; J. W. Goodison *et al.*, *Fitzwilliam Museum Cambridge. Catalogue of Paintings* (Printed for the Syndics of the Fitzwilliam Museum, Cambridge, 1960), I, pp. 165 f., repr. pl. 89; Escholier 1963, p. 42; *Mémorial*, under no. 363; Huyghe, pp. 204, 451, repr. fig. 129.

Though Robaut had listed this picture under 1825 and Escholier placed it in the years 1826–30, Joubin (*Journal* ref. cit.) suggested identifying it with a study *Femme au lit*, which Delacroix noted that he began in 1850. This suggestion seemed reasonable in view of the extraordinary suppleness combined with breadth of form and freedom of handling in the figure; a date *c.* 1845/50 (illogically broad in the circumstances) was consequently proposed in the Fitzwilliam Museum Catalogue of 1960. In the catalogue of the exhibition Edinburgh–London 1964, I proposed returning to a date closer to Robaut's, mainly because the exact pose of this nude appeared on a sheet of pen-and-ink drawings published by Huyghe and datable *c.* 1825/7 (repr. Huyghe, p. 131, where it is wrongly stated to be in the Louvre); but I also pointed out that the treatment of the white sheet on the right was comparable to that in the *Femme aux bas blancs* (J7); the handling of the scabbard of the yatagan, to the similar weapon in the *Turk Seated on a Sopha* (J35). I concluded that the characteristics of the nude which seemed inconsistent with other single nudes from the 1820s seemed best explained by placing this picture after the *Death of Sardanapalus* (J125), completed early in 1828, where such breadth of form and sensual abandon are found on a grand scale. The presence of this painting in the Coutan sale of 1830, a fact apparently unknown up to now, vindicates the earlier dating.

A *pentimento* in the lower right corner of the canvas clearly shows that the artist altered the perspective of the end board of the divan; and when the picture was cleaned in 1974 it appeared to the restorer that Delacroix might have painted the left arm of the nude, lying across her torso, before deciding to conceal it entirely.

It is wrongly stated in Robaut (under no. 175) that this picture is a sketch for the *Odalisque* lithographed by Debacq. The lithograph is of the *Odalisque* which Delacroix exhibited at the Salon of 1847 (R942; latterly Coll. Mme D. David-Weill, Neuilly, d. 1970; repr. *Mémorial*, no. 363)

1. *Odalisque reclining on a Divan* 36·8 × 46·4 cm (10)

and which has no direct connection with the Fitzwilliam nude.

[1] The title is supplemented by these comments: 'Tableau d'un joli ton et d'un effet très piquant. Les accessoires sont touchés avec une grande finesse.' In support of my identification of this lot with the Fitzwilliam picture, it may be pointed out that this is the only known painting of a woman on a bed from the 1820s which can properly be described as representing an odalisque (i.e. a member of a harem), by virtue of the oriental accessories on the floor in the foreground, to which the comments quoted above no doubt mainly refer.

[2] Confusing this picture with a *Bacchante* which passed in Delacroix's posthumous sale as an unfinished painting (lot 128), Moreau-Nélaton goes on to conclude that the signature must therefore be false. There seems to be no reason to doubt its authenticity, in spite of the fact that Moreau (followed, perhaps blindly, by Robaut) lists the picture as unsigned.

[3] The picture is stated in the catalogues of this sale and the Cheramy sale of 1913 to be 'signé du monogramme de la vente', meaning presumably that it then bore on the back the red wax monogram 'E.D.' of Delacroix's posthumous sale. Though there are traces of red sealing-wax on the stretcher, no initials remain.

Copies after the Masters

11 THE CHRIST CHILD,   Pl. 8
after RAPHAEL, detail from the 'BELLE JARDINIÈRE' (Louvre, RF1496)
$23\frac{5}{8} \times 19\frac{11}{16}$ in. (60×50 cm)[1]
Moreau p. 319. R24 (1819. No repr.)
Whereabouts unknown

Provenance: Delacroix's posthumous sale, Feb. 1864, lot 152, to M. Sourigues, 5,000 fr.; his sale (S . . .), 28 Feb. 1881, lot 13, to Haro, 5,700 fr.; sale Haro & fils, 30 May 1892, lot 78 (repr.), 12,000 fr.; sale Haro père, 2 Apr. 1897, lot 120, 6,000 fr.; Edouard Aynard; his sale, 1 Dec. 1913, lot 7, to Schoeller, 5,550 fr.

Exhibitions: *Bd Italiens*, Paris 1864, no. 309 (supp. to 3rd ed.; as 'Copie de Raphael', 64×52 cm, lent by M. Sourigues); *EBA*, Paris 1885, no. 98.

Literature: Silvestre *Delacroix* (1855), p. 83; Silvestre *Documents nouveaux* (1864), p. 20; Piron, p. 53; J. Gigoux, *Causeries sur les artistes de mon temps* (Calmann Lévy, Paris, 1885), p. 64; Robaut, p. 11, under no. 28; H. Houssaye, 'L'Exposition des œuvres d'Eugène Delacroix à l'Ecole des Beaux-Arts', *Revue des Deux Mondes*, LXVIII (1885), p. 667; *Journal* I. 474 n. 5; *Mémorial*, under no. 3; Huyghe, pp. 13, 109, 132; Maltese, p. 143; S. Lichtenstein, 'Delacroix's Copies after Raphael', *Burl Mag*, CXIII (1971), pp. 530, 599, no. 1, repr. fig. 37, p. 527.

This is a full-scale copy from the lower half of the *Virgin and Child with St. John*, known as the *Belle Jardinière*, the infant St. John being omitted by Delacroix from the area copied. It is assigned to 1819 by Robaut, who lists it immediately before the dated *Virgin of the Harvest* (J151), presumably on the reasonable assumption that it was painted in preparation for this altar-piece, so clearly influenced by Raphael's Florentine Madonnas. It seems to have disappeared without trace since the Aynard sale of 1913 and is known only from the heliogravure illustration for the catalogue of the Haro sale of 1892, reproduced here. Delacroix refers to it only once, late in life, and then very summarily to note a loan: 'Prêté à

Mme Halévy, en partant pour Champrosay, les deux copies de Raphaël, *l'Enfant* et *le Portrait à la main* [J(L)14.].' (*Journal* I. 474, entry for 6 July 1852.)

According to an anecdote recorded in Robaut (p. 11), Ingres saw this copy when it was in Haro's studio for restoration (at an unspecified date) and was struck by its beauty. On learning that it was by Delacroix, he is said to have cried: 'Le misérable! Et il fait sa peinture!'

[1] According to the catalogue of Delacroix's posthumous sale; 64×52 cm according to that of Exh. *Bd Italiens*, Paris 1864.

12 THE ENTOMBMENT,   Pl. 9
after TITIAN (Louvre, RF1584)
$15\frac{3}{4} \times 21\frac{7}{8}$ in. (40×55.5 cm)*
R Ann 32bis (c. 1821. No repr.)
c. 1819/21
Musée des Beaux-Arts, Lyon

Provenance: Bequeathed by Delacroix in 1863 to the painter Paul Chenavard (1807-95), who gave it to the Musée des Beaux-Arts, Lyon (B-286), 1881.

Exhibition: Bordeaux 1963, no. 47.

Literature: Silvestre *Delacroix* (1855), p. 83; Delacroix's will, dated 3 Aug. 1863, in *Correspondance* (Burty 1878), p. viii; M. Reymond, *Le Musée de Lyon. Tableaux anciens* (Libr. Fischbacher, Paris, 1887), pp. 181, 198; *Catalogue sommaire des Musées de Lyon* (Mougin-Rusand, Lyon, 1887), p. 42, no. 214 (1899 ed., p. 56, no. 275); L. Rosenthal, *La Peinture romantique* (A. Fontemoing, Paris, n.d. [1900]), p. 217 n. 3; P. Dissard, *Le Musée de Lyon. Les Peintures* (Laurens, Paris, 1912), p. 19; H. Focillon, *La Peinture au XIXe siècle* (Laurens, Paris, 1927), p. 175; C. Mauclair, *Le Palais Saint-Pierre* (Paris, n.d. [1929], Coll. 'Les Musées d'Europe'), p. 70; R. Régamey, *Eugène Delacroix* (Paris, 1930), pp. 71-2; M. Vincent, *Catalogue du Musée de Lyon*, VII, *La Peinture des XIXe et XXe siècles* (IAC Les Editions de Lyon, Lyon, 1956), p. 55, repr. pl. XV, fig. 2; K. E.

Maison, *Themes and Variations* (Thames and Hudson, London, 1960. German ed., *Bild und Abbild*, published Munich and Zurich, 1960), p. 123, fig. 157; L. Johnson, 'The Delacroix Centenary in France—I', *Burl Mag*, CV (1963), p. 302, repr. fig. 2.

This copy is stated in Delacroix's will to be from his own hand: 'Je lègue à M. CHENAVARD, sus-nommé, peintre, une copie de moi du *Christ au tombeau*, du Titien' (Burty, op. cit.). There is no indication in his writings when he painted it. Mlle Vincent (op. cit., 1956), the first cataloguer of paintings in the Museum of Lyon to venture a date, thinks that it was probably painted in 1850 at the earliest, on the grounds that entries in Delacroix's *Journal* suggest that he did not truly appreciate Titian until his later years. He seems, however, to have shown a marked interest in Titian by the early 1820s, since he owned three copies by Géricault (Clément nos. 179–81) after major paintings by this master which he presumably acquired at Géricault's posthumous sale in November 1824, from the two lots (20 and 23) that included copies after Titian (see Moreau, pp. xx f., for an account of Delacroix's purchases at the sale). Robaut lists this copy at the beginning of 1821 in R Ann, stating in his MS. entry: 'C'est vers ce temps qu'il faut placer [cette] copie'. In drawing attention to Robaut's entry for the first time, I accepted his dating as more convincing for stylistic reasons than a date *c.* 1850 (op. cit., 1963). While this small study, hardly more than a quarter of the original in size, is schematic in certain respects, it lacks the breadth and confidence of the late Delacroix, and an almost timid attention to detail in some passages suggests an early date, perhaps even earlier than Robaut's: the Virgin's neat row of carefully stacked fingers, for example, is comparable to the Christ's toes in the *Christ brought before Caiaphas* of 1818(?) (J150), as are other aspects of the two pictures, though the copy seems generally more assured and therefore likely to be a little later.

Literature: L. Johnson, 'The Delacroix Centenary in France—I', *Burl Mag*, CV (1963), p. 302, repr. fig. 6.

This is a copy, on the same scale as the original, of the left-hand figure in the so-called *Portrait of Two Venetians* in the Louvre. The original was catalogued as a Giovanni Bellini in 1816 (*Notice des tableaux exposés dans la Galerie du Musée royal* (Impr. Mme Hérissaut-Le Doux, Paris, 1816), p. 140), and by Frédéric Villot in 1849 (*Notice des tableaux exposés dans les galeries du Musée National du Louvre Ire partie. Ecoles d'Italie* (Vinchon, Paris, 1849), p. 23, no. 63). Both sources identified it as a portrait of Giovanni and Gentile Bellini. Therefore Delacroix may be assumed to have thought that he was here copying a self-portrait by Giovanni. In the second, 1852, edition of his catalogue of Italian paintings in the Louvre, Villot altered the attribution to Gentile Bellini because it had been assigned to him by Félibien in the seventeenth century. In 1871, Crowe and Cavalcaselle ascribed it to Cariani of Bergamo (*c.* 1485/90—post 1547), in their *History of Painting in North Italy* (see London 1912 ed., edited by T. Borenius, I, p. 134). This is the most generally accepted attribution today.

In 1963, I published drawings after both heads on a sheet contained in a sketch-book which Delacroix bought in England in 1825 (Louvre, RF9143, fol. 7^r. L. Johnson, op. cit., fig. 7), and suggested that this copy in oils followed closely on the drawings. That section of the sketch-book which was used in England appears to end on fol. 6^r, and the pages filled after Delacroix's return to Paris, about the end of August 1825, begin on fol. 7 with the studies after the Cariani. Since this copy in oils appears to have served as an inspiration for some of the heads in the *Execution of Marino Faliero* (J112), which was being completed in April 1826, it was most probably painted within six months of Delacroix's return from England.

The head of the figure with folded hands at the top of the ramp in the *Marino Faliero* is especially similar.

13 PORTRAIT OF A MAN,   Pl. 10
after CARIANI (Louvre, RF1156. Attr. to Giovanni Bellini when copied)

16$\frac{15}{16}$ × 14$\frac{9}{16}$ in. (43 × 37 cm) E.D.
R1932 (No repr.)
1825/6
Claude Roger-Marx, Paris

Provenance: Delacroix's posthumous sale, Feb. 1864, lot 157 (as 'Portrait d'homme [d'après le Bellin.]'), to M. Filhston, 600 fr.; present owner by 1934.

Exhibitions: Arts décoratifs, Paris 1934, no. 112; Bordeaux 1963, no. 7.

14 TWO BEARDED HEADS, after   Pl. 11
VERONESE, detail from THE MARRIAGE AT CANA (Louvre, RF1192)

25$\frac{3}{16}$ × 32$\frac{1}{4}$ in. (64 × 82 cm)[1] E.D.
R1930 (No repr.)
1820
Private collection, Paris

Provenance: Delacroix's posthumous sale, Feb. 1864, lot 155 (as 'Fragment des Noces de Cana [d'après Paul Véronèse]', 63 × 80 cm), to Haro, 400 fr.; M. Démellette, by 1927; Charles Lefèvre Démellette, Paris, by 1952.

Exhibitions: Bd Italiens, Paris 1864, no. 59; Paris 1927, no. 283; Salle Ren., Paris 1929, no. 90? ('Les Noces de Cana

(Copie d'après Véronèse, fragment)', without dimensions or owner); Wildenstein, London 1952, no. 54 (as 'The Violin Player (after Veronese)'); Bordeaux 1963, no. 62 (as 'Joueurs de Viole (. . . d'après . . . Véronèse)').

Literature: Silvestre *Delacroix* (1855), p. 83; Silvestre *Documents nouveaux* (1864), p. 20; L. Johnson, 'The Delacroix Centenary in France—I', *Burl Mag*, CV (1963), pp. 302, 305.[2]

Soulier recounts how in their youth he and Delacroix collaborated on a commission to do some coloured drawings of machines for inventors' patents. When he brought Delacroix his share of the earnings, he found him 'perché dans le Grand Salon du Louvre au haut d'une immense échelle, copiant des têtes dans *les Noces de Cana* de Paul Véronèse.' (*Correspondance* I. 37-8 n. 2.) This account is joined, by way of explanation, to a copy by Soulier of a letter that Delacroix wrote to him in English to arrange a meeting to 'resolve in what day we can to begin our undertaking of *colorage*, which I wish to see quickly termined.' (Ibid. 39.) According to this transcript (in the *Bib AA*), Delacroix's letter was dated 10 December 1818, but it appears that either Soulier copied the year inaccurately or filled it in wrongly from memory, and the year ought to be 1819; for in a letter to his sister which is definitely dated 30 May 1820 (original MS. in *Bib AA*), Delacroix writes of what is surely this same project: 'Voilà à peu un mois que j'ai entrepris un ouvrage qui me rapportera quelque petit bénéfice, Ce sont des dessins de machines que je copie avec un jeune homme de ma connaissance.' He proceeds, moreover, to inform her that he is working at the Louvre with a scaffold: 'je vais ensuite au Musée auquel je ne manque guère parce que j'y paie un échafaudage fort cher' (*Correspondance* V. 51). He also notes in his accounts for June 1820: 'Reçu le 10 de Soulier 85 frs. pour les dessins.' (*Journal* III. 340—Supp.)

There can thus be little doubt that it was on 10 June 1820 that Soulier found Delacroix up a ladder copying heads in the *Marriage at Cana*. The present, full-scale copy was most probably painted at that time. It does not represent musicians, as sometimes stated, but the heads of two men standing in the foreground to the left of the instrumentalists. The error may have originated with Robaut, who described lot 155 from the posthumous sale, without apparently having seen it, as 'Tête du joueur de viole des Noces de Cana'.

A water-colour study after the central group in the foreground is reproduced in Escholier (I. 93).

According to Thoré Ann ED, lot 156 in Delacroix's posthumous sale, listed in the catalogue as 'Autre fragment du même tableau' with dimensions 0.84 × 1.00 m, was in fact by Géricault and had been bought by Delacroix at the former's sale in 1824. It was sold to Lehmann for 250 fr. and

catalogued by Robaut without a reproduction as no. 1931. It may have been the copy shown at the Géricault exhibition at Winterthur in 1953, under no. 24 and at Bordeaux 1963, no. 289. In a private collection in Paris, it represents the same heads as Delacroix's copy, but also includes the head of the dwarf to the left and the six figures immediately above them.

Though only two copies of details from the *Marriage at Cana* are listed in the catalogue of the posthumous sale, three, all attributed to Delacroix, are contained in Inv. Delacroix (nos. 60, 78, 198). Thus if the identification of the subject was correct in all three cases, one study is lost (see J(L)17).

[1] These are the dimensions listed in the Cat. Exh. *Bd Italiens*, Paris 1864, which must be more accurate than those given in the catalogue of Delacroix's posthumous sale, 63 × 80 cm, and followed elsewhere; for the sight dimensions that I was able to take within the frame from the front at Bordeaux in 1963 were 63 × 79.9 cm.

[2] Where I referred to this copy as no. 63 in the Exh. Bordeaux 1963. It was in fact no. 62 in the exhibition catalogue, though listed with the wrong title, and the numbers 62 and 63 attached to the paintings had been accidentally interchanged when I was at the exhibition. The painting catalogued under no. 63 and illustrated pl. 13 is a smaller picture (32 × 40 cm) showing the group of musicians in the centre of the *Marriage at Cana* full-length. It is not by Delacroix, in my opinion.

15 JOB TORMENTED BY DEMONS, after RUBENS   Pl. 12

$24\frac{7}{16} \times 20\frac{1}{2}$ in. (62 × 52 cm) E.D.
Probably R1949 or 1954 (No repr.)
c. 1821
Musée Bonnat, Bayonne

Provenance: Delacroix's posthumous sale, Feb. 1864, probably part of lot 176 ('Six toiles contenant des fragments d'études d'après Rubens, Véronèse, Murillo, etc.'), to Gaultron, 100 fr. or 11 fr.;[1] Léon Bonnat, who placed it on extended loan to the Museum at Bayonne from *c*. 1901 and bequeathed it to the town on his death, 8 Sept. 1922.

Exhibition: *Exposition d'Œuvres originales d'Eugène Delacroix*, Musée Bonnat, Bayonne, 1963, no. 2, repr.

Literature: Possibly Inv. Delacroix, no. 193; G. Gruyer, *Ville de Bayonne. Musée Bonnat. Catalogue sommaire* (Impr. A. Lamaignère, Bayonne, 1902), p. 22, no. 70 (no. and description unaltered in Bayonne 1903 and Paris 1908 eds.); A. Personnaz and G. Bergès, *Le Musée de Bayonne* (H. Laurens, Paris, 1925), p. 20, no. 70; *Ville de Bayonne. Musée Bonnat. Catalogue sommaire* (Musées nationaux, Paris, 1930), p. 116, no. 768; *Journal* (1932 ed.), III, repr. opp. p. 168; B. White, 'Delacroix's Painted Copies after Rubens', *AB*, XLIX (1967), pp. 39, 45 f., repr. fig. 34.

This was not listed as a copy after Rubens in the catalogues of the Musée Bonnat before 1925, and the proper subject not given before 1930.

Rubens's painting of this subject was on the wing of a triptych executed for the church of St. Nicholas in Brussels and destroyed by fire in 1695. An old copy measuring 1.46 × 1.19 m, which, according to Rooses, was probably done after Vorsterman's engraving of the original, passed in the Henry sale, Paris, 23 May 1836 (lot 71); it was bequeathed to the Louvre by Louis La Caze in 1869 (*Notice des tableaux légués au Musée impérial du Louvre par M. Louis La Caze* (Paris, 1870), no. 107). Though Delacroix might have known that copy when it belonged to Henry, who was *commissaire expert du Musée royal*, Vorsterman's print is likely to have been more accessible to him and therefore the source of his own sketch in neutral tones. The Vorsterman is reproduced in M. Rooses, *L'Œuvre de P. P. Rubens* (Jos. Maes, Antwerp, 1886), I, pl. 39.

While this study contains a number of crudities that may at first sight appear uncharacteristic of Delacroix's authentic work, in overall technique and in details of handling it is remarkably similar to the oil sketch *Death of Drusus* (J99), which is datable to 1821 and closely related to drawings of certain authenticity in Delacroix's sketch-books. The theme of demons is, moreover, one that interested Delacroix around the period of the *Barque de Dante* (J100), and they are treated with some spirit here.

The red wax seal of Delacroix's posthumous sale is on the stretcher, and the back of the canvas is stamped with the trade-mark of Haro, Delacroix's colour merchant. Since this is the only known sketch after Rubens that both bears the E.D. seal and could reasonably be described as a grisaille, it may be the copy listed in Inv. Delacroix, no. 193 as '1 grisaille, *descente de croix d'après Rubens par Delacroix*'.

---

[1] There were two studies under this lot number which are stated in Burty Ann ED to be after Rubens, but are not given titles. One of them was knocked down to Gaultron for 100 fr., the other to the same buyer for 11 fr.

16 NEREID, after RUBENS,   Pl. 13
detail from the LANDING OF MARIA DE'
MEDICI AT MARSEILLES (Louvre, RF2090)

18 5⁄16 × 15 in. (46.5 × 38 cm) Relined. Indistinct E.D.
R1943 (No repr.)
c. 1822
Offentliche Kunstsammlung, Kunstmuseum, Basle

Provenance: Delacroix's posthumous sale, Feb. 1864, lot 172 (as 'Une des néréides dans l'embarquement de Marie de Médicis [d'après Rubens]. Musée du Louvre', 46 × 33 cm), to Philippe Burty, 130 fr.; his sale, 2 March 1891, lot 10, 480 fr.; mixed sale, Paris 20 Nov. 1922, lot 45 (as 'Copie d'après Rubens'), 5,300 fr.; Georges Aubry sale, 11 March 1933, lot 80 (repr.); Kunstmuseum, Basle (Inv. no. 1602),

1933, gift of friends of Professor Friedrich Rintelen in his memory.

Exhibitions: Paris 1927, no. 284; Louvre 1930, no. 227; Basle 1937, no. 15; Basle 1939, no. 229; Bremen 1964, no. 19; 'Art into Art', London 1971, no. 200.

Literature: Escholier I, repr. opp. p. 52; P. Fierens, 'Eugène Delacroix, admirateur et copiste de Rubens', *Pictura*, II (1946), p. 5; *Offentliche Kunstsammlung Basel, Katalog 1946*, Basle, p. 131; H. Wellington (ed.), *The Journal of Eugène Delacroix* (Phaidon, London, 1951), pl. 43; K. E. Maison, *Themes and Variations* (Thames & Hudson, London, 1960. German ed., *Bild und Abbild*, published Munich and Zurich, 1960), excellent full-page pl. p. 127; L. Johnson, 'The Etruscan Sources of Delacroix's *Death of Sardanapalus*', *AB*, XLII (1960), p. 298 n. 17; Johnson 1963, pl. 3; Maltese, p. 27; B. White, 'Delacroix's Painted Copies after Rubens', *AB*, XLIX (1967), pp. 37, 44, 44 n. 90 and 92, 48, repr. fig. 2; J. Thuillier and J. Foucart, *Le Storie di Maria de' Medici di Rubens al Lussemburgo* (Rizzoli, Milan, 1967; ed. in French, Paris, 1969), pp. 77, 146, repr. in colour fig. 98.

This is a greatly reduced study after the central figure in the group of three nereids in the foreground of Rubens's *Landing of Maria de' Medici at Marseilles*, one of the paintings from the Medici cycle which was originally commissioned for the Palais du Luxembourg and moved from there to the Louvre *c.* 1816. Delacroix must have studied this painting closely by 1822, to judge from his remarks, reported by Andrieu, about how the drops of water on the nereids influenced his own *Barque de Dante* (see J100). The technique seems consistent with a date of 1822 or earlier: it displays the same thick impasto scored with brushmarks, the pasty-coloured lights, the drab olive shadows and warm reflections in the breast that are to be found in parts of the *Barque de Dante*; it is Rubens handled in a manner that still owes much to Géricault.

I have suggested (1960) that the central nude in the foreground of the *Death of Sardanapalus* was partly influenced by this figure from Rubens (see J125).

Robaut proposed no date for this copy. Fierens (1946) placed it in the period 1822–4. It is listed as *c.* 1840 in the catalogue of the exhibition Basle 1939. Maison (1960) dates it to 1828 without argument, but presumably because that is where Robaut (no. 260) placed another copy after the same painting (see J(R)16).

Delacroix commented on the nereids in his *Journal* on two occasions. On 5 October 1847, he remarked (I. 242): 'Rubens est *lâché* dans ses Naïades, pour ne pas perdre sa lumière et sa couleur.' And on 1 June 1849, after visiting the Louvre, he wrote (I. 294): 'Les Sirènes . . . ne m'ont jamais semblé si belles. L'abandon seul et l'audace la plus complète peuvent produire de semblables impressions.' He also analysed Rubens's treatment of history in the Medici cycle, with reference to this painting among others, in his essay on Gros of 1848 (*Œuvres litt.*, II. 164).

Delacroix's original canvas is of an irregular shape on the left edge, as can be clearly seen in the reproduction. The exposed portion of the old canvas on which the original piece is laid down was repainted by the Kunstmuseum's restorer, who at the same time relined the entire surface.

17 CONCLUSION OF THE Pl. 15
PEACE, after RUBENS (Louvre, RF2103)

$12\frac{3}{4} \times 9\frac{5}{8}$ in. (32.4 × 24.4 cm)* E.D.
Moreau p. 320. R1948 (No repr.)
1820/5
Dr. H. R. Liebermann, Capetown

Provenance: Delacroix's posthumous sale, Feb. 1864, lot 170 (as 'Marie de Médicis fermant le temple de la Discorde [d'après Rubens]. Musée du Louvre', 40 × 32 cm), to M. Dejean, 310 fr.; M. C . . . sale, 13 Apr. 1865, lot 31 (same description and provenance from the posthumous sale noted), 160 fr.; with Lepke, Berlin, *c.* 1906; Georg Liebermann, Berlin, *c.* 1906 to his death in 1927; by descent to the present owner, having been hidden in Germany during the war and brought to South Africa by his mother in 1949.[1]

Exhibitions: None.

Literature: Planet *Souvenirs*, p. 35 and n.; B. White, 'Delacroix's Painted Copies after Rubens', *AB*, XLIX (1967), pp. 43 and n., 49, repr. fig. 11; J. Thuillier and J. Foucart, *Le Storie di Maria de' Medici di Rubens al Lussemburgo* (Rizzoli, Milan, 1967; ed. in French 1969), p. 90.

This study, about one-twelfth the size of the original painting in the Medici cycle, appears to date from the first half of the 1820s, and perhaps played a part in the development of the *Death of Sardanapalus* (J125), with its luminous diagonal contained between darker zones and its flares threatening incombustible objects. Later it was recommended to an assistant as a guide to colouring a scheme of decorations comparable in scale to the Medici cycle: Louis de Planet refers to it on 3 November 1841, when noting Delacroix's advice for painting the *Aristotle* pendentive in the library of the Palais Bourbon: 'Regarder les tons des jambes et des bras dans l'esquisse faite par M. Delacroix d'après le tableau de Rubens, *Marie de Médicis devant le petit temple*, et s'en inspirer pour les tons des jambes du jeune homme dans le pendentif d'*Aristote*.' The next day, he sheds further light on one of the uses to which Delacroix put his copies after Rubens: 'Quand on peint, avoir près de soi des études d'après Rubens, de manière à pouvoir les consulter, surtout pour les tons; on s'en inspirera

pour réchauffer sa palette qui doit être plus vigoureuse qu'on n'est habitué à l'avoir à l'atelier, où l'on n'a jamais vu le modèle vivant éclairé en vigueur, comme il le serait s'il était en plein air, dans les conditions que le tableau ou le sujet exige.' (Planet *Souvenirs*, p. 38).

Delacroix himself refers to this sketch on 2 October 1847: 'Prêté à Soulier petite esquisse, d'après Rubens, de la vie de Marie de Médicis, *la paix mettant le feu à des armes*: des monstres sur le devant, la Reine dans le fond entrant dans le Temple de Janus.' (*Journal* I. 241).

The surface is in poor condition, suffering from extensive craquelures and a small hole in the canvas in the neck of the figure of Peace. There is some retouching just above and extending slightly to the left of this figure where the canvas has been patched from behind.

---

[1] The history from 1906 was furnished by the present owner, who added the interesting fact that this copy was bought on the recommendation of Max Liebermann, his great-uncle. Its history between 1865 and 1906 is unknown, but a photograph of it, preserved in the archives of Messrs. Wildenstein in New York, appears to date from the nineteenth century and bears the number 3932, which is not a Wildenstein reference, but might be a Durand-Ruel photograph and inventory number, according to Mr. Fisher, Wildenstein's New York manager in 1966. The same photograph is reproduced by B. White from another print belonging to the Netherlands Institute for Art History.

18 SATYR EMBRACING A Pl. 16
NYMPH, after RUBENS, detail from DIANA AND HER NYMPHS DEPARTING FOR THE CHASE (Cleveland Museum of Art)

$6\frac{1}{2} \times 8\frac{5}{8}$ in. (16.5 × 22 cm) E.D.
R1945 (No repr.)
Probably 1825
Private collection, Germany

Provenance: Delacroix's posthumous sale, Feb. 1864, lot 174, to de Bellio, 330 fr.; Johan Lønberg, Denmark; mixed sale (including paintings from his collection), Bruun Rasmussen's, Copenhagen, 30 Apr. 1964, lot 1166 (repr.), to F. and P. Nathan, Zurich; sold by them to the present owner, 1965.

Exhibitions: None.

Literature: None, other than Robaut.

This powerful study, approximately half-scale, appears to have been done from the original painting that is now in Cleveland, Ohio, and not from either the James Ward engraving published in 1800 or the studio version that has been in Cassel since the eighteenth century. The Cleveland *Diana* was in England by 1800, and in 1825 was in the collection of Sir Simon Clarke at Oak Hill in East Barnet, Hertfordshire, where Delacroix could easily have gone to see it during his stay in London in the summer of that year. Though this study is exceptionally assured and vigorous for a work of 1825, it is not altogether inconsistent with a sketch such as that for the *Murder of the Bishop of Liège* from the latter half of the 1820s (J135), and from what is known of the history of the Rubens[1] it seems unlikely that Delacroix could have seen the original at any other time.

[1] For a history of the Rubens and related works, see H. S. Francis, 'Peter Paul Rubens, Diana and her Nymphs Departing for the Chase', *Bulletin of the Cleveland Museum of Art*, XLVII, no. 2 (Feb. 1960). A detail reproduced in colour on the cover includes the passage copied by Delacroix. For Sir Simon Clarke's full address, see G. E. C. [Cokayne] (ed.), *Complete Baronetage* (W. Pollard, Exeter, 1900), p. 112.

19 PORTRAIT OF SUZANNE FOURMENT, after RUBENS (Louvre, RF2114)   Pl. 17

$25\frac{5}{8} \times 21\frac{1}{4}$ in. (65 × 54 cm) E.D. ?

R259 (1828. No repr.)

c. 1825/8

A. K. Solomon, Cambridge, Mass.

Provenance: Delacroix's posthumous sale, Feb. 1864, lot 161 (as 'Portrait de la femme de Rubens [d'après Rubens]. Musée du Louvre', 65 × 54 cm), to Arosa, 380 fr.; his sale, 25 Feb. 1878, lot 43 ('Portrait d'une dame de la famille Boonen, d'après Rubens (Musée du Louvre)', 65 × 54 cm), to M. Hecht, 700 fr.; P. A. Cheramy; his sale, 5 May 1908, lot 185, to M. Renard, 1,700 fr.; anon. sale, Paris 21 June 1919, 2,355 fr.; R. Gerard; purchased from him by Bernheim-Jeune, 11 Oct. 1919, and sold to Hahnloser, 11 Nov. 1919 (Arch B-J); Dr. Arthur Hahnloser, Winterthur, d. 1938; Professor Hans Hahnloser, Berne, his son, to 1965; mixed sale (including his property), Sotheby's, 30 June 1965, lot 29, to Zurich agent for Objets d'Art International; with Spencer Samuels, their New York representative; bought from him by the present owner, Sept. 1967.

Exhibitions: *Bd Italiens*, Paris 1864, no. 157 (as 'Copie d'après Rubens', 64 × 55 cm, lent by M. Arosa); Winterthur 1922, no. 43; Louvre 1930, no. 255A; Basle 1937, no. 14; Lucerne 1940, no. 38; Wildenstein, London 1952, no. 53; Bordeaux 1963, no. 13; Berne 1963-4, no. 24; Bremen 1964, no. 20; Providence 1975, no. 80, repr.

Literature: Album of photolithographs of pictures in the Arosa collection (privately printed by 1878, never distributed commercially. Annotated copy in *Bib AA*, bound together with Arosa sale catalogue), repr. no. 21; Cat. Exh. Atelier Delacroix, Paris 1952, under no. 5; K. E. Maison, *Themes and Variations* (Thames & Hudson, London, 1960. German ed., *Bild und Abbild*, published Munich and Zurich, 1960), p. 131, fig. 168; B. White, 'Delacroix's Painted Copies after Rubens', *AB*, XLIX (1967), pp. 37, 50, repr. fig. 27; L. Johnson, 'Four Rediscovered Portraits by Delacroix', *Burl Mag*, CXII (1970), p. 4, repr. fig. 3.

This full-scale copy is dated to 1828 by Robaut and, while he gives no reasons for his opinion, the apparent influence of the design and of some details of handling on Delacroix's portrait of Madame Simon of 1829 (J91) makes a date of 1828 plausible, if a little narrow. In some aspects of the handling it seems, though generally freer, to have much in common with the copy painted in 1824 of the portrait of Charles II of Spain attributed to Carreño (J21), and could therefore be earlier than Robaut places it. It seems, in any case, most likely to have been painted in the years immediately following the English journey of 1825, a period when Delacroix was strongly influenced by Rubens.

20 HENRI IV ENTRUSTS THE REGENCY TO MARIA DE' MEDICI, after RUBENS (Louvre, RF2093)   Pl. 14

$35\frac{1}{4} \times 45\frac{7}{8}$ in. (0.895 × 1.165 m)* E.D.

Moreau p. 320. R1947 (No repr.) and R Ann 39bis (1821)

c. 1825/31

Los Angeles County Museum of Art

Provenance: Delacroix's posthumous sale, Feb. 1864, lot 169, to Thoré (Burty Ann ED), probably for Emile Pereire, 1,950 fr.; Emile Pereire sale, 6 March 1872, to A. Hulot, 2,650 fr.; his sale, 9 May 1892, 3,000 fr.; with Brame, Paris; with Durand-Ruel, Paris, New York, Paris, May 1892-Sept. 1896; they sold it to Edgar Degas, 4 Sept. 1896 (Arch D-R); his sale, 26 March 1918, lot 25 (repr.), 24,000 fr.; with P. Rosenberg by 1921; Boner, Berlin, by 1930; with F. and P. Nathan, Zurich, by 1956, to 1958; they sold it to Los Angeles County Museum (P.306.58-3), 1958.

Exhibitions: *EBA*, Paris 1885, no. 116; Basle 1921, no. 89; Louvre 1930, no. 226; Basle 1937, no. 16; Venice 1956, no. 19; Toronto-Ottawa, 1962-3, no. 10, repr.; Edinburgh-London 1964, no. 27; Providence 1975, no. 84, repr.

Literature: Silvestre *Delacroix* (1855), p. 83; Meier-Graefe 1922, repr. p. 124; Escholier I, repr. p. 91; C. Mauclair, 'Delacroix', *L'Art et les Artistes*, XVIII N.S. (1929), repr. p. 162; P. Fierens, 'Eugène Delacroix, admirateur et copiste de Rubens', *Pictura*, II (1946), p. 5; presumably P. Lemoisne, *Degas et son œuvre* (Paul Brame et C. M. de Hauke aux Arts et Métiers Graphiques, Paris, 1946, I, p. 259 (report of E. Moreau-Nélaton's visit to Degas in 1907, reprinted from the former's article in *L'Amour de l'Art*, XII (1931), p. 269);[1] R. Brown, 'A Study after Rubens by Delacroix', *Bulletin of the Art Division, Los Angeles County Museum*, X, no. 2 (1958), pp. 3-7, repr. in monochrome fig. 1, detail (the three woman) repr. in colour on cover; R. Brown, 'A Further Note on Delacroix's Study after Rubens', ibid., no. 3, p. 18, repr.; Johnson 1963, p. 101, detail (the King's head) repr. in colour pl. 51; B. White, 'Delacroix's Painted Copies after Rubens', *AB*, XLIX (1967), pp. 37, 41, 48 f., repr. fig. 22; J. Thuillier and J. Foucart, *Le Storie di Maria de' Medici di Rubens al Lussemburgo* (Rizzoli, Milan, 1967; ed. in French, Paris 1969), p. 80.

This free copy is from the lower half of Rubens's painting in the Medici cycle, and about half the scale of the original. A wide variety of dates has been proposed without supporting arguments: annotated Robaut, 1821, Meier-Graefe (1922), *c*. 1835(?), C. Mauclair (1929), 1822, P. Fierens (1946), 1822–4, R. Brown (1958), 'just before Delacroix's African journey of 1832'. Escholier, while not advancing a date, reproduced the copy in such a position in his book as to suggest that he believed it to date from about the mid-1820s. I originally proposed a date of *c*. 1838/41 (Cat. Exh. Toronto–Ottawa, 1962–3; Johnson 1963) because I thought this unusually large copy might have been done in preparation for a major mural scheme and because the palette used for the King's head was similar to one Delacroix composed for De Planet's use in the ceiling paintings in the library of the Palais Bourbon and was employed in the manner of colour modelling advised by Delacroix at the time (cf. Planet *Souvenirs*, pp. 72–4). I still believe these analogies are valid and that this copy may, like J17, have been consulted when the Library decorations were being painted in the early 1840s; but I revised my opinion of the dating in 1964 (Cat. Exh. Edinburgh–London), because it no longer seemed to me possible to support so late a dating, in view of the style of the picture as a whole. The handling of the costumes, ranging in the treatment of highlights from the precision of the armour through the rather timid speckling of the King's tunic to the broad schematic strokes in the women's skirts, now suggests to me a lack of unity, a concern with differences of detail rather than synthesis, that is more consistent with a copy from the 1820s than the late 1830s.

[1] Moreau-Nélaton reports that on leaving Degas's bedroom, 'nous saluons au passage, dans la pièce voisine . . . une copie [de Delacroix] d'après Rubens, devant laquelle mon compagnon [Degas] s'est arrêté en jetant: "Vous savez, Delacroix avait laissé ça chez Mme Sand."' It was probably to this copy that Degas referred, as held by R. Brown (op. cit. 1958, p. 4).

21 COPY OF A PORTRAIT
OF CHARLES II OF SPAIN (1661–1700) (now attributed to Juan Carreño de Miranda (1614–85); to Velazquez by Delacroix)

Pl. 18

$45\frac{3}{4} \times 35\frac{3}{16}$ in. (1.162 × 0.894 m)*
R Ann 204ter (1827)[1]
1824
Private collection, Paris

Provenance: Bequeathed by Delacroix in 1863 to Baron Charles Rivet, d. 1872; by descent to Mme de Catheu, by 1916; acquired from the de Catheu family, Château de

Fougeras (Haute-Vienne) by Fabius Frères, Paris, 1950; sold by them to the present owner, 1966.

Exhibition: Bd Italiens, Paris 1864, no. 108 (as 'Copie du portrait de Philippe IV d'après Vélasquez', 115 × 88 cm., lent by Baron Rivet).

Literature: Silvestre *Delacroix* (1855), p. 83; Delacroix's will, dated 3 Aug. 1863, in *Correspondance* (Burty, 1878), p. v; Moreau-Nélaton 1. 60, fig. 32; M. Florisoone, 'El Hispanismo de Delacroix', *Revista española de Arte*, 11 (1933), p. 389; G. H. Hamilton, 'Hamlet or Childe Harold? Delacroix and Byron', *GBA*, XXVI ('1944'; but article dated 8 Jan. 1945), pp. 372 ff., fig. 6 (wrongly indicated as in Coll. Rivet, Paris); G. Viallefond, *Le Peintre Léon Riesener* (Editions Albert Morancé, Paris?, 1955), p. 26; Johnson 1963, p. 20; M. Florisoone, 'La Genèse espagnole des *Massacres de Scio*', *Revue du Louvre*, 13 (1963), pp. 195–8, 200 n. 2; Huyghe, pp. 66, 87, fig. 55; Maltese, p. 133.

Copies: 1. Pencil study by Bonington, 14.6 × 9.8 cm, *c*. 1825 (Castle Museum and Art Gallery, Nottingham). 2. Léon Riesener, water-colour with gouache, gum in shadows, 21 × 17 cm, Cat. Exh. Léon Riesener, Couper Gallery, London Nov.–Dec. 1965, no. 31, repr. 3. Unidentified artist, full-scale copy in oils on canvas, inscribed lower left: 'Eug. Delacroix d'après Vélasquez/1850.' 1.165 × 0.897 m, Prince de Ligne, Château de Belœil, Belgium (withdrawn from sale Sotheby's, London 3 July 1968, for which catalogued as a Delacroix and repr. in colour, lot 17).

These three works appear to have been taken from Delacroix's copy and not from the original.

Of all Delacroix's copies, this portrait is the most completely documented in his writings. On 25 March 1824, he went with his friend Leblond to see some pictures, which included 'un Velasquez admirable, qui occupe tout mon esprit' (*Journal* 1. 63–4). On 11 April, he obtained permission to copy it (ibid. 72) and referred periodically to the progress he was making on the copy (ibid. 76, 78, 80, 82) until 7 May 1824, when he confided that his resolve was flagging: 'aujourd'hui je ne puis penser à l'achever que comme à une *seccatura*' (ibid. 94). In none of these references does Delacroix state the location or the subject of the painting he was copying. He did, however, leave the only copy in oils that he is known for certain to have painted after a so-called Velazquez[2] to Baron Rivet, describing it in his will as 'copie du portrait de Charles II, roi d'Espagne, d'après Velasquez' (Burty, op. cit.); and in an unpublished note of a loan, datable to 1829, he wrote: 'à Rivet le Charles II d'après Velasquez' (Louvre, RF 23355, fol. 42^v.). It is also described in the list of copies from his own hand published during his lifetime in Silvestre *Delacroix* (1855), as 'Grand portrait de Charles II, de Vélasquez.' In a letter of 21 August 1863, a week after Delacroix's death, Léon Riesener wrote to Baron Rivet referring to the bequest: 'Vous savez que notre ami vous a dédié sa belle copie d'après Vélasquez que vous aimiez tant' (G. Viallefond, op. cit.). Joubin was the first to identify the original as a portrait of Charles II of Spain (Fig. 5) which was in the Duke of Orleans's Gallery at the Palais Royal in 1824 and attributed to Juan Carreño de Miranda, a pupil of Velasquez (*Journal* III. 525–additions to I. 63 and 64; I. 72 n. 5). Hamilton (op. cit., p. 372) specified that it was recorded as being in the Palais Royal in 1825 by J. Vatout, *Catalogue historique et descriptif des tableaux appartenant . . . [au] Duc d'Orléans*, II, Paris 1825, no. 166, p. 423 (where no attribution is proposed). Hamilton added that it was odd Delacroix should have mistaken it for a Velazquez since it had been attributed to Carreño a year earlier in *Indicateur de la Galerie des Tableaux . . . au Palais Royal.* By 1836, it had been transferred to the Château d'Eu and listed as a Carreño in the catalogue of pictures in that royal residence (see J. Vatout, *Le Château d'Eu. Notices historiques*, IV (Impr. Félix Malteste, Paris, 1836), p. 101, no. 252). It was in the Duc de Vendôme sale, Paris, 4 Dec. 1931, lot 60, being now listed as only attributed to Carreño. Joubin (*Journal* I. 72 n. 5), followed by Florisoone (op. cit., p. 195), states that it was a copy after Carreño, which may well be

Fig. 5. *Charles II of Spain*, attr. to Carreño de Miranda.

true, but the original from which it is supposed to have been copied has not been convincingly identified.

Delacroix was painting this full-scale copy[3] concurrently with the *Massacres of Chios* (J105). He was fairly explicit about the qualities he admired in the Spanish portrait at the time: 'Voilà ce que j'ai cherché si longtemps, cet empâté ferme et pourtant fondu. Ce qu'il faut principalement se rappeler, *ce sont les mains*' (*Journal* I. 72, 11 April 1824). On 14 April, he noted: 'Ce matin au *Velasquez*. Recommencé la tête, qui était trop forte pour le corps' (ibid. 78). A ridge of paint visible along the outer contour of the hair at the top and left of the head may be a vestige of this alteration.

In terms of influence on Delacroix's own work, this copy probably affected the technique of some passages in the *Massacres of Chios* and it may have suggested the motif of a hand grasping a tentacular glove in a hat that is employed in the portrait of Louis Schwiter of 1826 (J82). Indeed, being a copy of a full-length male portrait on a large scale, it is in a sense the most relevant exercise that Delacroix had had in preparation for the Schwiter portrait. It has been suggested that this copy influenced the design of Delacroix's *Self-portrait as Ravenswood*, but if the influence is accepted on visual evidence, and there is none other, the traditional date of the Self-portrait would have to be changed (see J64).

[1] A MS. note on p. 60, accompanied by a small sketch, describes it as: 'Philippe IV, copié par E. Delacroix, d'après Velasquez sur toile de 40 environ. Donné par le Maître au Baron Rivet.' A larger copy by Robaut is contained in Tracings I.

[2] The following pictures are listed as copies by Delacroix after Velazquez in Inv. Delacroix, but no autograph copies after Velazquez are listed in his posthumous sale and the attributions in the inventory may therefore have all, like no. 99, been found to be inaccurate by the time of the sale: no. 64, '1 portrait de femme' (see J(L)32); no. 97, 'un portrait'; no. 99, '1 copie de l'infante d'après Velazquez' (attributed to Géricault in the posthumous sale, lot 234); no. 219, '1 portrait d'homme'.

[3] Its dimensions in fact slightly exceed those given by J. Vatout (op. cit., 1825) for the portrait in the Palais Royal, which were 39 × 31 'pouces'. Vatout may have recorded the sight measurements only. The size is listed as 1.25 × 1.53 m in the catalogue of the Duc de Vendôme sale of 1931, where the original canvas is said to have been enlarged.

22 COPY OF A ST.   Pl. 19
CATHERINE (attributed to Zurbarán; to Alonso Cano by Delacroix)

$32\frac{1}{8} \times 25\frac{5}{8}$ in. (81.5 × 65 cm)*

c. 1824/7

Musée des Beaux-Arts, Béziers

Provenance: Presumed to be the painting bequeathed by Delacroix in 1863 to Baronne de Rubempré;[1] M. Adalbert de Faniez, d. *c.* 1896; by his bequest to the city of Béziers.

Exhibition: Bordeaux 1963, no. 66.

Literature: Silvestre *Delacroix* (1855), p. 83; Delacroix's will, dated 3 Aug. 1863, in *Correspondance* (Burty, 1878), p. vi; Inv. Delacroix, no. 292; *Musée de la Ville de Béziers.*

Catalogue des peintures, aquarelles, dessins, sculptures, objets d'art, etc. (Imp. A. Bouineau, Béziers [1905]), p. 20, no. 54; L. Johnson, 'The Delacroix Centenary in France—I', *Burl Mag*, CV (1963), p. 302, repr. fig. 8; M. Florisoone, 'La Genèse espagnole des Massacres de Scio', *Revue du Louvre*, 13 (1963), p. 200 n. 2.

Delacroix described this picture in his will as 'une copie de Sainte en buste tenant une palme et une épée, d'après Alonzo Cano' (Burty, op. cit.); and he refers to the same work, no doubt, in some notes that he made on 21 June 1856, apparently with a view to drafting a will: 'Rubempré, portrait de sainte.' (*Journal* II. 458). Though it is not stated in his will to be from his own hand (nor indeed is the copy of the portrait of Charles II of Spain (J21), which is more fully documented in other sources), it was recorded in print by a well-informed source during the artist's lifetime as an autograph copy, being described in the list of copies by Delacroix in Silvestre *Delacroix* (1855) as 'Sainte avec une épée, par Alonzo Cano (galerie du maréchal Soult).' It is also listed as by Delacroix in Inv. Delacroix. The model appears in fact to have been a painting that, whatever its earlier attribution, was listed in the catalogue of the Soult sale, Paris 19–22 May 1852, as a Zurbarán and described thus (lot 40): '*Sainte Catherine.* Elle est représentée à mi-corps, tenant un glaive d'une main et une palme de l'autre'; canvas, 83 × 63 cm. The painting (Fig. 6) was bought by Barclay, and later passed into the collection of Lt. Col. William Stirling of Keir, Dunblane, Scotland, where it remained until *c.* 1963. It does not seem to be mentioned in the recent literature on Zurbarán (or Cano).

On 3 May 1824, Delacroix recorded seeing Marshal Soult's pictures and made a note to recall some of the female figures when painting the angels for his *Agony in the Garden* (J00), which was to be shown at the Salon in 1827 and for which a preliminary oil sketch had been painted in January 1824: 'Vu les tableaux du maréchal Soult.—Penser, en faisant mes anges pour le préfet, à ces belles et mystiques figures de femmes, une, entre autres, qui porte ses tétons dans un plat [the *St. Agatha* by Zurbarán, Musée Fabre,

Fig. 6. *St. Catherine*, attr. to Zurbarán.

Montpellier]' (*Journal* I. 91). It is highly probable that the *St. Catherine* was one of the mystic figures that he admired on that visit, and, as I suggested in 1963 (op. cit.), it seems likely that this copy was painted sometime between that visit to the Soult collection and the exhibition of the *Agony in the Garden* in 1827.

¹ The stretcher is inscribed in ink: 'Eugène Delacroix à la Baronne de Rubempré', and the canvas is stamped with the trade-mark of Haro, Delacroix's colour merchant; but it is not known how or when the painting came into the possession of its last private owner, M. de Faniez.

Costume, Accessories, Arms and Armour

23 A SEATED INDIAN,   Pl. 21
THREE-QUARTER VIEW

Cardboard on wood panel, 14⅜ × 10⅝ in. (36.5 × 27 cm)
Painted initials bottom right: *DC*
R1488 (1823. No repr. under this number, but the picture listed is wrongly used to illustrate R82—J23a)

c. 1823/4
Rijksmuseum Kröller-Müller, Otterlo

Provenance: Presumably Delacroix's posthumous sale, Feb. 1864, lot 183 ('Costume de Calcutta.—Le personnage qui le porte est assis, les jambes croisées, vêtu de marron, vu de trois quarts', 40 × 33 cm. Support not listed), to de Laage,

630 fr.; Philippe Burty, by 1885; his sale, 2 March 1891, lot 11 (as *attributed* to Delacroix: 'Nègre assis. Les jambes croisées, la tête couverte d'un chapeau rouge. Esquisse sur carton collé sur bois', without dimensions), to Bernheim-Jeune (Arch B-J, with dimensions: 37 × 26 cm), 420 fr.; sold by them to J. R. P. C. H. de Kuyper, The Hague, Apr. 1891 (ibid.); his sale, Amsterdam 30 May 1911, lot 34 (repr.); Mrs. H. Kröller-Müller, The Hague, 1911 (her collection became the Kröller-Müller Foundation in 1928, and the Rijksmuseum Kröller-Müller (Inv. no. 91-11) in 1938).

Exhibitions: *EBA*, Paris 1885, no. 38 (as 'Prince javanais assis.—Etude (1823)', 35 × 26 cm, lent by Ph. Burty);[1] Düsseldorf 1928, no. 29; Rotterdam 1935, no. 11 (as by Decamps); Arnhem 1936, no. 16 (as by Decamps); Edinburgh-London 1964, no. 9 (as by Decamps).

Literature: H. P. Bremmer, *Catalogus van de schilderijen verzameling van Mevrouw H. Kröller-Müller, 's Gravenhage, Lange Voorhout I*, 1917, no. 39 (as by Decamps); H. P. Bremmer, *Catalogus verzameling H. Kröller-Müller, 's Gravenhage, Lange Voorhout I*, I (1921), no. 66 (as by Decamps); *Catalogue of Nineteenth and Twentieth Century Painting—State Museum Kröller-Müller* (Otterlo, 1957. Ed. in Dutch, 1956), p. 34 no. 106 (as by Delacroix); M. Sérullaz, 'A Comment on the Delacroix Exhibition organized in England', *Burl Mag*, CVII (1965), p. 366.

The presence of the initials 'DC', with which Decamps (1803-60) often signed his paintings, in the lower right corner of this study is first recorded in the catalogue of the de Kuyper sale in 1911, where the picture was nevertheless listed and sold as a Delacroix. It was attributed to Decamps in all literature and in all exhibitions between the first and second World Wars—no doubt on the strength of these initials. It was reclaimed as by Delacroix in the post-war catalogue of the Kröller-Müller Museum, the initials being said to have been 'presumably added later'. In the Cat. Exh. Edinburgh-London 1964, I (1) questioned whether it was conceivable that anyone would have added the initials used by Decamps to a picture that had always been attributed to a greater artist; (2) suggested it was more probable that they were concealed by a frame or by dirt at the time of Delacroix's posthumous sale; and (3) re-attributed this study to Decamps, together with J25, which seemed to me, then as now, unquestionably by the same hand, though the attribution to Delacroix had not previously been challenged in print. The inclusion of this single seated figure as merely attributed to Delacroix (among other works by him for which no such reservation was made) in the catalogue of the Burty sale of 1891 seemed to confirm my doubts about its authenticity, the sale having occurred during the lifetime of Robaut and of Burty, the latter of whom had actually helped to classify the drawings in Delacroix's posthumous sale in 1864.

A third picture from the group of four paintings of apparently the same Indian, which are listed in the catalogue of the posthumous sale and by Robaut, has since come to light (J24) and is, in my view, by the same hand as the two under discussion, as is the fourth picture that has reappeared still more recently (J23a).

Sérullaz (op. cit., 1965, p. 366 and fig. 28), contesting the attributions to Decamps, reproduced a sheet of five pencil studies of heads which he had 'discovered' were in the Musée des Beaux-Arts at Besançon (D.2405), two of which appeared to be direct studies by Delacroix for the seated Indian in J25, and the other three, closely related to the Otterlo painting. That sheet, which bears the stamp of Delacroix's posthumous sale, was of course already known to me and fresh in my mind when I attributed the paintings to Decamps, but at the time the initials 'DC' on the Otterlo study seemed to me the overriding consideration and adequate evidence in themselves for contesting Delacroix's authorship of the two paintings from the series that were then known and of the sheet of drawings. I now believe that it is to attach undue weight to these lightly applied initials to allow them to serve as a basis for denying Delacroix's hand, not only in the Besançon sheet of drawings, but in four paintings which are listed as autograph in the catalogue of his posthumous sale and in Robaut. Rejection of these four painted studies of Indians would also imply rejection of the *Studies of a Pair of Babouches* (J26), which seems so closely related to them. New evidence which has contributed to the revision of my opinion is the following note of a loan in one of Delacroix's sketch-books used between 1825 and 1830: 'à Mr Rue.—une toile l'indie [*sic*, and this word struck through twice] / les deux études de l'indien en habit brun sur la même toile' [all struck through from 'Mr Rue' on, presumably upon return of the loan] (Louvre RF9144, fol. 22v). Though Delacroix does not specify that the picture is by him, he ordinarily notes the name of the artist when lending works that are not from his hand, and it may be reasonably assumed both that he is referring to the *Two Studies of an Indian, Standing* (J24), as the costume is brown, and that it is from his hand. His note could be taken further to imply the existence of a canvas with two studies of the Indian in a costume other than brown (i.e. J25, where the dress is white). Moreover, his striking through of his first description of the loan, which was evidently to read 'l'indien', suggests that he saw the possibility of confusion between the loan he was actually making and a painting of a single Indian—no doubt the Otterlo study or J23a. Thus the existence by the latter half of the 1820s of at least two paintings of Indians in Delacroix's studio, and seemingly from his own hand, is firmly documented.

The problem remains of how to account for the presence of the initials 'DC' on a painting which the main body of evidence indicates is by Delacroix, how explain Burty's apparent loss of confidence in its authenticity by 1891. The possibility of this being a copy by Decamps after a lost original by Delacroix can, in my opinion, be ruled out. It is also most improbable that the initials were added between 1891, when it was both bought and sold as a Delacroix by Bernheim-Jeune, and 1911 when it passed as a Delacroix, with mention of the initials 'DC', in the sale of the man who had bought it from Bernheim-Jeune. Nor are they likely to have been added between 1885, when Robaut published his *catalogue raisonné*, reproducing the picture as a Delacroix, and 1891. For reasons that remain obscure, it seems that they can only have been added sometime between 1864, when de Laage bought the picture at Delacroix's post-humous sale, and 1885, when it is recorded in Burty's possession. It was apparently also in that period that the picture was cut down from the size listed in the catalogue of Delacroix's posthumous sale for the lot that this is presumed to be, and affixed to a wood panel—a process which would have necessitated removing the seal of the posthumous sale from the back of the cardboard.

The initials 'DC', being perhaps covered by dirt or by a frame, appear to have been overlooked by Robaut and Burty up to 1885 at least, for Robaut notes that the picture was unsigned in his annotated copy of the 2nd edition of the Cat. Exh. *EBA*, Paris 1885 (*Bib AA*, MS. 298[ter]) and he neither notes nor reproduces the initials on his copy in coloured chalks contained in Tracings I. Burty may have uncovered them sometime after the exhibition; which could account for why the study was merely attributed to Delacroix in the Burty sale.

None of the studies in this series of Indians appears to have served Delacroix for a completed painting. The closest analogy in a finished work is the *Indian armed with a Kukri* (J39).

[1] The identification of this exhibit with the picture illustrated as R82 is confirmed in R Ann and in Robaut's annotated copy of the 2nd edition of the exhibition catalogue (*Bib AA*, MS. 298[ter]).

23a A SEATED INDIAN,   Pl. 21
PROFILE VIEW

$18\frac{3}{16} \times 14\frac{13}{16}$ in. (46.2 × 37.6 cm).* E.D.
Moreau p. 321. R82 (1823. History after 1864 confused with that of J23, by which it is also wrongly illustrated.)
c. 1823/4
Private collection, Paris*

Provenance: Delacroix's posthumous sale, Paris 1864, lot 184 ('Même personnage [as preceding lot—J23], vu de profil', 45 × 37 cm), to David Michau, 650 fr., d. *c.* 1877; his posthumous sale (D. M . . .), 11 Oct. 1877, lot 18 ('Costume de Calcutta', without further description), to Mme Edouard Michel(?),[1] his niece, 325 fr.; Mme Edouard Michel; by descent to M. Edouard Michel, her grandson, by 1978.

Exhibitions: None.
Literature: None.
In an unpublished letter to Moreau, dated 1 April 1873, Michau confirms that he bought an 'Indien de Calcutta' at Delacroix's posthumous sale, and gives a description of it that matches this picture. He also lists the support as canvas and the dimensions as those given in the catalogue of the posthumous sale (Moreau N). It is therefore clear that the Otterlo version (J23), which is painted on cardboard and has always had different dimensions from these, is not the one bought by Michau, as claimed by Sérullaz (op. cit., 1965, under previous number).

[1] According to Mme Michel's grandson, she inherited the picture from Michau. If so, she presumably had to buy it in at this sale.

24 TWO STUDIES OF   Pl. 20
AN INDIAN, STANDING

$14\frac{1}{2} \times 18$ in. (36.8 × 45.7 cm) Relined. E.D.
R1489 (1823. No repr.)
c. 1823/4
Mr. and Mrs. Paul Mellon, Upperville, Va.

Provenance: Delacroix's posthumous sale, Feb. 1864, lot 185 ('Deux études sur la même toile: le personnage, debout, est vu de face, et auprès, vu de dos', 37 × 45 cm), to Edouard Frère, 410 fr.; his sale, 29 Nov. 1889, lot 215 (as 'Grecs'[1]), 250 fr.; P. A. Cheramy; his sale, 5 May 1908, lot 182 ('Deux études d'Indiens. L'un de face, l'autre de trois quarts à droite et de dos.' Wrongly stated to be lot 144 (J(O)10) from Delacroix's posthumous sale), to Georges Petit, 500 fr.; sale estate P. A. Cheramy, 15 Apr. 1913, lot 36 (same description as for 1908 sale, and same error), to Cassirer, 1,700 fr.; Bloomingdale, New York; mixed sale, Galerie Charpentier, Paris 14 June 1957, lot 55 (as 'Deux études d'homme asiatique en costume de guerrier'), 2,500,000 fr.; with Gallery Moos Ltd., Toronto; with Eugene Thaw, New York; purchased from him by Paul Mellon, 1969.

Exhibitions: Galerie Godard Lefort, Montreal, Oct.–Nov. 1968, Gallery Moos, Toronto, Nov.–Dec. 1968, no. 6, repr. (mixed exhibition without title).

Literature: *Catalogue of Nineteenth and Twentieth Century Painting—State Museum Kröller-Müller* (Otterlo, 1957. Ed. in Dutch, 1956), p. 34, under no. 106; L. Johnson, in Cat. Exh. Edinburgh–London 1964, under no. 9.

Though Robaut did not reproduce this painting in his published *catalogue raisonné* and described it inaccurately, no doubt because it was unknown to him before the Frère sale of 1889, it is reproduced in coloured chalks on grey paper in Robaut Tracings I and the description is amended to read thus in R Ann: 'Ce sont deux personnages debout dont l'un est à gauche, vu de face; l'autre, vu de dos la tête détournée et de profil.'

It is evidently to this picture that Delacroix refers in noting a loan to M. Rue in a sketch-book used between 1825 and 1830 (see J23 for a transcription of the note and discussion of the series to which this study belongs).

A pencil drawing of a full-length Oriental figure with turban, datable *c.* 1823/4 (Louvre sketch-book, RF23355, fol. 27^v), is very similar in pose to the study on the left of this canvas and shows a similar abbreviation of the model's right hand which, as here, rests in mid-air as though supported by an invisible cane. It appears unlikely that this drawing and the oil studies of Indians are far apart in date.

[1] With no further details, but it is noted in R Ann (margin to R1489) that this study of an Indian passed in the Frère sale as lot 215.

25 TWO STUDIES OF   Pl. 20
AN INDIAN, STANDING AND SEATED

$14\frac{3}{4} \times 18$ in. (37.5 × 45.7 cm) Relined. E.D.

R1483 (1823)

c. 1823/4

Mr. and Mrs. Paul Mellon, Upperville, Va.

Provenance: Delacroix's posthumous sale, Feb. 1864, lot 186 ('Deux études sur la même toile: le même personnage [as preceding lot—J24], habillé de blanc, est assis; auprès, il est debout et vu de face', 37 × 45 cm), to Cadart & Luquet, 455 fr.; with Detrimont; purchased from him by Henri Rouart, Feb. 1844 (R Ann); his sale, 9 Dec. 1912, lot 190, to Lucien Henraux, 5,600 fr.; in his family to 1937, when sold to P. Rosenberg; Erich Maria Remarque, Porto Ronco, Ticino, Switzerland, by 1938; with Sam Salz, New York; purchased from him by Paul Mellon, Oct. 1960.

Exhibitions: *Bd Italiens*, Paris 1864, no. 311 (supp. to 3rd ed., as 'Les deux Indiens'); *EBA*, Paris 1885, no. 191; *Centennale*, Paris 1900, no. 223; Louvre 1930, no. 12; Amsterdam 1938, no. 114; Zurich 1939, no. 304; Remarque collection, Knoedler, New York Oct.-Nov. 1943, no. 3; Wildenstein, New York 1944, no. 1, repr.; (on loan from E. M. Remarque to the Metropolitan Museum, New York, 1949-56); Venice 1956, no. 3; (on loan from E. M. Remarque to the Kunsthaus, Zurich, 1957); Louvre 1963, no. 42, repr.

Literature: L. Johnson, 'Delacroix at the Biennale', *Burl Mag*, XCVIII (1956), p. 327; *Catalogue of Nineteenth and Twentieth Century Painting—State Museum Kröller-Müller* (Otterlo, 1957. Ed. in Dutch, 1956), p. 34, under no. 106; L. Johnson, in Cat. Exh. Edinburgh-London 1964, under no. 9; M. Sérullaz, 'A comment on the Delacroix Exhibition organized in England', *Burl Mag*, CVII (1965), p. 366; G. Brett, *Delacroix* (Knowledge Publications: 'The Masters' 15, London, 1965), repr. in colour pl. II.

See J23 for a full discussion of the group of studies of which this is a part.

Robaut lists as a variant of the standing figure here a water-colour, 23 × 15.5 cm, which passed in the Robert Caze sale, 30 April 1886, to Meyer, the '*expert*' for the sale, for 60 fr. (R Ann 1483bis). His reproduction of it in black and red chalks on tracing paper in Tracings I shows that in the position of the hands and the inclusion of a scarf across the shoulders it was closer to the figure on the left in J24.

26 STUDIES OF A PAIR OF   Pl. 22
BABOUCHES

Cardboard, $6\frac{1}{2} \times 8\frac{1}{8}$ in. (16.6 × 20.6 cm)* E.D.

R424 (1832)

c. 1823/4

Musée du Louvre

Provenance: Delacroix's posthumous sale, Feb. 1864, part of lot 221 ('Diverses toiles: études, esquisses et ébauches', without dimensions), to M. de Calonne, 165 fr., who gave it to the painter Gustave Ricard;[1] his sale, 20 June 1873, lot 37, to Alfred Sensier, 200 fr.; his sale, 10 Dec. 1877, lot 3, to Gauchez (probably for Wilson), 785 fr.; John Wilson; his sale, 14 March 1881, lot 147, to Malinet, 1,320 fr.; Auguste Courtin; his sale, 29 March 1886, lot 38, to P. A. Cheramy, 435 fr.; his sale, 5 May 1908, lot 153, to Wedel, 4,500 fr.; sale estate of P. A. Cheramy, 15 Apr. 1913, lot 22, to Schoeller, 3,050 fr.; Carle Dreyfus, by 1930; by his bequest to the Louvre (RF1953-4), 1953.

Exhibitions: Art Musulman, Paris 1893, no. 111; *Les Mains et les Pieds dans l'Art*, Galerie Sambon, Paris 1924, no. 39; Louvre 1930, no. 60; Orangerie, Paris 1933A, no. 177; Atelier Delacroix, Paris 1945, no. 43; *Collection Carle Dreyfus*, Cabinet des Dessins, Louvre 1953, no. 29; Bordeaux 1963, no. 18; Atelier Delacroix, Paris 1971 (no cat.); Marseille 1975, no. 52, repr. in colour.

Literature: J. Meier-Graefe and E. Klossowski, *La Collection Cheramy . . .* (R. Piper, Munich, 1908), p. 94, no. 174; E. Lambert, 'Delacroix et les Femmes d'Alger' (H. Laurens, Paris 1937), pp. 33, 54, repr. pl. IX. 19; Sterling-Adhémar, no. 677, pl. 238; R. Huyghe *et al.*, *Delacroix* (Hachette, Coll. Génies et Réalités, Paris, 1963), repr. p. 134.

Robaut catalogued this study among sketches from the North African journey, under the year 1832, but without connecting it with any specific painting. It was suggested in the catalogue of the exhibition Louvre 1930: 'Ces babouches ne sont pas sans rapport avec celles qui figurent dans les *Femmes d'Alger* [dated 1834] et peut-être conviendrait-il de les situer plus tard que Robaut, au moment des recherches pour le grand tableau.' In the catalogue of the Louvre exhibition in 1953, this study was dated to 1832 and claimed as 'Une des premières recherches pour les babouches que l'on voit dans "Les Femmes d'Alger".' There does not, however, appear to be any real connection between these slippers and any in the *Femmes d'Alger*. They seem very much more likely to be those worn by the Indian in J25, as noticed by Robaut in R Ann,[2] and in the other three paintings of the same model (J23, J23a and J24), in all of which the slippers are, as here, an olive-yellow on the outside, with scarlet trim. This study may also have served as a basis for the footwear in the *Indian armed with a Kukri*, shown at the Salon of 1831 (J39), but stylistically it is close to the series of Indians from the early 1820s.

Since 1864, when this picture passed in Delacroix's posthumous sale in a lot described as diverse canvases, its support has been variously listed as canvas, wood, and cardboard. These variations reflect errors in cataloguing and should not be taken as indicating that more than one version of this subject was painted by Delacroix.

[1] According to Robaut. However, a label on the back of the picture bears this inscription in ink: 'Peinture d'Eugène Delacroix avec le cachet de sa vente posthume en 1864. Achetée par Gustave Ricard le peintre et vendue après sa mort le 20 Juin 1873 à l'hôtel Drouot.

'Ricard avait cette peinture en son atelier et en parlait comme d'un morceau des plus éclatans, des plus vifs de Delacroix.'

Ricard is not recorded as a buyer of any pictures at the posthumous sale.

[2] Margin to R424: 'Ces mêmes babouches sont portées par le mulâtre qui pose pour la toile Nᵒ 186 de la Vente posth: Voir notre Nᵒ [1483].'

27 STUDIES OF A TURKISH FLINTLOCK GUN AND YATAGAN, Pl. 23

c. 1824

Paper laid down on canvas, $13\frac{3}{16} \times 20\frac{1}{16}$ in. (33.5 × 51 cm)* E.D.

Moreau p. 321. R1917 (No repr.)

c. 1824

Alfred Strolin, Neuilly-sur-Seine

Provenance: Delacroix's posthumous sale, Feb. 1864, lot 191, to Lemonnier, 900 fr.; sale M. G. C. [Chalupt], 26 March 1873, lot 12, 320 fr.; sale S[chwabacher], of Vienna, and L.R., 23 March 1875, lot 23, 500 fr.; Philippe Burty, by 1885; his sale, 2 March 1891, lot 6, 1,020 fr.; P. A. Cheramy, by 1892 (R Ann); his sale, 5 May 1908, lot 177, to Henri Haro, 500 fr.; his sale, 12 Dec. 1911, lot 213, to G. Bernheim, 450 fr.; Alfred Strolin; his sale ('Collection Strolin et succession de Mme Strolin-Vari, ayant fait l'objet de séquestres de guerre'), 7 July 1921, lot 11, bought back by him (conversation with his son, 1966), 550 fr.; by descent to the present owner, his son.

Exhibition: EBA, Paris 1885, no. 39 ('Etudes d'armes pour le "Massacre de Scio" (1823)').

Literature: J. Meier-Graefe and E. Klossowski, *La Collection Cheramy* ... (R. Piper, Munich, 1908), p. 114, no. 268; *Journal* I. 90 n. 3.

The study of the yatagan in its sheath evidently served for the *Turk Seated on a Sopha* (J35), which was probably painted no later than 1825 and where the same weapon is seen on the left.

Three pencil studies of the same gun as here are on a sheet of drawings in the Louvre (RF9823ʳ), which seems to date from *c.* 1824, since the verso contains one or more self-portrait studies where the artist does not appear to be older than twenty-five or twenty-six.

These are very possibly arms which Delacroix records on 1 May 1824 that he was expecting to receive: 'J'aurai, par le général Coëtlosquet, des armes de mameluk'. (*Journal* I. 90.) Joubin surmises in his note to this entry that all the studies R1917-19 (J27, J(O)5, J(O)4 and J(L)47a) may have been painted from arms lent by the General; but he apparently had no knowledge of the paintings when he composed the note, and of those extant it is only this picture which can be said to tally reasonably with the description 'Mameluk arms'.

28 STUDY OF A FIGURE IN GREEK COSTUME (Front view with foot raised on a socle) Pl. 27

$15\frac{3}{8} \times 10\frac{7}{16}$ in. (39 × 26.5 cm) E.D.

Moreau p. 320. R84 (1823. No repr.)

c. 1824/5

Whereabouts unknown

Provenance: Delacroix's posthumous sale, Feb. 1864, lot 177 ('Costume souliote. — Le personnage qui en est revêtu est vu de face, le pied posé sur une pierre', 40 × 26 cm. Burty Ann ED: 'Le visage est inachevé'), to Petit, 580 fr.; Jules Chéret, d. Nice 1932; Georges Bernheim sale, 7 June 1935, lot 49 (repr.), to Javal, 10,500 fr.

Exhibitions: None.

Literature: None, other than Moreau and Robaut.

This study is known to me only from the illustration in the catalogue of the Bernheim sale of 1935, reproduced here.

This picture, the three following numbers and J(L)38 form a coherent group of studies of Greek costume seen from a variety of view-points and as though worn by a native posing in dynamic attitudes. They were probably painted in close succession. They are dated variously 1822 or 1823 by Robaut; the commentary for this study and R85 (J(L)38) states, without supporting evidence, that these two were made 'en vue du *Massacre de Scio*' (J105), but they seem to be of no direct relevance to that painting and could well have been done after it had been completed or was nearing completion. The whole group has perhaps some connection with entries in the *Journal* (I. 116, 117) where Delacroix writes of seeing, wishing to copy and then borrowing costumes belonging to his friend, the painter Jules Robert Auguste. On 30 June 1824, he notes: 'Chez M. Auguste [. . .] Il serait trés avantageux d'avoir [. . .] et de les copier [. . .] les costumes grecs et persans, indiens, etc.' And on 8 July: 'Chez M. Auguste, chercher les costumes.' These studies could have been done from costumes borrowed from Auguste at that time; but they may also be nearer in date to the *Portrait of Count Palatiano in Suliot Costume* (J(L)80) where the subject wears the same type of costume as in this series—that is to say, they might have been painted around the latter half of 1825.

While this study and others in the group have traditionally been identified as Suliot costume (the dress of the inhabitants of the region of Suli in Albania (Epirus), who were noted for their sustained and courageous resistance to the Turks), I am unable to affirm that it should be narrowed down to that single region of Greece, and is not a more widely diffused national costume.

29 STUDY OF A FIGURE IN   Pl. 26
GREEK COSTUME (Back view)

$16\frac{1}{8} \times 12\frac{1}{4}$ in. (41×31 cm) E.D.
R Ann 85bis and R1486 (1823. No repr.[1])
c. 1824/5
Göteborgs Konstmuseum, Gothenburg

Provenance: Delacroix's posthumous sale, Feb. 1864, lot 179 ('Le même [personnage en costume souliote (lot 177; J28)], vu de dos, les bras étendus', 40×33 cm. Burty Ann ED 'Très clair & très vif'), to Isambert, 300 fr.; Dr. A. Tripier, by 1885; his sale, 31 May 1895, lot 14, to Diot and Tempelaere, 500 fr.; Edgar Degas; his sale, 26 March 1918, lot 30 (as 'Officier grec' and R80; J(L)41), 6,000 fr.; with a Munich dealer; with Svensk-Franska Konstgalleriet, Stockholm; purchased from them by the Göteborgs Konstmuseum (no. WL17), Sept. 1918.

Exhibition: *EBA*, Paris 1885, no. 221.

Literature: See P. Guigou, 'Eugène Delacroix', *Revue Moderniste*, No. 4 (Apr. 1885), p. 8;[2] A. W. [Alfred Westholm], 'Eugène Delacroix's Grekiska Dräkstudie', *Göteborgs Konst-Museum, Årstryck* 1953, pp. 61–3, fig. 27.

For discussion of the group to which this study belongs, see the preceding number.

   [1] It is, however, reproduced in Tracings 1.
   [2] Writing of the exhibition *EBA*, Paris 1885, Guigou mentions 'des Klephtes et des Turcs aux vestes brochées et ramagées d'or et d'émeraudes, au jupon blanc flottant, qui sont en même temps d'un pittoresque extrêmement vif et d'une habileté de facture rare.' This passage could refer to any, or all, of the studies of Greek costume that were shown, the others from this group being J30 and J(L)38. Klephtes were habitual rebels against Ali Pasha, Vizier of Epirus, and their cause was closely connected with the Greek struggle for independence from Turkish domination.

30 TWO STUDIES OF A FIGURE   Pl. 24
IN GREEK COSTUME (Front and side views)

$13\frac{7}{8} \times 18\frac{1}{4}$ in. (35.2×46.4 cm)* Relined. E.D.
R Ann 85ter (1823) and R1479 (1822. No repr.[1])
c. 1824/5
Musée du Louvre

Provenance: Delacroix's posthumous sale, Feb. 1864, part of lot 182 ('Deux autres études [de costume souliote] séparées', without dimensions), to Paul Huet, 205 fr. (Burty Ann ED), d. 1869; René Paul Huet, his son; by descent to M. Perret-Carnot, his son-in-law; recovered by Service français de récupération artistique following World War II, and deposited at the Louvre (MNR143/anc. Fr.239).

Exhibitions: *EBA*, Paris 1885, no. 113; Art Musulman, Paris 1893, no. 113; St. Petersburg 1912, no. 191; Louvre 1930, no. 10A; *Petit Palais*, Paris 1936, no. 239; (on deposit at the Musée national des Beaux Arts, Algiers, 1952–61); Venice 1956, no. 2 (wrongly identified as R1482); Athens 1963 (no cat.).

Literature: See P. Guigou ref. for 1885, under J29 (*Literature* and n. 2); R. P. Huet, *Paul Huet* . . . (H. Laurens, Paris, 1911), p. 381; L. Johnson, 'Delacroix at the Biennale', *Burl Mag*, XCVIII (1956), p. 327; J. A. Meletopoulos, 'L'Exposition sur "L'Insurrection hellénique et le philhellénisme français depuis le Directoire et jusqu'à 1830" au Musée national historique', *Messager d'Athènes — Le Progrès*, 17 May 1963 (unpaginated), mentioned on last page of text in the offprint, and a full-page repr.

For discussion of the group to which this study belongs, see J28.

   [1] It is, however, reproduced in Tracings 1.

31 TWO STUDIES OF A FIGURE   Pl. 25
IN GREEK COSTUME (Front views)

$16\frac{7}{8} \times 17\frac{15}{16}$ in. (42.9×45.5 cm[1])* Relined. E.D.
R1481 (1822. No repr.)
c. 1824/5
Musée du Louvre

Provenance: Delacroix's posthumous sale, Feb. 1864, lot 181 ('Deux autres figures [en costume souliote] sur la même toile', 42×43 cm), to M. Philippe Rousseau, 250 fr.;[2] Raymond Koechlin, by 1927;[3] by his bequest to the Louvre (RF3669), 1932.

Exhibitions: Paris 1927, no. 280; Louvre 1930, no. 14; Athens 1963 (no cat.); Kyoto-Tokyo 1969, no. H-3, repr.; Atelier Delacroix, Paris 1973 (no cat.); id., Paris 1974 (no cat.)

Literature: Sterling-Adhémar, no. 658, pl. 229; J. A. Meletopoulos, 'L'Exposition sur "L'Insurrection hellénique et le philhellénisme français depuis le Directoire et jusqu'à 1830" au Musée national historique', *Messager d'Athènes — Le Progrès*, 17 May 1963 (unpaginated), mentioned on last page of text in the offprint, and a full-page repr.

For discussion of the group to which these studies belong, see J28.

[1] The canvas has at some time been extended by 2 cm along the upper edge.
[2] This buyer and price are listed by Robaut and in M-Nélaton Ann ED; but they are entered alongside lot 180 (J(L)44) in Burty Ann ED, where no price or buyer is noted for lot 181.
[3] A label on the back of the picture bears the title 'Arabes (Esq.)', 'Nº 18602' and a price code 'Atdd', suggesting that it passed through a dealer's hands sometime between 1864 and 1927. The dealer was possibly Georges Aubry, for in 1930 he owned J(D) 9, which is similarly inscribed on the back, with the title 'Maures (Esq.)', 'Nº18601' and the price code 'Atdd'.

32 STUDY OF VICENTINI IN ARMOUR   Pl. 27

$9\frac{1}{2} \times 7\frac{1}{4}$ in. (24 × 18.5 cm)
R382 (1832)
c. 1825/6
Robert Lebel, Paris

Provenance: Duc de Trévise, by 1938; R. Lebel, by 1963.

Exhibitions: Knoedler, New York 1938, no. 54; Bordeaux 1963, no. 19.

Literature: See *Journal* ref. below.

Delacroix refers to an 'Etude d'après *Bastien en cuirasse*, chez Triqueti' in a list of paintings which he compiled in the 1840s (*Journal* III. 372—Supp.). Robaut evidently did not know the original study and took his illustration for it from a water-colour copy by Frédéric Villot. Though more detailed, his illustration corresponds in essentials to this oil study, and he adds in R Ann that Delacroix's painting was done after a model by the name of 'Visentini [*sic*], de Venise.' Delacroix refers to a Bastiano Vicentini, who appears to have served him as model and handyman, in a letter postmarked 18 June 1826 (*Correspondance* I. 184 and n. 2), and this is no doubt the person referred to in Robaut's note and Delacroix's list.

This study is assumed, in the absence of knowledge of any others, to be the canvas listed unseen by Robaut, though the very summary, and in places gauche, execution suggests that the assumption might have to be revised if a more detailed version came to light.

Robaut's date of 1832 cannot be considered reliable, since he had not seen the picture, and is probably several years too late. The study appears to be about contemporary with a water-colour known as *Le Chevalier blessé* and probably representing the *Death of Bayard*. The same model appears to have been employed in both instances and I should date the water-colour *c.* 1825/6 (Louvre, RF3374, repr. Escholier I. 240).

Miscellaneous Orientalia

33 SEATED FIGURE IN TURKISH COSTUME (J. B. PIERRET ?)   Pl. 28

$12\frac{5}{8} \times 9\frac{1}{2}$ in. (32 × 24.2 cm)* E.D.
Moreau p. 230. R123 (1825)
1824/5
Mme Bassuet, Paris*

Provenance: Delacroix's posthumous sale, Feb. 1864, lot 77[1] (as 'Turc assis, accoudé sur une table'. Burty Ann ED: 'Casaque verte — turban blanc.'); Louis Auguste Bornot, 600 fr., d. 1888; by descent to Jacques Béraldi, who had given it by 1930 to Dr. Bassuet, husband of the present owner.

Exhibitions: EBA, Paris 1885, no. 18; Louvre 1930, no. 24A; Atelier Delacroix, Paris 1932, no. 175.

Literature: Escholier I, repr. p. 117; P. H. Michel, *The Massacre of Chios* (Max Parrish, London, 1947), repr. pl. 10, and referred to on opp. p. (unnumbered); Huyghe, p. 166, 205, repr. pl. 132.

The picture was listed in the catalogue of Delacroix's posthumous sale as 'Turc assis, accoudé sur une table'; Moreau, followed by Robaut, called it a portrait of Pierret, it is not known on what grounds. Though Pierret's widow could have been the source of their information, it is less likely than in the case of the family portraits that remained in her possession. Pierret is known to have posed for the *Massacres of Chios* in May 1824 (*Journal* I. 97–8) and there is no reason to doubt that he would have willingly acted as a model for a study of Turkish costume at the same period or a little later; but the features seem too generalized to justify calling this study a portrait or to identify it surely as the artists's friend portrayed in J67. Here Delacroix is clearly less interested in the model's character as revealed by his features than in the costume and a nervous interplay of zig-zag lines and sparkling gold embroidery.

[1] The lot number was still affixed to the top left corner of the surface in 1966.

34 TURK SEATED BY A SADDLE　　　Pl. 29
(Known as 'LE TURC À LA SELLE')

$16\frac{1}{8} \times 12\frac{15}{16}$ in. (41×32.8 cm)*
Signed top left: *E. Delacroix*.
R265 (1828. Repr. in reverse.)
1824/5?
Musée du Louvre

Provenance: Acquired by Adolphe Moreau in 1843, d. 1859; by descent to his grandson, Etienne Moreau-Nélaton; he donated it to the Louvre in 1906 (RF1654). At Musée des arts décoratifs 1907-34; transferred to Louvre 1934.

Exhibitions: *Exposition du Cercle de la rue de Choiseul*, Paris 1864; *EBA*, Paris 1885, no. 153; Louvre 1930, no. 75.

Literature: Silvestre *Delacroix* (1855), p. 80; p. Burty, 'L'Exposition du Cercle de la rue de Choiseul et de la Société nationale des Beaux-Arts', *GBA*, XVI (1864), p. 369; *Catalogue de la collection Moreau . . .* (Frazier-Soye, Paris, 1907 and 1923), no. 58; Moreau-Nélaton I. 62, repr. fig. 40, II. 246; Brière 1924, p. 83; Escholier I. 121, 213, repr. p. 210; Hourticq 1930, pl. 26; Sterling-Adhémar, no. 681, pl. 241; Bortolatto, full-page colour repr., pl. XXXV.

Print: Lithograph in reverse by Eugène Le Roux for the *Galerie d'Amateurs*, after 1843 (Moreau p. 125).

Though this picture was dated 1835-40 in the catalogue of the Moreau collection, followed by the Louvre catalogues, Robaut seems to have been closer to the truth in assigning it to 1828—probably sight unseen, as he apparently reproduced it in his *catalogue raisonné* from Le Roux's lithograph and did not note the signature until after the publication of his catalogue. Stylistically, it can best be accommodated in a still earlier period: the sharp angularities of pose and of some accessories, the robust modelling of the hands assort better with the *Seated Figure in Turkish Costume* of 1824/5 (J33) than with the more delicately conceived *Young Turk stroking his Horse* (J38) shown at the Salon of 1827-8.

35 TURK SEATED ON A SOPHA　　　Pl. 30
SMOKING

$9\frac{3}{4} \times 11\frac{7}{8}$ in. (24.7×30.1 cm)*
Signed bottom left: *Eug. Delacroix*.
Moreau p. 266. R977 (1846. Repr. in reverse.)
Probably 1825
Musée du Louvre

Provenance: Baron de Mainnemare; his sale (posthumous), 21 Feb. 1843, lot 6, to Adolphe Moreau, 201 fr., d. 1859; by descent to his grandson, Etienne Moreau-Nélaton; he donated it to the Louvre in 1906 (RF 1656). At Musée des arts décoratifs 1907-34; transferred to Louvre 1934.

Exhibitions: Probably *Soc. Amis des Arts*, Paris 1825, no. 18 ('Un Turc se reposant sur son divan'); probably Douai 1827, no. 96 ('Un barbaresque fumant sur un sopha'); *EBA*, Paris 1885, no. 150; Louvre 1930, no. 46; Louvre 1963, *M* only, no. 73 (repr. in back of cat.); Atelier Delacroix, Paris 1967, no. 4.

Literature: Silvestre *Delacroix* (1855), p. 80; Moreau, p. 127; E. Feydeau, 'Collection de M. Adolphe Moreau', *l'Artiste*, 7th ser., III (1858), p. 295; Tourneux, p. 141; *Catalogue de la collection Moreau...*(Frazier-Soye, Paris, 1907 and 1923), no. 55; Moreau-Nélaton I. 62, repr. fig. 37, II. 246 Brière 1924, p. 82; Escholier I. 121, 212 f., repr. opp. p. 178, Hourticq 1930, pl. 116; Sterling-Adhémar, no. 672, pl. 236; L. Johnson, 'The Delacroix Centenary in France—II', *Burl Mag*, CVI (1964), p. 260; Maltese, pp. 33, 135, 146, repr. in colour pl. VII; Trapp, p. 111.

Print: Lithograph by L. Laroche, 1851.

In a note contained in R Ann and first published in the catalogue of the exhibition Louvre 1930, Robaut tentatively revised his dating of 1846 to 1827, on discovering that a painting of this subject was included in the exhibition Douai 1827. I proposed a still earlier date (op. cit., 1964), suggesting that it was probably also the picture shown by the Société des Amis des Arts in Paris in 1825 as 'Un Turc se reposant sur un divan'.

The yatagan on the left is the same weapon as in the study J27.

36 TURK IN A RED CAPE　　　Pl. 31

$14 \times 10\frac{1}{16}$ in. (35.5×25.5 cm)
Signed bottom right: *Eug. Delacroix*
c. 1825
Private collection, Paris

Provenance: Presumably Albert Picard, President of the Provincial Council of Brabant, at Brussels, in April 1873; Georges Viau; with Winkel & Magnussen, Copenhagen, 1918; H. G. Laroche, Paris; with Alfred Daber, Paris, by 1956.

Exhibitions: Exhibition of French art organized by Winkel & Magnussen, dealers of Copenhagen, Charlottenberg, Sweden, Oct. 1918, no 84, repr. (asking 25,000 Kr.); Daber, Paris 1956, no. 2, repr.; 'L'Héritage de Delacroix', Knoedler, Paris 1964, no. 4.

Literature: *Prisme des Arts*, no. 1 (15 March 1956), repr. p. 45.

It is here presumed that this is the picture of a 'Greek' described in a letter to Adolphe Moreau dated Paris 23 April 1873, from a correspondent with an illegible signature. The description mentions a signature at the bottom right, lists the owner as given above and the dimensions as 34×24 cm.

It continues: 'Ce Grec est représenté en pied, il marche, vu de trois quarts, son bras gauche relève un manteau d'un rouge écarlate; il porte un turban blanc. Fond de paysage' (Moreau N).

37 INDIAN WARRIOR WITH TETHERED HORSE

Pl. 32

$14\frac{9}{16} \times 18\frac{1}{2}$ in. (37 × 47 cm)
Signed bottom right: *Eugène Delacroix*
Moreau p. 101 (under no. 46). R610 (1835).
1825
Private collection, Paris

Provenance: Hippolyte Poterlet; bought from him by Paul Huet for 90 fr.; taken from him in 1828 by a dealer on the pretext of getting Delacroix to sign it and kept by the dealer, Paul Huet accepting 120 fr. in payment under protest; Amable Paul Coutan; his sale, 19 Apr. 1830, lot 30 ('Cheval attaché à un poteau; derrière lui est un guerrier arabe qui regarde les mouvemens qu'il fait pour se détacher'), to Paul Huet, 110 fr.,[1] d. 1869; René Paul Huet, his son; Maurice Perret-Carnot, his son-in-law, *c.* 1928-1941/2.

Exhibitions: *EBA*, Paris 1885, no. 115 ('Arabe syrien et son cheval au piquet'); St. Petersburg 1912, no. 193, repr.; Louvre 1930, no. 204A ('Cheval persan tirant au renard'); Petit Palais, Paris 1936, no. 238.

Literature: Silvestre *Delacroix* (1855), p. 80; R. P. Huet, *Paul Huet* (H. Laurens, Paris, 1911), pp. 26 f.; *Correspondance* III. 379 n. 1; Cat. Exh. Petit Palais, Paris 1936, *Errata and Addenda*, 2nd ed., p. 341.

Print: Etching by Félix Bracquemond, 1857, unpublished, no doubt because of Delacroix's severe and detailed criticism of it expressed in a letter to Champfleury, dated 19 March 1857 (*Correspondance* III. 378 ff.)

To the assortment of titles quoted above from sale and exhibition catalogues may be added that which René Paul Huet, according to R Ann, submitted with the picture when he lent it to the exhibition *EBA*, Paris 1885: 'Cheval arabe tirant au renard et guerrier persan'. And in a further variation Moreau dubbed the warrior a Turk. None of these exotic titles conforms with the one chosen by Delacroix, which, though less specific than it might be, has the merit of combining brevity with accuracy and is to be found in a list of works he compiled in the 1840s: '*Cheval et Indien* (id. [i.e. Angleterre]) à Huet.' (*Journal* III. 374—Supp.) In addition to providing the best clue to the subject, this brief note also makes it possible to date the picture precisely to the summer of 1825, for, since it obviously does not represent an English scene, the reference to England in the note can only mean that the picture was actually painted during the English journey. The title 'Cheval avec un Indien' is also given in Silvestre *Delacroix* (1855), and the reference in parentheses

to England repeated. Thus Robaut's dating of 1835 was rather wide of the mark, and while the compiler of the catalogue of the exhibition Louvre 1930 hit on the right period by speculating that the picture was given to Poterlet by Delacroix *c.* 1824 or 1825, there is evidence in Delacroix's own writings for dating it more precisely and, it should be noted, no documentary evidence at all to support the opinion that Poterlet received the picture as a gift.

Internal evidence corroborates the sources which connect the picture with the English journey and identify the figure as an Indian: several of the accessories, though apparently not the entire costume, are clearly based on objects in the Meyrick collection of arms and armour, which Delacroix is known to have visited at Cadogan Place in London on 8 and 9 July 1825 (see L. Johnson, in catalogue of exhibition Edinburgh-London 1964, nos. 95 and 96): the saddle lying on the ground is Mahratta (a warlike Hindu race occupying the central and south-western parts of India); the sword and shield, and probably the bamboo lance, are based on the weapons carried by a dummy dressed in the armour of a Polygar (tribe of southern India), the sword and shield having been copied in water-colour on a sheet of studies done in London, and for some reason used in 1963 to illustrate an article on Delacroix's *Battle of Nancy* (*Revue du Louvre*, XIII, p. 97, fig. 2). The Polygar manikin and the saddle are both reproduced in Joseph Skelton's work on the Meyrick collection, *Engraved Illustrations of Antient Arms and Armour . . . at Goodrich Court*, published in 1830 (pls. CXXXVII and CXXXVIII).

The horse is likely to have been modelled on one belonging to the horse dealer A. Elmore, who befriended Géricault and Delacroix during their English visits: in a letter from London dated 27 June 1825, Delacroix wrote to Pierret: 'Je me suis mis depuis peu de temps à travailler chez [M. Elmore].' (*Correspondance* I. 163.)

---

[1] Every detail of the picture's history down to this point is taken from the account by René Paul Huet (ref. cit. under *Literature*), except for the dates, Coutan's ownership and the identification of his sale as the one in which Paul Huet bought the picture back. According to this account, it was two years after the incident with the dealer that 'un catalogue de vente tombe sous les yeux de Paul Huet, il y voit: Delacroix — *Cheval persan tirant au renard* — avec figure. — Mais c'est mon tableau! Il va à la vente, le retrouve encadré et signé; le rachète cent dix francs.' In spite of the discrepancy between the title given by R. P. Huet and in the Coutan sale catalogue, there seems to be no other sale that would fit: the unnamed dealer would therefore have taken the painting from Paul Huet in 1828, and presumably sold it to Coutan.

38 YOUNG TURK STROKING HIS HORSE

Pl. 33

$12\frac{7}{8} \times 16$ in. (32.7 × 40.7 cm)* Red wax seal of the city of Luxembourg on the stretcher.[1]
Signed bottom, left of centre: *Eug. Delacroix*
Moreau p. 169 (1826). R172 (1826)

c. 1826

Musée J. P. Pescatore, Galerie municipale de peinture, Luxembourg

Provenance: J. P. Pescatore, d. Paris 5 Dec. 1855; by his bequest to his native city, Luxembourg, which came into possession of his collection in 1871 when it was relinquished by its usufructuaries; the Musée Pescatore was officially inaugurated on 10 Feb. 1872.

Exhibitions: Salon 1827–8, no. 296 ('Jeune Turc caressant son cheval'); Musée Colbert, Paris 1829A, no. 10 (as 'l'Arabe et son coursier'[2]); presumably also Musée Colbert, Paris 1829B, no. 158 (as 'l'Arabe et son cheval') and Musée Colbert, Paris 1830A, no. 193 (as 'Arabe bédouin et son cheval'—for sale); Louvre 1963, no. 93 and 96, repr.; Berne 1963–4, no. 12; Kyoto-Tokyo 1969, H-6, repr.

Literature: *Visite au musée du Louvre, ou Guide de l'amateur à l'exposition des ouvrages de peinture . . . des artistes vivants (Année 1827–1828) . . . par une Société de Gens de Lettres et d'Artistes* (Leroi, Paris, 1828), p. 107; A. Jal, *Esquisses, croquis, pochades, ou tout ce qu'on voudra, sur le Salon de 1827* (Ambr. Dupont, Paris, 1828), p. 511; F., review of Exhibition Musée Colbert, Paris 1829A, *Journal des Artistes et des Amateurs*, 22 Nov. 1829, p. 322; Silvestre *Delacroix* (1855), p. 80 (as 'Grec caressant son cheval'); Piron, p. 106; Moreau-Nélaton I. 86; Escholier I. 212, 216; M. Noppeney, 'Les Collections d'art de la ville de Luxembourg', *Société des Amis des Musées du Grand-Duché de Luxembourg — Annuaire 1949* (Impr. de la Cour Victor Buck, Luxembourg, 1949), p. 7; *Musée J. P. Pescatore . . . Guide du visiteur* (R. Mehlen, Luxembourg, 1960), no. 94[r] (no pagination); Escholier 1963, p. 40; Huyghe, p. 205, repr. fig. 137; L. Johnson, 'Eugène Delacroix et les Salons. Documents inédits au Louvre', *Revue du Louvre*, 16 (1966), p. 220.

This picture was accepted for the Salon on 12 October 1827 (L. Johnson, op. cit., 1966), which is the earliest firm date that can serve as a guide to when it was painted. On 2 May 1824, Delacroix noted in his *Journal*: 'J'ai coloré l'aquarelle du *Turc qui caresse son cheval*', and in Joubin's opinion this was probably 'la première pensée' for the painting of the same title (*Journal* I. 91 and n. 1); but since the water-colour has not come to light, there is no way of knowing how similar it was to the painting and whether it could be considered a preliminary study for it.

The saddle on the ground appears to be modelled on the same saddle in the Meyrick collection as is found in the *Indian Warrior with Tethered Horse* (J37) painted in England in the summer of 1825. The picture is not, therefore, likely to have been painted earlier than the second half of 1825, and Moreau should probably be believed when he states firmly: 'Peint en 1826'. It is dated without argument to 1825–6 by Huyghe, 'probably between 1824 and 1827' in *Mémorial*.

This small painting prompted only facetious comments from Jal when it was exhibited at the Salon. The severe, but more considered, remarks of an anonymous critic writing in the *Visite au musée du Louvre*, do not appear to have been previously noticed and are quoted here in full: 'Je ne conçois pas le ciel bleu de Prusse, *balayé*, de M. Delacroix. Son jeune Turc est presque un ci-devant jeune homme; il parait moins caresser son cheval que s'assoupir sur lui, comme un homme ivre. Que fait-il de sa main droite? Je le croirais un peu manchot.' The Prussian-blue sky is no longer visible.

[1] Wrongly stated to be the seal of Delacroix's posthumous sale in *Mémorial*.
[2] Cf. F. (loc. cit., under *Literature*, 1829): 'Vous connaissez déjà *l'Arabe et son coursier*, le Salon de 1828 en a été gratifié; c'est ce petit tableau où le soi-disant Arabe, qui caresse son cheval, est fait de manière que l'on chercherait en vain [...] à préciser la place de l'épaule, du coude et du poignet'.

39 INDIAN ARMED WITH A KUKRI   Pl. 34

16 × 12⅝ in. (40.7 × 32 cm)
Signed bottom right: *Eug Delacroix*.
Moreau p. 171 (1830). R325 (1830).
c. 1830
Kunsthaus, Zurich

Provenance: Painted in 1830 for [J. B.] Pierret, according to Moreau, d. 1854; Mme Pierret, his widow, to at least 1864; with Durand-Ruel, by 1873(?); with Laurent; bought from him by Boussod, Valadon & Cie, 16 Aug. 1878, 2,000 fr. (Arch Goupil/Boussod); sold by them to the dealer Hecht, 23 Jan. 1879, 2,500 fr. (ibid.); he sold it to Crouan Lagotellerie, 2,500 fr. (Dieterle R); bought by M. Fayard in 1913 (ibid.); by Rosenberg, 7 Oct. 1937 (ibid.); acquired through the Vereinigung Zürcher Kunstfreunde from the Rosengart Gallery, Lucerne, for the Kunsthaus, Zurich (Inv. no. 2476), 1939.

Exhibitions: Salon 1831, no. 513; *Bd Italiens*, Paris 1864, no. 169; ? Durand-Ruel, Paris 1878, *h.c.*;[1] Zurich 1939, no. 318; Zurich 1943, no. 85; Zurich 1950, p. 24; Wildenstein, London 1952, no. 17; Essen 1954, no. 33; Louvre 1963, no. 131, *M* no. 133, repr.; Berne 1963–4, no. 29, repr.; Bremen 1964, no. 27, repr.; Zurich 1965, no. 12; Munich 1972.

Literature: L. P. [Louis Peisse], review of Salon of 1831, *Le National*, 30 May 1831; Silvestre *Delacroix* (1855), p. 80; Moreau-Nélaton I. 118; Escholier I. 276; *Kunsthaus Zürich. Bilder nach Skulpturen und Gemälden der Sammlung. Nachtrag 1939* (Zürcher Kunstgesellschaft, Zurich, 1939), pl. 164; L. Johnson, 'Eugène Delacroix et les Salons. Documents inédits au Louvre', *Revue du Louvre*, 16 (1966), p. 220.

Print: Etching by Le Rat for the *Galerie Durand-Ruel*, 1873, no. 198.

This picture was exhibited at the Salon of 1831 with the following title and explanation:

Un Indien armé du Gourka-kree.

Les Indiens se servaient de cette arme pour couper les jarrets des chevaux, ou égorger les sentinelles avancées, en se traînant avec précaution près des camps anglais.

It was accepted by the Salon jury on 17 April (Johnson, 1966). Pierret is not listed as the owner in the Salon catalogue, as one might expect him to be if Moreau was right in stating that the picture was painted for him. It was ignored by all the critics except Peisse, who dismissed it as a 'petite pochade' that ought to have remained in the artist's studio.

Delacroix is said to have painted a copy for Alexandre Dumas after the Salon (see J(L)51).

A water-colour study for the vegetation above the Indian's head, including a summary brush drawing of the head and shoulders, was with Thaw, New York, in 1964 (23.5 × 21 cm. ED stamp bottom left), and passed in a mixed sale at Sotheby's, London, on 3 July 1974, lot 132 (repr.), to H. Brandon. A rapid brush drawing in brown wash of the Indian's profile in reverse, at the bottom of a sheet of unrelated studies, also appears to be a preliminary sketch for this painting (Louvre, RF9640; repr. here Fig. 26).

---

[1] According to Robaut, 'Il fut exposé de nouveau, en 1878, dans la galerie de M. Durand-Ruel.' It is not, however, listed in the catalogue of the retrospective exhibition of modern masters mounted by Durand-Ruel in 1878, and may simply have been on view at the Gallery as stock.

40 TURKISH HORSEMAN GALLOPING
Pl. 35

$5\frac{1}{2}$ × 13 in. (14 × 33 cm) E.D.[1]
Signature, mostly effaced and probably false,[2] bottom left

---

c. 1831/2?
Whereabouts unknown

Provenance: Delacroix's posthumous sale, Feb. 1864, lot 79 ('Cavalier turc au galop', 14 × 33 cm), to the dealer Cadart, 350 fr.; Louis Bazille; sale P. Leenhardt of Montpellier ('Ancienne Collection Louis Bazille'), 4 May 1922, lot 21 (repr.), to Gradt, 9,987 fr.; mixed sale (by Schoeller), 6 May 1925, lot 92, to Georges Aubry (?), 7,300 fr.; Georges Aubry, by 1930.

Exhibitions: Bd Italiens, Paris 1864, no. 111 ('Cavalier arabe', 14 × 32 cm, lent by Luquet, Cadart's partner); Louvre 1930, no. 202.

Literature: None.

This, rather than R46 (J(R)25), appears to be the painting which passed in Delacroix's posthumous sale as lot 79. Though it is difficult to date and may well have been painted in 1832 or later, it is included in this volume so that it can be conveniently referred to in connection with R46. It assorts fairly well with two small-scale paintings of a single oriental horseman, one dated 1832 and the other assigned to that year by Robaut: the signed and dated *Cavalier marocain chargeant* (14 × 21 cm) shown in the exhibition 'Peinture 1830–1940', Galerie Daber, Paris 1962, no. 4; and the *Cavalier turc au repos* (10 × 14 cm. R374).

The horse is black and the rider wears a white and blue costume.

---

[1] Posthumous sale seal recorded as being on the crossbar of the stretcher in the catalogues of the 1922 and 1925 sales.

[2] No signature is mentioned in the catalogue of Delacroix's posthumous sale, and the picture seems too unfinished to be likely to have been fully signed by the artist.

Horses and Other Animals

HORSES

(See also, *A Battlefield, Evening* (J104), *Indian Warrior with Tethered Horse* (J37) and *Young Turk Stroking his Horse* (J38).)

Of the thirty-six paintings of horses listed as by Delacroix in the catalogue of his posthumous sale, about half are missing. The ten studies which made up lot 211 were described as blocked in ('ébauchées'), and were therefore particularly vulnerable to later 'completion' by restorers for commercial or misguided aesthetic ends, making attribution and dating difficult. The lack of any description in the sale catalogue of the individual pictures in this lot and of the fourteen studies in lot 210 creates many problems of identification, problems which Robaut had scarcely begun to investigate when his catalogue was published.

Much of this section, therefore, is of necessity tentative. An attempt has been made to assemble more reproductions of authentic works than have previously been available and at the same time to provide as much information as possible about what is missing (J(L)52–65), in the hope that it may lead to some of the lost works. Also a group of dubious paintings, which have crept into the *œuvre* as a result of difficulties of identification, is reproduced and discussed (J(O)6–7, J(M)3–4, J(D)11, J(R)26, 28–31).

The dating also has to be tentative, apart from the two or three dated or datable pictures, around which the undated studies do not seem to coalesce with any consistency. All the known studies seem beyond question to belong in the pre-1830 period and it may well be that Delacroix did not paint horse studies in oils after 1830. It is in establishing an accurate chronology for the studies of the 1820s that the problem lies, and it cannot be satisfactorily solved until more of the missing studies come to light

41 HORSE STANDING IN A MEADOW, FACING LEFT   Pl. 36

$6\frac{5}{16} \times 8\frac{7}{8}$ in. (16.1 × 22.6 cm)* Relined. E.D.
R30 (1819)
1819?
Lady Keynes (on loan to the Fitzwilliam Museum, Cambridge)

Provenance: Delacroix's posthumous sale, Feb. 1864, lot 83, to Haro, 250 fr.; sale Haro & fils, 30 May 1892, lot 88, 95 fr.; sale Haro père, 2 Apr. 1897, lot 125, 125 fr.; Edgar Degas; his sale, 26 March 1918, lot 29, to John Maynard Keynes, 900 fr., d. 1946; Lady Keynes, his widow.

Exhibition: Bd Italiens, Paris 1864, no. 42.

Literature: None, other than Robaut.

According to the catalogue of the exhibition *Bd Italiens*, Paris 1864, this study was painted in the company of Géricault. It may have been on the basis of this evidence that Robaut dated it to 1819, thinking perhaps that Géricault would not have been painting horses with Delacroix during the years of ill health between his return from England at the end of 1821 and his death in 1824. Possibly for the same reason, Chesneau assumed in his commentary in Robaut that this was the first study of a horse painted from nature by Delacroix. The information that the study was done in the company of Géricault, printed in the year following Delacroix's death, cannot be lightly discounted and Robaut's dating is therefore plausible at least. The modelling is painstaking and rather stiff, the placing of the horse in space unsure—characteristics that seem consistent with a date as early as 1819.

42 STUDY OF A HORSE, FACING LEFT   Pl. 36

$5\frac{1}{8} \times 7\frac{1}{2}$ in. (13 × 19 cm)
Part of R1860 (No repr.)
Whereabouts unknown

Provenance: Delacroix's posthumous sale, Feb. 1864, part of lot 210 ('Quatorze études diverses de chevaux'); Victor Chocquet, d. 1891; Marie Chocquet, his widow; her sale 1 July 1899, lot 58 ('Etude de cheval, de profil à gauche',

12 × 18.5 cm, with mention also of the seal of the posthumous sale on the back), 240 fr.

Exhibitions: None.

Literature: J. Rewald, 'Chocquet and Cézanne', GBA, LXXIV (1969), p. 77.

The history of this study after the Chocquet sale of 1899 is uncertain, but to judge from the description and dimensions given in the catalogue of that sale, the old photograph reproduced here is probably a record of it, however inadequate. The original photograph, preserved in the Wildenstein archives in New York, bears the following MS. inscription: '6151. — Delacroix — Etude de cheval. L:5351 — 13 × 19 [cm]'.

I am unable to determine who bought this study at Delacroix's posthumous sale before it passed into Chocquet's collection (for a list of buyers and prices of studies in lot 210 that cannot be identified with specific pictures, see J(L)64).

43 STUDY OF A CHESTNUT STALLION   Pl. 39

$13 \times 9\frac{7}{8}$ in. (33 × 25 cm)
Part of R1860 (No repr.)
1822/3?
Whereabouts unknown

Provenance: Delacroix's posthumous sale, Feb. 1864, part of lot 210 ('Quatorze études diverses de chevaux', without dimensions), to de Balleroy, 460 or 405 fr. (Burty Ann ED); Baron d'Ivry; Marquis de Balleroy, by 1924.

Exhibitions: Géricault, Paris 1924, no. 325; Louvre 1930, no. 208.

Literature: None.

This and the following study were lent by the Marquis de Balleroy to the exhibition Louvre 1930, in the catalogue of which they are stated to have come from Delacroix's posthumous sale. Though I have seen neither, there appears to be no reason, judging from the good photographs available, to doubt their authenticity and provenance. Probably painted as a pair, they were apparently bought as a pair at the posthumous sale, for de Balleroy is recorded in Burty Ann ED as buying two studies in succession from lot 210, at 460 and 405 fr.

44 STUDY OF A GOLDEN CHESTNUT STALLION   Pl. 38

$13 \times 9\frac{7}{8}$ in. (33 × 25 cm)
Part of R1860 (No repr.)
1822/3?
Whereabouts unknown

Provenance: Delacroix's posthumous sale, Feb. 1864, part of lot 210 ('Quatorze études diverses de chevaux', without dimensions), to de Balleroy, 460 or 405 fr. (Burty Ann ED); Baron d'Ivry; Marquis de Balleroy, by 1924.

Exhibitions: Géricault, Paris 1924, no. 326; Louvre 1930, no. 208A.

Literature: None.

See the preceding entry.

45 A TEAM OF FOUR HORSES Pl. 37

$9\frac{9}{16} \times 12\frac{13}{16}$ in. (24.3 × 32.5 cm)* Relined. E.D.
Moreau p. 321. R73 (1823)
1822/3 ?
Private collection, Paris

Provenance: Delacroix's posthumous sale, Feb. 1864, lot 205, to Paul Verdé Delisle, 435 fr.; Didier Verdé Delisle, by 1930 (Dieterle R.), presumably by descent; with Tedesco, May 1930, in very bad condition (ibid.); bought from him in the same month by Jean Dieterle, 3,000 fr. (ibid.); sold by him to Bourgeat, Nov. 1930 (ibid.); mixed sale (by Laurin), Paris 24 June 1954, lot 17, to Jacques Dubourg for a private client, 180,000 fr.

Exhibition: EBA, Paris 1885, no. 30.

Literature: None, other than Moreau and Robaut.

While there is no reason to doubt that this is lot 205 from Delacroix's posthumous sale and hence the picture illustrated and catalogued by Robaut under no. 73, it has been so heavily restored as to make any judgement of its date particularly hazardous and the acceptance of Robaut's attribution an act of faith. But a likely time for Delacroix to have painted a study of this kind, showing post(?) horses in harness with blinkers is around October 1822, when he wrote in his *Journal* (I. 14): 'Voir à la poste pour étudier des chevaux'; and a week later (I. 19): 'J'ai entrevu un progrès dans mon étude de chevaux.' It could also, however, be about contemporary with the *Two Draught-Horses* (J46), datable some six months later.

46 TWO DRAUGHT-HORSES Pl. 37

$11\frac{1}{4} \times 15\frac{1}{2}$ in. (28.5 × 39.3 cm)* E.D.
R1867 (No repr.)
1823
Mrs. R. Peto, London

Provenance: Delacroix's posthumous sale, Feb. 1864, lot 203 (the original lot number, attached to the surface, is visible in the top left corner of the reproduction here), to de Hérédia, 250 fr.; present owner, by 1963.

Exhibitions: Bd Italiens, Paris 1864, no. 167^{his}; ?Charpentier, Paris 1948, no. 50 ('Deux chevaux de poste'); Edinburgh-London 1964, no. 6, repr.

Literature: L. Johnson, 'Delacroix Drawings at Bremen', *Master Drawings*, II (1964), pp. 418, 419 n. 5.

This unfinished picture was evidently composed from two pencil studies contained on a sheet in the Bremen sketch-book (fol. 56), one of which shows the whole of the nearer horse, and the other that portion of the hindquarters of the farther horse shown here (repr. L. Johnson, op. cit., fig. 6). These drawings are on a page opposite a sheet of early studies apparently related to the *Massacres of Chios* (J105), which Delacroix decided in May 1823 to paint for the Salon. They, and the painting, are likely therefore to be connected with Delacroix's resolution of 15 April 1823: 'Il faut absolument se mettre à faire des chevaux. Aller dans une écurie tous les matins; se coucher de très bonne heure et se lever de même' (*Journal* I. 25).

47 STUDY OF A BROWN-BLACK HORSE TETHERED TO A WALL Pl. 40

$20\frac{1}{2} \times 28\frac{5}{16}$ in. (52 × 71.9 cm)* E.D.
Part of R1860 (No repr.)
1823 ?
Mr. and Mrs. Paul Mellon, Washington, D.C.

Provenance: Delacroix's posthumous sale, Feb. 1864, part of lot 210 ('Quatorze études diverses de chevaux', without dimensions); Léon Suzor, Paris, by 1960, d. 1962; anon. sale, Hôtel Drouot, Paris 19 March 1965, lot 80 (repr.), to Claude Aubry, 36,000 fr.; with Nathan, Zurich; acquired from them by the present owners, Feb. 1967.

Exhibitions: Charpentier, Paris 1948, no. 48; Wildenstein, London 1952, no. 5.

Literature: None.

Though this study was apparently part of lot 210 of the posthumous sale, I am unable to determine who the buyer was. For a list of the buyers and prices of pictures in this lot that are not identified, see J(L)64.

48 THREE STUDIES OF A HORSE Pl. 41

$18 \times 14\frac{3}{4}$ in. (45.7 × 37.5 cm)* E.D.
R74 (1823)
1823 ?
The late Mme D. David-Weill, Neuilly-sur-Seine

Provenance: Delacroix's posthumous sale, Feb. 1864, lot 204 ('Cheval de charrue', without dimensions), to Baron Charles Rivet, 450 fr., d. 1872; by descent to Mlle de Catheu, his granddaughter; bought from her by Jean Dieterle, 10 March 1938; sold by him to D. David-Weill, 17 May 1938.

Exhibitions: None.

Literature: None, other than Robaut.

The lot number of the posthumous sale is still affixed to the surface, in the top left.

49 A BROWN HORSE, FACING   Pl. 42
LEFT

$18\frac{1}{8} \times 21\frac{15}{16}$ in. $(46 \times 55.7$ cm$)$* E.D.
R72 (1823)
c. 1823/4
Mme Boris Méra, Neuilly-sur-Seine

Provenance: Delacroix's posthumous sale, Feb. 1864, lot 207 ('Cheval dans une écurie', without dimensions), to Louis Auguste Bornot, 400 fr., d. 1888; by descent to the present owner.

Exhibition: *EBA*, Paris 1885, no. 19 (as 'Cheval rouan à l'écurie — Etude (1823)', dimensions wrongly listed as 30×40 cm)[1]

Literature: Escholier I, repr. p. 100.

Though Robaut lists the dimensions of R72 as 31×40 cm, there can be no doubt from its history that this is the same picture and that Robaut recorded the wrong measurements.

There are sketches on the back of the canvas drawn by the artist with a brush and bitumen(?) of the profile of a man with a moustache wearing a turban, of two horse heads and the hindquarters of a horse.

Robaut's unsupported dating of 1823, though it can be considered only approximate, seems reasonable. It is known from the *Journal* that Delacroix was working energetically on horse studies during parts of the years 1823 and 1824, and stylistically the modelling of the head here seems consistent with, for example, the *Seated Indian* of *c.* 1823/4 (J23).

A copy by Mlle Riesener is recorded in R Ann (margin to R72), without dimensions or location.

[1] The identification of this exhibit as R72 is confirmed by R Ann (marginal note to R72) and by the annotation '72' alongside the printed entry in Robaut's copy of the second edition of the exhibition catalogue (*Bib AA*, MS. 298ter). A small label printed with the number 19 used, furthermore, to be stuck in the lower left corner of our painting and is clearly visible in the reproduction in Escholier.

50 STUDY OF A CHESTNUT AND   Pl. 43
A GREY HORSE IN A STABLE

$12\frac{5}{8} \times 16\frac{1}{8}$ in. $(32 \times 41$ cm$)$* E.D.
(Area shown in photograph, taken in frame, 31.3×40 cm)
R76 (1823)
1823/4?
Private collection, Paris

Provenance: Delacroix's posthumous sale, Feb. 1864, part of lot 210 ('Quatorze études diverses de chevaux', without dimensions), to Louis Auguste Bornot, 430 fr., d. 1888; M. Gavet, his son-in-law, by 1885; by descent to the present owner.

Exhibitions: None.

Literature: See below.

It seems unlikely that this is the picture Delacroix lent to Célestin Nanteuil in April 1858, as claimed by Joubin, who based his opinion on this passage in the *Journal* (III. 189 and n.): 'Prêté hier à M. Nanteuil une étude de deux chevaux sur la même toile (de douze environ), faite autrefois aux gardes du corps; — de profil tous les deux.' It is difficult to accept that Delacroix would have described this canvas as roughly a No. 12, which measures 50×61 cm.

Four holes in the canvas have been patched, three being close to the bottom and causing little damage to the paint surface; the fourth and largest is on the chestnut's back close to the shoulder.

51 STUDY OF TWO BROWN   Pl. 44
AND BLACK HORSES IN A STABLE

Paper laid down on canvas, $10\frac{1}{4} \times 13\frac{1}{2}$ in. $(26 \times 34.3$ cm$)$* E.D.
Part of R1871 (No repr.)
1824?
Roger Hauert, Paris

Provenance: Delacroix's posthumous sale, Feb. 1864, part of lot 211 ('Dix études ébauchées'), to Paul Huet, 190 fr. (Burty Ann ED), d. 1869; René Paul Huet, his son; probably to M. Maurice Perret-Carnot, his son-in-law, by descent, to *c.* 1941; with Jacques Blot; purchased from him by the present owner, 1941.

Exhibition: *EBA*, Paris 1885, no. 114.

Literature: R. P. Huet, *Paul Huet* . . . (H. Laurens, Paris, 1911), p. 381.

In a letter to Sollier dated 17 April 1864, Paul Huet lists the works he bought at Delacroix's posthumous sale, referring to this picture as 'deux chevaux (étude qu'on peut croire de Géricault)' (R. P. Huet, ref. cit.). The study was dated to 1824 in the catalogue of the exhibition *EBA*, Paris, 1885. No reasons are given for the dating, but it may have been based on sound information (from talking to Paul Huet himself, for example) and, in the absence of firmer evidence on which to base an opinion, it is reasonable to think that this sketch may be connected with one of the several horse-studying projects that Delacroix refers to in his *Journal* in 1823 and 1824. Though not reproduced in Robaut, there is a chalk drawing of it in Tracings V (Supp.).

52 STUDY OF TWO HORSES Pl. 45

$12\frac{3}{8} \times 19\frac{1}{2}$ in. $(31.5 \times 49.5$ cm)
Part of R1860 (No repr.)
Whereabouts unknown

Provenance: Delacroix's posthumous sale, Feb. 1864, part of lot 210 ('Quatorze études diverses de chevaux', without dimensions), to Paul Verdé Delisle, 170 or 360 fr.; by descent to Pierre Verdé Delisle, his grandson, who consigned it to Jean Dieterle in June 1929; sold Jan. 1936, 9,000 frs.

Exhibitions: None.

Literature: None.

This picture is known to me only from the photograph reproduced here.

53 TWO HORSES FIGHTING IN Pl. 46
A MEADOW

$10\frac{5}{8} \times 12\frac{5}{8}$ in. $(27 \times 32$ cm)
Signed and dated bottom right: *Eug. Delacroix 1825*
Moreau p. 82. R130
Whereabouts unknown

Provenance: Delacroix's posthumous sale, Feb. 1864, lot 82 ('Chevaux en liberté', 27×32 cm; signature correctly given, but date misread as 1827.[1] Burty Ann ED: 'en gaîté & en folie'), to Paul van Cuyck, 1,605 fr.; his sale, 7 Feb. 1866, lot 9, 750 fr.; possibly the 'Combat de Chevaux' bought from Goldschmidt by Boussod & Valadon in Dec. 1879 and sold to Monnerot in the same month (Arch Goupil/Boussod, vol. 10, p. 70).

Exhibition: Possibly Douai 1827, under no. 97 ('Etudes de chevaux'); most probably the picture submitted to the Salon jury in 1827 with the title 'Deux chevaux en liberté', and refused on 12 October.

Literature: Possibly *Correspondance* v. 145 and n. 3;[2] Silvestre *Delacroix* (1855), p. 80; A Dumas père, 'Eugène Delacroix', *Le Monde illustré*, 22 Aug. 1863, p. 126; L. Johnson, 'Eugène Delacroix et les Salons. Documents inédits au Louvre', *Revue du Louvre*, 16 (1966), pp. 217, 220, 227 n. 6.

All trace of this picture has been lost since 1879 at the latest, and it is known only from the diminutive but clear print in Robaut and the old photograph reproduced here. It is one of only three oil paintings, all representing horses, which have some claim to have been painted in England (J37 and J(L)58 are the other two); for it is evidently to this picture, dated in the year of the English journey, that Delacroix refers in a list drawn up in the 1840s, as '*Chevaux au vert se battant* (Angleterre)' (*Journal* III. 374—Supp.), the parenthesis perhaps indicating not only that this is an English scene but

that, as supposed by Robaut (p. 480) in his addendum to R130, it was actually painted in England. Delacroix seems to allude to this same painting when noting a loan to his friend Chenavard in 1829: 'les chevaux qui jouent d'Angleterre et une autre peinture de cheval' (Louvre sketch-book, RF23355, fol. 42^v). It is further listed, during Delacroix's lifetime, in Silvestre *Delacroix* (1855), as 'Deux chevaux en liberté (Angleterre).' It may also be this picture (and not, as Joubin, followed in *Mémorial* (no. 506), assumes, the Louvre's *Arab Horses Fighting in a Stable* dated 1860) which Delacroix lists on 1 April 1857 as '*Chevaux qui se battent. Les mêmes que dans le Choc*' (Journal III. 90). For the position of the horses here, if not their colour, is virtually the same as in the two, post-1832 versions of *le Choc* (i.e. *Collision of Moorish Horsemen*; both reproduced in L. Johnson, 'Delacroix's "Rencontre de Cavaliers Maures" ', *Burl Mag*, CIII (1961), figs. 12 and 13), and not much like the 1860 picture, where the bodies of both horses are facing in the same direction.

Alexandre Dumas père (loc. cit., 1863) records having seen it in Delacroix's studio towards the end of his life, and refers to it as '*Chevaux anglais qui se mordent dans une prairie*'.

[1] The correct date, 1825, is recorded by Moreau, and can just be seen in the old photograph reproduced here, which also shows how easily the 5 could be taken for a 7.
[2] With a letter dated Tuesday 7 November [1826], Delacroix submitted an unidentified painting which he described as an '*Etude de chevaux*' to the Société des Amis des Arts, asking a price of 150 fr. As noted by Joubin, it does not appear to have been accepted by the Société. It could therefore have been available for exhibition at Douai in 1827 and might have been our painting.

54 TWO HORSES FIGHTING Pl. 46
IN THE OPEN

$14\frac{7}{16} \times 17\frac{15}{16}$ in. $(36.7 \times 45.5$ cm)* E.D.
R131 (1825)
c. 1828
R. Verdé Delisle, Paris

Provenance: Delacroix's posthumous sale, Feb. 1864, lot 81, to Paul Verdé Delisle, 2,400 fr.;[1] by descent to Pierre Verdé Delisle, his grandson, by 1929, d. *c.* 1960; then inherited by the present owner, his nephew.

Exhibitions: EBA, Paris 1885, no. 29; Charpentier, Paris 1948, no. 47, repr.

Literature: *Plaisir de France*, March 1948, repr. p. 11.

Robaut lists this picture under 1825, but his dating cannot be considered reliable since he confused the painting with lot 82 in the posthumous sale (J53)—an error he recognized in an addendum (p. 481)—, saying it was signed and dated. In composition and handling, it has much in common with the *Lion and Tiger* at Prague (J55), which can most reasonably be dated to 1828/9, and therefore appears to have been painted several years later than Robaut thought. In both these electric, sketchily treated pictures of animals antagonized, there is a comparable diagonal arrangement, stressed in a rather contrived way by the tail of one of the animals. In addition, the schematic handling of the white horse's mane, like bursting sparks, is very like the lion's mane in the other picture.

The same subject was treated in a not dissimilar manner by Géricault's first master, Carle Vernet, whose lithograph *Deux chevaux en liberté se battant* may have had an influence on this painting (repr. in A. Dayot, *Carle Vernet* (Le Goupy, Paris, 1925), p. 169).

[1] The original label bearing the lot number is still affixed to the surface of the canvas, in the top left corner. The present owner also has the receipt that was made out to his grandfather at the time of the sale.

OTHER ANIMALS

55 LION AND TIGER   Pl. 47

$9\frac{7}{16} \times 12\frac{5}{8}$ in. (23.9 × 32.1 cm)*
Signed bottom towards the right: *Eug Delacroix*
Moreau p. 279. R1304 (1856. No repr.)
1828/9
National Gallery, Prague

Provenance: Sale the late M.G., 24 Jan. 1859, lot 13, 900 fr.; Binder, by 1860; Dowager Duchess of Hamilton (widow of the 11th Duke; Princess Marie Amélie, cousin of Napoleon III), by 1873; presumably by descent to the 12th Duke of Hamilton, d. 1895 (Algiers); his(?) sale, Christie's, London 6 Nov. 1919 ('the late Duke of Hamilton'[1]), lot 126, to Knoedler's (in association with Bernheim-Jeune and Geo. Petit), £483; bought from Bernheim-Jeune by the Gallery of Modern Art of the Kingdom of Bohemia, Prague (later incorporated into the National Gallery), June 1923 (Arch B-J).

Exhibitions: Musée Colbert, Paris 1829B, no. 106 ('Le Lion et le tigre'); Bd Italiens, Paris 1860, no. 175; Basle 1921, no. 90; 'French Art from Delacroix to Picasso', National Gallery, Prague, no. 3, repr., National Gallery, Berlin, p. 40, Budapest, p. 12, 1965. (The picture has also been shown in several special exhibitions at the National Gallery, Prague.)

Literature: Y, 'Beaux-Arts. Des Expositions en France et en Angleterre. Musée Colbert', *Le National*, 20 Jan. 1830; Tourneux, p. 106; Escholier III, repr. opp. p. 216; V. Volavka, 'Francouzské malírství v pražské národní galerii', *Umění*, VII (1935), repr. fig. 217; id., *Die Französische Malerei und Grafik des XIX Jahrhunderts in der Tschechoslowakei* (Artia, Prague, 1953), p. 32, repr. p. 33, detail of the lion's head p. 35; L. Johnson, 'A Note on

Delacroix at Prague', *Burl Mag*, CXII (1970), p. 385, repr. fig. 50.

Robaut, who had evidently never seen this picture, dated it to 1856, a date which was not called in doubt till 1970 when I (op. cit.) identified this as the painting shown at the Musée Colbert in December 1829 under the title *Le Lion et le tigre*. It is thus Delacroix's first known oil painting of felines imagined in their wild state, and the only one he painted before 1830. Having characteristics in common with the lithograph *Cheval sauvage terrassé par un tigre* (Delteil 77) of 1828, it may well have followed on closely from Delacroix's experiment in the print with that new theme of animal combat. It passed almost unnoticed in reviews of the 1829 exhibition, being mentioned only by a critic who signed himself 'Y' and wrote: 'Le Lion et le Léopard [*sic*] [. . .] sont bien dessinés, mais la couleur de cette esquisse est trop sombre, et les tons verdâtres y dominent désagréablement.'

Copy: Oil on board by Henri Rousseau, 18 × 24 cm.

[1] The 13th Duke was still living in 1919, so this description presumably refers to the 12th Duke, though he had been dead for over two decades.

56 STUDIES OF LIONS   Pl. 48

$23\frac{7}{8} \times 19\frac{5}{8}$ in. (60.7 × 49.8 cm)* E.D.
Moreau p. 213. R264 (1828)
c. 1830
Mme M. de Boulancy, Paris

Provenance: Delacroix's posthumous sale, Feb. 1864, lot 213 ('Plusieurs études de lions sur la même toile', without dimensions), to Biedermann, 1,180 fr.; ? M. J. Nicolas, by Aug. 1864; Detrimont; Soultzener, who received it from Detrimont in exchange for a painting by Diaz and 1,000 fr. cash, 11 March 1873;[1] by descent to the present owner, Soultzener's great-granddaughter.

Exhibition: ? Bd Italiens, Paris 1864, no. 92 ('Têtes de lionnes. Etude', 61 × 47 cm, lent by M. J. Nicolas).

Literature: None, other than Moreau and Robaut.

These animated studies give every appearance of having been done from nature, and may have been painted in the Jardin des Plantes. The kind of rapid sketching with the brush seen in the study in the centre on the extreme left is found in drawings of felines and other subjects around 1830 (e.g. on a letter postmarked 19 January 1831, *Bib AA* MS. 243, fol. 18, and on a sheet datable to about April of the same year, ibid., fol. 23ʳ and 23ᵛ). This canvas may, therefore, be connected with a general programme for studying wild animals about the time when Delacroix was planning his first large-scale painting of felines, the *Young Tiger with its Mother* dated 1830 (J59). The following note to Pierret, postmarked 17 April 1830, could be relevant: 'As-tu des billets pour le Jardin des Plantes ? Je passerai demain dimanche chez toi vers 5 heures pour en prendre au moins un' (*Correspondance* I. 254).

The studies are all painted in ochres and browns, but three palettes are laid out on the back, each consisting of a row of 11 to 14 pigments. These perhaps reflect Delacroix's attempts to choose a bright range of colours for one of his later Lion Hunts.

Delacroix refers twice to this canvas: first, in a note of a loan made probably in 1849: 'Prêté à Lehmann, le 22 mars, la toile d'*Etudes de Lions*'; secondly, in an inventory he compiled in the 1840s, merely listing it, as 'Etudes de *Lions* sur une seule toile.' (*Journal* I. 251; III. 374—Supp.)

The study at the top and the seated lion in the centre are used almost without variation in a signed water-colour of two lions, which Robaut dates without argument to 1848 (R1053. Now in the Fogg Art Museum, Acc. no. 1943.352). The seated lion is also used alone in a signed water-colour in the Museum of Fine Arts, Budapest (no. 1918-462).

In the small print illustrating this picture in Robaut, the studies are not distributed in the same way as on the canvas. That is apparently because Robaut's tracing of it (Tracings 1) was not done in a piece but on two sheets, with alterations being made in the relative positions of the studies.

[1] Signed and dated receipt from Detrimont, in Dieterle R, between pp. 74-5.

57 STUDY OF A SLEEPING OR DEAD LIONESS
Pl. 49

$9\frac{7}{8} \times 14\frac{7}{8}$ in. (25.1 × 37.8 cm)* Relined. E.D.
Part of R1879 (No repr.)
c. 1830 ?
San Francisco Museum of Art

Provenance: Delacroix's posthumous sale, Feb. 1864, part of lot 214 ('Trois autres études d'animaux', without dimensions), to Prévost, 180 fr., or Moureau, 150 fr.; Gustave Guillaumet; his studio sale, 6 Feb. 1888, lot 443; Duc de Trévise, by 1938; with André Seligmann Inc.; gift of Mr. and Mrs. Maxine Hermanos to the San Francisco Museum of Art (51.6054), 28 Dec. 1951.

Exhibitions: Knoedler, New York and Chicago 1938-9, no. 53; Springfield, Mass. 1939, no. 20; San Francisco 1939, no. 31; *Masterworks of Five Centuries*, Golden Gate International Exposition, San Francisco 1939, h.c.[1] (On extended loan to the California Palace of the Legion of Honour, from Jan. 1969.)

Literature: Inv. Delacroix, no. 239.

In addition to the stamp of Delacroix's posthumous sale on the stretcher, the lot number 214 is still pasted to the surface in the top left corner. This study should no doubt be identified with the picture listed in Inv. Delacroix, no. 239, as by the master and under the title '*étude de lionne morte*'.

A pencil drawing of the lioness in virtually the same pose, with a study of the head and neck alone beneath it, is on a sheet which also bears the stamp of the posthumous sale (Louvre RF9685; repr. *Mémorial*, no. 472).

[1] Though this picture is not listed in the catalogue, a label printed with the name of this exhibition is stuck on the back. It was therefore presumably moved to this show after the one at the San Francisco Museum of Art closed in May.

58 STUDY OF A DEAD DOG
Pl. 49

$16\frac{3}{8} \times 34\frac{7}{16}$ in. (41.5 × 87.5 cm)* Relined
R379 (1832)
c. 1830 ?
Peter Staechelin, Basle

Provenance: Delacroix's posthumous sale, Feb. 1864, lot 212 ('Etude d'après un chien mort', without dimensions), to Baron Paul de Laage, 350 fr.; anon. sale (Escribe & Haro *experts*), Hôtel Drouot, 23 May 1873, lot 15 ('Chien mort', 40 × 85 cm), to Soutzo, 610 fr.; Sedelmeyer sale, 30 Apr. 1877, lot 26 (mention of provenance from the posthumous sale), to Perreau, 880 fr.; Rudolf Staechelin, Basle, d. 1946; Peter Staechelin, Basle.

Exhibitions: Bd Italiens, Paris 1864, no. 12 ('Chien mort', 42 × 87 cm); 'Sammlung Rudolf Staechelin', *Kunstmuseum*, Basle 1956, no. 2, repr.; 'Fondation Rodolphe Staechelin, de Corot à Picasso', *Musée national d'Art Moderne*, Paris 1964, no. 1, repr.

Literature: None known, other than Robaut.

Though this canvas, which has been both relined and attached to a new stretcher, does not bear the seal of Delacroix's posthumous sale, there appears to be no reason to doubt that it was the study which passed in that sale as lot 212. In pose and in some aspects of the technique, it has much in common with the study of a *Lioness* (J57) and may be about contemporary with it.

59 A YOUNG TIGER PLAYING WITH ITS MOTHER
Pl. 50

$51\frac{9}{16} \times 76\frac{9}{16}$ in. (1.31 × 1.945 m)*
Signed and dated bottom left: *Eug. Delacroix.*/*1830.*
Moreau pp. 47, 171. R323.
Musée du Louvre

Provenance: M. Auguste Thuret (painted for him according to Moreau, and sold to him for 1,500 fr. according to Piron), to at least 1862; with Francis Petit, asking 20,000 fr., by 1865 (Piron); Maurice Cottier, d. by 1885; by his bequest to the Louvre with a life interest to his wife; entered the Louvre in 1903 (RF1943).

Exhibitions: Luxembourg, Paris 1830, no. 55 ('Un jeune tigre jouant avec sa mère'); Salon 1831, no. 516 ('Etude de deux tigres'); *Bd Italiens*, Paris 1861–2 (no cat.); *EBA*, Paris 1885, no. 51; Geo. Petit, Paris 1892, no. 87, repr.; Louvre 1930, no. 51; Atelier Delacroix, Paris 1946A and B, no. 1; Belgrade 1950, no. 2; Atelier Delacroix, Paris 1951, no. 3, repr.; Tokyo, Fukuoka, Kyoto 1954–5, no. 32; Louvre 1963, no. 132, *M* no. 134, repr. (in back of cat.); Berne 1963–4, no. 30, repr.; Bremen 1964, no. 28; Moscow 1969, no. 30, repr.

Literature: [Louis Peisse] 'Exposition dans la Galerie du Luxembourg . . . au profit des blessés', *Le National*, 30 Oct. 1830; anon. review of the same exhibition, *Journal des Artistes et des Amateurs*, 4th year, 2nd vol., no. XIX (7 Nov. 1830), p. 324; E. Delécluze, review of the Salon of 1831, *Journal des Débats*, 7 May 1831; L. P. [Louis Peisse], id., *Le National*, 30 May 1831; anon., id., *Le Constitutionnel*, 4 June 1831; A. Jal, *Salon de 1831. Ebauches critiques* (Dénain, Paris, July 1831), p. 58; E. Fillonneau, 'Exposition de peinture du boulevard des Italiens. Changements du 15 au 30 novembre', *Le Courrier Artistique*, 15 Nov. 1861, pp. 41 f.; T. Gautier, 'Exposition du boulevard des Italiens', *Moniteur universel*, 6 March 1862; anon., list of paintings under title 'Société nationale des Beaux-Arts. Première Exposition des sociétaires fondateurs', *Le Courrier Artistique*, 15 June 1862; Piron, p. 107; Tourneux, pp. 109, 114, 115; M. Vachon, *Maîtres modernes. Eugène Delacroix à l'Ecole des Beaux-Arts, mars-avril 1885* (L. Baschet, Paris, 1885), photogravure pl. (unnumbered); R. Reboussin, 'Les animaux dans l'œuvre de Delacroix,' *L'Art et les Artistes*, Dec. 1913, p. 204; Moreau-Nélaton, I. 103, 118, repr. fig. 74, II. 205, 246; Brière 1924, p. 78, no. 212B; Escholier I. 249, repr. opp. p. 248; Hourticq 1930, pl. 32; Cassou 1947, pl. 9, full-page repr. of the mother tigress's head on opp. p.; Sterling-Adhémar, no. 671, repr. pl. 236; Escholier 1963, p. 64, repr. in colour p. 53; Maltese, pp. 41, 152, repr. pl. 27; L. Johnson, 'Eugène Delacroix et les Salons. Documents inédits au Louvre', *Revue du Louvre*, 16 (1966), p. 220; id., 'A Note on Delacroix at Prague', *Burl Mag*, CXII (1970), p. 385; Trapp, pp. 203, 206, repr. in colour p. 207.

Prints: Lithograph, reversed, by Delacroix, for *L'Artiste*, I (1831), 24ᵉ livraison (Delteil 91); etching by Charlotte Julien; wood engraving by Boetzel after Feyen-Perrin, for C. Blanc, *Les Artistes de mon temps* (Firmin-Didot, Paris, 1876), p. 49.

Though listed in the catalogue of the Salon of 1831 as 'Etude de deux tigres', this painting was submitted to the Salon jury with the title 'Un jeune tigre avec sa mère' (L. Johnson, 1966). Later, it was sometimes mistaken by critics for a tigress and her mate. It is the culmination, in Delacroix's early years, of an interest in wild animals that quickened about 1828 and found expression in several lithographs, in drawings and minor studies in oil; but nothing that precedes it leads one to expect an animal painting so masterly and on such a scale. It was admired without reservation, for its naturalism above all, by those critics who mentioned it in 1830 and 1831. Louis Peisse wrote (1830):

C'est un des meilleurs morceaux de l'exposition. La tigresse est admirablement peinte; la tête est superbe de vérité et d'expression; la pose de l'animal est rendue avec une énergie remarquable. Les belles nuances de la peau bandée sont exécutées de main de maître. La couleur, appliquée avec justesse et vigueur, n'est pas jetée avec la négligence que cet artiste avait mise presque à la mode. Elle n'est pas non plus fantastique, comme celle qu'il a souvent adoptée pour les chevaux; elle est vraie et prise sur nature. C'est une excellente étude, qui prouve que M. Delacroix pourra faire de belles choses quand il n'aura plus ses fantaisies systématiques.

And the anonymous critic of the *Journal des Artistes*:

Certes, ces deux quadrupèdes, de grandeur naturelle, sont peints avec talent, avec vérité; mais on peut s'étonner, à bon droit, de voir M. Delacroix peindre avec plus de soin [not 'force', as transcribed by Tourneux, followed in *Mémorial*], d'exactitude, de ressemblance enfin les animaux que les hommes. Jamais cet artiste singulier n'a peint un homme qui ressemblât à un homme, comme son tigre ressemble à un tigre.

Added to the exhibition at the Galerie Martinet in the boulevard des Italiens in the second half of November 1861, the painting was not less warmly praised by Théophile Gautier: 'C'est un morceau superbe, et jamais les redoutables félins n'ont été mieux reproduits dans leur grâce féroce et dans leur scélératesse moelleuse [. ...] Quoi-qu'il ne soit pas animalier de profession, Delacroix connaît son tigre aussi bien que Méry.'

A water-colour, measuring 28.5 × 19.2 cm and claimed to be a study for this painting, passed in a sale at the Galerie Charpentier, 8 Dec. 1953, lot 11A; on the verso was a pencil study of the young tiger alone. A highly finished pencil drawing in the Louvre was apparently done after the painting, in preparation for the lithograph (RF3380; *Mémorial*, no. 135, repr.). It is listed in R Ann as no. 322ᵇⁱˢ, Robaut having seen it on 29 March 1898 when it was with Tempelaere.

Portraits and Studies of Heads

60 HEAD OF ACTAEON   Pl. 52

$9\frac{7}{8} \times 8\frac{1}{4}$ in. (25.1 × 21 cm)* E.D.
R1509 (1825)
1817/18
Museum of Melun

Provenance: Delacroix's posthumous sale, Feb. 1864, lot 196 ('Figure d'Actéon.' Burty Ann ED: 'Sorte de fresque de Pompeia'), to Detrimont, 550 fr.; Count Horace de Choiseul; he gave it to the Museum of Melun (*Ancien inventaire* no. 31), 10 June 1866.

Exhibitions: None.

Literature: Silvestre *Delacroix* (1855), p. 80.

This study may be identified with a picture that Delacroix describes in a list of works that he compiled in later life as 'Tête d'Actéon, fort ancienne.' (*Journal* III. 374—Supp.) Robaut had evidently not seen the original when he reproduced it in the Supplement of his catalogue, from a sketch supplied by a M. Lhuiller, and dated it to 1825. A highly finished pencil study for the face is contained in a sketch-book (Louvre, RF9141, fol. 13ᵛ·) and separated by three pages from studies for the *Portrait of Elisabeth Salter* (J61), which is datable to the winter of 1817/18. Robaut's date may therefore be put forward by some seven years to a period when Delacroix was still in training.

The intensity of the expression, the dramatic chiaroscuro and vigorous brushwork distinguish this painting from those prize-winning entries by Delacroix's contemporaries for the competition for the *Tête d'expression* that are preserved at the Ecole des Beaux-Arts, yet it clearly stems from the same academic source, namely Le Brun's illustrations of the passions. For the most part, it derives from Le Brun's 'la Frayeur' (engraved in, e.g. *Methode pour apprendre à dessiner les passions . . . par Mr. Le Brun . . .*, Amsterdam, 1702, fig. 12), but the direction of the gaze appears to come from 'Le mepris A la Haine' (ibid., fig. 8), which is the basis of a study on the same sheet as the finished drawing for this painting. An expression dominated by fear and tinged with hatred or contempt is of course appropriate to the situation of Actaeon who, beginning to be transformed into a stag, with small horns sprouting from his head, is about to be torn to pieces by his own hounds.

The leaden flesh tones, thick impasto and *tenebroso* modelling suggest an influence of Géricault, who may have been painting preparatory studies for the *Raft of the Medusa* when this study was done.

There is some deterioration caused by the use of bitumen in the shadows, particularly in the hair and arm.

61 PORTRAIT OF ELISABETH SALTER   Pl. 53

Oils on paper laid on canvas
$9\frac{5}{8} \times 7\frac{1}{2}$ in. (24.4 × 19 cm)* E.D.
Part of R1904
Winter 1817/18
Le Comte Doria, Paris

Provenance: Delacroix's posthumous sale, Feb. 1864, part of lot 201, to Baron Aimé Seillière, 280 fr. (Burty Ann ED); Baron Ernest Seillière, his son; Baronne Seillière, his widow; the present owner, her son-in-law.

Exhibitions: Rosenberg, Paris 1928, no. 1; Louvre 1930, no. 1A; Atelier Delacroix, Paris 1932, no. 186; Drouin, Paris 1943, no. 73; Bernheim-Jeune, Paris 1948, no. 27 (with wrong dimensions and wrong provenance); Charpentier, Paris 1950, no. 27b; Wildenstein, London 1952, no. 2; Atelier Delacroix, Paris 1963, no. 38; Edinburgh–London 1964, no. 1; Atelier Delacroix, Paris 1969.

Literature: P. Burty, *Lettres de Eugène Delacroix* (Quantin, Paris, 1878), p. xvii; A. Joubin, 'Etudes sur Eugène Delacroix', *GBA*, xv (1927), pp. 164 f., repr. opp. p. 164; R. Escholier, 'A propos d'une exposition Delacroix', *L'Art Vivant*, IV (1928), p. 127; Hourticq 1930, pl. 1; J. Russell, ' "That devilish English tongue". Unpublished Letters of the Youthful Delacroix to Elisabeth Salter', *Portfolio and Art News Annual*, no. 6 (1962), pp. 76-8, 115-20, repr. p. 76; Escholier 1963, p. 12, repr. in colour p. 13; R. Escholier, *Delacroix et les Femmes* (Fayard, Paris, 1963), p. 40, repr. opp. p. 64; Huyghe, pp. 15, 88, repr. pl. 66.

The identity of the sitter was first proposed by Joubin (op. cit.) when he published this portrait in 1927, and has since won general acceptance. Delacroix twice mentions an 'Elisabeth Salter' in his writings, in 1822 and 1824 when recollecting the sound of her voice and re-reading her letters (*Journal* I. 3, 56). Joubin and others have reasonably assumed that this was the full name of the English girl 'Elisa' or 'Eliza', whom Delacroix had pursued with ardour during the winter of 1817-18 when she was living in Paris under the same roof as he and his sister, Henriette de Verninac. An amusing record of that adventure is preserved in the *Correspondance* (I. 11-14, 25) and in the more recently published drafts of Delacroix's messages in English to the girl (Russell, op. cit.; Huyghe, pl. 67; Cat. Exh. Edinburgh-London 1964, no. 1).

Joubin based his identification on the period of the costume and on a description presumed to be of Elisabeth in a letter from Delacroix to Pierret, which is postmarked 11 December 1817: 'Le nez est assez original: la narine est retroussée fièrement [. . .] La bouche est d'une élégance charmante mais le triomphe de cette tête c'est dans son contour. La joue, le petit double menton, la manière dont tout cela se pose sur le col vaut des autels.' (*Correspondance* I. 12.) The artist himself refers in 1824 to his portrait of 'Salter' (*Journal* I. 75) and is reported by his cousin Léon Riesener to have kept 'un petit portrait charmant d'une petite Anglaise, femme de chambre de sa mère' (read 'soeur') with whom he had been in love in his youth (Burty, op. cit., p. xvii). Both references may be to this picture. It is, moreover, known from one of Delacroix's drafts that he had arranged to paint Elisa's portrait: 'I dare to hope you have complaisance to go by Sunday for the agreed portrate.' (Russell, op. cit., p. 119.)

It has usually been said that Delacroix's English girl-friend was his sister's maid, and the contents of one of his letters in French do indeed leave little doubt that she worked for Mme de Verninac, as a cook (*Correspondance* I. 14.). But it appears from the drafts of his letters in English that she was chiefly dependent on a 'M^{ad} L.' (possibly Lambs: see *Bib AA* MS. 256, 38^r where the name is crossed out but remains partially legible), who had come to reside temporarily in Paris in connection with a lawsuit, and whom she intended to quit as soon as they returned to England. 'M^{ad} L.' may well have rented accommodation from Delacroix's sister and shared the services of the girl she had brought from England. She was in any event a major obstacle to be reckoned with when Delacroix was trying to arrange clandestine meetings in the house with Elisa.

Two small pencil studies for this portrait are to be found above a composition study for a *Cupid and Psyche* in a sketch-book (Louvre, RF9141, fol. 17^v). The sitter also seems to be represented in a full-length study, with a dancing satyr in attendance, in another sketch-book (Louvre, RF23356, fol. 31^r).

This type of three-quarter view portrait, with its incisive contours, smooth, uncomplicated modelling and plain background remains within the neo-classical conventions current in France during the first two decades of the nineteenth century. A remarkably similar precedent is Gros's portrait of his nephew, Jacques Amalric, as a child, dated 1804 (repr. in colour, R. Escholier, *Gros, ses amis et ses élèves* (Floury, Paris, 1936), frontispiece).

Moreau (p. 227), followed by Robaut (no. 13), records a larger portrait which he entitles *Elisabeth* and dates 1817–18 (see J(L)68). If his date and identification are correct, the references cited above from Delacroix's writings could apply as well to this lost portrait as to Count Doria's version.

61*a* PORTRAIT OF FOUGERAT   Pl. 54

12$\frac{7}{8}$ × 9$\frac{9}{16}$ in. (32.3 × 24.3 cm)* Relined
c. 1818

Hector Brame–Jean Lorenceau, Paris

Provenance: Possibly painted for the sitter, but later in the possession of Pierre Albert, nephew of the Verninacs' forester at Boixe, near Mansle, Charente; M. Duguet, notary or solicitor; M. Marie Duguet; Mme Naud; private collection, France;[1] with Hector Brame.

Exhibitions: None.

Literature: E. Biais, 'Note sur Delacroix', *Réunion des Sociétés des Beaux-Arts des départements*, 1891, p. 620.

According to Emile Biais (loc. cit.), Archivist of the city of Angoulême, who had known Pierre Albert, nephew of the Verninacs' forester and one of Delacroix's hunting companions in the Forest of Boixe, Delacroix painted a number of portraits of relatives and members of the Verninacs' staff when he visited their house in the Forest in his youth, but these early paintings had been either dispersed or destroyed by 1891. Biais had nevertheless recently found some 'aux murs d'un logis villageois, comme nous l'avions conjecturé'. This was presumably the home of the Albert family and somewhere in the region of Boixe, though the author does not specify. Biais continues: 'Dans le nombre des primitifs portraits peints par Eugène Delacroix en ce temps-là, on doit mentionner celui du garde-chasse Fougerat, puis le portrait de M. Charles de Verninac. Le premier est figuré de trois quarts, en buste, demi-nature; il porte un habit foncé; sa cravate rouge est d'une touche vibrante. Le portrait de M. Charles de Verninac est également en buste, mais de grandeur naturelle, a un habit bleu et d'une tonalité sombre.'

Since the portrait of Charles de Verninac (or rather its replica by Delacroix, which is what Biais must have seen) is unquestionably authentic and, though unknown to Moreau and Robaut, documented in Delacroix's correspondence (see J62), there is no reason to doubt the authenticity of this portrait, which has the same provenance and appears to have been identified by Pierre Albert, who must have seen it painted.

Delacroix's visits to the Forest of Boixe seem to have been limited to the autumn of each year from 1818–20 (see J62) and this portrait of the gamekeeper must therefore date from those years. It is probably earlier than the portrait of Charles de Verninac from the same years (J62), being somewhat harder and more meticulous in modelling, sharper in lighting, with less breadth and assurance in the handling of the cravat. It nevertheless reveals a precocious sensitivity to colour relationships, in the way Delacroix sets off the ruddy complexion against the bright red cravat and repeats the blue-grey of the eyes in the shirt.

An Antoine Fougerat, described as 'garde de la forêt de Boixe, âgé de soixante-deux ans', signed the death certificate of Raymond de Verninac, dated 25 April 1822 (published by Biais, op. cit., p. 622 n. 1), but, unless greatly flattered here, Delacroix's sitter appears to have been a younger man, possibly Antoine's son.

[1] The provenance from Dughet on was provided by M. Philippe Brame, before I brought Biais's article to his attention, and has not been independently corroborated. But it may be supposed that Duguet was the M. Adrien Duguet-Albert who communicated to Emile Biais in 1891 (op. cit., p. 620 n. 1) the letters Delacroix wrote to Pierre Albert, original owner of Delacroix's copy of the early portrait of Charles de Verninac (see J62) which apparently hung in the same village house as this portrait c. 1891. M. Adrien Duguet-Albert is therefore a likely person to have come into possession of both portraits.

62 PORTRAIT OF CHARLES DE VERNINAC   Pl. 55

$18 \times 14\frac{15}{16}$ in. (45.8×38 cm)* Relined
R Ann, listed c. 1885 in margin of R361. Also possibly R448 (No repr.) and Moreau p. 235[1]
c. 1819
M. Raoul Ancel, Hurtebise (Charente)*

Provenance: Henriette de Verninac?; Albert family, Forest of Boixe, c. 1823–1846 or 7; then restored to Delacroix, who bequeathed it in 1863 to Mme Duriez (*née* Zélie de Verninac); she probably gave it in 1864 to her sister, Mme Pierrugues (*née* Hyéronime de Verninac);[2] Senator Daniel Ancel (1812–1905) by 1885, second husband of Mme Pierrugues's daughter, Louise; by descent to the present owner.

Exhibitions: *Bd Italiens*, Paris 1864, no. 99 (as 'Portrait de jeune homme', 47×39 cm, lent by M. de Verninac[3]); *EBA*, Paris 1885, no. 105 (as 'Portrait du jeune de Verninac, neveu de Delacroix', $56[sic] \times 38$ cm, lent by M. Ancel[4]).

Literature: Probably Silvestre *Delacroix* (1855), p. 80 ('Deux portraits du neveu de l'artiste.'),[5] Delacroix's will, dated 3 August 1863, in *Correspondance* (Burty 1878), p. vi; L. Johnson, in Cat. Exh. Edinburgh–London 1964, under no. 18; L. Johnson, 'Eugène Delacroix and Charles de Verninac: an Unpublished Portrait and New Letters', *Burl Mag*, CX (1968), pp. 511–18, fig. 32.

Charles Etienne Raymond Victor de Verninac was born in Paris at 97 rue de Grenelle on 29 November 1803 (L. Johnson, op. cit., 1968, p. 512) and died in New York on 22 May 1834, of yellow fever contracted at Vera Cruz (*Correspondance* I. 376). He was the only child of Delacroix's sister, Henriette de Verninac. After a chequered scholastic career, when his conduct caused his parents and teachers some concern, he graduated *bachelier-ès-lettres* from the Lycée Louis-le-Grand in July 1821 (*Correspondance* v. 86, 90); then, leaving Delacroix, who had supervised his schooling since 1819, joined his parents at their country property, the Forest of Boixe, near Mansle, Charente, where he remained till his father died in 1822 (ibid. 91, 111 and *passim*). By the autumn, he had returned to Paris and to a

lukewarm reception from Delacroix, his senior by only five years, who confided in his *Journal* (I. 20): 'Je ne vois pas sans un sentiment d'envie la beauté de mon neveu.' For his subsequent career, see J83 and J92.

Delacroix had painted a small portrait of his nephew before 6 April 1824, for he notes in his *Journal* (I. 69) on that date: 'Tâcher de retrouver la naïveté du petit portrait de mon neveu.' Five days later, in discussing his ideal of modelling heads softly and smoothly without excess of detail or sacrifice of firm contour, he remarks (ibid. 74–5): 'Il y avait de cela dans ce petit portrait de Géricault . . . [unidentified], dans ma Salter un peu et dans mon neveu.' The coupling of, presumably, the portrait of Elisabeth Salter of 1817/8 (J61) and the portrait of the nephew may mean that they were not far apart in date. Be that as it may, ours is the only portrait of Delacroix's nephew that can be reasonably dated before 1824 and it plainly portrays an adolescent, perhaps fifteen or sixteen years old—Charles's age in 1818-19. It reveals not only the qualities of modelling and the naïveté noted by Delacroix in his *Journal*, but a laboured modelling of the head that suggests an early date, though probably not so early as the Salter portrait with its egg-shell finish and less unctuous impasto.

In 1847, Delacroix was painting a copy of a small portrait of his nephew in exchange for the original which had been returned to him from the Forest of Boixe by M. Pierre Albert, nephew of the Albert who was forester to the Verninacs when Charles and Delacroix used to shoot in the Forest (*Correspondance* v. 178, 182. *Journal* I. 174). This copy reappeared recently and was shown at the exhibition Atelier Delacroix, Paris 1973. It is signed top right: *Eug. Delacroix*, and measures 46×38 cm (repr. in colour, M. Sérullaz, 'A propos de l'exposition *Delacroix et la Peinture Libérée*', *Revue du Louvre*, XXIII, no. 6 (Nov.–Dec. 1973), p. 363[6]). Delacroix spent part of the autumn of each year from 1818-20 in the Forest of Boixe with his nephew and sister (see *Correspondance* and *Lettres intimes* at the relevant periods), and seems never to have returned afterwards. It is in these years that the portrait is most likely to have been painted and left at Boixe, perhaps first as a gift for Charles's mother, who might, when she relinquished the estate in 1823, have allowed Albert to keep it as a memento of the boy he had taught to fence and, no doubt, to shoot (L. Johnson, op. cit., 1968, p. 515). A timely moment to present a portrait of her son to Henriette de Verninac would have been at the end of the long vacation of 1819 when, instead of returning as usual to reside in Paris, she remained at the Forest while Charles travelled to the capital with Delacroix to resume his education at the Lycée as a boarder (*Correspondance* v. 3 ff.).

This type of bust portrait of a youth seen full-face against a plain background and wearing a broad open collar is found in David, *Portrait d'un jeune inconnu*, signed and dated 1786, Musée Granet, Aix-en-Provence (repr. L. Johnson, op. cit.

1968, fig. 37)[7] and in Géricault, *Buste de jeune homme*, which Clément (p. 309, no. 129) dates between 1818 and 1820 (repr. L. Johnson, op. cit., 1968, fig. 38). In both these examples painted by Delacroix's predecessors the features are more animated, the pose less rigid and the gaze less fixed than in this portrait painted by a future master when still in training. Yet there is a dash of lively colour technique here that the others do not contain, in the jaunty cravat with its pink stripes and floral pattern in red and green.

[1] Robaut says the 'Portrait de M. de Verninac' that he lists under no. 448 was bequeathed by Delacroix to Mme Duriez de Verninac. Following Moreau, he records the dimensions as 55 × 40 cm and dates it 1833. While there is a marked difference between these dimensions and the measurements of the three portraits of Charles de Verninac presumed to be those left to Mme Duriez, they are very close to the (wrong) dimensions given for our portrait, which is one of the three, in the catalogue of the exhibition *EBA*, Paris 1885 and repeated in R Ann. Robaut does not reproduce or describe his no. 448, but Moreau had given a description which is consistent with its being our portrait: 'simple étude de la tête jusqu'aux épaules'.

[2] Delacroix's bequest to Mme Duriez de Verninac (as he named Mme Duriez, *née* de Verninac) included three portraits of his nephew, Charles de Verninac. This portrait can be identified as the third, which is described in the will as 'un petit buste de face, la tête grandeur de nature'. In the next clause of the will, the legatee is requested to share the things left to her with 'M. son frère [François de Verninac] et son excellente soeur, Mme Pierrugues' (see transcript of the will in *Correspondance* (Burty 1878), p. vi, where 'Pierrugues' is misspelt, the 'i' being omitted). It is not entirely clear how the legacy was eventually divided up, but that this portrait was part of Mme Pierrugues's share is suggested by the fact that it was lent to the exhibition at the Ecole des Beaux-Arts in 1885 by her son-in-law.

[3] This cannot be taken as a sure indication of ownership, since the loan may simply have been arranged through François de Verninac, acting for one of his sisters—Mme Duriez or Mme Pierrugues.

[4] In spite of the vertical measurement given in the exhibition catalogue, there can be no doubt that this is our portrait, for a copy in chalks from the portrait lent by Ancel is contained in Robaut Tracings II (repr. L. Johnson, op. cit. under *Literature*, 1968, fig. 33). Furthermore, Robaut lists Ancel's address as 'rue Bellechasse 17' [Paris] in his annotated copy of the second edition of the exhibition catalogue (*Bib AA* MS. 298*ter*, no. 105) and an apparently contemporary pencil inscription on the back of the frame of our portrait reads: 'Ancel 17 Bellechasse'.

[5] This entry in the list of works by Delacroix in Silvestre probably refers to this portrait and to the Sachs version (J83), since the Javal version (J92) is unfinished, and only completed portraits were included in the list, the *George Sand and Chopin*, for example, being omitted.

[6] The author claims (p. 362 n. 5) that he brought the first version of this portrait to my attention. I discovered it quite independently in 1966 by tracing M. Raoul Ancel, the descendant of Senator Daniel Ancel, the last known owner, with the help of the Librarian of the Senate and the Mairie of Dirac, and sending him a sketch of Robaut's drawing of the portrait for purposes of identification. I published it with the permission of M. Ancel after inspecting it at Hurtebise and understanding from conversation with him that I was the first to recognize its authenticity. All my correspondence on the subject is preserved in my files.

[7] The attribution of this painting to David and the authenticity of the signature have been disputed.

63 HEAD OF A WOMAN   Pl. 56

17$\frac{5}{16}$ × 12$\frac{13}{16}$ in. (44 × 32.6 cm)* E.D.
Probably part of R1904 (No repr.)
1821
Mme Léonardo Bénatov, Paris

Provenance: Delacroix's posthumous sale, Feb. 1864, probably part of lot 201 ('Onze études de têtes et portraits'), to ?;[1] anonymous sale, 8 May 1953, lot 161 (repr.); resold immediately by the purchaser to M. Léonardo Bénatov.

Exhibitions: Gobin, Paris 1937, no. 16, repr.; Wildenstein, London 1952, no. 3; Louvre 1963, no. 7, repr.; Berne 1963–4, no. 2, repr.; Bremen 1964, no. 1, repr.; Edinburgh–London 1964, no. 4.

Literature: M. Florisoone, *Delacroix* (Braun, Paris, 1953), fig. 13.

Florisoone (op. cit., caption to fig. 13) thought this might be a study for *The Virgin of the Harvest* of 1819 (J151), but it has since been more plausibly connected with *The Virgin of the Sacred Heart* of 1821, J153 (Cat. Exh. Wildenstein, London 1952, no. 3; *Mémorial*, no. 7). It was most probably done in the early months of 1821 from one of the models Delacroix is known to have hired for the latter painting (*Correspondance* v. 79), as a preliminary study from the life for the Virgin. For a full discussion of the painting to which it is related, see J152 and J153.

A strip of canvas just over 4 cm high has been added across the bottom of the picture, and a triangular section reaching to the hair fills the top right corner. Although these areas are evidently not part of the original study, they were possibly added during the artist's lifetime, since the picture is on a stretcher bearing the seal of his posthumous sale and is relined with a canvas stamped with the trademark of his colour merchant, Haro.

It has been convincingly held that a very similar charcoal study of a head, now in the Louvre, represents the same model (Cat. Exh. Wildenstein, London 1952, no. 3; Cat. Exh. Louvre 1963, no. 7. Repr. in Escholier I. 35 and Cat. Louvre: *Dessins* 1963, pl. 1).

[1] If it was part of lot 201, I am unable to determine who bought it at the sale. For a list of the buyers and prices which cannot be attached to individual items in this lot, see (J(L)82.

64 SELF-PORTRAIT AS   Pl. 58
RAVENSWOOD

16$\frac{1}{8}$ × 12$\frac{3}{4}$ in. (40.9 × 32.3 cm)*
R40 (1821)
1821 ?
Musée du Louvre

Provenance: Said by Robaut to have been given by Delacroix upon 'completion' to [Joseph Auguste] Carrier, the miniaturist (1800–75); his sale 5 May 1875, *h.c.* (R), to a dealer, 50 fr.; purchased the next day by Alfred Robaut; acquired from him by P. A. Cheramy, May 1885 (R Ann); his sale 5 May 1908, lot 165 (repr.), to Vedel, 7,500 fr.; sale estate of P. A. Cheramy 15 Apr. 1913, lot 26, to Paul Jamot,

3,100 fr.; by his bequest to the Atelier Delacroix, 1941; acquired by the Louvre (RF 1953-38), 1953.

Exhibitions: Durand-Ruel, Paris 1878, no. 167; *EBA*, Paris 1883, no. 59; *EBA*, Paris 1885, no. 179; Cassirer, Berlin 1907, no. 1; Charpentier, Paris 1923, no. 81; Paris 1927, no. 273; Copenhagen, Stockholm, Oslo 1928, nos. 50, 42 and 43; Rosenberg, Paris 1928, no. 2; Charpentier, Paris 1929, no. 277; Arts décoratifs, Paris 1930, no. 1704; Louvre 1930, no. 5, repr. *Album*, p. 7; R.A. London 1932, no. 375; Atelier Delacroix, Paris 1932, no. 1; Atelier Delacroix, Paris 1934, no. 53; Brussels 1935, no. 940; Bernheim-Jeune, Paris 1936, no. 39; Atelier Delacroix, Paris 1937B, no. 2; Amsterdam 1938, no. 113; Knoedler, New York and Chicago 1938-9, no. 52; Springfield, Mass. 1939, no. 15; Atelier Delacroix, Paris 1939, no. 52; Orangerie, Paris 1941, no. 28; Atelier Delacroix, Paris 1945, no. 32; Atelier Delacroix, Paris 1946A and B, no. 33; Atelier Delacroix, Paris 1947, no. 24, repr.; Atelier Delacroix, Paris 1948, no. 35; Atelier Delacroix, Paris 1950, no. 11; *Bib. nat.*, Paris 1951, no. 468; Atelier Delacroix, Paris 1951, no. 112; Wildenstein, London 1952, no. 7, repr. frontispiece; Melendez y Pelayo, Institut français, Madrid 1957; London 1959, no. 110; Chopin Exh., Warsaw 1960; Recklinghausen 1961; Amsterdam 1961, no. 35, repr.; Rome-Milan 1962, no. 74; Atelier Delacroix, Paris 1963, no. 3; Berne 1963-4, no. 3, repr. pl. 3; Bremen 1964, no. 2, repr. p. 12; Edinburgh-London 1964, no. 15; Atelier Delacroix, Paris 1967, no. 1; Moscow 1969, no. 28; Kyoto-Tokyo 1969, H-1, repr.; Atelier Delacroix, Paris 1969-70 (no cat.); Bourg-en-Bresse 1971, no. 13, repr.; Atelier Delacroix, Paris 1972 (no cat.); id., Paris 1973 (no cat.)

Literature: L. Rouart, 'La Collection de M. Cheramy', *Les Arts*, no. 64 (Apr. 1907), p. 22, repr. p. 26; J. Meier-Graefe and E. Klossowski, *La Collection Cheramy* . . . (R. Piper, Munich, 1908), no. 143 (repr.); J. L. Vaudoyer, 'L'Exposition de "L'Art et la Vie Romantiques" ', *GBA*, VII (1923), p. 196, repr.; L. Benoist, 'La Collection Paul Jamot', *L'Amour de l'Art*, VII (1926), p. 170, repr. p. 168; Escholier I. 55, repr. opp. p. 50; R. Escholier, 'A propos d'une Exposition Delacroix', *L'Art Vivant*, IV (1928), p. 127, repr. p. 130; P. Jamot, 'Delacroix', in *Le Romantisme et l'Art* (Henri Laurens, Paris, 1928), pp. 122 f., repr. pl. XX; J. L. Vaudoyer, ' "Cent Ans de Vie Française." A propos du Centenaire de la "Revue des Deux Mondes" ', *L'Art Vivant*, VI (1930), p. 87; Hourticq 1930, pl. 1; C. Roger-Marx, 'Géricault, Delacroix et l'Angleterre', *L'Art Vivant*, VIII (1932), p. 245; P. Jamot, 'Eugène Delacroix en costume d'Hamlet', *BSHAF* 1935, pp. 41-4; A. Joubin, 'Les Modèles de Delacroix', *GBA*, XV (1936), p. 351; G. H. Hamilton, 'Hamlet or Childe Harold? Delacroix and Byron', *GBA*, XXVI ('1944'; but article dated 8 Jan. 1945), pp. 365-86, repr. fig. 1; Sterling-Adhémar, no. 657, pl. 229;

P. Courthion, *Romanticism* (Skira, 1961), pp. 25 f., repr. in colour p. 23; R. Huyghe *et al.*, *Delacroix* (Hachette, Coll. Génies et Réalités, Paris, 1963), repr. p. 46, detail of head p. 47; Huyghe, pp. 66, 87, 457, 520 n. 16, repr. pl. 56; Maltese, pp. 23, 133, repr. in colour pl. II; R. Rosenblum, 'Ingres' (review of exh. at Petit Palais 1967-8), *Revue de l'Art*, no. 3 1969, p. 103; E. Haverkamp-Begemann and A.-M. Logan, *European Drawings and Watercolors in the Yale University Art Gallery 1500-1900*, vol. I, *Catalogue raisonné* (Yale University Press, New Haven and London, 1970), p. 54 n. 2.

Print: J. de Tarade, 1883, in *Annuaire illustré des Beaux-Arts* . . ., ed. F. G. Dumas (Librairie d'Art, L. Baschet, Paris, 1883), p. 243.

This portrait poses a problem as to the role in which Delacroix has chosen to represent himself and the date of execution.

Robaut records that the stretcher was inscribed in pencil by the artist: 'Raveswood', for Ravenswood, the hero of Walter Scott's *Bride of Lammermoor*; and in the nineteenth-century exhibition catalogues, all compiled in the years when Robaut owned the portrait, it was in that role the artist was said to have cast himself here. In 1907, the character was identified as Hamlet, without argument of any sort, under the reproduction in Rouart's article on the Cheramy collection. This identification was uncritically repeated almost without exception for nearly forty years: in the catalogues of the two Cheramy sales and in exhibition catalogues, but not by Meier-Graefe and Klossowski (1908), who confined themselves to calling it a self-portrait; nor by Escholier (1926), who rejected Hamlet in favour of Ravenswood, on the ground of the inscription on the stretcher. Jamot, in a lecture at the Sorbonne in 1927 (published 1928: P. Jamot, loc. cit.), claimed, without adducing any evidence at all, that Ravenswood was Delacroix's nickname for Carrier: the inscription therefore applied to the original recipient of the picture, not to the identity of the character portrayed, which was Hamlet. He repeated these opinions in 1935, still without any kind of corroboration. As I pointed out, however, in 1964 (Cat. Exh. Edinburgh-London, no. 15), even if it were true that Delacroix called Carrier Ravenswood, for which there is no evidence, why should the name written alone on the stretcher without a dedication have applied rather to Carrier than to the guise assumed by Delacroix in the portrait?

The first serious discussion of the problem was contributed by Hamilton in his basic article of 1945. He rejected the Hamlet opinion on the ground that the costume was unlike any employed for the Prince of Denmark that Delacroix would have seen within the period when the portrait was presumably painted. Nor, it may be added, do the hair-style and costume correspond to other representations of Hamlet by Delacroix. With less reason, Hamilton also rejected the Ravenswood identification, accepting Jamot's 'fact' concerning Delacroix's nickname for Carrier and arguing: 'This XVII Century Spanish dress would ill become the fictional Ravenswood, since the novel is laid in early XVIII Century Scotland' (p. 368). He goes on to propose, on the basis of a tenuous comparison with an illustration by Richard Westall to *Childe Harold's Pilgrimage*, which Delacroix is known to have read in 1824, that the artist has here represented himself as Childe Harold (pp. 384 f.). But seventeenth-century Spanish dress would surely be more inappropriate for Childe Harold, a nineteenth-century hero, than for Ravenswood, who in Scott's novel is called a 'd-d son of a Spaniard', said to look 'like a Spanish grandee', and described as wearing a 'dark-coloured riding cloak' that hung in 'the ample folds of the Spanish mantle'[1]—reason enough, it would seem, for an impressionable young artist, who was never to be over-scrupulous about dates, to select a Spanish style of costume for Ravenswood.

Robaut's date of 1821, which may well have been based on information given by Carrier, was altered without argument to *c.* 1824 in the Cat. Exh. Atelier Delacroix, Paris 1937. Hamilton also proposed revising it to 1824, mainly because of the similarity between this small portrait and Delacroix's large copy, known to have been done in 1824, after a Spanish portrait of Charles II of Spain (J21). Huyghe (p. 520 n. 16) accepts this later date, on the grounds of the picture's 'bold and developed technique' and the thin features of Delacroix who 'in 1824 . . . had been emaciated by his first attacks of fever'. However, Delacroix had a severe bout of fever in the autumn of 1820, which, by his own account, emaciated him.[2] The appearance of bold handling is largely due to the unfinished state of the portrait, and the perspective of the fireplace(?) on the left, for example, hardly supports the opinion that the technique is 'developed'. The cool and lugubrious harmony, particularly the icy blue-greens of the setting, accords better with the *Winter* of 1821 and the *Barque de Dante* of 1822 (J94 and J100) than with works of 1824. Hamilton's comparison with Delacroix's copy of the Charles II of Spain is shrewd but inconclusive as a dating argument, for Delacroix could very well have known the design of the Spanish portrait by 1821: for instance, either this very portrait with minor variations, or a version of it, is reproduced in the centre background of Ingres's *Philippe V décore le Maréchal de Berwick* (Salon 1819. Coll. Duchess of Alba, Madrid. Repr. Cat. Exh. Ingres, Petit Palais, Paris 1967-8, p. 143. The copy of the Spanish portrait cannot be distinguished clearly in reproductions). Finally, Delacroix is more likely to have identified himself with Ravenswood, 'a youth about twenty years of age',[3] in 1821, when he was himself twenty-two to -three, than in 1824. In asking why he should have done so, it may be recalled that by 1821 he, his brother and sister

were already threatened with financial ruin through the loss to creditors of the estate in the Forest of Boixe that had belonged to their mother (see e.g. *Lettres intimes*, pp. 183 ff.). He might easily have made a Romantic association between his fate and that of Scott's hero as described at the beginning of the novel. After the funeral of his father, Edgar Ravenswood stands alone in the deserted hall of his residence, Wolf's Crag, brooding over the loss of the ancestral Castle of Ravenswood to the lawyer Ashton, after long litigation. 'But its space was peopled by phantoms, which the imagination of the young heir conjured up before him—the tarnished honour and degraded fortunes of his house, the destruction of his own hopes, and the triumph of that family by whom they had been ruined. To a mind naturally of a gloomy cast, here was ample room for meditation.'[4]

[1] *Waverley Novels* (Boston, 1827 ed.), vol. 13, part i, p. 225, part ii, pp. 18, 23.
[2] Delacroix to Guillemardet, Oct. 1820: 'Ce n'est que depuis hier qu'elle [la fièvre] m'a quitté . . . Je suis maigre d'une façon qu' il est bien difficile de concevoir'. (*Lettres intimes*, p. 111.)
[3] As in note 1, part i, p. 25.
[4] Ibid. 28.

65 PORTRAIT OF MADAME LOUIS CYR BORNOT   Pl. 57

$25\frac{5}{8} \times 21\frac{1}{8}$ in. (65×53.7 cm)*
Signed and dated top right: *Eug. Delacroix/1818*
R1460
1822
Private collection, Paris

Provenance: Louis Auguste Bornot, d. 1888, grandson of the sitter and owner of the Abbey of Valmont from 1841; by descent to the present owner through the successive proprietors of the Abbey: Camille Bornot, d. 1921, his son; Jacques Béraldi, d. 1963, his great-nephew.

Exhibitions: Louvre 1930, no. 2; Charpentier, Paris 1950, no. 27c, repr.; Atelier Delacroix, Paris 1963, no. 30.

Literature: Moreau-Nélaton I. 32, repr. fig. 8; II. 156; Escholier I. 42, repr. opp. p. 42; L. Johnson, 'The Delacroix Centenary in France—I', *Burl Mag*, CV (1963), p. 301, n. 1; L. Johnson, 'Eugène Delacroix et les Salons. Documents inédits au Louvre', *Revue du Louvre*, 16 (1966), p. 228, n. 7.

Anne Françoise Bornot (*née* Delacroix) was the artist's aunt on his father's side. She was born at Givry-en-Argonne (Champagne) on 26 November 1742 and died at Epinay-sous-Sénart on 16 May 1833. Her husband, Louis Cyr Bornot, *receveur des domaines du Roi*, died in 1787 (*Journal* III. 519, addition to I. xxiii, line 36).[1]

Robaut, having presumably received the information from Auguste Bornot himself, states that Delacroix signed and dated this portrait at the request of his cousin Auguste, during one of his last visits to Valmont. All writers, struck by the high degree of skill for a twenty-year-old student, followed Robaut in wondering whether Delacroix had recalled the date correctly; Joubin (1938) resolved the problem beyond reasonable doubt by publishing a letter of 7 June 1822 from Delacroix to his sister and identifying the portrait mentioned in it with this one: 'J'ai vu tout récemment la bonne tante Bornot dont je viens de faire le portrait qu'elle me demandait depuis longtemps' (*Correspondance* v. 127 and n. 1).

During a visit to the Abbey of Valmont in October 1849, after a long absence, Delacroix expressed immense satisfaction with this work on comparing it with portraits by his uncle Henri Riesener, and it may have been then that, misjudging his own precocity, he dated it four years too early:

Au fond, je sens bien que cette facilité dans le grand maître n'est pas la qualité principale; qu'elle n'est que le moyen et non le but, ce qui est le contraire dans les médiocres. J'ai été confirmé avec plaisir dans cette opinion en comparant le portrait de ma vieille tante avec ceux de l'oncle Riesener. Il y a déjà, dans cet ouvrage d'un commençant, une sûreté et une intelligence de l'essentiel, même une touche pour rendre tout cela qui frappait Gaultron lui-même [Auguste Bornot's half-brother]. Je n'attache d'importance à ceci que parce que cela me rassure. Une main vigoureuse, disait-il, etc. (*Journal* I. 315.)

¹ All details regarding Mme Bornot are taken from a biographical note compiled by a member of the family and attached to the back of the portrait.

66 PORTRAIT OF GENERAL   Pl. 59
CHARLES DELACROIX

Panel. $15\frac{3}{8} \times 11\frac{7}{16}$ in. (39 × 29 cm)
Moreau p. 228. R51
1822
Mme J. Famin, Nieul-sur-mer (Charente-Maritime)

Provenance: Bequeathed by the artist in 1863 to his cousin Léon Riesener,¹ d. 1878; Mme Alexandre Lauwick, his daughter, d. 1932; Mme Georges Itasse,² her daughter; the present owner, her daughter.

Exhibitions: *Bd Italiens*, Paris 1864, no. 142; *Universelle*, Paris 1878, no. 785; *EBA*, Paris 1885, no. 125; Rosenberg, Paris 1928, no. 3; Louvre 1930, no. 10; Atelier Delacroix, Paris 1938, no. 2; Wildenstein, London 1952, no. 4; Atelier Delacroix, Paris 1963, no. 32.

Literature: Silvestre *Delacroix* (1855), p. 80 ('Petit portrait en pied du frère de l'artiste.'); Eugène Delacroix's will, dated 3 Aug. 1863, in *Correspondance* (Burty 1878), p. iii; Inv. Delacroix, no. 328; E. Chesneau, *L'art et les artistes modernes* (Didier, Paris, 1864), pp. 340 f.; Moreau-Nélaton 1. 49 f., fig. 18; Escholier 1. 72 f., repr. p. 71; R. Escholier, 'A propos d'une Exposition Delacroix', *L'Art*

Vivant, IV (1928), p. 127, repr. p. 130; P. Jamot, 'Delacroix', in *Le Romantisme et l'Art* (Henri Laurens, Paris, 1928), p. 122; Hourticq 1930, pl. 2; Maltese, pp. 27, 134, repr. in colour pl. IV.

Charles Henri Delacroix, the artist's elder brother, was born in Paris on 9 January 1779 and died at Bordeaux on 30 December 1845. He spent three years in the Navy, from the age of fourteen. In 1799 he was commissioned in the Ninth Regiment of Light Cavalry (*Chasseurs à cheval*), wounded several times during the Italian campaign, and promoted in the field at the Battle of Novi. He won the rank of Colonel on the field of Eylau, in 1807. Serving in the *Grande Armée* as aide-de-camp to Prince Eugène, he participated in the Russian campaign and, wounded by a shot which fractured his right thigh, was taken prisoner at Wilno in December 1812. He was repatriated in July 1814 and the following year retired to a life of inactivity with the honorary rank of Field Marshal. He also held the title of *Baron de l'Empire*.³

By 1820 he had settled in the village of Le Louroux, about twenty-five kilometres south of Tours, where the artist visited him and painted this portrait. Eugène admired his brother's courage and frank character and was always steadfast in his loyalty to him, but disapproved of his marriage to an innkeeper's daughter in 1822⁴ and was concerned at the low company he had fallen into since his retirement (see e.g. *Journal* I. 11 f.). He is known to have stayed with his brother at Le Louroux for about ten days in 1820 (*Correspondance* I. 71) and again in the summer of 1822 for a month or more (ibid. 143; *Journal* I. 10, 12). After that, they did not see each other again for five years (*Correspondance* I. 196).⁵ It was during the second visit that Delacroix began his *Journal* and though he does not write of this portrait there is no reason to doubt that, as first recorded by Moreau, it represents the General in 1822 reclining in his garden, with his house in the background. Joubin discovered that this building, converted into a post office, still existed after World War II (*Journal* III. 519—addition to I. 1 n. 1). Though somewhat altered since 1822, it survives to this day as the village post office. The Etang du Louroux, also painted by Delacroix (*Journal* I. 333) and in which his brother risked his life to save two boys from drowning in 1825 (*Correspondance* I. 172; *Lettres intimes*, p. 188), lies at a point out of sight in the portrait, not far behind the house.

The detached realism and informality of this portrait, painted in the same year as the more turbulent and ambitious *Barque de Dante* (J100), are worth stressing since they are qualities that tend to be overlooked in the work of an artist who is generally noted for emotive departures from a relaxed naturalism. This unadorned image of a valiant soldier reduced to idleness by the fall of Empire is in sober contrast to the portrait of the same subject, resplendent and erect in the uniform of a Captain of Hussars, painted by his uncle Henri Riesener in 1804, and later owned by his brother Eugène (Cat. Exh. Atelier Delacroix, Paris 1938, no. 17, belonging to Mme Malvy, *née* de Verninac, who in 1966 still retained it in the family Château de Croze). The landscape setting has been compared by Escholier (1928) to the early Corot. Delacroix also drew a bust portrait of his brother at a more advanced age (R991. Repr. Moreau-Nélaton II, fig. 260; Escholier II, p. 305; and *Album Exhibition Louvre* 1930, p. 73).

¹ Described in the will as 'le petit portrait de mon frère couché.'
² It is recorded as being in the Itasse collection by Moreau-Nélaton, I. 214 (1916), and by Escholier, I. 287 (1926), but Mme Lauwick is given as the owner in the catalogue of the exhibition Louvre 1930. Thus it seems that Mme Lauwick was the actual owner till her death, though the portrait may have been in her daughter's possession earlier.
³ This summary of the sitter's career and his dates are based on the following sources: General Delacroix's *Etat des Services*, Archives of the Ministère de la Guerre, Vincennes; the inscription on his tomb at Bordeaux, transcribed in Moreau-Nélaton II. 46; and *Journal* I. 1 n. 1. See also Piron, pp. 34–6.
⁴ *Journal* III. 521—correction to I. 11 n. 1.
⁵ The date of 1823 given for this portrait in the catalogue of the Exhibition *Universelle*, Paris 1878, and on a label on the back of the frame may therefore be discounted.

67 PORTRAIT OF JEAN BAPTISTE PIERRET   Pl. 60

$10\frac{1}{4} \times 7\frac{7}{8}$ in. (26 × 20 cm)
Moreau p. 228. R64
1823?
Whereabouts unknown (destroyed in 1944?)

Provenance: Mme J. B. Pierret, widow of the sitter, presumably from his death in 1854; Mme C. F. Vila of Chaumont (Haute Marne), their daughter, by 1885; Mme E. Carlier (*née* Vila), her daughter, by 1916, d. *c.* 1920 at Rennes; by her bequest to Mme Jouanneau (*née* Carlier), her daughter, d. 1944; possibly destroyed with the rest of her possessions in a bombing of Rennes in 1944.¹

Exhibition: EBA, Paris 1885, no. 239^quater.

Literature: Moreau-Nélaton I. 68, fig. 38.

Jean Baptiste Pierret was born in Paris on 21 November 1795 and died there on 7 June 1854. In 1820 he married Marguerite Jeanne Aimée Heydinger, by whom he had seven children; three of their four sons died in infancy; Delacroix was godfather to the youngest child, Marie (for portraits of the two elder daughters, see J85 and J86).

Pierret was one of Delacroix's earliest and closest comrades. The artist's letters to him, beginning in 1817, are particularly copious and affectionate in the early years, but bear witness to a lifelong friendship. By 1819 he aspired to become a painter and received generous encouragement from Delacroix: 'Tu seras peintre, ami: nous marcherons ensemble.' (*Correspondance* I. 80. See also ibid. 42, 52 f., 75

f., 104; and *Lettres intimes*, pp. 98, 114, 119.) In 1824 he resolved, with Delacroix's approval, to be a portrait painter (*Journal* I. 78). Though his profession is given as 'artiste peintre' as late as 1826, on his eldest daughter's baptismal certificate (see J85), he failed to make a career as an artist and followed his elder brother, Claude, into the Ministry of the Interior where he became a 'Chef de Bureau' and 'Chevalier de la Légion d'Honneur.'²

Pierret's widow was still living when Moreau and Robaut compiled their catalogues and may, with certain knowledge, have supplied their date of 1823. Otherwise, one might judge the portrait, from reproductions, to belong in the latter half of the 1820s, because the costume appears to belong in those years and the sitter could well be over twenty-eight.

Moreau records that the waistcoat was yellow; Robaut, the cravat black.

¹ In a letter from Rennes dated 13 April 1967, Mme Jouanneau's daughter, Mme Oberthür, states that she knows her mother owned this portrait and everything by Delacroix that she had kept 'a disparu avec tout ce qu'elle possédait au cours d'un bombardement sur Rennes en 1944 qui a anéanti l'immeuble dans lequel elle habitait.' In the same letter, however, she says that Mme Jouanneau disposed of some of her possessions following the death of her husband in World War I, and she does not seem to be absolutely sure that the portrait was not among them.
² All biographical details, for which references are not cited, are based on family papers, particularly J. B. Pierret's *Etat civil*, in the possession of his descendant, Maurice Vila.

68 PORTRAIT OF HENRI DE VERNINAC   Pl. 61

$23\frac{1}{4} \times 19\frac{3}{16}$ in. (59 × 48.8 cm)*
Signed bottom right: *E. Delacroix*
c. 1824
Maurice Lehmann, Paris

Provenance: By descent to Mme J. L. Malvy (*née* de Verninac), granddaughter of the sitter's brother, to 1948; de Verninac sale, 8 Dec. 1948, lot 16 (repr.), to the present owner.

Exhibitions: Wildenstein, London 1952, no. 16; Atelier Delacroix, Paris 1963, no. 25bis (wrongly listed as Charles de Verninac, on a loose sheet in the catalogue).

Literature: M. Zahar, 'La Collection Verninac', *Arts*, 19 Nov. 1948 (repr. and wrongly identified as François de Verninac).

Henri de Verninac (1801–1829¹) was the nephew of Delacroix's brother-in-law, Raymond de Verninac. The issue of the marriage of first cousins, François and Marie-Anne de Verninac, he had an older brother François, possibly portrayed later by Delacroix (see repr. in Cat. de Verninac Sale, 8 Dec. 1948, pl. VII) and two sisters, Zélie (Mme Duriez) and Hyéronime (Mme Pierrugues). His father was a Marseillais shipowner with banking interests in

Paris and proprietor of the Château de Croze (Lot), whence this portrait was brought for sale in 1948. Henri lived in Paris where he attended to his father's banking business and had been brought up, visiting Croze only for holidays.[2] Nothing is known in detail of his contacts with Delacroix or of the circumstances in which his portrait was painted. The costume and cut of the hair point to a date in the years 1823-6; the style of painting suggests that it should be placed about the middle of that period. In the dreamy expression tinged with melancholy and harmonized with a background of dark clouds lowering over a hilly landscape, it contains more characteristics that are normally associated with Romanticism than any earlier portrait by Delacroix.

[1] De Verninac family tree, in the possession of M. Raoul Ancel, Hurtebise (Charente).
[2] Conversation with M. Charles Malvy, great-grandson of Henri's brother François.

69 PORTRAIT OF A YOUNG MAN   Pl. 62
(NEWTON FIELDING?)

$15\frac{3}{4} \times 12\frac{5}{8}$ in. (40×32 cm)
Moreau p. 233. R361
1823/4?
Whereabouts unknown

Provenance: Delacroix's posthumous sale, Feb. 1864, lot 74,[1] to Eugène Lecomte, 1,250 fr.; his sale 11 June 1906, lot 42, to Raymond Lecomte, 11,100 fr.; Paul Cocteau, who is said to have sold it to Jacques Dubourg *c.* 1939;[2] it may have left Paris for Germany during the war.[3]

Exhibitions: None.

Literature: *Journal* III. 435 (Supp.)?; L. Johnson, in Cat. Exh. Edinburgh–London 1964, mentioned under no. 18; L. Johnson, 'Eugène Delacroix and Charles de Verninac: an Unpublished Portrait and New Letters', *Burl Mag*, CX (1968), p. 512 n. 12, fig. 36.

Although the sitter was not identified in the catalogue of Delacroix's posthumous sale, Moreau presumed that it was 'M. de Verninac' and dated this portrait to 1831. Robaut followed Moreau's identification and dating and, apparently confusing this picture with one of the three portraits of Charles de Verninac (see J62, J83, J92), specified further that it represented the artist's nephew and belonged to Mme Duriez. It seems improbable that, having taken the pains to leave three portraits of his beloved nephew to his family, Delacroix would have left a fourth to pass, unidentified, at public auction after his death, in a sale that contained no other family portraits, unless the *Head of an Old Woman* (J87) represents Mme Bornot. Moreover, this is not a face that is likely to have moved Delacroix to remark: 'Je ne vois pas sans un sentiment d'envie la beauté de mon neveu.'

(*Journal* I. 20); nor can it be said to bear much resemblance to the portraits that can be certainly identified as Charles.

It may be mere coincidence that this painting is the item before the portrait of Thales Fielding (J70) in the catalogue of the posthumous sale, but the fact that the sitter wears a kind of Tam o'Shanter suggests that he might be someone proud of Scottish origins, as one of the Fielding brothers with whom Delacroix shared accommodation for a while during his youth is said to have been. 'Mais un jour', recounts Léon Riesener, 'les deux amis partageant ce déjeuner se fâchèrent. Fielding disait très sérieusement qu'il descendait du roi Bruce; Delacroix l'appelait "sire". Mais Fielding ne pouvait, sur ce sujet, admettre la plaisanterie' (*Correspondance* (Burty 1878), p. xvii). It may indeed have been one of the Fieldings who introduced Delacroix to Burns's poem *Tam o'Shanter* (see J109). The exact relationship of Delacroix with the Fielding brothers remains obscure, partly because of his failure to mention their Christian names in his *Journal*. No less than two of them were residing in Paris by May 1823, for Delacroix records visiting them in his *Journal* (I. 28) at that time: 'Le soir chez les Fielding'. He is probably referring to Newton and Thales, as stated by Joubin (*Journal* III. 523—correction to I. 28 n. 1). Thales returned to England in October 1824 and it was then that Delacroix evidently moved to the accommodation vacated by his friend at 20 rue Jacob (see letter from Delacroix to Achille Devéria, 8 Oct. 1824 (in Escholier I. 108) and to Soulier, Oct. 1824 (*Correspondance* I. 150 f.). For discussion of the misdating of the latter see J70). He possibly shared it with Newton, who was to reside permanently in Paris, where he died in poverty. There is no evidence to support the view that Delacroix lived at 20 rue Jacob when Thales was there, as some writers have suggested.

If this portrait represents Newton Fielding (1799-1856: *DNB*), it should not be dated later than 1824 because of the youth of the sitter, who is surely not beyond his early twenties.

[1] As 'Portrait de jeune homme à mi-corps, coiffé d'un béret bleu.' An early photograph of our portrait in M-Nélaton Port. V shows the original lot number still affixed to the top left-hand corner of the canvas.
[2] Conversation with Jean Dieterle.
[3] Conversation with Jacques Dubourg.

70 PORTRAIT OF THALES   Pl. 63
FIELDING

$12\frac{5}{8} \times 9\frac{5}{8}$ in. (32.1×24.5 cm)* Relined. E.D.
Moreau p. 229, 313. R60 (1823)
c. 1824
Private collection, Paris

Provenance: Delacroix's posthumous sale, Feb. 1864, lot 75, to Achille Piron, 390 fr.; his sale 21 Apr. 1865, lot 8, to Baron

Charles Rivet, 165 fr., d. 1872; by his bequest to Mme Lajudie, his daughter; by descent to the present owner.

Exhibitions: None.

Literature: *Journal* III. 435 n. 1—Supp.; L. Johnson, 'Four Rediscovered Portraits by Delacroix', *Burl Mag*, CXII (1970), pp. 4–7, repr. fig. 6.

The identity of the sitter is first recorded in the catalogue of Delacroix's posthumous sale, though there is evidence in one of his own undated notes suggesting that he painted the portrait of at least one of the Fielding brothers: 'A qui ai-je prêté le portrait de Fielding?' (*Journal* III. 435—Supp.)

Thales Fielding (1793–1837), the British artist, appears to have been a close friend of Delacroix in the years 1823–5 and there is reason to believe that the two painters sometimes helped one another with their work. Delacroix probably refers to Thales when writing of the *Massacres of Chios* (J105) on 7 March 1824: 'Fielding m'a arrangé mon fond.' (*Journal* I. 60.) And when he notes on 11 May 'Travaillé chez Fielding à son *Macbeth*' (ibid. 100), he is most likely referring to the water-colour which Thales exhibited at the Salon of 1824 under the title: 'Macbeth rencontrant les sorcières sur la bruyère' (no. 647). But owing to the possibility of confusion with other members of the Fielding family—four brothers, all artists—and to the scarcity of facts regarding their movements, it has so far proved impossible to trace the history of the friendship in detail.

Thales's permanent residence was in Newman Street, London, where he died and is recorded as living in the catalogues of the Royal Academy Exhibitions for 1822 and, after a gap of two years when he is not listed, from 1825. He was probably living in Paris in 1823, as it is reasonable to suppose, with Joubin, that he was one of the Fieldings whom Delacroix records visiting in May of that year: 'Le soir chez les Fielding.' (*Journal* I. 28 and III. 523—correction to I. 28 n. 1); and he was certainly there in 1824, for his address is given as 'rue Jacob 20' in the official catalogue of that year's Salon, and Delacroix, in a letter to Soulier, wrote with regret of his departure in October and planned to visit him in England the following year, which indeed he did (*Correspondance* I. 150 f.[1]).

Moreau dates this portrait to 1824, while Robaut places it in 1823, doubtless on the strength of Delacroix's letter to Soulier deploring Thales's departure, which was published after Moreau's catalogue and wrongly dated 1823 (see n. 1). Certainly the parting of the two friends would have furnished Delacroix with a good motive for painting the portrait about Autumn 1824 and there can be no objection to Moreau's date on the grounds of style or of the sitter's age, which was thirty-one in 1824.

The picture was cleaned and restored *c.* 1963, when it was brought to Paris from the country; at the same time it was

relined, the stretcher removed and the seal of Delacroix's posthumous sale transferred to the new stretcher.[2]

Thales Fielding also painted a portrait of Delacroix, which was hung at the Royal Academy Exhibition of 1827 (no. 269) but has not come to light since. A lithograph that is thought to reproduce it is illustrated here in Fig. 1 (see also Escholier I. 118 n. 2, 143).

---

[1] The date of this letter to Soulier is given as 'mardi 11 octobre 1823' in Burty's 1878 edition of the Letters (p. 68) and in Joubin's edition (1935), but there can be no doubt, as Escholier (I. 91 n. 1) pointed out in 1926, that it actually dates from October 1824. It may be added that 11 October did not fall on a Tuesday in either 1823 or 1824, so there is a mistake in the day of the week or the day of the month as well as in the year. Escholier's argument for revising the date to 1824 was based primarily on the contents of a letter dated 8 October 1824 from Delacroix to Achille Devéria (published in neither the Burty nor the Joubin editions of the *Correspondance*), in which the writer notifies his friend that he has changed his address to 'rue Jacob, 20' (Escholier I. 108), just as in the letter to Soulier he reports what is clearly the same move: 'Je t'écris, mon bon ami, de la rue Jacob où je suis installé. Nous avons vu partir samedi le bon Thalès.' Since Escholier's correction, the misdated letter to Soulier has caused further error. Dupont, for example, publishes two letters from Delacroix to Soulier discussing the same matter as the misdated one and dates them to 1823 (*Lettres intimes*, pp. 165–7). Delacroix, however, dated the first of these, 'vendredi 22 octobre' and 22 October was a Friday in 1824, not in 1823.

[2] Conversation with the owner.

THE GOUBAUX PORTRAITS (1824–30)

Prosper Parfait Goubaux (1795–1859) was a genial schoolmaster and man of letters with a wide variety of intellectual interests, a translator of Horace and a playwright who collaborated with Alexandre Dumas the Elder, Ernest Legouvé and Eugène Sue. In 1820 he founded the Institution Saint-Victor, a boys' secondary school. He sold it in 1846 to the city of Paris, remaining its director; it developed into the Collège Chaptal.

Goubaux had attended the same lycée as Delacroix; the latter records that they saw one another on 1 January 1824 and recalled their schooldays (*Journal* I. 42). Perhaps about that time, they came to an agreement whereby Delacroix was to paint portraits for 100 fr. each of pupils at Goubaux's school who won prizes in the *Concours général*. Robaut lists ten such portraits, painted between 1824 and 1834. They were hung in the reception room at the school. Six were painted before 1832; all trace of three of these has been lost since 1885 (see J71–J76). The entire series seems to have remained at the school till Goubaux's death in August 1859,[1] then Charles Rigault, a former pupil at the Institution Saint-Victor,[2] returned some of the portraits to the original sitters or members of their families;[3] others, no less than five, had found their way into the possession of Georges Arosa by 1873,[4] and may well have belonged to him much earlier, since two of those that are later recorded in his collection were said to be unavailable when reclaimed by

Eugène Berny d'Ouville, one of the sitters, on Goubaux's death (see J75, n. 1). It is also likely that a picture lent by Arosa to the exhibition *Bd Italiens*, Paris 1864, and listed in the catalogue (no. 156) as 'Un portrait d'homme', with dimensions 60 × 49 cm, was one of the Goubaux portraits, probably that representing Bellinger, which was the only one of the four Goubaux portraits in the Arosa sale of 17 December 1895 that was not identified by name (lot 14: 'Portrait d'homme'.).

Literature: (Goubaux and his school. References to specific portraits are given under the individual entries.) G. Vapereau, *Dictionnaire universel des contemporains* (Paris, Hachette, 1858; and 3rd ed., 1865); M. du Camp, *Souvenirs littéraires* (Hachette, Paris, 1882) I. 36 ff. (for recollections of the school by a former pupil); E. Legouvé, *Soixante ans de souvenirs* (Hetzel, Paris, 1886, 4th ed.) II. 16–46 (for the most complete and sympathetic account of Goubaux's appearance and personality and the fortunes of his school), English translation by A. D. VanDam, *Sixty Years of Recollections* (Eden, Remington & Co., London and Sydney, 1893) II. 9–45; *Journal* I. 338 n. 2.

¹ In 1867 Louis Judicis, who had himself sat to Delacroix for one of the Goubaux portraits in the 1830s (R380), listed the ten portraits in the series that were known to him (the same ten later catalogued by Robaut) and stated: 'Jusqu'en 1860, époque de la mort de M. Goubaux, ils ont décoré le parloir du collège Chaptal (ancienne institution Saint-Victor).' (Joc'h d'Indren—misprint of Judicis's pseudonym Indret—, not in *L'Intermédiaire*. IV, no. 87–90 (Aug. and Sept. 1867), col. 317. For information about this, see letter dated 25 June 1877 from Judicis to Robaut in R Ann, p. 105.)

Though it is just possible that a few of the portraits by Delacroix escaped Robaut's notice, Ernest Legouvé's claim in the preface to the catalogue of the Paul Huet sale, 15–16 April 1878, that there were more than sixty of them can be discounted. Robaut calls it a 'monstrueuse erreur qu'il a volontairement commise' (R Ann, p. 119).

² See letter dated 24 June 1877 from Alfred Robaut to [Eugène] Berny d'Ouville in R Ann between pp. 72 and 73.

³ Writing of the series as a whole, Moreau (p. 231), 1873, says: 'Ces portraits, payés 100 francs au peintre, étaient destinés à orner le parloir de la célèbre maison d'éducation; ils y sont restés jusqu'à la mort de son chef, et ont été remis à ce moment aux familles des lauréats.' For evidence that not all were returned to the prize-winners or their representatives, and that Charles Rigault was involved in the distribution, see the individual entries below.

⁴ Moreau (p. 231), 1873, states without specifying: 'M. Arosa possède aujourd'hui six de ces portraits.' Robaut, however, records Arosa as the owner of five only: Abel Widmer (J71), Eugène and Amédée Berny d'Ouville (J75 and J76), Heurtaux (R447) and Bellinger (R553; Arosa's ownership is recorded in a marginal note to this number in R Ann).

71 ABEL WIDMER   Pl. 64

23½ × 19 in. (59.7 × 48.3 cm) Oval. Relined
R115
1824
The National Gallery, London

Provenance: Prosper Parfait Goubaux, d. 1859; G. Arosa, probably before 1873;¹ his sale, 17 Dec. 1895, lot 15, to

Degas, 390 fr.;² his sale, 26 March 1918, lot 33, purchased by special grant for the British Nation. At the Tate Gallery; transferred to the National Gallery, 1956.

Exhibition: Edinburgh–London 1964, no. 13.

Literature: Joc'h d'Indren [Louis Judicis], note in *L'Intermédiaire*, IV, nos. 87–90 (Aug. and Sept. 1867), col. 317; E. Degas, conversation of 22 Dec. 1895, reported in D. Halévy, *Degas parle...* (La Palatine, Paris and Geneva, n.d. [1960]), p. 85 (English translation by M. Curtiss, *My Friend Degas* (Rupert Hart-Davis, London, 1966), p. 72); A. Robaut, note requesting information about Abel Widmer and others, *L'Intermédiaire*, XXXIII, no. 716 (10 Feb. 1896), cols. 164–5; E. Pélicier, reply to inquiry about Widmer, ibid., no. 727 (30 May 1896), cols. 625–6; *National Gallery Millbank, Catalogue Modern Foreign School* (London, 1926), no. 3287; M. Davies, *National Gallery Catalogues, French School* (London, 1957, 2nd ed., revised), no. 3287, pp. 76 f.

Abel Widmer won a second prize in mathematics in the *Concours général* of 1824.³ Born at Chantemerle, Hautes-Alpes, on 12 December 1805, he came to Goubaux's school after leaving the Lycée Louis-le-Grand at the end of September 1822. He went on to take two years at the Ecole polytechnique (November 1825 to November 1827), then entered the cotton spinning plant run by his uncle at Essonnes, Seine-et-Oise. In 1832, he was director of a spinning-mill at Rouval, acquired by his uncle, but owing to a heart disease retired prematurely and died at the age of thirty-three on 16 January 1838.

Though this is the only unsigned portrait of the ten catalogued by Robaut, there is no reason to doubt that Delacroix initiated the series in 1824 with this picture. It is recorded in 1867, by one of the other prize-winners, Louis Judicis (loc. cit.), as one of the portraits by Delacroix that hung in the school. In the pose of the head and handling it is, moreover, much like the *Portrait of Henri de Verninac* of c. 1824 (J68), if somewhat more leaden in spirit—a reflection perhaps of the sitter's personality.

¹ See the general history above, *The Goubaux Portraits*.

² Marginal note to R115 in R Ann.

Daniel Halévy (op. cit.) reports a conversation that he had during a visit to Degas on 22 December 1895, when the artist showed him two Goubaux portraits, which, it seems clear from the text, he had acquired at an auction a few days earlier. Degas, according to Halévy, introduced one of them as 'M. Bussy d'Hédouville' (plainly an error for Berny d'Ouville—see J75 and J76) and the other simply as a winner of a second prize for Latin translation. Heurtaux was the only pupil awarded this prize whose portrait is recorded as passing in the Arosa sale and that was bought by M. Fouretaine, according to R Ann (R447). Degas (or Halévy) evidently made a mistake about the prize and was actually referring to the portrait of Abel Widmer, which is noted in R Ann as purchased by Degas at the sale.

³ This is stated in Robaut under the entry for Désiré Pellerin (R120) and, apparently independently, by E. Pélicier in his detailed biographical note of 1896 (loc. cit.), from which all details of the sitter given in the present entry have been taken.

72 DÉSIRÉ PELLERIN   Pl. 65

$23\frac{5}{8} \times 19\frac{11}{16}$ in. (60 × 50 cm)[1]
Signed lower left[2]
R120
1825
Whereabouts unknown

Provenance: Prosper Parfait Goubaux, d. 1859; Ch. Rigault, probably from 1859 to *c*. 1877;[3] Alfred Robaut; Baron de Beurnonville; his sale, 24 March 1883, lot 158 (apparently bought in or withdrawn); his sale (baron de B.), 21 May 1883, lot 158, 510 fr.; Th. Leroy, by 1885.[4]

Exhibition: EBA, Paris 1885, no. 233.

Literature: Joc'h d'Indren [Louis Judicis], note in *L'Inter-médiaire*, IV, nos. 87-90 (Aug. and Sept. 1867), col. 317; A. Robaut, note requesting information about Désiré Pellerin and others, ibid. XXXIII, no. 716 (10 Feb. 1896), cols. 164-5 (no reply concerning Pellerin was published).

Désiré Pellerin, a sixth-form pupil at Goubaux's school, won the second prize for geography in the *Concours général* of 1825. According to Louis Judicis (loc. cit.), also a Goubaux pupil portrayed by Delacroix, he became a mining engineer. He died young, at the end of 1837 (R Ann between pp. 36 and 37).

This portrait has not been heard of since 1885. It is known only from the sketch after it in Robaut Tracings I and the small illustration in Robaut, reproduced here. Some details of colour are also published in Robaut:'. . . yeux bleu foncé . . . Habit noir-bleu, gilet jaune á raies brunes, gants gris-ardoise.'

[1] According to Robaut; 60 × 48 cm, according to the catalogue of the Baron de Beurnonville sale, 24 March 1883, lot 158.
[2] According to Robaut. A signature is visible, though illegible, in the small illustration in Robaut, but none appears on the larger sketch after this portrait in Robaut Tracings I.
[3] R Ann contains copious notes, numbered pp. 36a–d, giving information about the names of the prize-winners at Goubaux's school, the dates of their awards and the subjects. In addition, some biographical details of the sitters are included together with an account of what happened to certain of the portraits. These notes for the most part were apparently furnished in 1877 by Rigault, who took charge of some of the portraits on Goubaux's death (see e.g. J73, n. 2 and J74), and were a source of much information published in Robaut. A note on Pellerin states: 'la toile originale est entre mes mains', meaning presumably Rigault's hands, though Robaut as well as Rigault (misspelt Rigaut) is recorded as an owner in R and the note could refer to him.
[4] The owner recorded in Robaut's annotated Cat. Exh. EBA, Paris 1885, no. 233 (Bib AA, MS. 298ter).

73 AUGUSTE RICHARD DE LA HAUTIÈRE   Pl. 65

$23\frac{5}{8} \times 19\frac{11}{16}$ in. (60 × 50 cm)
Signed and dated top left: *Eug. Delacroix 1828*[1]
R258
Whereabouts unknown

Provenance: Prosper Parfait Goubaux, d. 1859; returned to the sitter by M. Charles Rigault in 1859.[2]

Exhibitions: None.

Literature: Joc'h d'Indren [Louis Judicis], note in *L'Inter-médiaire*, IV, nos. 87-90 (Aug. and Sept. 1867), col. 317; A. Robaut, note requesting information about Richard de la Hautière and others, ibid. XXXIII, no. 716 (10 Feb. 1896), cols. 164-5 (no reply concerning de la Hautière was published); Escholier I. 251; Escholier 1963, p. 54.

Richard de la Hautière was awarded the second prize for Latin translation in the *Concours général* of 1828. He appears to have settled at Vendôme, near Blois, as a barrister *c*. 1847.[3] According to his own account, written from an address at Blois at the age of sixty-four in correspondence with Robaut, he sat for Delacroix when he was fifteen and a half in 1828; the portrait had never resembled him and was a sketch ('ébauche') rather than a finished work.[4]

This portrait is known only from the small photograph (8.2 × 6.4 cm) contained in R Ann and reproduced here; and from the smaller print in Robaut. Some colour notes are contained in Robaut: 'Les cheveux sont châtain clair, le teint blanc et rose, l'habit noir, le gilet blanc, la cravate jaune avec des rayures.' The picture is last recorded in the possession of the sitter in 1877, in the correspondence referred to above.

[1] Though the signature and date are not visible in the old photograph reproduced here from R Ann p. 72e, a note on the back of the photograph states: 'Signé et daté en haut à gauche sur une ligne horizontale', and both can be seen in the small illustration in Robaut.
[2] Note on the back of the photograph referred to in n. 1: 'Mr Auguste Richard de la Hautière . . . à qui ce portrait a été rendu par M. Rigault en 1859.' Also note in R Ann, p. 36c, apparently from Rigault: 'de la Hautière (Richard) . . . je lui ai renvoyé en 1859 son portrait original.'
[3] Note in R Ann, p. 36c, apparently from Rigault 1877: 'de la Hautière (Richard) fixé depuis 30 ans à Vendôme, comme avocat.'
[4] Letter dated 14 July 1877 from de la Hautière to Robaut, in R Ann, between pp. 72 and 73. The sitter gives his age at the time of writing and confirms the details of the prize he won in another letter to Robaut, dated 28 July 1877 and preserved in the same place. He also gives his profession, 'avocat', with his signature.

74 ACHILLE DOMINIQUE SCHMITZ   Pl. 65

$23\frac{5}{8} \times 19\frac{11}{16}$ in. (60 × 50 cm)
Signed and dated lower left: *Eug. Delacroix/1829*[1]
R293
Whereabouts unknown

Provenance: Prosper Parfait Goubaux, d. 1859; returned to the sitter's two brothers by Charles Rigault in 1859;[2] last recorded in the possession of the sitter's brother, 'M. Schmitz, intendant militaire à Orléans', by Robaut, 1885.

Exhibitions: None.

Literature: Joc'h d'Indren [Louis Judicis], note in *L'Inter-médiaire*, IV, nos. 87-90 (Aug. and Sept. 1867), col. 317; A. Robaut, note requesting information about 'Schmitz (devenu Intendant militaire)' and others, ibid. XXXIII, no. 716 (10 Feb. 1896), cols. 164-5; A.Y., note concerning 'L'intendant général Schmitz' in reply to Robaut's inquiry, ibid. no. 722 (10 Apr. 1896), col. 440; Escholier I. 251; Escholier 1963, p. 54.

Achille Schmitz, a fourth-form pupil[3] at Goubaux's school, won the second prize for Latin translation in the *Concours général* of 1829. Born in Paris on 17 November 1813, he went on from the Institution Saint-Victor to the Ecole poly-technique in November 1833, and then into a career as an officer in the Engineers. After serving nearly twelve years in Africa and attaining the rank of Captain, he was posted to the Crimea and killed by cannon-fire at Sebastopol on 6 October 1854.[4]

This portrait is known only from Robaut's drawing after a purported copy of it by one of the sitter's brothers in Robaut Tracings I (see nn. 1 and 2 below) and from the small illustration in Robaut, reproduced here.

References to money owed to the artist by Goubaux in letters of 28 October and 19 November 1829 from Delacroix, at Valmont, to Pierret may apply to the fee for this portrait (*Correspondance* I. 246, 248), though it is also possible that Delacroix had not yet received full payment for his portraits of earlier prize-winners and was claiming that.

In a letter addressed to Goubaux at the rue Blanche and dated merely 'Ce dimanche 2', Delacroix writes: 'M. Judicis a été très exact et son portrait [R380] est très avancé [. . .].

'Si tu veux m'envoyer M. Schmitz mardi, je serai à ses ordres' (*Correspondance* I. 338-9). In a footnote, Joubin argues that the letter was written in September 1832 because (1) Goubaux's address in the rue Blanche is not listed in the *Almanach des 20.000 adresses* before 1833 and therefore, according to Joubin, he must have moved there in 1832; and (2) Judicis won a prize for Greek translation in the *Concours général* of 1832. He goes on to conclude that Achille Schmitz's portrait must have been painted three years after he won a prize in 1829 and that Robaut therefore dated it inaccurately. These opinions fail to take account of the following points: (1) Robaut records that this portrait of Schmitz actually bore the date 1829; (2) the portrait of Judicis is stated to have been painted in 1834, in the entry for it in the catalogue of the posthumous sale of the sitter's collection at Fontainebleau, 8 November 1893; and (3) Achille Schmitz is stated in Robaut (no. 293) and in R Ann (p. 36a) to have won the second prize in special mathematics at the *Concours général* of 1833, in addition to the award he received in 1829.

If all these facts are accurate Delacroix's letter to Goubaux should be dated 1834 and there was apparently a second portrait of Schmitz, which has never come to light, painted in that year.

[1] It is stated to be signed and dated 1829 in Robaut; an illegible signature and date are also visible in the illustration to the entry. Though neither is reproduced on his drawing after a purported copy of the portrait by one of the sitter's brothers in Robaut Tracings I, Robaut notes the full form of the signature and date on the back of the drawing.

[2] Note in R Ann p. 36c, apparently from Rigault 1877: 'Schmitz (Achille) [. . .]. Le portrait original a été remis par moi à ses frères dont l'aîné Mr le Baron Isidore Schmitz est aujourd'hui intendant militaire à Orléans, lequel en a fait une copie pour son autre frère le G.al Schmitz.' The Christian names of the elder brother and commissary were in fact François Xavier Léon, and it was the younger brother, the General, whose name was Isidore. The former was born on 10 November 1816 (see his *Etat des Services* (65, 995/3), Archives of the Ministère de la Guerre, Vincennes) and died at La Rochelle, where he had retired on 4 February 1890 (his 'Acte de décès', Mairie of La Rochelle). The latter, Isidore Pierre Schmitz, was born on 21 July 1820 and died in Paris on 2 February 1892 (see his *Détail des Services*, Archives of the Ministère de la Guerre, Vincennes).

[3] R Ann p. 36a.

[4] All details, except those concerning his record at Goubaux's school, are from Achille Schmitz's dossier (no. 7,905/Nu) in the Archives of the Ministère de la Guerre, Vincennes.

75 EUGÉNE BERNY D'OUVILLE   Pl. 66

$24\frac{1}{4} \times 19\frac{7}{8}$ in. (61.6 × 50.5 cm: visible oval surface. Overall dimensions of canvas: 64 × 52 cm)
Signed and dated lower right: *Eug Delacroix/1828*
R257
Henry P. McIlhenny, Philadelphia

Provenance: Prosper Parfait Goubaux, d. 1859; G. Arosa, from 1859? to at least 1885;[1] probably anonymous sale, 4 December 1897, lot 37, to Vincent Noto (dealer), 800 fr.;[2] Dr. Georges Viau by 1926 to at least 1930; with Jacques Seligmann, from whom it was purchased by the present owner in 1933.

Exhibitions: Charpentier, Paris 1926, no. 47; Paris 1927, no. 276; Louvre 1930, no. 47, repr. *Album*, p. 28; (at the Fogg Art Museum, Cambridge, Mass., for part of 1934. Possibly shown in conjunction with the Exh. 'French Drawings and Prints of the Nineteenth Century', 21 March-28 Apr., but not catalogued); Philadelphia 1937 (no cat.); Hartford 1952, no. 28, repr. pl. V; Philadelphia 1958 (no cat.); San Francisco 1962, no. 21, repr.; Cleveland 1963, no. 74; Philadelphia 1968.

Literature: Joc'h d'Indren [Louis Judicis], note in *L'Inter-médiaire*, IV, nos. 87-90 (Aug. and Sept. 1867), col. 317; A. Robaut, note requesting information about Eugène Berny d'Ouville and others, ibid. XXXIII, no. 716 (10 Feb. 1896), cols. 164-5 (no reply concerning Berny d'Ouville was published); Escholier I. 251, repr. opp. p. 253; W. George, 'Genèse d'une crise', *L'Amour de l'Art*, XIII (1932), p. 268, repr. p. 271; Escholier 1963, p. 54.

Eugène Berny d'Ouville, a fourth-form pupil[3] at Goubaux's school, won the second prize for Latin composition in the *Concours général* of 1828, when he would have been about fourteen. He stayed on at the school as a teacher till the age of twenty-eight, then joined the Ministry of Justice as a drafter ('rédacteur').[4] He confirmed the identification of the portrait when Robaut saw him in June 1877 and clearly recalled that he had been to pose several times for Delacroix at his address in the *passage* Saulnier,[5] whence the artist moved at the end of 1828.

This portrait is set apart from the others in the series by its refined blend of physical and spiritual beauty.

The commentary in Robaut implies that the picture was cut down from a rectangular to oval shape whereas the Richard de la Hautière (J73) had retained its original form. The opinion is hard to accept in view of the general design, which seems to have been conceived for an oval frame; the position of the signature and the comparative dimensions of the two paintings also argue against it.

[1] It is recorded as Arosa's in Robaut (1885) and was probably one of the group of Goubaux portraits stated earlier by Moreau (1873) to belong to Arosa (see general history above, *The Goubaux Portraits*). Robaut, however, noted on the back of his drawing of the portrait in Tracings I, after seeing the sitter: 'A la mort de Mr Goubaux, il réclama son portrait qu'on ne pût lui remettre pas plus que celui de son frère Amédée [J76].' A possible explanation of why they could not be returned is that both portraits had already been acquired by Arosa.

[2] All these details, except the lot number, are applied in R Ann (margin of R328) to the portrait of the sitter's brother, Amédée (J76); and the present portrait is recorded in R Ann as lot 16 in the sale 'succession G. Arosa (17 Dec. 1895)', with a note giving Degas as the purchaser which was later defaced in an attempt to erase it. Lot 16 was indeed described in the Arosa sale catalogue as 'Portrait d'Eug. Berny d'Ouville. Signé et daté 1820', but there was almost certainly a confusion between the two portraits, the dates on both of which are imperfect and could both be mistaken for '1820'. For Robaut records in R Ann (margin of R553) that Degas purchased two out of the four portraits in the Arosa sale: one of the two, it is known from R Ann, was the Abel Widmer (J71); the other, it is clear from Degas's conversation with Halévy a few days after the sale, was a portrait of one of the Berny brothers (see J71, n. 2). It was apparently the portrait of Amédée, which passed in Degas's sale in 1918, and not that of his brother Eugène, which there is no firm evidence for thinking ever belonged to Degas. The only alternative explanation would be that the portrait of Eugène was in fact in the Arosa sale of 1895 and bought by Degas, but disposed of before his death. In that case, it would be hard to understand why Robaut tried to efface the note in R Ann recording Degas as the purchaser.

The details of lot 37 in the catalogue of the anonymous sale of 4 Dec. 1895 could apply to either picture: 'Portrait d'homme. Toile ovale, signée à droite'.

[3] Note in R Ann p. 36*a*, apparently from Rigault 1877, and also giving details of the prize as published later in Robaut.

[4] Both details are noted on the back of Robaut's drawing of the portrait in Tracings I.

[5] As n. 4 for all facts in this sentence.

76 AMÉDÉE BERNY D'OUVILLE   Pl. 67

$24\frac{1}{4} \times 19\frac{3}{4}$ in. (61.6 × 50.2 cm) Oval
Signed and dated lower right: *Eug. Delacroix/1830*
R328
Senhor A. de Medeiros e Almeida, Lisbon

Provenance: Prosper Parfait Goubaux, d. 1859; G. Arosa, from 1859?; probably his sale ('Collection de feu M. A . . .'),

17 Dec. 1895, lot 16, (as 'Portrait d'Eug. Berny d'Ouville') to Degas;[1] his sale, 26 March 1918, lot 28; Dr. Viau, by 1923; Jakob Goldschmidt, New York, by 1940; his sale (with other owners), London (Sotheby's), 28 Nov. 1956, lot 123 (repr.), to Drown, £8,500.

Exhibitions: Charpentier, Paris 1923, no. 87; New York 1940, no. 245 (as 'Portrait of a Boy'), repr. p. 169; Wildenstein, New York 1944, no. 5, repr.; Wildenstein, New York 1945, no. 27; Edinburgh-London 1964, no. 22, pl. 11.

Literature: Joc'h d'Indren [Louis Judicis], note in *L'Intermédiaire*, IV, nos. 87-90 (Aug. and Sept. 1867), col. 317; E. Degas, conversation of 22 Dec. 1895, reported in D. Halévy, *Degas parle . . .* (La Palatine, Paris and Geneva, n.d. [1960]), p. 85 (English translation by M. Curtiss, *My Friend Degas* (Rupert Hart-Davis, London, 1966), p. 72); Moreau-Nélaton I. 98, repr. fig. 68; J. L. Vaudoyer, 'L'Exposition de "L'Art et la Vie romantiques" ', *GBA*, VII (1923), pp. 195 f.; Escholier I. 251; *Art News*, XLIII, no. 14 (Nov. 1944), full-page repr. p. 8; J. Siegfried, 'The Romantic Artist as a Portrait Painter', *Marsyas*, VIII (1957-9), p. 38; Escholier 1963, p. 54.

Amédée Berny d'Ouville, a sixth-form pupil at Goubaux's school, won the second prize in Latin composition in the *Concours général* of 1830. He died during an Atlantic crossing—by 1867, since he is recorded as deceased by Louis Judicis (loc. cit.), who also states that he was a merchant. The entry in Robaut reports that the painting was recognized by the sitter's brother Eugène, presumably when Robaut saw him in 1877 (see J75); he commented: 'C'est bien mon frère, il avait tout à fait cette petite tête de fouine.'

[1] J75 n. 1 applies also to this portrait up to 1885; after 1885, see J75 n. 2,

77 HEAD OF A WOMAN (Study for   Pl. 68 the *Massacres of Chios*)

$15\frac{1}{2} \times 12\frac{1}{2}$ in. (39.4 × 31.8 cm)
Moreau p. 168. R95
1824
Private collection, Paris

Provenance: Frédéric Leblond,[1] d. 1872; Mme Leblond, his widow; Dr. E. Gebauer, Mayor of Cléry (Loiret), his nephew, by 1885; his sale, Cléry, 31 May 1904, lot 15; Mme Albert Esnault-Pelterie (mauve wax seal of the collection on the stretcher), by 1906 (probably acquired 1904), d. *c*. 1938; Mme J. Meunié (*née* Popelin), her granddaughter.

Exhibitions: Probably Salon 1824, as part of no. 451;[2] *Bd Italiens*, Paris 1864, no. 102; *EBA*, Paris 1885, no. 88; Geo. Petit, Paris 1910, no. 73; Louvre 1930, no. 16, repr. *Album*, p. 10 (on loan to the Philadelphia Museum of Art, Apr. 1937-Jan. 1963); Louvre 1963, no. 54, repr.

Literature: *Journal* III. 371—Supp.;[1] Silvestre *Delacroix* (1855), p. 80 ('Tête de vieille femme pour le Massacre de Scio.'); Tourneux, p. 44; L. Rouart, 'Collection de Madame Esnault-Pelterie', *Les Arts*, June 1906, p. 4; P. Dorbec, 'L'Exposition des "Vingt Peintres du XIXᵉ Siècle", à la Galerie Georges Petit', *GBA*, 4ᵉ période, IV (1910), p. 16; Escholier I. 114, 124, repr. p. 125; Johnson 1963, p. 20, repr. pl. 7; M. Florisoone, 'La Genèse espagnole des Massacres de Scio de Delacroix', *Revue du Louvre*, 13 (1963), p. 202; Maltese, p. 145, under no. 5; L. Johnson, 'Eugène Delacroix et les Salons. Documents inédits au Louvre', *Revue du Louvre*, 16 (1966), p. 227 n. 5, 228 n. 7; Trapp, p. 36.

This is a study, evidently done from the life, for the old woman seated on the right in the foreground of the *Massacres of Chios* (J105). The position of the head and the expression are unchanged in the final figure, though the woman is made to seem older and is more freely and colouristically modelled than is this highly sculpturesque, smoothly constructed head which, despite its expressiveness, has some of the qualities of a plaster cast.

There is no record of when the head of the old woman was painted on the final canvas, but Delacroix notes that he retouched 'la vieille' on 26 April 1824 (*Journal* I. 87), by which time this study had presumably been completed. On 12 May, he refers specifically to the head in the large picture when recalling with pleasure and approval the comments of Cogniet, who had visited his studio that afternoon: 'Et puis combien ce pauvre Géricault aimerait cette peinture! La vieille, sans bouche grande ouverte, ni exagération dans les yeux.' (ibid. 101).

[1] In a list of works contained in the so-called 'Carnet héliotrope' and probably compiled in the 1840s, Delacroix notes: '*Les 2 études* qu'il [Leblond] a à moi, *la Vieille et la jeune fille.*' (*Journal* III. 371—Supp.) Joubin (ibid. 317 n. 2) thought that entry probably referred to an *Education of the Virgin*, but, as pointed out in *Mémorial* (no. 54), he was unquestionably mistaken and it applies to our picture and the *Girl seated in a Cemetery* (J78), both of which are recorded as belonging to Leblond in Cat. Exh. *Bd Italiens*, Paris 1864. It is not known when Leblond acquired the two pictures nor if they were a gift from the artist, though he was a good friend of Delacroix's by the end of 1823 (*Journal* I. 39) and might well have owned them as early as 1824.

[2] This number is described in the official catalogue of the Salon as: 'Etudes, *même numéro*'; and it immediately follows the entry for the *Massacres of Chios*, the only other work by Delacroix listed in the catalogue. According to Moreau (pp. 167 f.), these studies comprised our picture and the *Girl seated in a Cemetery* (J78). While there is every likelihood that he was right, it should be borne in mind that they are not identified in reviews of the Salon, nor are they listed in the register of works Delacroix submitted to the Salon jury in 1824 (see L. Johnson, op. cit. (1966), p. 227 n. 5).

78 GIRL SEATED IN A CEMETERY

Pl. 69

25¹³⁄₁₆ × 21¼ in. (65.5 × 54.3 cm)
Moreau p. 168. R66 (1823)
1824
Musée du Louvre

Provenance: Same as the preceding number till 1904; Dr. Gebauer sale, Cléry, 31 May 1904, lot 12, to Bernheim-Jeune for Etienne Moreau-Nélaton (Arch B-J no. 13.698); he donated it to the Louvre in 1906 (RF1652). At Musée des arts décoratifs 1907-34; transferred to Louvre 1934.

Exhibitions: Probably Salon 1824, as part of no. 451;[1] *Bd Italiens*, Paris 1864, no. 103 (as 'Une jeune fille vue à mi-corps'); *EBA*, Paris 1885, no. 87 (as 'Femme souliote, orpheline au cimetière'); Louvre 1930, no. 15; Atelier Delacroix, Paris 1945, no. 2; id., Paris 1947, no. 2; id., Paris 1949, no. 31; id., Paris 1950, no. 12, repr.; Bernheim-Jeune, Paris 1952, no. 19; Louvre 1963, no. 55, repr.; Atelier Delacroix, Paris 1973 (no cat.)

Literature: *Journal* III. 371—Supp.;[2] Silvestre *Delacroix* (1855), p. 80 ('Tête de jeune fille pour le Massacre de Scio'); W. Bürger [Théophile Thoré], 'Eugène Delacroix. Exposition de ses œuvres à Paris', *L'Indépendance Belge*, 28 Aug. 1864; Tourneux, p. 44; *Catalogue de la Collection Moreau . . .* (Frazier-Soye, Paris, 1907 and 1923), no. 52; Moreau-Nélaton I. 53, repr. fig. 22, II. 246; Brière 1924, p. 82; Escholier I. 112, 116, 124, repr. p. 119; Hourticq 1930, pl. 6; Cassou 1947, pl. 4 and full-scale detail of head on opp. p.; P. H. Michel, *The Massacre of Chios* (Max Parrish, London, 1947), repr. pl. 11 and referred to in unpaginated text; Christoffel 1951, pl. 14; Sterling-Adhémar, no. 662, pl. 232; P. Courthion, *Romanticism* (Skira, 1961), p. 30, repr. in colour p. 28; Escholier 1963, repr. in colour p. 32; M. Florisoone, 'La Genèse espagnole des Massacres de Scio de Delacroix', *Revue du Louvre*, 13 (1963), p. 202, repr. fig. 6; Huyghe, pp. 135, 451, repr. fig. 104; Maltese, pp. 27, 32, 145, 149, repr. pl. 5; T. Prideaux *et al.*, *The World of Delacroix* (Time Inc., New York, 1966), repr. in colour p. 52; L. Johnson, 'Eugène Delacroix et les Salons. Documents inédits au Louvre', *Revue du Louvre*, 16 (1966), p. 227 n. 5; Trapp, p. 36, repr. in colour p. 38.

On 17 February 1824, Delacroix, presumably referring to this study, lists a payment of 7 francs 'A la mendiante qui m'avait posé pour l'étude dans le cimetière.' (*Journal* I. 52). On the same date he recalls that four days ago 'Je faisais le jeune homme du coin d'après la mendiante' (ibid.), referring no doubt to the Greek youth whose head is in a similar pose on the extreme left of the *Massacres of Chios* (J105). In the light of these entries, it seems unlikely that the study was painted as early as 1823, where Robaut places it; more probably Delacroix employed the same model for the two figures within a period of a few weeks. Thoré noted (1864) that artists showed a lively interest in this picture when it was shown at the exhibition in the boulevard des Italiens in 1864.

Since 1885 writers have generally followed Robaut in calling this figure an orphan and sometimes, because of the connection with the *Massacres of Chios*, a Greek, but she is not referred to as either in any source before 1885 and these identifications have no factual basis. The pose of the head and the gaze upturned in an expression of pathetic bewilderment recall Géricault's *Wounded Cuirassier* (Salon 1814. Louvre). The theme and mood were perhaps inspired as much by Géricault's death in Paris on 26 January 1824, which deeply affected Delacroix (ibid. 50), as by any thoughts of the victims of Chios or the misfortunes of orphans. At the same time, the remarks quoted at the end of the entry for the preceding number suggest that Delacroix may have come to believe a few months later that Géricault would have found the expression of eye and open mouth overstated—just as he considered the head of his own *Wounded Cuirassier* a 'tête de veau avec un grand œil bête.' (Clément, p. 67.)

The variety of freely handled textures and rough edges of the draperies contrast with the more Ingres-like finish of the head, with its porcelain texture and cameo-like precision of contour. Such diversity in a single study reflects something of the range of technical experiment in the *Massacres of Chios*.

[1] See n. 2 under the preceding number.
[2] See n. 1 under the preceding number.

79 PORTRAIT OF ASPASIE   Pl. 70

$31\frac{7}{8} \times 25\frac{5}{8}$ in. (81 × 65 cm)* E.D.
Moreau p. 231 (1826). R47 (1821), also under 162 and addition p. 479
c. 1824
Musée Fabre, Montpellier

Provenance: Delacroix's posthumous sale, Feb. 1864, lot 192 ('Etude d'après une mulâtresse, figure à mi-corps'), to Andrieu, 550 fr.; Alfred Bruyas, by Aug. 1864; he gave it to the town of Montpellier in 1868.

Exhibitions: *Bd Italiens*, Paris 1864, no. 302 (Supp. to 2nd ed.); Algérie, Paris 1930, no. 178; Louvre 1930, no. 7; Paris and Berne 1939, no. 36 and 30; Brussels 1947-8, no. 29; Louvre 1963, no. 43 (as 'Aline la mulâtresse'; 2 repr.).

Literature: Cat. of M. F. V. [Villot] Sale, 11 Feb. 1865, under entry for lot 5,[1] Silvestre *Delacroix* (1855), p. 80; Théophile Silvestre, in A. Bruyas *et al.*, *La Galerie Bruyas* (Quantin, Paris, 1876), pp. 271 f.; G. Lafenestre and E. Michel, *Musée de Montpellier*, in *Inventaire général des richesses d'art de la France. Province. Monuments civils* (Plon, Paris, 1878), I, p. 204; Vincent van Gogh, letter to Theo, Dec. 1888, in *The Complete Letters of Vincent van Gogh* (New York Graphic Society, Greenwich, Conn., 1958) III. 109; L. Gonse, *Les Chefs d'œuvre des musées de France. La Peinture* (Société française d'Editions d'Art, Paris, 1900), p. 216; *Catalogue des peintures et sculptures exposées dans les*

galeries du Musée Fabre . . . (Imp. Serre et Roumégous, Montpellier, 1904), no. 143; Meier-Graefe 1922, repr. p. 93; Escholier I. 110, repr. opp. p. 104; A. Joubin, *Catalogue des peintures et sculptures exposées dans les galeries du Musée Fabre de la ville de Montpellier* (Blondel La Rougery, Paris, 1926), no. 459, repr. pl. LX; Hourticq 1930, pl. 2; Sérullaz *Dessins* 1952, p. 36; L. Johnson, 'The Early Drawings of Delacroix', *Burl Mag*, XCVIII (1956), p. 23; Escholier 1963, repr. in colour p. 33; R. Huyghe *et al.*, *Delacroix* (Hachette, Coll. Génies et Réalités, Paris, 1963), repr. p. 71, detail p. 70; Huyghe, pp. 281, 525 n. 26 and 27; Cat. Exh. Bremen 1964, p. 160; L. Johnson, 'Delacroix Drawings at Bremen', *Master Drawings*, 2 (1964), p. 417; Maltese, pp. 33, 147, repr. pl. 13.

Copy: Paul Gauguin, canvas 45 × 37 cm, before 1878, repr. in G. Wildenstein, *Gauguin* (Les Beaux-Arts, Paris, 1964) I, p. 13.

In the course of the past century, there has been much confusion over the identity of the sitter and the dating of this portrait, the two following numbers, and J88. As early as 1865, however, the model for this painting and the next two was identified as a 'mulâtresse' by the name of Aspasie in the catalogue of the sale of Frédéric Villot, who was not only the owner of the next picture but collaborated in compiling the catalogue of his sale and was, by his own account, a good friend of Delacroix's by 1827 (letter of 5 July, 1864, in R. P. Huet, *Paul Huet* (Laurens, Paris, 1911), p. 386). Furthermore, this portrait was convincingly identified in the first edition of the *Journal* with an entry dated 4 October 1857: 'puis [read Pour] l'*Aspasie* jusqu'à la ceinture grande comme nature, voir un bon croquis dans un album du temps'. (*Journal* (1893-5 ed.) III. 292 and n.) Joubin, in his edition of the *Journal*, first published in 1932, repeated this identification, adding that the sketch-book containing the drawing that Delacroix was evidently referring to was in the Louvre, and published a further reference to the painting by Delacroix himself, dated 1 April 1857: '*Aspasie* grande comme nature jusqu'aux genoux'. (*Journal* III. 128 n. 5, 91.) Sérullaz finally published the drawing, as a study for this portrait, together with another of the same model in the same sketch-book, dating them convincingly *c.* 1824 (*Dessins* 1952, nos. 45 and 46, both repr.pl. XXIX. Louvre, RF23355, fols. 29[r], 35[r]. The study for this portrait is also repr. in *Mémorial*, no. 44.).

A basis for apparent error originated with Silvestre who, in his entry for *La Galerie Bruyas*, stated that the sitter was a model known in the Paris studios as 'Aline la mulâtresse', and the confusion was compounded by Robaut who failed to recognize two out of the three portraits said to be of Aspasie in the catalogue of the Villot sale, grouping all three of them under a single number in 1826 as 'Aspasie', when he had already catalogued this version as 'La Mulâtresse' under

1821 and J81 as 'Aline la mulâtresse' under 1824. Moreau had introduced another complication, reflected in some of the subsequent literature, by calling Aspasie a 'Mauresque'. In view of the evidence of identity from Delacroix's *Journal*, from the sale catalogue of his friend Villot, from the inscription by his cousin Léon Riesener on the stretcher of the next picture, and from a comparison of the similarity of features of the sitter, there appears to be no doubt that this three-quarter length portrait and the next two bust-portraits are of one and the same model, a mulatress by the name of Aspasie, and not Aline or Aspasie 'la Mauresque'. If J88 represents the same model and, as seems likely, is also the *Tête d'étude d'une Indienne* shown at the Salon of 1827, Aspasie was probably an Indian mulatress. Delacroix never mentions an Aline; he does, however, include a 'Steline, négresse, rue pavée St. Sauveur n° 2' in a list of names and addresses of models contained in a sketch-book that he was using in 1821 (Louvre, RF9151, fol. 30ᵛ).

As for the problem of dating, this portrait and the next two numbers were, according to the catalogue of the Villot sale, which is followed by Moreau, all painted in the year 1826. Silvestre (1876), presumably relying on the earlier opinions rather than on independent evidence, places it 'entre son *Massacre de Scio* et sa *Mort de Sardanapale*', i.e. 1824/7. In Lafenestre and Michel's 1878 catalogue of the Musée de Montpellier it is dated 1821 without argument. Robaut follows this date uncritically, as do Meier-Graefe, Escholier and Joubin, but it is unconvincing on stylistic grounds and further suspect because Robaut had evidently not examined the picture when he catalogued it, a reproduction that he had not himself taken from the original being included only in the additions and corrections at the end of his catalogue. While it might seem unlikely that Villot, the conscientious author of one of the Louvre's catalogues of paintings, would have specified that the portraits were done in 1826 unless he had sound reasons for thinking so, it is quite possible that he remembered correctly that they had all been painted in the same year but failed to recall the right date when thinking back some forty years—to a period before he knew the artist. The three pictures seem indeed to form a homogeneous group not far apart in date, but, equally, the most acceptable date for the two studies related to this portrait and published by Sérullaz is *c.* 1824, a principal reason being that they are in a sketch-book containing several drawings securely datable to 1823/4 (see J101 and J104), and none certainly later, though notes in the back of the book were written as late as 1829 (see date on fol. 43ʳ). It may be added that Delacroix evidently had a coloured girl ('nera'), with whom he was on intimate terms, modelling in his studio in the course of May 1824 (*Journal* I. 105). All in all, the evidence of style, of the related studies and of the presence in Delacroix's studio of a coloured woman to whom he was not indifferent, points, if inconclusively, to a date of 1824 rather than 1826 for this

portrait and the two following numbers. The interest in an exotic, possibly Indian, type and the handling of such a detail as the striped cloth may be compared to the series of studies of a male Indian that appear to date from the same period (J23-J25). Huyghe (p. 325 n. 26) dates it *c.* 1823 without argument; Sérullaz (*Mémorial*, no. 43), *c.* 1823/4, on the basis of comparison to, 'entre autres', the old woman in the *Massacres de Scio* (J105).

A possible variant of this painting, of one of the two following numbers or of J88 is listed in R Ann as no. 47ʰⁱˢ (see J(L)72a).

¹ Where it is described as 'grande comme nature, avec des bras' and specified as lot 192 in Delacroix's posthumous sale.

80 PORTRAIT OF ASPASIE   Pl. 71

10⅝ × 8½ in. (27 × 21.5 cm)*
Moreau p. 231 and 272. R162 (1826)
c. 1824
Mrs. Walter Feilchenfeldt, Zurich

Provenance: Frédéric Villot; his sale, 11 Feb. 1865, lot 5, to M. Chocquet,¹ 141 fr.; Léon Riesener, by 1873; his sale, 10 Apr. 1879, lot 223, to Henri Rouart,² 150 fr.; his sale, 9 Dec. 1912, lot 183, to Devillez (for Louis Rouart?), 5,500 fr.; Louis Rouart, by 1937; purchased from him by Walter Feilchenfeldt, Zurich, 1950.

Exhibitions: EBA, Paris 1885, no. 192; Gobin, Paris 1937, no. 8; Zurich 1939, no. 308; Basle 1939, no. 215; Venice 1956, no. 8; Louvre 1963, no. 45, repr.; Berne 1963-4, no. 15, repr. pl. 2; Bremen 1964, no. 14, repr. p. 95; Edinburgh-London 1964, no. 8, repr. pl. 1.

Literature: Silvestre *Delacroix* (1855), p. 80; Escholier I, repr. opp. p. 106; J. Siegfried, 'The Romantic Artist as a Portrait Painter', *Marsyas*, VIII (1957-9), p. 39, fig. 14; Huyghe, p. 281; Maltese, pp. 147 f. (under no. 13); K. Lankheit, *Revolution und Restauration* (Holle Verlag, Baden-Baden, 1965. Ed. in French, Albin Michel, Paris, 1966), repr. in colour p. 135.

This is one of three studies which, according to the catalogue of Frédéric Villot's sale in 1865, was painted in 1826 of a mulatress called Aspasie, the others being J79 and J81. The date, which is presumed to have been given by Villot himself, and was followed by Moreau and Robaut, has been generally accepted without question, despite the fact that it was recorded some forty years after the event and without documentary support. Sérullaz (*Mémorial*, no. 45), though apparently under the illusion that the 1826 date originated with Robaut in 1885, thought however that this portrait should be dated, like the Montpellier picture (J79) and for 'the same reasons of style and technique', in the years 1823-4. I find this earlier date more probable, especially if it is accepted that Villot was right in thinking that the three portraits were a series painted in the same year. It may be added that a crimson background as here is found in the *Studies of a Turkish Flintlock Gun and Yatagan* (J27), which is datable *c.* 1824 for other reasons.

¹ According to Robaut's annotation in his copy of the sale catalogue (*Bib AA* MS. 299), where the name is misspelt 'Choquet'.

² An apparently old pen inscription on the stretcher runs: 'Vente Riesener 1879 M. Rouart.' The picture is recorded in Rouart's possession by 1885 (Cat. Exh. *EBA*, Paris 1885, no. 192). The stretcher also bears an earlier ink inscription signed L. Riesener: 'Aspasie peinte par Eugène Delacroix'.

Though Robaut's annotation concludes with the comment, 'C'est l'une des très rares œuvres supportables de cette Vente Andrieu', it may be doubted whether the painting, which is untraced, was a genuine Delacroix.

This picture is curiously, and without argument, said to have been painted in 1821 in the *Errata and Addenda* in the second edition of the catalogue of the exhibition Petit Palais, Paris 1936 (p. 342).

¹ Where it is described as 'de dimension à peu près égale à celle-ci [lot 5; J80], mais le fond n'est pas rouge' and specified as lot 193 from Delacroix's posthumous sale.

81 PORTRAIT OF ASPASIE   Pl. 71

$12\frac{3}{4} \times 9\frac{5}{8}$ in. (32.4 × 24.5 cm)* E.D.
Moreau pp. 231 and 321. R99 (1824), also under 162
c. 1824
Mrs. Walter Feilchenfeldt, Zurich

Provenance: Delacroix's posthumous sale, Feb. 1864, lot 193 ('Autre étude de mulâtresse, buste'), to Baron Charles Rivet, 380 fr., d. 1872 (the back of the canvas is inscribed in black ink: 'C. Rivet'); Baronne Rivet, his widow; Comte de Salvandy, their son-in-law, after 1885; by descent to Mlle de Catheu, by 1936; with Brame, before Jan. 1960; purchased from him by the present owner, 1964.

Exhibitions: *EBA*, Paris 1885, no. 173 (as 'Aspasie la Moresque' [*sic*]); Petit Palais, Paris 1936, no. 244 (as 'Aline la mulâtresse').

Literature: Silvestre *Delacroix* (1855), p. 80; Cat. of M. F. V. [Villot] sale, 11 Feb. 1865, under entry for lot 5;¹ Escholier I. 110; *Mémorial*, under no. 45; Maltese, p. 148 (under no. 13).

This is the sketchiest and, being virtually a grisaille study, the least coloured of the three paintings said in the catalogue of Frédéric Villot's sale of 1865 to represent a mulatress by the name of Aspasie and to date from 1826 (see J79, for discussion of this dating, and J80). Having failed to identify it as one of the versions mentioned in Villot's sale catalogue, Robaut, taking it instead for a portrait of the model in the *Woman in a Blue Turban* (J88), which Moreau had listed under 1824 and called *Aline* (*La Mulâtresse*), gave it this same date and title derived from Moreau. Later, however, he recognized that it might represent the same sitter as the version that passed in Villot's sale (J80) (marginal annotations to no. 99 and 162 in R Ann).

Robaut listed as no. 162bis in R Ann a painting which passed in Pierre Andrieu's posthumous sale, 6 May 1892, for 66 fr. as 'Etude de femme' by Delacroix, without further description (lot 175); in so doing, Robaut apparently mistook it for the painting mentioned in Villot's sale catalogue which was without question the present portrait.

82 PORTRAIT OF LOUIS AUGUSTE SCHWITER   Pl. 72

$85\frac{3}{4} \times 56\frac{1}{2}$ in. (2.18 × 1.435 m)
Signed bottom left: *Eug Delacroix*.
Moreau p. 231. R190
1826– ?30
The National Gallery, London

Provenance: Louis Auguste (later Baron) Schwiter; his sale, 26 March 1890, lot 4,¹ to the dealer Montaignac (R Ann), 2,600 fr.; he probably sold it shortly thereafter to Edgar Degas, in whose collection it is recorded in 1907;² his sale, 26 March 1918, lot 24 (repr.), purchased by special grant for the National Gallery.

Exhibitions: Louvre 1963, no. 72, *M* no. 75, 2 repr.; Edinburgh–London 1964, no. 17.

Literature: A. Jal, *Esquisses, croquis, pochades, ou tout ce qu'on voudra, sur le Salon de 1827* (Ambr. Dupont et Cie, Paris, 1828), p. 14; A. D. Vergnaud, *Examen du Salon de 1827. Novembre, première partie* (Roret, Paris, 1828), p. 10; Silvestre *Delacroix* (1855), p. 80; Moreau-Nélaton I. 76 f., 84; II. 235; R. Fry, 'The Sale of Degas's Collection', *Burl Mag*, XXXII (1918), p. 118; R. Fry, 'Recent Acquisitions for Public Collections—VII', ibid. XXXIV (1919), p. 23, repr. p. 21; Escholier I. 142, 168, 212, 216, repr. opp. 168; *National Gallery Millbank, Catalogue Modern Foreign School* (London, 1926), no. 3286; A. Joubin, 'Documents inédits. Haro entre Ingres et Delacroix', *L'Amour de l'Art*, XVII (1936), p. 87; *National Gallery, Illustrations, Continental Schools* (London, 1937), repr. p. 89; P. Lemoisne, *Degas et son œuvre* (Paul Brame et C. M. de Hauke aux Arts et Métiers Graphiques, Paris, 1946), I, p. 259 (report of E. Moreau-Nélaton's visit to Degas in 1907, reprinted from the former's article in *L'Amour de l'Art*, XII (1931), p. 269); *Journal* II. 370 n. 2; *National Gallery Catalogues, French School, Plates* (London, 1950), pl. 35; K. Garlick, *Sir Thomas Lawrence* (Routledge & Kegan Paul, London, 1954), p. 15; M. Davies, *National Gallery Catalogues, French School* (London, 1957), no. 3286 p. 75 f.; J.

Siegfried, 'The Romantic Artist as a Portrait Painter', *Marsyas*, VIII (1957-9), p. 41; Escholier 1963, pp. 23, 32, repr. in colour p. 25; Huyghe, p. 168, repr. in colour pl. VIII, full-page black-and-white detail of head, pl. 173; Maltese, pp. 33, 124, 148, repr. pl. 14; L. Johnson, 'Eugène Delacroix et les Salons. Documents inédits au Louvre', *Revue du Louvre*, 16 (1966), p. 220; R. Rosenblum, *Ingres* (Harry N. Abrams, New York, 1967), p. 120, fig. 108.

Louis Auguste Schwiter was not, as usually supposed, a Baron when this portrait was painted. Born at Nienburg on 1 February 1805, he was the only son of the French general Henry César Auguste Schwiter (b. Rueil 1768, d. Nancy 1839), who was created a Baron of the Empire in 1808.[3] He was related to Delacroix's intimate friend Pierret, whose mother-in-law was a Schwiter by birth; it was perhaps through this relationship that he met and was befriended by Delacroix. He became a portrait painter, exhibiting at the Salon from 1831 till 1859. Among his earliest Salon pictures were portraits of Pierret (Salon 1831), of his father Baron Schwiter and of Delacroix (Salon 1833; the latter listed as 'Portrait de M. Eugène D.' and presumably the painting repr. in Meier-Graefe 1922, p. 251).[4] He died while on holiday at Salzburg on 20 August 1889.

There is no reason to doubt that this picture was painted, for the most part anyway, in 1826, where it is placed by Moreau and Robaut. Joubin (1936) added support to that date by suggesting that a canvas measuring 6 ft. 6 in. by 4 ft. 4 in. delivered to Delacroix by his colour merchant in July 1826 was for this portrait. It was submitted to the Salon jury of 1827, as 'Portrait en pied de Mr S.', and refused at their fourth session, on 9 October 1827 (L. Johnson, 1966). As indicated by Martin Davies, the perspective of the balustrade was once different and, it may be added, is still incompletely resolved. If the picture was reworked after the refusal, as implied by Moreau who says it was not finished till 1830, it seems most likely to have been in that area, where the faulty perspective alone might well have sufficed to cause an academically dominated jury to turn down the portrait. The refusal did not pass without comment among the Salon critics. Jal wrote: 'Vous avez refusé un portrait de M. Delacroix, et vous ne persuaderez à personne que ce morceau ne valût pas celui de M. Gros que vous acceptiez de droit [Equestrian portrait of Charles X, Musée de Versailles, repr. in R. Escholier, *Gros, ses amis et ses élèves* (Floury, Paris, 1936), pl. 32].' Vergnaud objected on similar grounds, saying: 'nous avons au salon, comme portraits, une foule de peintures plus que médiocres, et dues aux pinceaux d'artistes qui jadis ont fait de bons tableaux.' The balance was later redressed, privately, by Degas, who hung this canvas in his own collection close to Ingres's portrait of Count de Pastoret, which had been accepted for the Salon of 1827 (Moreau-Nélaton II. 235. The Ingres now belongs to

the Art Institute of Chicago; repr. Cat. Exh. Ingres, Petit Palais, Paris 1967-8, p. 203).

Moreau states: 'le fond de paysage a été en partie peint par M. Paul Huet.' This may simply mean that Huet helped to block in the landscape, as one of the Fielding brothers is known to have assisted Delacroix in preparing the background of the *Massacres de Scio* (J105). On the other hand, the middle distance and parts of the background are very similar in style to some of Huet's landscape paintings, and not consistent with the more nervous and energetic handling of the leaves and flowers on the terrace. As late as 1847, Delacroix sought advice from Corot about how to paint trees (*Journal* I. 207) and at this early stage of his career may very well have invited the actual collaboration of his friend Huet in painting them.

Writers in the present century have often remarked on the influence of Sir Thomas Lawrence in this portrait. Delacroix was struck by Lawrence's portraits at the Salon of 1824 (*Journal* III. 352); the following year, he met the artist in person in England and saw further works by him (*Correspondance* I. 165-6); and in 1829 devoted a sympathetic essay to him in the *Revue de Paris* (reprinted in *Œuvres litt.* II. 157-62). In addition to painting a type of portrait Lawrence favoured—an elegant member of the upper classes seen full-length against a park, Delacroix seems here to have emulated less tangible qualities that he admired in the English painter and mentions in his essay: 'Ses personnages [. . .] prennent [. . .] cet air noble et cette tournure distinguée qu'il sait donner à presque tous.' And: 'Il saisit sur les traits la nuance la plus délicate de mélancolie ou de gaieté' (*Œuvres litt.* II. 159).

Though Lawrence is clearly the dominant influence, the hand holding hat and glove suggests that Delacroix referred as well to his copy after the Spanish portrait of Charles II (J21), from which he may also have learnt something about the handling of blacks in the costume.

A sheet of four pen drawings in an album in the Louvre (RF10464) were presented as studies of Schwiter in the Exh. Louvre 1930 (no. 770), one being in the same pose as this portrait. Martin Davies, followed by Sérullaz (*Mémorial*, no. 75), appeared unconvinced by this identification and thought the drawing 'may not have been executed in view of the portrait', though he did not question its attribution to Delacroix. In my opinion, the whole sheet was drawn by Pierret, either from drawings by Delacroix or at a session when Delacroix was taking sketches of Schwiter in preparation for this portrait. Robaut mentions three 'croquis préparatoires' for the portrait (R Ann, marginal note to R190) and reproduces them on a single sheet in Robaut Tracings I. Two of them are identical in pose to two of the drawings on the Louvre sheet, including the one that is in the same pose as the painted portrait; the third shows Schwiter from the back standing at an easel with brush and palette. Even in Robaut's copy, these sketches, whose present whereabouts are unknown, are superior in quality to those on the Louvre sheet, and there can be no real doubt that they represent Schwiter.

Besides these sketches and the portrait, Delacroix made a lithograph of Schwiter in 1826 (R188; Delteil 51) and a pen-and-ink drawing, which Robaut also dates to 1826 (R189).

[1] As 'Portrait de M.X.', but otherwise described in full. Also, a label with the lot number is still affixed to the bottom right corner of the surface, and its passage in the sale is recorded in R Ann.

[2] By Etienne Moreau-Nélaton, who, recalling a visit he paid to Degas in the rue Victor Massé on 26 December 1907, states that on leaving the bedroom 'nous saluons au passage, dans la pièce voisine, le *Schwiter* de Delacroix' (see P. A. Lemoisne, *Degas et son œuvre*, I. 259).

[3] For details of General Schwiter's career, see G. Six, *Dictionnaire biographique des généraux et amiraux français de la Révolution et de l'Empire (1792-1814)* (G. Saffroy, Paris, 1934) II.

[4] For further details about Schwiter's work, see Thieme-Becker and Bellier-Auvray. See also D. Meyer, 'Un jubilé oublié à l'occasion du 150ᵉ anniversaire de la naissance de Schwiter', *Pays Lorrain*, no. 2, 1955, p. 69 f., which is a brief but informative biographical note on General Schwiter and his son, based on family papers.

83 PORTRAIT OF CHARLES DE VERNINAC (presumed)

Pl. 73

$24\frac{1}{4} \times 19\frac{7}{8}$ in. (61.5 × 50.5 cm)*[1]

c. 1826

Arthur Sachs, Paris

Provenance: Probably the portrait of his nephew that hung at the head of Delacroix's bed and which he bequeathed in 1863 to Mme Duriez (*née* Zélie de Verninac);[2] Vicomte Bernard d'Hendecourt, Paris; his sale, Sotheby's, 8 May 1929, lot 140, repr. (as 'Portrait of a Young Man'), to Durlacher for Arthur Sachs; sale Arthur Sachs and Marian François-Poncet (his daughter, joint owner), New York 28 Nov. 1973, lot 8 (as 'Henri de Verninac'. Repr. in colour), bought in, at $95,000.

Exhibitions: Bd Italiens, Paris 1864, no. 98? (as 'Portrait d'homme', 62 × 51 cm, lent by M. de Verninac);[3] Louvre 1930, no. 200B (as 'Portrait de Jeune Homme'); (removed from France to California by the owner *c*. 1942 till 1950. On extended loan to the California Palace of the Legion of Honour, San Francisco, from *c*. 1947 to 1950); Orangerie, Paris 1956, no. 33 (as 'Portrait de jeune homme'); Paris 1961, no. 42 (as 'Portrait de jeune homme'); Atelier Delacroix, Paris 1973 (no. cat.)

Literature: Probably Silvestre *Delacroix* (1855), p. 80 ('Deux portraits du neveu de l'artiste.');[4] presumably Delacroix's will, dated 3 August 1863, in *Correspondance* (Burty 1878), p. vi; *The Art News*, XXVII (1929), p. 5, repr. p. 7 (announcement of the d'Hendecourt sale); *Arts*, 12-18 July 1961, p. 14 (notice of Exh. at Musée Jacquemart-André); R. Huyghe *et al.*, *Delacroix* (Hachette, Coll. Génie et Réalitiés, Paris, 1963), repr. in colour opp. p. 89 (as

'Portrait de jeune homme'); Huyghe, better repr. in colour pl. X; L. Johnson, 'Eugène Delacroix and Charles de Verninac: an Unpublished Portrait and New Letters', *Burl Mag*, CX (1968), p. 512 n. 12, fig. 34 (as 'Portrait of Charles de Verninac').

The identity of the sitter is established beyond reasonable doubt by a comparison of his features and the colour of his eyes to the two portraits which certainly represent the artist's nephew (J62 and J92).

The portrait is datable from the costume and style of hair cut in the period 1823/6. The handling suggests that it was painted towards the end of that period, the streaks of heavily dragged impasto in the backdrop being very similar to passages in an oil sketch of 1826 for *Justinian Drafting his Laws* (J120). A date of 1826 accords well with the apparent age of the presumed sitter, who was then twenty-two to twenty-three.

Huyghe (caption to pl. X) surprisingly identifies the sitter as Henri de Verninac, whose distinctive and quite dissimilar features are portrayed in J68, and dates the picture to *c*. 1827 without giving his reasons.

In 1825 Charles de Verninac set his heart on entering the Consular Service and directed his studies towards that end.[5] He achieved his ambition when he was appointed a student vice-consul in April 1829; meanwhile he earned his living by working in the *Caisse d'amortissement* in Paris, where he was employed for four years before joining the Consular Service.[6] For details of his career as a consular official, see J92.

[1] A modern, metallic backing had been applied to the canvas and a new stretcher with a metal brace provided before the picture was acquired by Arthur Sachs in 1929.

[2] Of the three portraits of Charles de Verninac included in the legacy that Delacroix requested Mme Duriez to share with her brother and sister, two can be satisfactorily accounted for as part of their share (J62 and J92). The first mentioned by Delacroix in his will, and identified simply as 'l'un se trouvant à la tête de mon lit', was most probably kept by Mme Duriez, who no doubt had first choice and selected the best of the three. Though it cannot be certainly identified with the present portrait, which came to light in 1929 at the d'Hendecourt sale, the high quality of our picture and the almost certain identity of the sitter make it reasonable to suppose that it was the portrait chosen by Delacroix to hang at the head of his bed.

[3] This exhibit cannot be positively identified, as several of the de Verninac family portraits correspond almost equally well to this description, e.g. J68 and J92, and might have been lent to the exhibition by François de Verninac, either from his own collection or acting as an intermediary for one of his sisters. The dimensions of this portrait are, however, fractionally the closest to those listed in the exhibition catalogue and it seems, in addition, a likely choice from the family's point of view because of Delacroix's special affection for his nephew and of its finished quality, as compared to J92.

[4] See J62, n. 5.

[5] Dossier Charles de Verninac, Archives of the Ministère des affaires étrangères, document 4: Charles de Verninac to Foreign Minister, 25 December 1828: '[. . .] j'ai dirigé toutes mes études vers les connaissances exigées [. . .]: de plus j'ai suivi les cours de droit, et je n'ai plus que ma thèse à soutenir pour avoir le grade d'avocat.

'Depuis 1825, époque à laquelle je conçois quelque espoir d'entrer dans les Consulats, tous mes efforts ont été tournés vers ce but.'

[6] L. Johnson, op. cit., p. 515 n. 26.

84 PORTRAIT OF JENNY LE GUILLOU'S DAUGHTER

Pl. 74

$18\frac{1}{8} \times 15\frac{1}{16}$ in. (46×38.2 cm)*
Moreau p. 238. R716 and p. 491 (1840)
c. 1826
Musée du Louvre

Provenance: Jeanne-Marie Le Guillou, d. 1869; by her bequest to M. Duriez till the fall of the Second Empire,[1] then to the Louvre; Louvre (RF26), Aug. 1872.

Exhibitions: Louvre 1930, no. 99A; Bordeaux 1963, no. 25.

Literature: Moreau-Nélaton I. 205, fig. 200, II. 245; Escholier II. 211–14; Sterling-Adhémar, no. 689, pl. 245; *Mémorial*, mentioned under no. 243; Huyghe, p. 518 n. 17; Maltese, pp. 33, 149, pl. 16.

Jeanne-Marie (Jenny) Le Guillou (1801–69) was Delacroix's housekeeper and had been in his service for at least twenty-eight years at the time of his death.[2] When this portrait went to the Louvre in 1872, in compliance with her wishes, it was entered in their inventory anonymously as 'Portrait de jeune fille en buste, robe verte à fleurs, col de tulle', and it was excluded from their official catalogues altogether until 1930, when it was listed in the catalogue of the Delacroix exhibition at the Louvre as a portrait of her daughter. It had been so identified publicly for the first time in Moreau, which was published in the year after its acquisition by the Louvre, and this identification was retained by Robaut, after he had examined it in the reserves of the Louvre with the co-operation of the curator. Thus, though the Louvre seem to have discreetly guarded the reputation of their unwed benefactor, her relation to the sitter was evidently well established by word of mouth at an early date. A more controversial question, to which a final answer is unlikely to be found, is whether the father was Delacroix.

Several letters written by Delacroix to Pierret in the latter half of 1819 leave little doubt that a domestic servant by the name of Caroline was pregnant by him and had recently entered Pierret's household where she was being cared for (*Correspondance* I. 41–3, 46, 52, 58, 61, 65). In notes communicated to Philippe Burty in 1880, Gustave Lassalle-Bordes, who had been closely associated with Delacroix between 1838 and 1850 as his pupil and chief assistant, claims Jenny told him that (1) her real name was Caroline, (2) she had worked for Mme Pierret before coming to Delacroix, (3) she would never have lost her daughter, who apparently died in childhood, had he allowed them to stay together. He goes on to relate how Jenny led the way to her bedroom and showed him the portrait of her daughter, which she said Delacroix had painted for her, and he saw 'les traits d'une enfant chétive, le teint bistré, les cheveux châtains et, le dirai-je ? des traits en partie semblables à deux

portraits de Delacroix jeune homme faits par lui.'[3] Moreau-Nélaton, who published extracts from the alleged conversation (I. 34 n. 1, 205), found Lassalle-Bordes's evidence credible. Escholier (I. 44 f.; II. 211–14) vehemently rejected it, denying that Jenny's Christian name could have been Caroline since it was given as Jeanne-Marie in Delacroix's will and refusing to admit that the child looked at all like Delacroix, or indeed that the portrait was by him. Joubin subscribed to the view that the sitter was the daughter of Jenny and Delacroix, and published an undated letter delivered by hand to an unknown destination, which he suggested Delacroix had written concerning this girl to the director of a children's home about 1830: Delacroix discusses how a female child he had recommended to the recipient of his note had had to be withdrawn by her mother from the care of someone who had treated her so badly as to affect her health (*Correspondance* I. 42 n. 1; V. 147 f., 147 n. 2). Huyghe, while accepting the authenticity of the portrait, dismissed Lassalle-Bordes's account as 'malicious gossip' and the source of 'legend'. Maltese, though remaining non-committal about the child's parentage, finds a surprising likeness to Delacroix in some of her features.

There can be no doubt of Lassalle-Bordes's ill feeling towards Delacroix, who had dismissed him, or of his malice and the inaccuracy of some of the information he gave to Burty. Moreover, by the time he recorded his alleged conversation with Jenny, he could have known something about the misfortunes of Caroline, from the fragments of Delacroix's correspondence with Pierret that had been published in Burty's first edition of the Letters (1878), and might have fabricated his story accordingly. The arguments for disbelieving it are nevertheless more emotional than rational. An unprejudiced observer cannot deny the resemblance between this child and Delacroix. And the fact that he gave Jenny's name as Jeanne-Marie in his will does not rule out the possibility that she also had the Christian name of Caroline, by which she might have been known earlier: knowing that Pierret had compromising early letters from him that might be published, Delacroix may well, to protect Jenny's reputation, have deliberately omitted the name of Caroline from this legal document.[4] It also seems suggestive that Jenny should have left Delacroix's *Self-Portrait* and this picture to the Louvre (see n. 1), but not her own portrait (R715), which was acquired by the Louvre many years later: the self-effacing mother wishes the great man and his daughter to enter the national museum of France side by side and for ever?

Maltese (1965) revises the date of this picture to *c.* 1826 on stylistic grounds, rejecting Moreau's and Robaut's date of 1840, which had not been contested earlier, though it was probably based on the false assumption that Delacroix's portrait of Jenny was contemporary with that of her daughter. A close parallel in style and pose is to be found in the *Portrait of Anne Claire Pierret* (J85), which can be more securely dated to 1826. It may be recalled that Delacroix appears to have lived with the Pierret family at 46 rue de l'Université for some time around the end of 1825 (*Correspondance* V. 144, 211). Was Caroline still in their household, now with a daughter six or seven years old who is portrayed here?

A small hole in the top of the canvas, mentioned by Robaut and since repaired, is visible in the reproduction in Moreau-Nélaton, as is a damaged area of about the same size to the left of the painting in the hair. There is extensive *craquelure*, which Maltese finds, unscientifically, to be of a pattern that supports his dating.

[1] By a letter of 1 March 1872, Pierre Andrieu, Delacroix's chief assistant from 1850, notified the Ministre de l'Instruction publique of the rights of the Administration des Musées to two portraits—this one and the famous *Self-Portrait* (R295, Louvre)—which Jeanne-Marie Le Guillou had 'laissés en jouissance sous la condition qu'ils reviendraient aux Musées à la chute de l'Empire'. (An abstract of the letter is preserved in the archives of the Bibliothèque de la conservation at the Louvre and was published in *Mémorial*, under no. 243.) Delacroix left his *Self-Portrait* to Mlle Le Guillou with, according to Robaut (R295), a verbal stipulation that it be given to the Louvre the day the Orleans family returned to the throne of France. It was probably for that reason that she did not leave the portraits to the Louvre directly upon her death, but stipulated, perhaps verbally like her master, that they should go there upon the fall of the Second Empire, which she no doubt thought would coincide with the restoration of the Orleans. As for the question of whom she bequeathed them to in the interim, Moreau (p. 237) states that she left the *Self-Portrait* to Mme Durieu, and Robaut (R716), that the portrait of her daughter went to M. Duriez. In fact, she most probably left both portraits to M. and Mme Duriez, the latter, *née* Zélie de Verninac, being related to Delacroix through his sister's marriage and having already inherited from him most of the family portraits mentioned in his will.
[2] Writing in Feb. 1864, Théophile Silvestre (*Documents nouveaux*, p. 44) says that Jenny had become 'par vingt-huit ans de dévouement presque un autre lui-même [Delacroix].' This has generally been interpreted as meaning that Jenny entered Delacroix's service about 1835, but Silvestre does not specify which year of the artist's life he is writing about and, as far as his evidence goes, there is nothing against supposing that she had been in Delacroix's employment since well before 1835.
[3] *Nouvelles notes reçues de M. Lassalle-Bordes le 16 9bre 1880*, MS. copy by M. Tourneux, BN Estampes (Yb³975), p. 49.
[4] Since this entry was written, I have found Jenny's death certificate, on which her Christian names are given as Jeanne Marie only. Discovering from this document that she was born at Pleyben (Finistère), I passed the information on to M. J. L. Debauve, suggesting that he might wish to search for her birth certificate while spending the summer in Brittany. He promptly turned up the document in the archives of Finistère at Quimper and kindly sent me a copy: Jenny is registered as Jeanne Marguerite le Guillou. Though she did not die with the same second name that she was given at birth, these documents greatly reduce the possibility that she was ever known as Caroline.

85 PORTRAIT OF ANNE CLAIRE PIERRET   Pl. 74

16⅛ × 12¾ in. (41 × 32.4 cm)
Moreau p. 230. R121 (1825)
1826
Wildenstein & Co., New York

Provenance: Mme J. B. Pierret; presumably inherited by her daughter Mme C. F. Vila, the sitter; Mme E. Carlier (*née* Vila), her daughter; she gave it to Mme Nicour, her stepdaughter, d. 1925; by her bequest to Mme Madeleine Oberthür of Rennes (*née* Jouanneau), great-granddaughter of the sitter, to 1958; Wildenstein & Co.

Exhibition: Wildenstein, London 1960, no. 32.

Literature: Moreau, p. 232; Escholier I, repr. p. 191; Huyghe, p. 32, pl. 31.

The sitter was the second child and first daughter of Delacroix's intimate friend, J. B. Pierret (J67). She was born in Paris on 26 August 1821 and baptized there on 28 August 1826.[1] Moreau, who may have had the information from her mother, says that she was painted 'vers l'âge de 5 ans', but lists the portrait under the year 1825, for the greater part of which she was not yet four years old. Two pages later (p. 232), however, he is inconsistent in saying that it was done the year before that of her sister Juliette (J86), which he dates 1827. If we regard Moreau's listing of the picture in 1825 as a slip and allow everything else he says about it, 1826 is the correct date and indeed an acceptable one, given the sitter's date of birth. There is a good possibility that both portraits, which Moreau describes as pendants, were painted to commemorate the baptism of the two children, which took place on the same day in 1826.[2] Claire's portrait could have been painted first, close to the time of her christening, and Juliette's, more complex in pose and more expressive, might have been delayed a few months owing to the fatal illness of their brother Jean Baptiste, who died at the age of six on 18 November 1826;[3] it would thus fall into the succeeding year, where Moreau puts it.

In later life, the sitter married an architect, Corneille Frédéric Vila, in Paris on 10 May 1843. He died at Sèvres in March 1877. In October 1879, his widow was appointed provisional Director of the municipal infants' school at Chaumont and by December 1884 had risen to the post of Departmental Inspector of nursery schools for Haute-Marne. She was buried in the family plot in the 'Cimetière du Nord' in Paris on 17 October 1904.[4]

The picture has been relined, the stretcher renewed and some damage to the paint surface and original canvas repaired, apparently since 1958. Archives photographiques negative MOR-NEL 74 records the condition before restoration.

Robaut records two further painted portraits of Anne Claire Pierret as a child, but in neither case can the identity of the sitter be taken as certain (see J(L)78 and J(L)79).

[1] Both dates are given on her baptismal certificate, in the possession of her great-grandson, Maurice Vila.
[2] *Etat civil* of J. B. Pierret in the possession of Maurice Vila.
[3] Same reference as n. 2. See also *Correspondance* I. 187.
[4] All facts in this paragraph are based on family papers in the possession of Maurice Vila.

86 PORTRAIT OF MARGUERITE JULIETTE PIERRET   Pl. 75

$15\frac{5}{16} \times 12\frac{5}{8}$ in. (39 × 32 cm)

Moreau p. 232. R215

1827

Mr. and Mrs. Severance A. Millikin, Cleveland, Ohio

Provenance: As for the preceding number till 1958; Mrs. Walter Feilchenfeldt, Zurich; purchased from her by the present owners, 1958.

Exhibition: Louvre 1963, no. 68, repr.

Literature: Escholier I, repr. p. 190.

Marguerite Juliette Pierret was born in Paris on 17 November 1822, and died a spinster at Sèvres on 28 April 1878.[1] This portrait was probably painted early in 1827 when she was just over four years old (for further details see the preceding number).

Robaut (no. 70) records an earlier portrait of the sitter under 1823, but, given the date of her birth, either his identification or date is wrong (see J(L)78).

[1] All biographical details are from family papers in the possession of Maurice Vila.

87 HEAD OF AN OLD WOMAN (MADAME BORNOT?)   Pl. 78

$15\frac{1}{2} \times 12\frac{3}{4}$ in. (39.4 × 32.4 cm)

Moreau p. 192, 313. R788 (1843)

1826/7

Philadelphia Museum of Art (anonymous loan, since April 1937)

Provenance: Delacroix's posthumous sale, Feb. 1864, lot 73, to Haro, 830 fr.; his sale 30 May 1892, lot 79 (repr.), to P. A. Cheramy before the public sale for about 6,000 fr. (R Ann); his sale 5 May 1908, lot 171 (repr.), to Haro, 17,000 fr.; Mme Albert Esnault-Pelterie (mauve wax seal of the collection on the stretcher), by 1910, d. *c.* 1938; Mme Jacques Meunié (*née* Popelin), her granddaughter.

Exhibitions: *Universelle*, Paris 1855, no. 2940; *Bd Italiens*, Paris 1864, no. 45; *EBA*, Paris 1885, no. 97; Alsace-Lorraine, Paris 1885, no. 111; Petit, Paris 1892, no. 91; Cassirer, Berlin 1907, no. 29; Petit, Paris 1910, no. 71; Louvre 1930, no. 164.

Literature: C. Baudelaire, 'Exposition universelle 1855. Beaux-Arts', *Le Pays*, 3 June 1855; reprinted in *Curiosités esthétiques*, 1868 (*Œuvres* II, Pléiade ed., Paris, 1932, p. 162); M. du Camp, *Les Beaux-Arts à l'Exposition universelle de 1855* (Librairie nouvelle, Paris, 1855), pp. 114 f.; T. Gautier, 'Exposition universelle', *Le Moniteur universel*, 25 July 1855; reprinted in *Les Beaux-Arts en Europe* (M. Lévy, Paris, 1856) Ière série, ch. XIV; E. Gebauer, *Les Beaux-Arts à*

l'Exposition universelle de 1855 (Librairie Napoléonienne, Paris, 1855), p. 42; C. Vignon, *Exposition universelle de 1855. Beaux-Arts* (Fontaine, Paris, 1855), p. 205; Silvestre *Delacroix* (1855), p. 80 ('Autre tête de vieille femme'); Inv. Delacroix, no. 116; Moreau p. 76, 131, 153; L. Rouart, 'La Collection de M. Cheramy', *Les Arts*, no. 64 (Apr. 1907), p. 22, repr. p. 26; J. Meier-Grafe and E. Klossowski, *La Collection Cheramy . . .* (R. Piper, Munich, 1908), p. 22 and no. 186, repr.; P. Dorbec, 'L'Exposition des "Vingt Peintres du XIXe siècle" à la Galerie Georges Petit' *GBA*, 4e période, IV (1910), pp. 16 f., repr. p. 15; L. Roger-Milès, *Vingt peintres du XIXe siècle. Chefs-d'œuvre de l'école française* (Imp. Geo. Petit, Paris, 1911), p. 92, repr. p. 67 (M. Roux etching); Moreau-Nélaton II. 156, fig. 376; O. Benesch, 'Rembrandts Vermächtnis', *Belvedere*, 6 (Aug.-Dec. 1924), p. 173; Escholier II, repr. opp. p. 286, III. 220; Johnson 1963, p. 50, pl. 2; L. Johnson, 'Eugène Delacroix et les Salons. Documents inédits au Louvre', *Revue du Louvre*, 16 (1966), pp. 217, 220, 227 f., n. 7, fig. 1; E. Benesch (ed.), Otto Benesch, *Collected Writings. Volume I. Rembrandt* (Phaidon, London, 1970), p. 80, 278 n. 20 (reprint in English translation of O. Benesch, 1924).

Prints: F. Villot woodcut, *c.* 1843; E. Saint-Marcel etching; A. Robaut lithograph, 1872; A. Sirouy lithograph; Marcel Roux etching, 1911.

Robaut's date of 1843, which was evidently based on Moreau's (p. 76) dating of Villot's woodcut after this picture, remained uncontested till 1963, when I revised it to *c.* 1822/6 on stylistic grounds. Several years later I found and published (1966) documentary evidence that Delacroix had had a 'Tête d'étude d'une vieille femme', measuring 54 × 47 cm with frame, refused for the Salon on 8 October 1827 and I suggested that our study was the rejected work, probably painted in 1826.

Moreau-Nélaton had rightly pointed out that this picture 'n'est pas sans ressemblance avec la vieille tante Bornot peinte par l'artiste dans sa jeunesse' (J65) and, the revised date bringing it within the lifetime of Mme Bornot, I concluded (1966, p. 228 n. 7) that it might indeed represent her. Delacroix, however, could not have intended it to be identified publicly as an image of his aunt, for it is listed in the register of paintings submitted to the Salon jury in 1827 simply as a 'tête d'étude' and he showed it under the title 'Tête de vieille femme' at the *Exposition universelle* in 1855. Moreover, a 'Tête de vieille femme', listed without further identification in an inventory of pictures that he compiled for his own use on 1 April 1857 probably refers to this study (*Journal* III. 90). Though his aunt may have served as the model, he apparently considered it a character study of old age rather than a portrait of a specific person. Neither Delacroix's choice of title nor the costume justifies calling it a study of a nun, as it has been named by some writers, beginning with Vignon, ever since it was first exhibited in 1855. It was also listed as 'portrait d'une religieuse' in Inv. Delacroix, but not in the catalogue of the posthumous sale, where it was described simply as 'Tête de vieille femme'.

The majority of critics who commented on it in 1855 were unfavourably impressed by its realism. Gautier, however, while considering it one of the most eccentric productions of the artist, admired the boldness of handling and remarked with approval: 'tout le travail hideux de la sénilité est rendu en quelques coups, plus exactement que ne le fait Denner étudiant au microscope le derme flétri de ses vieux et de ses vieilles.' The same author also noted an influence of Bonington. More recently, I have drawn attention (1966, p. 228 n. 7) to the similar type of elderly woman found specifically in two water-colours of Bonington dated 1826 and in a painting by the same artist developed from one of the water-colours: *The Meditation*, Wallace Coll.; *The Visit*, Louvre: and *The Use of Tears*, Museum of Fine Arts, Boston. It is interesting in this connection that a note in Burty Ann ED records that the Delacroix was said to represent 'La servante de Bonington'. The same note continues, however: 'Mr Haro prétend que c'est le portrait d'une parente de Delacroix'; by which Haro no doubt meant Mme Bornot.

A similarity in technique and spirit to Rembrandt's portraiture has been noted by Meier-Graefe, Klossowski, Dorbec and Benesch. It may be added that there is evidence of an interest in Rembrandt in Delacroix's circle some months before the Salon of 1827: his close friend Hippolyte Poterlet had been in Holland copying Dutch masters for an undetermined period by August 1827 and had sent copies back to Paris, including some after Rembrandt which Delacroix admired (*Correspondance* I. 193). Escholier's opinion that this study recalls Raeburn more than Rembrandt is puzzling.

Klossowski draws a further comparison with one of Géricault's portraits of a mad woman (now *Musée des Beaux-Arts*, Lyon; repr. Berger, pl. 94), but in order to stress differences more than similarities between the conceptions of the two artists, particularly in the lighting and the handling of pigment. In my opinion, the naturalistic intentions of both, expressed by means of a thick and rough impasto, outweigh the differences.

88 PORTRAIT OF A WOMAN IN A BLUE TURBAN   Pl. 76

$23\frac{1}{4} \times 19$ in. (59.1 × 48.3 cm)
Signed right centre (at level of shoulder): *Eug Delacroix*.
Moreau p. 229 (1824) and ?169. R98 (1824) and ?184
1827
Philadelphia Museum of Art (anonymous loan, since April 1937)

Provenance: Given by the artist to Frédéric Leblond, d. 1872; Mme Leblond, his widow; Dr. Gebauer, Mayor of Cléry (Loiret), his nephew, by 1885; his sale, Cléry, 31 May 1904, lot 13; Mme Albert Esnault-Pelterie (mauve wax seal of the collection on the back), by 1906 (probably acquired 1904), d. *c.* 1938; Mme J. Meunié (*née* Popelin), her granddaughter.

Exhibitions: Probably Salon 1827–8, no. 298 (as 'Tête d'étude d'une Indienne'); Bd Italiens, Paris 1864, no. 104 (as 'Une tête de femme mulâtre'); EBA, Paris 1885, no. 86 (as 'Aline la Mulâtresse'); Petit, Paris 1910, no. 72; Louvre 1930, no. 19, repr. *Album*, p. 10.

Literature: *Visite au Musée du Louvre, ou Guide de l'amateur à l'exposition . . . (Année 1827–1828) . . . par une Société de Gens de Lettres et d'Artistes* (Paris, 1828), p. 220 (if it is the 'Tête d'étude d'une Indienne' shown at the Salon); probably Silvestre *Delacroix* (1855), p. 80; L. Rouart, 'Collection de Madame Esnault-Pelterie', *Les Arts*, June 1906, p. 4, repr.; P. Dorbec, 'L'Exposition des "Vingt Peintres du XIXe Siècle" à la Galerie Georges Petit', *GBA*, 4e période, IV (1910), p. 16; L. Roger-Milès, *Vingt peintres du XIXe siècle, Chefs-d'œuvre de l'école française* (Imp. Geo. Petit, Paris 1911), p. 92, repr. p. 55 (M. Kamm etching); Moreau-Nélaton I. 86, fig. 59; Escholier I. 110, p. 216, repr. opp. p. 108; *Bulletin of the Philadelphia Museum of Art*, XXXIII, no. 176 (Jan. 1938), repr. (a typographical error on the title-page gives this issue as vol. XXXII, no. 174. The pages and plates are unnumbered); Johnson 1963, p. 51, pl. 17; *Mémorial*, under no. 43; L. Johnson, 'Eugène Delacroix et les Salons. Documents inédits au Louvre', *Revue du Louvre*, 16 (1966), pp. 220, 228 n. 8; Maltese, p. 148 (under no. 13).

Print: M. Kamm etching, 1911.

Moreau (p. 169) and Robaut (no. 184) were unable to identify the 'Tête d'étude d'une Indienne' exhibited at the Salon of 1827–8 with any painting that they knew, or to give any particulars but the title. Moreau-Nélaton affirmed, plausibly but without argument or documentary proof, that the present portrait, which Moreau and Robaut had called 'Aline la mulâtresse' and dated to 1824, was the Salon painting of an Indian. This opinion has received no support in subsequent literature, except from myself (1963 and 1966). A reason that has not been hitherto proposed for believing the Philadelphia picture may portray an Indian is, that the list of Delacroix's works in Silvestre *Delacroix* (1855) includes an 'Indienne avec turban' that cannot be identified with any other recorded painting. The sole comment on the Salon picture in contemporary reviews (op. cit., 1828) is too general to confirm the identification beyond doubt, being merely: 'Portrait assez remarquable, surtout sous le rapport des couleurs et de la ressemblance, premiers mérites dans une composition de ce genre.' But the opulent colouring, the glazing and full, rotund forms are consistent with the style of the *Death of Sardanapalus* (J125), and therefore with a date of 1827. The concern with the interplay of ovals (turban, face, eyes, shawl) may also be compared to the *Young Woman in a Large Hat* (J89), datable *c*. 1827. If it is the 'Tête d'étude d'une Indienne', it was accepted by the Salon jury on 8 October 1827 (see L. Johnson, 1966, p. 220).

This figure is close not only in style and colouring (the blue head-dress and deep red shawl) to the concubine and crimson cushion on which she reposes at the foot of the bed in the *Death of Sardanapalus*, but actually bears a marked physical resemblance to her. According to Silvestre, the model for the Montpellier portrait of a mulatress, whom he called Aline, also appears in the *Death of Sardanapalus* (*La Galerie Bruyas*, p. 271; see J79). He could only have meant the recumbent figure I have just mentioned.

If the four portraits of a mulatress from the 1820s do not represent a single model named Aspasie, then this one is the most likely to represent a different person known as Aline (see J79-J81 for the others). Evidence has been cited (J79) to indicate that Silvestre was probably wrong to identify the sitter of the Montpellier picture as Aline instead of Aspasie, but he may have been right in saying that 'Aline la mulâtresse' was to be found in the *Death of Sardanapalus*; in which case the subject of the present portrait was surely also 'Aline la mulâtresse', as stated by Moreau in the first catalogue of Delacroix's *œuvre*.

Moreau (p. 229) was the first to record a variant, which he states was also given to Leblond by Delacroix, measuring 35 × 22 cm, and where the sitter is shown in the same costume as here but without the brooch. Robaut, amending the dimensions to 35 × 27 cm, questions its authenticity in his entry for the present portrait; and his drawing of it is contained in Tracings I (no. 98*bis*), inscribed: 'pas à reproduire, très douteux d'abord'. It appears therefore to have been a copy, with a slight variation, after Delacroix, or a portrait taken by another artist from the same model at the same time. It was listed among the paintings by Delacroix in the catalogue of the Gebauer sale at Cléry, 31 May 1904, lot 14, as: 'Tête de femme Souliote au turban bleu, dite Aline la mulâtresse', 36 × 25 cm.

89 YOUNG WOMAN IN A LARGE HAT   Pl. 77

$10\frac{5}{8} \times 8\frac{11}{16}$ in. (27 × 22 cm)

R207 and part of R1904

c. 1827

Whereabouts unknown (formerly Musée du Louvre)

Provenance: Delacroix's posthumous sale, Feb. 1864, part of lot 201 ('Onze études de têtes et portraits'), to ?;[1] Moureau; he sold it to Ernest Christophe,[2] sculptor, d. 1892; Joseph

Reinach, 1892-d. 1921;[3] Louvre 1921 (RF 2323), by his bequest; disappeared from the Louvre in unknown circumstances during World War II.

Exhibitions: EBA, Paris 1885, no. 46; Louvre 1930, no. 39.

Literature: M. Tinayre, 'Un Portrait de George Sand', *GBA*, XXXIV (1905), pp. 326 f., litho. by J. Tinayre repr. opp. p. 326; Brière 1924, no. 3068 (p. 80); A. Rothmaler, 'Les Portraits de George Sand par Delacroix', *GBA*, XIV (July 1926), p. 77; Escholier I. 154 f., 214, repr. opp. p. 166; II. 138; Hourticq 1930, pl. 27; A. Joubin, 'Les Modèles de Delacroix', *GBA*, XV (June 1936), p. 358, repr. p. 350, fig. 6; H. Wellington (ed.), *The Journal of Eugène Delacroix* (Phaidon, London, 1951), p. 491, repr. pl. VI; Escholier 1963, pp. 24 f.; R. Escholier, *Delacroix et les femmes* (Fayard, Paris, 1963), p. 56; Trapp, p. 59.

Prints: Lithograph by Julien Tinayre (*c*. 1905) repr. in *GBA*, XXXIV (1905), opp. p. 326; in *L'Instantané* (illustrated supplement of *La Revue hebdomadaire*), 20 Feb. 1909, pl. 19840; and in *Die Musik* IX (Feb. 1910), p. and pl. unnumbered.

Since Robaut prudently catalogued this spirited sketch-portrait as 'Jeune femme au grand chapeau' in 1885, the sitter has been inconclusively identified with no less than four women whom Delacroix admired. It was bequeathed to the Louvre in 1921 as a portrait of George Sand, having been so called as early as 1905 when it was published by Marcelle Tinayre in the *Gazette des Beaux Arts* and held to represent 'l'illustre romancière à cette période de sa vie où elle s'incarnait elle-même dans le personnage de Lélia [i.e. 1833]'. Samuel Rocheblave, who was known for his writings on art history as well as on George Sand, apparently endorsed this opinion, since he is credited with communicating Julien Tinayre's lithograph, bearing the caption 'Portrait de George Sand', to *L'Instantané* in 1909 (ref. under *Prints*). The identification was contested by de Rothmaler in 1926, on the grounds that the features are quite unlike those in authentic early portraits of George Sand and she did not settle in Paris before 1831, being an unknown provincial at the date assigned to the picture by Robaut. In the same year, Escholier (I. 154 f.; II. 138) substituted the name of Mme Dalton, a French dancer known to Bonington and Delacroix in the 1820s, for George Sand. By 1930, Joubin had claimed that the sitter was Mme de Conflans, sister of the artist's friend Félix Guillemardet, apparently on no firmer evidence than mention of her in the *Journal* in 1824 as wearing a round hat with feathers (see Cat. Exh. Louvre 1930, no. 39; *Journal* I. 76 n. 2). He withdrew this identification in 1936 (though it remained unchanged in subsequent editions of the *Journal*) and argued that it was a portrait of the painter Elise Boulanger *c*. 1833-5, on the basis of unconvincing comparisons with known portraits of the newly proposed sitter. Escholier retains his original opinion that it is Mme Dalton in Escholier 1963, but in his *Delacroix et les femmes* of the same year accepts Joubin's outdated suggestion of Mme de Conflans.

The very attractive sitter, who remains anonymous in the face of so much conjecture, was probably an actress, for she wears not contemporary dress but seventeenth-century period costume, which was frequently worn for theatrical productions in the early nineteenth century, regardless of the period of the action. Robaut's date of 1827 seems about right, from the style and technique, as far as they can be judged in reproduction, and because a pencil study of the same woman in the same costume is contained in a sketch-book that was in use about that time (Louvre, RF9150, fol. 16ʳ). The same model may have served for the *Lady and her Valet* (J8).

¹ According to Robaut (no. 1904), it was part of lot 201, but I am unable to determine who bought it at the sale and for what price. For a list of the buyers and prices which cannot be attached to individual items in this lot, see J(L)82.
² An inscription dated Oct. 1880 on the back of Robaut's drawing of this picture in Robaut Tracings I states that Christophe 'l'a achetée autrefois 100 fr. à Moureau — (après la vente [posthume de Delacroix])'. Moureau is not recorded as a direct purchaser of any paintings at the posthumous sale.
³ According to the account given by Marcelle Tinayre in 1905 (op. cit., under *Literature*), when Christophe died 'une de ses amies [. . .] signala le tableau à M. Joseph Reinach', who thereupon visited Christophe's atelier with the Minister of Fine Arts, M. Bourgeois, and M. Roujon. Reinach 'acheta le tableau, et déclara, le jour même, qu'il le léguerait au musée du Louvre'. The source of this circumstantial account was presumably Reinach himself, who is recorded as the owner of the painting on the illustration to Tinayre's article.

90 HEAD OF DANTE   Pl. 79

Oils on paper laid on canvas
$10\frac{13}{16} \times 9\frac{1}{16}$ in. (27.4 × 23 cm)* E.D.
Probably part of R1904
1827
Henri Galland, Paris

Provenance: Probably Delacroix's posthumous sale, Feb. 1864, part of lot 201 ('Onze études de têtes et portraits'), to ?;¹ Paul Huet ?, d. 1869; René Paul Huet to 1928, his son; Maurice Perret-Carnot, 1928²—c. 1938, his son-in-law; said to have belonged to Maurice Gobin in 1955; anonymous sale, Hôtel Drouot, Room 7, 7 March 1955, lot 141 (repr.), to the present owner.

Exhibitions: None.

Literature: L. Johnson, 'The Formal Sources of Delacriox's *Barque de Dante*', *Burl Mag*, C (1958), p. 232, fig. 24.

This painting is closely based on a cast of Dante's 'death-mask', now considered spurious but no doubt thought to be genuine by Delacroix (repr. L. Johnson, op. cit., fig. 26). There is a rapid pen-and-ink study for it on the recto of a

sheet of drawings whose verso contains studies for the *Death of Sardanapalus* (J125), painted in 1827 (Louvre drawing, RF5276; recto repr. here, Fig. 24). Three pencil drawings from the cast, one of which is a full preliminary study for our painting, are contained in a sketch-book in the Louvre (RF9150, fol. 14ʳ), two pages before a drawing connected with the *Young Woman in a Large Hat* (J89), which Robaut dates 1827, and one page after studies that are apparently for the *Death of Sardanapalus* (fol. 13ʳ).

The firmly accented bone structure and the predominantly ochreish and brown colouring recall Géricault's manner at the period of the *Raft of the Medusa*, a picture which was certainly in Delacroix's mind when he conceived this study, since two sketches from it are in the same sketch-book as the drawings from the Dante cast and separated from them by only two sheets (fol. 17ʳ; repr. Huyghe pl. 83, but in my opinion wrongly dated to *c*. 1820).

¹ If it was part of lot 201, I am unable to determine who bought it at the sale. For a list of buyers and prices which cannot be attached to individual items in this lot, see J(L)182.
² The stretcher is inscribed: 'Etude du Dante, donnée par M. Eugène Delacroix à M. Paul Huet et timbrée après coup à la vente [posthume de Delacroix].' A label on the stretcher has a further inscription relating to the provenance: 'Collection Paul Huet 1822-1869.—Collection René-Paul Huet, 1869-1928.—Collection Maurice Perret-Carnot, 1928.'
When I published this study in 1958, I accepted these inscriptions at face value. Now, in light of further knowledge of related drawings and of how inscriptions were added to other works in the Perret-Carnot Collection, I regard them with some scepticism. It seems improbable that Paul Huet would, or could, have simply had a picture that Delacroix had given him stamped with the seal of the posthumous sale when it had not passed in the sale. On the other hand, this study is not in the list which Paul Huet himself gives of the several paintings that he bought at the posthumous sale (see letter to Sollier d. 7 Apr. 1864, in R. P. Huet, *Paul Huet* (Paris, H. Laurens, 1911), p. 381). The most likely explanation for the presence of the seal on the stretcher is that the picture did pass in the sale, but was acquired only later by the Huet family.
As for the inscribed label, Paul Huet could not have been given the study in 1822 if it was painted in 1827 and, since it no doubt passed to someone else in Delacroix's sale of 1864, he may not even have acquired it before his own death five years later. There is no reason to doubt that it belonged to René Paul Huet, though he may not have come into possession of it as early as 1869.

91 PORTRAIT OF MADAME   Pl. 80
FRANÇOIS SIMON

$24 \times 20\frac{1}{16}$ in. (61 × 51 cm, before relining)* Relined 1969
Signed top left: *Eug. Delacroix*.
R294
1829
Staatliche Kunsthalle, Karlsruhe

Provenance: M. François Louis Sylvain Simon, the sitter's husband, d. 30 Nov. 1877 at Crécy-en-Brie; Mme Cinot, their daughter, to at least 1885; Mme Maisonnale, who acquired it from her,¹ to 1906; Mme de Valcourt, to 15 June 1907, when it was purchased, by M. Bischoffsheim(?), for the collection that later belonged to Marie Laure,

Vicomtesse de Noailles,[2] Vicomtesse de Noailles, Paris, to at least 1937; Sig. Frua de Angeli, Italy; his daughter, New York, by 1968; with Mrs. Walter Feilchenfeldt, Zurich, June 1969; bought from her by the Staatliche Kunsthalle, Karlsruhe, 1970.

Exhibitions: Probably Musée Colbert, Paris 1829A and B, no. 83 and 201 (as 'Portrait de Madame *****'); *Bd Italiens*, Paris 1864, no. 314 (supp. to 3rd ed., as 'Portrait de Mme S . . .'); *Universelle*, Paris 1878, no. 857; *EBA*, Paris 1885, no, 47 (as 'Mme Cinot');[3] Atelier Delacroix, Paris 1937B, no. 16, repr. frontispiece.

Literature: E. Véron, *Eugène Delacroix* (Librairie de l'Art, Paris and London, 1887), p. 40; Escholier I. 214; A. Joubin, 'L'Appartement et l'atelier de Delacroix, rue de Furstenberg', *GBA*, XIX (1938), p. 293, repr. alone fig. 4, and in a general view of Delacroix's salon as arranged for the 1937 exh., fig. 3; M. Ledivelec, *Delacroix* (Gibert Jeune, Paris, n.d.), pl. 8; Escholier 1963, p. 42; L. Johnson, in Cat. Exh. Edinburgh–London 1964, mentioned under no. 33; L. Johnson, 'Four Rediscovered Portraits by Delacroix', *Burl Mag*, CXII (1970), pp. 3 f., repr. in colour frontispiece (after cleaning).

The sitter was first identified in the catalogue of the exhibition *Universelle*, Paris 1878, as 'Louise-Thérèse-Victoire Damoiseau, dame Simon (1799–1874), femme d'un premier sujet de l'Opéra', the date of the portrait being given as 1829, as it had already been given in the exhibition *Bd Italiens*, Paris 1864, when it still belonged to M. Simon and the sitter was still living. Robaut added that she was the daughter of a veterinarian, 'inspecteur général du département de la Seine', and that her husband died at Crécy-en-Brie in 1877. I added (1970) some biographical details about the husband, including his Christian names and precise dates (b. Paris 5 April 1800). It is further stated in Robaut that the velvet bodice worn by Mme Simon was taken from Delacroix's studio costumes. There appears to be no reason to doubt this, or that the portrait was painted in Delacroix's studio in 1829, which Robaut notes on his drawing of this picture in Tracings I; for the information probably came direct from the sitter's husband, whom Robaut visited at Crécy no more than two years before Simon's death in 1877 (R Ann, p. 147). In support of the date 1829, I have suggested (1970) that there can be little question that the five asterisks in the entry for the female portrait exhibited at the Musée Colbert in December 1829 stand for the letters of Mme Simon's surname.

Robaut was struck by the Englishness of this portrait, which he described as 'peinture absolument *manière anglaise*' (Tracings I). Though there may be some influence of English techniques, there appears to be a more potent overall influence, on both design and handling, of Rubens's portrait of Suzanne Fourment in the Louvre, which

Delacroix had copied (J19). While employing essentially the same design as Rubens, in reverse, Delacroix enlarges the scale of the sitter in proportion to the size of the canvas, thus increasing at once the breadth of form and the sense of communication with the subject. The eccentric placing of the head adds to the feeling of mobility, enhancing the effect of a fugitive expression caught in the shy half-smile and warm brown eyes, helping to animate a face characterized more by pliant docility than ready wit. The similarity of the chain necklaces in the two portraits raises the question whether Delacroix may not have adorned his sitter with jewellery from his own collection (or painted from his own imagination under the influence of Rubens), as well as with clothing. The brooch may have belonged to him, for it could well be the same one, more impressionistically treated, as worn by the sitter in *Woman in a Blue Turban* of 1827 (J88).

The canvas, which had been attached to an American stretcher of recent make, was very thin and the varnish had deteriorated when I examined this picture shortly before it was relined and cleaned by Miss Buschor, restorer at the Kunsthaus, Zurich, in 1969. Otherwise, the paint surface was in good condition. The violet bodice has probably darkened with age, thus attenuating some of the original contrast with the yellow silk shawl which introduces its colour complement.

Robaut lists under the year 1834 (no. 555) a small, unsigned full-length portrait of Mme Simon seated in a domestic interior. That picture is recorded in the collection of Victor Chocquet by 1880 (in *Correspondance* (Burty 1880), II, p. 295) and passed in his widow's sale, 1 July 1899, lot 50, as a portrait of Mme Frédéric Villot. It was purchased by the City Museum and Art Gallery, Birmingham, in 1963. Though it was in the exhibition Louvre 1930 (no. 70A) and I included it in the exhibition Edinburgh–London 1964 (no. 33) before seeing the 1829 version, I am now inclined to doubt the attribution to Delacroix, but not the identity of the sitter. A full-page colour reproduction is contained in P. Pool, *Delacroix* (Paul Hamlyn, London, 1969), pl. 21.

Delacroix drew several water-colour studies of the husband in theatrical costume, catalogued by Robaut under nos. 275, 276, and 556. The first and last of these are in the Musée de l'Opéra, Paris, and are respectively illustrated in L. Johnson, op. cit. 1970, fig. 2, and in Cat. Exh. Bordeaux 1963, pl. 67.

[1] Letter from Emile Mare, brother of Mme Maisonnale, to the Curator of the Louvre, Paris 22 Oct. 1906. It is clear from the context that the picture had belonged to her for some years by 1906. According to the same letter, '[Delacroix] disait à son ami Simon en le [le portrait] lui offrant: "Je ne ferai assurément jamais mieux." ' (Archives du Musée du Louvre, p 30 (DELACROIX, Eugène).) Since M. Mare's motive for writing was to sell the portrait on his sister's behalf, the evidence of Delacroix's opinion may not be reliable.

[2] A catalogue card from the collection of the Vicomtesse de Noailles records the date of purchase and the name of the seller, but I have been

unable to confirm the name of the buyer, who was presumably M. Bischoffsheim, the Viscountess's grandfather from whom she inherited other paintings by Delacroix.

[3] Despite the wrong identification in the exhibition catalogue, confusing the sitter with the owner, there can be no doubt that this is our portrait, as its presence in this exhibition is recorded in R Ann, margin to no. 294, as well as in the MS. letter referred to in note 1 above.

92 PORTRAIT OF CHARLES DE VERNINAC

Pl. 81

$24\frac{1}{8} \times 19\frac{3}{4}$ in. (61.2 × 50.2 cm)*

c. 1829

Fernand Javal, Paris

Provenance: Bequeathed by Delacroix in 1863 to Mme Duriez (*née* Zélie de Verninac), who probably gave it upon settlement of the will to her brother, François de Verninac, d. 1871;[1] by descent to Mme J. L. Malvy (*née* Louise de Verninac), his granddaughter, to 1948; de Verninac sale, 8 Dec. 1948, lot 15 (repr. pl. v), to the present owner.[2]

Exhibitions: Atelier Delacroix, 1973B, no. 3; Amsterdam 1938, no. 116, Wildenstein, London 1952, no. 15; Venice 1956, no. 6; Atelier Delacroix, Paris 1963, no. 25; Edinburgh–London 1964, no. 18.

Literature: Delacroix's will, dated 3 August 1863, in *Correspondance* (Burty 1878), p. vi; A. Joubin, Preface to Cat. Exh. Atelier Delacroix, Paris 1937A; A. Joubin, 'L'Appartement et l'atelier de Delacroix, rue de Furstenberg', *GBA*, XIX (1938), p. 298, repr. fig. 2 (in general view of the artist's bedroom as arranged for 1937 exh.); *Arts*, 29 Dec. 1950 (article, with repr., on litigation following the de Verninac Sale in 1948); Huyghe, p. 32, repr. fig. 27; L. Johnson, 'Eugène Delacroix and Charles de Verninac: an Unpublished Portrait and New Letters', *Burl Mag*, CX (1968), p. 512 n. 12, fig. 35.

There is general agreement, though no documentary evidence, that this portrait of Delacroix's nephew was painted between 1825 and 1830.[3] The discovery of Charles de Verninac's true date of birth (1803 instead of 1800) and of the details of his movements as a consular official (L. Johnson, 1968) has not required this dating to be drastically revised, but the sitter appears to be closer to twenty-six than twenty-two years of age and a possible reason why the portrait was left unfinished is that Charles left Paris for Malta sooner than Delacroix says he expected him to, in September 1829 (*Correspondance* I. 241); therefore a date towards the end of the agreed period seems most acceptable, but not as late as 1830, since Charles was then in Malta.

On the one hand, this picture is closely related to the Portrait of Schwiter (J82), in its imperious hauteur and its affinities with Lawrence (it is comparable to, e.g., Lawrence's Portrait of Sir Alexander Mackenzie of *c.* 1800—Fig. 7). On the other hand, in its blend of forceful

characterization and sketchiness, it adumbrates Delacroix's two most renowned portraits, both from the 1830s, and in the Louvre: the Self-Portrait and the Portrait of Chopin.

Charles de Verninac was appointed a student vice-consul to Malta in July 1829 and, leaving Paris in September, arrived on the island in November. He served there with distinction till the end of June 1831, when he returned to France in readiness to depart for a new post, as Vice-Consul to Chile. Arriving in Paris about the middle of June, he sailed for Valparaiso from Toulon on 28 November 1831, never to return. A conflict of personalities between Charles

Fig. 7. *Alexander Mackenzie*, Thomas Lawrence.

and the Consul General, Ragueneau de la Chainaye, with whom he endured the arduous voyage to South America, led to the latter's demanding his subordinate's recall upon their arrival at Valparaiso on 11 May 1832. The Foreign Minister appears to have justly sided with Charles in the dispute, and Delacroix's nephew continued in his post at Valparaiso till January 1834, when he sailed for Lima on the first leg of his return journey to France. Making his way to the United States, whence he intended to cross the Atlantic, he contracted yellow fever at Vera Cruz and died in quarantine in New York on 22 May 1834, at the age of thirty. (For a full account of his career and Delacroix's letters to him, see L. Johnson, op. cit. See also J62 and J83.)

1 Delacroix's bequest to Mme Duriez included three portraits of his nephew, of which this may be presumed to be the second, described in the will as 'le second en ébauche dans mon atelier'. As stated under J62, n. 2, the terms of the will required Mme Duriez to share her legacy with her brother, François de Verninac, and sister, Mme Pierrugues, and it is not certain how it was divided up. But the emergence of this portrait in this century in the possession of the granddaughter of François de Verninac suggests that he was allotted this one.

2 After the bidding was completed, the State's right of pre-emption was exercised through a curator of the Louvre. The pre-emption was lifted in December 1948, and the original successful bidder, M. Javal, was now asked to pay. He refused, on the grounds that the particulars of the portrait given in the sale catalogue were inaccurate, and a lawsuit followed, which he lost. (For an account of the litigation and the events leading to it, see *Arts*, 29 Dec. 1950.) Though the portrait has rightly been accepted as authentic, the entry in the catalogue of the de Verninac sale certainly contained some glaring inaccuracies, several of which have been repeated in much of the subsequent literature, notably that (1) the picture was bequeathed by Delacroix to his sister, who had been dead thirty-six years when he drew up his will; (2) it is listed by Robaut, who evidently had no firsthand knowledge of the de Verninac family portraits when his *catalogue raisonné* was published, and included nothing in it that can be identified with this picture; and (3), following Joubin (op. cit., 1937 and 1938), that it was the portrait stated in the will to be at the head of Delacroix's bed (see J83). There is no reason to suppose that this is the picture that hung by the artist's bed, since it is the only unfinished portrait of Charles de Verninac, and the only portrait in the will that corresponds to that description is explicitly stated to be 'dans mon atelier' (see also n. 1 here).

3 Exhibitions London 1952 and Venice 1956: 1825/30. Paris 1973B, *c*. 1825; Amsterdam 1938, 1825/9; Edinburgh-London 1964, 1826/9. Huyghe, op. cit., *c*. 1830; L. Johnson, op. cit., 1829?.

93 PORTRAIT OF NICOLÒ PAGANINI   Pl. 79

Cardboard. $17\frac{3}{4} \times 12$ in. $(45 \times 30.4$ cm$)^1$
R386 (1832)
1831?
The Phillips Collection, Washington, D.C.

Provenance: Said to have been painted for Achille Ricourt;[2] Adolphe Herman; his sale 10 Feb. 1879, lot 10, to Perreau, 1,600 fr.; he sold it to Boussod, Valadon et C[ie], 24 Oct. 1881, and they sold it to Champfleury, 29 March 1882 (Arch Goupil/Boussod); his sale 28 Apr. 1890, lot 5, to Cheramy (R Ann), 2,305 fr.; his sale 5 May 1908, lot 158 (repr.), to Dikran Khan Kelekian, 8,200 fr.; his sale 30 Jan. 1922, New York, lot 115 (repr.), to Kraushaar Galleries for Duncan Phillips.

Exhibitions: EBA, Paris 1883, no. 58; EBA, Paris 1885, no. 44; R.A. London 1896, no. 48; Cassirer, Berlin 1907, no. 15; Zurich 1917, no. 95; Brooklyn 1921, no. 89; Chicago 1930, no. 13, repr.; Louvre 1930, no. 60A; Portraits, Philadelphia 1937, p. 15; Knoedler, New York and Chicago 1938-9, no. 43; Wildenstein, New York 1943, no. 423; Washington 1945, no. 13; Richmond, Virginia 1947, no. 14; Detroit 1950, no. 31; Orangerie, Paris 1955, no. 24, repr.; Toronto-Ottawa 1962-3, no. 4, 2 repr. (one in colour as frontispiece); Louvre 1963, no. 150, repr.; *Berlioz and the Romantic Imagination*, Victoria and Albert Museum, London 1969, no. 258, repr.

Literature: C. Pissarro, letter of 19 Oct. 1891, in J. Rewald (ed.), *Camille Pissarro, Lettres à son Fils Lucien* (Albin Michel, Paris, 1950), p. 263; L. Rouart, 'La Collection de M. Cheramy', *Les Arts*, no. 64 (Apr. 1907), p. 22, repr. p. 24; J. Meier-Graefe and E. Klossowski, *La Collection Cheramy . . .* (Munich, R. Piper, 1908), pp. 92 f., repr. frontispiece; *Collection Kélékian. Tableaux de l'école française moderne* (Paris, New York, Cairo, 1920), pl. 38; R. Fry, 'Modern Paintings in a Collection of Ancient Art', *Burl Mag*, XXXVII (1920), p. 309, repr. pl. III p. 308; Meier-Graefe 1922, repr. p. 118; Escholier II. 168, repr. p. 167; H. Tietze (ed.), *Masterpieces of European Painting in America* (George Allen & Unwin Ltd., London, 1939), p. 327, repr. p. 266; J. Barzun, 'Romanticism: Definition of a Period', *Magazine of Art*, XLVII (1949), repr. p. 244; *Journal* II. 423 n. 2; *The Phillips Collection Catalogue* (Thames and Hudson, New York and London, 1952), p. 29, repr. pl. 16; J. Siegfried, 'The Romantic Artist as a Portrait Painter', *Marsyas*, VIII (1957-9), p. 36; J. Starzynski, 'Delacroix et Chopin', *Académie polonaise des Sciences*, fasc. 34 (Paris, 1962), repr. fig. 1; G. Mras, 'The Delacroix Exhibition in Canada', *Burl Mag*, CV (1963), p. 71; L. Johnson, 'Delacroix in Canada' (Letter), ibid., p. 213; Johnson 1963, pp. 39, 49 f., repr. pl. 27; Huyghe, pp. 198, 208, repr. fig. 168; Maltese, pp. 33, 37, 154, repr. pl. 32; T. Prideaux *et al.*, *The World of Delacroix* (Time Inc., New York, 1966), p. 136, full-page colour repr. p. 137; M. Kemp, 'Ingres, Delacroix and Paganini: Exposition and Improvisation in the Creative Process', *L'Arte*, N.S. III (1970), pp. 49, 50, 53, 56, 57, 61, 62, repr. fig. 2, p. 52.

Though Robaut records in an annotation to a copy of the catalogue of the exhibition *EBA*, Paris 1885 that this portrait was widely contested at the time of the show,[3] its authenticity has never been called in doubt since and it has come to be one of the most generally admired of Delacroix's portraits for its expressive intensity, its complete evocation, despite its sketchiness, of Paganini's physical appearance and musical talent. Camille Pissarro (1891) singled it out as one of several 'esquisses superbes de Delacroix' in the Cheramy collection. Even Roger Fry (1920), who shared the Englishman's congenital lack of appreciation of Delacroix, conceded: 'However, I can come to terms with regard to so profound and dramatic an interpretation of character as the little *Paganini* discovers. It is indeed a marvellously intense and imaginative conception.' More recently, after recalling Paganini's state of physical decrepitude when he came to Paris, I emphasized the spiritual content of the picture: 'Delacroix makes him seem like a soul which has met a body by accident [. . .] By means of expressive distortion and suppression of sharp detail, he stresses his spiritual force, his deep concentration, his assurance and vitality as a musician, rather than the physical accidents of his debilitated frame.

More than that, he conveys [. . .] a sense of the satanic power that many felt in Paganini who heard him play.' (Johnson 1963, p. 49.)

Robaut's dating of 1832 was either accepted or altered without argument[4] until 1962 when I argued (Cat. Exh. Toronto-Ottawa 1962-3, no. 4) that the style and colouring did not seem inconsistent with the *Interior of a Dominican Convent* (J148) and the *Boissy d'Anglas at the Convention* (J147), both of which are dated 1831; also, that the sketchy nature of the portrait suggested it was rapidly painted under a vivid and comparatively recent impression of Paganini performing, and these conditions were most likely to have occurred in 1831 after Delacroix attended Paganini's first concert in Paris,[5] at the Opéra on 9 March, since he was in North Africa when the violinist gave his series of ten recitals in the capital in 1832 and opportunities to see him play in Paris would thereafter have been exceedingly limited. These arguments were accepted in *Mémorial* and by Maltese. Mras, however, dissented, holding that the sketchy character of the picture was too assured and calculated for such an early date but not proposing an alternative.

The first visit of Paganini (1782-1840) to Paris in 1831 caused a sensation. Apart from his unique virtuosity, through which he made his major contribution to the history of music by extending the range of his instrument, his cadaverous appearance, the legend of his league with the Devil and the myth that he was a persecuted genius who had perfected his art while languishing in prison for murdering his mistress were of irresistible appeal to French Romantic artists, who created many images of him in the first two or three years of the 1830s. Louis Boulanger drew a lithograph of Paganini playing the violin in prison, which was published in *L'Artiste* in the spring of 1831, and a series of unpublished pen-and-ink sketches of him at rehearsal (*BN Estampes*. Fig. 8); Dantan made a full-length statuette dated 1832 (Musée Carnavalet, Paris); and two comic watercolours by Grandville and Tony Johannot are contained in the Paganini Collection in the Library of Congress, Washington, D.C. These works are mostly caricatures of an exceptional musician and trivial in sentiment. Delacroix's image, though perhaps not free from influence of the caricaturist's devices, stands apart, with David d'Angers's noble bronze bust of Paganini (Salon 1834; Musée d'Angers), as the most elevated interpretation by French artists in the 1830s of this picturesque and gifted personality.

On the two occasions when Delacroix is recorded as speaking of Paganini, he remarked on his prodigious technique and drew analogies with his own art of painting. In conversation with the violinist Ernst in January 1856: 'Comme je lui parlais de mon souvenir de Paganini, il me dit que c'était sans doute un homme incomparable. Les difficultés et les prétendus tours de force que présentent ses œuvres sont encore, pour la plupart, indéchiffrables pour les violons les plus habiles: voilà l'inventeur, voilà l'homme propre à la chose. Je pensais à tant d'artistes qui sont le contraire, dans la peinture' (*Journal* II. 423). And, in advising his pupil Lassalle-Bordes: 'Il faudrait', me disait [Delacroix], 'que ce dont on a la vision pût être rendu sans peine; il faut que la main acquière également une grande prestesse, et l'on n'y arrive que par de semblables études.

Fig. 8. *Paganini*, Louis Boulanger.

Paganini n'a dû son étonnante exécution sur le violon qu'en s'exerçant chaque jour pendant une heure à ne faire que des gammes. C'est pour nous le même exercice.' (Lassalle-Bordes quoted by Robaut under R386).

Robaut states (R386) that some pencil sketches of Paganini passed in Delacroix's posthumous sale, and adds in R Ann: 'J'en ai offert au moins un croquis à Ad Hermaint [*sic*, for Adolphe Herman] le violoniste.'

[1] Robaut gives the dimensions as 41 × 28 cm and states in R Ann: 'Mr Champfleury fait agrandir la toile [*sic*] en 1885.' The size is listed as 45 × 31 cm in Cat. Exh. *EBA*, Paris 1885, but it was already recorded as larger than Robaut states in Cat. Exh. *EBA*, Paris 1883: 44 × 31 cm. At my request, the picture was taken out of its frame in 1958, re-measured and examined for

evidence that it had been enlarged. No conclusive signs that the original board had been extended were found, though I was informed by the Phillips Gallery that 'possible additions were made at top and bottom .9cm. each.' I can add nothing to this from my own later examination of the original, except to say that it seems more likely Robaut's original measurements were at fault than the picture was subsequently enlarged.

2 In the entry for R386: 'Delacroix passe pour avoir peint ce sujet pour Ricourt, ancien directeur du journal *l'Artiste*.' Achille Ricourt was editor of *L'Artiste* from 1831–8. It was a periodical which ardently supported

Delacroix, an occasional contributor, and other members of the Romantic School.

3 *Bib AA*, MS. 298ter, annotation to no. 44: 'a été très contesté'. Robaut specifies in R Ann, margin to R386, that Philippe Burty did not accept it: 'L'appréciation de Burty est que ce n'est pas de Delacroix.'

4 Meier-Graefe-Klossowski and Phillips Collection Cat., c. 1832; Escholier, 'évidemment postérieur à la date que lui assigne Robaut'; Tietze, c. 1830.

5 G. I. C. de Courcy, *Paganini, the Genoese* (University of Oklahoma Press, 1957), II, p. 14.

Allegory and Decorations

THE FOUR SEASONS: DECORATIONS FOR TALMA'S DINING-ROOM

R1451–4 (1863. No repr.) and under R332–5 (1830)

1821

Mme F. Jouët-Pastré, Paris

Provenance: Painted in 1821 as over-doors for Talma's dining-room at 9 rue de la Tour des Dames, Paris; M. Frédéric Jouët (a subsequent owner of the house at that address), by 1864; by descent to M. Frédéric Jouët-Pastré, d. 1965; the present owner, his widow.

Exhibitions: Bd Italiens, Paris 1864, no. 152–5; Louvre 1963, nos. 14–17, all repr.

Literature: Silvestre *Delacroix* (1855), p. 80; L. Clément de Ris, *Critiques d'art et de littérature* (Didier, Paris, 1862. Chapter on Delacroix dated April 1857), pp. 381 f; Escholier I. 282; L. Johnson, 'Four unknown Paintings by Delacroix', *Burl Mag*, XCVII (1955), p. 85, repr. figs. 27–30; L. Johnson, 'Delacroix's Decorations for Talma's Dining-room', *Burl Mag*, XCIX (1957), pp. 78–87, repr. figs. 25 (*Summer*), 27 (*Spring*), 29 (*Winter*), 31 (*Autumn*); Sérullaz *Peintures murales*, p. 21; Huyghe, pp. 201, 376, 420, 523 n. 35, 526 n. 7; L. Johnson, 'The Delacroix Centenary in France—II', *Burl Mag*, CVI (1964), p. 263; Maltese, p. 133, *Winter* repr. in colour, pl. 1; Trapp, p. 17 and n. 28; L. Johnson, 'Some Early Murals by Delacroix', *Burl Mag*, CXVII (1975), pp. 650, 653 and n., 654, 657 and n., 658 and n.

In cataloguing these pictures, without illustrations, under the year 1863, Robaut confused them with the *Seasons* which Delacroix was painting in his late years for the banker Frédéric Hartmann's drawing-room and left uncompleted on his death; under the year 1830, he illustrated and catalogued four studies as *Les Saisons* (R332–5), three of which are advanced studies for the *Spring*, *Summer* and *Winter* paintings reproduced here, commenting 'ces quatre sujets ont été exécutés, dit-on, en peinture pour la salle à manger de Talma.' The history of Delacroix's earliest extant decorations rested at that stage till 1955, when the four paintings, their correct attribution having by now been lost

even to their owner, were rediscovered in the house built in Paris in 1821 by the architect Lelong for the famous French tragedian Talma (L. Johnson, op. cit., 1955). Though they were no longer in the positions for which they had been designed, having been removed, and presumably extended for framing, some time before they were exhibited in 1864, it was established by early plans and a sectional elevation of the house (Fig. 9) that they had originally been in the dining-room: *Winter* and *Autumn* were clearly visible, in their original semicircular shape, over the two doors in the west wall; it could be assumed that *Spring* and *Summer* were their respective counterparts over the two corresponding doors in the wall opposite (L. Johnson, op. cit., 1957). The chronological sequence of the Seasons thus ran counterclockwise in the room; the sequence of execution is unknown. The date of construction of Talma's house and the date of a sketch-book shown to contain studies connected with these decorations, combined with a remark by Delacroix in a letter to his sister dated 29 June 1821, that he would perhaps have some pictures to paint during the holidays in a house that was being built (*Correspondance* V. 87), proved beyond reasonable doubt that the four paintings had been executed in the summer of 1821 (L. Johnson, op. cit., 1957). I have since found further confirmation of this dating in Clément de Ris, who wrote in 1857 (op. cit.), during the artist's lifetime: 'En 1821, après avoir quitté l'atelier de Guérin, Talma lui [à Delacroix] demandait, pour la salle à manger de son hôtel de la rue de la Tour-des-Dames, quatre dessus de porte existant encore. Composées assez habilement, mais d'une exécution timide et sèche, ces toiles sont loin de faire présenter la fougue et l'éclat du peintre de la *Médée* et du *Trajan*.'

From preliminary studies and notes in a Louvre sketch-book (RF9151), it appears that Delacroix first planned to paint nine semicircular pictures to be distributed evenly on the three inner walls of the dining-room, so as to repeat on each wall the triple rhythm of the round-headed windows in the fourth wall (L. Johnson, op. cit., 1957, p. 85, figs. 18, 19, 22); but the final scheme was almost certainly reduced to just these four paintings of the Seasons over the

Fig. 9. *Talma's House.*

four doors of the room. The most advanced studies for the final paintings, developed from a multitude of preliminary sketches, are represented by detailed, semicircular water-colour compositions in the Louvre (RF9240, *Winter*, squared for transfer, repr. ibid. fig. 30; RF9246, *Autumn* and an earlier stage of *Spring*, repr. ibid. fig. 33 and *Mémorial* no. 18; RF9244, *Summer*, repr. in same sources, fig. 26 and no. 21; RF9239, *Spring*, repr. in same, fig. 28 and no. 20).

Designed for a classical tragedian's house built in a classical style, Delacroix's *Seasons* are developed from studies of Graeco-Roman paintings from Herculaneum and its environs, of Antique statuary and of seventeenth-century French decorative paintings (for a full discussion and illustrations of these influences, see L. Johnson, op. cit., 1957[1]). There may also be some influence of Michelangelo, as suggested by Maltese. The handling, though stiff and uncertain in some parts, has a spontaneity and freshness in others and reveals a delight in the qualities of freely applied impasto; in this, the influence seems to stem from Gros and Géricault.

[1] The studies after seventeenth-century French decorative paintings, reproduced as fig. 10, have since been identified by one of my students, Paul Denis, as from decorations by Cotelle de Meaux in the Chambre des Reines-Mères at Fontainebleau. For a colour reproduction of one of the figures copied by Delacroix, see P. Gélis-Didot, *La Peinture décorative - France du XVIe au XVIIIe siècle* (C. Schmid, Paris, 1897-9), un-numbered pl.

94 WINTER
Pl. 82

Canvas laid down on wood panel, $17\frac{1}{2} \times 33\frac{3}{8}$ in. (44.5 × 84.8 cm)*; original lunette, approximately $16\frac{1}{2} \times 31\frac{7}{8}$ in. (42 × 81 cm)*

The dog appears to be closely based on an engraving of a Graeco-Roman wall painting (in *Le Pitture antiche d'Ercolano e contorni* (Royal Press, Naples, 9 vols., 1757-92), II (1760), p. 209). The free handling of the snow recalls Gros's in *Napoleon on the Field of Eylau* of 1808; the overloaded water carrier, an angel from Delacroix's own *Virgin of the Sacred Heart* (J153). The cold, blue-green hues of *Winter*'s drapery look forward to Dante's robe in the *Barque de Dante* (J100) of the following year; the hand clutching beneath the cloth, to the right hand of the dead mother in the foreground of the *Massacres of Chios* (J105) of 1824.

Though the most lively of the four pictures in spirit and execution, this is also the most damaged by tears in the canvas, the two worst ones running from the eye of *Winter* towards the left, and above his knee across the spilling water.

95 AUTUMN
Pl. 83

Canvas laid down on wood panel, $17\frac{5}{8} \times 33\frac{3}{8}$ in. (44.7 × 84.8 cm)*; original lunette, approximately $16\frac{11}{16} \times 32\frac{11}{16}$ in. (42.3 × 83 cm)*

96 SUMMER Pl. 82

Canvas laid down on wood panel, $17\frac{3}{4} \times 33\frac{1}{2}$ in.
(45×85 cm)*; original lunette, approximately $16\frac{1}{2} \times 32\frac{1}{4}$ in. (42×82 cm)*

97 SPRING Pl. 83

Canvas laid down on wood panel, $17\frac{5}{8} \times 33\frac{3}{8}$ in.
(44.7×84.8 cm)*; original lunette, approximately $16\frac{1}{2} \times 32\frac{11}{16}$ in. (42×83 cm)*

This classicizing figure of Spring combines elements from Graeco-Roman painting, including the famous *Maiden Gathering Flowers* from Stabiae, and from an Antique *Crouching Aphrodite* in the Louvre, copied by Delacroix in a sketch-book.

98 GREECE ON THE RUINS OF MISSOLONGHI Pl. 84

$82\frac{1}{4} \times 57\frac{7}{8}$ in. (2.09×1.47 m)
Signed bottom left: *Eug. Delacroix.*
Moreau p. 199 (1827). R205 (1827)
1826
Musée des Beaux-Arts, Bordeaux

Provenance: Bought from the artist by the City of Bordeaux, Feb. 1852 (*Correspondance* III. 107 n. 2).

Exhibitions: *Gal. Lebrun*, Paris 1826, *h.c.*; Hobday's Gallery, London 1828;[1] Musée Colbert, Paris 1829A, no. 7 ('La Grèce. (Allégorie.) Elle est représentée sous les traits d'une femme pleurant sur les ruines'); id., Paris 1829B, no. 138 (with same title and description, but wrongly attributed to Belloc); id., Paris 1830A, no. 90 (same title and description)—for sale; id., Paris 1830B, no. 195 (same title and description)—for sale; *Soc. Amis des Arts*, Bordeaux 1851, no. 142 ('La Grèce sur les ruines de Missolonghi; allégorie.')—for sale at 2,500 fr.; *Centennale*, Paris 1900, no. 214, repr.; Basle 1921, no. 65, repr.; Paris 1927, no. 262bis; Rosenberg, Paris 1928, no. 6; Copenhagen, Stockholm, Oslo 1928, no. 52, repr., 44, repr., 45, repr.; Louvre 1930, no. 38, repr. *Album*, p. 23; Amsterdam 1938, no. 118, repr.; Belgrade 1939, no. 46; Buenos Aires 1939, no. 46, repr. *Album*, p. 20; San Francisco 1940-2, no. 34, repr.; New York 1941, no. 41, repr.; Atelier Delacroix, Paris 1946B, F; Bristol 1950, no. 14; Wildenstein, London 1952, no. 11, repr.; Brussels 1953, no. 85; New Orleans 1953-4, no. 55, repr.; Amsterdam 1961, no. 37, repr.; Louvre 1963, no. 108, *M* no. 111, 2 repr.; Berne 1963-4, no. 21; Bremen 1964, no. 17, repr.; Bordeaux 1964, no. 115, repr.; Munich 1964-5, no. 92, repr. in colour; Moscow-Leningrad 1965, no. 14; Montreal 1967, no. 114, repr.; Ghent 1970, no. 45, repr. in colour; Atelier Delacroix, Paris 1973 (no cat.); London 1974, S68, repr.; Paris,

Detroit, New York 1974-5, no. 39, repr. (not exhibited in New York); Marseille 1975, no. 50, repr. in colour.

Literature: V. Hugo, 'Exposition de tableaux au profit des Grecs: la nouvelle école de peinture', August 1826 (not published till 1967, in *Œuvres complètes de Victor Hugo* (Le Club Français du Livre, Paris), II, p. 984); M. B. [Boutard], 'Seconde Exposition en faveur des Grecs', *Journal des Débats*, 2 Sept. 1826; F., 'Musée Colbert. Novembre', *Journal des Artistes*, II, no. XXI (22 Nov. 1829), p. 322; *Biographie . . . des contemporains* (chez F. G. Levrault, Paris 1834), III, p. 39; T. Thoré, 'Artistes contemporains. M. Eugène Delacroix', *Le Siècle*, 24 Feb. 1837; *L'Artiste*, 5th s., VIII (1852), p. 64; T. Silvestre, *Les Artistes français*, 1855 (1926 ed., I, pp. 28 f.); Silvestre *Delacroix* (1855), p. 80; P. Lacour and J. Delpit, *Catalogue des Tableaux . . . du Musée de Bordeaux* (Imp. Duviella, Bordeaux, 1856), p. 37, p. 96, no. 106; A. Busquet, 'Exposition de la Société des Amis des Arts de Bordeaux', *L'Artiste*, N.S., I (1857), p. 164; L. de Pesquidoux, *Voyage artistique en France* (Michel Lévy, Paris, 1857), pp. 130-2; A. Houssaye, 'Les Musées de Province. Le Musée de Bordeaux', *Moniteur universel*, 24 March 1858; L. Clément de Ris, *Les Musées de Province* (Vᵛᵉ J. Renouard, Paris, 2 vols., 1859-61), II (1861), p. 362; W. Bürger [Th. Thoré], 'Eugène Delacroix. Exposition de ses œuvres à Paris', *L'Indépendance Belge*, 28 Aug. 1864; E. Vallet, *Catalogue des Tableaux . . . du Musée de Bordeaux* (Impr. G. Gounouilhou, Bordeaux, 1881), p. 148, no. 440; Moreau-Nélaton I. 91, 163, repr. fig. 65, II. 114; Escholier I. 213 f., 276, repr. opp. p. 212, II. 276, III. 173; Hourticq 1930, pl. 23; *Correspondance* I. 407, III. 84 n. 1, 112 n. 1, IV. 24 n. 1, 59 n. 1, 277 n. 1; A. Joubin, 'Modèles de Delacroix', *GBA*, XV (1936), p. 355, repr. p. 349, fig. 5; Cassou 1947, pl. 8, full-page detail of head and bust on opp. p.; G. Hamilton, 'Delacroix's Memorial to Byron', *Burl Mag*, XCIV (1952), pp. 257-61, repr. p. 259, fig. 16; L. Johnson, in Cat. Exh. Toronto-Ottawa 1962-3, p. 71 and n.; Huyghe, pp. 178, 181, 183, 199, 282, 302, detail of head and bust, fig. 214, repr. in colour, pl. V; L. Johnson, 'The Delacroix Centenary in France—II', *Burl Mag*, CVI (1964), p. 261; Maltese, pp. 39, 124, 151, 152, repr. pl. 26; L. Johnson, in Cat. Exh. Montreal 1967, no. 114; Trapp, pp. 66 and n., 69 and n., 83 n. 27, 93, 101, 324 n. 66, 333, repr. in colour, pl. VI; L. Johnson, 'Pierre Andrieu, un "polisson"?', *Revue de l'Art*, No. 21 (1973), p. 68. (Some further bibliography will be found under no. 39 in the Cat. Exh. Paris, Detroit, New York 1974-5.)

Copies: Canvas by Pierre Andrieu, 42×27.5 cm, *c*. 1850?: J(R)35.

Canvas by Odilon Redon, 46×33 cm, *c*. 1870, Ari Redon Collection, Paris. Repr. Cat. Exh. Bordeaux 1963, pl. 56.

Prints: Lithograph by Alfred Robaut. Etching by Charles Manciet.

In May 1825 the Turks besieged Missolonghi on the Gulf of Patras, having made several attempts to reduce it since the Greek insurrection broke out in 1821. For almost a year the Greeks withstood the siege, but finally famine and disease achieved what Turkish arms had failed to accomplish and, following a final desperate sortie by some of the garrison, the Turks entered the city on the night of 22 April 1826. As a final gesture of defiance, the remaining defenders fired their mines on 25 April and died in the explosion, together with a number of the victors. It is no doubt to this dramatic climax that the arm of a dead man emerging from rubble alludes.

Though in 1826 Victor Hugo and Boutard both noted the presence of this picture in the replenished exhibition for Greek relief at the Galerie Lebrun, it is not listed in the second catalogue of that exhibition, for which Delacroix submitted a description of his *Combat of the Giaour and Hassan* (J114) on 14 June (*Correspondance* I. 185). Writing on 2 September, Boutard remarks that the new exhibition has already been open for several weeks. Thus the *Greece* was presumably finished sometime between the middle of June and the middle of August. It is not known when it was begun, but it cannot have been before May.

Lord Byron arrived at Missolonghi during a breathing space between sieges, to support the Greek cause and died there, apparently of uraemic poisoning, in April 1824. It has been suggested Delacroix painted this canvas as a memorial to the English poet and that certain *motifs*, such as the dead hand, may have been inspired by passages in his poetry (Hamilton, op. cit., 1952). The fall of Missolonghi can hardly have failed to evoke thoughts of Byron in Delacroix's mind as in the public's; and it is perceptive to see in that eloquent hand a possible influence of an image of the dead Selim's hand, much admired by Delacroix in 1824 (*Journal* I. 99):

> That hand—whose motion is not life—
> Yet feebly seems to menace strife—
>
> (*The Bride of Abydos*, ii, 26)

But there is no firm evidence for believing that this picture was intended to be more than a tribute to Greece alone, conceived in much the same circumstances as Picasso's *Guernica*, under the shock of recent catastrophic war news. It is Delacroix's second major painting inspired by the Greek War of Independence, the first being the *Massacres of Chios* of 1824 (J105). It is the first time Delacroix uses allegory in a painting with a contemporary political theme. He was to employ it only once more in a modern topical context: in the *Liberty leading the People* of 1830 (J144), where the principal figure is also a female personification.

According to Joubin (op. cit., 1936), the model Laure, who is mentioned in the *Journal* in 1824, posed for the figure of *Greece*, but there is no certain record of Laure's features and no document to substantiate this opinion. Whoever the live model may have been, the antique model, as usefully

suggested by Trapp (p. 66), is the antique Tyche, which in the Hellenistic age was a protective personification of the city, represented wearing an architectural crown of a sort that appears in preliminary studies for Delacroix's *Greece*, to be replaced in the painting by a less severe floral head-dress. If the head has much in common with the Tyche of Antioch, for example, the pose, with arms outstretched in a gesture of entreaty, and bared breast seem to find a more immediate, neo-classical source in the woman in the centre foreground of David's *Sabines* of 1799. The most pervasive influence of all, for both pose and expression, seems however to have been a Christian, High Renaissance one, namely, the *Virgin mourning over the Body of the Dead Christ* engraved by Marcantonio after Raphael, as pointed out by Sara Lichtenstein ('Delacroix and Raphael', unpublished Ph.D. dissertation, University of London, 1973, pp. 96 f.). The severed heads resting on the wall at the upper left introduce a less ideal note and recall similar studies by Géricault. The victorious and exotic soldier in the right background, usually called a Turk though black, is described as an Egyptian by Victor Hugo (op. cit., 1826), who was the first person to write about this picture and may be supposed to have been well informed. It will be recalled that thousands of Egyptians reinforced the Turks towards the end of the siege.

A long, blue velvet coat embroidered in gold, which Delacroix apparently used as a model for the costume of *Greece*, has been exhibited at the Atelier Delacroix from the Collection Cournault. Delacroix bequeathed some of his exotic studio accessories to Charles Cournault.

Hugo (op. cit., 1826) was impressed most by the pathos of the scene: 'M. Eugène Delacroix vient de livrer [. . .] un nouveau tableau. [. . .] C'est *la Grèce sur les ruines de Missolonghi*. Nous n'aimons pas les allégories; mais celle-là est d'un profond intérêt. Cette femme, qui est la Grèce, est si belle d'attitude et d'expression! Cet Egyptien qui triomphe, ces têtes coupées, ces pierres teintes de sang, tout cet ensemble a quelque chose de si pathétique!' Boutard (op. cit., 1826), on the other hand, was unsympathetic and condescending: 'Le talent inné se laisse apercevoir et lutte d'une manière singulière avec la bizarrerie systématique et le faire désordonné de l'artiste, dans [. . .] *la Grèce encore debout sur les ruines de Missolonghi*.' Whether or not Delacroix had painted a suitably classical image of Greece was still in dispute in the 1850s. Pesquidoux (op. cit., 1857) thought: 'Tout est correct, juste, modéré, tout est contenu et puissant: les qualités du maître apparaissent dans leur application saisissante, et sans le contraste des défauts qu'on lui a si souvent reprochés'. While Arsène Houssaye (op. cit., 1858), claiming to quote a critic in Bordeaux, wrote: 'Je ne m'arrêterai pas à critiquer des détails, comme l'imitation par trop réaliste du sang répandu sur les pavés. Certes, il y a dans cette figure de belles qualités de couleur et de poésie; mais ni dans ce ciel furieux ni dans ce personnage un peu mélo-dramatique, je ne puis reconnaître la Grèce, même expirante; car n'est-elle pas, jusqu'à son dernier soupir, la mère harmonieuse de Pindare, d'Hésiode et d'Homère ?'

The picture was usually called *Greece expiring on the Ruins of Missolonghi* between 1885, when Robaut, unlike Moreau, catalogued it under that title, and 1964, when I pointed out (op. cit.) that this was a misnomer, there being no mention of the word 'expirant' in Delacroix's several written references to the work or in Boutard's notice of 1826. The picture was not listed under that title in any of the known catalogues of exhibitions held during the artist's lifetime, and Delacroix submitted the title '*La Grèce sur les ruines de Missolonghi* (allégorie)' for the exhibition at Bordeaux in 1851 (*Correspondance* III. 84). The misnomer seems nevertheless to have gained currency shortly after the painting was bought by the City of Bordeaux and may have originated with the Museum, which was in any case responsible for disseminating the error through its cata-logues from 1856 on. The point is not merely academic, for Greece and her cause of independence were not to die, in spite of this defeat: three years after the fall of Missolonghi the Turks evacuated the city. Though Delacroix could not have foreseen this, his allegorical figure of Greece, however tragic, is surely not expiring. There is, on the contrary, every reason to believe the painting was conceived specially for the exhibition for Greek relief, as a direct and mute appeal for help, not as an image of a lost cause.

A number of preliminary studies for the theme are contained in the Louvre sketch-book RF9145, on fols. 8ʳ, 11ᵛ and 12ʳ (both repr. *Mémorial*, no. 112), 12ᵛ, 13ʳ and ᵛ, 14ʳ, 15ᵛ and 16ʳ; studies on fols. 7ᵛ, 11ʳ, 21ᵛ, 36ᵛ, 37ʳ, 39ᵛ and 40ʳ may also be connected with the subject. The studies in this sketch-book show that Delacroix first considered a more crowded pyramidal composition, dominated by a less stable and more agitated figure of Greece in despair over children lying at her feet. Among several rough single studies of a

wildly gesticulating Greece is to be found a full-page rapid pencil drawing (fol. 15ᵛ) which fixes the essentials of her final, restrained pose, but endows her with a heavy, square torso and head, which contrast with the subtly tapered shoulders and face of the finished figure and recall the more massive proportions of the early *Virgin of the Sacred Heart* (J153).

Further studies for this painting were included in lot 312 of Delacroix's posthumous sale (R1526. No repr.), but none of certain authenticity has to my knowledge come to light. I reserve judgement on two sheets that have been claimed to derive from this source: one was in a private collection in Paris in 1964 (repr. Cat. Exh. Bremen 1964, p. 96), and the other was with Arthur Kauffmann in London in the same year, having been acquired from Claude Aubry.

A highly finished pencil drawing of a Greek or Turkish soldier holding a musket, signed and dated 1826, has been thought to be a study for the 'Turk' standing in the background. Although the pose is almost identical and there is obviously a close connection between the two figures, it is unlikely that this self-sufficient, signed drawing of a white soldier is a study for the black warrior in a completely different costume in the painting (R1528. Louvre, RF9217. Repr. *Mémorial*, no. 113, where its identification as a Turk is questioned).

---

[1] Though it has often been said that the *Greece* was exhibited in London in 1828 and well received by the English, I have been unable to find certain proof of either statement. Delacroix recalled in a letter dated 31 December 1858: 'Deux ou trois ans après mon voyage en Angleterre [1825], j'y envoyai plusieurs tableaux, entre autres *la Grèce sur les ruines de Missolonghi*' (*Correspondance* IV. 59); and it has been deduced from this slim evidence that the picture was shown with the *Marino Faliero* (J112), at the British Gallery in March 1828. But unlike J112 it is neither listed in the catalogue of the British Institution's exhibition held there at that time, nor mentioned in notices of the show in the London papers. It may well have been included in the exhibition of British and French pictures that opened at Hobday's Gallery on 3 June 1828 (see advertisement in *Morning Post* on that date), but it has proved impossible to trace a copy of the catalogue of that exhibition, and the picture is not mentioned in notices contained in the London daily and weekly papers in the month of June.

Historical and Literary Subjects

99 THE DEATH OF DRUSUS, SON OF GERMANICUS
Pl. 86

Paper laid down on canvas, dimensions unknown. E.D.[1]
Probably R1462 (No repr.)
Probably 1821
Whereabouts unknown

Provenance: Delacroix's posthumous sale, Feb. 1864, probably part of lot 150 ('Trois compositions datant de la

jeunesse du maître', without dimensions), to ?, 80 fr. (Burty Ann ED); with Hector Brame, *c.* 1952.

Exhibitions: None.

Literature: Sérullaz *Dessins* 1952 (on *Addenda* sheet, under pl. II no. 3); L. Johnson, 'The Early Drawings of Delacroix', *Burl Mag*, XCVIII (1956), p. 24; L. Johnson, 'The Delacroix Centenary in France—I', *Burl Mag*, CV (1963), p. 301.

Sérullaz (op. cit., pl. II. 3, pp. 14 f.) published a more

complete, pencil study for this composition, showing all the figures full-length, from a Louvre sketch-book (RF9146, fol. 33ʳ) and suggested plausibly that the subject was that noted by the artist in another Louvre sketch-book as 'Drusus fils de Germanicus mourant de faim enfermé dans son palais' (RF9151, fol. 43ʳ); on the *Addenda* sheet to this publication, the author announced, referring to this oil sketch: 'La peinture représentant la Mort de Drusus, a été récemment retrouvée dans une collection particulière.' He dated the drawing *c*. 1817–18, and it is certainly in a sketch-book that was used primarily in that period. However, in reproducing a less advanced composition drawing for the same subject and contained in the same sketch-book as the note of the subject (RF9151, fol. 40ᵛ; repr. L. Johnson, op. cit. (1956), fig. 34), I pointed out (op. cit., 1956) that the drawing is on a sheet opposite a preliminary study for the *Barque de Dante* (J100), a painting shown at the Salon of 1822; the note is also on a page containing family accounts datable to the summer of 1821. I concluded that this painted sketch was therefore probably executed in the autumn or winter of 1821 and, both theme and general conception being of a conventionally Poussinesque, neo-classical character, that Delacroix may have considered it as a subject to be painted for the Salon of 1822, instead of the more daring and original *Barque de Dante*.[2] My publication of the drawing and my dating arguments pass unnoticed in *Mémorial*, where the drawing is catalogued under no. 2. A study for the figure of Drusus only, mentioned but not reproduced by Sérullaz (op. cit., pp. 14 f.), is to be found on fol. 32ᵛ of the Louvre sketch-book RF9146.

Drusus Julius Caesar (A.D. 7–33), as the second of the surviving sons of Germanicus and Agrippina, was considered, following the deaths of his father in 19 and of Drusus, son of Tiberius, as a likely successor to Tiberius after his elder brother Nero. He was arrested in 30 and died, imprisoned in the palace, in 33.

The theme and design fit snugly into the French classical tradition. Though the precise subject is unusual, this type of death-bed scene abounded in French neo-classical painting, and the subject of the death of Drusus' father Germanicus had been treated in a famous painting by Poussin (Palazzo Barberini, Rome), copied from an engraving after the Poussin by Géricault (Clément, no. 160), and painted on a small scale (32 × 53 cm) by Guérin, the master of both Géricault and Delacroix (Musée Magnin, Dijon).

---

[1] M. Sérullaz, to whom I am indebted for the photograph, recalled that the original canvas was approximately a No. 12 (50 × 61 cm). M. Paul Brame, however, who had handled it, thought it measured approximately 19 × 30 cm. Both agreed in thinking it had the seal of Delacroix's posthumous sale on the back.

[2] I later revised my opinion of the date of the drawing to September or October 1820 ('The Formal Sources of Delacroix's *Barque de Dante*', *Burl Mag*, C (1958), p. 228 n. 5), but on further reflection it seems to me that my first dating was more probably correct.

100 THE BARQUE OF DANTE   Pl. 87

$74\frac{7}{16} \times 96\frac{7}{8}$ in. (1.89 × 2.46 m) Relined
Signed and dated, on the bow of the boat: *Eug.
    Delacroix/1822*
Moreau pp. 167, 188, 206. R 49
Musée du Louvre

Provenance: Acquired by the State at the Salon of 1822 for the Musée du Luxembourg (opened in 1818 for the display of works by living artists), 2,000 fr. (decision of 16 July 1822: archives du Louvre DDc 4), paid in two instalments, 29 October 1822 and 1 July 1823, according to unpublished notes by Philippe Burty (cf. Moreau-Nélaton I. 47 n. 1); transferred to the Louvre (Inv. 3820), November 1874.

Exhibitions: Salon 1822, no 309 ('Dante et Virgile conduits par Phlégias, traversent le lac qui entoure les murailles de la ville infernale de Dité.

Des coupables s'attachent à la barque, ou s'efforcent d'y entrer. Dante reconnait parmi eux des Florentins.'); *Universelle*, Paris 1855, no. 2914; *Bd Italiens*, Paris 1864, no. 39; Louvre 1930, no. 8, repr. *Album* p. 11; Petit Palais, Paris 1936, no. 228, repr. *Album* pl. 53; Atelier Delacroix, Paris 1945, no. 1; Petit Palais, Paris 1946, no. 152; Atelier Delacroix, Paris 1947, no. 1; id., Paris 1952, no. 14; Louvre 1963, no. 26, *M* no. 27, 2 repr.; Bremen 1964, no. 3, repr.; Edinburgh–London 1964, no. 5, repr.; Atelier Delacroix, Paris 1967, no. 2; Moscow 1969, no. 27, repr.

Literature: Anon., 'Chuchotements au Salon de Peinture', *Le Miroir*, 1 May 1822, p. 3; A. T . . . rs [A. Thiers], review of Salon of 1822, *Le Constitutionnel*, 11 May 1822 (reprinted with some changes in *Salon de mil huit cent vingt-deux, ou collection des articles insérés au Constitutionnel sur l'Exposition de cette année* (Maradan, Paris, 1822, pp. 56–8); E. J. D. [Delécluze], review of Salon of 1822, *Le Moniteur universel*, 18 May 1822; C. P. Landon, *Annales du Musée de l'Ecole moderne des Beaux-Arts. Salon de 1822* (Imp. royale, Paris, 1822), pp. 87 f., repr. (Réveil line engraving) pl. 55; A. de Loève Veimars, 'Salon de 1822', *Album*, 10 June 1822, pp. 262 f.; P. A. [Coupin], 'Exposition des tableaux en 1822', *Revue encyclopédique*, XVI (Oct. 1822), p. 19; M., *Revue critique des productions exposées au Salon de 1824* (Dentu et Blosse, Paris, 1825), p. 338; anon., review of Salon of 1831, *La Quotidienne*, 15 May 1831; *Biographie . . . des Contemporains* (Levrault, Paris, 1834), III, p. 39; T. Thoré, 'Artistes contemporains. M. Eugène Delacroix', *Le Siècle*, 24 Feb. 1837; C. Baudelaire, *Salon de 1846* (M. Lévy, Paris 1846) and 'Exposition universelle', *Le Pays*, 3 June 1855, both reprinted in *Curiosités esthétiques*, 1868 (*Œuvres*, Pléiade ed. Paris 1932, II, pp. 73, 74, 78, and 158, 159); T. Gautier, 'Exposition universelle de 1855', *Le Moniteur universel*, 19 July 1855; M. du Camp, *Les Beaux-Arts à l'Exposition universelle de 1855* (Librairie nouvelle, Paris, 1855), p. 94; E. and J. de Goncourt, *La Peinture à*

11. *The Barque of Dante* (100), detail

l'Exposition de 1855 (E. Dentu, Paris, 1855), p. 44; E. J. Delécluze, *Les Beaux-Arts dans les deux mondes en 1855* (Charpentier, Paris, 1856), pp. 199, 214 (for a fuller list of reviews of the Exposition universelle of 1855 not considered worth mentioning here, see Tourneux pp. 95-8); T. Silvestre, *Histoire des artistes vivants* (Blanchard, Paris, n.d. [1855], p. 51; T. Silvestre, *Les Artistes français, 1855* (1926 ed., I, p. 28); F. Villot, *Notice des peintures, sculptures et dessins de l'école moderne de France exposés dans les Galeries du Musée impérial du Luxembourg* (Mourgues frères, Paris, 1858), p. 10, no. 39; L. Clément de Ris, *Critiques d'art et de littérature* (Didier, Paris, 1862. Chapter on Delacroix dated April 1857), pp. 382-4; C. Blanc, 'Eugène Delacroix', *GBA*, XVI (1864), pp. 8-12, repr. (Pisan engraving) p. 9 (reprinted in *Les Artistes de mon temps*, 1876, pp. 27-33, repr. (same engraving) p. 29); A. Cantaloube, *Eugène Delacroix, l'homme et l'artiste* (Dentu, Paris, 1864), pp. 18-20; L. Chardin, 'Retour à Eugène Delacroix', *L'Artiste*, 7th ser. II (1864), p. 147; E. Chesneau, *L'Art et les artistes modernes* (Didier, Paris, 1864), pp. 342, 345 f.; Silvestre, *Documents nouveaux* (1864), p. 22; [F. Villot], Introduction to catalogue of his sale (M.F.V.), 11 February 1865, p. v; Piron, pp. 9, 50 f., 57, 62, 105; C. Blanc, 'Grammaire des arts du dessin', *GBA*, XX (1866), p. 382 (reprinted in *Grammaire des arts du dessin* (Renouard, Paris, 1870), p. 609); E. de Mirecourt [pseudonym of C. J. B. Jacquot], *Eugène Delacroix* (Lib. des Contemporains, Paris, 1870 (4th ed.; 1st ed., 1856)), pp. 23-32; P. Andrieu, in A. Bruyas *et al.*, *Musée de Montpellier. La Galerie Bruyas* (Quantin, Paris, 1876), pp. 361-3 (abridged reprint of Andrieu's essay in R. Piot, *Les Palettes de Delacroix* (Lib. de France, Paris, 1931), pp. 71 f.); B. de Tauzia, *Notice supplémentaire des tableaux exposés dans les galeries du Musée national du Louvre* (Paris, 1878), no. 753; J. Tripier Lefranc, *Histoire de la vie et de la mort du Baron Gros* (chez J. Martin, Paris, 1880), pp. 373-5; G. Lafenestre and E. Richtenberger, *Le Musée national du Louvre* (Anc. Maison Quantin, Paris, n.d. [1893], p. 267, no. 207; Boyer d'Agen, 'Un supplément au *Journal* d'Eugène Delacroix', *Revue des Revues*, XV, no. 24 (15 Dec. 1895), pp. 499 ff.; L. Rosenthal, *La Peinture romantique* (A. Fontemoing, Paris, n.d. [1901]), pp. 91-3; Moreau-Nélaton I. 42-7, repr. fig. 15; Meier-Graefe 1922, pp. 15, 18, 19, 20 and n., 21, 22, 24, 29, repr. p. 95; O. Redon, *A soi-même* (Paris, 1922), p. 165; Brière 1924, p. 77, no. 207, repr. pl. LIV; I. de Vasconcellos, *L'inspiration dantesque dans l'art romantique français* (Picart, Paris, 1925), pp. 35-46, repr. fig. 3; Escholier I. 58-68, 60 n. 1, repr. opp. p. 66; Hourticq 1930, pls. 3, 4 (detail, woman right foreground), 5 (detail, horizontal figure left foreground); [Mme L. Chamson], 'Quatre lettres d'Eugène Delacroix au comte de Nieuwerkerke (1859-1861)', *BSHAF*, 1934, pp. 169-72; Cassou 1947, pl. 3, followed by full-page details: head of Virgil; occupants of boat (across two pages), woman right foreground; head and shoulders of

horizontal figure, left foreground; whole of same figure (across two pages); W. Friedlaender, *David to Delacroix* (Harvard University Press, Cambridge, Mass., 1952), pp. 110 f., repr. fig. 67; Sérullaz *Dessins* 1952, pp. 24-30 (studies); *Lettres intimes*, p. 140 n. 1; L. Johnson, 'The Formal Sources of Delacroix's *Barque de Dante*', *Burl Mag*, C (1958), pp. 228-32, repr. fig. 5; Sterling-Adhémar, no. 660, pl. 230; Johnson 1963, pp. 17-19, repr. pl. 4, colour detail of water drops on woman's torso, pl. 5; Huyghe, pp. 111 f., 176, 464 f., repr. fig. 86, colour pl. II; Maltese, pp. 22-4, 26 f., 134, repr. in colour pl. III; T. Prideaux *et al.*, *The World of Delacroix* (Time Inc., New York, 1966), repr. in colour pp. 50-1, colour detail of water drops on woman's torso, p. 51; Trapp, pp. 18-28, 18 n. 32, 26 n. 41 and 45, repr. in colour pl. I; S. Lichtenstein, 'Cézanne's Copies and Variants after Delacroix', *Apollo*, CI (1975), p. 117, repr. p. 116, fig. 2.

Prints: Line engraving by Réveil, 1822; etching by Henriet, published in *L'Artiste*, N.S. IV, 6th livraison (13 June 1858), opp. p. 96 (Moreau, p. 89, no. 10); etching by Bouruet (ibid. 89, no. 11); lithograph by C. Nanteuil, 1849 (ibid. 132, no. 65); wood engraving by Pisan after Masson, first published *L'Illustration*, 23 June (not January) 1855 (for other states and other places of publication, see Moreau, p. 138, no. 5); wood engraving after Nanteuil (ibid. 139, no. 6); wood engraving by Blaupain after J. Laurens, 1867 (ibid. 139, no. 7).

Copies: 1. BY KNOWN ARTISTS

    (a) Pierre Andrieu (his sale, 6 May 1892, lot 142: 'La Barque du Dante [d'après Eugène Delacroix]', without dimensions or further description). Possibly *3a* below.

    (b) Courbet, 1840s (cf. G. Riat, *Gustave Courbet* (Floury, Paris, 1906), p. 28).

    (c) Manet, canvas, 38 × 46 cm, 1850s. Musée des Beaux-Arts, Lyon (A. Tabarant, *Manet et ses œuvres* (Gallimard, Paris, 1947), p. 19, p. 533, no. 6, repr. p. 602. Larger repr. *Catalogue du Musée de Lyon*, 1956, pl. LIII. 4, and A. Boime, *The Academy and French Painting in the Nineteenth Century* (Phaidon, London, 1971), fig. 111).

    (d) Manet, canvas, 33 × 41 cm. Metropolitan Museum, New York (Tabarant, op. cit., p. 19, p. 533, no. 7; repr. Boime, op. cit., fig. 112).

    (e) Pringal (sculptor), c. 1866 (cf. *Barque de Dante* file, Service de documentation, Louvre).

    (f) Adolphe Felix Cals (1810-80), oils on cardboard, 11.5 × 16.5 cm (sale G. Viau, 24 Feb. 1943, lot 45).

    (g) Cézanne, canvas, 25 × 33 cm, 1870/3. Collection Lady Clark (Venturi, no. 125, repr.; repr. also in

S. Lichtenstein, op. cit. 1975 (under *Literature* above), p. 116, fig. 1).

(*h*) Paul Rivemale, canvas, 1.80 × 2.38 m. Signed and dated 1885. Musée Fabre, Montpellier.

2. BY UNIDENTIFIED ARTISTS AND RECORDED IN THE NINETEENTH CENTURY

(See also J(R)36)

(*a*) Sale Ary Scheffer, 15 March 1859, lot 13 ('Delacroix (d'après Eugène). Virgile et le Dante dans la barque', canvas, 31 × 39 cm).

(*b*) Canvas, 34.4 × 39.5 cm, Art Institute of Chicago. Provenance: Samuel Colman; John Taylor Johnston; his sale, New York, 19 Dec. 1876; Mrs. Potter Palmer, Paris. Exhibitions: Chicago 1930, no. 1; Louvre 1930, provisional cat. no. 9 (excluded from final version). Repr. Art Institute of Chicago Bulletin, XV (1921). For long incorrectly identified as R50 (J(R)36).

(*c*) Catalogue Exhibition *EBA*, Paris 1885, no. 118 ('Le Dante et Virgile dans la barque. Toile de 10 [46 × 55 cm]', lent by M. Hulot.) Removed between first and second editions of the catalogue: entry marked 'supprimer' by Robaut in first edition (*Bib AA*, MS. 298). Cat. Exh. Durand-Ruel, Paris 1878, no. 162 ('La Barque du Dante — Esquisse', lent by same owner). Withdrawn (cf. MS. notes in *BN Estampes* annotated catalogue: 'copie', 'non exposée').

(*d*) Head only of figure in left foreground, described in R Ann (margin to R49–50) as 'Une horrible copie de la tête du premier personnage de gauche tout nu, les deux bras relevés et les mains se rejoignant', left with Robaut in 1894 for several years by its owner, 'M^r B d'A'.

3. BY UNIDENTIFIED ARTISTS AND OF UNCERTAIN PROVENANCE

(*a*) Canvas, 33 × 41 cm*, Bührle Foundation, Zurich. Provenance: French private collection; Museum der Stadt, Ulm; purchased by Emil Bührle from a Swiss dealer, 1953. Repr. *Kunsthaus Zürich, Sammlung Emil G. Bührle . . .* (Zurich, 1958), pl. 33, as a study for the *Barque de Dante*. Possibly 1*a* above.

(*b*) Canvas, 24.1 × 30.5 cm. City Art Museum of St. Louis, purchased from the Marie Sterner Gallery, New York, 1934. Repr. *Bulletin of the City Art Museum of St Louis*, XIX (1934), p. 33, as a study for the *Barque de Dante*.

(*c*) Canvas, 53 × 72 cm. M. Moras le Puy bought it at Bourges in 1939 from a dealer who said he had bought it from the estate of the Marquis de Saint Venon, former curator of the Musée de Nevers.

Photographs in *Barque de Dante* file, Service de documentation, Louvre. Known to me only in reproduction.

(*d*) Sale G. Viau, 24 Feb. 1943, lot 94 ('La barque du Dante (d'après Delacroix)', canvas, 32 × 40 cm).

(*e*) Mixed sale, Christie's, London 29 Nov. 1946, lot 106 ('Dante and Virgil crossing the Styx', support not listed, 38.1 × 48.3 cm).

(*f*) Paper laid down on canvas, 35.4 × 25.3 cm. With R. M. Light, Boston, Mass., 1962.

(*g*) Horizontal figure in the water, left foreground, canvas, 64 × 78 cm, Kunstmuseum der Rumänischen Volksrepublik (from Collection Peles-Schlosser). Repr. in colour *Meister der Universellen Malerei in den Museen Rumäniens*, preface by G. Oprescu (Bucharest, 1960).

(*h*) The same, dimensions unknown, apparently false signature bottom left, formerly Savile Gallery, London. Repr. *International Studio*, May 1930, p. 27.

(*i*) The same, canvas, 24 × 32 cm (sale M.X. 26 June 1937, lot 5 (repr.), as by Delacroix: 'Le damné du Styx. Etude pour la barque de Dante et Virgile. Cadre d'époque', 9,200 fr.) Appears from reproduction to be possibly by Andrieu, but not by Delacroix. It is perhaps an early copy of J(L)93.

(*j*) The same, pen and ink on paper, 27.5 × 48.5 cm. False(?) E.D. National Museum of Western Art, Tokyo. Listed as a study by Delacroix for the Salon painting in their 1961 catalogue, no. P-91, repr.; but appears from photogaphs to be by Pierre Andrieu. Photo Archives photographiques BAP 14321.

Delacroix's first Salon painting, the *Barque de Dante* (as it is most generally known) immediately established his reputation as a major talent. As early as 26 July 1821, Delacroix had expressed in a letter to his sister a desire to paint a picture for the Salon of 1822 (*Correspondance* V. 91), but had evidently not decided on the subject, as he wrote to Soulier on 15 September, saying: 'Je me propose de faire pour le Salon prochain un tableau dont je prendrai le sujet dans les guerres récentes des Turcs et des Grecs' (ibid. I. 132). In addition to a subject from contemporary history, he may also, more conventionally, have considered a classical subject, the *Death of Drusus*, as a way of making his mark at the Salon (see J99). By 16 January 1822, he had apparently begun work on the *Barque de Dante*, returning to a theme that had occupied him during a spell of fever when he was staying with his sister at the Forest of Boixe in Charente in the autumn of 1820; for on that date he told his sister: 'J'ai des frais pour le tableau que je fais' (ibid. v. 104), and on 11 March 1822, in reply to her inquiry about the subject: 'Le sujet de mon tableau [. . .] est tiré du Dante. C'est celui dont je fis le dessin pendant ma fièvre à la Forêt (ibid. v. 109). The canvas was finished by 15 April (perhaps as early as the beginning of the month if it was started in mid-January), and Delacroix announced to Soulier: '[. . .] je sors d'un travail de chien qui me prend tous mes instants depuis deux mois et demi. J'ai fait dans cet espace de temps un tableau assez considérable qui va figurer au Salon. Je tenais beaucoup à m'y voir cette année, et c'est un coup de fortune qui je tente' (ibid. 1. 140).

The Salon opened on 24 April. Delacroix recounts that he had shown the picture to his master, Guérin, before submitting it to the Salon, but 'il n'en fit guère que des critiques, et [. . .] je ne pus jamais tirer de lui son assentiment à mon désir de l'exposer' (quoted in Piron, pp. 50 f.). According to the same account, however, it attracted the attention of other professors from the Ecole des Beaux-Arts at the Salon, particularly of Gros, who, in a compliment that has since become famous, characterized it as *'du Rubens châtié'*, and seemed inclined to take Delacroix under his wing in order to groom him for the Prix de Rome, an overture which the younger artist rejected because he felt he had now set out on an independent path (ibid. 51 f.). Though the picture is relatively academic, in the sense that it gives the impression of a group of separately studied figures, nude and draped, displayed in a wide variety of poses designed to impress an academically biased jury, the freedom and boldness of handling were immediately recognized by the more reactionary critics as a threat to the classical standards of the French school. Delécluze (op. cit., 1822) labelled it 'une vraie *tartouillade*', while conceding however that it contained figures 'dont les contours et la couleur sont pleins d'énergie'; and Landon (op. cit., 1822) lamented: 'Vu de près, la touche en est si hachée, si incohérente, quoiqu'exempte de timidité, qu'on ne saurait se persuader qu'au point où le talent d'exécution est parvenu dans notre école.'

The most favourable criticism, traditionally thought to reflect the opinion of Gérard, came from Adolphe Thiers (op. cit., *Constitutionnel*, 1822), then a provincial lawyer newly arrived in Paris:

Dans ce sujet, si voisin de l'exagération, on trouve cependant une sévérité de goût, une convenance locale en quelque sorte, qui relève le dessin, auquel des juges sévères, mais peu avisés ici, pourraient reprocher de manquer de noblesse. Le pinceau est large et ferme, la couleur simple et vigoureuse quoique un peu crue.

L'auteur a, outre cette imagination poétique, qui est commune au peintre comme à l'écrivain, cette imagination de l'art, qu'on pourrait en quelque sorte appeler l'imagination du dessin, et qui est tout autre que la précédente. Il jette ses figures, les groupe, les plie à volonté avec la hardiesse de Michel-Ange et la fécondité de Rubens. Je ne sais quel souvenir des grands artistes me saisit à

l'aspect de ce tableau; j'y retrouve cette puissance sauvage, ardente mais naturelle, qui cède sans effort à son propre entraînement.

[. . .] Je ne crois pas m'y tromper, M. de Lacroix a reçu le génie.

If Théophile Silvestre was perhaps unduly severe in dismissing this review as 'une paraphrase prudhommesque de l'opinion du baron Gérard' (in *Galerie Bruyas*, 1876, p. 408), there is no doubt that Thiers's prescience has been much overrated, and it may be pointed out in this connection that he deleted the final sentence quoted above from the reprint published later in 1822. The anonymous and forgotten critic of *Le Miroir* (op. cit., 1822) had shown himself to be at least as perceptive, earlier, in writing: 'je parie [. . .] que si jamais il devient coloriste, [M. Delacroix] prendra un rang distingué dans l'école.'

In a letter of 31 May 1822, Count de Forbin showed interest in purchasing the picture for the State and asked the price. Delacroix replied that he would like to have 2,400 fr., but left it up to the Count to make a fair offer (*Correspondance* 1. 143), and in the event received 2,000 fr. He happily learnt from Guillemardet at the beginning of September, while on holiday in the country, that his picture was hanging in the Luxembourg (*Lettres intimes*, p. 140).

It was not until 1876, with the publication of the essay by Delacroix's pupil, Pierre Andrieu, in the *Galerie Bruyas*, that discussion of the formal sources of the *Barque de Dante* moved beyond such generalities as 'Rubens châtié' and 'la hardiesse de Michel-Ange et la fécondité de Rubens'. Andrieu (op. cit., p. 363) remarked that the woman clinging to the boat on the right 'rappelle sensiblement la *Nuit* de Michel-Ange', and reported Delacroix as saying (p. 362): 'Suisse a posé seul pour tous les personnages du tableau, sauf toutefois pour le *Caron* [read *Phlégias*]. Ce *Caron*, je l'ai fait d'après le torse antique.' In 1958 (op. cit.), I supported Andrieu's account by illustrating the similarity between Delacroix's boatman and the torse Belvedere (of which there is a study of the back view in a sketch-book containing drawings for the painting, Louvre RF9151, fol. 39ᵛ), and between the woman in the water and Michelangelo's statue of *Night*. I showed in addition, through preparatory drawings, how a single model had apparently posed for several of the principal figures, and proposed further sources, notably a combination of the pose of *God the Father* in Michelangelo's first Creation scene on the Sistine ceiling and of a head in Géricault's *Raft of the Medusa* for the horizontal figure on the left; the arrangement of the drapery folds in Michelangelo's statue of *Rachel* (*Vita contemplativa*) for the Dante; and a figure in Rubens's *Hero and Leander* (Dresden Gallery) for the central figure in the water. Since then, Maltese (p. 134) has pointed to a convincing similarity between the raised arm of the woman in the water and Michelangelo's *Dying Slave* in the Louvre; and I (Cat. Exh. Edinburgh–London 1964, no. 5) have suggested that the damned soul peering over the far side of the boat derives from the figure of Cavalcante in Flaxman's line engraving *The Fiery Sepulchres*, pl. 11 of his illustrations to the *Divine Comedy* of 1807. Delacroix considered it the best head in his painting and recalled in 1853: 'La meilleure tête de mon tableau du *Dante* a été faite avec une rapidité et un entrain extrêmes, pendant que Pietri me lisait un chant du Dante, que je connaissais déjà, mais auquel il prêtait, par l'accent, une énergie qui m'électrisa. Cette tête est celle de l'homme qui est en face, au fond, et qui cherche à grimper sur la barque, ayant passé son bras par dessus le bord' (*Journal* II. 136 f., III. 530 (Addition and Correction to II. 136)).

It is the fusion of these many separate elements, none of which in itself marks a specially original choice (the life model, the Antique, Flaxman, Géricault and, with particular emphasis, Michelangelo) into a painting which, sometimes 'electrified' by inspiration, expresses with fresh energy a vision of damned souls writhing in torment in a lugubrious setting that makes the *Barque de Dante* an early masterpiece of French Romanticism, in spite of its debt to the academic tradition. Delacroix's immediate predecessors, Gros, Girodet, Géricault and Ingres, had all treated subjects from Dante's *Inferno* during the first two decades of the nineteenth century, but always in drawings or small paintings. Delacroix's painting, inspired by canto viii of the *Inferno*, is the first large painting of a Dantesque subject by a major French artist exhibited at a Salon in the nineteenth century, and it forcefully asserts a new faith in the 'poetry of torture' (as Chateaubriand, in the *Génie du christianisme*, had referred to Dante's *Inferno*) and in Michelangelesque and Rubensian energy, as opposed to the strained and brittle late neo-classicism of Guérin.

Though Delacroix characteristically chooses his turbulent water-scene from literature, his debt to Géricault's painting of a contemporary shipwreck, the *Raft of the Medusa*, shown at the Salon of 1819, is so marked that as late as the 1850s many people still attributed the figure stretched out in the left foreground to Géricault (cf. Baudelaire, op. cit., 1855, p. 159 and Clément de Ris, op. cit., 1862, p. 383). It is hard to follow Friedlaender (op. cit., 1952, p. 111) in thinking that the colour of the painting 'represents a decisive step away from Géricault's plastic, Caravaggiesque chiaroscuro', since the tonal modelling of this figure, as of others in the picture, with heavily impasted, ochreish lights and black or brown shadows, is virtually indistinguishable from Géricault's colouring in the *Raft of the Medusa*. The only significant colour innovation, in my opinion, is to be found in the drops of water on some of the figures in the foreground, of which Andrieu reports (op. cit., 1876, pp. 361-2): '[Delacroix] se sentit, dit-il, fort embarrassé pour rendre en toute vérité naturelle "les gouttes d'eau qui découlent des figures nues et renversées." Ces gouttes d'eau le firent chercher. Le souvenir des Sirènes de

Rubens, dans le "Débarquement de Marie des Médicis à Marseille", et l'étude des dégradations de l'arc-en-ciel, cette palette de la création, lui firent trouver l'effet vivant de ces gouttes d'eau. Ce fut là son point de départ.' These drops are constructed with unfused dabs of pigment: white for the highlights, then green and yellow juxtaposed, and strong red cast shadows. In some respects they are very similar to the drops on the nereids in the Rubens and it is easy to accept the truth of Andrieu's account, but, as I have pointed out (op. cit., 1963), the colours are brighter than Rubens's and Delacroix extends their range. It is therefore possible that Andrieu was right in saying that he also found inspiration in the rainbow. The importance of these drops does not lie in any use of complementary contrasts (as Trapp (p. 23 and n.) incomprehensibly takes me to believe), but in their being an early example of a preoccupation which was to become central to Delacroix's later colour technique: the search for a rational analysis and division of form into its colour components, instead of following accepted conventions such as 'Caravaggiesque chiaroscuro' in modelling form. Nor is it possible to accept Trapp's suggestion (p. 24) that the drops may be 'impure evidence' added or retouched in the 1850s, since the colour modelling appears far too immature and obtrusive to allow that Delacroix added or materially altered it in his late years; and he would surely not have permitted his assistant to do so in a work that had been in the most important public collection of modern art in Paris since 1822.

If the drops of water provide an early example of the rational analysis of form into coloured components, Delacroix's affective or emotive use of colour, equally important for his influence on later colourists, was noted as early as 1822 by Veimars (op. cit.), who wrote of the contrast between the 'couleur méditative' of Dante's head and 'la couleur livide, l'exécution heurtée des damnés' which 'laissent dans l'âme je ne sais quelle impression funeste'. Charles Blanc, an author of more influence in forming the attitudes of later generations of painters towards Delacroix, also emphasized this aspect of the Romantic master's colour and, drawing a musical analogy, thought he saw the seeds of it in the *Barque de Dante* (op. cit., 1866, p. 382): 'Dans un tableau sinistre, le rôle du blanc resserré est celui que joue en plein orchestre un coup de tam-tam. Ainsi la touche de linge blanc qu'on aperçoit sur le manteau de Virgile dans la *Barque du Dante* [. . .] est un réveil terrible au milieu du sombre; elle brille comme un éclair qui sillonne la tempête.'

By 1859, the surface of the painting had suffered so badly from blisters ('gerçures') that Delacroix, in a letter to Count de Nieuwerkerke dated 13 December 1859, expressed his concern that the picture would be entirely lost if some radical repair such as a relining or even a transfer were not undertaken without delay (*Correspondance* IV. 133 f.). On 15 February 1860, he again wrote to the Count stressing that he wished to retouch the painting himself, 'et en parlant de retouches je n'ai en vue que la réparation des gerçures malheureusement trop nombreuses qui seront restées après le rentoilage' (ibid. 151). Granted this privilege, he had the painting taken to his studio and thought the restoration complete by about the middle of the summer of 1860, when fresh blisters appeared; others developed towards the end of the year, but Delacroix had finished the retouching by 8 February 1861 and the canvas was ready to be collected (letters to the same, 20 January and 8 February 1861, ibid. 232 f., 239 f.). Andrieu (op. cit., 1876, p. 363) gives the following account of the condition and restoration: '*Dante et Virgile*, fort détérioré en 1857 [*sic*], était tout craquelures; une couture traversait les figures d'en bas, notamment la femme [. . .] [The seam is still visible]. C'était une restauration délicate et difficile à faire. Soit que M. Delacroix fut trop absorbé pour le moment, soit qu'il ne voulût pas se donner le souci de réparer les dégâts de son tableau, il me confia le soin de le faire à sa place.' Given Delacroix's insistence and extreme concern, seen in the letters to Nieuwerkerke, that he be allowed personally to undertake the restoration, it may be wondered how reliable is Andrieu's claim to have been entrusted with it. In the same essay, Andrieu states that the use of 'massicot', a lead oxide, is 'assez sensible' in the *Barque de Dante*, especially in the horizontal figure in the left foreground.

In 1819, Delacroix was already translating passages from the *Inferno* and drawing sketches inspired by it: the Louvre sketch-book RF23356 contains studies illustrating the episode in canto i where Dante is frightened by a lion and wolf standing side by side in his path (fols. 18ᵛ and 19ʳ, repr. Sérullaz *Dessins* 1952, pl. XVI), and, accompanied by the artist's own translation of the text, the scene from canto iii where Charon loads his boat with the damned. The latter choice is closer to Michelangelo, in both theme (bottom right of *Last Judgement*) and style (e.g. a figure inspired by the *Dying Slave*), as well as to the Salon painting of 1822 (fols. 34ᵛ and 35ʳ, text and studies repr. ibid., pl. XV). I have suggested (op. cit., 1958, p. 228 n. 5 and fig. 6) that an advanced composition drawing in wash for the subject chosen for the Salon, now in the National Gallery of Canada, was probably the drawing referred to as having been done in the Forest of Boixe in the autumn of 1820, in Delacroix's letter to his sister of March 1822 cited above (see also Cat. Exh. Toronto–Ottawa 1962–3, no. 26, repr.). There the position of the three figures in the boat is reversed, the Virgil is less calm than in the painting, and the figures in the water are not spread across the foreground. The authenticity of the drawing has not been universally accepted, but, though certain crudities of execution cannot be denied, these seem to me consistent with the Dante studies in the sketch-book RF23356 and with the drawing's having been done in adverse conditions in a remote region of

France. Moreover, two sheets of undisputed studies show Dante and Virgil in the same position and pose, and a third has the bow of the boat, with Phlegyas standing on it, facing towards the left (Louvre, RF9151, fols. 41ʳ and ᵛ (repr. L. Johnson, 'The Early Drawings of Delacroix', *Burl Mag*, XCVIII (1956), figs. 32 and 31), 42ʳ). No drawing of a comparable stage of development for the whole composition has, to my knowledge, come to light, and the many preliminary studies for the final picture may perhaps best be classified here according to individual figures or setting (no pretence is made to account for all forty of the sheets of drawings that passed under lot 305 in Delacroix's posthumous sale as studies for the *Barque de Dante*):

Figure biting stern
1. Pen and ink, 20 × 32.5 cm, E.D., Louvre, RF9186 (repr. Trapp, fig. 19).
2. Pencil, 28.5 × 20.5 cm, E.D., Louvre, RF9182.
3. Pen and ink, 26.7 × 34.3 cm, E.D., Metropolitan Museum, New York (repr. *Mémorial*, no. 31).

Nude left foreground (see also study in oils J(L)93)
1. Pencil, 44.5 × 29.5 cm, E.D., Louvre, RF9173.
2. Conté crayon heightened with white chalk, squared, 23.7 × 28.5 cm, E.D., Louvre, RF9174 (repr. *Mémorial*, no. 34). Verso: two sketches in white chalk of a right hand gripping, apparently for the figure on the far side of the boat.
3. Head only, pierre noire, 17 × 19.3 cm, E.D., Louvre, RF9164 (repr. ibid., no. 32).

Nude centre foreground
1. Conté crayon, 21 × 22.7 cm, E.D., Louvre, RF9180.
2. Conté crayon heightened with white chalk, 26 × 36.9 cm, E.D., Louvre, RF9166 (repr. *Mémorial*, no. 33). Verso: Dante and Virgil in the barque conducted by Phlegyas, nude study of Phlegyas from the back.
3. Conté crayon heightened with white chalk, squared, 20.2 × 27 cm, E.D., Louvre, RF9176 (repr. L. Johnson, op. cit., 1958, fig. 10).

Nude right foreground
1. With centre nude, Conté crayon and black lead, 27.7 × 40 cm, E.D., Louvre, RF9188 (repr. *Mémorial*, no. 38; better detail repr. Sérullaz *Dessins* 1952, pl. XIX.28).
2. With centre nude, Conté crayon heightened with white chalk, 26.6 × 40.7 cm, E.D., Louvre, RF9191 (repr. *Mémorial*, no. 37; better repr. Sérullaz *Dessins* 1952, pl. XIX.29).
3. Studies for upraised left arm, Conté crayon, 26.5 × 35.7 cm, E.D., Louvre, RF9187 (repr. L. Johnson, op. cit., 1958, fig. 13).

Group right foreground and figure on far side of the boat (for latter, see also verso of *Nude left foreground*, no. 2)
1. Conté crayon, 21.1 × 30 cm, E.D., Louvre, RF9181 (repr. ibid., fig. 11).

Dante

1. Nude, for final pose, Conté crayon, 30 × 44 cm, E.D., Louvre, RF9167 (repr. ibid., fig. 9).
2. Nude, same pose, same model, pencil, 17 × 24.3 cm, E.D., Louvre, RF9184.
3. Nude and draped, for final pose, E.D., Coll. Daragnès (1926) (repr. Escholier I. 67).
4. Bust, head facing left (Arosa sale 27 Feb. 1884, lot 140 ('En buste, la tête de profil, tournée vers la gauche. Dessin à l'estompe, rehaussé de blanc, finement exécuté', 22 × 19 cm), to M. G. Pereire. Listed by Robaut under R1478, and in R Ann (margin to R49).
5. Study of head (with head of Virgil), charcoal, Conté crayon, some touches of brown ink, 20.4 × 30.7 cm, E.D., R1476, Louvre, RF9193 (repr. *Mémorial*, no. 30; better repr. Sérullaz *Dessins* 1952, pl. XVII.24).
6. Dante frightened, Virgil faintly indicated beside him, black lead, quarto size, owned by A. Bouvenne *c.* 1885, R Ann 48*ter* (repr. Tracings I).

Virgil

1. Studies for the figure and drapery (Arosa sale 27 Feb. 1884, lot 129 ('Il est debout, drapé dans un ample manteau. Sur la gauche, une étude de draperie pour le même personnage. A la sépia, rehaussé de blanc, sur papier gris', 27 × 18 cm). R Ann 48*bis*. Repr. Robaut Tracings I and stated to be part of lot 305 in Delacroix's posthumous sale.

Phlegyas

1. Six nude studies, full-length, Conté crayon, 30 × 43.5 cm, E.D., Louvre, RF9179.
2. Single nude study, full-length, pencil, E.D., Louvre, RF9189. Verso: faint composition study in white chalk close to final design, showing Dante and Virgil in the boat and some figures in the water.
3. Single nude study, full-length, Conté crayon heightened with white chalk, 26 × 21.9 cm, E.D., Louvre, RF9190 (repr. *Mémorial*, no. 35; also L. Johnson, op. cit., 1958, fig. 12).

The background

1. Two studies, grey wash, 24.3 × 43.5 cm, E.D., Louvre, RF9177 (repr. *Mémorial*, no. 40).
2. Four studies, grey wash, 32 × 45.7 cm, E.D., Louvre, RF9178.
3. Single study, water-colour, 14 × 19 cm, E.D., Louvre, RF9163 (repr. *Mémorial*, no. 41; in colour, Sérullaz *Dessins* 1952, pl. XXII].

Five pen and ink drawings on tracing paper in the Louvre, though all bearing the stamp of Delacroix's posthumous sale, do not appear to be from his hand:

1. Dante, as in the composition study in the National Gallery of Canada, and apparently traced from it, 17.5 × 12.5 cm, RF9172.

2. Phlegyas, posed as in Louvre sketch-book RF9151, fol. 42ʳ, 10.1 × 6.1 cm, RF9168.
3. Phlegyas, 18 × 8.7 cm, RF9171 (repr. Huyghe, fig. 87).
4. Nude centre foreground, 9.7 × 19 cm, RF9175 (repr. Trapp, fig. 17).
5. Figure on far side of boat, 10 × 9 cm, RF 9170.

101 THE NATCHEZ   Pl. 88

$35\frac{1}{2} \times 46\frac{1}{16}$ in. (0.902 × 1.17 m)* Relined
Signed lower right: *Eug. Delacroix*
Moreau pp. 160, 175, 252. R108 (1824)
1823–?1835
Lord Walston, Thriplow, Cambridge

Provenance: Shown in the exhibition of the Société des Amis des Arts de Lyon in 1837, which was organized as a lottery, and said to have been won by M. Paturle, Delacroix receiving 1,200 fr.;[1] sale Paturle 28 Feb. 1872, lot 7 (repr., Bracquemond etching), to Febvre, 19,000 fr.; sale Sedelmeyer ('comprenant ses tableaux modernes et ceux des Galeries de San Donato [i.e. estate at Florence of the Demidoff family] et de San Martino'), 30 Apr. 1877, lot 25 (repr., Bracquemond etching), 7,100 fr.; Prince Demidoff, 1878; M. Perreau; purchased from him by Boussod, Valadon & Cⁱᵉ, 24 Oct. 1881, 6,000 fr. (Arch Goupil/Boussod); sale liquidation Goupil & Cⁱᵉ, 25 May 1887, lot 44 (repr.), 5,000 fr., to Escribe, according to Arch Goupil/Boussod, bought in and sold at this price to Edmond Guillout, according to R Ann (therefore Escribe probably acting for Boussod, Valadon & Cⁱᵉ); Edmond Guillout; purchased from him by Boussod, Valadon & Cⁱᵉ, 31 Dec. 1888, 6,560 fr., and sold to F. Michel the same day, 8,400 fr. Arch Goupil/Boussod); Philippe George [*sic*] d'Ay; his sale 2 June 1891, lot 17 (repr.), 15,600 fr.; with Durand-Ruel in Dec. 1900 (R Ann); M. Bessonneau, Angers, by 1916; M. Frappier (his son-in-law?), by 1923; sale Bessonneau d'Angers, 15 June 1954, lot 31 (repr.), to Messrs. Reid and Lefevre, London, 3,700,000 fr.; the present owner, by 1959.

Exhibitions: Salon 1835, no. 556; Moulins 1836, Supp. no. 266; Exposition de la Société des Amis des Arts de Lyon, Lyon 1837, no. 72; Durand-Ruel, Paris 1878, no. 156 (Prince Demidoff listed as owner in cat.); *EBA*, Paris 1885, no. 32; Exposition d'Œuvres d'Art des 18, 19 et 20 siècles au profit du Comité National d'Aide à la Recherche Scientifique, Paris Apr.–May 1923, no. 187; Rosenberg, Paris 1928, no. 5; Venice 1956, no. 4; Louvre 1963, no. 220, *M* no. 217, repr.; Edinburgh–London 1964, no. 7, repr.; (on occasional loan to the Fitzwillian Museum, Cambridge.)

Literature: W., 'Exposition de 1835', *Le Réformateur*, 15 March 1835; A. T. [Tardieu], 'Salon de 1835', *Le Courrier français*, 30 March 1835; E.S., 'Exposition de 1835 (Septième article)', *La Tribune Politique et Littéraire*, 6 Apr. 1835; F.P., 'Salon de 1835 (Huitième article)', 13 Apr. 1835; A., review of Salon of 1835, *Le Constitutionnel*, 26 Apr. 1835 (everything on *The Natchez*, except its title, reprinted in Tourneux, p. 61); L. P . . . e [Peisse], 'Salon de 1835', *Le Temps*, 30 Apr. (*not* Aug.) 1835; anon., 'Salon de 1835. (IIIᵉ Article.) Les Peintres et les poètes', *L'Artiste*, IX, 8ᵉ livraison (1835), p. 90; G. de F. [Guyot de Fère], review of Salon of 1835, *Journal spécial des Lettres et des Beaux-Arts*, 2nd year, vol. I (1835), p. 204 (comments on *The Natchez* transcribed in full in Tourneux, p. 62); C. Lenormant, 'De l'école française en 1835. Salon annuel', *Revue des Deux-Mondes*, II, 4th series (1835), p. 197; V. Schoelcher, 'Salon de 1835. Deuxième article', *Revue de Paris*, XVI, N.S. (1835), pp. 58 f.; *L'Artiste*, XII (1836), p. 24; ibid., XIV (1837), p. 212; T. Thoré, 'M. Eugène Delacroix', *Le Siècle*, 25 Feb. 1837; Silvestre *Delacroix* (1855), p. 80; A. de Vienne, 'La Galerie de M. Paturle', *L'Artiste*, 6th series II (1856), p. 76; Piron, p. 107; *Correspondance* (Burty 1880) I. 222 f.; H. Houssaye, 'L'Exposition des œuvres d'Eugène Delacroix à l'Ecole des Beaux-Arts', *Revue des Deux Mondes*, LXVIII (1885), p. 668; Tourneux, pp. 61, 62, 63; Moreau-Nélaton I. 154, 163, repr. fig. 121; J. Meier-Graefe 1922, repr. p. 99; Escholier I, repr. p. 131; Hourticq 1930, repr. pl. 7; *Journal* I. 15 n. 2 (addition: III. 521), III. 375 and n. 6, 523 (addition to I. 39, para. 3); *Correspondance* I. 409, II. 3 n. 5; Sérullaz *Dessins* 1952, p. 44; *Art News Annual*, XXIV (1954), repr.; L. Johnson, 'The Early Drawings of Delacroix', *Burl Mag*, XCVIII (1956), p. 23 and n. 5; L. Johnson, 'Delacroix at the Biennale', ibid., p. 327; Johnson 1963, p. 120, repr. pl. 6; Huyghe, pp. 187, 282, 302, detail (whole group) repr. pl. 216; M. Sérullaz, 'A Comment on the Delacroix Exhibition Organized in England', *Burl Mag*, CVII (1965), p. 366; L. Johnson, 'Eugène Delacroix et les Salons. Documents inédits au Louvre', *Revue du Louvre*, 16 (1966), p. 223; Trapp, p. 194 n. 33.

Print: Etching by Bracquemond, 1872.

The subject and its source were described as follows in the official catalogue of the Salon of 1835: '*Les Natchez*. Fuyant le massacre de leur tribu, deux jeunes sauvages remontent le Meschacébé [Mississippi]. Pendant le voyage, la jeune femme a été prise des douleurs de l'enfantement. Le moment est celui où le père tient dans ses bras le nouveau-né qu'ils regardent tous deux avec attendrissement.

(Chateaubriand, épisode d'*Atala*)'

The couple were wrongly identified as Chactas and Atala by Houssaye (op. cit., 1885) and in R Ann (see Johnson, op. cit., 1956, p. 23 and n. 5); and more recently the title given to the picture by Delacroix misled Sérullaz (op. cit., 1952) into citing Chateaubriand's *Les Natchez* as the source. I identi-

fied the scene as from the epilogue of the novel *Atala*, published in 1801, and communicated my findings, with an account of the characters depicted, in the course of a lecture at the Courtauld Institute in 1957 and almost annually in university lectures from then on. The epilogue was noted as the source in my book, *Delacroix* (p. 120), issued in February 1963. The characters are unnamed by Chateaubriand: they are the half-breed granddaughter of Chateaubriand's French hero, René, and her Red Indian husband, who are fleeing from the massacre of his tribe by the French. The infant soon died because the mother's milk had been spoilt in labour.

According to Moreau (p. 160), the picture was 'plus qu'à moitié ébauchée' when Delacroix had to interrupt its progress to work on the *Massacres of Chios* (J105), which was submitted to the Salon jury by the first week of August, 1824. Moreau's information seems to be partially corroborated by an entry made in Delacroix's *Journal* (I. 39) on 23 December, 1823: 'Je travaille à mes sauvages'; which has been convincingly taken by Joubin (ibid. III. 523) to apply to *Les Natchez*. The first mention of the subject is found in the *Journal* (I. 15) on 5 October, 1822: '*Une jeune Canadienne traversant le désert avec son époux est prise par les douleurs de l'enfantement et accouche; le père prend dans ses bras le nouveau-né.*' Further support of Moreau's statement that work on the canvas was well-advanced by 1824 comes from two preparatory drawings, which are datable to 1823/4: a full composition-study in pencil and brown wash in the Louvre, bearing a study for the *Massacres of Chios* on the verso (RF9219, probably R1497; repr. Sérullaz *Dessins* (1952), pl. XLI and *Mémorial*, no. 218) and a powerful study in black and white chalks for the figure of the husband, identical in pose to the final version except for the position of the left hand (Louvre sketch-book, RF23355, fol. 9ᵛ; repr. Cat. Exh. Edinburgh-London 1964, pl. 45). Finally, the wife is so similar in type and conception to the dead mother in the right-hand corner of the *Massacres of Chios* that they were surely conceived, if not actually painted, at almost the same time.

Unfortunately, there is no certain evidence of the progress of the painting between December 1823 and 19 February 1835, the date when it was accepted for the Salon, but everything points to the conclusion that it was conceived and probably mostly painted during the first half of the 1820s. Had it existed in its present state that early, however, it seems inconceivable that Delacroix would not have submitted it to one of the Salons before 1835. The execution of the landscape seems of early date and so is the conception of the main figures, but the flesh passages may have been finished or reworked shortly before the Salon. This could account for the curious detachment of the figures from their setting, to which they seem unrelated by atmospheric 'liaison'.

No Salon reviewer, in any event, seemed aware that this was anything but a recent work, and Thoré, writing in 1837 (op. cit.), saw in it new signs of a change of manner, characterized by tighter handling ('execution plus serrée') and more concentrated effects. Reactions at the Salon were mixed. Typical of the adverse criticism were Tardieu's objections (op. cit., 1835) to the 'faulty drawing', 'earthy colour of the flesh', 'ugly heads', 'sad and desolate background'. The most sympathetic and sensitive analysis of the painting was written by Schoelcher (op. cit., 1835), who, having observed how in general the air around Delacroix's figures seems to be permeated with the passions that animate them, goes on to demonstrate this quality in *The Natchez*:

rien de plus triste que cette savane immense et unie, que ce fleuve coulant avec lenteur et sans murmure; rien de plus mélancolique que cette nature calme, que cet air de solitude dont sont enveloppés les deux êtres vivants qui fuient les persécutions, qui souffrent et qui aiment [. . .] A cela, M. Delacroix joint une puissance et une propriété d'expression rares à trouver, même chez les grands maîtres. *Les Natchez*, sous ce rapport, nous semble un véritable chef-d'œuvre.

It was not until recently that a strong influence of Raphael on the figures was noted and specified, by Sara Lichtenstein, who made a convincing comparison between the pose of the mother and that of Cleopatra in the print of 1528 by A. Veneziano, *Death of Cleopatra*, long believed to reflect Raphael's design, and between the husband and the kneeling angel, with drapery hanging from folded arms, in the *Baptism of Christ* in the Vatican Loggia ('Delacroix and Raphael', unpublished Ph.D. dissertation, University of London, 1973).

This is the only picture inspired by the writings of Chateaubriand that Delacroix is known to have painted. At the Salon of 1808, Girodet had shown his famous *Burial of Atala* (Louvre), which depicts another scene from the same novel and stresses its religious character more than does the Delacroix.

---

[1] In publishing a letter of thanks dated 15 February 1838 from Delacroix to his friend Charles Rivet, who was Prefect of the Department of the Rhône and a member of the Administrative Council of the Société, Philippe Burty added the following note: 'Le tableau auquel il est fait allusion paraît avoir été payé à Delacroix 1,200 francs. C'était, croyons-nous, un épisode tiré des *Natchez*.' (*Correspondance*, Burty 1880, I. 222 f.) Though Delacroix refers to both the painting and the lottery inexplicitly, saying only 'Que j'aurais désiré que mon triste tableau, s'il vous a plu le moins du monde, vous fût échu!', Burty was no doubt correct in identifying the picture as *The Natchez*, but did not give the source of his information that Delacroix received 1,200 francs for it. Statements in later sources that Paturle won it in 1838 are probably deduced from the date of this letter and from the fact that the picture passed in Paturle's sale in 1872. The exhibition appears to have opened in December 1837, since the catalogue contains a list of members of the Society on 1 December of that year, and the draw may have been held before the end of the year. A note in the catalogue states: 'On trouve chez le concierge [du Palais St-Pierre] des billets d'un franc, qui donnent droit au tirage des objets acquis par la Société à l'Exposition de cette année [1837].'

---

102 DON QUIXOTE IN HIS LIBRARY   Pl. 90

$15\frac{3}{4} \times 12\frac{5}{8}$ in. (40×32 cm)* Relined
Signed bottom, left of centre: *Eug. Delacroix*
Moreau pp. xx, 243 f. R138 (1825)
1824
Dr. Schaefer, Obbach über Schweinfurt, Germany

Provenance: Placed for sale with Mme Hulin, rue de la Paix, in 1824 at a price of 300 fr. (Moreau); Prince d'Esling; his sale ('Monsieur le Prince d'Esl.') 4 March 1833, lot 1 ('Don Quichotte, entouré de livres de chevalerie, médite sur les prouesses des anciens chevaliers errants, et rêve au moyen de les imiter.'); Du Sommerard; his sale 11 Dec. 1843, lot 23 ('Scène de Don Quichotte', without dimensions or further description), 100 fr.; anon. sale (by Ridel, of works largely from the Durand-Ruel gallery) 28 Jan. 1845 (not 1854), lot 29, 400 fr.; P. Barroilhet, 1852; Arsène Houssaye; his sale (A.H.) 29 March 1854, lot 63 ('Don Quichotte', without dimensions or further description), 590 fr.; Bouruet-Aubertot, by 1864; his sale 22 Feb. 1869, lot 8 ('Don Quichotte', 40×31 cm), 6,850 fr.; sale Liebig and Frémyn ('Collections de M.L. et de M.F.') 8 Apr. 1875, lot 22, bought in at 6,200 fr.; anon. sale (by Haro) 28 Apr. 1883, lot 31 ('Don Quichotte rêvant à la chevalerie. Signé en bas de la toile', 40×32 cm), 2,000 fr.; with Durand-Ruel in May 1892 (R Ann); with Bernheim-Jeune in June 1892 (ibid.); with Durand-Ruel, 1893; with Georges Bernheim, 1920 (Dieterle R); mixed sale, Galerie Charpentier, Paris 3 Dec. 1959, lot 48, repr., to Nathan, Zurich, 1,600,000 fr.; the present owner, by 1963.

Exhibitions: Gal. Beaux-Arts, Paris 1852, no. 131 ('Don Quichotte', without dimensions or further description, lent by P. Barroilhet); Bd Italiens, Paris 1864, no. 127; New York 1893, no. 57 ('Don Quichotte', without dimensions or further description, lent by Durand-Ruel); Berne 1963–4, no. 5; Bremen 1964, no. 5; Edinburgh–London 1964, no. 10, repr.

Literature: *Bulletin de l'Ami des Arts*, III (1845), p. 245; Silvestre *Delacroix* (1855), p. 80; Tourneux, p. 140; anon., 'The Loan Exhibition at the Fine Arts Building', *Art Amateur*, XXVIII, no. 5 (Apr. 1893), p. 126; Moreau-Nélaton I. 59, repr. fig. 31; C. Mauclair, 'Delacroix', *L'Art et les Artistes*, XVIII N.S. (1929), repr. p. 147; Escholier I. 96, repr. opp. p. 96; *Journal* I. 69 n. 1, 78 n. 2.

This scene does not actually occur in *Don Quixote*. Delacroix combines elements from two separate passages in Cervantes's novel: that in which Don Quixote's housekeeper expresses to the curate her fear that her master's addiction to reading books of chivalry must have turned his brain (chapter v); and the inspection of the volumes in Don Quixote's library by the curate, with the help of the barber and housekeeper (chapter VI). On neither occasion was the hero in the room, but Delacroix introduces him with obvious advantages for a pictorial narrative.

At least five illustrated editions of *Don Quixote* in French were published in Paris between 1820 and 1824, three of which included illustrations by well-known Romantic artists: Florian's translation with some illustrations by Tony Johannot (1820); a translation illustrated by Achille Devéria and published by Desoer (1821); and Bouchon Dubournial's translation illustrated by Eugène Lami and Horace Vernet (*Œuvres complètes de Cervantes*, vols. VI-IX, 1821). Of the five editions known to me, only the last-named contains an illustration of the inspection of the library. It is by Lami. Don Quixote is not present and the style is quite unlike Delacroix's. A parallel in style and spirit to Delacroix's picture is to be found less in contemporary French book illustrations than in a small, undated painting (15 × 11 cm) of Don Quixote in his library by Bonington, which belonged to Baron Rivet (private collection, Paris), and in another of the same subject, showing the hero alone but for his dog, attributed to Bonington and close in size to the Delacroix (40.6 × 33 cm. Castle Museum and Art Gallery, Nottingham, repr. in catalogue of Bonington exhibition held there, 1965, pl. 48).

According to Robaut, this painting was completed, after an interruption, only in 1825, but that is apparently incorrect, because Delacroix writes on 20 April 1824: 'J'ai presque fini le *Don Quichotte*.' And three days later: 'Travaillé et comme fini le petit *Don Quichotte*' (*Journal* I. 81, 83). In May he states firmly: 'Plus de *Don Quichotte* et de choses indignes de toi', suggesting not only that he thought his true bent lay in large-scale history paintings, but that the *Don Quixote* had been finished (ibid. 97). He had begun it on 6 April and worked on it steadily in the following weeks (ibid. 69, 70, 77-9).

103 THE PENANCE OF JANE   Pl. 91
SHORE

Wood panel, 10⅝ × 8¼ in. (27 × 21 cm)*
Signed lower left: *Eug. Delacroix*
R Ann 211*bis* (1827)
1824
Dr. W. F. Schnyder, Solothurn, Switzerland

Provenance: Probably painted for Amable Paul Coutan;[1] Coutan-Hauguet sale 16 Dec. 1889, lot 9 (support wrongly listed as canvas), repr., to Bernheim-Jeune, 1,300 fr.; acquired from them by Gadala 9 Jan. 1891, returned by him 23 March 1893, and acquired by Lippmann 24 March 1893 (Arch B-J); his sale (M. Maurice L.) 22 Apr. 1899, lot 9, 860 fr.; Seff (?) 1899 (ink inscription on back); Dr.

Hans Graber, Zurich, by 1939; the present owner, by 1963.

Exhibitions: Zurich 1939, no. 306; Berne 1963-4, no. 4; Bremen 1964, no. 4; Edinburgh-London 1964, no. 12, repr.

Literature: Moreau-Nélaton I. 59, repr. fig. 30; Escholier I. 94; P. Pool, *Delacroix* (Paul Hamlyn, London, 1969), p. 31, full-page colour repr. pl. 9; Trapp, p. 158 n. 45.

Jane Shore was the wife of a London merchant. In 1470 she left her husband to become the mistress of Edward IV, on whose death she was accused of witchcraft by Richard III. She was condemned to wander about in a sheet, holding a taper in her hand, and it was decreed that anyone who offered her food or shelter should be put to death. She continued an outcast for three days. Then her husband came to her assistance, but was seized by Gloucester's men, and Jane died.

There were performances of two different plays on this theme in Paris in 1824: Népomucène Lemercier's tragedy *Jane Shore*, in which the great Talma created the part of Gloucester on 1 April (see H. Collins, *Talma* (Faber & Faber, London, 1964), p. 387), and Liadière's play of the same title, which was performed at the Théâtre de l'Odéon on 2 April. But it is probable that the text of Nicholas Rowe's tragedy (1713, Act V, sc. i) was Delacroix's initial source of inspiration. A French translation of Rowe's *Jane Shore* appeared in *Chefs-d'œuvre du théâtre anglais*, vol. I, Paris 1822, and in a volume on its own in 1824. Delacroix cites Rowe's text on his lithograph *Jane Shore*, depicting the moment in the following scene when Jane's husband vainly tries to help her, and which, though dated to 1828 by Delteil (no. 76), was apparently designed in April 1824 (see *Journal* I. 79).

Delacroix first mentions his interest in the theme, which had been treated earlier by Blake and by some of his contemporaries, on 6 March 1824: 'Pensé à faire des compositions sur *Jane Shore* et le théâtre d'Otway' (ibid. 59); on 23 March he began 'une *Jane Shore*' (ibid. 63), possibly the water-colour R211, said to be dated 1827 but redated 1824 in R Ann; on 3 April he notes: 'Le soir, *Jane Shore*' (ibid. 79), leaving it unclear whether he attended a play that evening or advanced his own designs. On 15 April he definitely began to paint this picture: 'commencé à peindre la *Pénitence de Jane Shore*' (ibid. 79). Further progress on 'la *Jane Shore*', probably this painting, is reported on 17 and 20 April (ibid. 78, 81).

---

[1] The collector Coutan bought an *Ivanhoe* (J(L)94) from Delacroix at the end of 1823 and promised to take more pictures from him (*Journal* I. 40). Delacroix saw him on several occasions at the very period when he was concerned with the subject of Jane Shore or actually painting this picture (ibid. 60, 62, 66, 89) and, though there appears to be no firm evidence to support Joubin's statement that it was executed for Coutan (ibid. 63 n. 4), this seems very likely.

104 A BATTLEFIELD, EVENING   Pl. 94

19 × 22¼ in. (48.3 × 56.5 cm)* Relined
Signed bottom right: *Eug Delacroix*
Moreau pp. 283, 312. R166 (1826)
1824
Rijksmuseum H.W. Mesdag, The Hague

Provenance: Delacroix's posthumous sale, Feb. 1864, lot 66 ('Le Soir d'une bataille', with further description, mention of signature, dated *c*. 1826, 46 × 55 cm), to Baron de Laage, 3,100 fr.; Prince Paul Demidoff; his sale 3 Feb. 1868, lot 3, to Gauchez, 5,800 fr.; sale La Rocheb . . . [Marquis de la Rochebousseau] (a fictitious name, according to Lugt, attached to a sale of paintings brought together by Léon Gauchez) 5 May 1873, lot 7 (repr.), to Laurent Richard, 6,200 fr.;[1] Sale L. [Liebig] & F. [Frémyn] 8 Apr. 1875, lot 23, bought in at 2,400 fr.; Théodore Melot, Brussels, by 1887; bought by Arnold, Tripp & Cⁱᵉ 25 Feb. 1891, and sold by them 1 June 1891, to Hendrik Willem Mesdag, The Hague (Arch A. Tripp); he presented his collection to the State, 1903, d. 1915.

Exhibitions: Bd Italiens, Paris 1864, no. 7; Edinburgh-London 1964, no. 14, repr.; *Fantasie en Werkelijkheid*, Dordrecht 1967, *h.c.*; *French Paintings from the Mesdag Museum, The Hague*, Wildenstein, London 1969, no. 14 (repr. in colour p. 5)

Literature: Silvestre *Delacroix* (1855), p. 82; Silvestre *Documents nouveaux* (1864), pp. 5 f., 13; H. Perrier, 'De Hugo van der Goes à John Constable — II', *GBA*, 2ᵉ période, VII (1873), p. 372, Martial etching repr. opp. this p.; E. Véron, *Eugène Delacroix* (Librairie de l'Art, Paris and London, 1887), reduction of Martial's etching repr. p. 23; *Catalogue des collections du Musée Mesdag. Ecoles étrangères XIX siècle* (1964), p. 44, no. 112, repr. pl. 29; T. Crombie, 'The Mesdag in Mayfair', *Apollo*, LXXXIX (1969), p. 144, repr. fig. 2; W. Gaunt, 'French pictures from the Mesdag Museum', *The Times*, 25 Feb. 1969.

Prints: Etching, with the title *Waterloo*, by A. P. Martial, *GBA* 1873, loc. cit.; Cat. Sale La Rocheb . . . 1873; reduction in E. Véron 1887, loc. cit.

Though Robaut, following Silvestre *Delacroix* (1855) and the catalogue of the posthumous sale, dated this painting to 1826, Joubin was most probably right in identifying it as the picture Delacroix blocked in on 21 June 1824: 'Ebauché les deux *Chevaux morts*' (*Journal* I. 115 and n. 4); and therefore presumably finished well before 1826. It is no doubt to the same work that Delacroix refers much later, in a list of paintings compiled in 1857, as: '*Les Deux chevaux morts sur le champ de bataille* (ancien)' (ibid. III. 89 n. 1, 90). Neither reference seems to justify the title *Waterloo*, appended in 1873, with the publication of Martial's etching; nor does the mountainous background.

The picture was much admired by Silvestre, who noted (op. cit., 1864, p. 6) that it was painted 'à l'instar de Géricault' and concluded: 'Ce noir Montfaucon, étudié d'après nature et ennobli par un grand esprit, restera l'un des épisodes les plus navrants de la peinture militaire.' Montfaucon was a region on the outskirts of Paris between La Villette and the Buttes-Chaumont, the heights from which Paris was defended in 1814. It is traditionally associated with the massive gibbet that was erected there in the thirteenth century, but in Delacroix's day it was a centre for knackers' yards and it is no doubt to the slaughtered horses that Silvestre was chiefly alluding when he wrote of 'this gloomy Montfaucon, studied from nature.' But since that was also the region where Marshal Marmont put up a final, desperate resistance to the allies in 1814, before they occupied Paris, Silvestre—and Delacroix in his painting—may have intended a wider allusion to the collapse of the First Empire at that time. In any event, Delacroix mentions going to Montfaucon with Pierret and Fielding two days before 'blocking in the two dead horses' (*Journal* I. 115). The purpose of the visit is not stated, but certainly the dead horses are based on studies from nature, wherever they were done: there is a series of drawings of dead horses on fols. 1ᵛ to 5ʳ, on fols. 12ʳ and 13ʳ, in a sketch-book that was partly used in 1824 (Louvre, RF23355); those on fols. 5ʳ and 13ʳ seem particularly to have served for the farther horse in the painting. The whole series may have been done on the visit to Montfaucon in June 1824, but could also date from as early as May 1823, when Delacroix noted specifically: 'Hier, je fus avec Champmartin étudier les chevaux morts' (*Journal* I. 30). Some details for the farther horse are explored rapidly in pen-and-ink sketches, intermediate between the sketch-book drawings from nature and the painting, on a sheet of drawings in the Louvre (RF9713) which includes studies for a *Mazeppa*; Delacroix was planning in March 1824 to do a *Mazeppa* (Journal I. 60, 62).

As for the relationship to Géricault, the theme, a wounded cuirassier, naturally invites comparison with Géricault's more famous *Wounded Cuirassier*, shown at the Salon of 1814 and now in the Louvre. But Delacroix's treatment is quite different. Though pathetic in his bewilderment and anonymous, Géricault's cuirassier was a heroic figure, monumental in scale, and dominated a large canvas. Delacroix makes the horrors of battle more explicit, the situation of his fallen soldier more tragic, by stressing the dead horses and the desolate expanse of the battlefield. Géricault's picture heralded the fall of Empire; Delacroix's is its epitaph. Yet the Delacroix is also more colourful, with the bold blue, red and yellow in the horses. The blue colouring of the nearer horse, a choice likely influenced by Delacroix's study of Persian manuscript illuminations at this period, adumbrates his use of this hue for horses in several of his major paintings, for example the fallen horse

III. *Scenes from the Chios Massacres* (105), detail

on the left of the *Battle of Taillebourg* of 1837 (Musée de Versailles).

Robaut lists a sepia drawing of a dead horse (R167) which he considers to be a study for this painting, but which seems more closely related to the dead horse in the *Scene from the War between the Greeks and Turks* (J115).

The painting, as well as being relined, has a new stretcher.

Another version, listed under R Ann 166^(bis) as a 'Répétition sans changement. Esquisse', passed as a Delacroix in the sale of his assistant Pierre Andrieu, 6 May 1892, lot 179 ('Le guerrier blessé', without dimensions), 435 fr. It was in an anonymous sale in Paris, 22 June 1910, lot 3, 145 fr. (Dieterle R); was shown under the title *Waterloo* in the exhibition Paris 1927, no. 3, when it belonged to M. Demelette; and as 'Les Chevaux morts' in Atelier Delacroix, Paris 1963, no. 139. It is painted on millboard, measures 30.2 × 36.2 cm, bears on the front and back the stamp of the sale of Andrieu, by whose hand it was probably painted.

---

[1] According to the catalogue of this sale, the picture had belonged to Prince Paul Galitzin as well as to Prince Demidoff. It is not listed in the catalogues of the Galitzin sales of 18 Dec. 1826 or 17 Jan. 1870 (Brussels), nor is Galitzin mentioned as an owner by Moreau or Robaut. His compatriot Demidoff might, however, have acquired it from him privately some time between 1864 and 1868.

105 SCENES FROM THE CHIOS MASSACRES   Pl. 89

164 3/16 × 139 3/8 in. (4.17 × 3.54 m)
Signed bottom left: *Eug. Delacroix*
Moreau pp. 160, 167, 190, 205. R91
1824
Musée du Louvre

Provenance: Acquired by the State in 1824 for the Musée du Luxembourg, 6,000 fr.; transferred to the Louvre (Inv. 3823), November 1874.

Exhibitions: Salon 1824, no. 450 ('Scènes des massacres de Scio; familles grecques attendent la mort ou l'esclavage, etc. (Voir les relations diverses et les journaux du temps)'; *Universelle*, Paris 1855, no. 2924; *Bd Italiens*, Paris 1864, no. 38; Louvre 1930, no 18, repr. *Album* p. 13; Petit Palais, Paris 1936, no. 229; id., Paris 1946, no. 154; London 1959, no. 111, repr.; Louvre 1963, no. 46, 2 repr.; Petit Palais, Paris 1968–9, no. 267.

Literature: A. Thiers, review of Salon of 1824, *Le Constitutionnel*, 25 and 30 Aug. 1824 (reprinted in *Salon de mil huit cent vingt-quatre* (Paris, n.d.), pp. 6 f., 16–19; S., review of id., *Le Diable Boiteux*, 28 Aug. 1824; anon., 'Beaux-Arts. Exposition de 1824', *L'Etoile*, 29 Aug. 1824; anon., review of Salon, *Journal du Commerce*, 4 Sept. 1824; Chauvin, review of id., *Gazette de France*, 1 and 9 Sept. 1824

(reprinted in *Salon de mil huit cent vingt-quatre* (Pillet, Paris, 1825), pp. 13–15, 23, repr. (Langlumé line lithograph) opp. p. 14; F., review of id., cast in form of letter to 'M.B., à Rome', *Le Drapeau Blanc*, 7 Sept. 1824; D., review of id., *Le Moniteur universel*, 8 Sept. 1824; M., review of id., *L'Oriflamme*, 8th livraison (Sept. 1824), pp. 345–7 (reprinted in *Revue critique des productions de peinture, sculpture, gravure exposées au Salon de 1824* (Dentu et Blosse, Paris, 1825), pp. 4–6); anon., review of id., *L'Aristarque français*, 12 Sept. and 28 Oct. 1824; Y. [said to be A. Thiers, cf. Tourneux p. 46], review of id., *Le Globe*, 26 and 28 Sept. 1824; D. [Delécluze], review of id., *Journal des Débats*, 5 Oct. 1824; A. [Stendhal], review of id., *Journal de Paris et des départements*, 9 Oct. 824 (reprinted in *Mélanges d'art et de littérature* (Michel Lévy, Paris, 1867), pp. 179 f.); review of id., *Annales des Arts ... par une Société d'artistes et de Gens de Lettres*, I (1824), pp. 326 f.; anon., review of id., *Mercure du dix-neuvième siècle*, VII (1824), pp. 199–205; F. Flocon and M. Aycard, *Salon de 1824* (Leroux, Paris, 1824), pp. 11–18; A. Jal, *L'Artiste et le philosophe, entretiens critiques sur le Salon de 1824* (Ponthieu, Paris, 1824), pp. 47–53, repr. (Blanchard (?) line lithograph (printer C. Motte), opp. p. 47); C. P. Landon, *Annales du Musée et de l'Ecole moderne des Beaux-Arts. Salon de 1824* (Ballard, Paris, 1824), I, pp. 53–5, repr. (Réveil line engraving) opp. p. 53; N., review of Salon of 1824, in form of letter to 'Madame de X, à Arcis-sur-Aube', *Lettres Champenoises*, XVIII (1824), pp. 79 f.; A.N., review of Salon of 1827–8, *L'Observateur*, II, no. 95 (8 Dec. 1827), p. 468; P., review of id., *La Quotidienne*, 24 Apr. 1828; D., 'Peinture. Considérations sur le Romantisme', *L'Observateur des Beaux-Arts*, I, no. 5 (24 Apr. 1828), p. 19; anon., *Revue française*, no. 1 (1828), pp. 200 f.; T. Thoré, 'Artistes Contemporains. M. Eugène Delacroix', *Le Siècle*, 24 and 25 Feb. 1837; C. Baudelaire, *Salon de 1846* (Michel Lévy, Paris, 1846), reprinted in *Curiosités esthétiques*, 1868 (*Œuvres*, Pléiade ed. Paris 1932, II, pp. 74 and n. 85); C. Perrier, 'Exposition universelle des Beaux-Arts', *L'Artiste*, XV, 6th livraison (10 June 1855), p. 73; T. Gautier, 'Exposition Universelle de 1855', *Moniteur universel*, 19 July 1855; M. Du Camp, *Les Beaux-Arts à l'Exposition universelle de 1855* (Lib. nouvelle, Paris, 1855), pp. 98 f.; E. and J. de Goncourt, *La Peinture à l'Exposition de 1855* (E. Dentu, Paris, 1855), p. 43; E. J. Delécluze, *Les Beaux-Arts dans les deux mondes en 1855* (Charpentier, Paris, 1856), p. 214 (for a fuller list of reviews of the Exposition universelle of 1855 not considered worth mentioning here, see Tourneux pp. 95–8); T. Silvestre, *Histoire des artistes vivants. Etudes d'après nature. Ingres* (Blanchard, Paris, 1855), p. 1 (Ingres quoted); id., *Delacroix* (n.d. [1855]), pp. 47, 58, 63 (reprinted in T. Silvestre, *Les Artistes français*, 1855 (1926 ed., I, pp. 17, 25, 28)); F. Villot, 'John Constable', *Revue universelle des Arts*, IV (1856), p. 302; F. Villot, *Notice des peintures, sculptures et dessins de l'école moderne de France exposés dans les Galeries du*

Musée impérial du Luxembourg (Mourgues frères, Paris, 1858), p. 10, no. 40; E. Chesneau, 'Le Mouvement moderne en peinture. Eugène Delacroix', *Revue européenne*, XVIII (1861), pp. 489 f., 517 n. 1 (reprinted in *La Peinture française au XIXe siècle. Les Chefs d'école* (Didier, Paris, 1862), pp. 335 f.); C. Blanc, 'Eugène Delacroix', *GBA*, XVI (1864), pp. 14 f., repr. (Pisan engraving) p. 13 (article reprinted in *Les Artistes de mon temps*, 1876, pp. 34-6); A. Cantaloube, *Eugène Delacroix, l'homme et l'artiste* (Dentu, Paris, 1864), pp. 24 f.; L. Chardin, 'Retour à Eugène Delacroix', *L'Artiste*, 7th ser. II (1864), p. 148; E. Chesneau, *L'Art et les artistes modernes* (Didier, Paris, 1864), p. 347; A. Dumas, *Causerie sur Eugène Delacroix*, lecture of 10 Dec. 1864, pp. 32-6 of MS. in *BN Estampes* (see *Literature* for J112 and Tourneux p. 27 for further details); [F. Villot], Introduction to catalogue of his sale (M. F.V.), 11 February 1865, p. v; Piron, pp. 64-7, 105; C. Blanc, 'Grammaire des arts du dessin', *GBA*, XX (1866), p. 388 (reprinted in *Grammaire des arts du dessin* (Renouard, Paris, 1870), p. 616); C. Blanc, 'Ingres', ibid. XXIII (1867), p. 456; E. de Mirecourt [pseudonym of C. J. B. Jacquot], *Eugène Delacroix* (Lib. des Contemporains, Paris, 1870 (4th ed.; 1st ed., 1856)), pp. 33 ff.; P. Andrieu, in A. Bruyas *et al.*, *Musée de Montpellier. La Galerie Bruyas* (Quantin, Paris, 1876), pp. 363 f. (this passage complete in abridged reprint of Andrieu's essay in R. Piot, *Les Palettes de Delacroix* (Lib. de France, Paris, 1931), pp. 73 f.); L. Riesener, in Delacroix *Correspondance* (Burty 1878), p. xvi; B. de Tauzia, *Notice supplémentaire des tableaux exposés dans les galeries du Musée national du Louvre* (Paris, 1878), no. 754; G. Lassalle-Bordes, 'Notes Supplémentaires' in Delacroix *Correspondance* (Burty 1880), II, p. xviii; E. Chesneau, *La Peinture anglaise* (Quantin, Paris, undated new ed. [1st ed. 1882]), p. 142; E. Chesneau, Introduction to Robaut, pp. xix f., xxviii f., xxviii n. 1; G. Lafenestre and E. Richtenberger, *Le Musée national du Louvre* (Anc. Maison Quantin, Paris, n.d. [1893]), p. 282, no. 208; Boyer d'Agen, 'Un Supplément au *Journal* d'Eugène Delacroix' (record of recent conversation with Delacroix's friend Paul Chenavard, d. 1895), *Revue des Revues*, XV, no. 24 (15 Dec. 1895), pp. 505-7 (reprinted in Boyer d'Agen, *Ingres d'après une correspondance inédite* (Daragon, Paris, 1909), pp. 168-71); P. Signac, *D'Eugène Delacroix au Néo-Impressionnisme* (Editions de la Revue Blanche, Paris, 1899), pp. 29-32, 35; L. Rosenthal, *La Peinture romantique* (A. Fontemoing, Paris, n.d. [1901]), p. 97; Moreau-Nélaton I. 52 f., 62-5, repr. fig. 39; J. Gasquet, 'Delacroix et les Massacres de Scio', *L'Amour de l'Art*, II (1921), pp. 129-35, repr. p. 130; Meier-Graefe 1922, pp. 22-4, repr. p. 101; Brière 1924, p. 77, no. 208, repr. pl. LV; H. Verne, 'Ingres et Delacroix au Salon de 1824', *La Renaissance*, VII (1924), p. 232, repr. p. 231; Escholier I. 109, 111, 114 ff., repr. opp. p. 128, detail of woman tied to horse, opp. p. 132; Hourticq 1930, pls. 8, 9 (detail, man and woman

left foreground), 10 (detail, old woman), 11 (detail, woman tied to horse); M. Florisoone, 'El Hispanismo de Delacroix', *Revista Española de Arte*, II, no. 7 (Sept. 1933), pp. 389, 390, 398, repr. p. 387; A. Joubin, 'Modèles de Delacroix', *GBA*, 6th per. XV (1936), p. 355; A. Joubin, 'Delacroix au Salon de 1824', *BSHAF*, 1937, pp. 150-2 (publication of paper read at meeting of 5 Apr. 1935, cf. résumé *BSHAF*, 1935, pp. 40 f.); A. Joubin, 'Logis et Ateliers de Delacroix', *BSHAF*, 1938, p. 63; Cassou 1947, pl. 5, followed by full-page details: right-hand group from waist of old woman to head of Turk; left-hand group; woman left foreground from waist up; dead mother and child (across two pages); woman tied to horse; head of dead mother; P. H. Michel, *The Massacre of Chios* (Max Parrish, London, 1947), illustrated with three poor colour repr., some black-and-white details and some related studies; W. Friedlaender, *David to Delacroix* (Harvard University Press, Cambridge, Mass., 1952), pp. 111 f., repr. fig. 69; Sérullaz *Dessins* 1952, pp. 36-9 (studies); R. B. Beckett, 'Constable and France', *The Connoisseur*, CXXXVII (1956), pp. 249-50, repr. p. 253; M. Florisoone, 'Constable and the *Massacres de Scio* by Delacroix', *JWCI*, XX (1957), pp. 180-5, repr. pl. 13*a*; Sterling-Adhémar, no. 661, pl. 231; Escholier 1963, repr. in colour p. 21, colour detail of centre middleground, p. 22; M. Florisoone, 'La Genèse espagnole des *Massacres de Scio* de Delacroix', *Revue du Louvre*, 13 (1963), pp. 195-208, repr. p. 197; M. Hours, 'Quelques tableaux de Delacroix sous les rayons X', *Bulletin du Laboratoire du Musée du Louvre*, 8 (1963), pp. 5-9, X-ray of heads of couple left foreground fig. 3, of old woman from waist up fig. 5; Johnson 1963, pp. 19-26, colour detail of old woman's arm and skirt, pl. 9; Huyghe, pp. 118-31, repr. in colour pl. III; L. Johnson, 'Two Sources of Oriental Motifs copied by Delacroix', *GBA*, 6th per. LXV (1965), p. 164; Maltese, pp. 29-32, 135, repr. in colour pl. V, colour detail of man and woman left foreground, pl. VI; L. Johnson, 'Eugène Delacroix et les Salons. Documents inédits au Louvre', *Revue du Louvre*, 16 (1966), p. 217 and n., 220; T. Prideaux *et al.*, *The World of Delacroix* (Time Inc., New York, 1966), repr. in colour p. 54, colour detail of old woman's arm and skirt, pp. 54-5; Trapp, pp. 29-47, repr. in colour pl. II.

Prints: Line lithograph by Langlumé, 1824; id., for A. Jal *Salon de 1824*; line engraving by Réveil, 1824; etching by A. Masson (Moreau, p. 93); lithograph by P. Blanchard for *Voyage d'un jeune Grec à Paris* (ibid. 117); wood engraving by Pisan after Masson, *L'Illustration*, 23 June 1855, p. 392, and *GBA*, XVI (1864), p. 13; engraving by La Guillermie for the Chalcographie of the Louvre, 1883/4.

Copies: I. BY KNOWN ARTISTS

   (*a*) A. Devéria (attributed), 17 × 14 cm, Delacroix's posthumous sale, Feb. 1864, lot 243, to Marchal de Calvi, 125 fr.

(b) Louis de Planet, canvas, 98 × 80 cm, c. 1842–3. Musée du Vieux Toulouse, Toulouse. (Planet *Souvenirs*, pp. 65 and n., 107 and n. Exhibited Bordeaux 1963, no. 336.)

(c) Pierre Andrieu, canvas, 41 × 32 cm, signed bottom left: *P. Andrieu*. 1850. Musée du Vieux Toulouse, Toulouse. (Exhibited Bordeaux 1963, no. 197.)

(d) Dead mother and child, by Fantin-Latour, canvas (?), 23 × 26 cm, dated 8 September 1854. Private collection, Paris. Exhibited Galerie Tempelaere, Paris, Jan. 1905, no. 4.

2. BY UNIDENTIFIED ARTISTS AND RECORDED IN THE NINETEENTH CENTURY

(a) Sketch, canvas, 46 × 36 cm, Musée d'art et d'histoire, Geneva (Inv. No. 1888-18, acquired in 1888 from the collection of the Marquis de Saint-Aubin, Paris. Cf. M.-T. Coullery-Mira, 'Delacroix et le Massacre de Scio. A propos d'une esquisse du Musée de Genève', *Bulletin du Musée d'Art et d'Histoire, Genève*, N.S. II (1955), pp. 88 ff., repr. fig. 36, as by Delacroix). Listed in provisional catalogue for Exhibition Louvre 1930, no. 17 (excluded from final version). Exhibited Bordeaux 1963, no. 5, as by Delacroix.

(b) Anonymous sale, Hôtel Drouot, Room 6, 15 March 1895, lot 19 ('Les Pestiférés. Etude. Signée à droite', without support or dimensions. R Ann, margin to R91: 'pauvre petite toile de 3 [27 × 22 cm] ou 4 [33 × 24 cm]'. Possibly 2c below.

(c) Sketch, canvas, 24.5 × 19 cm,* painted initials 'ED' bottom right. Collection late Mme David-Weill, Neuilly-sur-Seine. Provenance: Marquis de Montferrier (red wax seal of his collection on stretcher). According to Escholier (I. 99 n. 1), Delacroix gave this sketch to Gérard's pupil, Julie Duvidal de Montferrier, later Countess Abel Hugo, and thence it came into the possession of her descendant, the Marquis de Montferrier. But its quality suggests that it may have had a less distinguished provenance and should perhaps be identified with 2b above. Repr. Escholier I, opp. p. 126, and M.-T. Coullery-Mira, op. cit. *supra* (2a), fig. 35.

(d) Dead mother and child, canvas, 0.955 × 1.32 m, false signature bottom left: *Eug. Delacroix*. R92 (no repr.). National Gallery, Prague. Provenance: Hartmann of Mulhouse; his sale (M.X.) 11 May 1876, lot 16, as a copy by Delacroix, to Auguste Vacquerie, d. 1895; Mme E. Lefèvre,

widow of his nephew; her sale (Veuve E.L.) 7 June 1899, lot 5 (repr.), to Haro; P. A. Cheramy, d. 1913; he left it to the National Gallery, London: bequest refused; Pierre Dubaut; he sold it in 1923 to the Gallery of Modern Art, Prague, later incorporated into the National Gallery.

Shown in various exhibitions as a Delacroix, including *EBA*, Paris 1885, no. 226, Cassirer, Berlin 1907, no. 24, repr., and Prague, p. 11, repr. p. 18, Budapest and Berlin 1965.

This copy has been attributed to Delacroix as late as 1967 (cf. R. Jullian, 'Un Tableau de Delacroix à la Galerie Nationale de Prague', *BSHAF*, 1967, pp. 160-7, repr. fig. 1; but the attribution was rightly contested as early as 1885 and cannot be sustained (cf. L. Johnson, 'A Note on Delacroix at Prague', *Burl Mag*, CXII (1970), p. 382, repr. fig. 48).

(e) The same, canvas, 40 × 50 cm. R93 (no repr.). Whereabouts unknown. Provenance: Léon Charly, by 1885 (previous owners according to Robaut: Jeanron, Niel, Martin, Burty, Barbedienne); P. A. Cheramy; sale his estate 15 Apr. 1913, lot 31, to Strolin. Exhibited *EBA*, Paris 1885, no. 155.

Though this study was attributed to Delacroix by Robaut and by Meier-Graefe and Klossowski in their 1908 catalogue of the Cheramy collection (no. 146), a note in R Ann, stating that the attribution was widely doubted at the 1885 exhibition, suggests that it was recognized to be a copy at an early date and that Robaut probably revised his opinion. Repr. L. Vauxcelles, 'La Collection Cheramy', *L'Art et les Artistes*, I (1905), p. 126, and R. Jullian, op. cit. *supra* (2d), fig. 2.

(f) Woman tied to horse, far right, canvas laid down on wood panel, 20 × 11 cm Musée d'Ixelles, Belgium (bequeathed to the Museum by Gauchez c. 1895. Cf. P. Domène, 'Les Galeries publiques belges', *Beaux-Arts* (Brussels), no. 44 (1933), p. 6, repr.)

See also J(L)95.

3. BY UNIDENTIFIED ARTISTS AND OF UNCERTAIN PROVENANCE

(a) Dead mother and child, canvas, 0.825 × 1.022 m, falsely signed bottom left: E^gD^x. Smith College Museum of Art, Northampton, Mass. (Gift of Col. Walter Scott, 1921). According to A. V. Churchill, the picture was purchased by S. Vose of the Westminster Art Galleries,

Providence, R.I., about 1864 ('Three Unpublished Paintings by Eugène Delacroix', *Bulletin of Smith College Museum of Art*, No. 11 (Apr. 1930), p. 3, repr. p. 13, as by Delacroix *c*. 1838. Also repr. ibid., No. 13 (May 1932), p. 16, and Catalogue Exhibition Chicago 1930, no. 6).

(*b*) The same, canvas, 73 × 92 cm. Musée des Beaux-Arts, Lyon (bequeathed to the Museum in 1957 by M. Herriot, as a Delacroix; formerly in the collection of Baron Vitta. Cf. R. Jullian, op. cit. *supra* (2*d*), p. 164, repr. fig. 3).

(*c*) Old Woman, oil sketch. Formerly Collection Joachim Gasquet (repr. J. Gasquet, op. cit. *supra*, 1921, p. 131, as by Delacroix).

(*d*) Right-hand group, from lap of old woman to head of Turkish horseman, canvas, 73.7 × 50.2 cm. Memorial Art Gallery, University of Rochester, New York. Said to have been bought by S. Vose *c*. 1850 (see 3*a* for another copy from Vose).

(*e*) Whole picture, canvas, 2.083 × 1.715 m. Collection Dudley Wallis, London, 1949, formerly Collection Baron H. Rothschild. Photograph in *Massacres de Scio* file, Service de documentation, Louvre.

The Chios massacres were sparked off by an attack on the island by insurgents from Samos, though the inhabitants of Chios appear to have given no support to the raiders. On 11 April 1822, a week after the Samians had landed, ships of the Turkish fleet arrived in force before the town of Chios and several thousand men were disembarked to relieve the citadel. 'From that time', according to a Greek eyewitness, 'till the day of our departure [10 May] it was one continued scene of murder, conflagration, and plunder, both in country and town' (*The Star*, 6 July 1822). 'A letter in the French papers from a young Greek at Smyrna', dated 19 May and published in the same edition of *The Star*, states:

Throughout [the town of] Chios only fifteen houses are standing, containing our mothers, our sisters, and our daughters, reduced to the most dreadful slavery [. . .] Upwards of forty villages have been consumed by the flames.

The ferocious incendiaries then scoured the mountains and the forests, and they are now at the twenty-fourth village of Mastic.

[. . .] Every day women of the first families in the island are exposed for sale in the public markets.

With the arrival of fresh contingents of Turks, the atrocities lasted for more than two months in all. A census taken in the first week of July found that only nine hundred inhabitants out of a population of nearly ninety thousand were left on the island (F. C. H. L. Pouqueville, *Histoire de la Régénération de la Grèce*, 2nd ed., Paris 1825, III. 532). The protracted period of the slaughter helps to explain Delacroix's choice of title: he is not depicting a single

incident from a particular day in the history of the Greek War of Independence, but rather an amalgam of impressions gained from reading or listening to accounts of the events. Thus, Joubin has suggested (op. cit., 1937) that the group of the dead mother with an infant clutching her breast was inspired by the following passage in the *Mémoires sur la guerre actuelle des Grecs* of 1823 by Colonel Voutier, whom Delacroix met on the day he began his painting: 'Un voyageur témoin des désastres de Chio m'a dit que rien n'avait produit sur son âme une impression plus douloureuse que la vue du cadavre d'une jeune femme dont un enfant prenait de ses mains avides les mamelles flétries.' Since this motif was a commonplace in pictures of plagues, as Stendhal (op. cit., 1824) was the first to point out, Delacroix was here able to develop a perfect correspondence between actuality and pictorial tradition. Further historical facts which have received little or no attention in discussions of Delacroix's picture may be mentioned as being of apparent relevance to it. Plague broke out on the island about one month after the massacres began (Pouqueville, op. cit., p. 492). This suggests that Delacroix may have intended to show the effects of disease as well as Turkish barbarity, and it no doubt partly accounts for his obvious debt to Gros's *Plague at Jaffa*. Certainly the resemblance to a plague scene, as though it were unintentional, was widely remarked on at the Salon of 1824 (cf. Y., op. cit., 28 Sept. 1824: 'Tout le monde sans exception a pris ce massacre pour une peste'), and later both Baudelaire (op. cit., 1846) and Silvestre (op. cit., 1855, p. 58), perhaps informed by Delacroix of his true intentions, judged the symptoms of pestilence to be deliberate.

Another, more cheerful consequence of the misfortunes of Chios was the triumph on the night of 18 June of the Greek leaders Constantine Canaris and George Pepinis in destroying, with two fireships which they personally commanded, the Turkish flagship, when it was lying off Chios with the admiral and more than two thousand men on board, and the Capitan Bey's vessel (Pouqueville, op. cit., pp. 523 ff.). Though the blaze had subsided by dawn, the fire in the harbour in the left background of the picture may well allude to it (Delacroix mentioned the incident in his *Journal* (I. 43 f.) on the day he began the painting), and if so a note of hope is introduced into a scene of otherwise unrelieved despair.

As early as September 1821, Delacroix had considered painting a subject from the Greek War of Independence, for the Salon of 1822, but abandoned the idea in favour of the *Barque de Dante*. The disasters of Chios rekindled his interest in the Greek cause and in May 1823 he noted in his *Journal* (I. 32): 'Je me suis décidé à faire pour le Salon des scènes du *Massacre de Scio*.' On Sunday 9 November of the same year, he recorded: 'J'ai arrêté cette semaine une composition de *Scio*' (ibid. 35); and on 1 December he announced in a letter to Guillemardet: 'J'ai là dans mon atelier depuis plusieurs jours une grande toile encore toute fraîche et vierge, il faut pour la couvrir tout le suc que je possède' (*Lettres intimes*, p. 148). Uncertainty about the location of the studio where Delacroix painted the *Massacres de Scio* has caused much confusion in the later literature, but it appears, from early sources, to have been situated in the rue des Maçons, between the Sorbonne and what is now the Boulevard St Michel.[1]

Evidently stimulated by his conversation earlier in the day with Voutier, a Frenchman who had risen to the rank of Colonel in the service of the Greek insurgent army, Delacroix declared on 12 January 1824: 'C'est donc proprement aujourd'hui *lundi 12* que je commence mon tableau' (*Journal* I. 45); by which he appears to have meant, to judge by other entries, that he began to make drawings from the life for his painting. Setting to work on the actual canvas later in the week, he began with the couple in the left foreground and, with some interruptions for smaller pictures, worked more or less regularly for the next five months, employing a wide variety of models, making frequent revisions and enlisting the help of his friends Soulier and Fielding (probably Thales), both more versed in English landscape methods than he, to prepare the background. Of all Delacroix's major Salon paintings, this is the most fully documented in his *Journal*, and it is possible to follow his progress and hesitations exceptionally closely (all references in the *Journal* to the evolution of the painting are conveniently extracted and arranged in chronological order in *Mémorial*, with the exception of those for 27 January, 30 March, 13 June and 19 July 1824). On the whole, however, the *Journal* entries are more useful in indicating the areas of the canvas that Delacroix was painting at a given time than in elucidating his stylistic intentions and changes of technique, these often being cryptically referred to as 'reworking', 'retouching' or 'repainting' of a particular passage. But from the many entries made between January and late June, one major problem emerges: how to combine a strongly accented contour with an internal modelling that is uncomplicated yet firm. Still very much concerned with plastic problems, Delacroix seems nevertheless to be trying to break away from the truculent plasticity and academic enumeration of muscles that are characteristic of the *Barque de Dante*. He turns for guidance not so much to the colourists, as to Géricault, Ingres, Michelangelo, Raphael and the Spaniards. His preoccupation with these difficulties is reflected in the incisive contour and unexaggerated modelling of two studies connected with the *Massacres de Scio*, *Head of a Woman* (J77) and *Girl Seated in a Cemetery* (J78). But the final painting itself is less unified in style than either of these studies, bearing witness as it does to the multitude of influences that the young artist was trying to assimilate and transmute into an original work of art. The

flesh modelling varies from the head of the dying Greek in the foreground, clearly influenced in the red-rimmed eyes by a figure in Gros's *Plague at Jaffa* but more freely and more colouristically modelled; through the schematic modelling, Veronese-like, of the infant; to the uncolouristic nude tied to the horse, tonally modelled in accordance with the ideal of a 'firm yet blended impasto' that Delacroix had found in the Spanish portrait he was copying (J21). In a special study, Florisoone (op. cit., 1963) has brought attention to the importance of the Spanish influence, overestimating it in my opinion and making some far-fetched comparisons, while not mentioning what appears to be an almost literal copy from Murillo's *Beggar Child* in the Louvre, in the right leg and foot of the child on the extreme left.

Charles Blanc states (op. cit., 1864) that the *Massacres de Scio* was conceived under the influence of the *Plague at Jaffa*, Alexandre Dumas (op. cit., 1864) that Delacroix told him the first idea for it came to him in front of Gros's picture. Though neither statement should perhaps be taken literally, there can be no doubt that Gros's painting, first shown at the Salon of 1804, was the most important contemporary precedent for a Near-Eastern scene of suffering of this kind, treated on a grand scale and with some feeling for the sensuous painterly qualities of the medium, for sunshine and the lustre of exotic costume. The more the pity that Gros should have so far renounced the implications of his own early creative gifts as to disapprove of Delacroix's picture and, if Alexandre Dumas is to be believed (op. cit., 1864, p. 35), denounce it as the 'massacre of painting'.

From the moment it was hung at the Salon, in the grande galerie of the Louvre (*Journal du Commerce*, 26-7 Aug. 1824), the *Massacres de Scio* was interpreted as making a new departure, as posing a threat to the accepted standards of the neo-classical school, and Delacroix himself looked back on it as marking the point where, he supposed, 'je commençai à devenir pour l'école un objet d'antipathie et une espèce d'épouvantail, et je me demande encore comment j'ai pu remonter un pareil courant' (quoted in Piron, p. 66). In Thiers's opinion (op. cit., 1824) 'M. Delacroix [. . .] a levé tous les doutes en faisant succéder le tableau des Grecs à celui du Dante.' For the first time a painting by Delacroix was labelled romantic in contrast to the classicism of David: Chauvin (op. cit., 9 Sept. 1824), after arguing that the classicist satisfies both heart and mind by drawing on 'la belle nature' whereas the romantic 'a je ne sais quoi de forcé, de hors nature, qui choque au premier coup d'œil', concluded: 'J'appelle classique *Léonidas* [. . .] et romantique le *Massacre de Scio*.' And D. sententiously declared (op. cit., 8 Sept. 1824): 'Il faut élever le cœur et non le déchirer [. . .] M. Delacroix a un très beau talent, mais qu'il se souvienne que le goût français est noble et pur, et que nous mettrons toujours une grande différence entre les peintures touchantes de Racine et les drames sanglants de Shakespeare.' Characteristics which were now, as later, judged most commonly to part from the French classical ideal were lack of unity (Landon: 'on ne trouve ici qu'un assemblage confus de figures'; M.: 'je cherche en vain cette pensée unique'); bold handling at the expense of 'correct' drawing (*Journal du Commerce*: 'Nous ne saurions faire l'éloge du dessin de M. Delacroix; mais il y a dans le faire une hardiesse qui saisit'); the sacrifice of beauty and restraint for the sake of expressiveness (M.: 'l'expression y est poussée jusqu'à l'énergie la plus repoussante'; Delécluze: 'ce peintre met de la prétention à faire laid'); and colour that was either too brilliant or too gruesomely real (e.g. M. and Delécluze). Ingres, congratulating himself on the superior qualities of his *Vœu de Louis XIII* shown at the same Salon, was to distil the classic-academic camp's hostile criticism of the *Massacres de Scio* into a single drop of venom by singling it out as an example of the 'fever and epilepsy' of modern art (quoted in Silvestre, op. cit., 1855).

On the other hand, Flocon and Aycard, in a sympathetic review (op. cit., p. 16), defended Delacroix's departure from the accepted canons of the French school and interpreted the term 'romantic' as a compliment:

Il serait difficile de dire sous quel maître il a étudié, mais il est évident qu'il n'a voulu suivre la méthode d'aucun de ceux de notre école. Aussi on l'accuse d'être romantique, car on emploie ce mot en peinture aujourd'hui, comme on s'en sert déjà depuis quelque temps en littérature sans avoir pu encore en donner une définition précise. Il me paraît qu' [...] on l'applique à ceux qui sortent du chemin battu pour arriver au but par des voies inconnues que leur audace leur a fait découvrir. S'il en est ainsi, au lieu d'en faire un terme de proscription, ne serait-il pas mieux d'applaudir à leurs essais, surtout lorsqu'ils sont heureux.

The unidentified Y. (said to be Thiers) also stands out for his extraordinarily intelligent and prophetic rebuttal of the reactionary critics (*Le Globe*, 28 Sept. 1824[2]): 'S'il n'y a pas d'arrangement dans son tableau, il y a un dérangement bien volontaire. Il n'existe sans doute rien de plus petit, de plus pauvre que la symétrie introduite dans les arts par les imitateurs de David [...] Tout cela [les expressions] tient à la recherche du terrible. C'est une autre espèce de genre classique, dont les modèles, au lieu d'être Virgile et Racine, seraient Shakespeare et le Dante.' Going on to defend Delacroix against accusations of 'une improvisation irréfléchie', he justly affirms: 'M. Delacroix a profondément étudié toutes les manières; on le sent à son tableau [...] Cette négligence de pinceau n'est qu'apparente: l'auteur, profondément dégoûté de tout ce qu'on fait aujourd'hui, s'est jeté dans les contraires, avec préméditation [...] Veut-on du génie de couleur et d'exécution, le tableau entier en est plein, et quand l'auteur aura terminé ses expériences, il sera le plus habile coloriste de notre école.'

In spite of his detractors, Delacroix won official recognition in the form of a medal, second class, awarded at the Salon and in having his picture bought for a generous sum by the State.

Delacroix's debt to Gros was noted at the Salon, by the anonymous critic of the *Mercure* who observed (op. cit., p. 203): 'Dès la première vue, on reconnaît à la couleur de M. Delacroix, un élève de M. Gros, le coloriste de l'école actuelle'; but went on to compare it unfavourably with the *Plague at Jaffa*, where there were 'point de mensonges ou de fictions de couleurs, point d'incohérence de tons et de fatigue pour les yeux éblouis par la disposition de la lumière.' What is surprising is that neither in 1824 nor later were the links beyond Gros, with the founder of the French neo-classical school, David, remarked on. With the passage of time, it is the essential continuity of the Davidian tradition in the *Massacres de Scio* that seems ever more striking; which is not to deny the originality of Delacroix's contribution in setting this forceful and boldly conceived monumental painting against the stream of late neo-classical affectation and pedantry, or in marking an advance on David and Gros in freedom of handling, the use of colour, and perhaps also in the humane observation of varieties of mute suffering. With a restraint that seems almost Davidian to generations that have known *Guernica*, Delacroix has, as surely as David crystallized the aspirations of his age in the *Horatii*, found a pictorial equivalent for the intense feelings aroused in a whole generation of Europeans by the Chios massacres, and summed up in the words of Pouqueville (op. cit., p. 481): 'Il n'y aura jamais assez de larmes pour pleurer les malheurs de Chios.' He does not celebrate the virility of Roman warriors, as does David in the *Horatii*, or the bogus humanity of Bonaparte, as Gros in *Jaffa*, yet his dying Greek, while owing much to Gros, seems also to be the direct descendant of the stricken figure, with beard and turban, in the foreground of David's early *St. Roch interceding on behalf of the Plague-stricken* at Marseille; the Greek's companion, to be derived from the Camilla in David's *Horatii*. There is a precedent for the old woman in the centre of David's *Sabines* and, in the same picture, though different in spirit, for a rearing horse mounted by a rider with a partially sheathed sword on the far right of the composition.

An unresolved question, that of how far the *Massacres de Scio* may have been retouched at a late stage under the influence of Constable, did not originate until over thirty years after the picture was painted. Constable was not mentioned in connection with Delacroix's work in any review of the Salon of 1824. Frédéric Villot, who did not know Delacroix in 1824, was the first to discuss the influence of Constable, claiming in 1856 (op. cit.): 'M. Delacroix, qui avait été à même de voir ses [Constable] paysages avant l'exposition, frappé de leur éclat et de leur texture [...], rentre dans son atelier, reprend son *Massacre de Scio* presque terminé, empâte ses lunières, introduit de riches demi-teintes, donne par des glacis de la transparence aux ombres, fait circuler le sang et palpiter la chair.' Théophile Silvestre says simply (op. cit. [1855], p. 63), without mentioning Constable: 'Delacroix obtint la permission d'y faire, avant l'exposition publique, quelques retouches dans la Salle des Antiques du Louvre.' Villot, in a second version (op. cit., 1865) and by now having presumably read Silvestre, changes the time and place of the retouching, while repeating, and adding to, the types of repainting that he claims were done: 'Après avoir passé à l'examen du jury, il descend sa toile dans une des salles des antiques, empâte les lumières [. . .]' Villot's accounts fail to inspire complete confidence not only because of their inconsistency as to the time and place of the retouching but also because so many types of revision are mentioned it is hard to see how these could derive from Constable's influence or to believe Villot had any exact knowledge of what was done.

Though Delacroix had seen and admired an oil sketch by Constable as early as November 1823 (*Journal* I. 35), it was not until 19 June in the following year, when the *Massacres de Scio* was probably nearing completion, that he saw the works that may have led him to retouch his own picture: 'Vu les Constable [. . .] Ce Constable me fait un grand bien', he records in the *Journal* (I. 115) on that date; and six days later: 'Revu les Constable' (ibid. 116). But from that time until the opening of the Salon on 25 August, there is no record of specific progress on the *Massacres de Scio* or of the influence the Constables may have exerted. The pictures Delacroix saw were no doubt the *Hay Wain* (National Gallery), the *View on the Stour* (San Marino, California), and a small picture of Yarmouth, all of which the Paris dealer Arrowsmith had just received from Constable; the first two were to be exhibited at the Salon (for a history of Constable's dealings with Arrowsmith, see H. Isherwood Kay, 'The Hay Wain', *Burl Mag*, LXII (1933), pp. 281-9). Since Delacroix evidently had an opportunity of studying major works by Constable over two months before the Salon opened, it seems strange indeed that he would not have retouched his picture under their influence until it had been accepted by the Salon jury. Perhaps it was only after it had been removed from his 'dark, damp' studio that he fully realized how far it lacked that special gift of Constable's for spreading the light of the sky over his landscapes by means of small, vibrant touches of pigment. But it is more important to know what changes, if any, Delacroix made after seeing the Constables than when they were made, and in the absence of adequate documentary proof these can only be deduced from internal evidence in correlation with accounts by people who knew Delacroix and which seem more or less untrustworthy. I believe the account by Delacroix's assistant, Pierre Andrieu, to deserve special attention, as he claims to quote Delacroix on the subject and publishes his report in a book edited by Théophile Silvestre, who is the only person Delacroix is known for certain to have spoken to about the impression Constable made on him in 1824 (cf. Delacroix to Silvestre, 31 Dec. 1858: 'Je vous en ai déjà parlé et de l'impression qu'il m'avait produite au moment où je peignais le *Massacre de Scio*': *Correspondance* IV. 60). Andrieu states (loc. cit., 1876), after quoting Delacroix as saying that the picture very nearly turned out to be grey and drab:

Très frappé, au Salon de 1824, par les paysages de Constable, M. Delacroix s'était mis à repeindre de pied en cap, sous cette impression, son *Massacre de Scio*, quinze jours avant de l'exposer. Le Comte de Forbin lui avait permis cette reprise dans la salle des Antiques du Louvre. 'Ah! disait-il, je m'en donnai là, toute cette quinzaine, employant les couleurs les plus vives et me rappelant mon point de départ, c'est-à-dire les gouttes d'eau tant cherchées pour *Dante et Virgile*.'[3]

If 'de pied en cap' is doubtless a hyperbole that should be discounted, evidence recently discovered, which shows that the *Massacres de Scio* was admitted by the jury on 6 August, nineteen days before the opening of the Salon (Johnson, op. cit., 1966), leaves no doubt at least that Delacroix did have a fortnight in which he could have done some retouching in the Louvre. I find it plausible that he could have been recalling his starting-point, the drops of water in the *Barque de Dante*, at a late stage after studying Constable and been fortified by his example in the use of a divided touch: touches of pure green and red, similar in size and colour to touches in those drops, are placed over the flat brown shadow on the old woman's forearm. Orange particles and rarer dots of blue are flecked over her skirt; colour apart, the former are exactly like the dry, broken crumbs of impasto that add the sparkle of reflected light to trees and fields and water in Constable's *Hay Wain* (see colour details of *Scio*, Johnson 1963, Prideaux 1966). To repeat my earlier summary of the problem (Johnson 1963, pp. 25 f.):

Unless new evidence comes to light, general agreement on the precise limits of the retouching may never be reached; it is likely that it was mostly concentrated in the foreground where it would have been most apparent to visitors to the Salon. But if the small, brightly coloured touches that have been indicated are admitted to have been inspired by Constable, then the meaning of his influence is clear. They serve to scatter, not the 'cool tint of English daylight' as do Constable's less variegated touches, but the bright hues of a Mediterranean sky; they introduce colour and transparency into dark shadows; and they help to bind separately studied passages into a subtly animated chromatic harmony. Delacroix's innovation is to have used a generally wider range of spectral hues for his touches and to have applied them to a monumental figure painting instead of to landscape.'[4]

After discussing the retouching, Andrieu goes on to report Delacroix as saying: ' "Je n'étais pas riche [. . .] et je n'avais employé que des couleurs de qualité commune: aussi ai-je revu avec peine plus tard que plusieurs d'entre elles ont disparu, les laques par exemple. Les bleus ont tourné au vert. Il n'y a que les couleurs Mars et le Jaune Indien qui se soient bien comportées." ' According to Lassalle-Bordes (loc. cit., 1880): '[Delacroix] trouva que les tons avaient poussé au jaune et fut pris de la fantaisie de le retoucher, ce qu'il fit en 1847, au moment où nous terminions la coupole du Luxembourg. Je voulus l'en détourner, mais inutilement.' But no confirmation of a later retouching has been found in other sources, and if one did indeed take place it seems most likely to have been after varnish was removed in 1854, an operation viewed with apprehension by Delacroix, who noted in the *Journal* (II. 206): '[Arnoux] dit que le *Massacre* n'a pas gagné au dévernissage, et je suis presque de son avis, sans avoir vu. Le tableau aura perdu la transparence des ombres comme ils ont fait avec le Véronèse et comme il est presque immanquable que cela arrive toujours.'

Twenty-three sheets of drawings and sketches listed as 'Scènes du Massacre de Scio (1824)' passed under lot 308 in Delacroix's posthumous sale in 1864 (R1491). Many of these remain to be traced, but all those listed below bearing the E.D. stamp are probably from that lot.

In addition to two composition studies for the *Massacres de Scio* contained in a sketch-book, four on separate sheets are preserved in the Louvre. Those in the sketch-book, being a mass of delicate, tangled *pentimenti* and placed eight pages before some sheets of copies dated 5 January 1824, are probably the earliest of the group (RF9142, fols. 18 and 19ʳ). That on fol. 18, though indeterminate in detail, is remarkably close to the final picture in the disposition of the main masses: the Turkish horseman is lightly indicated on the right, possibly a woman and child are below him in the corner of the frame; standing figures dominate on the left, with a figure, eventually to develop into the wounded Greek, stretched out at their feet. On fol. 19 the horseman is on the left, a seated couple embracing below him. This arrangement, though later discarded, is explored in a small pen-and-ink sketch which is hardly less tangled in its turbulent, dynamic forms but begins to develop on the left the Turk's captive nude with upraised arm who appears with her abductor on the right of the painting (23.4 × 37.8 cm (entire sheet), E.D., RF9203, repr. Huyghe fig. 107, Trapp fig. 22 and, with studies of separate figures on left of sheet, *Mémorial* no. 48). A more studied and deliberate attempt to organize the composition in a manner suited to a 'grande machine' is found in a large water-colour, where the main differences from the final design lie in the disposition of the mother and child, of the old woman, and of the landscape background (33.8 × 30 cm, R Ann 93ᵇⁱˢ, Louvre, RF3717, repr. in colour Escholier I, opp. p. 122, Trapp pl. III). This study shows some influence of Persian miniatures (see L. Johnson, op. cit., 1965). It is closely related to a drawing in the Louvre on the verso of a study for the *Natchez* (J101) (black lead, 19.8 × 30.5 cm, RF9219, repr. Sérullaz *Dessins* 1952, pl.

xxx-47, Huyghe fig. 106. To the right of this study and not reproduced in Sérullaz or Huyghe is a schematic drawing in brown ink for the wounded Greek in the left foreground). Robaut also records a drawing heightened with sepia, 23 × 19 cm, which passed in the same sale as the water-colour (Coutan-Hauguet, 16 Dec. 1889, lot 151) and differed from it in minor details only (R Ann 93ᵗᵉʳ, repr. Tracings I. Present whereabouts unknown). A sheet of black lead drawings in the Louvre includes what is almost certainly a preliminary study for the woman seated in the right foreground of the water-colour; an inscription in pencil at the top, '30 decembre 1823. Le jour du carton de Michel Ange', suggests that the water-colour was not completed before the beginning of 1824 and is not therefore, as sometimes suggested, the composition which Delacroix said he fixed in the first week of November 1823 (20.4 × 27.7 cm, E.D., Louvre, RF9199).

Finally, the sixth composition study in the Louvre introduces the dead mother and child in the right foreground and consolidates the two main pyramidal groups of figures in a manner close to the final design (black lead, 25 × 20 cm, E.D., RF9201ʳ, repr. Sérullaz *Dessins* 1952, pl. xxx-48, *Mémorial* no. 49, Huyghe fig. 106a).

Studies for individual figures that appear in the final painting are as follows:

Adolescents embracing far left
1. Black lead, 25 × 20.2 cm, E.D., Louvre, RF9205.

Woman seated left foreground
1. Two studies, black lead, 30.2 × 23 cm, E.D., Louvre, RF9202 (repr. Sérullaz *Dessins* 1952, pl. xxxi-49, *Mémorial* no. 50). On same sheet, a study for the group of combatants in centre background, and a head in *profil perdu*, which seems more likely to be connected with the woman tied to the horse on the right than, as suggested in *Mémorial*, with the adolescent on the far left.
2. Three studies, black lead heightened with white chalk, 37.3 × 30.5 cm, E.D., Louvre, RF9208 (repr. P. H. Michel, op. cit. 1947, fig. 7).

Centre figure seen from back
1. Detailed study of back and drapery, black lead, 24.9 × 20.3 cm, E.D., Louvre, RF9206.

Old Woman (see also study in oils J77)
1. Black lead, with colour notes for her costume, 28.3 × 20.3 cm, E.D., Louvre, RF9209 (repr. *Mémorial* no. 51, notes transcribed). On same sheet, studies for the man with back turned seated in the centre of the composition.

Woman tied to horse
1. Four studies, black lead, 27.2 × 19.3 cm, E.D., Louvre, RF9207 (repr. Sérullaz *Dessins* 1952, pl. xxxii-52, *Mémorial* no. 52).

Turk on horse

1. Studies of pose, right hand, head. Black lead, 25.1 × 19.6 cm, E.D., Louvre, RF9212 (repr. Sérullaz *Dessins* 1952, pl. XXXII-51).
2. Three studies of pose, black lead, 25 × 20.3 cm, E.D., Louvre, RF9213 (repr. *Mémorial* no. 53).
3. Miscellaneous studies, including one for Turk on horse with woman attached, horse's legs, three of a woman with a child, a group fighting. Black lead on tracing paper, 18.5 × 33 cm, E.D., Louvre, RF9204.

Infant far right

1. Sheet of studies, black lead, 17.1 × 11.7 cm, E.D., Louvre, RF9210.

A further sheet of pencil drawings in the Louvre bears miscellaneous studies on the recto and verso, especially for a woman seated (23.5 × 18.7 cm, E.D., RF9211).

Slight pencil studies that appear to be connected with this painting are contained in Louvre sketch-book RF23355: fol. 17ᵛ, wounded Greek left foreground (?); fol. 38ʳ, woman with two dead infants. A sheet in the Museum of Art of the Romanian Academy at Bucharest contains two studies in black chalk, apparently done from a female model, related to the figure on the extreme left of the Louvre water-colour, one is a study of drapery and legs from the waist down, the other shows the head in profile, shoulders and bare breasts, basically establishing the pose that was to be used for the dead mother on the far right of the painting (21.8 × 32 cm, E.D., Inv. no. 336). Robaut reproduces in Tracings 1 a sheet of three studies of the old woman seated holding a dead child, a motif that was carefully explored in these three variations but finally abandoned (pen-and-ink and sepia wash on tracing paper, dimensions not given, E.D., passed in Féral sale 21 Oct. 1885 as 'Etudes de plusieurs figures pour le Massacre des innocents' and in Eugène Charavay sale, May 1890. A sheet with replicas of two of these studies, in brush and sepia ink over pencil, 21.6 × 31.8 cm, which was with Sotheby's in 1972, appears to be a forgery based either on the lost original or on Robaut's copy.

Neither the water-colour of an old woman listed by Robaut under no. 94 as a study for the *Massacres de Scio* (repr. Escholier I. 121) nor the pencil drawing related to it (repr. ibid. 120) seems to have any connection with the painting.

See also *Girl seated in a Cemetery* (J78) for a study in oils related to this painting; and *Three Life Studies of a Female Nude* (J(O)3).

---

[1] E. de Mirecourt, op. cit., 1870 (1st ed. 1856), p. 36: 'Il avait, rue des Maçons-Sorbonne, un atelier sombre, humide, ouvert aux souffles de la bise.' T. Silvestre, op. cit., 1855, p. 47: '[Delacroix] a fait à la diable le *Massacre de Scio* dans un petit atelier humide du quartier de la Sorbonne.' G. Lassalle-Bordes, loc. cit., 1880, p. xviii: 'Il me conta qu'il avait

commencé [le *Massacre de Scio*] dans une chapelle d'église en réparation (à la Sorbonne, je crois).' Léon Riesener, the artist's cousin: 'dans un atelier situé place Saint-Michel; l'atelier était une des chapelles de côté d'une vieille église' (quoted by A. Joubin, op. cit., 1938).

I cannot find that there was any church in the rue des Maçons at the relevant period, but there were several former colleges on the west side and Delacroix may have used a chapel in one of those as a studio.

[2] Though much more favourable than the earlier review in the *Constitutionnel*, which was certainly by Thiers, this article appears on internal evidence to be very possibly by the same author. Both criticisms refer, for example, to Delacroix's 'search for the terrible' and, alone among the Salon reviews, mention that the Greeks are shown after wandering for several days in the countryside.

[3] Other nineteenth-century versions of the retouching by people who were close to Delacroix, but which inspire little or no confidence, come from Piron (p. 74); Lassalle-Bordes (loc. cit., 1880); and Chenavard (loc. cit., 1895).

[4] I first localized Constable's influence in the foreground, drawing attention to the coloured touches on the sandy ground, on the arm of the old woman and on the infant on the right, in public lectures delivered at Cambridge University and the Courtauld Institute on 21 November 1955 and 29 May 1956, the text of the second lecture being still in my possession. My conclusions were partially based on knowledge of Andrieu's account, not referred to in the lectures.

---

106 TASSO IN THE HOSPITAL   Pl. 92
OF ST. ANNA, FERRARA

19¹¹⁄₁₆ × 24 in. (50 × 61 cm)* Signed top left: *E. Delacroix*.[1]
Moreau pp. 92, 145, 160, 191, 257. R88
1824
Mrs. Hortense Ande-Bührle, Zurich

Provenance: Painted in 1824 for M. Formé, according to Moreau (p. 92); bought by Alexandre Dumas from M. Susse, place de la Bourse, *c.* 1833; sold by Dumas to Etienne Arago; he sold it to Susse, who in turn resold it to Dumas; he sold it to M. Petit, a cloth merchant; bought from him by Alexandre Dumas fils;[2] his sale ('Collection de M. Al. D . . . fils'), 28 March 1865, lot 2 (dimensions wrongly listed as 48 × 32 cm), to M. Delaroche, 14,000 fr.; Khalil Bey; his sale, 16 Jan. 1868, lot 18, to Haro, 16,500 fr.; Carlin; his sale, 29 Apr. 1872, lot 5, to M. J. C. Candamo, 40,000 fr.; sale M. C. G. de Candamo, 14 Dec. 1933, lot 10 (repr.), to Kenneth Clark, 46,000 fr., to at least 1952; Emil Bührle, Zurich, d. 1956; the present owner, his daughter.

Exhibitions: Salon 1824, *h.c.*; Musée Colbert, Paris 1830B, no. 40; *Gal. Beaux-Arts*, Paris 1846A, no. 97 (in 'Suites du Supplément'); *Universelle*, Paris 1855, no. 2929; *Bd Italiens*, Paris 1860, Supp. no. 346; *Bd Italiens*, Paris 1864, no. 16 (lent by Alexandre Dumas fils); Alsace-Lorraine, Paris 1885, no. 110; London 1936, no. 5; Paris 1937, no. 317; London 1942, no. 4; Wildenstein, London 1952, no. 8; Bremen 1964, no. 6; Petit Palais, Paris 1968–9, no. 270.

Literature: M., *Revue critique des productions de peinture, sculpture, gravures exposées au Salon de 1824* (Dentu et Blosse, Paris, 1825), pp. 339 f.; F., 'Musée Colbert. Quatrième Exhibition', *Journal des Artistes et des Amateurs*,

4ᵉ année, no. XXII, 1ᵉʳ vol. (30 May 1830), pp. 593 f.; *Biographie . . . des contemporains* (chez F. G. Levrault, Paris, 1834), III, p. 39; Silvestre *Delacroix* (1855), p. 80; C. Baudelaire, 'Exposition universelle', *Le Pays*, 3 June 1855, reprinted in *Curiosités esthétiques*, 1868 (*Œuvres*, Pléiade ed. Paris 1932, II, p. 160); C. Perrier, 'Exposition universelle des Beaux-Arts', *L'Artiste*, 5ᵉ série, XV, 6ᵉ livraison (10 June 1855), p. 73; *Correspondance* I. 407, III. 253, 253 n. 3; T. Gautier, 'Exposition universelle de 1855', *Le Moniteur universel*, 25 July 1855; M. Du Camp, *Les Beaux-Arts à l'Exposition universelle de 1855* (Librairie nouvelle, Paris, 1855), pp. 112 f.; T. Gautier, review of Exhibition *Bd Italiens*, Paris 1860, *Le Moniteur universel*, 5 May 1860; Z. Astruc, *Le Salon intime. Exposition au Boulevard des Italiens* (Poulet-Malassis & De Broise, Paris, 1860), p. 44; A. Dumas, 'Eugène Delacroix', *Le Monde illustré*, 22 Aug. 1863, p. 124 (reprinted from *Mes mémoires* M. Lévy, Paris), vol. IX (see Tourneux, p. 27); A. Cantaloube, *Eugène Delacroix, l'homme et l'artiste* (E. Dentu, Paris, 1864), p. 49; L. Chardin, 'Retour à Eugène Delacroix', *L'Artiste*, 7th ser. II (1864), p. 149; T. Gautier, Introduction to catalogue of sale Alexandre Dumas fils, 28 March 1865, p. 3; A. Hermant, 'La Collection de Khalil-Bey', *Le Monde Illustré*, XXII (Jan.-June 1868), p. 26, full-page repr. (Maurand print), p. 25; C. Yriarte, notice on Khalil Bey sale, ibid. 50; Haro, letter of protest dated 25 January 1868, ibid. 75; A. Dumas fils, letter of protest to the Editor, ibid. 114; *L'Art*, 16 (1879), p. 250, repr. (Flameng etching), opp. p. 250; C. Yriarte, Introduction to catalogue of sale Alexandre Dumas fils, 12 May 1892, pp. 8 f.; Moreau-Nélaton I. 59, 163, Mouilleron litho. repr. fig. 28, II. 58, 156, 194; Escholier I. 93, II. 209, III. 219; A. Joubin, 'A propos du *Tasse dans la Maison des Fous*', *GBA*, XI (1934), pp. 247-9, repr. p. 247; G. Rouchès, *Delacroix et la littérature italienne* (Les Presses françaises, Paris, 1934), p. 601; A. Joubin, 'Delacroix au Salon de 1824', *BSHAF*, 1937, pp. 149 f. (publication of paper read at meeting of 5 Apr. 1935, cf. résumé, *BSHAF*, 1935, pp. 40 f); J. Laver, *French Painting and the Nineteenth Century* (Batsford, London, 1937), p. 28, repr. in colour pl. 15; *Journal* I. 35 n. 4 (corrected III. 523), III. 520 (addition and correction to I. 4 n. 1), 525 (addition to I. 71); Huyghe, pp. 173, 176, 206, 463, 489, repr. pl. 335; L. Johnson, Cat. Exh. Edinburgh-London 1964, under no. 98; Maltese, pp. 34, 147; J. Pommier and C. Pithon (eds.), *Les Fleurs du Mal par Charles Baudelaire* (Club des Libraires de France, Paris, 1966 ed.), pp. 378 f., repr. p. 379; L. Johnson, 'Eugène Delacroix et les Salons. Documents inédits au Louvre', *Revue du Louvre*, 16 (1966), pp. 220, 227 n. 5; Trapp, p. 345.

Prints: Lithograph in reverse by Mouilleron, 1844; wood engraving by Charles Maurand, 1868; etching by Léopold Flameng, 1879; etching by Achille Devéria of the figure of Tasso alone with some variations in the costume and

background (example of first state in M-Nélaton Port., vol. I).

Copy: Canvas, 18.4 × 24.4 cm. A contemporary copy, possibly by Poterlet. Private collection, Paris.

Delacroix planned to do a painting of this subject with life-size figures in September 1822 (*Journal* I. 4), but abandoned the project and painted this smaller version. Though the composition appears to have been determined by November 1823 ('J'ai arrêté cette semaine une composition de *Scio* et presque celle du *Tasse*', *Journal* I. 35, entry for 9 November), it is known from M.'s Salon review that the picture was hung at the Salon of 1824 only 'dans les derniers temps de l'exposition'. It is therefore unlikely to have been completed before the winter of 1824 (the Salon opened on 25 August). M. was the only reviewer to comment on it at the time, criticizing the artist for not placing the distasteful madmen at a greater distance from Tasso. While conceding 'ceux qui mettent avant tout la verve et la chaleur, trouveront de tout cela chez cet artiste, et avec la plus grande originalité de composition', M. concludes in a typical reactionary vein, 'mais ceux dont la raison veut être satisfaite avant tout, trouveront que ce jeune homme n'a qu'un goût déréglé, sans frein, et qu'il est, avec toutes ses belles qualités, trop voisin du bas et de l'ignoble.' The picture was more harshly attacked for not conforming to academic standards in F.'s review of 1830: 'Y a-t-il une seule proportion anatomique exactement rendue ?' By 1855 it won general admiration from the critics, Charles Perrier, for example, finding it 'd'une finesse et d'une beauté que M. Delacroix a malheureusement sacrifiées trop souvent' and contrasting it with the work of its owner, Alexandre Dumas père, who 'comprendra peut-être un jour combien une telle sobriété est préférable à la diffusion et à la multiplicité des détails'.

Delacroix first notes down the subject 'Tasse à l'hôpital des fous' *c*. 1820, in a list of prospective themes for pictures contained on the inside of the front cover of a Louvre sketch-book (RF23357; for a transcript of the note in context, see *Journal* III. 343—Supp.). There was much interest in the life and work of Torquato Tasso (1544-95) in the early nineteenth century: Byron's poem *The Lament of Tasso* appeared in 1817; Goethe's play *Torquato Tasso* was available in French translation by 1823; Fleury Richard (1777-1852), a founder of the School of Lyon, exhibited a *Montaigne visiting Tasso in the Hospital* at the Salon of 1822 (Musée des Beaux-Arts, Lyon); Delacroix's close friend Pierret was collaborating in 1819 with Baour-Lormian on a new edition of his French translation of the *Gerusalemme liberata*; and John Black had published his scholarly *Life of Torquato Tasso; with an Historical and Critical Account of his Writings* in two volumes in 1810.

Tasso was confined in the Hospital of St. Anna, where lunatics were usually imprisoned, on the orders of his patron

Alphonso d'Este, Duke of Ferrara, from 1579 to 1586. Though the poet was genuinely deranged, the myth that he had been locked up because of his passion for Leonora d'Este, the Duke's sister, had already gained currency by the end of the sixteenth century and received an extra fillip during the Romantic era, notably in Byron's poem, in spite of the fact that it had already been competently discredited in Black's biography of 1810.

While it is indisputable that Delacroix knew of Byron's *Lament of Tasso* by 1819, without having read it (*Correspondance* I. 54: letter to Pierret), there is no evidence, either visual or documentary, to show that his painting was inspired by Byron, as claimed by Moreau-Nélaton (I. 59) and by later authorities. There is, however, no doubt that he shared the prevalent Romantic view of Tasso as a persecuted genius unjustly accused of madness, expressing it in such phrases as: 'Qu'on est rempli d'indignation contre ces indignes protecteurs qui l'opprimaient sous le prétexte de le garantir contre ses ennemis [. . .]! Que de pleurs de rage [. . .] il a dû verser en voyant que pour lui enlever plus sûrement [ses chers manuscrits] on l'accusait de folie' (*Correspondance* I. 54); and 'Le Tasse expie le beau en prison' (*Journal* III. 357). Delacroix consequently presents Tasso as a spiritual and contemplative figure surrounded by coarse-grained madmen, implying that he is the only sane person in a mad world. His attitude to insanity here is thus very different from Géricault's, as manifested in his series of objective portraits of the insane painted c. 1822-3, which reflect a new attitude to mental illness as something to be treated clinically and with humanity. Delacroix treats the madmen as grotesques unworthy of sympathy and his compassion for Tasso lies not in the fact of his alienation, but in his plight as an exceptional being supposed to be in complete possession of his faculties imprisoned with lunatics. Since Tasso was, in spite of his mental illness, perfectly conscious of his miserable situation, there is much historical justification for Delacroix's interpretation of the scene, which cannot be dismissed as mere Romantic fancy. In a letter written shortly after his confinement, for example, Tasso complained: 'But, above all, I am afflicted by solitude, my cruel and natural enemy' (quoted in Black's biography of 1810, II. 59).

According to Léon Riesener, the model Vicentini posed for 'le fou du Tasse', no doubt the second madman from the left, as for the executioner in the *Marino Faliero* (J112) (quoted in Escholier II. 209).

Robaut dated a second painting of this subject, now in the Reinhart Collection at Winterthur, to 1827, in spite of the fact that it is dated 1839 and was known by him to have been rejected by the Salon jury of 1839. Though I discussed this error in detail and rectified it in 1966 (op. cit., p. 227 n. 5), it has continued to prove very persistent. It may have originated with hearsay (and false) evidence, reported by F.

in 1830 (op. cit.), that Delacroix had had a *Tasso in the Madhouse* rejected by the Salon jury of 1827. Also, Piron had later (1865, p. 106) wrongly listed 'Un Tasse dans la Maison des Fous' as one of the pictures Delacroix showed at the Salon of 1827. It was the 1839 version which inspired Baudelaire's sonnet 'Sur *Le Tasse en prison*' (cf. Pommier and Pichon, op. cit., 1966). Van Gogh saw in Delacroix's conception of Tasso an ideal that he wished to attain in his own portraits during his Arles period: in a letter (531) to his brother Theo, he declares:

I want to paint men and women with that something of the eternal which the halo used to symbolize, and which we seek to convey by the actual radiance and vibration of our colouring.
Portraiture so understood [. . .] would be more in harmony with what Eug. Delacroix attempted and brought off in his 'Tasso in Prison', and many other pictures, representing a *real* man. Ah! portraiture, portraiture with the thoughts, the soul of the model in it, that is what I think must come.

It is not known which version Van Gogh refers to, since he could have seen prints of both.

An early pencil study of the subject, showing Tasso meditating in a reclining position, is in the collection of Claude Roger-Marx, Paris (repr. *Mémorial*, no. 56). A highly finished pencil drawing, signed and dated 1825, of the same design as this painting but with the addition of two inmates on the left and a crucifix on the wall in the background, is in the collection of Peter Nathan, Zurich (repr. ibid., no. 57; R135).

[1] At a distance of 3.5 cm below this signature, there is another, apparently faked, of the same form but smaller and underlined. It was no doubt added at a time when the genuine signature, already recorded in R Ann as 'à peine visible', had become obscured by dirt or was covered by a frame.

[2] The history of the picture from the time it was bought by Dumas père down to this point is given by Dumas fils, unfortunately without dates, in his letter to the editor of *Le Monde illustré* of 1868, which, though intended to rectify published inaccuracies in the provenance, has gone unheeded in the subsequent Delacroix literature. Dumas fils states in the letter that his father bought the painting 'thirty-five years ago', and that he himself finally sold it to M. Delaroche, a dealer in curios—meaning, it is here presumed, at his sale in 1865.

107 MACBETH AND THE WITCHES
Pl. 93

Oils over lithograph laid down on canvas, $13 \times 10\frac{1}{4}$ in. $(33 \times 26$ cm$)$
Signed top left: *Eug. Delacroix.*
R118 (1825. No repr.)
c. 1825
Messrs. Wildenstein, London

Provenance: Mme Louise Babut (?),[1] by 1864; Hartmann, of Mulhouse; his sale (M.X.), 11 May 1876, lot 12, 1,700 fr.; Albert Hecht, by 1878; Pontremoli; with Wildenstein, by 1970.

Exhibitions: *Bd Italiens*, Paris 1864, Supp. to 2nd ed., no. 294 (?); Durand-Ruel, Paris 1878, no. 158; *EBA*, Paris 1885, no. 111.

Literature: E. Bergerat, Introduction to catalogue of Hartmann sale, 11 May 1876; Delteil, under no. 40; Escholier I. 205 n. 1.

This picture is painted in mostly brown tones over the lithograph by Delacroix, parts of which were left to show through. The print is dated to 1825 by Moreau (p. 40), followed by Robaut (no. 117) and Delteil (no. 40), and while it is not known when Delacroix made this experiment in painting over it, it does not seem likely to have been attempted long after the lithograph had been completed. It may have been made with a view to judging whether or not to paint a version on canvas.

In a list of pictures compiled in the 1840s, Delacroix includes without comment a '*Macbeth et les sorcières*', which Robaut identifies as R118 (*Journal* III. 372 and n. 15), but it could equally well be R Ann 118*bis* (J108).

The lithograph was probably Delacroix's earliest work of substance inspired by Shakespeare. Delacroix shared to the full the interest in Shakespeare in French Romantic circles of the 1820s and the excitement over English productions of his plays. He wrote enthusiastically of productions he saw in London in 1825 and of the English company's famous visit to Paris two years later. Yet very few of his many works of Shakespearian subjects date from this decade, and he is not known to have seen a production of *Macbeth*. The *Macbeth* lithograph is one of Delacroix's most striking prints, in expression and technique, and is reported by Philippe Burty to have been one of the artist's favourites. Drawn from Act IV, scene i, it bears in certain states the caption:

> Toil and trouble;
> Fire burn, and cauldron bubble.

---

[1] A painting of this subject was among the four pictures lent by Mme Babut to the exhibition *Bd Italiens*, Paris 1864, and was listed in the Supplement to the 2nd edition of the catalogue simply as 'Macbeth et les sorcières', without dimensions. I find it impossible to determine whether it was this work or J108, or yet a third version that has since disappeared (see J108 n. 3).

108 MACBETH AND THE WITCHES   Pl. 93

Paper laid down on canvas, $10\frac{5}{8} \times 13\frac{3}{4}$ in. (27 × 35 cm)
Signed bottom right (and dated 1825 or 1832 ?[1]):
    Eug. Delacroix.
R Ann 118*bis* (1825)
Whereabouts unknown

Provenance: Given by the artist to the banker Alfred Tattet or his wife (?),[2] he died 1856; Jules Carayon-Talpeyrac; his sale 27 March 1893, lot 16, to Baron Joseph Vitta, of Lyon,

620 fr.; his sale 15 March 1935, lot 3 (repr.), to Rodière, 25,000 fr.

Exhibitions: Nice 1930, no. 2; Louvre 1930, no. 25A.

Literature: ? Silvestre *Delacroix* (1855), p. 81; ? P. de Saint-Victor, 'Eugène Delacroix', *La Presse*, 4 Sept. 1863;[3] J. Guiffrey, Preface to catalogue of Vitta sale, 15 March 1935, p. 7.

This work is known to me only from Robaut's tracing and from the illustration in the catalogue of the Vitta sale, reproduced here. Unlike the lithograph of the same subject (see J107), the design is horizontal with a view of the sea at the upper right.

---

[1] Said to be dated 1825 in the catalogue of the exhibition Louvre 1930 (when apparently unseen by the compiler), 1832 in the catalogue of the Vitta sale. No date is reproduced beside the signature on Robaut's tracing in Tracings I, and none is noted in his annotations to the tracing.

[2] Robaut notes on his tracing of this picture: 'N'est-ce pas cette toile que Delacroix aurait offerte à M^r ou Mme Tattet ?' He also records that an old label bearing an inventory number, 6606, that he was unable to identify was stuck at the upper left.

It is also possible that this was the picture lent by Mme Babut to the exhibition *Bd Italiens*, Paris 1864. See J107 n. 1.

[3] 'De *Macbeth* il a illustré deux pages: la *Rencontre avec les sorcières*, où le geste du Thane tirant son épée révèle en lui, par un trait de génie, la subite conception du crime qui réalisera la prophétie des trois monstres. — *Lady Macbeth*.' Of the two known versions of the subject (see also J107), this is the only one that could conceivably be interpreted as showing Macbeth about to draw his sword, but the passage may well refer to a third version that has not come to light since the 1860s.

109 TAM O'SHANTER PURSUED BY WITCHES   Pl. 95

$10\frac{5}{16} \times 12\frac{1}{8}$ in. (26.2 × 30.8 cm)*
Signed bottom right: *ED*
See Moreau pp. 172 and 248. See R136 and 197 (No repr. of this version)
Probably 1825
Private collection, Switzerland*

Provenance: Probably the version said to have been painted for Mme Dalton in 1825, d. Algiers 1859; ? returned to Delacroix by her daughter, Mme Charlotte Turton;[1] Marquis de Lambertye; his sale (Marquis de L.) 4 Feb. 1865, lot 14 ('Ballade écossaise. A la lumière de la lune voilée par les nuages, un cavalier presque mort de peur et tenant sa monture par le cou, franchit un pont à demi ruiné; des ombres sont accrochées à la queue de son cheval', 25 × 31 cm. Moreau-Nélaton annotated copy of sale cat., *BN Estampes*: 'Vieux tableau faible ressemblant à un Scheffer'), to Daru (Dieterle R), 2,300 fr.; Khalil Bey; his sale 16 Jan. 1868, lot 19 ('Légende écossaise. Signé à droite: E. Delacroix',[2] 26 × 30 cm), to Verdier, 3,750 fr.; Ricardo Hérédia, Comte de Benahavis; his posthumous sale, 20 June 1900, lot 3 ('Légende écossaise. Signé à droite', 26 × 30 cm., with mention of provenance from Khalil Bey), 3,100 fr.;

Fig. 10. *Tam o'Shanter*, J. Rogers after A. Cooper.

Baron Joseph Vitta, of Lyon, by 1930; Terlindern, Zurich, d. 1968; the present owner, from 1968.

Exhibitions: ?*Gal. Lebrun*, Paris 1829, no. 44 (see J139, under *Exhibitions*, for full catalogue entry); Nice 1930, no. 11; Louvre 1930, no. 38A.

Literature: Probably Silvestre *Delacroix* (1855), p. 82; T. Gautier, Preface to catalogue of Khalil Bey sale, Jan. 1868 (previously published in *Le Moniteur universel*, 14 Dec. 1867 and *La Liberté*, 13 Jan. 1868); Escholier I, p. 153, repr. opp. p. 160; *Journal* I. 296 n. 1; C. Bernard, 'Une liaison orageuse. Correspondance inédite entre Eugène Delacroix et Eugénie Dalton', *Nouvelles Littéraires*, numéro spécial: *Delacroix*, 9 May 1963, p. 8; *Mémorial*, mentioned under no. 399; Huyghe, p. 15; L. Johnson, 'Eugène Delacroix et les Salons. Documents inédits au Louvre', *Revue du Louvre*, 16 (1966), p. 229 n. 12.

The scene is taken from Robert Burns's poem *Tam o'Shanter* (1791). Returning home late one night, the hero passes some witches celebrating their Sabbath in a ruined church and, having taunted a young one dressed in a brief chemise with the words 'Weel done, Cutty Sark!', is pursued to the point illustrated here, the offended witch well in the lead:

> A running stream they darena cross.
> But ere the key-stane she [the mare] could make,
> The fient a tail she had to shake!
> For *Nannie*, far before the rest,
> Hard upon noble *Maggie* prest,
> And flew at *Tam* wi' furious ettle;
> But little wist she *Maggie*'s mettle—
> Ae spring brought off her master hale,
> But left behind her ain gray tail.
> The carlin claught her by the rump,
> And left poor *Maggie* scarce a stump.

In a letter of June 1831, Delacroix informed Feuillet de Conches: 'J'ai lu l'histoire de Tam O'Shanter dans la

ballade même de Burns, écrite en écossais avec le patois très difficile à comprendre, qui m'était expliqué à mesure par une personne du pays [perhaps one of the Fielding brothers]' (*Correspondance* I. 277 f.[3]).

Pictorially, Delacroix's conception of the subject seems to have been strongly influenced by Abraham Cooper's painting *Tam o'Shanter*, exhibited at the British Institution in 1813 (no. 36) and probably known to Delacroix through J. Rogers's engraving (Fig. 10 here).

It has been recognized in recent years (*Mémorial*, no. 399; L. Johnson, op. cit., 1966) that Moreau's account of Delacroix's several versions of this subject, followed in most respects by Robaut, who had evidently seen only one version (J139) when he published his catalogue, is so confused as to be of little use in sorting out their history. Indeed, Robaut had already shown himself puzzled by Moreau's dating of the same picture to 1825 and 1827 on different pages of his catalogue. It is therefore necessary to depend primarily on other sources in attempting to reconstruct the history of these pictures. It has never been suggested that more than three were painted. Only two versions are extant, this one and the Bührle picture (J139), but the general appearance of a third version which belonged to Charles Blanc is known from a line drawing taken from it with a pantograph by Paul Chenay, who gave this drawing to Robaut in 1886 (R Ann, marginal note to R197; Tracings I, no. 197. Note and drawing published in L. Johnson, op. cit., 1966, p. 229 n. 12, fig. 3. Fig. 11 here). According to R Ann, the stretcher of this last version measured 38.75 × 46 cm. The problem is to decide, on admittedly inconclusive evidence, which of the three pictures was reputedly painted for Mme Dalton in 1825, which exhibited at the Salon of 1831, and which referred to by Delacroix at Champrosay on 17 June 1849 as being among a group of pictures in progress: 'J'ai ébauché

Fig. 11. *Tam o'Shanter*, P. Chenay after Delacroix.

depuis mon arrivée et jusqu'au 26, jour où je retourne à Paris pour deux jours: *Tam O'Shanter*' (*Journal* I. 296).

The dimensions of the Salon painting, almost certainly including the frame, are recorded in the Salon register as 38 × 43 cm (L. Johnson, op. cit., 1966, p. 220). These would seem to rule out the Blanc version, which is too large, leaving the present picture and the Bührle version as possibilities for the Salon of 1831. The latter is the more mature composition and the more likely to have been selected for exhibition at a Salon. The present picture thus emerges as the version supposed to have been painted for Mme Dalton in 1825. This seems a reasonable probability not only on stylistic grounds, but because the initials with which it is signed are an appropriate form of signature for a gift to an intimate friend. Though Moreau was apparently the first to record (p. 172) that the subject was painted for Mme Dalton in 1825, there is confirmation during Delacroix's lifetime, if not of Mme Dalton's ownership, at least that a version was done in 1825, Silvestre *Delacroix* (1855) listing (p. 82): 'Tam O'Shanter et les Sorcières, d'après la ballade de Burns [probably the Blanc version]. — Même sujet, plus petit, fait en 1825.'

A pencil drawing in the Fitzwilliam Museum, Cambridge, supports this sequence: close to the Bührle version, for which it is apparently a study—in the pose of the witch on Maggie's tail, in the position of Maggie's legs and of the bridge arching under her belly—it nevertheless retains elements of the presumed earlier version that do not appear in the finished Bührle picture—the cast of Maggie's head, her reins, the witch directly behind Nannie (repr. Cat. Exh. Edinburgh–London 1964, pl. 50).

It has been argued (L. Johnson, op. cit., 1966, p. 229 n. 12) that an undated letter which Delacroix addressed to a friend to announce that he was sending him a painting of this subject was very possibly written to Charles Blanc about the end of June 1849 and applied to the version Delacroix is known to have painted at Champrosay in that year. (Robaut thought (R197 and marginal note in R Ann) that the letter was probably addressed to Charles Blanc in 1827 (when Blanc, however, was only fourteen); Joubin, to Feuillet de Conches, who is not recorded anywhere as an owner of a *Tam o'Shanter*, in 1830 or 1831 (*Correspondance* I. 264, V. 273).) The 1849 version would thus be the one known from the pantograph drawing (Fig. 10), and probably the picture which passed in the B. (Blanc?) sale in Paris, 30 March 1855, lot 20 (as 'Tristam O'Shanty', 37 × 46 cm)—a lot wrongly identified as one of the smaller versions by Moreau and Robaut.

See also J139.

¹ Mme Turton wrote to Delacroix from Algiers in 1859, informing him that she had been called to her dying mother's bedside and asking permission to visit him in Paris in ten or twelve days' time. She wished him to return a portrait of her mother which Mme Dalton had given him long ago and also wrote: 'J'ai retrouvé près d'elle tous les dessins et peintures qu'elle avait eu de vous.' As stated in the same letter, Mme Turton had lost her father and been abandoned by her husband: she may well have needed to sell, to Delacroix or with his help, the works by him that had belonged to her mother. (The letter was published by C. Bernard, op. cit. *infra*, 1963). Mme Dalton had settled in North Africa in 1839.

² This is apparently a mistake or a deliberate attempt to deceive on the part of the cataloguer. No version with a full signature on the right is known, and it will be noted that the cataloguer of the Hérédia sale in 1900 avoids describing precisely how the picture is signed.

³ In my opinion, this letter is more likely to have been written to Feuillet, who published a series of 'Lettres sur le Salon de 1831' in *L'Artiste* under the pseudonym Leaves de Conches, in reply to an inquiry about the *Tam o'Shanter* Delacroix exhibited at the Salon of 1831 than as an explanation of a version which Joubin supposes, with insufficient reason, Delacroix had sent to Feuillet in the same year.

110 CHARLES VI AND ODETTE DE CHAMPDIVERS   Pl. 96

14 × 10¹³⁄₁₆ in. (35.5 × 27.5 cm)
Signed bottom right: *Eug. Delacroix*
Moreau p. 116. R137 (1825)
Probably 1825
La Comtesse T. de Vigneral, Paris

Provenance: Duval le Camus, painter and dealer; his sale (anon.), 17 Apr. 1827, lot 38 ('Charles VI et Odette, sujet tiré des amours des Gaules'), 110 fr.; Frédéric Leblond, by 1832, d. 1872; Dumas-Descombes, by 1885; his widow or son-in-law, M. Bouriel (R Ann); the present owner, by 1963.

Exhibitions: Musée Colbert, Paris 1832, no. 144 (listed as lent by M. Leblond); *EBA*, Paris 1885, no. 73; Edinburgh–London 1964, no. 11, repr.; Bourg-en-Bresse 1971, no. 15, repr.

Literature: Silvestre *Delacroix* (1855), p. 80; Moreau-Nélaton I. 141; anon., 'Un Delacroix réapparaît grâce à l'exposition du Louvre', *Connaissance des Arts*, no. 137 (July 1963), p. 21, repr. p. 21; M. Sérullaz, 'A Comment on the Delacroix Exhibition organized in England', *Burl Mag*, CVII (1965), p. 366; L. Johnson, 'Some Historical Sketches by Delacroix', ibid. CXV (1973), p. 672 and n. 1.

Print: Full-scale lithograph by Maurin, March 1826 (*Bibliographie de la France*, 11 March 1826, p. 205, gravure 156).

Odette de Champdivers, a young Burgundian lady, became Charles VI's mistress during the first decade of the fifteenth century, when his madness had become pronounced and he was virtually separated from his wife, Queen Isabeau of Bavaria. Odette nursed the King with devotion and came to be popularly known as 'la petite reine'. She had a daughter by him. Charles VI died in 1422, having become King in 1380 at the age of twelve.

The name of Leblond, for whom Moreau says this picture was painted in 1825, is still inscribed on the back of the canvas, but it seems that he could have acquired it only at or after the Duval le Camus sale of 1827. It once seemed to me, on the grounds of stylistic characteristics which the painting shares with the *Penance of Jane Shore* (J103) and *Don Quixote in his Library* (J102), both of 1824, that Moreau's date of 1825 might be a little too late, but the discovery since of the date of Maurin's lithograph (see L. Johnson, op. cit. 1973, p. 672 n. 1), which it seems unlikely would have been done many months after the painting, leads me to think that Moreau was most probably right, and that the *Charles VI and Odette* was painted within a few months of Delacroix's return from London in August 1825, when he was in close touch with Bonington.

Though attention has been drawn to the fact that in 1843 Halévy composed an opera *Charles VI*, it is perhaps more pertinent that Delaville's play of the same title, with Talma as the King, opened in Paris on 6 March 1826 (see H. Collins, *Talma* (Faber & Faber, London, 1964), p. 360).

A signed drawing of the same subject passed in the Poterlet sale on 7 December 1840 (see Tourneux, p. 140).

This painting has suffered from extensive craquelures and lack of cleaning.

111 LOUIS D'ORLÉANS   Pl. 97
SHOWING HIS MISTRESS

$13\frac{7}{8} \times 10\frac{9}{16}$ in. (35.2 × 26.8 cm)* Relined
Signed bottom left, on the base of the bed:
   EUG. DELACROIX[1]
Moreau p. 254. R139 (1825. Repr. of nude only, in reverse, after Villot's etching) and p. 538.
c. 1825/6
Messrs Reid & Lefevre, London

Provenance: Frédéric Leblond, by 1832; anon. sale (by Schroth), 6 March 1843, lot 30 ('Le duc d'Orléans montrant le corps de sa maîtresse', without dimensions), 300 fr.; Frédéric Villot; his sale (M. F.V.) 25 Jan. 1864, lot 12 ('Le duc de Bourgogne montrant sa maîtresse au duc d'Orléans', with further description but no dimensions), 1,200 fr.; Jérôme, Prince Napoleon, d. 1891; Count Duchâtel, by 1885; Alfred Beurdeley, by 1916; his sale 6 May 1920, lot 34 ('Le duc de Bourgogne montrant sa maîtresse au duc d'Orléans', repr.), to Nunès et Fiquet, for M. Schwob d'Héricourt, 25,250 fr.; with Paul Brame, 1967; Mr. B. E. Bensinger, Beverly Hills, California, by 1968; with Messrs Reid & Lefevre, London, 1974.

Exhibitions: Musée Colbert, Paris 1832, no. 145 ('Un jeune seigneur montre à son courtisan le corps de sa maîtresse'); *EBA*, Paris 1885, no. 71 ('Le duc de Bourgogne montrant sa maîtresse', 30 × 20 cm²); St. Petersburg 1912, no. 198 ('Le duc de Bourgogne montrant sa maîtresse au duc d'Orléans'); Lefevre, London 1974, no. 8 ('Le duc d'Orléans, montrant sa maîtresse au duc de Bourgogne'), repr. in colour.

Literature: Anon., 'Exposition du Musée Colbert au profit des familles des indigens cholériques', *L'Artiste*, III (1832), 18e livraison, p. 198; Silvestre *Delacroix* (1855), p. 80; G. Dampt, *Eugène Delacroix. A propos de la dernière exposition de ses œuvres* (Tresse, Paris, 1885), p. 21; F. Monod, 'L'Exposition centennale de l'art français à Saint-Pétersbourg', *GBA*, 4th per. VII (1912), p. 307; Moreau-Nélaton I. 141, repr. fig. 106; Escholier I. 214, repr. p. 213; *Journal* III. 372 n. 5—Supp.; Escholier 1963, p. 42; Huyghe, p. 166; L. Aragon, ' "Qu'est-ce que l'art, Jean-Luc Godard?" ', *Les Lettres Françaises*, no. 1096 (9-15 Sept. 1965), p. 8; L. Aragon, 'Deux remarques purement historiques', ibid., no. 1097 (16-22 Sept. 1965), p. 1, repr. p. 1; K. Roberts, review of exhibition Lefevre, London 1974, *Burl Mag*, CXVII (1975), p. 58, repr. p. 59, fig. 55.

Print: Etching by Frédéric Villot of the nude only.

The significance of this scene and the correct identity of the participants seem to have been lost to writers on Delacroix from the time it was first exhibited in 1832 till 1965, when the poet Aragon elucidated the subject. The anonymous critic of the exhibition at the Musée Colbert in 1832 could not reasonably have read a mischievous character ('un caractère de malice') into the expression of the woman had he been aware of her true plight, nor could Moreau have described her as 'endormie'. The misnomer 'Le duc de Bourgogne montrant sa maîtresse au duc d'Orléans' originated with the catalogue of the Villot sale in 1864 and persisted, with one or two equally inaccurate variations, down to Huyghe a century later. Louis Aragon (2nd ref. cit.) drew attention to a passage in a nineteenth-century edition of Barante's *Histoire des ducs de Bourgogne*, where it was related, in volume III published in 1824, how the Duke of Orleans (1372-1407) had offended his former chamberlain, Aubert le Flamenc, seigneur de Cany, by taking his wife (Mariette d'Enghien) as his mistress, and on one occasion playing a trick on the still unwitting cuckold by showing him her naked body, covering only her face so that she would not be recognized. Aragon calculated that the scene painted by Delacroix would have occurred sometime between 1388 and 1390, when the Duke of Orleans was still Duke of Chartres. While Aragon is unquestionably right about the subject-matter, it may be doubted whether the summary account of the episode in Barante was Delacroix's primary source. The story is recounted in greater detail (on such a point as a sheet concealing the woman's face, for example), and with more humour, in Brantôme's *Les Vies des dames galantes*, as part of the First Discourse, *Sur les dames qui font l'amour et leur maris cocus*, reissued in the complete works in 1822:

Louis, duc d'Orléans, tué à la porte Barbette à Paris, fit bien au contraire, grand débauscheur des dames de la Cour, et tousjours des plus grandes; car, ayant avec luy couché une fort belle et grande dame, ainsi que son mary vint en sa chambre pour luy donner le bon-jour, il alla couvrir la teste de sa dame, femme de l'autre, du linceul, et luy descouvrit tout le corps, luy faisant voir tout nud et toucher à son bel aise, avec defense expresse sur la vie de n'oster le linge du visage ny la descouvrir aucunement, à quoi il n'osa contrevenir, luy demandant par plusieurs fois ce qui luy sembloit de ce beau corps tout nud : l'autre en demeura tout esperdu et grandement satisfait. [. . .]

Elle, après son mary party, fut interrogée de M. d'Orléans si elle avoit eu l'allarme et peur. Je vous laisse à penser ce qu'elle en dist, et la peine et l'altere en laquelle elle fut l'espace d'un quart-d'heure. [. . .]

Et le bon fut de ce mary, qu'estant la nuict d'amprès couché avec sa femme, il luy dit que M. d'Orléans luy avoit fait voir la plus belle femme nue qu'il vit jamais, mais, quant au visage, qu'il n'en sçavoit que rapporter, d'autant qu'il luy avoit interdit.

[. . .] Et cette dame tant grande, et de M. d'Orléans, on dit que sortit ce brave et vaillant bastard d'Orléans [comte de Dunois, 1403–68], le soustien de la France et le fléau de l'Angleterre, et duquel est venue cette noble et généreuse race des comtes de Dunois. (*Œuvres complètes du Seigneur de Brantôme, accompagnées de remarques historiques et critiques. Nouvelle édition . . .*, ed. L. J. N. Monmerqué, Foucault, Paris, 1822–3, 8 vols., VII (1822), pp. 60 f.)

This particular text was probably the immediate source of Delacroix's painting. Since the husband and wife are not openly named, it is possible that Delacroix did not know who they were, and that might explain why in his only reference to the picture he called it simply: 'Le duc d'Orléans montrant sa maîtresse' (*Journal* III. 372).

The picture is stated to have been painted in 1825 in the Villot sale catalogue, which Villot himself helped to compile, and although the title of the painting is wrongly listed the date may well be accurate, especially since Villot had apparently copied the painting as early as the 1820s and done an etching of part of it. While it is reasonable to accept that it was painted around the end of 1825, when Delacroix returned to Paris from England and was working with Bonington, certain features of the colouring suggest that it could be somewhat closer in date to the *Death of Sardanapalus* (J125) and that some latitude in interpreting Villot's date, recorded almost forty years after the event, should therefore be allowed.

According to Robaut, Villot did a copy of this painting in 1829 which hung alongside the original in the collection of Prince Napoleon and was wrongly attributed to Decamps. It was perhaps this copy which passed in the Baron Lepic sale on 18 June 1897, in the catalogue of which it is listed as attributed to Delacroix (lot 9, 32 × 26 cm, to Michel Lévy, 100 fr.). A replica that I saw in Paris in 1962 in the collection of M. Léon Suzor was listed in the inventory compiled after his death in the same year, by M. Strolin, as the copy by Frédéric Villot of 1829. It was unsigned and its dimensions, which I took myself, were 36.2 × 28.4 cm. Its present location is unknown to me.

A copy in pastels by an unknown artist, 28.5 × 22.5 cm, was shown as by Delacroix in the Exhibition Berne 1963–4, no. 104 (Coll. Peter Nathan, Zurich).

[1] The signature does not appear to be mentioned anywhere in print before 1974 (Cat. Exh. Lefvre, London 1974), but is noted by Robaut in an annotation to no. 71 in the 2nd edition of the Cat. Exh. *EBA*, Paris 1885: 's.b.g.' (signé bas gauche) (*Bib AA*, MS. 298*ter*).

[2] The dimensions are recorded for the first time in the catalogue of this exhibition, without doubt inaccurately, as in the case of the painting shown under the preceding number, *Marine.—Dieppe*, which was lent by the same owner, Count Duchâtel, was also later in the Beurdeley collection and was listed as measuring 30 × 50 cm, instead of 36 × 52 cm, its true dimensions.

112 THE EXECUTION OF THE DOGE MARINO FALIERO   Pl. 98

$57\frac{5}{8} \times 45$ in. (1.464×1.143 m)

Signed bottom left: *Eug Delacroix f*[bat]

Inscribed on the open volume held by the winged lion:

PAX TIBI MARCE EVANGELISTA MEUS

Moreau pp. 168, 189. R160.

1826

The Wallace Collection, London

Provenance: Sold by Delacroix in March 1856 for 12,000 fr. (*Journal* II. 442), to M. Bouruet-Aubertot (Moreau, pp. xviii n. 1, 189 n. 3);[1] he sold it to Isaac Pereire for 20,000 fr. (W. Bürger, op. cit. *infra*, 1864, p. 198 n. 1, and F. Villot, 1865), before Aug. 1863; he sold it for 60,00 fr. (Moreau, p. xviii n. 1), probably to Monjean; Monjean sold it for 80,000 fr. in 1868 (Moreau N), to Lord Hertford, d. 1870; Richard Wallace, his heir, d. 1890; Lady Wallace, his widow, d. 1897; by her bequest to the British nation as part of the Wallace Collection, which opened as a national museum at Hertford House, London, in June 1900.

Exhibitions: Gal. Lebrun, Paris 1826A, no. 45; Salon 1827–8, no. 294; British Institution, Pall Mall, London 1828, no. 102; Gal. Beaux-Arts, Paris 1844—for sale at 1,000 fr. (Moreau, p. xviii n. 1); *Universelle*, Paris 1855, no. 2921; Bd Italiens, Paris 1864, no. 151; (lent by Sir Richard Wallace to the Museum at Bethnal Green for public exhibition, June 1872–April 1875, no. 371); R.A. London 1896, no. 65.

Literature: L. V. [Vitet], 'Exposition de tableaux au bénéfice des Grecs (IIᵉ article). M. Delacroix', *Le Globe*, 3 June 1826; anon. review of id., *Le Constitutionnel*, 5 June 1826; V. Hugo, 'Exposition de tableaux au profit des Grecs: la nouvelle école de peinture', August 1826 (not published till 1967, in *Œuvres complètes de Victor Hugo* (Le Club Français du Livre, Paris), II, p. 984); anon., 'Salon de 1827. La Nouvelle Ecole', *La Pandore*, 24 Nov. 1827; D. [Delécluze], review of Salon, *Journal des Débats*, 20 Dec. 1827; Anon., review of Salon, *Le Figaro*, 21 Dec. 1827; A. Béraud *et al.*, *Annales de l'Ecole française des Beaux-Arts* (Pillet aîné, Paris, 1827), p. 74; A. Jal, *Esquisses, croquis, pochades ou tout ce qu'on voudra sur le Salon de 1827* (Ambr. Dupont, Paris, 1828), pp. 111–13; *Visite au Musée du Louvre, ou Guide de l'amateur à l'exposition . . . (Année 1827–1828) . . . par une Société de Gens Lettres et d'Artistes* (Leroi, Paris, 1828),

p. 106; [A. Vergnaud], *Examen du Salon de 1827. Novembre, première partie* (Roret, Paris 1828), p. 10; anon., 'Fine Arts. British Gallery', *Literary Gazette*, 16 Feb., 1828 (quoted in W. T. Whitley, *Art in England, 1821–1837* (University Press, Cambridge, 1930), p. 142); anon., 'French Pictures', *The Times*, 20 June 1828; *Biographie . . . des Contemporains* (chez F. G. Levrault, Paris, 1834), III, p. 39; Alexandre D.[Decamps], *Le Musée, revue du Salon de 1834* (Ledoux, Paris, 1834), p. 54; [A. de la Fizelière], 'Promenades dans les galeries des Beaux-Arts', *Bulletin de l'Ami des Arts*, II (1844), Supp. to the 2nd livraison (20 Jan.), p. 42; A. de la Fizelière, 'Galeries des Beaux-Arts. Coup d'œil sur la peinture moderne', ibid. III (1845), p. 4; C. Baudelaire, 'Salon de 1845' (*Œuvres* Pléiade ed., Paris 1932, II, p. 26); P. Pétroz, 'Exposition universelle des Beaux-Arts', *La Presse*, 5 June 1855; T. Gautier, 'Exposition universelle de 1855', *Le Moniteur Universel*, 19 July 1855; M. du Camp, *Les Beaux-Arts à l'Exposition universelle de 1855* (Librairie nouvelle, 1855), pp. 113 f. and n.; E. Gebauer, *Les Beaux-Arts à l'Exposition universelle de 1855* (Librairie napoléonienne, Paris, 1855), pp. 33 f.; E. Loudun [Alph. Balleyguier], *Exposition universelle de 1855* (Ledoyen, Paris, 1855), p. 116; T. Silvestre, *Les Artistes français*, 1855 (1926 ed., I, pp. 26, 29); E. Delécluze, *Les Beaux-Arts dans les deux mondes en 1855* (Charpentier, Paris, 1856. Reprint of articles published in the *Journal des Débats* in 1855), pp. 221, 224; A. de la Forge, *La Peinture contemporaine en France* (Amyot, Paris, 1856), p. 64; A. Dumas père, 'Eugène Delacroix', *Le Monde illustré*, 22 Aug. 1863, pp. 124–6; C. Blanc, 'Eugène Delacroix', *GBA*, XVI (1864), pp. 22 f., 127 (reprinted in *Les Artistes de mon temps* (Firmin-Didot, Paris, 1876), pp. 44 f., 86); W. Bürger [T. Thoré], 'Galerie de MM. Pereire', ibid. 198 and n., 199, 200, repr. opp. p. 198 (Flameng etching); id., 'Eugène Delacroix. Exposition de ses œuvres à Paris', *L'Indépendance Belge*, 28 Aug. 1864; A. Dumas père, *Causerie sur Eugène Delacroix*, lecture delivered at the salle Martinet, where the exh. *Bd Italiens*, Paris 1864 was being held, on 10 Dec. 1864, p. 49 of MS. in *BN Estampes* (Yb³ 977; this passage summarized in Moreau-Nélaton I. 182 f.; lecture reprinted in serial form in *La Presse* from 29 Dec. 1864 to 12 Jan. 1865. For further details of the publication of the contents of this lecture before 1865, see Tourneux, p. 27); F. Villot, catalogue of his sale [M.F.V.], 11 Feb. 1865, p. 3; Piron, pp. 73, 81, 105; Moreau, pp. xvii f., xviii n. 1, 94; G. Lassalle-Bordes, in *Correspondance* (Burty 1880), II. xxiii; Moreau-Nélaton I. 79, 80, 84, 87, 91, 161, 163, 182, repr. fig. 54, II. 113, 156, 167; Escholier I. 142, 176–8, 180, repr. opp. p. 180, 182, 195, 214, 217, II. 209; Hourticq 1930, pl. 13; *Correspondance* I. 177 n. 2, 213 f., 214 n. 1, 407, 426, II. 192, 192 n. 1, 411, III. 83 n. 3, 255, 255 n. 3, IV. 59 n. 1, V. 176 n. 4, 177; G. H. Hamilton, 'Eugène Delacroix and Lord Byron', *GBA*, XXIII (1943), p. 103 n. 12, repr. p. 104, fig. 3; *Journal* I. 57 n. 1, II. 442 n. 7; W. Friedlaender, *David to*

Delacroix (Harvard University Press, Cambridge, Mass., 1952), p. 116; G. Busch, 'Die Enthauptung des Dogen Marino Faliero von Eugène Delacroix', *Festschrift Kurt Badt zum siebzigsten Geburtstag* (Berlin, 1961), pp. 184 ff.; L. Johnson, 'The Delacroix Centenary in France—I', *Burl Mag*, CV (1963), p. 302; Johnson 1963, p. 27, repr. pl. 13; L. Johnson, 'The Delacroix Centenary in France—II', ibid. CVI (1964), p. 260; Huyghe, pp. 166, 173, 176, 178, 204, 343, repr. fig. 120, in colour pl. VI; L. Johnson, 'Bonington at Nottingham', *Burl Mag*, CVII (1965), p. 319; Maltese, pp. 37, 77, 124, 136, 148, 152; L. Johnson, 'Eugène Delacroix et les Salons. Documents inédits au Louvre', *Revue du Louvre*, 16 (1966), p. 220; T. Prideaux *et al.*, *The World of Delacroix* (Time Inc., New York, 1966), full-page colour repr. p. 73; J. Schultze, '"Voir Jean Duvet pour les Anges"', *Kunstgeschichtliche Studien für Kurt Bauch 1967*, p. 280, repr. fig. 2; *Wallace Collection Catalogues. Pictures and Drawings. Text with Historical Notes and Illustrations*, 16th ed. (London, 1968), pp. 85 f., no. P 324, repr. (repr. in separate volume of illustrations to earlier editions, p. 57); Trapp, pp. 59, 60, 63, 66, 69, 77, 79, 83, 93, 93 n. 8, 193, 300, 346, repr. in colour pl. v.

Print: Etching by Léopold Flameng, dated December 1863.

Copy: A sketch-copy in oils on canvas (33 × 27.5 cm*) by an unidentified artist, formerly in the Roberts, 1913, and Georges Aubry collections, was sent to Christie's as a Delacroix from South America in 1970 (Photo: Archives photographiques, BAP 7691235822; Cooper, 723093). Lent by Georges Aubry, it was shown as by Delacroix in the exhibition Paris 1927, no. 265.

Lassalle-Bordes reports (loc. cit., 1880) that when he asked Delacroix, in the 1840s, which of the pictures he had painted was his favourite he replied he had always had a weakness for this one. Lamenting its early withdrawal from the exhibition for Greek relief in 1826, Victor Hugo (op. cit.) records that it was also a favourite with the public: 'La foule se passionnait pour ce tableau.'

In a letter dated 21 April 1826, Delacroix wrote of it to his friend Soulier: 'Je finis un *Marino Faliero*, tableau assez considérable qui sera, je pense, à cette exposition pour les Grecs dont je t'ai parlé.' (*Correspondance* I. 179.) It was included in the catalogue of the exhibition for Greek relief, which opened at the Galerie Lebrun on 15 May, with a description of the subject which is the artist's own, presumably, and the fullest he was ever to provide:

Marino Faliero.
Le Doge de Venise Marino Faliero, ayant, à l'âge de plus de 80 ans, conspiré contre la république, avait été condamné à mort par le Sénat. Conduit sur l'escalier de pierre où les doges prêtaient serment avant d'entrer en charge, on lui trancha la tête, après l'avoir dépouillé du bonnet de doge et du manteau ducal. Un membre du conseil des Dix prit l'épée qui avait servi à l'exécution, et dit en l'élevant en l'air: *La justice a puni le traître*. Aussitôt après

la mort du doge, les portes avaient été ouvertes, et le peuple s'était précipité pour contempler le corps de l'infortuné Marino Faliero. (Voir la tragédie de Lord Byron.)

Byron's play was published in 1820, the author disclaiming that it was written to be performed. Delacroix departs from his text in only one basic respect, which is however essential to the development and final effectiveness of the composition: in the play, the execution takes place at the top of the staircase to the Doges' Palace, the patricians forming a circle round the condemned man (cf. stage directions at the beginning of Act v. iii; iv. 18–20); and as the curtain falls, the foremost member of the populace to rush into the court turns to those behind and exclaims: 'The gory head rolls down the "Giant's [sic] Steps"!' Preliminary studies show the corpse of Marino Faliero lying at the feet of the patricians at the top of the staircase (Louvre RF9216, 9996, repr. Mémorial, nos. 92 and 93; larger repr. of former in Maltese, pl. 15). The final arrangement was therefore a deliberate departure from Byron's text, prompted no doubt by a combination of pictorial, psychological and historical considerations. To have left the body at the top of the staircase would have made for a top-heavy composition, congested with figures above, dominated by steps below. The solution chosen, with the bare expanse of steps above the corpse instead of below it, is as pictorially effective in this glittering scene as the stark wall that stretches above the murdered Marat in David's severe masterpiece of 1793, and has the psychological advantage of isolating the beheaded Doge from his aloof peers and bringing him closer to the plebeians, with whom he had conspired. Historically also, there is some justification for placing the point of execution below the patricians, if not precisely at the point selected by Delacroix; for in his *Lives of the Doges* Marin Sanuto gives this account, published in Italian and English as an appendix to Byron's tragedy, where it was very likely consulted by Delacroix:

judgment was also given [. . .] that the execution should be done on the landing-place ['pato'] of the stone staircase, where the Dukes take their oath when they first enter the palace. On the following day, the seventeenth of April [1355], the doors of the palace being shut, the Duke had his head cut off, about the hour of noon. And the cap of estate was taken from the Duke's head before he came down stairs. (Lord Byron, *Marino Faliero*, 2nd ed., 1821, p. 192.)

Delacroix must also have been aware that the Council of Ten stand at a point in the palace higher from the court than the single flight of stairs he has depicted, and a preliminary composition study in brown ink, known to me only from the tracing by Robaut reproduced here (Fig. 12), shows that he initially tried to overcome this difficulty by suggesting that a second flight descended at right angles to the one painted here. The final solution gives the staircase an aspect of completeness, with the lion of St. Mark at the end of the ramp, while at the same time suggesting that the populace

are ascending from a lower point: the problem of having a distracting flight of steps visible below the body is again avoided, and the viewer who is familiar with Byron's tragedy is free to imagine that the 'gory head' has rolled down the 'Giant's Steps'. Though Maxime du Camp (op. cit., 1855) charged Delacroix with representing the so-called 'Giants' Staircase', built by Sansovino some two centuries after the execution of the Doge, the anachronism in this instance is Byron's, not Delacroix's, and the ignorance the critic's: the staircase in the painting is quite unlike Sansovino's and was surely not intended to emulate it. At the same time, it cannot be said that Delacroix was concerned to paint an accurate reconstruction of the place of execution as it existed in 1355.

Fig. 12. *Execution of Marino Faliero*, study. A. Robaut after Delacroix.

In its richness of hue and variety of texture, in the splendour of translucent glazes unmatched in the earlier works, the painting exemplifies the style that Delacroix developed shortly after the English journey, probably in collaboration with Bonington and no doubt partly under his influence. It is his masterpiece in the manner. While a debt to Venetian painting has often been noticed, the influence has been evoked in such general phrases as Thoré-Bürger's 'aussi fort qu'un Véronèse' (op. cit., 1864, p. 198) and Gautier's 'Cette toile [. . .] pourrait tenir son rang dans une galerie vénitienne, entre Vittori Carpaccio et Paris Bordone' (op. cit., 1855). An indication of some specific borrowings will therefore not be out of place. Some of the heads, particularly that of the figure with folded hands at the top of the ramp are clearly inspired by Cariani's *Portrait of Two Venetians* in the Louvre, formerly thought to represent Giovanni and Gentile Bellini (for Delacroix's copies from this portrait, see J13). The heads around that figure also have some analogies in arrangement, head-dress and features with the ambassador's entourage in the *Reception of an Ambassador* from the school of Gentile Bellini, also in the Louvre—a group copied in pencil by Delacroix in the same sketch-book bought in England in 1825 as contains on the previous page a copy of the Cariani (Louvre, RF9143, fol. 8ʳ). The greybeard dressed in black, standing at the head of the staircase behind Faliero's ducal robe derives from Titian's *Self-portrait* of *c.* 1550, of which Delacroix did a brown wash study after a reversed engraving on a sheet which contains two further studies of heads for the *Marino Faliero* (Louvre, RF10599). Despite these noble prototypes, the most common reproach made by French critics in the 1820s, apart from inept criticism of the prominence of the staircase, was for the ugliness of the figures, Louis Vitet, for

example, pointing out in a not wholly unsympathetic notice (op. cit., 1826) that in following a different path from David, Delacroix had here sacrificed 'l'art à la réalité, au lieu de le sacrifier à l'idéal'; and protesting: 'Il est des degrés intermédiaires entre le type d'Adonis et celui de l'Orang-Outang.'

Another sort of Venetian influence lies in the lunette above the entrance, which is apparently a free adaptation of the sculpture of the Doge Francesco Foscari kneeling before the lion of St. Mark, above the early fifteenth-century door to the Palace on ground level known as the *Porta della Carta*. The Doge Foscari, it will be recalled, was also the subject of a tragedy by Byron and, in the 1850s, of a painting by Delacroix.

The likelihood of a Flemish influence in the repoussoir figure holding a sword in the left foreground must also be considered, for there is reason to believe that Delacroix knew Johannes Stradanus's *Entry into Casulum* (Fig. 13. Cf. note in Delacroix sketch-book, Louvre, RF9150, fol. 1ʳ: 'Voir Johannes Stradanus flamand gravures de combats des Medicis', which may not however have been written before 1827).

No certainly authentic oil sketches have come to light (see

Fig. 13. *Entry into Casulum*, J. Stradanus.

J(D)16), but there is a fine water-colour study of the executioner, for whom the model Vicentini is said to have posed (Léon Riesener, quoted in Escholier II. 209. R1517, 23.2 × 17.4 cm, signed and dated 1826, Lyman Allyn Museum, New London, Conn. Repr. *Mémorial*, no. 92). Two very summary pencil studies, one showing the executioner, right arm upraised without a sword, the decapitated Doge and severed head before an arch, the other just the head lying beneath an architectural frame, are on facing sheets five pages after studies dated 5 January 1824 in the Louvre sketch-book RF9142 (fol. 32ᵛ, 33ʳ), and therefore seem likely to be connected with Delacroix's note in the *Journal* (I. 57) on 3 March 1824: 'Composé, ne sachant que faire, les *Condamnés à Venise*.' A note in English, 'Exec. at Venice', inside the back cover of a sketch-book that was in use both before and after the English journey probably refers also to this picture (Louvre, RF23355). Another summary pencil study, probably drawn after the English journey, shows the headless body of the Doge with three or four figures standing nearby. It is on a sheet of studies of Greek costume formerly attributed to Bonington (27.3 × 22.8 cm, Castle Museum, Nottingham; repr. L. Johnson, op. cit., 1965, p. 321, fig. 52). A sheet of pen-and-ink studies contained in an album in the Louvre is a doubtful attribution (RF10513; repr. *Mémorial*, no. 94).

The final work was well received when first exhibited in London, where it was to find a permanent home shortly after the artist's death. The critic of the *Literary Gazette* named it first among seventy works selected for mention in the British Institution show of 1828, and judged it to be 'in a noble and elevated style of art'.[2] Sir Thomas Lawrence is said to have been interested in acquiring it at the time (*Correspondance* IV. 59), but settled for a Bonington. In France, the Duke of Orleans wished to offer it as a gift to Victor Hugo, but Delacroix refused to let it go (cf. Tourneux, p. xi).

Asked to lend the picture to an exhibition at Bordeaux in 1851, Delacroix reported: '*Le Doge* a de nouvelles craquelures qui le déshonorent et demandent le mastic, le repeint, etc.' (*Correspondance* III. 83 f.)

Robert Fleury exhibited a painting of the same subject at the Salon of 1845 (no. 1449). Of horizontal format, it showed the Doge descending the staircase to the place of execution (engraved repr. in C. Yriarte, *Venice . . .*, translated from the French by F. J. Sitwell (Geo. Bell & Sons, London, 1880), where it is said to be in the possession of Sir Richard Wallace. Present location unknown.). It was compared unfavourably to Delacroix's picture by Baudelaire (op. cit., 1845): '[Il] rappelle imprudemment un magnifique tableau qui fait partie de nos plus chers souvenirs. [. . .] La composition était analogue; mais combien plus de liberté, de franchise et d'abondance!'

---

[1] According to Lassalle-Bordes (loc. cit. *infra*, 1880), followed by Robaut, the picture was originally sold by Delacroix for 1,800 fr. and

bought back for 3,000 fr. If this is true, the transactions must have occurred before 1844 when the picture was exhibited for sale at the Galerie des Beaux-Arts, for Moreau reports (pp. xvii f.) that for ten years from the time Delacroix moved into his studio in the rue Notre-Dame-de-Lorette in 1845, it remained 'sur l'escalier au-dessus de la porte d'entrée' and 'n'avait pu trouver acquéreur à aucun prix'. But Frédéric Villot (loc. cit. *infra*, 1865), who in this matter is probably a more reliable source than Lassalle-Bordes, records that Delacroix sent it to London [in 1828] hoping to sell it for 2,500 fr., but after waiting several months was offered only 1,500 fr. by a collector, and it was returned to him. Villot continues: 'Il ne se sépara de cette toile que dans les dernières années de sa vie.'

Alexandre Dumas (op. cit., 1863) reports that in 1836 he visited the Duke of Orleans who was about to send Victor Hugo an *objet d'art* by way of thanking him for a volume of his poems. Dumas claims he suggested sending a painting instead, having the (unsold) *Marino Faliero* in mind. The Duke is supposed to have authorized him to offer up to 6,000 fr. for it, but Delacroix refused, not being allowed to know who was to receive the gift.

[2] Léonor Mérimée must also have been referring to it when, in a letter dated 11 March 1828 to the painter S. J. Rochard, he wrote: 'Je ne suis pas surpris que le tableau de Lacroix ait du succès à Londres. Il y a vraiment de la couleur dans ce tableau, et une entente générale d'effet qui rappelle Paul Véronèse; mais j'aurais été bien surpris si les amateurs des tableaux de Wilkie avaient trouvé les détails de Lacroix assez terminés.'

---

113 A TURKISH OFFICER KILLED IN THE MOUNTAINS   Pl. 99

13 × 16⅛ in. (33 × 41 cm)*
Signed bottom left: *Eug. Delacroix*
Moreau p. 244 (1827). R201 (1827)
1826
Emil Bührle Foundation, Zurich

Provenance: H. Didier; his sale (anon.) 3 May 1849, lot 46 (as 'Grec mort (Guerre de la Délivrance)'), 500 fr.; M. J. Leroy; Arsène Houssaye; his sale (A.H.) 29 March 1854, lot 65 (under same title), 550 fr.; ? anon. sale 8 May 1861, lot 18 (under same title), 950 fr.; Barthélemy; his sale (B.) 14 Dec. 1871, lot 3 (as 'La Mort d'Hassan', 32 × 40 cm. Leroy the only previous owner listed), to M. Brun-Rodrigues, 5,600 fr.; Ad. Liebermann of Wahlendorf; his sale 8 May 1876, lot 25 (under same title), 7,100 fr.; Baron de Beurnonville; his sale 29 Apr. 1880, lot 15 (under same title), 7,900 fr. (apparently bought in); his sale 24 March 1883, lot 154 (apparently bought in or withdrawn); his sale (baron de B.) 21 May 1883, lot 154, bought in at 4,000 fr. (R Ann); Baron d'Erlanger; Sale Leo d'Erlanger and Commodore Gerald d'Erlanger, London 25 March 1946, lot 35a (as 'The Dead Moor'), to Messrs. Tooth, £1,800; sold by them to the Hon. Mrs. A. E. Pleydell-Bouverie, London, 1949; bought from an English dealer by Emil Bührle of Zurich, 1952, d. 1956.

Exhibitions: *Gal. Lebrun*, Paris 1826A, no. 47 ('Un officier turc tué dans les montagnes'); ? *Société des Amis des Arts*, Paris 1826/7, *h.c.*;[1] Tooth, London 1949, no. 9 (as 'Mort de Hassan', 1827); R.A., London 1949-50, no. 190 (under same title and date); Wildenstein, London 1952, no. 10 (under same title, 1824-6), repr.; Winterthur 1955, no. 68 (under same title, 1824); Venice 1956, no. 5 (under same title, 1824–6); Zurich 1958, no. 112 (under same title, 1826), repr.; Louvre 1963 (under same title), no. 60, *M* no. 74, repr.

Literature: L. V. [Vitet], 'Exposition de tableaux au bénéfice des Grecs (11ᵉ article). M. Delacroix', *Le Globe*, 3 June 1826; Silvestre *Delacroix* (1855), p. 80; Escholier I. 182; *Correspondance* I. 177, V. 145 n. 2; D. Cooper, 'French Pictures in London Galleries', *Burl Mag*, XCI (1949), p. 205, repr. p. 204, fig. 28; G. H. Hamilton, 'Delacroix, Byron and the English Illustrators', *GBA*, XXXVI (1949), pp. 263 f., 264 n. 5, 266 f., repr. (after Robaut), p. 264; *Journal* I. 99 n. 3; G. S. Whittet, 'London Commentary', *The Studio*, CXLIV (1952), p. 90, repr. p. 90; L. Johnson, 'Delacroix at the Biennale', *Burl Mag*, XCVIII (1956), pp. 327 f.; *Sammlung Emil G. Bührle. Festschrift zu Ehren von Emil G. Bührle zur Eröffnung des Kunsthaus-Neubaus und Katalog des Sammlung Emil G. Bührle* (Zurich, 1958), p. 86, no. 112, repr. pl. 34; L. Johnson, 'The Delacroix Centenary in France—II', *Burl Mag*, CVI (1964), pp. 260 f.; Trapp, pp. 120, 120 n. 32.

Though this picture has more generally been known as the *Death of Hassan* since Moreau and Robaut catalogued it under that title, there seems to be no evidence that it was ever called that by Delacroix or by anyone during his lifetime, and it seems indeed improbable that Delacroix would have represented the death of Hassan without placing his killer, the Giaour, in a prominent position. Also, the burning village in the background suggests that this is an episode from the Greek War of Independence rather than from Byron's poem, *The Giaour*, in which the artist could have found no hint of a fire. There is, however, no denying the close relationship, in pose and features, between this dead Turk and the fallen Hassan in works certainly inspired by *The Giaour* (J138 and Delteil no. 55); and in one detail of costume, the flowered palampore, it has an extra point in common with Byron's description of Hassan's dress (line 666 and n.). It therefore seems probable that Byron's poem was very much in Delacroix's mind when he painted this picture and was a direct inspiration, but is not actually intended to be illustrated here.

In view of the picture's inclusion in the show for the benefit of the Greeks in 1826, Hamilton's dating of it to that year, sight unseen (op. cit. 1949, p. 264), is the most acceptable; Delacroix's comment in a letter of May 1826, 'J'irai bientôt remettre *aux Grecs* ce que je finis en ce moment', could indeed refer to this work, among others shown (J112, J114 and J(L)101). In addition to that exhibition, it was at least submitted to the *Société des Amis des Arts* by Delacroix on 7 November 1826, with the title '*Un Turc mort, dans un paysage*' and at an asking price of 300 fr. (*Correspondance* V. 145).

It excited scarcely any comment on the one occasion it is

known to have been exhibited in the nineteenth century, and that was unfavourable, Vitet writing acidly in 1826 (op. cit.): 'quand on ne fait qu'une simple étude [. . .] on risque de passer pour un faiseur de croûtes. Si, pour le malheur de M. Delacroix, nos lecteurs découvrent son *Turc mort* et son *Don Juan*, dans les coins obscurs où ils sont cachés, ils verront se justifier la vérité de cette observation.' Later comment has been more appreciative and is summarized in Cooper's epithet (op. cit., 1949): 'a masterpiece in miniature'.

¹ Joubin (*Correspondance* V. 145 n. 3) thought that it had not been accepted because it was not listed in the Society's catalogue for 1826–7, but that may not be conclusive proof of the picture's refusal (which would surely be odd on the part of a society designed to help artists), because the catalogue includes a supplement with numbers printed on otherwise blank pages, which may have been intended for handwritten titles of pictures that were submitted late.

114 THE COMBAT OF THE GIAOUR AND HASSAN   Pl. 100

23½ × 28⅞ in. (59.6 × 73.4 cm)
Signed bottom left: *Eug. Delacroix*
R202 (1827, revised to 1826 in Addition, p. 481)
1826
The Art Institute of Chicago (Gift of the heirs of Mrs. Potter Palmer Jr.)

Provenance: Alexandre Dumas père, c. 1827 to May 1848;¹ Charles Mahler, May 1848 to at least 1885; Mr. Potter Palmer of Chicago, by 1889, d. 1902; Mrs. Berthe Honoré Palmer, his widow, d. 1918 (apparently kept at the Palmers' Paris address between 1892 and 1910 at least²); Mr. Potter Palmer Jr., d. 1943; Mrs. Pauline Kohlsaat Potter Palmer, his widow, d. 1956; inherited by her four heirs, who over a period of years donated their shares in the picture to the Art Institute of Chicago; entered the permanent collection of the Institute (62.966) in 1962, having been on loan there since 1930.

Exhibitions: Gal. Lebrun, Paris 1826B, no. 44 ('Combat du Giaour et du pacha Hassan'); Douai 1827, no. 94; (rejected twice for the Salon, on 14 and 28 January, 1828³); Musée Colbert, Paris 1829A, no. 8; Musée Colbert, Paris 1829B, no. 107; Gal. Beaux-Arts, Paris 1846A, no. 98 (in 'Suites du Supplément'); Bd Italiens, Paris 1860, Supp., no. 345; Bd Italiens, Paris 1864, no. 78; EBA, Paris 1885, no. 135; Barye, New York 1889–90, no. 613; Petit, Paris 1910, no. 62; Chicago 1930, no. 3, repr.; Louvre 1930, no. 40; Chicago 1934, no. 187; Knoedler, New York and Chicago 1938–9, no. 41, repr.; Wildenstein, New York 1944, no. 3, repr.; Washington 1945, no. 2; Toledo-Toronto 1946–7, no. 21, repr.; Pittsburgh 1951, no. 101, repr.; Baltimore 1954, no. 89, repr.; Orangerie, Paris 1955, no. 23, repr.; London 1974, S69, repr.

Literature: MM. Chenoux, *Notice sur l'Exposition des produits de l'industrie et des arts qui a eu lieu à Douai en 1827* (Impr. Wagrez aîné, Douai, 1827), p. 82; D. [Delécluze], 'Ouverture du Musée Colbert', *Journal des Débats*, 7 Nov. 1829; *Biographie . . . des contemporains* (chez F. G. Levrault, Paris, 1834), III, p. 39; Silvestre *Delacroix* (1855), p. 82; T. Gautier, *Les Beaux-Arts en Europe—1855* (Michel Lévy, Paris, 1855), p. 184; id., review of replenished Exhibition *Bd Italiens*, Paris 1860, *Moniteur universel*, 5 May 1860; Z. Astruc, *Le Salon intime. Exposition au Boulevard des Italiens* (Poulet-Malassis et De Broise, Paris, 1860), pp. 40-2; A. Dumas père, 'Eugène Delacroix', *Le Monde illustré*, 22 Aug. 1863, p. 124; Piron, p. 106; Moreau, pp. 82, 169, 275 n. 1; H. Galli, review of Exhibition *EBA*, Paris 1885, *L'Evénement*, 7 March, 1885; P. Burty, 'Eugène Delacroix à l'Ecole des Beaux-Arts', *L'Illustration*, no. 2195 (21 March 1885), p. 199; P. Dorbec, 'L'Exposition des "Vingt peintres du XIXe siècle", à la Galerie Georges Petit', *GBA*, IV (1910), p. 17; M. Hamel, 'Exposition de Chefs-d'œuvre de l'école française. Vingt peintres du XIXe siècle', *Les Arts*, no. 104 (Aug. 1910), repr. p. 8; L. Roger-Milès, *Vingt peintres du xixe siècle. Chefs-d'œuvres de l'école française* (Impr. Geo. Petit, Paris, 1911), p. 148, repr. p. 51 (Borrel etching); Moreau-Nélaton I. 59, 82, 84, 163, repr. fig. 56, II. 58, 194; Escholier I. 186 f., repr. p. 177, II. 101; Hourticq 1930, pl. 24; *Correspondance* I. 184 n. 1, 407, IV. 160, 160 n. 1; G. H. Hamilton, 'Eugène Delacroix and Lord Byron', *GBA*, XXIII (1943), p. 104 and n. 13, repr. p. 106, fig. 5; Cassou 1947, pl. 6, full-page repr. of the Giaour and his mount on opp. p.; G. H. Hamilton, 'Delacroix, Byron and the English Illustrators', *GBA*, XXXVI (1949), p. 263 and nn. 3 and 4, repr. p. 261, fig. 1; Christoffel 1951, p. 57; B. Farwell, 'Sources for Delacroix's *Death of Sardanapalus*', *AB*, XL (1958), p. 66 n. 3; *Annual Report 1962-63, Art Institute of Chicago*, p. 13; *Mémorial*, under no. 220; Huyghe, pp. 77, 167, 271, 279, 452, repr. fig. 204; *The Art Institute of Chicago Quarterly*, LVIII (1964), no. 1, 5th page (unpaginated), repr.; Maltese, p. 140; L. Johnson, 'Eugène Delacroix et les Salons. Documents inédits au Louvre', *Revue du Louvre*, 16 (1966), pp. 217, 220, 228 nn. 9 and 11; T. Prideaux *et al.*, *The World of Delacroix* (Time Inc., New York, 1966), repr. in colour pp. 96-7; Trapp, pp. 64, 69, 119 ff., 120 n. 36, repr. fig. 60.

Prints: Etching by Bouruet, 1836. Etching by Borrel, 1910/11.

Copy: Sketch-copy in oils with some variations, particularly in the more mountainous background, by Hippolyte Poterlet (1804-1835), wood panel, $7\frac{1}{2} \times 9\frac{7}{16}$ in. (19 × 24 cm). Provenance: Théophile Gautier; his sale 14 Jan. 1873, lot 25, to Mme Ozy Pilloy; Alexandre Dumas fils; ?his sale, 2 March 1896, h.c., to P. A. Cheramy, about 600 fr.[4]; sale his estate 15 Apr. 1913, lot 20, to Dikran Khan Kélékian; his sale, New York 30 Jan. 1922, lot 93 (repr.); with Knoedler, New York; with C. G. Boerner, Düsseldorf, 1972. Repr. in colour in their *Neue Lagerliste Nr. 21 (1972)*, no. 11.

According to Moreau (p. 275 n. 1), this sketch was 'due au pinceau de Poterlet', but 'avait été reprise presqu'entièrement par le maître, et peut bien, suivant nous, passer pour une œuvre d'Eug. Delacroix.' Though it is a sketch of remarkable quality in its own right, there are no stylistic reasons for believing that it is not entirely from the hand of Poterlet, who was a painter of considerable talent profoundly influenced by his friend Delacroix.

The subject is taken from Byron's poem, *The Giaour, a Fragment of a Turkish Tale*, first published in 1813. The setting is Greece in the late seventeenth century, the hero a Venetian warrior known only by the name of Giaour, a term of reproach applied by Turks to non-Mussulmans, especially Christians. Leila, a slave who had fled Hassan's harem to become the Giaour's mistress, having been thrown, in the Muslim manner, into the sea for infidelity, is about to be avenged by her lover: with a band of followers, and 'now array'd in Arnaut garb', he has ambushed Hassan and his escort in a craggy defile. Engaging Hassan in single combat, he kills him, then bends over his enemy in a scene also painted by Delacroix (J138). The account of the ambush and death of Hassan is contained in lines 567-674 of the poem. The fullest contemporary description of the subject that was (presumably) supplied by the painter is contained in the catalogue of the exhibition Douai 1827: 'Combat du Giaour et du Pacha, dans un défilé où l'escorte de ce dernier est attaquée par les albanais embusqués dans les montagnes (sujet tiré de lord Byron).' And Delacroix referred to the subject by the same title on other occasions. But Hassan, though a Turk of high rank, does not seem strictly speaking to have been a pasha, otherwise Byron would surely not have described the 'pistols which his girdle bore' as 'those that once a pasha wore' (lines 529-30). Several striking pictorial motifs, such as Hassan's upraised mace and the Albanian about to hamstring his horse, find no literal equivalent in the poem; and there it is the Giaour's not Hassan's horse, as here, that is black. If the mace may seem an un-Byronic weapon, it was certainly an arm used by the Turkish cavalry as late as the present century, and Delacroix might have been inspired to use it here by Gros's lithograph of 1817, *Chef des Mameluks demandant secours*, where a similar mace hangs from the Mameluke's saddle.

Delacroix is known to have read part of *The Giaour*, most probably in Pichot's French rendering, as shown by Hamilton, as early as 10 May 1824 (*Journal* I. 98) and it has sometimes been supposed, by Joubin among others, that an entry in his *Journal* on 11 May 1824, 'Commencé le *Combat d'Hassan et du Giaour*', refers to this painting (ibid. 100 and n. 2); but it might refer to a project that was abandoned at an early stage and was perhaps connected with such ink drawings of the theme as the *Combat of the Giaour and Pasha* in the Louvre (RF22715. Exh. Edinburgh-London 1964, no. 87; Exh. Kyoto-Tokyo 1969, D-5, repr.) and *The Giaour on horseback* in Lord Clark's collection (Exh. Edinburgh-London 1964, no. 88, repr.). There is, in any event, no compelling reason on stylistic grounds to suppose that this painting was begun before the English journey of 1825, and very good reason on documentary grounds to think it was not finished till May or early June 1826. In a letter to Soulier written in May 1826 Delacroix, referring to the exhibition for the benefit of the Greeks that opened at the Galerie Lebrun on 15 May, wrote: 'J'irai bientôt remettre *aux Grecs* ce que je finis en ce moment.' (*Correspondance* I. 181.) This painting was not listed in the first catalogue of the exhibition, but was included in the second catalogue issued some weeks later; in a letter from the country postmarked 13 June 1826,[5] Delacroix informed Pierret: 'L'encadreur doit apporter le cadre de mon tableau du *Giaour* avant le 15' and instructed him to have the picture delivered to the Galerie Lebrun, 'en *spécifiant que c'est pour le renouvellement de l'exposition*' (ibid. 184); and in a letter postmarked the following day, he sends the same friend an entry for the picture for 'le prochain Catalogue' (ibid. 185). It seems, therefore, that the picture was probably not finished in time for the opening in mid-May, but was certainly ready a month later. It is also worth noting that it was dated to 1826 during the artist's lifetime, in Silvestre *Delacroix* (1855).

For a picture of such energy and which has become so famous, *The Combat of the Giaour and Hassan* attracted surprisingly little notice during the artist's lifetime, perhaps because it was never accepted for the Paris Salon. It must, however, have been largely on the strength of this painting that Delacroix was awarded a silver medal for his contribution to the Salon at Douai in 1827 (cf. L. Johnson, op. cit., 1966, p. 228 n. 11, and *Journal des Artistes*, 11 November 1827), and there at least it won some critical acclaim, tempered by the common academic prejudice of the time against freedom of handling: Chenoux, in a full notice (op. cit., 1827), praised the pose of Hassan (whom he mistook for the Giaour), found the figure on the ground to be 'dessiné et peint avec une chaleur et une énergie remarquables' and concluded: 'Cex deux parties suffiraient pour donner beaucoup de prix à ce tableau, devant lequel on passe souvent sans chercher ce qu'il a de mérite, parce qu'il n'est pas d'un faire qui attire, qui plaise à la plus grande masse d'individus.'

The Giaour was among the first works by Byron that Delacroix read and, with *The Bride of Abydos*, a theme not treated in oils until the 1840s, the one which inspired the most pictures by him (see J133 and J138). Another version of this combat is dated 1835 (Petit Palais, Paris; repr.

Mémorial, no. 220) and shows the two horses and riders completely interlocked in a furious struggle instead of striking *en passant*; it appears to be strongly influenced by Rubens's drawing in the Louvre after Leonardo's *Battle for the Standard*. A third, lost version may have been done in the latter half of the 1830s, for Thoré reports in *Le Siècle* on 25 February 1837 that Delacroix is working on 'une autre composition du *Giaour et du Pacha*'. It is possible, however, that he was referring, rather loosely, to *The Giaour's Confession*, inspired by the same poem, and dated to 1838 by Robaut (no. 683; now National Gallery of Victoria, Melbourne).

Finally, a painting dated 1856 in the Fogg Art Museum is clearly related to the so-called *Combat of the Giaour and Pasha* and has generally been known by that title since Robaut so listed it (no. 1293); but it departs so far from Byron's text, by showing a Hassan-like figure kneeling on the ground surrendering his gun to a Giaour-like warrior on horseback drawing a pistol, that it must be considered, like the *Turkish Officer Killed in the Mountains* (J113), to be a scene from the Greek War of Independence influenced by Byron's poem but not actually illustrating it. There can be no real doubt that Joubin was right in identifying it with a no. 25 canvas (81 × 65 cm), which Delacroix called '*Cavalier grec et turc*' and delivered to Tedesco in April 1856 (*Journal* II. 442 and n.); but, as Joubin also implies, it may, at the same time, have been the outcome of a project to paint a '*Giaour foulant aux pieds de son cheval le pacha*', mentioned in July 1854 (ibid. 210 and n.). It is reproduced in Trapp, fig. 62, as '*Two Arabs in Combat*.'

[1] Moreau (p. 275 n. 1), thinking wrongly that the picture was painted in 1827 and exhibited at the Salon in that year, states: 'Il a appartenu dès l'origine à M. Alexandre Dumas père qui, en mai 1848, le céda à M. Mahler.' Since it was exhibited as late as December 1829 at the Musée Colbert without being listed as owned by Dumas, it may be doubted whether 'dès l'origine' should be taken literally to mean that the novelist acquired it as soon as it was ready for sale.
Moreau N specifies that the picture was bought from Dumas for 2,500 fr., with a water-colour of a lion (R985).
[2] Dieterle R: 'Appartenait en 1892 à Mme Potter Palmer 6 rue Fabert, Paris (vu en 1909 chez elle).'
[3] See L. Johnson, op. cit. *infra*, 1966. Moreau and Robaut, as well as most later authors, confusing this picture with the *Scene from the War between the Turks and Greeks* (J115), mistakenly record that it was exhibited at the Salon of 1827-8.
[4] According to R Ann (margin to R202), it was bought by Cheramy for about 600 fr. at the posthumous sale of Alexandre Dumas fils in 1895. No such sale is listed in Lugt, and no such picture is listed in the catalogue of the posthumous Dumas sale of 1896, in which it may however have passed *hors catalogue*.
[5] Joubin gives the date of the postmark as 18 June, but it is clear from the context of this and the following letter in the *Correspondance* that Moreau-Nélaton (I. 81) was right in reading it as 13 June.

115 SCENE FROM THE WAR Pl. 101
BETWEEN THE TURKS AND GREEKS

$25\frac{5}{8} \times 32\frac{1}{8}$ in. (65×81.5 cm)*
Signed bottom to the left: *Eug. Delacroix*.

R200 (1827. Repr. in reverse.)
1826/7
Oskar Reinhart Collection, Winterthur

Provenance: Bequeathed by the artist to the dealer Tedesco;[1] G. de L. sale 20 Apr. 1874, lot 15, 25,500 fr.; Comte Daupias; his sale 16 May 1892, lot 106, to Boussod, Valadon & C[ie] (Arch Goupil/Boussod), 10,200 fr.; they sold it to Bernheim-Jeune, 19 Feb. 1898 (ibid.), 7,500 fr. (Dieterle R); Louis Sarlin, by 1900; his sale 2 March 1918, lot 33 (repr. The public sale did not take place, as the collection was sold *en bloc* to a Dane); Oskar Reinhart, Switzerland, 1921.

Exhibitions: Salon 1827, no. 299 ('Scène de la guerre actuelle des Turcs et des Grecs'); *Centennale*, Paris 1900, no. 225, repr.; Geneva 1918, no. 67; Winterthur 1922, no. 36; Zurich 1939, no. 315, repr. Berne 1939-40, no. 83, repr.

Literature: P., 'Salon de 1827', *Journal de Paris*, 8 and 24 Nov. 1827; anon., 'Salon de 1827', *Courrier des Théâtres*, 25 Nov. 1827; A. Vergnaud, *Examen du Salon de 1827. Novembre, première partie* (chez Roret, Paris, 1828), p. 10; *Visite au Musée du Louvre ... (année 1827-28) ... par une société de gens de lettres et d'artistes* (Leroi, Paris, 1828), p. 158; Silvestre *Delacroix* (1855), p. 80; Delacroix's will, dated 3 Aug. 1863, in *Correspondance* (Burty 1878), p. viii; Inv. Delacroix, no. 291; Piron, p. 106; Moreau, pp. 81, 272; Moreau-Nélaton I. 84, 85, repr. fig. 55, II. 166; Escholier I. 186 and n. 2, repr. p. 174; G. H. Hamilton, 'Eugène Delacroix and Lord Byron', *GBA*, XXIII (1943), p. 104 and n. 15; id., 'Delacroix, Byron and the English Illustrators,' *GBA*, XXXVI (1949), p. 266 n. 10; Christoffel 1951, repr. in colour pl. II; B. Farwell, 'Sources for Delacroix's *Death of Sardanapalus*', *AB*, XL (1958), p. 66 n. 3; Huyghe, pp. 167, 205, repr. fig. 136; L. Johnson, 'Eugène Delacroix et les Salons. Documents inédits au Louvre', *Revue du Louvre*, 16 (1966), pp. 217, 220, 228 n. 9; Maltese, p. 140; Trapp, pp. 76 f., 120, 121 n. 36; R. Koella, *Collection Oskar Reinhart* (Bibliothèque des Arts, Paris, 1975), pp. 132, 334, repr. in colour pl. 51.

Print: Etching in reverse by Bouruet, *c*. 1827 (Delteil, Section 4, no. 1).

This painting was accepted by the Salon jury on 8 October 1827 (L. Johnson, op. cit., 1966). It is likely to have been finished after the summer of 1826, when Delacroix apparently sent his last pictures to the exhibition held at the Galerie Lebrun for the benefit of the Greeks (see J114 and J98); for it is most improbable that, had it been ready, he would have failed to include in the show a subject so appropriate for the occasion—an episode from the current Greek War of Independence.

It attracted little notice from the critics at the Salon. The stiff white stallion was criticized by Vergnaud (op. cit., 1828)

as 'mauvais de forme et de couleur' but, he conceded, 'il y a du mouvement dans l'ensemble'. The 'gens de lettres' (op. cit., 1828) regarded the painting as little more than a sketch and added the dubious compliment: 'Le cheval mérite d'être placé à côté de ceux de Carle Vernet, et les têtes ne dépareraient pas un tableau d'Horace.'

There is an uneasy mixture of contrivance and realism in this composition: the wooden rocking-horse convention of the galloping steed contrasts with the more naturalistic dead horse (probably based on studies from nature of the kind that served for *A Battlefield, Evening*—see J104), as does the easy posture of the Greek horseman with the complex angularities of the dead Turk, the latter so reminiscent of figures in that most manneristic piece by Gros, *The Battle of Aboukir* (Versailles, Salon of 1806). In a later version, of the same design and dimensions, dated 1856, the rigidities of pose and handling are greatly reduced by a use of suppler forms and more animated brushwork (R1296, repr. Huyghe, fig. 138).

According to Moreau (p. 81), this early version was painted entirely with copal varnish—varnish, that is, being presumably mixed with the pigments.

A sepia study of a dead horse, which Robaut (no. 167) identifies as a study for *A Battlefield, Evening* (J104), is closer in pose to the dead horse here.

---

[1] 'A. M. Tedesco, un tableau sur toile de 30 [92 × 65 cm] à 40 [100 × 73 cm], représentant un Grec à cheval et un Combat dans le fond' (Delacroix's will, loc. cit. *infra*), described in Inv. Delacroix as '*épisode de la guerre des Grecs*'. The picture left to Tedesco seems to have been this early version rather than the version dated 1856 referred to below, since Piron, whose dates are often out by a few years but not by decades, lists the version that belonged to Tedesco in 1865 under the year 1831.

116 MEPHISTOPHELES APPEARS BEFORE FAUST — Pl. 102

$18\frac{1}{8} \times 15$ in. (46 × 38 cm)
Signed bottom left: *Eug. Delacroix*
Moreau pp. 170, 247. R159 (1826), R226 (1827), and addition to R226, p. 481 (Catalogued twice by mistake.[1] No repr.)
1826/7
The Wallace Collection, London

Provenance: Charles Motte (?); he sold it to Achille Devéria (?);[2] anon. sale (by Couteaux), 26 Feb. 1853, lot 20 ('Sujet tiré de Faust (Goëthe)', without dimensions or further description, but this painting according to Moreau, p. 247); Paul Meurice, by 1864; anon. sale (by Petit), 22 March 1869, lot 19, 7,600 fr., to Lord Hertford (?), d. 1870; Richard Wallace, his heir, d. 1890; Lady Wallace, his widow, d. 1897; by her bequest to the British nation as part of the Wallace Collection, which opened as a national museum at Hertford House, London, in June 1900.

Exhibitions: Salon 1827–8, 2nd Supp. no. 1631; Hobday's Gallery, London 1828, no. 25 ('Dr. Faustus in his Study'); *Bd Italiens*, Paris 1864, no. 138; (lent by Sir Richard Wallace to the Museum at Bethnal Green for public exhibition, June 1872–April 1875, no. 589).

Literature: A. Jal, *Esquisses, croquis, pochades ou tout ce qu'on voudra sur le Salon de 1827* (Ambr. Dupont, Paris, 1828), p. 445; anon., 'French Artists: Hobday's Gallery', *Literary Gazette*, 7 June 1828; Silvestre *Delacroix* (1855), p. 80; Piron, p. 106; Moreau-Nélaton I. 94, 163; Escholier I. 217 n. 1, repr. opp. p. 208; *Correspondance* I. 407; W. Friedlaender, *David to Delacroix* (Harvard University Press, Cambridge, Mass., 1952), pp. 115 f.; L. Johnson, 'Eugène Delacroix et les Salons. Documents inédits au Louvre', *Revue du Louvre*, 16 (1966), pp. 218, 220, repr. p. 221 fig. 2; *Wallace Collection Catalogues. Pictures and Drawings. Text with Historical Notes and Illustrations*, 16th ed. (London, 1968), p. 86, no. P324 (repr. in separate volume of illustrations to earlier editions, p. 57); Trapp, pp. 77, 146, repr. fig. 73.

This picture was rejected by the Salon jury on 12 October 1827, and accepted, possibly after some reworking, on 14 January 1828 (L. Johnson, op. cit.). It was described in the second supplement to the official Salon catalogue thus: 'Le docteur Faust dans son cabinet. Méphistophélès, le démon sous une forme humaine, lui apparaît pour la première fois.' Though virtually identical in composition to Delacroix's lithograph of the same subject (Delteil no. 62), published in Albert Stapfer's French translation of Goethe's *Faust* in February 1828, it is far less cluttered by detail in the lower part, especially in the costumes and stuffs, and the table-cloth is extended down to cover an awkward gap in the centre—all changes suggesting that the painting was developed from the print rather than the other way round. Delacroix began work on the project to illustrate *Faust* as early as 1825 (see *Correspondance* I. 201), no doubt after the summer journey to England, where he saw a musical adaptation of the play which, according to his own account, was his main stimulus in resolving to do some illustrations (ibid., IV. 303 f.); and the final plate was not finished till December 1827. It is not known at precisely what point between these terminal dates the lithograph *Mephistopheles Appears before Faust* was drawn, but the painting is most unlikely to be earlier than 1826 and cannot be later (except for some possible reworking) than the beginning of October 1827, when it was submitted to the Salon.

The attitude of Faust and some parts of his costume are, though shown from a different angle, very close to those of Knox in David Wilkie's oil sketch for *John Knox Preaching before Mary Stuart* (Petworth House), a sketch greatly admired by Delacroix when he saw it in London in 1825 (*Correspondance* I. 160).

Delacroix's painting passed unnoticed by the Salon

critics, except for Jal who commented briefly: 'Ce petit tableau, d'un caractère très-original, est remarquable par la richesse du ton.'

When it was shown in London in 1828, the critic of the *Literary Gazette* remarked: 'We noticed a picture by this artist in the late Exhibition at the British Gallery, and praised its Venetian tone of colouring [*Execution of Marino Faliero* (J112)]. The same may be said of the present performance; but the characters are not equally well sustained. Indeed, who can take Faustus or Mephistopheles out of the hands of Retsch?'

[1] Robaut also catalogues the same canvas a third time, under the wrong title, *Méphistophélès dans les airs* (R223).

[2] According to Moreau (p. 170), followed by Robaut (under no. 239), the picture was painted for Motte, the lithographic printer, and he sold it to Devéria (presumably Achille rather than his brother Eugène, since it was the former who designed the cover of, and a poster to advertise, the 1828 edition of *Faust* illustrated by Delacroix and published by Motte, who also became Achille's father-in-law in 1829). The previously unnoticed fact that it was shown at Hobday's Gallery in London in June 1828, where pictures were exhibited for sale on commission (cf. 'Mr. Hobday's Picture Gallery', *Morning Advertiser*, 5 June 1828), would seem to prove that it could not have been painted for Motte, though he may well have acquired it on its return from London.

117 THE CAPULET BALL, unfinished   Pl. 103

$18\frac{9}{16} \times 14\frac{5}{8}$ in. (47.2 × 31.1 cm)* E.D.
R1492 (1824. No repr.)
c. 1826/8
Claude Roger-Marx, Paris

Provenance: Delacroix's posthumous sale, Feb. 1864, lot 146 ('[Esquisse] — Le bal chez les Capulets', without dimensions), to Philippe Burty, 80 fr.; ? Victor Chocquet, d. 1891; ? his widow's sale, 1 July 1899, lot 62 (as 'Faust. Esquisse. Cadre en bois sculpté. Toile, $46\frac{1}{2} \times 36$ cm.'), 300 fr.;[1] Aubry, by 1912; the present owner, by 1930.

Exhibitions: St. Petersburg 1912, no. 196; (lent to Galerie Druet, 20 rue Royale, Paris, by M. Aubry at an unknown date—label on back); Louvre 1930, no. 21, repr. *Album*, p. 16; Zurich 1939, no. 305; Louvre 1963, no. 63, *M* no. 62, repr.

Literature: Moreau-Nélaton I. 59, repr. fig. 29; Escholier I. 93 f., repr. opp. p. 94; *Correspondance* I. 365 n. 3; J. Rewald, 'Chocquet and Cézanne', *GBA*, LXXIV (1969), p. 76 (the 'Faust', which was probably this painting wrongly identified in the Chocquet inventory).

The scene is from *Romeo and Juliet*, I. v. Romeo disguised as a pilgrim, having just seen Juliet for the first time, approaches and takes her hand, saying:

> If I profane with my unworthiest hand
> This holy shrine, the gentle sin is this,—
> My lips, two blushing pilgrims ready stand
> To smooth that rough touch with a tender kiss.

The masked figure on the right is no doubt Tybalt, who recognized Romeo at the ball and wished to run him through.

Joubin thought this picture was perhaps the 'Roméo' which Delacroix offered to Mme Elise Boulanger in November 1833, apparently in exchange for a pastel copy that she made of it, and insisting that it seemed to him (as this painting undoubtedly is) 'point achevé'. (*Correspondance* I. 365 and n. 3, 366 and n. 1.) Sérullaz (*Mémorial*, no. 62) found it difficult to see how that could be so when this picture passed in Delacroix's posthumous sale. But Mme Boulanger may very well have either declined the gift or returned it to Delacroix later, perhaps in exchange for something else from his hand.

The style and figure types seem to fit better in the period of the *Faust* illustrations than as early as 1824, which is Robaut's date, followed almost without exception by later cataloguers, despite the fact that Robaut had probably never seen the picture, since he neither listed the dimensions nor reproduced it.

A drawing in brown ink and wash was identified as a study for the group of Romeo and Juliet in this picture by Sérullaz, who at the same time wrongly stated that I, like himself, had connected it with a subject from the *Bride of Lammermoor* (*Mémorial*, no. 63, repr. Louvre, RF9233, 11.9 × 9.4 cm). A connection with this picture had already been suggested, more tentatively, in the catalogue of the exhibition Louvre 1930, p. 161, no. 275.

Possibly Delacroix's first illustration of a Shakespearian subject was taken from *Romeo and Juliet*; it is a slight water-colour study of the farewell scene on the balcony done *c.* 1820 (Louvre sketch-book RF23357, fol. 5ʳ. Repr. Escholier I, p. 155). The scene represented here headed a long list of possible subjects for pictures from the play which Delacroix compiled towards the end of his life, on 29 December 1860: 'La scène du bal': Roméo en pèlerin [not 'pélerine', as transcribed in *Mémorial*] baise la main de Juliette; promeneurs, musiciens, etc.' (*Journal* III. 313.) But this is the only treatment of the scene at the ball that he is known to have attempted.

¹ A blue crayon inscription of unknown origin on the stretcher reads: 'Nᵒ 62 Vente Choquet [*sic*] Juillet 99'. And no painting from *Faust* that corresponds with this description is recorded elsewhere. On the other hand, no mention is made in the sale catalogue of the 'E.D.' seal on the stretcher, whereas it is recorded in the descriptions of some other works by Delacroix which had passed in his posthumous sale.

118 THE POOR GIRL   Pl. 104

$16\frac{1}{8} \times 14\frac{9}{16}$ in. (41 × 37 cm)¹
Signed bottom, right of centre: *Eug Delacroix*
R67 (1823)
1826/9?
Whereabouts unknown

Provenance: Stolen from the artist; Garnier (?) by 1855;² M. de Villars; his sale (M. de V.) 1 May 1874, lot 16 ('L'Orpheline au cimetière'), bought in by Haro at 1,100 fr.;³ M. H.G., by 1885 (initials of owner given in Cat. Exh. Alsace-Lorraine); MM. Haro, by 1930.

Exhibitions: Musée Colbert, Paris 1829A, no. 82 ('La pauvre fille'); Alsace-Lorraine, Paris 1885, no. 513 (1st Supp.; as 'L'Orpheline'); Louvre 1930, no. 11; Zurich 1939, no. 303, repr. (wrongly (?) listed as belonging to the Musée de la Ville de Paris, Petit Palais).

Literature: *Journal* I. 352; Silvestre *Delacroix* (1855), p. 80 ('Jeune fille dans un cimetière'); Huyghe, p. 135, repr. fig. 105; Maltese, p. 145 (under no. 5).

The composition was inspired by an obscure elegy by Alexandre Soumet, who is chiefly remembered for his *Divine Epopée*. La Pauvre Fille was first published in 1814⁴ and is now accessible only in Mme d'Altenheym-Gabrielle Soumet, *La Croix et la lyre* (E. Ducrocq, Paris, 1858), pp. 359–61. The lines in (my) italics below are quoted in the entry for Delacroix's painting in the catalogue of the exhibition at the Musée Colbert in 1829:

> J'ai fini ce pénible sommeil
> Qu'aucun songe heureux n'accompagne;
> J'ai devancé sur la montagne
> Les premiers rayons du soleil.
> S'éveillant avec la nature
> Le jeune oiseau chantait sous l'aubépine en fleurs,
> Sa mère lui portait la douce nourriture,
> Mes yeux se sont mouillés de pleurs.
> Oh! pourquoi n'ai-je pas de mère,
> Pourquoi ne suis-je pas semblable au jeune oiseau,
> Dont le nid se balance aux branches de l'ormeau?
> Rien ne m'appartient sur la terre;
> Je n'eus pas même de berceau;
> Et je suis un enfant trouvé sur une pierre,
> Devant l'église du hameau.
> Loin de mes parents exilée,
> De leurs embrassements j'ignore la douceur;
> Et les enfants de la vallée
> Ne m'appellent jamais leur sœur.
>
> .   .   .   .
>
> Souvent je contemple la pierre
> Où commencèrent mes douleurs;
> J'y cherche la trace des pleurs,
> Qu'en m'y laissant, peut-être, y répandit ma mère.
> *Souvent aussi mes pas errants*
> *Parcourent des tombeaux l'asile solitaire;*
> *Mais pour moi les tombeaux sont tous indifférents:*
> *La pauvre fille est sans parents,*
> *Au milieu des cercueils ainsi que sur la terre.*
> J'ai pleuré quatorze printemps,
> Loin des bras qui m'ont repoussée;
> Reviens, ma mère, je t'attends
> Sur la pierre où tu m'as laissée.

The commentary in Robaut suggests that this picture developed out of the *Girl Seated in a Cemetery* (J78):

Delacroix wished here to treat the theme for its own sake, having initially grafted it on to a study made for another purpose, namely, in preparation for the *Massacres of Chios*. This opinion, and hence Robaut's dating, is not entirely convincing in view of the literary source in Soumet; and the presence of the picture in the exhibition Musée Colbert, Paris 1829A, unrecorded by Robaut, suggests that it may have been painted a few years later than he placed it.

¹ According to Robaut. 39 × 31 cm according to the Cat. Exh. Alsace-Lorraine, Paris 1885.
² *Journal* I. 352 (Augerville, 12 July 1855): 'Trouvé cet affreux Garnier qui me dit effrontément avoir la *Jeune fille dans le cimetière*, je lui dis qu'elle m'avait été volée, en le regardant d'une manière qui l'a fait rougir.' The name of the 'owner' is not clearly legible, but Joubin thinks it is probably Garnier.
³ In a note to his drawing after this painting in Tracings I, Robaut writes: 'Dessiné chez M. Haro le 13 mai [18]74. Il l'avait fait passé en vente il y a 15 jours à l'H.D. [Hôtel Drouot] et, faute d'amateurs, il l'a retiré à 1100fr.'
⁴ According to Quérard, *La France Littéraire*.

119 JUSTINIAN, sketch   Pl. 105

11¹³⁄₁₆ × 8¼ in. (30 × 21 cm)*
R158
1826
Dr. Max Bangerter, Montreux

Provenance: Philippe Burty, by 1880; his sale 2 March 1891, lot 9, 540 fr.; P. A. Cheramy; his sale 5 May 1908, lot 176, not sold; sale his estate, 15 Apr. 1913, lot 38, to Jacobi, 520 fr.; Ernest Rouart, by 1926 to at least 1939; Duc de Trévise; his sale 8 Dec. 1947, lot 14, 90,000 fr.; the present owner, by 1951.

Exhibitions: *EBA*, Paris 1885, no. 41; Gobin, Paris 1937, no. 32; Zurich 1939, no. 310; Basle 1939, no. 214; (on extended loan to the Kunsthalle, Basle, July 1951 to Nov. 1963); Berne 1963–4, no. 20.

Literature: *Correspondance* (Burty 1880), I. 124 n. 1; Escholier I, repr. opp. p. 174.

Possibly the first oil sketch for the figure of Justinian seated, this study lacks the rich colouring of the more advanced studies and of the lost final version (J123) as it was described by eyewitnesses, and the secondary figures of scribe and angel are not included.

120 JUSTINIAN DRAFTING HIS   Pl. 106
LAWS, sketch

21¹¹⁄₁₆ × 17¹⁵⁄₁₆ in. (55 × 45.5 cm) E.D.
Moreau pp. 188 n. 1, 304, 311. R157
1826
Musée des arts décoratifs, Paris

Provenance: Delacroix's posthumous sale, Feb. 1864, lot 53, to Corot, 560 fr., d. 1875; Alfred Robaut; he sold it to Cheramy in May 1885 for 1,000 fr. (R Ann); his sale 5 May 1908, lot 175, not sold; sale his estate 15 Apr. 1913, lot 25, to Raymond Koechlin, 5,200 fr.; by his bequest to the Musée des arts décoratifs, Dec. 1931.

Exhibitions: *EBA*, Paris 1885, no. 175; Paris 1927, no. 279; Copenhagen, Stockholm, Oslo 1928, no. 51, 43, 44; Louvre 1930, no. 31, repr. *Album* p. 19; Petit Palais, Paris 1936, no. 232; *Cent cinquantième anniversaire du Conseil d'Etat*, Palais-Royal, Paris June 1950, repr. *Album* p. 19; Wildenstein, London 1952, no. 12; Venice 1956, no. 9; London 1959, no. 113, repr.; Louvre 1963, no. 73, *M* no. 76, 2 repr.; Berne 1963–4, no. 19; Bremen 1964, no. 16; Petit Palais, Paris 1968–9, no. 268; Kyoto–Tokyo 1969, H-5, repr.; Atelier Delacroix, Paris 1971 (no cat.)

Literature: J. Meier-Graefe and E. Klossowski, *La Collection Cheramy . . .* (R. Piper, Munich, 1908), p. 89, no. 153; Moreau-Nélaton I. 79, repr. fig. 49; Escholier I. 175 f., repr. in colour opp. p. 176; Hourticq 1930, pl. 12; R. Huyghe, 'L'Exposition Delacroix au Musée du Louvre', *Bulletin des Musées de France*, II (1930), repr. p. 131; T. Sauvel, op. cit. *infra* (J123), 1952, p. 39 n. 15; Huyghe, pp. 167, 461, 489, full-page repr. pl. 341; F. Trapp, op. cit. *infra* (J123), 1964, repr. fig. 16; Trapp, repr. fig. 43.

This sketch appears to represent an intermediate stage between J119 and J121 in the development of the final composition.

121 JUSTINIAN DRAFTING HIS   Pl. 107
LAWS, sketch

12⅝ × 9½ in. (32 × 24 cm)
R156
1826
Whereabouts unknown

Provenance: Joseph Auguste Carrier; his sale 5 May 1875 (R), *h.c.*, to Alfred Robaut; acquired from him by P. A. Cheramy (R Ann).

Exhibitions: None.

Literature: *Journal* III. 90 (if not J119, J120 or J122); J. Meier-Graefe and E. Klossowski, *La Collection Cheramy . . .* (R. Piper, Munich, 1908), p. 88, no. 152.

This work is known to me only from the small print in Robaut, reproduced here. Though Robaut was of the opinion that a water-colour, which he listed under no. 154, was of all the composition studies for the *Justinian* the most like the final version (J123), this oil sketch seems in fact to have been the closest, on the evidence of the photograph of J123, and was probably Delacroix's working model for the large canvas. Robaut records that the curtain in the background of this sketch was yellow, as opposed to red in the sketch now in the Musée des arts décoratifs (J120).

122 JUSTINIAN DRAFTING HIS   Pl. 107
LAWS, sketch

$9\frac{5}{8} \times 7\frac{1}{2}$ in. (24.5 × 19 cm)
Whereabouts unknown

Provenance: Sale Robert and Sensier (anon.), 10 Feb. 1882, *h.c.*

Exhibitions: None.

Literature: None.

This sketch, which was apparently in oils and is unlisted by Robaut, is known to me only from the copy in coloured chalks contained in M-Nélaton Port. vol. 2 and reproduced here. An inscription on the back of this drawing gives the dimensions and the following details: 'Esquisse Justinien, partie Vente Robert et Sensier février 1882. Communiqué par Charly.'

Since Delacroix is known to have drawn several preparatory studies showing Justinian standing instead of seated as in the final version (see J123), there is good reason to suppose that this drawing was taken from a genuine oil sketch for that alternative idea.

123 JUSTINIAN DRAFTING HIS   Pl. 107
LAWS

$146 \times 108\frac{5}{8}$ in. (3.71 × 2.76 m)
Signed and dated 1826, according to Moreau p. 209
Moreau pp. 188 and n., 209. R153 (1826)
1826–7
Destroyed in 1871

Provenance: Commissioned by the Government in 1826 for the third room of the Conseil d'Etat in the Palais du Louvre; presumably hung in the Hôtel Molé when the Conseil d'Etat moved there in 1832; destroyed in the burning of the Palais d'Orsay (seat of the Conseil d'Etat since 1840) by the Communards in May 1871.

Exhibitions: On view to the public *in situ*, January 1828;[1] *Universelle*, Paris 1855, no. 2917; *Bd Italiens*, Paris 1864, no. 97.

Literature: Official catalogue of Salon of 1827, p. 21 (not a numbered Salon entry); Letter from Léonor Mérimée to S. J. Rochard, August 1827 (published by C. Ephrussi, 'Simon-Jacques Rochard', *GBA*, 3rd per. VI (1891), p. 459); anon., *Annales de la littérature et des arts*, XXXI (1828), p. 23; 11 Jan. 1828; E. Delécluze, review of Salon of 1827–8, 8th article, *Journal des Débats*, 14 Jan. 1828 (section on the *Justinian* reprinted in Tourneux, p. 50); Ch. [Chauvin?], review of id., 6th article, *Moniteur universel*, 29 Jan. 1828; L.N., 'Musée du Louvre. — Salle du Conseil d'Etat', *L'Observateur*, III, no. 101 (2 Feb. 1828), p. 55; Ch., *L'Observateur des Beaux-Arts*, I, no. 5 (24 Apr. 1828), p. 18; anon., *Annales de la littérature et des arts*, XXXI (1828), p. 23; A. Jal, *Esquisses, croquis, pochades ou tout ce qu'on voudra sur le Salon de 1827* (Ambr. Dupont, Paris, 1828), pp. 443–5; anon., *L'Artiste*, II (1831), p. 180; A. Deschamps, 'Justinien, à Eugène Delacroix', in *Poésies* (Delloye, Paris, 1842 ed.), p. 175 (whole poem in Tourneux, p. 170); Silvestre *Delacroix* (1855), p. 80; C. Baudelaire, 'Exposition universelle', *Le Pays*, 3 June 1855, reprinted in *Curiosités esthétiques*, 1868 (*Œuvres*, Pléiade ed. Paris 1932, II, p. 160); T. Gautier, 'Exposition universelle', *Moniteur universel*, 25 July 1855, reprinted in *Les Beaux-Arts en Europe* (Michel Lévy, Paris, 1856); M. du Camp, *Les Beaux-Arts à l'Exposition universelle de 1855* (Librairie nouvelle, Paris, 1855), p. 110; E. Gebauer, *Les Beaux-Arts à l'Exposition universelle de 1855* (Librairie Napoléonienne, Paris, 1855), p. 33; L. Chardin, 'Retour à Eugène Delacroix', *L'Artiste*, 7th ser. II (1864), p. 148; Piron, p. 106; Letter from Edmond Maître to his father, 3 June 1871 (published by F. Daulte, *Frédéric Bazille et son temps* (Geneva, 1952), p. 86; Tourneux, pp. 48, 49; Moreau-Nélaton I. 78, 79, 86, 89, II. 125, 222; Escholier I. 174–6, 216, 217, III. 219; *Correspondance* I. 217 n. 2, 407, III. 246 and n. 254; *Journal* II. 211 and n.; T. Sauvel, 'Du Palais de la Cité au Palais-Royal', in *Le Conseil d'Etat, livre jubilaire publié pour commémorer son cent cinquantième anniversaire, 4 Nivôse An VIII — 24 Décembre 1949* (Recueil Sirey, Paris, 1952), pp. 39 n. 15, 40, 41; Sérullaz *Dessins* 1952, pp. 42, 48; Huyghe, pp. 167, 176, 461; F. Trapp, 'An Early Photograph of a Lost Delacroix', *Burl Mag*, CVI (1964), pp. 267–9, repr. in photograph of Exh. *Universelle*, Paris 1855, fig. 18, detail of the *Justinian* only from that photograph, fig. 17; Maltese, pp. 77, 124; Trapp, pp. 53 n. 21, 59, 72, 77, 81–3, 82 nn. 17 and 18, 93, 345, repr. (from photograph of Exh. *Universelle*, Paris 1855) fig. 44 (repr. of whole photograph fig. 205). See also Literature for J119, J120 and J121.

This painting was commissioned in 1826 as part of a scheme to decorate the third of four adjoining rooms set aside for the Conseil d'Etat in the Louvre. The third room was that of the Comité du contentieux (T. Sauvel, op. cit., 1952, p. 39 n. 15), and the principal paintings in the scheme were a rectangular ceiling by Martin Drolling, representing *Le Triomphe de la Loi* (repr. Sterling-Adhémar, pl. 278), and four large paintings of legislators on the two longer walls of the room: Delacroix's *Justinian* at the west end of the north wall; Ary Scheffer's *Charlemagne présente ses premiers capitulaires à l'assemblée des Francs* (Musée de Versailles. Fig. 14 here), opposite that; Marigni's *Moses* (whereabouts

Fig. 14. *Charlemagne*, Ary Scheffer.

unknown; destroyed ?) at the other end of the wall bearing the *Justinian*; and Cogniet's *Numa donnant les lois aux Romains* (whereabouts unknown; destroyed ?) on the same wall as the *Charlemagne*, opposite the *Moses*. The curved space of the ceiling between the frame of Drolling's painting and the cornice was filled with painted ornaments which included two imitation reliefs, *La Sagesse inspirant la Loi* and *La Justice dirigeant la Force*, over the centre of the long walls, and four medallions, each held by two winged genii and inscribed with the name of one of the four legislators, identifying the paintings below them. The medallions were painted by Caminade (L.N., op. cit., 1828), as presumably were all the ornaments. In the course of reconstruction around 1965, the whole ceiling down to the cornice was concealed, the position of the doors changed and the room divided by a partition wall. The two rooms thus formed now contain the Rothschild Collection and the Schlichting Donation. (Photographs of the original ceiling are preserved by the Archives photographiques, no. 62. P. 326-7.)

Citing letters preserved in the archives of the Louvre, Moreau-Nélaton (I. 78) showed that Delacroix was probably allowed some latitude in the choice of subject and was supplied with the stretcher for the *Justinian* in August 1826 (letter of 19 August 1826); he was required to deliver the completed painting by 1 November 1827 at the latest (letter of 29 July 1826), and no doubt finished it earlier since the full payment of 4,000 fr. for the commission was ordered on 18 September 1827 (letter of that date). The official, unpublished receipt for the payment, signed by Delacroix on 24 September 1827, is in M-Nélaton Doc. (Box IX). The picture was indeed probably completed by the end of August, as this payment is already requested in an unpublished letter dated 31 August 1827 from the Comte de Forbin, Directeur Général des Musées Royaux, to the Vicomte de la Rochefoucauld, chargé du Département des Beaux-Arts à l'intendance de la Maison du Roi (Archives nationales O³ 1419). Since it was dated 1826, according to Moreau, it may be assumed to have been begun in that year, and certainly the final oil sketch must have been completed and approved by about the end of August, for not only had the stretcher for the large canvas been provided by then, but in an unpublished letter dated 26 August 1826 Comte de Forbin wrote to the Garde des Sceaux: 'Le travail de la décoration des salles du Conseil d'Etat au Louvre, étant arrêté, je prie Votre Grandeur de vouloir bien m'indiquer le jour où je pourrai avoir l'honneur de le lui présenter.' (Archives nationales BB¹⁷ A 49 d^r 1.)

From the time of its destruction in 1871 till 1964, when Trapp published the photograph reproduced here, the appearance of the final work could be deduced only from the preliminary sketches that were known and from verbal descriptions by those who had seen it. Falling in the period between the completion of the *Marino Faliero* (J112) and the

execution of the *Sardanapalus* (J125), pictures remarkable for their richness of colouring and splendid accessories, the *Justinian* was from all accounts of equal opulence. Auguste Jal, for example, wrote (op. cit., 1828, p. 445): 'Ce qu'il y a de plus louable dans l'ouvrage, c'est la vive couleur des velours, les ornements d'or et les pierres précieuses qui parent les volumes dont le devant du tableau est garni.' And later, Maxime Du Camp (op. cit., 1855): 'avec quelle science de joaillier amoureux de ses bijoux le peintre a rendu les pierreries sorties dans l'or émaillé, avec quel soin sans pareil il a brodé les brodequins impériaux et orné de pierres précieuses le collet de la tunique: rubis, émeraudes, saphirs, aigues marines, turquoises, tout est imité jusqu'à l'illusion.' As summed up in Gautier's well-known comment (op. cit., 1855): 'Tout le Bas-Empire est résumé dans la figure de Justinien; aux larges draperies antiques commence à succéder les brocarts constellés de pierreries, le luxe asiatique de Constantinople.' But there was a general feeling among critics, in 1828 as in 1855, that the figure of Justinian was affected, ugly or badly drawn, that the artist had allowed himself to be carried away by his delight in the accessories at the expense of the main subject.

Some of the official disfavour incurred by the exhibition of the *Sardanapalus* at the Salon in the early weeks of 1828 seems to have rubbed off on the *Justinian*, for in a letter to Soulier dated 26 April 1828 Delacroix, reporting on his failure to get any recognition at the distribution of Salon honours on that day, added: 'La mystification a été plus loin encore dans la lecture qu'on a faite des travaux exécutés précédemment pour le Conseil d'Etat. On n'a fait mention ni de mon nom ni de ce que j'avais fait' (*Correspondance* I. 217).

Of the lot of ten sheets of preparatory studies that passed in Delacroix's posthumous sale (314), three are generally known: 1. a full-length charcoal study of the Emperor seated, very similar to the oil sketch J120 (Musée des arts décoratifs. Repr. *Mémorial*, no. 77); 2. a powerful study in Conté crayon for the angel pointing to the book of Roman laws which Justinian was shown in the process of codifying in the final canvas (Louvre, RF3411. Repr. Sérullaz *Dessins* 1952, pl. XLVIII; less good repr. *Mémorial*, no. 79); 3. a sheet of pen-and-ink drawings containing a study for the Emperor seated full-length, without a head, a study for the head of the scribe in the bottom left of the final picture, and an inscription in the artist's hand: 'les grands génies sont dans les hommes qui conservent le plus l'instinct ou en sont le plus guidés' (R155. Coll. Claude Roger-Marx, Paris. Repr. *Mémorial*, no. 78). The head of the scribe, incidentally, reappears in the bottom right corner of a sheet of studies for the *Sardanapalus*, and it is no doubt to the scribe in the *Justinian* that Delacroix refers in a note on the same sheet: 'Se souvenir du caractère du Juif qui a posé le scribe' (Louvre, RF5278. Repr. *Mémorial*, no. 104). Old photographs of the other drawings in lot 314 of the posthumous sale are contained in M-Nélaton Port. vol. II and comprise: two studies of Justinian seated in approximately the final pose, one full-length and one half-length; a sheet with two drawings showing Justinian seated full length, draped and in the nude; three sheets of studies for the alternative composition of Justinian standing; and an advanced study for the head of Justinian (Fig. 15 here), which is perhaps the surest indication of how the Emperor's features appeared in the final painting.

Fig. 15. *Justinian*, Delacroix.

In addition to the oil sketches already listed, and the separate sheets of drawings from the posthumous sale, there was the highly developed water-colour composition catalogued by Robaut under no. 154 and last recorded in the Cheramy collection, and some pencil sketches of Roman emperors, including Justinian, from Byzantine coins, contained in a Louvre sketch-book (RF9142, fols. 10ʳ—repr. Moreau-Nélaton I, fig. 50—and 11ʳ). While the existence of these last drawings would seem to lend credence to the statement contained in the *Moniteur universel*'s review of 29 January 1828, that the head of Justinian 'est fidèlement reproduite d'après les médailles de l'époque', the evidence of the photograph of the finished painting and the advanced drawing for the head reproduced here suggests that the final head owed little, if anything, to Byzantine images of the Emperor.

¹ Though the *Justinian* is listed in the catalogue of the Salon of 1827, as located in the third room of the Conseil d'Etat, it does not appear to have actually been on view to the public in time for the opening of the Salon in November, for the anonymous author of a special article on the paintings for the Conseil d'Etat which was published in the *Journal du Commerce* on 11 January 1828 began by announcing: 'Depuis trois ou quatre jours le public est admis à parcourir les salles du conseil d'état: c'est une faveur dont il faut se hâter de profiter. Les portes seront probablement fermées le 15; le conseil reprendra le cours de ses séances à huis-clos.' And the painting is not mentioned in any earlier reviews of the Salon. The period for viewing may have been extended beyond 15 January, since L.N. writes in *L'Observateur* of 2 February (p. 55): 'Et libres maintenant d'entrer dans la troisième salle du conseil d'état, élevons nos regards vers le plafond de M. Drolling.'

124 THE DEATH OF SARDANAPALUS, sketch   Pl. 108

31⅞ × 39⅜ in. (0.81 × 1.00 m) Relined Dec. 1955
Moreau p. 170. R168 (1826)
1826/7
Musée du Louvre

Provenance: Baron Charles Rivet, by 1849, probably given to him much earlier by Delacroix,¹ d. 1872; Baronne Rivet, his widow, to at least 1885; Comtesse de Salvandy, their daughter; by her bequest to the Louvre (RF2488), 1925.

Exhibitions: Bd Italiens, Paris 1864, no. 106; *EBA*, Paris 1885, no. 174; Copenhagen, Stockholm, Oslo 1928, no. 54, 45, 47; Arts décoratifs, Paris 1930, no. 1705; Louvre 1930, no. 34, repr. *Album*, p. 20; Petit Palais, Paris 1936, no. 233; Belgrade 1939, no 45; Atelier Delacroix, Paris 1947, no. 6; id., Paris 1948, no. 55; id., Paris 1951, no. 2; Venice 1956, no. 7; *Bib. nat.*, Paris 1957-8, no. 357; Agen, Grenoble, Nancy 1958, no. 17; London 1959, no. 112; Louvre 1963, no. 97, *M* no. 100, repr.; Berne 1963-4, no. 14, repr.; Bremen 1964, no. 13, repr.; Edinburgh-London 1964, no. 19, repr.; Montauban 1967, no. 216, repr.; Atelier Delacroix, Paris 1968, no cat.; Kyoto-Tokyo 1969, H-7, colour repr.; Atelier Delacroix, Paris 1971, no cat.; id., Paris 1973, no cat.; Marseille 1975, no. 51.

Literature: Journal III. 372; Silvestre *Delacroix* (1855), p. 80; Piron, pp. 70 f.; anon. [P. Burty], 'Chronique du Jour', *La République française*, 23 March 1873; P. Burty, 'Eugène Delacroix à l'Ecole des Beaux-Arts', *L'Illustration*, LXXXV, no. 2195 (21 March 1885), p. 198; Moreau-Nélaton I. 87, repr. fig. 61, II. 222); J. Guiffrey, 'La "Mort de Sardanapale" d'Eugène Delacroix au Musée du Louvre', *GBA*, 5th per. IV (1921), p. 199 n. 2; id., 'Une Esquisse du "Sardanapale" de Delacroix au Musée du Louvre', *Beaux-Arts*, III (1925), pp. 135 f., repr. p. 135; Escholier I. 224, 225, repr. opp. p. 226; P. Jamot, 'Deux Esquisses d'Eugène Delacroix au Musée du Louvre', *Art Vivant*, II (1926), pp. 725 f., repr. p. 724; id., 'Delacroix', in *Le Romantisme et l'art* (Laurens, Paris, 1928), p. 114; Hourticq 1930, pl. 18; Sterling-Adhémar, no. 666, pl. 234; L. Johnson, 'The Etruscan Sources of Delacroix's *Death of Sardanapalus*',

AB, XLII (1960), p. 298 n. 17; Maltese, p. 137; K. Lankheit, *Révolution et restauration* (A. Michel, Paris, 1966. German ed., Holle Verlag, Baden-Baden, 1965), repr. in colour, p. 130; J. Spector, *Delacroix: the Death of Sardanapalus* (Allen Lane, London, 1974), *passim*, repr. pl. 24, detail pl. 24A.

Baron Rivet, a close friend of Delacroix's and the first owner of this sketch, gives the following account of its origin and its relation to the final work:

En lisant le drame assez peu lisible de lord Byron, [Delacroix] avait été frappé du côté pittoresque du dénoûment. Un despote farouche et blasé qui s'ensevelit sous les débris de son palais, sacrifiant avec insouciance à son orgueil les objets de son affection, les instruments de ses plaisirs et les trésors de son luxe oriental: c'était une scène qui s'était d'abord présentée à son imagination, empreinte de deuil et d'horreur. Il avait pris la palette sous cette impression; en quelques heures, une esquisse d'un caractère énergique et sombre avait apparu sous son pinceau.

Quand il en vint à l'exécution, et que, sur la toile, la plus grande qu'il eût abordée, il entreprit de peindre, d'après le modèle, cette esclave à moitié nue qui se jette sur le lit de son maître, [. . .] il se laissa entraîner par les séductions de l'imitation. Il fit palpiter l'opale et l'or sur ce torse aux reflets éclatants, sur ces épaules, sur ces bras d'une couleur dont les aspects chatoyants l'enivrèrent d'enthousiasme. Il fit alors une des plus ravissantes études qui aient charmé les yeux; mais il perdit le ton général du tableau, pour conserver ce qu'il avait fait avec tant de verve et de bonheur. Il modifia donc peu à peu tous les accessoires, et la scène entière prit un effet tout différent de celui qu'elle devait d'abord exprimer.

Quelques années après, quand il revit l'esquisse et que je lui rappelai les émotions dont il avait subi l'influence:

— Savez-vous ce que cela prouve? me dit-il. C'est que je n'étais qu'un écolier; la couleur, c'est la phrase, c'est le style. On n'est un écrivain que lorsque l'on en est maître, et qu'on la fait obéir à sa pensée.

Aujourd'hui, ajouta-t-il, ma palette n'est plus ce qu'elle était. Elle est moins brillante peut-être, mais elle ne s'égare plus. C'est un instrument qui ne joue que ce que je veux lui faire jouer.' (From an unpublished article written for the *Revue des Deux Mondes*, quoted in Piron, pp. 70 f.)

This account of the sketch's being conceived under the impression of the dénouement of Byron's play, *Sardanapalus*, cannot be accepted without reservation, as Delacroix must have drawn on additional sources, even at this early stage (see J125). It is also hard fully to accept Rivet's claim that Delacroix's painting the nude on the bed from a model necessitated radical changes between sketch and final version, because the alterations that were made seem to have been purposefully aimed towards stabilizing the composition, stressing its main lines and filling gaps, rather than to adjusting the general tone of the picture to suit that single figure. But Rivet's account nevertheless serves to illustrate a general truth about Delacroix's reluctance to work too closely from the model lest the temptation to copy nature spoil the artist's imagined conception of his subject; and although the final picture as a whole does not appear to be keyed to the 'opale et or' of the nude on the bed, it may well

be due to an excessive reliance on posed models that the principal nudes tend to stand out as figures studied in isolation. It is interesting in this connection that Thénot, who helped with the perspective of the architecture, says that all the figures were done from nature (see J125).

On 4 February 1849, Delacroix commented on the sketch in his *Journal* (I. 258), having apparently not seen it for some time: 'Revu dans le cabinet de Rivet l'esquisse du *Sardanapale* qui ne m'a pas déplu malgré quelques excentricités.' It was perhaps on that occasion that he made the remarks attributed to him by Rivet.

According to Moreau, this sketch was painted at the end of 1826. The final painting was not, however, begun before the first half of July 1827, and Moreau's date for the sketch seems therefore to be too early by at least six months.

[1] This sketch is not mentioned in Delacroix's will and was not bequeathed to Baron Rivet, as sometimes stated. Philippe Burty writes (op. cit. *infra*, 1873) that Delacroix gave it to Rivet, and further (in 1885): 'Delacroix l'avait donnée au baron Rivet [. . .] La revoyant nombre d'années après, il s'écria: "Voilà ce que je voulais faire!"'; and goes on to give an account similar to but shorter than Rivet's quoted below, claiming to have heard it from Rivet himself.

125 THE DEATH OF SARDANAPALUS   Pl. 109

$155\frac{3}{8} \times 194\frac{3}{4}$ in. (3.95×4.95 m) Relined
Moreau pp. 169 f., 259 f. R198 (1827)
1827–8
Musée du Louvre

Provenance: Sold by the artist to John Wilson in 1846 for 6,000 fr. (Piron),[1] died Sept. 1849 at Ecoublay (nr. Fontenay-le-Vicomte), where the picture was hanging, in the dining-room of his home, at the time (*Journal* I. 304 f.); probably inherited jointly by Daniel Wilson, his son, and Mme Pelouze, his daughter;[2] their sale (M. D.W.) 21 March 1873, lot 4 (photo repr.), to Durand-Ruel, 96,000 fr.; he sold it to James Duncan of Benmore for about 46,000 fr.;[3] his sale (Duncan, de Londres), 15 Apr. 1889 (Paris), lot 9 (photo repr.), to Haro, 34,000 fr.; sale Haro et fils, 30 May 1892, lot 76, failed to fetch reserve of 100,000 fr. (R Ann); Baron Vitta bought it from the Haro family in 1893 for 80,000 fr. (*Le Temps*, 23 July 1921); he sold it to the Louvre (RF2346) in 1921 for 700,000 fr.

Exhibitions: Salon 1827–8, 2nd Supp., no. 1630 ('Mort de Sardanapale. "Les révoltés l'assiégèrent dans son palais . . . Couché sur un lit superbe, au sommet d'un immense bûcher, Sardanapale donne l'ordre à ses eunuques et aux officiers du palais, d'égorger ses femmes, ses pages, jusqu'à ses chevaux et ses chiens favoris; aucun des objets qui avaient servi à ses plaisirs ne devait lui survivre . . . *Aïscheh*, femme bactrienne, ne voulut pas souffrir qu'un esclave lui donnât la mort, et se pendit elle-même aux colonnes qui supportaient la voûte . . . *Baleah*, échanson de Sardanapale, mit enfin le feu au bûcher et s'y précipita lui-même." '); *Bd Italiens*, Paris 1861-2 (installed between 15 and 31 Dec. 1861—cf. *Courrier artistique*, 1 Jan. 1862-, on view to at least March 1862. Lent by M. E. Pelouze); Society of French Artists 6, London 1873, no. 13; Durand-Ruel, Paris 1878, no. 141; Durand-Ruel, New York 1887; according to R Ann, also shown by gaslight at the Durand-Ruel gallery in Paris during a Puvis de Chavannes exhibition in 1887 [20 Nov.-20 Dec.]; Copenhagen 1888, no. 100 (wrongly illustrated with the 1844 version);[4] Louvre 1930, no. 36, repr. *Album* p. 21; Lóuvre 1963, no. 96, *M* no. 99, 2 repr.; Petit Palais, Paris 1968-9, no. 514.

Literature: *Correspondance* I. 196 and n., 200 n. 1, 201 and n.; 213, II. 107; A. Béraud *et al.*, *Annales de l'Ecole française des Beaux-Arts* (Pillet, Paris, 1827 [*sic*]), pp. 73 f.; anon., review of Salon 1827-8, *Le Figaro*, 7 and 18 Feb. 1828; anon., id., *Journal du Commerce*, 7 Feb. 1828; anon., id., *La Pandore*, 9 Feb. 1828, p. 2; anon., id., *L'Observateur*, III, no. 103 (16 Feb. 1828), p. 89; anon., id., *La France chrétienne*, 22 Feb. 1828, p. 4; Ch. [Chauvin ?], id., *Moniteur universel*, 27 Feb. 1828 (extensively quoted, with slight variations, in Tourneux, pp. 48 f.); L.V. [Louis Vitet], id., *Le Globe*, 8 March 1828, pp. 253 f.; L. Mérimée, letter to S. J. Rochard, 11 March 1828 (published by C. Ephrussi, 'Simon-Jacques Rochard', *GBA*, 3rd per. VI (1891), p. 459); E. J. Delécluze, review of Salon 1827-8, 21 March 1828 (comments on the *Sardanapalus* quoted in full in Tourneux, p. 49); anon., id., *Gazette de France*, 22 March 1828 (quoted in Tourneux, p. 52); V. Hugo, letter to Victor Pavie, 3 Apr. 1828 (*Victor Hugo Correspondance 1815-1835* (C. Lévy, Paris, 1896), p. 79, wrongly dated to 1829); anon., review of Salon 1827-8, *L'Observateur des Beaux-Arts*, I, no. 4 (20 Apr. 1828), p. 16; P., id., *La Quotidienne*, 24 Apr. 1828 (extensively quoted in Tourneux, pp. 51 f.); D., id., *L'Observateur des Beaux-Arts*, I, no. 10 (8 May 1828), p. 33; anon. [Stendhal], 'Literary Letter from Paris', *The Athenaeum*, no. 31, 28 May 1828, p. 490; anon., *L'Observateur des Beaux-Arts*, no. 24 (29 June 1828); anon., review of Salon 1827-8, *Annales de la littérature et des arts*, XXXI (1828), pp. 19 f.; A. Jal, *Esquisses, croquis, pochades . . . sur le Salon de 1827* (A. Dupont, Paris, 1828), pp. 310, 312-14, 315 n. 2; T. Thoré, 'Artistes contemporains. M. Eugène Delacroix', *Le Siècle*, 24 Feb. 1837; Thénot, *Les Règles de la perspective pratique* (Danlos, Paris, 1853 ed.), pp. 18 f. (See also the 1834 ed. of Thénot's *Traité de perspective pratique*, p. 27, where the author gives the same account of assisting with the perspective in the *Sardanapalus*, but without actually naming the painting or Delacroix); G. Planche, *Portraits d'artistes* (M. Lévy, Paris, 1853), II, pp. 52, 53; C. Baudelaire, 'Salon de 1846'; and 'Exposition universelle', *Le Pays*, 3 June 1855, both reprinted in *Curiosités esthétiques*, 1868 (*Œuvres* Pléiade ed.,

Paris 1932, II, p. 745 n. 17; and p. 161); T. Silvestre, *Histoire des artistes vivants. Eugène Delacroix* (Blanchard, Paris, n.d. [1855]), p. 64; id., *Les Artistes français*, 1855 (1926 ed., I, p. 29); E. Fillonneau, *Le Courrier artistique*, 15 Jan. 1862, p. 59; anon. [Baudelaire], untitled review of Exhibition *Bd Italiens*, Paris 1861-2, *Revue anecdotique*, Jan. 1862 (*Œuvres* Pléiade, Paris 1961 ed., pp. 1112-13); T. Gautier, 'Exposition du Boulevard des Italiens', *Moniteur universel*, 6 March 1862; L. Clément de Ris, *Critiques d'art et de littérature* (Didier, Paris 1862; chapter on Delacroix dated Apr. 1857), pp. 387 f.; A. Dumas, 'Eugène Delacroix', *Le Monde illustré*, 22 Aug. 1863, p. 126; L. Chardin, 'Retour à Eugène Delacroix', *L'Artiste*, 7th ser. II (1864), p. 148; Piron, pp. 69-73, 106; T. Silvestre, 'Mort de Sardanapale', in catalogue of Wilson sale (D.W.) Paris, 21 March 1873, pp. 7-25; anon. [A. Vacquerie], *Le Rappel*, 20 and 21 March 1873; anon., *Le Temps*, 21 March 1873; anon. [P. Burty], *La République française*, 21 and 23 March 1873; anon. [J. Castagnary], *Le Siècle*, 22 March 1873; P. Andrieu, in A. Bruyas *et al.*, *Musée de Montpellier. La Galerie Bruyas* (Quantin, Paris, 1876), pp. 366 f. (section on the *Sardanapalus* reprinted in R. Piot, *Les Palettes de Delacroix* (Lib. de France, Paris, 1931), pp. 75-7, and from there in J. Spector, op. cit. *infra* 1974, pp. 113 f.; G. Lassalle-Bordes, in Delacroix *Correspondance* (Burty 1880), II, p. xviii; M. Vachon, *Eugène Delacroix à l'Ecole des Beaux-Arts* (Baschet, Paris, n.d. [1885]), pp. 27 f., repr. 5th pl.; A. Michel, *Notes sur l'art moderne* (A. Colin, Paris, 1896), pp. 89 f., 89 n. 1; Moreau-Nélaton I. 86-90, repr. fig. 62; A. Rigaud, 'Au Musée du Louvre. "La Mort de Sardanapale" ', *Comoedia*, 27 Aug. 1921, repr. in general view of the Salle des Etats; Thiébault-Sisson, 'Le *Sardanapale* d'Eugène Delacroix au Musée du Louvre. Le nouvel ménagement de la Salle des Etats', *Le Temps*, 31 Aug. 1921; J. Guiffrey, 'La "Mort de Sardanapale" d'Eugène Delacroix au Musée du Louvre', *GBA*, 5th per. IV (1921), pp. 193-202, repr. opp. p. 196; J. Vaudoyer, 'E. Delacroix et le "Sardanapale" ', *Feuillets d'Art*, II (1922), pp. 139-42; Meier-Graefe 1922, pp. 41-3, repr. p. 106; Brière 1924, p. 80, no. 3067, repr. pl. LVI; Escholier I. 192, 217-30, repr. opp. p. 228, details pp. 227, 228; M. Barrès, *Le Mystère en pleine lumière* (1927. Quoted in Huyghe, p. 178); P. Jamot, *La Peinture au Louvre, I, XIX siècle, 2e. partie* (Paris, 1929), p. 15; Hourticq 1930, pl. 19, details pls. 20 and 21; A. Joubin, 'Documents inédits. Haro entre Ingres et Delacroix', *L'Amour de l'Art*, XVII (1936), p. 87; id., 'Logis et ateliers de Delacroix', *BSHAF*, 1938, p. 63; Cassou 1947, pl. 7, full-page detail of head of woman on near side of bed, opp. p., followed by two-page detail of whole of same woman; G. Hamilton, 'Delacroix, Byron and the English Illustrators', *GBA*, 6th per. XXXVI (1949), pp. 271 f.; W. Friedlaender, *David to Delacroix* (Harvard University Press, Cambridge, Mass., 1952), pp. 112 f., repr. fig. 70; B. Farwell, 'Sources for Delacroix's

Death of Sardanapalus', *AB*, XL (1958), pp. 66–71, repr. fig. 1; Sterling-Adhémar, no. 667, pl. 234; L. Johnson, 'The Etruscan Sources of Delacroix's *Death of Sardanapalus*', *AB*, XLII (1960), pp. 296–300, repr. fig. 1; L. Simon, 'Delacroix aujourd'hui', *Europe*, XLI (1963), no. 408, pp. 70 f.; J. Cau, 'Un génie consacré plus à peindre qu'à vivre', in R. Huyghe *et al.*, *Delacroix* (Hachette, Paris, 1963), p. 13 (this book also contains outstanding details of the heads of the Negro and nude in the foreground, pls. X. 1, XI. 2); Johnson 1963, pp. 27 f., 37 f., repr. in colour pl. 14, detail of foot of man in right foreground repr. in colour pl. 16; P. Jullian, *Delacroix* (A. Michel, Paris, 1963), pp. 71–8; Huyghe, pp. 173–81, repr. in colour pl. XI, detail of lower left quarter, fig. 140; A. Brookner, 'Art Historians and Art Critics—VII: Charles Baudelaire', *Burl Mag*, CVI (1964), p. 276, repr. fig. 21; A. Chastel, 'L'Année Delacroix', *Art de France*, IV (1964), p. 334 n. 40; J. Seznec, *John Martin en France* (Faber & Faber, London, 1964), pp. 44–6, repr. pl. 10; L. Johnson, 'Two Sources of Oriental Motifs copied by Delacroix', *GBA*, 6th per. LXV (1965), p. 164; Maltese, pp. 32, 33, 34, 35, 36, 37, 38, 136 f., repr. pl. 23, detail of horse and Negro repr. in colour pl. X; L. Johnson, 'Eugène Delacroix et les Salons. Documents inédits au Louvre', *Revue du Louvre*, 16 (1966), pp. 217, 220; T. Prideaux *et al.*, *The World of Delacroix* (Time Inc., New York, 1966), repr. in colour pp. 76–7; H. Bessis, 'Delacroix et la Duchesse Colonna', *L'Œil*, no. 147 (March 1967), pp. 24 f.; B. White, 'Delacroix's Painted Copies after Rubens', *AB*, XLIX (1967), p. 44; L. Johnson, 'An Early Study for Delacroix's *Death of Sardanapalus*', *Burl Mag*, CXI (1969), pp. 296–9; M. Roskill, *Van Gogh, Gauguin and the Impressionist Circle* (London, Thames and Hudson, n.d. [1969]), p. 144, nude on left of bed repr. pl. 122 (compared to Gauguin's *Woman in the Hay with Pigs*, pl. 123); Trapp, pp. 83–92, repr. in colour pl. VII; J. Spector, *Delacroix: The Death of Sardanapalus* (Allen Lane, London, 1974), colour plate of whole in end of book, nine black-and-white details; P. Joannides, review of Spector's book, *Burl Mag*, CXVIII (1976), pp. 324–7.

Prints: Lithograph by A. Sirouy, 1860 (Salon 1861). Etching by A. Greux for *Galerie Durand-Ruel*, II, pl. 247, 1873. Wood engraving for *Le Monde illustré*, before 1885.

Copies: Reduced copy by H. Poterlet, 50 × 61.8 cm, before 1835, private collection, France.

Reduced copy, with slight variations, by Delacroix, 74 × 93 cm, 1844 (R791), McIlhenny Coll., Philadelphia (repr. in W. Friedlaender, 1952, pl. 71, and Spector, 1974, pl. 56; colour details in Escholier 1963, pp. 48, 49).

A painting after this reduced copy, by F. Villot in the same dimensions, 1844, Louvre (RF1962-26).

Four full-scale copies of details, by Delacroix, *c*. 1846 (see below, STUDIES).

Two paintings by Pierre Andrieu: (1) 37.5 × 46 cm,

private collection, Paris (repr. in H. Bessis, 'Pierre Andrieu', *Médecine de France*, May 1971); (2) full-scale copy painted for Daniel Wilson (R Ann), 1873 (?), and given to the Municipality of Tours by Mme D. Wilson (R Ann) or by Mme Pelouze in 1879, after being kept at the Château de Chenonceaux (F. Laurent and A. de Montaiglon, *Inventaire des richesses d'art de la France: Province, monuments civils*, V (Paris, 1891), p. 321). The latter source also states that it was exhibited for a while on the staircase of the old Town Hall. Now in store, rolled, in the Museum at Tours.[5]

Painting by an unidentified artist, possibly Andrieu (sometimes attributed to Delacroix), of the woman on the near side of the bed and the one reclining at the base, brought closer together, the elephant's head eliminated, 1 × 1.40 m. Whereabouts unknown (repr. in *Les Arts*, 1907, no. 64, p. 23 (Coll. Cheramy); Meier-Graefe and Klossowski, Catalogue Collection Cheramy, 1908, no. 150; Escholier I. 230; *Art News*, Summer 1963 (Private coll.; Photo Bulloz, no. 69505).

Painting by an unidentified artist of the standing nude in the foreground, down to the level of her wrist, 81.5 × 65 cm. National Museum of Western Art, Tokyo (listed as a study by Delacroix for the Salon painting in their 1961 catalogue, no. P-90, repr.; also repr. Bortolatto, no. 903).

Water-colour of the horse by the Duchesse Colonna, 1873, private collection, Switzerland (repr. in H. Bessis, op. cit., 1967, p. 26, fig. 1).

The Death of Sardanapalus provoked more general hostility from the critics and state officials, even from his friends, than any other major work painted by Delacroix; yet he, while sensitive to its 'defects' when he first saw it hanging at the Salon (*Correspondance* I. 211), regarded it as 'one of the finest feathers in my cap' (Silvestre, loc. cit., 1873, p. 13). Accepted by a majority of only one vote (*Correspondance* II. 300) on 14 January 1828 (Johnson, op. cit., 1966), by a Salon jury which included Ingres and Gros, it is Delacroix's largest and most Rubensian painting of the 1820s. Seen in the context of his work as a whole and beside Ingres's stately and decorous tribute to the classical tradition, the *Apotheosis of Homer*, shown at the same Salon and which Delacroix perhaps set out deliberately to rival (Johnson, op. cit., 1969), it may also be considered his most uninhibited reaction against neo-classical constriction, a counterpart in painting to Victor Hugo's famous manifesto of Romanticism in literature, the preface to *Cromwell*, published in December 1827. In this unabashed tribute to Rubens, in the convulsive movement, the violence, the frank sensuality, the orientalism, the opulent colouring, Delacroix challenged the principles embodied in the Raphaelesque *Apotheosis* as firmly as Picasso was to defy Matisse's *Bonheur de Vivre* with the *Demoiselles d'Avignon*—and in a composition containing as many discordant elements uneasily combined. From a distance of over thirty years, Gautier (op. cit., 1862) was to observe realistically of the *Sardanapalus*: 'On ne pouvait marchait d'un pied plus hardi sur la queue de l'école davidienne.' But Delacroix had naïvely expected to be decorated for treading on that tail with what he termed this 'prouesse *asiatique* contre les pastiches *spartiates* de l'école de David' (Escholier I. 220), and, as Manet was to be over the reception of his works, was bewildered and hurt by the antagonism shown towards a painting which, while owing much to tradition, offended by its very novelty in reinterpreting tradition and by flying in the face of prevailing canons. As with Manet's *Déjeuner sur l'herbe* and *Olympia*, the offence was no doubt complicated by the power of shock lent to the erotic by setting it within a context that was new yet recombined features from respected conventions of the past. Though the *Death of Sardanapalus* is original in iconography and one of Delacroix's most personal masterpieces, it combines a remarkable variety of sources, both literary and pictorial, ranging from classical legend to Romantic drama, from Etruscan sculpture to Indian architecture, from the greatest of Baroque masters to the least renowned of Romantics.

Sardanapalus, besieged by his rebellious subjects in his palace at Nineveh, lies on a huge bed at the top of a funeral pyre. Rather than fall captive with his retinue, he has ordered all his women and horses to be slaughtered, all his treasures to be heaped on the pile and burnt with him. Byron's play *Sardanapalus*, published in 1821, apparently provided the initial stimulus for the painting, as related by Delacroix's friend Baron Rivet in his account of how the oil sketch came to be painted (see J124). But in more recent years it has been stressed (Farwell, op. cit., 1958; Johnson, op. cit., 1960) that Delacroix is unlikely to have painted the sketch under the immediate impression created by reading the dénouement of Byron's play, as claimed by Rivet, because the sketch, like the final canvas, includes a scene of general slaughter, whereas the play ends with Sardanapalus seated alone on a pyre which is fired by his favourite concubine Myrrha as the curtain falls; there is no suggestion of a preliminary massacre. Farwell (ibid.) first drew attention to how the description of the scene in the Salon catalogue is printed within inverted commas, with ellipses and explains that Aïscheh, a Bactrian woman (who does not appear in any known versions of the Sardanapalus legend, including Byron's), is hanging herself rather than be put to death by a slave. Thus there arose the important question, still unanswered, of whether Delacroix also took inspiration from some ephemeral contemporary version of the story, perhaps a spectacle mounted in Paris and itself adapted from Byron. Farwell, trying to account for the gap between Byron's finale and Delacroix's painting in terms more concrete than sheer artistic licence, proposed that the idea of the barbaric massacre of slaves and concubines on the

occasion of a king's death might have had its origin in Herodotus' description of a royal Scythian burial. At the same time, she held that Delacroix must have looked into the same classical source as Byron acknowledged, Diodorus, who describes how Sardanapalus 'built an enormous pyre in his palace, heaped upon it all his gold and silver [. . .] and consigned [his concubines and eunuchs] and himself and his palace to the flames.' I (op. cit., 1960), working from one of Delacroix's notes on a sheet of preliminary drawings (Louvre, RF5278ʳ), 'étrusques de toutes façons', suggested, while illustrating other Etruscan influences on the picture, notably for the pose of Sardanapalus, that an engraving of a pseudo-Etruscan relief representing a slaughter scene (repr. ibid., fig. 2) could not only account in part for the difference between play and painting, but was a primary inspiration for the design as a whole. This opinion has not won universal favour, but, though the Etruscan influences are perhaps not so pervasive as a paper devoted to that subject may imply, I can only maintain that the points of similarity between the engraving and painting are too many to be coincidental, and that the nude kneeling on the tasselled cushion on the far left of the engraving is directly linked to the corresponding study on a preparatory sheet of drawings for the *Sardanapalus* (Louvre, RF6860). In deciding on the preliminary carnage, could Delacroix also, one wonders, have had any knowledge, from descriptions or studies, of David's Baroque *Funeral of Patroclus* of 1779, with its massacre of twelve princes to be placed on the gigantic pyre (Repr. Cat. Exh. Paris, Detroit, New York 1974–5, p. 56 Fr. ed., p. 54 U.S. ed.)?

Quintus Curtius is a historical source which has not attracted the notice of later scholars and may account for some of the mood of the *Sardanapalus*, as well as for notes that were made in preparing it. Silvestre reports (loc. cit., 1873, p. 15): 'Pour exprimer le faste et la volupté des mœurs asiatiques dans la *Mort de Sardanapale*, Eugène Delacroix se rappelait [. . .] quelques passages de Quinte-Curce sur les magnificences, les orgies babyloniennes et les fabuleux trésors des rois.' Quintus Curtius' account of the destruction of Persepolis and its riches, which 'surpassed all that had gone before' (*Historia Alexandri Magni*, Rolfe ed., 1946, I. 379), may well have led Delacroix to add 'peintures persepolitaines' to the list of works of art he wished to look at (Louvre, RF5278ʳ.); in this he would have been frustrated, for none existed. More important, the Roman historian's colourful descriptions of India and the riches of its kings could have turned Delacroix's attention to things Indian, an interest which is reflected in notes on the same sheet of drawings ('Voir les types des Indiens et leurs monuments, leurs divinités'; 'Peintures licencieuses de Delhi'), and in the final painting, most strikingly perhaps in the use of heavy, bulbous capitals inspired by the cave temple at Elephanta, which complement the elephant heads on the couch.[6] In details, a passage such as Quintus Curtius' description of the Indian king Sopithes, who surpassed 'all other barbarians in physical attractiveness', could have broadly influenced Delacroix: 'His robe, which covered his legs as well as the rest of his body, was embroidered with gold and purple, [. . .] from his ears hung pearls conspicuous for whiteness and size' (ibid. II. 373).

The legend of Sardanapalus, 'last king of the Assyrian empire of Nineveh', supposed to have died in 876 B.C., was fabricated by Ktesias in the *Persika* at the beginning of the fourth century B.C., and repeated by Byron's source, Diodorus, and other later chroniclers. The essence of Sardanapalus' character as given by Ktesias is its duality. He is represented as an improbable mixture of effeminate hedonist and dauntless warrior: an idle and debauched monarch who, when attacked, placed himself at the head of his troops and twice defeated the rebels, but eventually had to withdraw to his palace, where he withstood a siege for two years before cremating himself, the trappings of his power and the instruments of his pleasure. His attributes were probably made up out of the character of the god Sandon, who was widely worshipped in Asia, both as a heroic and a female divinity (a connection first made, curiously enough in 1829, by K. O. Müller). Thus Byron, in attributing, as he did, some dignity and virility to Sardanapalus, instead of dwelling on his depravity and moralizing about it, as so many commentators, both pagan and Christian, had done before him, was not being gratuitously inventive so much as returning to the original myth.[7]

Delacroix, too, lends some dignity and manliness to his Sardanapalus. It has been argued that the haughty and chill isolation of the king here, as in Byron's play, is typical of the individualistic mood of Romanticism in the 1820s and related to the attitudes of disdain and proud isolation found in the early writings of Stendhal, Vigny, Hugo and of the young Delacroix (Spector, op. cit., 1974, p. 62). The same author finds (p. 78) that the aims of the French anti-classical writers, in wishing to abolish the Unities for example, seem to correspond loosely to the disjunction of mood, scale and space in the painting: the convulsive movement of large figures in the foreground against the still, unnaturally diminished figure of Sardanapalus; the anomalies of the spatial structure, which combines a largely frieze-like foreground, steeply tilted into the picture-plane, with the dominant diagonal wedge thrusting deep into space. It is useful to consider the painting in relation to contemporary attitudes in literature, and certainly more helpful than trying to explain its highly charged erotic content in terms of Delacroix's sexual anxieties, seeing it as a reflection of impotence, which is a misguided interpretation mooted by Escholier in 1926 (I. 229), bruited by Cau in 1963 (loc. cit.) and, with voyeuristic variations, by Simon in the same year, to be finally elaborated by Spector in 1974 (op. cit.). But it

should be remembered that there are equally striking anomalies of scale and space in the *Plague at Jaffa*, painted by Delacroix's precursor Gros, long before Stendhal and Hugo formulated the principles of Romantic literature in France. Moreover, to ignore purely technical questions, apparently unrelated either to literature or sex, is to risk missing the root causes of the disjunctions and also, perhaps, of Delacroix's concern lest the Salon public see the picture with his critical eye.

I have held (1960, 1963, pp. 28, 37), and still believe, that the spatial disunity between foreground and background reflects the artist's struggle with a primarily formal problem, that of fusing the neo-classical methods of his training with the Baroque style to which he was drawn by temperament. It may be that this spatial disjunction contributes, as Spector feels (p. 23), 'to the picture's peculiar and disturbing power in displaying the opposed moods of pensive melancholy and animal energy', but only accidentally: the same 'detachment of the mental from the physical' is preserved in the *Christ on the Sea of Galilee* from the 1850s, where, as I have attempted to show (ibid.), the specific formal problem of the *Sardanapalus* has been resolved by fully synthesizing the two modes.[8]

Delacroix's assistant of later years, Gustave Lassalle-Bordes, reports moreover (loc. cit., 1880) that Delacroix could not bring himself to master the rules of perspective and practised it intuitively ('de sentiment'); that, he continues, 'fut cause de l'insuccès de son tableau de *Sardanapale*, qui parut si choquant par l'absence de ces règles, tout en ayant de très belles parties.' Disregard for the rules of perspective was certainly not the only reason why the *Sardanapalus* seemed so shocking when first exhibited, but it may well have been one of the major reasons for its apparent lack of success among painters, as well as for a disjunction of scale that was unintentional and therefore different in kind from the doctrinaire rejection of rules by anti-classical writers. The perspectivist Thénot (op. cit., 1853) is a qualified and telling witness of Delacroix's involuntary ineptitude while painting the *Sardanapalus*:

M. Eugène Delacroix me pria de lui tracer quelques lignes monumentales dans [. . .] *la Mort de Sardanapale*. Toutes les figures étaient peintes, il ne restait plus à faire que l'architecture. Toutes ces figures avaient été dessinées de la même place et à la même hauteur, sans qu'il se fût occupé de l'horizon dans le tableau ni dans la nature; alors on voyait le dessus de la tête quand on devait voir le dessous du menton, et ainsi de suite pour toutes les autres parties de ces figures. Cependant il les croyait exactes de dessin puisqu'il les avait dessinées d'après nature; il aurait dû savoir que lorsque le modèle est élevé de cinq pieds, il n'est pas vu de même que s'il était de quinze ou vingt pieds, quoique dans la même position l'aspect soit tout différent.

Thénot gives this as an illustration of how, if the models are not placed at the height corresponding to the position they will occupy in the pictorial space, 'il y a dans le tableau un désaccord dont l'œil ne peut se rendre compte.'

Another factor that may have contributed to the disjunction of scale and to the spatial anomalies is the influence of a seventeenth-century Persian miniature copied by Delacroix and depicting a cremation scene with an Indian woman immolating herself on the funeral pyre of her betrothed (see Johnson, op. cit., 1965, for repr. and discussion).

The painters to whom Delacroix here owes most are Rubens and Gros, who was perhaps the most Rubensian of Delacroix's immediate predecessors in the French school. In general, the painting's controlled turbulence and rich colouring, its emphasis on voluptuous nudes and its cornucopia of sparkling accessories, its composition dominated by a luminous diagonal all relate it to the manner of the Baroque master. In particular, the standing nude in the foreground, though done from life, derives from a nereid in Rubens's *Landing of Maria de' Medici at Marseilles* in the Louvre and the foremost nude in his *Rape of the Daughters of Leucippus*, a picture more similar in spirit to the *Sardanapalus* (for a discussion of these sources, see Johnson, op. cit., 1960, p. 298 n. 17, J16 for a copy of the nereid); the shoulder and upper arm of the man stabbing her appear to have been influenced in form and technique by the triton in the left foreground of the *Landing*. It has been suggested (White, op. cit., 1967) that the nude reclining at the foot of the couch is derived from the caryatid in the same picture. The link between Delacroix's painting and the Rubens can already be seen in the oil sketch (J124), where the nude is immersed in smoke and flames corresponding to the waves in which the nereids play. Over and above these adaptations of Rubens's forms, the diagonal wedge that contains the major figures seems to owe its very brilliance largely to methods learnt from Rubens, in the way this is brought out by the dark values to either side of it and by the Negro's arm cutting into it. In 1827 John Burnet's *Practical Hints on Colour in Painting*, containing hand-coloured illustrations, was published in London. Referring to the plate of Rubens's *Descent from the Cross*, composed in a diagonal, the author writes: 'Rubens has given great brilliancy to his light by bringing his strongest dark in contact with it in the most cutting manner'; and of the next plate (setting crucifixion beside sex in a way that has been held to be of special significance as a key to Delacroix's psyche but not to Rubens's or Burnet's), the *Rape of the Sabines* in the National Gallery: 'We find [. . .] the strong colour surrounding the light [. . .] With Rubens this is generally the case.' Delacroix knew this treatise, whether by 1827 is not certain, and was interested enough in it to make notes in French which included a rough translation of the latter passage.[9] See also Delacroix's copy of Rubens's *Conclusion of the Peace* (J17).

In addition to the debts to Rubens of form and technique, and in some ways more important because it shows how

Delacroix could have thought of himself as a propagator of a truer classicism than Ingres's even in a work that seemed to his contemporaries and may still seem to us the epitome of 'Romanticism', is Delacroix's particular interpretation of Rubens as a truly 'Homeric' artist in contrast to the painter of the *Apotheosis of Homer*, whom he considered Homeric 'only in pretension'. The Homeric quality (surely in this sense embodied in the *Sardanapalus*) he defined as: 'the true cry of suffering, the sweat of the fighter or of the labourer, the atrocious detail often carried to an extreme, the blood, the tears, which make us men.'

Gros's influence emerges most powerfully in the group of the Negro and horse, which appears to owe much, both in spirit and arrangement, to the black tugging at the bridle of a startled, rearing horse on the far right of the *Battle of Nazareth* (Musée des Beaux-Arts, Nantes), an oil sketch much admired by Delacroix.

A lesser painter who may have played a modest role in the development of the picture is Hippolyte Poterlet. Robaut reports hearsay evidence that, in a moment of discouragement while seeking his composition, Delacroix turned to Poterlet and asked him to paint it on a canvas as he conceived it; Poterlet then did a small oil sketch which departed from Delacroix's design mainly in the figures to the right of the bed.[10] Spector (p. 126) makes the interesting suggestion that the idea for the man extending his arm on the far right and, above all, for the figure of Aïscheh hanging herself may have come from the corresponding figures in this sketch, since it 'is the only place before the final painting where they appear.' Delacroix records that Poterlet was working alongside him on 21 November 1827 when, though 'notable progress' had been made on the *Sardanapalus*, it was far from finished (*Correspondance* I. 205 f., 207), and he may have incorporated some of the younger painter's ideas at that late stage.

Delacroix had been billed for the canvas and stretcher on 12 July 1827 (Joubin, op. cit., 1936. The actual bill is in M-Nélaton Doc., bound in *Lettres à Pierret*, II); preparations to cover it must have begun about then, since it was accepted for the refurbished Salon in mid-January and he wrote that six months' work had gone into it (*Correspondance* I. 211); but most of the colouring seems to have been done in the months of November and December, after the Salon had opened early in November: on 29 October Delacroix placed a large order for colours, to be prepared more liquidly than usual, and a further one on 16 December (*Correspondance* I. 200, 207). The fluidity of the colours makes itself felt in the wide use of rich glazes, probably the result of the combined influence of Rubens and English painting. More individual, though related to this, was Delacroix's desire, reported by Andrieu (loc. cit., 1876), to match the variety of hue, the 'blondeur et fraîcheur' of pastel and distemper. To this end, he drew from the life the three beautiful pastel studies in the

Louvre and fully succeeded in translating one of them into oils, in the foot of the man in the foreground (see analysis and juxtaposition of colour details in Johnson 1963, p. 37 and pls. 15, 16). Some other parts of the picture, the arm of the foremost nude, for example, are in a manner as sculpturesque as David's, but alongside it that foot, brought into relief by means of thin colour hatchings, instead of opaque impasto, illustrates what Cézanne must have meant when, speaking of his own career, he declared it had taken him forty years to discover that painting was not sculpture.

The adverse criticism of the *Sardanapalus* at the Salon, revolving a little more ferociously than usual around lack of taste, of grace and 'noblesse', of order, 'good' drawing and finish, is too well known to require extended comment here.[11] It is, however, worth noting from Vitet's familiar attack in *Le Globe* (8 March 1828) the physical position of the painting in the Salon, hung rather high: 'Ses touches sont tellement heurtées, ses couleurs si peu fondues, que, si son tableau était placé seulement quelques pieds plus bas, on aurait en vérité beaucoup de peine à en supporter la vue'; and from Léonor Mérimée's uneasy letter written three days later, the position it was feared it might take in altering the course of French art: 'je ne crois pas qu'il puisse pervertir notre École. Il faudrait, pour faire révolution, commencer par savoir imiter avec vérité au moins les parties essentielles.' Two rarer beings who defended the picture were the anonymous critic of the *Figaro* (18 February 1828) and Victor Hugo. The former, protesting at the injustice of the critics, admitted that the painting might have its faults, but 'ce sont les défauts d'un homme qui travaille de verve et d'inspiration. Pourquoi fermer les yeux sur les beautés consolantes qui les rachètent? On ne peut lui refuser cette finesse de couleur, cette originalité de style qui lui appartiennent.' And Hugo (loc. cit., 3 April 1828): 'ne croyez pas que Delacroix ait failli. Son *Sardanapale* est une chose magnifique, et si gigantesque qu'elle échappe aux petites vues. [. . .] ce bel ouvrage [. . .] n'a point eu de succès près des bourgeois de Paris: *sifflets des sots sont fanfares de gloire*.'

STUDIES: Most of the known studies for the *Sardanapalus*, none of which is dated, are handily reproduced in a tentative chronological order and described by Spector (op. cit., 1974). All the notes on the recto of the sheet Louvre RF 5278 (his pl. 12), several of which have been referred to above, are transcribed in French in *Mémorial* (no. 104), in English by Trapp (p. 87). The Louvre's three pastel studies are all reproduced in black and white by Spector; a full-page colour reproduction of the pastel for the foremost nude is in Huyghe, p. 124, and Trapp, pl. VIII; the sheet for the Negro and woman on the left of the bed is illustrated (poorly) in colour in T. Prideaux *et al.*, *The World of Delacroix* (1966), p. 76; and the foot in Johnson 1963, as referred to above. A

pastel, not mentioned by Spector, passed in the same sale as these (Decock, 12 May 1948, lot 2, 24 × 31 cm): for the woman lying against the far side of the bed, it is reproduced by G. Bazin in 'Pastels de Delacroix pour le *Sardanapale*', *L'Amour de l'Art*, XXV (1945), p. 71. Lot 5, described as a pastel study of an arm and foot, 14 × 27 cm, which I have not seen, may also have been for the *Sardanapalus* (see J. Bouchot-Saupique, *Bulletin des Musées de France*, Dec. 1948, p. 284). Three rough sketches connected with the early stages of the composition, notably a preliminary idea for the pose of the arms of Sardanapalus, have recently come to light, on the back of a sheet of drawings which includes studies after Andrea del Sarto and Goya (Sale Christie's, London, 25 June 1976, lot 10, repr.).

Lot 318 in Delacroix's posthumous sale is described in the catalogue as twelve sheets of drawings and sketches for the *Sardanapalus* (not thirty as stated under R1519). Burty Ann ED gives only eleven, noting that nine went to Sabattier [*sic*] for 30 fr., two to Moureau for 53 fr. A few of these are not accounted for and might, assuming the description in the catalogue to be accurate, shed further light on the development of the painting.

Four paintings, described as 'fragments de figures pour le Sardanapale', passed as lot 198 in the posthumous sale: (1) to an anonymous buyer, 160 fr.; (2) to Guerrier [Burty Ann ED; R: Garnier], 100 fr.; (3) to Rederon [Burty Ann ED; R: Riduon; Thoré Ann ED: Redon], 140 fr.; (4) to Saint-Maurice, 28 fr. They were listed without dimensions and were evidently unknown to Robaut, who put them in his Supplement under no. 1520, without illustrations or measurements, dating them to 1826, no doubt because they were described as studies *for* the *Sardanapalus* in the posthumous sale catalogue. Nothing that can be certainly identified with any of these studies has, to my knowledge, come to light since 1864, but, rather than preparatory studies for the Salon painting, they were most likely the copies done from it shortly before it was delivered to Wilson in 1846, according to Andrieu, who describes them (loc. cit., 1876) as 'une suite d'études à l'huile et de même dimension que les figures du tableau primitif de *Sardanapale*, M. Delacroix les avait faites pour lui-même avant de le céder [. . .] à M. Wilson.'

See also the portraits of *Aspasie* and *Woman in a Blue Turban* (J79 and J88).

CONDITION: The *Sardanapalus* was strip-lined ('remmargé') and the varnish cleaned in Haro's workshop in 1846 before being dispatched, rolled, to Wilson (*Correspondance* II. 276). A horizontal seam in the canvas, still visible across the full width of the surface at the height of the horse's ear, had come unstitched by 1849, when Delacroix, seeing his masterpiece at Ecoublay at the time of John Wilson's death, lamented: 'l'état pour le moment est déplorable: la toile détendue, la couture du bas fendue dans toute sa longueur et retenue ça et là par des points de couture.' (A horizontal seam is also visible across the full width at the level of the right wrist of the woman against the far side of the bed.) There is, however, no record of any steps being taken to restore it before 1856: on 2 September of that year Delacroix wrote to an unknown correspondent (Haro ?): 'J'ai vu M. Fould qui devant quitter Paris la semaine prochaine, désirerait auparavant s'entendre avec vous sur la restauration du *Sardanapale*' (unpublished letter, Coll. late M. R. Leybold). How Fould (no doubt Achille Fould, who as Minister of State had been in charge of organizing the Exposition universelle of 1855) was involved is not clear, but it is presumably to this restoration arranged in 1856 that Burty (loc. cit., 23 March 1873) and Andrieu (loc. cit., 1876) refer without establishing the date. Burty reports that, having been blocked in with distemper then lightly covered with oils, the *Sardanapalus* was not resistant and had to be restored some years after it was sold to Wilson: 'il fallut procéder à un rentoilage. Il fut exécuté avec les soins les plus minutieux par M. Haro [. . .] Andrieu répara les blessures sous les yeux du maître, qui, l'opération menée à bien, vint lui-même renforcer par quelques touches vigoureuses ce que la peinture primitive avait d'un peu lanterneux. Ces retouches, mâles et dans le système des larges hachures [. . .] ne se dérobent point à un examen attentif. Le tableau a été reverni tout récemment.' Andrieu, adding a few technical details about condition but failing to mention Delacroix's final retouching, confirms that it was to him, under the Master's close supervision, that fell the task of 'cette difficile et scabreuse restauration.'

¹ According to Haro, followed by others down to the present day, the picture was sold to Wilson in 1845 (Introduction to Cat. Sale D. W. [Wilson], p. 6), but letters of 19 May and 9 August 1846 from Delacroix to Mme Haro seem to confirm Piron's date, or show at least that the picture was not delivered before the summer of 1846 (*Correspondance* II. 271, 276). In the latter he writes: 'Je suis obligé de partir sans être présent au roulement du *Sardanapale* pour l'emporter chez elle et le remarger [. . .] Elle a l'adresse de M. Wilson à qui le tableau est destiné et s'entendra pour l'expédition aussitôt après le remargement.'
² Since the picture was lent to the exhibition *Bd Italiens*, Paris 1861-2 by M. Pelouze, owner of the Château de Chenonceaux (through his wife ?), it was presumably housed by Mme Pelouze and her husband (at the Château ?—see under *Copies*, by Andrieu, and n. 5) until the time of the Wilson sale in 1873. Daniel Wilson was in any case probably a joint owner of the Château (he is listed as owner in the 1880 ed. of Vapereau's *Dictionnaire des contemporains*). But it is not known for certain where the *Sardanapalus* was kept between 1849 and 1873.
³ According to a press cutting in the catalogue of the Duncan sale preserved in *BN Estampes*, Adolphe Thiers, President of the Republic at the time, ordered the picture to be bought for the Musée du Luxembourg at the Wilson sale in 1873, 'et le fit pousser jusqu'à 90.000 fr., il fut adjugé à un marchand de tableaux [Durand-Ruel] qui le paya 96.000 fr. Ce marchand ne put s'en défaire, il l'exposa un peu partout et finit par le céder à M. Duncan, en perdant 50.000 fr.' *Le Rappel* of 20 March 1873 reports that Thiers had come to Paris the day before and visited the sale room, where 'il a longtemps admiré le *Sardanapale* de Delacroix.' Within a fortnight of buying the picture at the Wilson sale, Durand-Ruel had shipped it to England (cf. Théophile Silvestre to Alfred Bruyas, 2 Apr. 1873 (Bib *AA*

MS. 215, doc. 58): 'c'est 96 mille que le *Sardanapale* a été vendu à Durand-Ruel, qui déjà le promène en Angleterre.').
    James Duncan (1834-1905) made a fortune in the sugar refining industry, bought a large estate at Benmore in 1875 and had a picture gallery specially built alongside the house. He remained there until 1882 and, having lost much money as a result of the German Sugar Bounty, was declared bankrupt in 1885. Hence, though he is not listed as the owner in Robaut's *catalogue raisonné* of 1885 and it is not known exactly when he bought the *Sardanapalus* or where he kept it, he had presumably acquired it by 1882 and perhaps hung it in his gallery at Benmore. The fact that it was shown by Durand-Ruel, or lent in his name, three times in the two years before it was auctioned at the Duncan sale in 1889, suggests that Durand-Ruel had it back on consignment from Duncan, but failed to find a buyer.
⁴ In the *Kunstbladet* of 31 July 1888, Karl Madsen, later director of the State Museum of Art in Copenhagen, refers to the picture exhibited as a 'big painting' and, in a footnote, mentions the later, small version. In November, the painting in the exhibition is described in the same journal as 'the gigantic canvas'. Hence there appears to be no doubt that it was the 1827 version which was shown.
⁵ The Museum appears to have no record of when or by whom the gift was made (letter from M. Jean-Marie Girard, 24 Dec. 1969). The copy may have been commissioned as a replacement for the original shortly before it was sold in 1873, and later given to the Museum jointly by Mmes Wilson and Pelouze, who were sisters-in-law and probably both used the Château de Chenonceaux.
⁶ Farwell (op. cit., 1958, p. 71) suggested that the capitals were derived from Elephanta and mentioned that Thomas Daniell did an aquatint of the interior of the temple in 1799. Her point is strengthened by an unpublished note in the Louvre sketch-book RF9146 (fol. 4), used by Delacroix some ten years earlier: 'Vues de l'Inde par Daniel [*sic*]'.
⁷ See Spector (op. cit., 1974, chap. 3) for a summary of attitudes to Sardanapalus from antiquity down to the nineteenth century, and for various treatments of his end in the visual arts and music before and after Delacroix's painting. To these may be added A. Fantuzzi's Mannerist engraving, after Rosso (?), showing a nude Sardanapalus on a flaming pyre surrounded by his anguished retinue in various states of undress (Bartsch XVI. 348.26).
⁸ For a brief summary, with references, of other interpretations of the space in the *Sardanapalus*, see Spector, p. 23 and n.
⁹ The passages quoted are from pp. 46 and 47 of the 4th edition, 1835. See *Journal* III. 380 for Delacroix's undated translation.
¹⁰ See R Ann, under no. 198, for his account and for a small drawing after part of the sketch. The note, save for a descriptive passage, was published in Johnson (op. cit., 1960, p. 298 n. 17), and the sketch identified at the same time as that reproduced in Meier-Graefe and Klossowski's catalogue of the Cheramy collection, 1908, no. 155, and in Christoffel 1951, pl. 26. Poterlet's sketch, still attributed to Delacroix, is now in a private collection in England. Spector (op. cit., 1974, pp. 125 f. n. 68) gave the note with slight variations, overlooking its earlier appearance in print and ignoring the published reproductions of the sketch.
¹¹ See Spector (op. cit., 1974, chap. 5) for an excellent summary in English of critical opinion from 1828 to the present day; Tourneux for more extensive Salon criticisms in French.

126 HENRI III AT THE DEATH-BED OF MARIE DE CLÈVES   Pl. 110

14 × 10¹³⁄₁₆ in. (27.5 × 35.5 cm)*
Signed lower left, on the table-cover: *Eug. Delacroix.*
1826/7
Private collection

Provenance: Mme Alexandrine de Rothschild, Paris, d. 1965.

Exhibitions: None.

Literature: Probably Silvestre *Delacroix* (1855), p. 80; L. Johnson, 'A New Delacroix: *Henri III at the Death-Bed of Marie de Clèves*', *Burl Mag*, CXVIII (1976), pp. 620–2, repr. in colour, fig. 1, detail of signature, fig. 2.

It was suggested in 1976 (op. cit.) that this painting is most probably a picture which, though not mentioned in later catalogues or other literature, is listed under the title 'Henri III et la princesse de Rohan morte' among works from the 1820s in the catalogue in Silvestre *Delacroix* (1855); but that the dead woman must in fact be Marie de Clèves, Princesse de Condé, whom Henri III 'aimait uniquement' according to Pierre Matthieu. She died in childbirth in Paris at the age of twenty-one, in 1574, the year of Henri III's accession to the throne of France, leaving the King, who Brantôme tells us was determined to marry her, inconsolable. The other man in the picture may be Henri de Bourbon, Prince de Condé, whom Marie de Clèves had married in 1572 and who was in fact in Germany at the time of her death, but could have been included by Delacroix for dramatic emphasis.

The stance and costume of the King, who anachronistically wears the Order of the Holy Ghost which he instituted five years after the event depicted, is based primarily on a water-colour copy of a contemporary portrait of Henri III in the eighteenth-century *Recueil de Gaignières* in *BN Estampes* (repr. ibid., fig. 3). The profile of Marie de Clèves is apparently taken from a drawing by Bonington after the Virgin in Sebastiano del Piombo's *Visitation* in the Louvre, a study Bonington himself used for the sick girl in his water-colour *The Visit* (Louvre), which is dated 1826 (both works repr. ibid., figs. 4, 5). This connection with Bonington, combined with the fact that Delacroix is known to have lent a head of Henri III to the English artist by 1828, points to a date of 1826/7.

127 HENRI IV AND GABRIELLE D'ESTRÉES   Pl. 111

$15\frac{1}{8} \times 20\frac{11}{16}$ in. (38.5 × 52.5 cm)*
Signed bottom left: *Eug Delacroix*
R1515 (1826)
c. 1827–8
Private collection, W. Germany

Provenance: Claye, before 1885; Hodgson, London; Charles Sedelmeyer; his sale 12 June 1907, lot 32 (repr.), to Oppenheimer, 5,300 fr.; apparently the painting which belonged to Charles Peccatte, curator of the Musée de Saint-Dié-des-Vosges (d. 1964), and was reported looted from his collection in November 1944 by the retreating German troops;[1] the present possessor, by 1963.

Exhibitions: Berne 1963–4, no. 13; Bremen 1964, no. 12.

Literature: L. Johnson, 'Some Historical Sketches by Delacroix', *Burl Mag*, CXV (1973), p. 672, and n. 2, 675, repr. fig. 49.

This painting was known to Robaut only from a drawing done from memory by Bracquemond, which no doubt served as the basis for the inaccurate engraving used to illustrate it in Robaut's catalogue. While he was therefore in no position to date the picture on style, his unsupported dating of 1826 cannot be far out. The picture seems more likely, however, to have been painted a year or two later, on the grounds of stylistic analogies with other works: the delicate proportions of the Gabrielle are close to those of the *Woman with Parrot*, dated 1827 (J9); a preliminary pencil study for the Gabrielle, in the Louvre (RF9565, repr. L. Johnson, op. cit., 1973, fig. 51), is in certain details very similar to a drawing of Mme Pierret dated 13 April 1827 in the Museum Boymans, Rotterdam (repr. *Mémorial*, no. 114); and this painting has a number of features in common with the handling and composition of the *Cromwell at Windsor Castle* (J129), which cannot be earlier than 1826 and is unlikely to have been painted before 1828. Finally, the remarkable points of similarity—limp hand holding feathered fan, white satin draperies—between our picture and Bonington's *Henri III and the English Ambassador* (Wallace Collection), which Delacroix recalled was one of the English artist's last paintings (*Correspondance* IV. 288), therefore probably done early in 1828, suggests that the two works may be almost contemporary, rather than some two years apart.

Gabrielle d'Estrées (1573–99) was the mistress of Henri IV and bore him two sons. In the words of Péréfixe whose *Histoire du roi Henry le Grand* of 1661 was known to Delacroix by 1828 (*Correspondance* I. 233): 'Henry conceived a violent passion for Gabrielle d'Estrées, a young Lady of accomplished beauty, and noble birth, who got such an ascendant over his affection, that, whilst she lived, she always held the first place in his heart; insomuch that having had three or four children by her, he was almost resolved to marry her' (M. Le Moine's English translation of Péréfixe, Paris 1785, p. 171).

The profile of the King is probably based on that painted by Rubens in his *Henri IV entrusts the Regency to Maria de' Medici*, copied by Delacroix around the latter half of the 1820s (J20); the features of Gabrielle d'Estrées on an engraved portrait by Thomas de Leu, her contemporary (repr. L. Johnson, op. cit., 1973, fig. 50).

The theme of Henri IV and Gabrielle d'Estrées had already been treated in painting by Richard (Salon 1810), and Gabrielle had been represented next to this popular king in an engraving as early as April 1791, in the *Mercure de France* (cf. Cat. Exh. Bourg-en-Bresse 1971, p. 42).

---

[1] 'Déclaration de spoliation' submitted by M. Peccatte after the war to the Service français de récupération artistique, described as '*Henri IV et Gabrielle d'Estrées*', attributed to Delacroix. See also: *Commandement en chef français en Allemagne. Groupe Français de Conseil de Contrôle: Répertoire des biens spoliés en France durant la guerre 1939–1945*, II (Berlin-Frohnau, 1947), Item no. 103.

128 MILTON DICTATING   Pl. 112
PARADISE LOST TO HIS DAUGHTERS

$31\frac{11}{16} \times 25\frac{3}{8}$ in. (80.4 × 64.4 cm)*
Signed lower left: *Eug. Delacroix*
Moreau p. 170. R87 (1824) and p. 538
1827/8?
George Heard Hamilton, Williamstown, Mass.

Provenance: Duc de Fitz-James, by 1828 (?); with the heir to the title to at least 1885; anon. sale 31 Jan. 1887, lot 20, to Durand-Ruel, 8,200 fr.; Erwin Davis, New York; his sale, New York, 19 March 1889, lot 107, $4,500; H. B. Davis; he consigned it to Durand-Ruel, New York, from 7 March 1907 to 25 May 1908—unsold (Arch D-R); Katharine M. Berwind, New York; her sale, New York, 22 March 1946, lot 282 (repr.), to the present owner.

Exhibitions: Salon 1827-8, 2nd Supp. no. 1632 ('Milton et ses filles'); *Bd Italiens*, Paris 1863; *EBA*, Paris 1885, no. 78; Toronto-Ottawa 1962-3, no. 1, repr.; Louvre 1963, no. 105, *M*. no. 108, repr.; Edinburgh-London 1964, no. 16.

Literature: A. Béraud *et al.*, review of Salon 1827-8, *Annales de l'Ecole française des Beaux-Arts* (Pillet, Paris, 1827 [*sic*]), p. 75; D., review of Salon 1827-8, *L'Observateur des Beaux-Arts*, I, no. xiii (23 May 1828), p. 50; A. Jal, *Esquisses, croquis, pochades, ou tout ce qu'on voudra, sur le Salon de 1827* (A. Dupont, Paris, 1828), p. 445; Silvestre *Delacroix* (1855), p. 80; X. Feyrnet, 'Courrier de Paris', *L'Illustration*, XLI, no. 1052 (25 Apr. 1863), p. 259; Piron, p. 106; E. Charavay (ed.), *Lettres autographes composant la collection de M. Alfred Bovet* (Paris 1885), p. 595 (Letter dated 20 March 1828 from Constant Dutilleux to Théodore Laches; comments on this painting reprinted in Cat. Exh. Toronto-Ottawa 1962-3, p. 9, and *Mémorial*, p. 73); G. Dampt, *Eugène Delacroix. A propos de la dernière exposition de ses œuvres* (Tresse, Paris, 1885), p. 16; Moreau-Nélaton I. 68, 101, repr. fig. 36; J. Guiffrey, 'La "Mort de Sardanapale" d'Eugène Delacroix au Musée du Louvre', *GBA* 5th per. IV (1921), p. 195; Escholier I. 217 n. 1; *Journal* I. 21 n. 1; Sérullaz *Dessins* 1952, p. 44; Huyghe, p. 173; Maltese, p. 124; T. Prideaux *et al.*, *The World of Delacroix* (Time Inc., New York, 1966), repr. in colour p. 75; L. Johnson, 'Eugène Delacroix et les Salons. Documents inédits au Louvre', *Revue du Louvre*, 16 (1966), pp. 218, 220; Trapp, pp. 77 f., repr. fig. 40.

This picture was unknown to Robaut in the original when he compiled the entry for his *catalogue raisonné* and he therefore illustrated his entry with a reproduction of a markedly different pen-and-ink drawing (now Musée des Beaux-Arts, Lyon; repr. Cat. Exh. Edinburgh-London 1964, pl. 43), thinking that it gave an idea of this canvas but which in fact appears to be connected with the *Goetz von Berlichingen* lithographs of 1838-43. Robaut also followed

Moreau in dating it to 1824, but with the reservation that had it not been for Moreau's dating he would have placed it after Delacroix's journey to England in 1825. I suggested that since it was included in the second supplement of the catalogue of the Salon of 1827-8 with the *Death of Sardanapalus* (J125), it might, like the larger picture, not have been completed until after the Salon had opened, in November; and argued that on the grounds of stylistic analogy (the groping left arm of Milton, for example, is virtually the same motif as the right arm of Cromwell) and other correspondences, it should be dated as closely as possible to the *Cromwell at Windsor Castle* (J129), which could not be earlier than 1826 and was unlikely to be earlier than 1828 (Cat. Exh. Toronto-Ottawa 1962-3, no. 1). This opinion appeared to be somewhat strengthened by my discovery that the *Milton* was not presented to the Salon jury till 14 January 1828, when it was rejected, being accepted only at the following session, on 28 January, possibly after being reworked (L. Johnson, op. cit., 1966, pp. 218, 220). Moreau's statement that it was painted in 1824 for the Société des Amis des arts, which cannot be confirmed from known sources, should probably be discounted; it may have been based on knowledge of Delacroix's note in his *Journal* (I. 21), on 22 October 1822: 'Je veux faire, pour la Société des Amis des arts, *Milton soigné par ses filles*', a project which appears, however, to have come to nothing until it was realized some five years later in the form of this painting.

While Delacroix seems never to have produced a picture inspired by Milton's poetry and this painting is unique in his *œuvre*, Milton was generally admired by the Romantics. He is included with Dante and Shakespeare as a model for the new school of literature in Victor Hugo's Preface to *Cromwell* of 1827. Two new editions of translations of *Paradise Lost* were published in France in the first half of the 1820s: Dupré de Saint-Maur's translation, at Avignon in 1823; and Jacques Delille's, at Paris in 1824. The former contains a translation of an essay on Milton by Addison. There is no evidence that Delacroix read this particular essay, but he is known to have been reading Addison as early as 1820 (*Journal* I. 32) and it could have fired his interest in the subject. There are, however, pictorial precedents for the subject that could have been known to Delacroix in reproduction, notably Fuseli's painting of 1793 for the *Milton Gallery* (no. 40. Fig. 16 here). George Romney had also done a painting of the subject, in a very different manner, and had it engraved. And Decaisne showed a painting, known from Léon Noel's lithograph of 1830 reproduced here (Fig. 17), of the same subject in the same Salon as Delacroix's picture (no. 273). The two compositions have so many points in common, in spite of the contrast of an indoor and open-air setting, that it is difficult to believe that one was not influenced by the other—the

Delacroix by the Decaisne, if the sequence of their appearance at the Salon is any indication of their chronology.

In contrast to the expressive distortions of the Fuseli, Delacroix's painting is outstanding for its *naturalism* and sensitive interpretation of the scene without dramatic exaggeration. Milton's blindness is not only expressed by his unseeing eyes, but implied in the suggestion of the senses he can still enjoy: touch, by the hand on the rich Turkish carpet covering the table; smell, by the flowers; hearing, by the mandolin held by his daughter. Unlike Fuseli, Delacroix conveys by purely pictorial means an idea of the work Milton is dictating, by placing on the wall a picture of the *Expulsion of Adam and Eve from Paradise*, derived from Raphael's fresco in the Vatican Loggia. According to a note

Fig. 16. *Milton*, Fuseli.

Fig. 17. *Milton*, L. Noel after H. Decaisne.

by Robaut in the second edition of the catalogue of the exhibition *EBA*, Paris 1885 (*Bib AA*, MS. 298ter), this representation of the *Expulsion* 'est un morceau rapporté dans la toile coupée à cet effet', but no separate insertion is apparent to the naked eye, nor is this passage visibly later in execution than the rest of the picture; an X-ray examination might prove helpful. According to the same source (repeated in R Ann), the figure of the girl seated next to Milton was painted by Ary Scheffer. This seems possible, on grounds of style and expression, though no other instance of another artist painting a figure in an early easel painting by Delacroix is recorded. Guiffrey (1921) sees a strong influence of Wilkie in the picture as a whole.

A sheet of pencil studies for the legs and left hand of the Milton is preserved in the Musée des Beaux-Arts, Besançon (Cat. Exh. Edinburgh-London 1964, no. 91, repr. pl. 47). Sérullaz (op. cit., 1952) has suggested with some plausibility that a pen-and-ink study of the head and shoulders of a woman (Louvre, RF10374), probably Mme Pierret, may have served for the daughter on the far left of this painting.

The painting attracted little notice from the Salon reviewers. Those who did mention it were brief but complimentary: Béraud, 'le coloris est chaud et vigoureux'; D., 'mérite [. . .] une mention particulière'; Jal, 'une production agréable, l'expression du poëte plaît par sa simplicité; une de ses filles est jolie.' When it was on show at the Galerie Martinet in April 1863, Feyrnet mentioned it, with David's *Sacre* and *Marat*, as one of the pictures that excited the most curiosity.

129 CROMWELL AT WINDSOR CASTLE   Pl. 113

13$\frac{11}{16}$ × 10$\frac{11}{16}$ in. (34.8 × 27.2 cm)* Relined
Signed bottom left: *Eug Delacroix*
Moreau p. 171. R320 (1830) and Additions, p. 483
1828/30
Dr. J. Tadion, Lausanne

Provenance: Duc de Fitz-James, by 1831; Bernheim *aîné*; sale his estate, Brussels 18 March 1884, lot 55, to the dealer Rothschild, 5,200 fr.; anon. sale, Hôtel Drouot, salle 2, 1 Apr. 1889, lot 24, bought in at 2,000 fr.; consigned to Bernheim-Jeune by Rothschild, 10 Apr. 1889 (Arch B-J); bought from Rothschild by Robaut soon after and sold to P. A. Cheramy for 7,000 fr. (R Ann, pp. 89, 483); his sale 5 May 1908, lot 166 (repr. and wrongly described as the sketch for the painting shown at the Salon of 1831), to Simon Oppenheimer, 3,000 fr.; O. Gerstenberg, Berlin; bought from him by Peter Nathan, Zurich, *c.* 1966, and sold to Mr. and Mrs. Robert Benjamin, Great Neck, N.Y., by 1969; mixed sale (including their property), Christie's, London 3 July 1973, lot 3 (repr. in colour), to the present owner.

Exhibitions: Salon 1831, no. 514 (mentioned in the catalogue as owned by the Duc de Fitz-James); 'XIX and XX Century French Paintings and Drawings', Lefevre Gallery, London Nov.-Dec. 1966, *h.c.*

Literature: L. P. [Peisse], 'Salon de 1831', *Le National*, 30 May 1831; A. Jal, *Salon de 1831. Ebauches critiques* (A. J. Dénain, Paris, 1831), p. 131; C. P. Landon, *Annales du Musée et de l'École moderne des Beaux-Arts. Salon de 1831 ... par Ambroise Tardieu pour servir de suite et de complément aux Salons Landon* (Pillet *aîné*, Paris, 1831), p. 47; L. Rouart, 'La Collection de M. Cheramy', *Les Arts*, no. 64 (Apr. 1907), p. 22, repr. p. 20; J. Meier-Graefe and E. Klossowski, *La Collection Cheramy . . .* (R. Piper, Munich, 1908), pp. 91 f., no. 165, repr.; Moreau-Nélaton I. 102, 118, repr. fig. 71; Escholier I. 276; *Correspondance* I. 266 n. 3; L. Johnson, Cat. Exh. Toronto-Ottawa 1962-3, p. 10 and n. 2; L. Johnson, 'Eugène Delacroix et les Salons. Documents inédits au Louvre', *Revue du Louvre*, 16 (1966), p. 220; K. Roberts, review of Lefevre Gallery Exhibition, *Burl Mag*, CVIII (1966), p. 645, repr. p. 644, fig. 55.

This painting was accepted for the Salon of 1831 on 17 April. The scene was described as follows in the official catalogue: 'Cromwell dans le château de Windsor.

Ayant retourné par hasard un portrait de Charles Ier, il tombe à cette vue dans une méditation profonde; il oublie qu'il a un témoin qui l'observe: c'est un espion du parti royaliste qui a obtenu accès auprès de lui. (*Woodstock*, de Walter Scott)'

The episode is from Chapter VIII in Scott's novel, first published in 1826:

Wildrake [the cavalier] stood a silent, inactive, and almost a terrified spectator, while Cromwell, assuming a firm sternness of eye and manner, as one who compels himself to look on what some strong internal feeling renders painful and disgustful to him, proceeded, in brief and interrupted expressions, but yet with a firm voice, to comment on the portrait of the late King. His words seemed less addressed to Wildrake, than to be the spontaneous unburdening of his own bosom, swelling under recollection of the past and anticipation of the future.
'That Flemish painter,' he said—'that Antonio Vandyke—what a power he has! Steel may mutilate, warriors may waste and destroy—still the King stands uninjured by time.' (*Woodstock*, Everyman ed. 1969, p. 99.)

Delacroix's image of the King is not a replica of any of Van Dyck's portraits of Charles I. It most resembles the upper half of the full-length portrait of the King in Garter robes preserved, appropriately enough, at Windsor Castle. Wildrake's satin-clad left arm is also very similar to the King's right arm in the Van Dyck.

Though this picture is unlikely to have been painted by January 1828, for had it been completed by then it would probably have been submitted to the Salon of 1827-8, it may be doubted whether it is as late as 1830, the year in which, according to Moreau who cites no supporting evidence, it was painted for the Duc de Fitz-James. It seems likely, on the grounds of style and of the period from English history chosen, to be closer in date to the *Milton dictating 'Paradise Lost'* (J128), which was probably completed around the end of 1827, and certainly no later than January 1828. Two French stage adaptations of *Woodstock*, which could have provided Delacroix with a stimulus for painting the subject in 1828, were performed in Paris in March of that year (cf. H. A. White, *Sir Walter Scott's Novels on the Stage*, New Haven and London, 1927, p. 245).

The picture attracted little attention from critics of a Salon which included the *Liberty*: Jal found the figure of Wildrake 'fort bien'; Tardieu noted tersely, 'bonne composition, exécution faible'; and Peisse thought the painting should have remained in the artist's studio.

A summary sketch for the pose of Cromwell with three alternative poses for Wildrake, some very close to the final stance, are on a sheet of studies covered mostly with felines, in the Art Institute of Chicago (1971.309, black lead, pen and ink, water-colour, 38 × 48.5 cm). Two of the studies of tigers are related to the lithograph *Tigre royal* of 1829 (Delteil 80).

About 1831 Delacroix painted a large water-colour of *Cromwell before the Coffin of Charles I* (R368; more accurately reproduced in Robaut Tracings II), which was intended as an improvement on Delaroche's interpretation of the subject in his highly successful painting exhibited at the Salon in that year (Musée des Beaux-Arts, Nîmes). For a full account of the circumstances in which Delacroix painted it, see R. P. Huet, *Paul Huet* (H. Laurens, Paris, 1911), pp. 381-3.

130 CARDINAL RICHELIEU   Pl. 114
SAYING MASS, sketch

$14\frac{13}{16} \times 10\frac{5}{8}$ in. (37.6 × 27 cm)*
Moreau pp. 170 n. 1, 210. R255 (repr. in Additions, no. 255, p. 482)
1828
The late Mme David-Weill, Neuilly

Provenance: M. Mahler, by 1873; he had probably disposed of it by 1885;[1] M. D. David-Weill; Mme D. David-Weill, his widow, d. 1970.

Exhibition: Louvre 1963, no. 128, *M* no. 130, repr.

Literature: Silvestre *Delacroix* (1855), p. 81.

According to Moreau, this sketch was presented to the Duc d'Orléans for approval as a design for the large painting of 1828 (J131). Except for minor variations in the setting and grouping, it establishes the final composition.

---

[1] It was not included in the exhibition *EBA*, Paris 1885, to which Mahler lent two other paintings, and Robaut noted in R Ann, perhaps shortly after the exhibition, that it used to belong to Mahler, without naming the new owner.

131 CARDINAL RICHELIEU   Pl. 115
SAYING MASS IN THE CHAPEL OF
THE PALAIS-ROYAL

$89\frac{3}{8} \times 51\frac{3}{16}$ in. (2.27 × 1.30 m)[1]
Signed, dated 1828[2]
Moreau pp. 170, 209 f. R253
1828
Destroyed in 1848

Provenance: Commissioned by the Duc d'Orléans for his gallery in the Palais-Royal, paid 4,000 fr.;[3] destroyed in the burning and pillage of the Palais-Royal by the revolutionaries on 24 Feb. 1848.

Exhibited: Salon 1831, no. 512 ('Le cardinal de Richelieu dans sa chapelle du Palais-Royal. Il dit la messe entouré de la compagnie de ses gardes, le mousquet sur l'épaule et la mèche allumée. (Palais-Royal)').

Literature: L. P. [Peisse], review of Salon of 1831, *Le National*, 30 May 1831; anon., review of id., *Le Constitutionnel*, 4 June 1831; F.P., 'Salon de 1831', *Moniteur universel*, 4 June 1831; anon., *L'Observateur aux Salons de 1831* (Gauthier, Paris, n.d.), p. 5; C.P. Landon, *Annales du Musée et de l'Ecole moderne des Beaux-Arts. Salon de 1831 ... par Ambroise Tardieu pour servir de suite et de complément aux Salons Landon* (Pillet aîné, Paris, 1831), pp. 42 f., line engraving by Normand fils, pl. 19; T. Thoré, 'M. Eugène Delacroix', *Le Siècle*, 25 Feb. 1837; J. Vatout, *Histoire lithographiée du Palais-Royal* (C. Motte, Paris, n.d. [1845]), Jourdy lithograph with commentary, pl. 3; id., *Le Palais-Royal, son histoire et sa description* (Didier, Paris, 1852), p. 338; Piron, p. 106; G. Dampt, *Eugène Delacroix. A propos de la dernière exposition de ses œuvres* (Tresse, Paris, 1885), p. 9; Moreau-Nélaton I. 118, 163, Jourdy lithograph repr. fig. 70, II. 72, 125; Escholier I. 231, 276; *Correspondance* I. 220 n. 1, 222 n. 2, 260 n. 1; Huyghe, pp. 191, 206; L. Johnson, 'Eugène Delacroix et les Salons. Documents inédits au Louvre', *Revue du Louvre*, 16 (1966), pp. 219, 220; Trapp, pp. 93 and n. 9, 193.

Prints: Line engraving by Normand fils, for Landon-Tardieu *Salon de 1831*. Lithograph by Jourdy, for *Histoire lithographiée du Palais-Royal*, 1845 (Moreau pp. 18 f. Repr. here).

The appearance of this painting can only be deduced from prints, preliminary sketches and contemporary descriptions. It is not known when Delacroix received the commission, but he evidently finished the work about the end of September 1828, for it is to it that he no doubt refers in a letter to Félix Guillemardet dated 4 October 1828, saying 'le duc d'Orléans est content de ma peinture' (*Lettres intimes*, p. 151); and in another to Soulier in the same month: 'Je te dirais que le maudit tableau du duc d'Orléans m'a tenu trois grands mois' (*Correspondance* I. 222). He also states in letters to Thoré that it was painted in 1828 for 'la galerie du Palais-Royal' (Moreau-Nélaton I. 163, *Correspondance* I. 407). This 'Galerie historique', which served as a family ballroom and occasional theatre, was decorated with paintings representing scenes from the life of Richelieu and the history of the Palais-Royal down to the nineteenth century, commissioned by the Duc d'Orléans, who continued his patronage as King from 1830. No fewer than six other paintings for the same gallery were shown at the Salon of 1831, by Steuben, Ary Scheffer, Gosse, Eugène Devéria (2) and Drolling. Like Delacroix's picture, they are all illustrated by Normand fils line engravings in the Landon-Tardieu *Salon de 1831* (pls. 5, 21, 23, 26-8 respectively). A richly coloured oil sketch for Heim's *Richelieu reçoit les premiers Académiciens* in the series is preserved in the Musée Fabre at Montpellier.

The commentary on Delacroix's picture in Vatout's *Histoire lithographiée du Palais-Royal* places the scene in 1635, and, citing an unidentified historical source, explains: 'à l'exemple du cardinal de Lorraine, [Richelieu] avait des gardes dont l'ordre était "de ne l'accompagner pas seulement jusque dans le Louvre, mais même de ne pas le quitter à l'autel, et de mêler ainsi l'odeur de la poudre à canon et de la mèche parmi l'odeur de l'encens et des autres parfums secrets".' Richelieu built himself the Palais-Cardinal, later much enlarged and known as the Palais-Royal, in 1629.

The head of Richelieu seems to have been based on Philippe de Champaigne's portrait of the Cardinal in the Louvre, from which Delacroix asked his friend Louis Schwiter, in an undated letter, to make a copy of the head, presumably with a view to using it as a model in this painting (*Correspondance* I. 220). It is perhaps Schwiter's copy that is listed in Inv. Delacroix, no. 61, as 'I tableau représentant la tête de Richelieu, d'après Philippe de Champaigne, auteur inconnu.'

The critics in general regarded the picture at the Salon of 1831 as both monotonous and carelessly finished, but agreeable in colour. F.P. (op. cit.) complained:

On n'y trouve rien d'original, rien de hasardé: l'expression même, cette partie de l'art dans laquelle M. Delacroix s'est souvent montré supérieur, est ici d'une froide nullité. L'ordonnance est sage et d'un effet calme [. . .]. Un épisode heureusement imaginé, une circonstance accidentelle aurait [. . .] pu rompre cette monotonie. Quant à l'exécution pratique, ce n'est pas en y apportant des soins trop minutieux que M. Delacroix a refroidi sa verve: les têtes sont à peine modelées. Toutefois le ton général est harmonieux.

Louis Peisse (op. cit.) added a criticism which could be levelled with equal justice at the variant (J132): 'Toutes les têtes des personnages, prêtres et hallebardiers, sont fondues dans le même moule.' Tardieu (op. cit.) repeated this criticism but conceded 'le petit page est jeté avec grace; le diacre agenouillé est bien ajusté.' However, 'l'air ne circule

pas entre ces personnages; ceux du fond sont aussi *faits* que ceux des premiers plans.'

Lot 321 in Delacroix's posthumous sale comprised eight sheets of 'Aquarelles, dessins et croquis' connected with this subject (R1543). One, probably the water-colour now at Chantilly (R254. See J132), went to Jacques Leman for 105 fr. and the others to the same buyer for a total of 26 fr. (Burty Ann ED). All eight of them passed in the Leman sale of 14 March 1874, in the catalogue of which they are individually described (lots 41-8). One, a pencil study for the priest kneeling at the altar (lot 44), was lent to the exhibition Louvre 1963 from the Warburg Collection, New York (repr. *Mémorial*, no. 132). Lot 43 was described as a pencil study, after the same model, of Cardinal Richelieu; lots 45 and 46 were single pencil studies for each of the two guards on the left; lot 47, 'Etude de figures pour les trois soldats de droite. Au milieu, étude de main avec une crosse d'arquebuse. Mine du plomb', 19 × 30 cm; lot 48 was a pencil study for the costume of one of the soldiers, the two boots being different, 21 × 12.5 cm; finally, lot 42 was a composition study: 'Les fonds sont seulement indiqués au crayon; les groupes de soldats de droite et de gauche sont étudiés en détail. L'officier de droite, qui dans l'aquarelle tient son épée, porte ici une hallebarde. Au crayon et au pinceau', 40 × 30 cm. The principal variation between this study (of which a faded photograph is preserved in the *Bib AA* copy of the Leman sale catalogue) and the final composition is that the page stands closer to the centre of the picture, as a more isolated figure and with the halberdiers at his back. A pencil drawing lent from a private collection in Amsterdam to the exhibition Zurich 1939, no. 144, may have been one of these Leman studies. A sheet of Louis XIII costume studies in pencil, mostly of heads adorned with plumed hats, which Huyghe connects with the destroyed painting, must have been part of another lot in Delacroix's posthumous sale, of which it bears the stamp (Louvre. Repr. Huyghe, fig. 164). Another sheet of pencil studies of full-length figures in costume of the same period, also from the posthumous sale, appear likewise to be connected with this subject, the largest and most complete figure seeming to have served particularly for the halberdier on the left of the variant J132 (Louvre, RF9895). Three of the drawings on the sheet, though not that one, are taken from Wilhelm Baur's etching, *Francesi*, in his series *Costumes of Different Nations* published in 1636, and Baur is no doubt the inspiration for the whole sheet.

---

[1] Moreau, followed by Robaut, listed the dimensions as 4.20 × 3.00 m, but those given here are converted from the measurements recorded in C. P. Landon in 1831 (op. cit. *infra*) as '7 pieds' by '4 pieds 9 pouces', which are also the dimensions listed in Landon for the six other paintings commissioned for the same gallery and shown in the same Salon. The dimensions, including frame, given in the register for the Salon of 1831 are 2.40 × 1.80 m (cf. Johnson, op. cit. *infra*, 1966). See also n. 3 for a further indication, in Delacroix's correspondence, that the canvas was

much smaller than Moreau supposed, closer to the size of the *Battle of Poitiers*.

² According to Moreau (p. 209), followed by Robaut.

³ In a letter dated 1 November 1830, Delacroix, seeking payment for the *Battle of Poitiers* (J141) and clearly referring to the precedent of the *Richelieu*, as pointed out by Joubin, recalls: 'je [. . .] demandai le prix de 4,000 francs. C'était celui que je venais d'obtenir de Mgr le duc d'Orléans pour un tableau à peu près de la même importance' (*Correspondance* I. 260).

132 CARDINAL RICHELIEU   Pl. 115
SAYING MASS, variant

15¾ × 12¾ in. (40 × 32.4 cm)

Signed lower right: *Eug. Delacroix*

Inscribed on back of canvas: *T* (?) *Babut B/g*
                                La Rochelle.

R Ann 254 (1828. No repr. Water-colour study R 254 altered to 254bis)

Probably 1828

J. P. Durand-Matthiesen, Geneva

Provenance: Bought from the artist by Mme Louise Rang-Babut of La Rochelle, a former pupil, for 200 fr., about 1846 (*Journal* I. 250); by descent to Mme Brumauld des Houlières, La Rochelle, her granddaughter, by 1887 (R Ann) to at least 1930; with Matthiesen, London, by 1958; with Durand-Matthiesen, Geneva, by 1963.

Exhibitions: *Bd Italiens*, Paris 1864, Supp. to 2nd ed., no. 292 ('Le cardinal de Richelieu disant la Messe au Val-de-Grâce. Esquisse', lent by Mme Louise Babut); Louvre 1963, no. 129, *M* no. 131, repr.; Berne 1963-4, no. 23; Bremen 1964, no. 18; Edinburgh-London 1964, no. 21.

Literature: ? Silvestre *Delacroix* (1855), p. 81 ('Deux esquisses avancées du *Richelieu* exposé en 1831 et détruit en 1848 au Palais-Royal.'); A. Joubin, 'Deux amies de Delacroix, Madame Elisabeth Boulanger-Cavé et Madame Rang-Babut', *Revue de l'Art ancien et moderne*, LVII (1930), p. 82, repr. p. 93; *Journal* I. 250 n. 1; Huyghe, p. 207, repr. fig. 163.

Having been sold about 1846, this picture raises the problem of whether it is contemporary with the large painting destroyed in the Palais-Royal and the oil sketch for it (J131 and J130) or was painted independently shortly before being sold. Sérullaz (*Mémorial*, no. 131) favours the later date on the grounds of the style, which he does not analyse, and of the signature, which could well have been added shortly before the picture was delivered to Mme Babut. Huyghe lists it as a preparatory sketch of 1828, without discussion. I have argued (Cat. Exh. Edinburgh-London 1964, no. 21) that it was painted, with the possible exception of minor retouching, in 1828, probably as an alternative sketch for the large canvas. It has greater dramatic tension (closer in spirit to the *Death of Sardanapalus* (J125) completed at the beginning of 1828) in the form of the twisted columns and the halberdier on the left, a less rigidly balanced foreground,

less particularized features in the head of Richelieu, and a more rudimentary setting in the background on the right than either the final painting as it is known from the Jourdy lithograph or the oil sketch that eventually served as a model. It would be hard to account for these characteristics in a variant painted nearly twenty years after the larger canvas, and for the technique of rendering highlights, as in the Cardinal's chasuble and the gold trim of the canopy, with dry crumbs of impasto, often found in smaller paintings of the latter half of the 1820s. Also, a composition study in water-colour, which apparently served for this painting, belongs stylistically in the late 1820s rather than the 1840s (R254. Musée Condé, Chantilly. Repr. Moreau-Nélaton I, fig. 73; Escholier I, p. 232).

It is possible, then, that this represents Delacroix's first idea for the painting for the Palais-Royal, an idea modified, by official demand or perhaps on the painter's own initiative following criticism of the *Sardanapalus*, into something more static and 'official'. An unresolved difficulty arises, however, because of uncertainty about the lost 'esquisse peinte' mentioned by Robaut as belonging to Charles Nuitter (J(L)103) and its relationship, in time, design and style, to this variant: a pencil tracing in Robaut Tracings I reproduces a picture identical in design to this variant, but it is inscribed with the dimensions '35 × 24½', without further particulars. Is that the Nuitter sketch? And if so, is it a reduced copy of this variant or was the variant copied from it?

The coupled, twisted columns of the altar, which contrast with the single straight column of the large canvas, seem to be loosely based on Roman Baroque models and to have nothing to do with the actual appearance of the chapel in the Palais-Cardinal. Comparable twisted columns seem to have first appeared in Paris in the 1660s, after the death of Richelieu, on the altar of the Val-de-Grâce; which may account for why the setting is identified as that church in the catalogue of the exhibition *Bd Italiens*, Paris 1864.

See also J131.

133 THE MURDER OF THE   Pl. 116
BISHOP OF LIÈGE, sketch

23⅝ × 28⁹⁄₁₆ in. (60 × 72.5 cm) E.D.

Moreau pp. 171 n. 3, 246 n. 1 ?¹ R196

1827

Musée des Beaux-Arts, Lyon

Provenance: Delacroix's posthumous sale, Feb. 1864, lot 55 ('L'Évêque de Liége. [. . .] Variante du tableau appartenant à M. Frédéric Villot', 59 × 72 cm), to Petit, 2,125 fr.; ? the 'esquisse de l'*Evêque de Liège*' sold by him to P. Durand-Ruel, Feb. 1872, 18,000 fr., who returned it 16 June 1877 (Toupet, op. cit. *infra*, 1963, p. 90 n. 28); M. Roederer, Le

Havre; M. Binant, by 1885; his sale 20 Apr. 1904, lot 27 (repr.), to the Musée de Lyon (Inv. B—682), 20,000 fr.

Exhibitions: *EBA*, Paris 1885, no. 11; *Centennale*, Paris 1889, no. 265; Liège 1955, no. 522; London 1959, no. 115; Louvre 1963, no. 135, *M* no. 137, repr.

Literature: Silvestre *Documents nouveaux* (1864), pp. 6, 13; A. Cantaloube, *Eugène Delacroix* (E. Dentu, Paris, 1864), p. 56; [F. Villot], *Catalogue de la vente du cabinet de M. F.V.* [Villot] (Paris, 11 Feb. 1865), under entry for lot 1; P. Dissard, *Le Musée de Lyon. Les Peintures* (H. Laurens, Paris, 1912), p. 19, repr. pl. 106; Moreau-Nélaton I. 105, 106; Cat. Exh. Louvre 1930, under no. 41; Hourticq 1930, pl. 28; ? P. Durand-Ruel, 'Mémoires', in L. Venturi, *Les Archives de l'impressionnisme* (Durand-Ruel, Paris, New York, 1939), II, p. 188; M. Vincent, *Catalogue du Musée de Lyon*, VII, *La Peinture des XIXe et XXe siècles* (IAC Les Editions de Lyon, Lyon, 1956), pp. 43-6, repr. pl. VII[2]; M. Toupet, 'L'Assassinat de l'Evêque de Liège par Eugène Delacroix', *Revue du Louvre*, 13 (1963), pp. 90 f., repr. fig. 9; M. Gauthier, *Delacroix* (Oldbourne Press, London, 1964), repr. in colour, pl. XI (a less selective bibliography of secondary twentieth-century sources than is given here will be found in the entries for this picture in M. Vincent's catalogue of the Musée de Lyon, 1956, and the catalogue of the exhibition London 1959).

Though this work has sometimes been called a variant (e.g. posthumous sale) or a reduction (e.g. Moreau p. 171 n. 3) of the picture painted in 1829 (J135), there appears to be no reason to doubt that Villot was right in stating (loc. cit., 1865) that it was a preliminary sketch painted in 1827 for that version, to be modified, notably in the disposition of the architecture, in the finished painting: stylistically it fits well in the third quarter of the 1820s; it is closely related to a composition drawing which clearly precedes the painting of 1829 (Nathan Collection, Zurich); and the architecture is arranged in the opposite direction from the setting of the 1829 version, where it is made to recede from right to left, parallel to the table.

    The condition is listed as good in the 1956 catalogue of the Musée de Lyon, but Silvestre wrote of it already in 1864 (op. cit.) as 'une esquisse qui malheureusement va tomber en écailles', and there are evident signs of repainting in parts, most painfully perhaps in the mask-like head of William de la Marck.

    For another version of this sketch, probably a student's copy, see J(R)41.

---

[1] 'Réduction (H.58^c, L.72^c), aujourd'hui à M. Petit.' Whether or not this is the picture described p. 171 n. 3 as 'Réduction (H.59^c, L.72^c) [...] Vente Delacroix après décès, n° 55' is unclear; but they may well be one and the same since Petit bought lot 55 at the posthumous sale. Durand-Ruel (loc. cit. *infra*, 1939) records that Francis Petit sold him 'la réduction de "l'Evêque de Liège".'

---

134 THE MURDER OF THE BISHOP OF LIÈGE, laid-in fragment   Pl. 118

$12\frac{3}{16} \times 17\frac{15}{16}$ in. (31×45.6 cm)* E.D.
R Ann 291bis (1829) and probably R1471 (1821. No repr.)[1]
1827/9
Musée du Louvre

Provenance: Delacroix's posthumous sale, Feb. 1864, probably lot 147 ('[Esquisse] Sujet puisé dans un roman de Walter Scott', without dimensions), to Isambert, 350 fr. (Burty Ann ED); Durand-Ruel; Legrand; Alfred Robaut (R Ann lists these three owners); Carle Dreyfus, by 1927; by his bequest to the Louvre (RF1953-5), 1953.

Exhibitions: Paris 1927, no. 278; Louvre 1930, no. 42; *Collection Carle Dreyfus*, Cabinet des Dessins, Louvre 1953, no. 28; Louvre 1963, no. 138, *M* no. 138, repr.; Kyoto-Tokyo 1969, H-8, repr.; Atelier Delacroix, Paris 1971 (no cat.).

Literature: Sterling-Adhémar, no. 668, pl. 233; M. Toupet, 'L'Assassinat de l'Evêque de Liège par Eugène Delacroix', *Revue du Louvre*, 13 (1963), p. 91 and n. 31, repr. p. 94, fig. 14.

Although this fragment has always been considered a preparatory sketch for either the Louvre or Lyon version of the *Murder of the Bishop of Liège* (J135 and J133), it was not strictly speaking a preliminary sketch at all, but rather the partial lay-in on a canvas that appears to have originally been as large as the finished Louvre version, and, being uncovered except for this section at the time of the artist's death, was cut down to its present size before his posthumous sale in 1864. Robaut reports on the operation and the reason for it in his hand-written entry under R Ann 291bis:

Première esquisse peinte à dimension égale de la grande composition ci-après [R292; J135]. Toile H o^m 30, L o^m 45.

    C'est seulement le quart de droite de cette composition (voir N° 292 [J135]) Vente posthume ED. L'autre moitié ou quart [meaning 'trois quarts' ?] de la toile étant tout-à-fait nue, la commission des exécuteurs testamentaires de Delacroix décide qu'on reporterait la partie peinte sur un châssis. (Affirmation de C. Dutilleux qui n'était point de l'avis de ses collègues et qui eût voulu voir vendre tout l'atelier dans l'état où le Maître l'avait laissé. C^t Dutilleux voulait ainsi qu'on ne pût jamais soupçonner que la moindre retouche était passée sur cette peinture de E. D^x)

    It seems likely, therefore, that this fragment represents a false start on what was intended to be the final canvas, and was painted at some point between the Lyon sketch (J133) and the completed painting in the Louvre. The very summarily indicated figure on the extreme left may be intended to represent the Bishop, in which case there would have been a more direct confrontation between him and Guillaume de la Marck than in the large canvas as completed, but he would have had his back turned to the viewer of the picture, instead of being presented in the far more dramatic and eye-catching position finally chosen.

¹ It is under the latter number that Robaut catalogues lot 147 from Delacroix's posthumous sale, apparently without having seen it, since he neither illustrates it nor lists the dimensions.

135 THE MURDER OF THE   Pl. 117
BISHOP OF LIÈGE

$35\frac{13}{16} \times 45\frac{11}{16}$ in. (0.91 × 1.16 m)
Moreau pp. 171 f., 246. R292
1829
Musée du Louvre

Provenance: Duc d'Orléans, by 1836;¹ sale Duchesse d'Orléans, 18 Jan. 1853, lot 17, to Frédéric Villot, 4,800 fr.; his sale (M. F.V.) 11 Feb. 1865, lot 1, bought in by Villot at 35,000 fr. and sold by him to Durand-Ruel for 33,000 fr., 19 Aug. 1866 (M. Toupet, op. cit. *infra*, 1963, p. 88); he sold it to Khalil Bey, 39,000 fr.; his sale 16 Jan. 1868, lot 17, to Durand-Ruel, 46,000 fr.; Francis Petit bought it from Durand-Ruel for Mme de Cassin, April 1868, 50,000 fr. (ibid.); sale Marquise Landolfo-Carcano (formerly Mme de Cassin), 30 May 1912, lot 23 (repr.), to M. L. Tauber, 205,100 fr.; bought from his heirs by Gérard in 1944 (Dieterle R); M. L. Salavin; acquired from him by the Louvre (RF1961-13), Feb. 1961.

Exhibitions: Musée Colbert, Paris 1829B, no. 108; id., Paris 1830A, no. 58;² R.A., London (Somerset House) 1830, no. 328;³ Salon 1831, 3rd Supp. no. 2949; *Universelle*, Paris 1855, no. 2923; Universal Exhibition, London 1862, no. 156; Alsace-Lorraine, Paris 1874, Supp. no. 782; Petit, Paris 1884, no. 16; Paris 1927, no. 277; Louvre 1930, no. 50, repr. *Album*, p. 27; Paris 1937, no. 316; Durand-Ruel, Paris 1938, no. 23; Liège 1955, no. 521, repr.; Venice 1956, no. 13; Charpentier, Paris 1957, no. 24, repr.; Louvre 1963, no. 134, *M* no. 136, 2 repr.; Petit Palais, Paris 1968-9, no. 269; Atelier Delacroix, Paris 1972 (no cat.).

Literature: Correspondance I. 236 n. 1, II. 411, III. 165, IV. 299 and n., 314 and n.; anon., 'Album', *Revue de Paris*, IX (12 Dec. 1829), p. 131; F., *Journal des Artistes et des Amateurs*, 20 Dec. 1829, p. 396; Y., *Le National*, 20 Jan. 1830; anon., 'Musée Colbert', *La Silhouette*, 2 Feb. 1830, p. 49; anon., review of R.A. Exhibition, *The Gentleman's Magazine*, May 1830, p. 447; anon., id., unidentified cutting, May 1830; Leaves de Conches [pseudonym of Feuillet de Conches], 'Cinquième lettre à M. William Allan . . . à Edimbourg' [dated Paris, 10 June 1831], *L'Artiste*, I (1831), p. 249 n. 1; Melchior F.S., review of Salon, *Le Voleur*, 30 June and 31 July 1831; anon., review of Salon, *La Gazette de France*, 14 July 1831; F.P., 'Salon de 1831 (13e article)', *Le Moniteur universel*, 15 July 1831; anon., 'Salon de 1831', *La Quotidienne*, 28 July 1831; anon., *L'Artiste*, II

(1831), p. 180; G. Planche, *Salon de 1831* (Pinard, Paris, 1831), pp. 114 f. (reprinted in *Etudes sur l'Ecole française* (M. Lévy, Paris, 1855), I, pp. 66 f.); A. Tardieu, *Annales du Musée de l'Ecole moderne des Beaux-Arts. Salon de 1831* (Pillet aîné, Paris, 1831), pp. 46 f.; C. Baudelaire, 'Exposition universelle de 1855', *Le Pays*, 3 June 1855 (reprinted in *Curiosités esthétiques*, 1868 (*Œuvres* Pléiade ed., Paris 1932, p. 160)); P. Pétroz, *La Presse*, 5 June 1855; J. Lecomte, 'Exposition universelle de 1855', *L'Indépendance belge*, 20 June 1855; T. Gautier, 'Exposition universelle de 1855', *Le Moniteur universel*, 19 July 1855; M. Du Camp, *Les Beaux-Arts à l'Exposition universelle de 1855* (Libr. nouvelle, Paris, 1855), pp. 111 f.; E. Gebauer, *Les Beaux-Arts à l'Exposition universelle de 1855* (Libr. Napoléonienne, Paris, 1855), pp. 35 f.; E. and J. de Goncourt, *La Peinture à l'Exposition de 1855* (E. Dentu, Paris, 1855), p. 42; E. Loudun [A. Balleyguier], *Exposition universelle de 1855* (chez Ledoyen, Paris, 1855), p. 115; P. Mantz, *Revue française*, II (1855), p. 174; T. Silvestre, *Les Artistes français*, 1855 (1926 ed., I, p. 26); C. Vignon, *Exposition universelle de 1855* (Fontaine, Paris, 1855), pp. 202 f.; A. de la Forge, *La Peinture contemporaine en France* (Amyot, Paris, 1856), pp. 60 ff.; T. Thoré, 'Exposition internationale de Londres en 1862', *Le Temps*, 1862, review with same title published at same time in *L'Indépendance belge* (both reprinted in *Salons de W. Bürger* [Thoré's pseudonym] *1861 à 1868* (Libr. ve J. Renouard, Paris, 1870), I, pp. 192, 211, 289, 322); P. de Saint-Victor, 'Eugène Delacroix', *La Presse*, 4 Sept. 1863; F. de Lasteyrie, *La Peinture à l'Exposition universelle [de Londres]* (Castel, Paris, 1863), p. 128; A. Cantaloube, *Eugène Delacroix* (E. Dentu, Paris, 1864), pp. 53 f.; [F. Villot], *Catalogue de la vente du cabinet de M. F.V.* [*Villot*] (Paris, 11 Feb. 1865), entry for lot 1; Piron, p. 106; T. Gautier, *Le Moniteur universel*, 14 Dec. 1867; C. Hugo, *Victor Hugo en Zélande* (M. Lévy, Paris, 1868) (the relevant passage, quoting Victor Hugo's recollection of a conversation with Delacroix, is reprinted in Tourneux, p. 34); P. de Saint-Victor, 'Eugène Delacroix', *Le Moniteur universel*, 27 June 1881; E. Chesneau, Introduction to Robaut, pp. xx ff.; P. Burty, 'Eugène Delacroix à l'Ecole des Beaux-Arts', *L'Illustration*, 21 March 1885, p. 199; Tourneux, pp. 103-4, *passim*; Moreau-Nélaton I. 94, 105, 106, 118, 120, 149, 160, 163, repr. fig. 80, II. 88, 114, 156, 204, 222; Meier-Graefe 1922, p. 44; O. Benesch, 'Rembrandts Vermächtnis', *Belvedere*, 6 (1924), p. 173, repr. pl. 29; Escholier i. 196 and n., 240 ff., 263, 276, repr. p. 245; R. Huyghe, 'L'Exposition Delacroix au Musée du Louvre', *Bulletin des Musées de France*, 11 (1930), repr. p. 123; Hourticq 1930, pl. 27; L. Venturi, *Les Archives de l'impressionnisme* (Durand-Ruel, Paris and New York, 1939), II, p. 165, repr. p. 64; Christoffel 1951, p. 63, repr. p. 64; L. Johnson, 'Delacroix at the Biennale', *Burl Mag*, XCVIII (1956), pp. 327, 328 and n.; O. Benesch, 'Rembrandt's Artistic Heritage—II—From

Goya to Cézanne', *GBA*, LVI (1960), p. 109; L. Johnson, Cat. Exh. Toronto–Ottawa 1962–3, p. 10 n. 2; Johnson 1963, p. 27, repr. pl. 18; M. Toupet, 'L'Assassinat de l'Evêque de Liège par Eugène Delacroix', *Revue du Louvre*, 13 (1963), pp. 83–94, repr. fig. 2, details p. 83 (Bishop) and p. 86 (de la Marck and surrounding area); Huyghe, pp. 187–91, 369, 455, 522 nn. 25 and 26, repr. in colour pl. XV, p. 178; Maltese, pp. 17, 37, 77, 151 f., repr. pl. 24; L. Johnson, 'Eugène Delacroix et les Salons. Documents inédits au Louvre', *Revue du Louvre*, 16 (1966), p. 220; T. Prideaux *et al.*, *The World of Delacroix* (Time Inc., New York, 1966), repr. in colour, pp. 98–9; Trapp, pp. 54 n. 25, 55, 93, 107, 173 and n., 335 n. 3, repr. fig. 96; C. Gordon, 'The Illustration of Sir Walter Scott: Nineteenth-Century Enthusiasm and Adaptation', *JWCI*, XXXIV (1971), p. 307.

The scene is based on chapter XXII of Sir Walter Scott's first historical novel with a foreign setting, *Quentin Durward*, which was immensely popular in France from the time it was published in 1823 (see J137). William de la Marck, the Wild Boar of Ardennes, having incited the citizens of Liège to revolt, has with their aid and with his own soldiery stormed the Bishop's palace, the Castle of Schonwaldt, and installed himself on the episcopal throne in the castle-hall to preside over a riotous banquet on the evening of the assault. Announcing 'with one stroke of a cleaver, will I consecrate myself Bishop of Liège', he has the Prelate, Louis de Bourbon, brought before him and slaughtered by Nikkel, a butcher: 'the tyrant slowly raised himself in his chair [. . .], he looked to Nikkel Blok, and raised his finger, without speaking a word. The ruffian struck, as if he had been doing his office in the common shambles, and the murdered Bishop sunk, without a groan, at the foot of his own episcopal throne.' (Everyman ed., 1960, p. 282.) An author's note at this point admits the historical inaccuracy of having the Bishop's murder occur in 1468, when he was only taken prisoner by the insurgents of Liège, instead of in 1482, when he was actually killed by Guillaume de la Marck—in a combat on horseback.

According to Frédéric Villot (loc. cit., 1865), Delacroix did the oil sketch for this painting (J133) in 1827, by which stage he had already hit on the idea of having the Bishop and his murderer at opposite sides of the table, instead of following the text, which puts William de la Marck on the throne at the head of the table and has the Prelate 'brought before the footstool of the savage leader'. Two composition drawings, which probably reflect earlier ideas than the oil sketch, follow the novel closely in this respect (part of lot 324 in Delacroix's posthumous sale and part of R1548; Champfleury sale 25 Jan. 1891; repr. Robaut Tracings 1; see also Cat. Exh. Louvre 1930, no. 274H). It was not until Delacroix moved into Carle Vernet's studio on the quai

Voltaire (at the end of January 1829[4]), Villot continues, that he began the final picture:

Il y commença presque immédiatement l'évêque de Liége, fit des modifications très importantes à l'esquisse et éprouva de grandes difficultés à réaliser l'effet de cette scène tel qu'il l'avait conçu. Aussi abandonna-t-il à plusieurs reprises une œuvre qui ne le satisfaisait pas. Enfin il s'y remit définitivement; l'homme debout, vu de dos, à gauche, le préoccupait beaucoup et il le recommença sept ou huit fois. Quant à la nappe blanche, c'était, suivant lui, le point capital du tableau. Un soir, en dessinant chez son ami, il lui dit: 'Demain j'attaque cette maudite nappe qui sera pour moi Austerlitz ou Waterloo. Venez à mon atelier à la fin de la journée.' M. V. [Villot] fut exact au rendez-vous. Delacroix [. . .] lui dit [. . .]: 'Eh bien, mon cher, c'est Austerlitz; vous allez cela.' En effet, la nappe flamboyait et illuminait la sanglante orgie. 'Je suis sauvé ajouta Delacroix; le reste ne m'inquiète plus; je vais me mettre à l'architecture, je changerai ma disposition première et m'inspirerai, pour la charpente de la voûte, des croquis que j'ai faits au Palais-de-Justice de Rouen.' [. . .]
Dans la pensée de Delacroix l'*Evêque de Liége* devait surtout être vu à la lumière, éclairé par un réflecteur.

It does not seem to have been previously noted that the main reason why Delacroix was so concerned over the figure standing on the left with its back turned, is surely that it must represent the hero, Quentin Durward, an archer in Louis XI's Scottish Guard, identified by his attribute, a quiver full of arrows, held by the boy next to him, who may in turn represent De la Marck's natural son, whom Quentin stayed close to by design and seized as a hostage in order to prevent further bloodshed following the murder of the Bishop.

Analogies between the effects of artificial light in this painting and those of Rembrandt were justly drawn as early as 1855 (T. Gautier and M. Du Camp, op. cit.); in 1924 Otto Benesch (op. cit.) compared the work specifically to a picture such as Rembrandt's *Conspiracy of the Batavians under Claudius Civilis* (National Museum, Stockholm; repr. M. Toupet, op. cit., 1963, fig. 4), and has been followed by others. But the influence of English art and architecture has perhaps been insufficiently noticed. The ceiling was not inspired by a vault in the Palais de Justice at Rouen, as suggested by Villot, but is a reproduction of the hammer-beam roof of Westminster Hall (cf. L. Johnson, op. cit., 1956, p. 328 n. 4, and later references to the borrowing), detailed pencil sketches of which are contained in an unpublished sketch-book used by Delacroix during his English visit in 1825. The armour worn by William de la Marck ('His head was unhelmeted, but he wore the rest of his ponderous and bright armour') is based on a suit which Delacroix also drew, very fully and precisely, in London in 1825, when visiting the Meyrick collection (Louvre, RF9837; the original armour is reproduced in Skelton's catalogue of the Meyrick collection, pl. 17, where it is dated 1495; it is now in Eastnor Castle and dated *c.* 1530). In addition to these exact references to ancient artefacts seen during the English journey, there is an apparent influence of Wilkie's oil sketch for *John Knox Preaching* (Petworth House; repr. Trapp fig. 28), which Delacroix had admired in the Scottish artist's studio in London in 1825 and feared would be spoilt in being developed into a finished painting: in both pictures the principal heretic, square-faced, bearded and of ferocious mien, is placed on the far right beneath a canopy, and in both his forceful gesture motivates the reactions of the group on the left, which includes a bishop with mitre and crozier (Johnson 1963, loc. cit.). And if there is a clear influence of Rembrandt in the emotive use of lighting, the massing of small-scale figures perhaps owes more to the example of lesser Dutch masters of the kind who also influenced Wilkie. But Delacroix rises above these lesser masters, both Dutch and British, in the dramatic force of his conception, in his mastery of pantomime and variety of pose and expression without loss of unity or surfeit of realistic detail.

This has generally been considered one of Delacroix's masterpieces, and was recognized to be of exceptional importance in his development as soon as it was completed, the anonymous critic of the *Revue de Paris* writing in 1829: 'votre tableau [. . .] vous sépare violemment du parti qui vous appelait son chef. Tout ici est mouvement, chaleur, naturel et vérité. Point de négligences de dessin, point d'effets bizarrement produits par le choc inattendu des couleurs. [. . .] Ceci est une protestation contre la secte pittoresque qui vous compromettait.' Given Delacroix's lifelong preoccupation with the problem of retaining the spontaneity of a sketch in a finished painting (a problem central to the development of French nineteenth-century painting as a whole), and his recent concern that Wilkie would spoil his *John Knox Preaching* in finishing it, it is interesting that as early as 1830 the critic of *Le National* noted the relatively sketchy handling of the picture and commented: 'Il y a vingt ans, le Massacre de l'évêque de Liége aurait été une jolie esquisse; maintenant c'est un tableau.' Later, Gautier (op. cit., 1855), calling it 'un des plus étonnants chefs-d'œuvre de l'artiste', neatly summarized this characteristic: 'moins fait qu'un tableau, plus fini qu'une esquisse, [il] a été quitté par le peintre à ce moment suprême où un coup de pinceau de plus gâterait tout.'

The *Bishop of Liège* was well received at the R.A. exhibition in London in 1830, the critic of *The Gentleman's Magazine* finding the 'savage and exulting aspects of the barbarous assassins' to be 'admirably contrasted with the trembling but placid features of their miserable victim'; the colouring 'bold and massy'. Another English critic declared it to be 'very elaborately painted, and with remarkable success. The story is extremely well made out, and although the place allotted to it is below its merit, enough of it may be seen to justify the belief that the artist

will soon force himself into a better situation.' (I owe both these quotations to Catherine Gordon, the latter is from an unidentified cutting dated May ?4, 1830, contained in a book of cuttings preserved at the Courtauld Institute.)

Widely discussed at the Salon of 1831, the picture did not induce favourable reactions only, as Melchior F.S. reported (op. cit., 30 June 1831): 'Vous dire qu'autour de ce tableau on discutait, on criait; que pour les uns tout était sublimité, génie; pour les autres tout barbarie et stupidité; c'est vous apprendre qu'il s'agit de l'une de ces œuvres qui font la gloire et le désespoir d'un homme.' Among the more sympathetic comments that have attracted little or no notice, are those by F.P. (op. cit., 1831): 'quoiqu'il y ait dans ce tableau un très-grand nombre de figures, l'unité d'action et d'intérêt y est assez habilement observée pour qu'on embrasse tout l'ensemble au premier coup-d'œil. Cette nouvelle production ne peut qu'ajouter à la réputation de l'auteur, qui dans aucun autre de ses ouvrages, n'a montré autant de talent pour l'ordonnance d'une grande machine'. Another anonymous critic records in 1831 (*L'Artiste*, II, p. 180) that the picture's admirers were not limited to members of the avant-garde: 'je me souviens d'avoir entendu les vétérans de l'école de l'empire, ceux à qui David a transmis l'héritage de ses traditions et de sa gloire, rendre à cette œuvre une éclatante justice.'

It is appropriate that the Duke of Orleans should have been the first owner of this painting, since his fifteenth-century namesake plays a prominent role in the novel which inspired it, as Quentin Durward's rival for the hand of the Countess of Croye.

Of the two drawings connected with this composition in *Mémorial*, one tentatively, the first (no. 139) appears to be unrelated to it, and the second (no. 140) is a most doubtful attribution.

[1] Delacroix to Thoré, 18 Jan. 1836: '[. . .] 1829: *Le sanglier des Ardennes ayant pris d'assaut le château de l'évêque de Liége le fait amener devant lui au milieu d'une orgie. (Ce tableau fait partie de la galerie de Mgr le duc d'Orléans, prince royal.)*' (*Correspondance* I. 407.) Beginning with Moreau (p. 172), the picture is usually stated to have been painted *for* the Duc d'Orléans, who in 1829 was of course the future King Louis-Philippe, but this cannot be so, because it was exhibited at the Musée Colbert in 1830 and all the paintings by Delacroix are listed as for sale in the catalogue. Also, the Duke is not mentioned as being the owner in the catalogues of the R.A. exhibition in 1830 and the Salon of 1831. He may have bought it at the time of the Salon. The origin of the belief that it had been painted for the Duke lies no doubt in the entry for this picture in the catalogue of the Villot sale in 1865, where it is stated: 'Le tableau achevé, M. V. [Villot] voulut l'avoir. "Je ne puis ni vous le donner ni vous le céder, lui répondit Delacroix, il appartient au duc d'Orléans qui me le paye 1,500 francs."' But it appears that if Delacroix's reply is correctly reported Villot must have asked for the picture some time after its completion, and not immediately upon completion as the phrasing in his catalogue implies.

[2] G. Planche (op. cit. *infra*, 1831) writes of the Salon picture: '*Le Meurtre de l'évêque de Liège* est placé de manière à n'être pas vu. Heureusement nous avons pu le juger à l'aise au Musée Colbert.'

[3] De Conches (op. cit. *infra*, 1831), referring to the Salon picture, writes: '*l'Assassinat de l'évêque de Liége*, que vous avez vu á Londres, est placé à

faux jour près d'une fenêtre, tout au bout de l'immense galerie.' There appears to be no doubt therefore that the version exhibited at the R.A. was the one shown later at the Salon.

⁴ Delacroix to Soulier, 28 January 1829: 'Je suis dans les horreurs du déménagement. [. . .] Tu voudras bien m'écrire dorénavant, quai Voltaire n° 15. [. . .] En attendant que je sois complètement établi, je mène une vie pitoyable'. (*Correspondance* I. 235 f.)

136 THE MURDER OF THE　　　Pl. 118
BISHOP OF LIÈGE, variant

Approx. 11 × 15⅜ in. (28 × 39 cm)[1]
Possibly signed[2]
Moreau pp. 113, 171 n. 3, 246 n. 1. R195 (1827)
Begun *c.* 1827 ?, completed 1844 ?
Whereabouts unknown

Provenance: Exchanged by the artist for a landscape by Diaz (Villot, loc. cit. *infra*, 1865), *c.* 1844; Diaz, to at least 1860; sold for 8,000 fr. (Piron), by 1865; with Durand-Ruel, by 1872; he probably sold it to John Saulnier of Bordeaux in 1872; sale John Saulnier, 5 June 1886, lot 36, to E. Lecomte, 7,500 fr.; his sale 11 June 1906, lot 43, to Arnold, Tripp & Cie, 3,300 fr.; they sold it to Durand-Ruel the next day, 4,000 fr. (Arch A. Tripp); sold by Durand-Ruel to C. A Jung, Germany, 8 Nov. 1910, 15,000 fr. (Toupet, op. cit. *infra*, 1963, p. 93).

Exhibitions: Gal. Beaux-Arts, Paris 1844;[3] Bd Italiens, Paris 1860, no. 166 ('L'Assassinat de l'évêque de Liége', 27 × 38 cm); probably Society of French Artists 4, London 1872, no. 10 ('Assassination of the Bishop of Liège (l^{ère} pensée)');[4] ? *Société des Amis des Arts*, Marseille 1877 ('Le Massacre de l'évêque de Liège', without further description); *EBA*, Paris 1885, no. 199; Paris 1886, no. 76; Cassirer, Berlin 1907, no. 11.

Literature: *Correspondance* v. 174; [A. de la Fizelière], 'Promenade dans les galeries des Beaux-Arts', *Bulletin de l'Ami des Arts*, II (1844), Supp. to 2nd livraison (20 Jan.), p. 42; ibid., 10th livraison (10 Apr.), p. 283 (notice of works lately received for sale at the Galerie des Beaux-Arts); T. Gautier, 'Exposition de tableaux modernes au profit de la Caisse de secours des artistes peintres', *GBA*, v (1860), p. 202; [F. Villot], *Catalogue de la Vente du Cabinet de M. F.V.* [*Villot*] (Paris, 11 Feb. 1865), under entry for lot 1; Piron, p. 106; Moreau-Nélaton II. 194; Escholier I, repr. p. 244 (the 'esquisse' mentioned on p. 240 seems also to refer to this picture); M. Toupet, 'L'Assassinat de l'évêque de Liège par Eugène Delacroix', *Revue du Louvre*, 13 (1963), pp. 91–3, repr. fig. 13.

Prints: Lithograph in reverse by Mouilleron, published in *Les Beaux-Arts* (L. Curmer, Paris), III (1844), 16th livraison, and in *Souvenirs d'artistes* (repr. Toupet, op. cit. *supra*, 1963, fig. 10). Etching by Charles Courtry, for the

Galerie Durand-Ruel, 1 (1873), 2nd livraison, pl. 16, d. 1872 (repr. ibid., fig. 11).

Though this has frequently been called a sketch since Piron and Moreau so described it, there can be no doubt that it is, rather, a small variant of the painting of 1829 in the Louvre (J135), which, if Frédéric Villot (loc. cit., 1865) is to be believed, was painted long after the principal picture from a small drawing, 'où [Delacroix] supprima les trois quarts des figures et le fond', and exchanged for a landscape by Diaz (perhaps lot 240 in Delacroix's posthumous sale: 'Intérieur de forêt' by Diaz). Delacroix refers to it in a list of pictures compiled in the 1840s, as '*L'évêque de Liège*, en petit, à Diaz' (*Journal* III. 373-Supp.), a description which conforms better to a small variant than to a sketch. The problem lies less in deciding whether it is a sketch or a variant than in dating it on the basis of inadequate photographs and inconclusive documentary evidence. Villot's account, combined with the fact that it was shown at the Galerie des Beaux-Arts in 1844 (loc. cit., 1844) as well as being lithographed in that year, suggests that it may not have been painted earlier than 1844. On the other hand, Delacroix did not show only recent works at the Galerie des Beaux-Arts (the *Marino Faliero* of 1826, for example, was shown there in 1845). Were it not for the evidence of Villot, who, though not infallible (he was apparently mistaken about Delacroix's intentions for the setting in J135), cannot be lightly discounted, there could be little hesitation in thinking that it preceded the final Louvre version in both conception and execution; in spite of Villot, it seems possible that it could have been begun *c.* 1827, abandoned when Delacroix decided to base the interior on Westminster Hall, and completed or reworked in 1844. But a final opinion cannot be given unless the original work or new evidence comes to light. An earlier Durand-Ruel photograph than the one reproduced here reveals severe and extensive craquelures over most of the surface, and the painting must have undergone a fairly drastic restoration before the later photograph was taken. This does not, however, appear to be the cause of the stiffness of the two principal figures.

---

[1] There is much variation in the dimensions recorded for this picture, ranging from 22 × 27 cm (Saulnier and Lecomte sales) to 30 × 40 cm (early Durand-Ruel photograph). The former measurements are almost certainly inaccurate, since they are amended to 29 × 40 cm in the entry in Arnold & Tripp's books recording their purchase of the painting at the Lecomte sale. Those given here are taken from the catalogue of the exhibition Cassirer, Berlin 1907.

[2] The picture is said to be signed in the catalogue of the Saulnier sale, but no other source records a signature.

[3] The *Bulletin de l'Ami des Arts*, official organ for this Gallery, reports in the supplement to its issue of 20 January that the 'Massacre de l'évêque de Liége' is on show, but in the issue of 10 April it is listed as one of the pictures that has been added to the exhibition within the past few days. The latter report is probably a mistake, and not an indication that two versions were exhibited in 1844.

[4] Marked as sold in a copy of the catalogue preserved in Arch D-R (communicated by Ronald Pickvance).

137 QUENTIN DURWARD AND LE BALAFRÉ
Pl. 119

$15\frac{15}{16} \times 12\frac{3}{4}$ in. (40.5 × 32.4 cm)*

Signed bottom left: *Eug Delacroix*

R1714 (No repr. 1842, revised in R Ann to 1838–9) and
R Ann 760*bis* (1842)

1828/9

Musée du Louvre (on deposit at the Mobilier national, Paris)

Provenance: Duchesse de Berry; her sale 8 Dec. 1830, lot 11 (injunction against the sale of his works perhaps obtained by the artist to recover debts owed him by the Duchess now in Exile—see J141 and L. Johnson, op. cit. *infra*, p. 569); Delacroix had regained possession of the picture by May 1831; M. Frémyn, by 1842; Edmond Bapst, a relative, by 1902, d. 1932; recovered by the Service français de récupération artistique following World War II and allotted to the Louvre (M.N.R. 144), 1950.

Exhibitions: *Bd Italiens*, Paris 1864, no. 168 ('Scène de Quentin Durward', 40 × 32 cm. Lent by M. Frémyn); Copenhagen 1914, no. 81 (lent by Edmond Bapst, French Minister in Copenhagen 1913–17).

Literature: *Journal* III. 372—Supp.; Silvestre *Delacroix* (1855), p. 80; H. Thirria, *La Duchesse de Berry* (Paris, 1900), p. 29; *Correspondance* I. 283 n. 2, 295 n. 3; D. Cooper, 'Bonington and *Quentin Durward*', *Burl Mag*, LXXXVIII (1946), p. 117 n. 25; L. Johnson, 'A Delacroix recovered: *Quentin Durward and Le Balafré*', ibid. CVIII (1966), pp. 568–70, full-page repr. fig. 1; M. Kemp, 'Scott and Delacroix, with some Assistance from Hugo and Bonington', in *Scott Bicentenary Essays* (ed. A. Bell, Scottish Academic Press, Edinburgh and London, 1973), p. 221 and n.

The subject is taken from chapter v of Walter Scott's novel *Quentin Durward*, which was published in 1823 and issued in French translation the same year. Quentin Durward, who will later join the Scottish Body-Guard of Louis XI, has arrived from Scotland at the Fleur-de-Lys, a tavern close to the Castle of Plessis-les-Tours. His uncle Ludovic Lesly, known as Le Balafré because of a ghastly scar across his face, and already a seasoned member of the Guard, has come from the Castle to greet him and seek news of his family in Scotland. On learning that they were all killed in a feud with the Ogilvies, he summons Andrew, his *coutelier*, and handing him a length of gold chain, instructs him: 'Tell my gossip [Father Boniface] that my brother and sister, and some others of my house, are all dead and gone, and I pray him to say masses for their souls as far as the value of these links will carry him, and to do on trust what else may be necessary to free them from Purgatory.'

Scott's first novel on a foreign theme, *Quentin Durward* enjoyed an immediate and exceptional popularity in Paris;

French editions appeared every year between 1826 and 1830. The Duchesse de Berry, daughter-in-law of King Charles X and the first owner of this picture, was an ardent admirer of Scott's novels and gained a reputation for wishing to emulate his historical romances in real life.

Until 1902, when he took a tracing of it (repr. L. Johnson, op. cit. 1966, fig. 35), Robaut knew of this picture only from a description of the subject in a letter which Delacroix had written on Friday 11 November [1831] to M. Paillet, *commissaire-expert des Musées Royaux*, who had undertaken to place it for him (*Correspondance* I. 295 f. The original letter passed in a sale at Sotheby's on 27 April 1971, lot 303). Knowing neither the year of the letter nor that the picture referred to had belonged to the Duchesse de Berry, Robaut was very wide of the mark in his dating. Between the first and second World Wars the picture was thought to be lost; it was not until 1966 that it was reproduced and Robaut's date amended. In publishing it at that time, I argued that a passage in a letter which Joubin dates to December 1828 or January 1829, where Delacroix writes of having 'quelqu' espoir d'arranger quelque chose avec la duchesse de Berry' (*Correspondance* I. 234), could well apply to this picture, which in that case would most probably have been painted in the early months of 1829 and would thus be contemporary with the *Murder of the Bishop of Liège* (J135), inspired by the same novel and painted in 1829. The almost identical features of Le Balafré and the highest placed figure on the extreme right of the *Bishop of Liège*, and the equally similar handling of their armour suggest that the two pictures were very close in date if not exactly contemporary.

Having recovered the painting in circumstances which remain obscure, following the Duchess's flight to England after the July Revolution of 1830, Delacroix intended to exhibit it at the Salon of 1831 (*Correspondance* I. 283—letter postmarked 28 May 1831), but there is no evidence that he actually did so.

The picture was restored in Copenhagen in 1914 and bears the following inscription on a label affixed to the stretcher: 'Restauré ce jour par moi, E. M. Benoit, artiste peintre restaurateur aux Musées Nationaux de France. Copenhague le 16 Juillet 1914 [signed] E. M. Benoit.' It has suffered considerably since then, the paint surface being abraded in the top left corner and in a smaller area between Le Balafré and his *coutelier*. There is also some loss of paint along the four edges of the picture where the canvas has deteriorated and, in places, broken away from the stretcher.

138 THE GIAOUR CONTEMPLATING THE DEAD HASSAN
Pl. 120

$8\frac{11}{16} \times 11\frac{1}{8}$ in. (22 × 28.2 cm)*

Signed bottom right: *Eug. Delacroix*.

R Ann 201*bis* (1828–30)

1829?
Rudolf Graber, Zurich

Provenance: Tabourier, by 1885; with Brame in 1895 (Dieterle R); P. A. Cheramy; his sale, 5 May 1908, lot 161 (repr.), to Georges Petit, 4,500 fr.; Dr. Hans Graber, Zurich, by 1939; the present owner, by 1963.

Exhibitions: Musée Colbert, Paris 1830A, no. 192 ('Le Giaour contemplant son ennemi mort'); Musée Colbert, Paris 1830B, no. 152 (under same title);[1] *EBA*, Paris 1885, no. 213 ('Mort d'Hassan'); Zurich 1939, no. 314 (as 'Officier turc tué dans la montagne'); Berne 1963–4, no. 22.

Literature: M. Vachon, *Maîtres modernes. Eugène Delacroix à l'École des Beaux-Arts, mars-avril 1885* (L. Baschet, Paris, 1885), repr. (unnumbered photogravure pl.); Moreau-Nélaton I. 163; Escholier I, repr. p. 179 (as 'Officier turc tué dans la montagne'); G. H. Hamilton, 'Delacroix, Byron and the English Illustrators', *GBA*, XXXVI (1949), p. 267, repr. p. 266, fig. 6 (after Escholier); L. Johnson, 'The Delacroix Centenary in France—II', *Burl Mag*, CVI (1964), pp. 260 f., repr. p. 265, fig. 12.

The subject is taken from Byron's poem, *The Giaour*, being the sequel to the combat between the Venetian Giaour and Turkish Hassan painted by Delacroix in 1826 (J114):

> Fall'n Hassan lies—his unclos'd eye
> Yet lowering on his enemy,
> As if the hour that seal'd his fate,
> Surviving left his quenchless hate;
> And o'er him bends that foe with brow
> As dark as his that bled below.—
> (lines 669–74)

The scene is also recalled later by the Giaour, in this couplet:

> "I gazed upon him where he lay
> And watched his spirit ebb away."
> (lines 1085–6)

Because of an apparent immaturity in the drawing and brushwork, I used to think (op. cit., 1964) that this was probably the earliest of Delacroix's paintings inspired by *The Giaour* and likely to be contemporary with these reflections in the *Journal* on 11 May 1824 (I. 99 f.): 'Le poète est bien riche: rappelle-toi, pour t'enflammer éternellement, certains passages de Byron; il me vont bien. [. . .] Je sens ces choses-là comme la peinture les comporte. La *Mort d'Hassan*, dans le *Giaour*. Le Giaour contemplant sa victime [. . .] Commencé le *Combat d'Hassan et du Giaour*.' But it now seems to be improbable that Delacroix would not have shown it publicly before the end of the decade, and particularly at the exhibition for the benefit of the Greeks in 1826, had it been painted as early as 1824.

Also, some of the ornamented details of the costumes and accessories, though imperfectly handled, are no more so than in some of the less polished pictures of the latter half of the 1820s (e.g. J7, J129 and J132); others may be the result of repainting by a later hand.

A signed water-colour of the same subject, with the Giaour standing in profile, sword poised over his victim, may very well be as early as 1824 (colour repr. Escholier I, opp. p. 182). A lithograph of the Giaour on horseback glowering at the dead Hassan is dated to 1827 by Moreau (p. 30), followed by Robaut (No. 203) and Delteil (No. 55).

---

[1] In a list of exhibited works compiled in 1836, Delacroix recorded that *le Giaour après le combat* was shown at the Galerie Colbert in 1829 (cf. Moreau-Nélaton I. 163), but no picture answering to that description is listed in the catalogues of the gallery's exhibitions before February 1830. It may, however, have been hung some months before it appeared in a catalogue. Robaut does not mention its inclusion in any of the shows.

---

139   TAM O'SHANTER PURSUED   Pl. 121
BY WITCHES

$10\frac{1}{16} \times 12\frac{1}{2}$ in. (25.6 × 31.7 cm)* E.D.
Moreau p. 248 n. 1. See R136 and 197 (repr. under R136)
c. 1829?
Mrs. Charlotte Bührle, Zurich

Provenance: Delacroix's posthumous sale Feb. 1864, lot 67 ('Sujet inspirée par une ballade écossaise', 25 × 32 cm), to de Laage, 540 fr.; G. Arosa; his sale 25 Feb. 1878, lot 35 ('Daté 1825'.[1] Repr. in special album of photolithographs of the collection, no. 23—*Bib AA*), to Collot (Dieterle R), 690 fr.; E. P. Turner, London (Bührle Cat., 1958); Collection Rouart (Alexis Rouart's wax seal on back); Henri Rouart, by 1926; with Mme Salvator, Oct. 1945 (Dieterle R); W. Walter, Paris (Bührle Cat., 1958); bought from an English dealer by Emil Bührle of Zurich, 1952, d. 1956; the present owner, his widow.

Exhibitions: ? Gal. Lebrun, Paris 1829, no. 44 ('Sujet tiré d'une ballade du poëte écossais Burns. Tam O'Shanter, en passant tard près d'une église abandonnée, est poursuivie par des sorciers [*sic*] qui y faisaient le sabbat. Sur le point de franchir un petit pont au-delà duquel il ne pouvait plus être suivi, une des sorcières prend la queue de la pauvre jument qui la lui laisse en manière de trophée; trop heureuse d'en être quitte à si bon marché.'); probably Salon 1831, 3rd Supp. no. 2950 ('Tam O'Shanter, ballade de Burns. Ce villageois écossais, en revenant le soir sur sa jument, est poursuivi par des sorcières qui faisaient le sabbat.'); Paris 1927, no. 269; Zurich 1958, no. 111; Louvre 1963, no. 139, *M* no. 399, repr.; Edinburgh-London 1964, no. 52, repr.

Literature: F., 'Galerie Lebrun. Seconde exposition au profit de l'extinction de la mendicité', *Journal des Artistes et des Amateurs*, 12 July 1829, p. 19, and 26 July, p. 62 (if Gal. Lebrun, Paris 1829, no. 44); anon., review of Salon 1831,

Gazette de France, 14 July 1831 (if Salon version); M. Tourneux, 'Lettres inédites de Eugène Delacroix', *L'Artiste*, N.S. IV (1901), Supp., p. 7; Moreau-Nélaton I. 118 (Salon painting); Escholier I, repr. p. 153; *Journal* I. 296 n. 1; *Kunsthaus Zürich, Sammlung Emil G. Bührle, Festschrift zu Ehren von Emil G. Bührle zur Eröffnung des Kunsthaus-Neubaus und Katalog der Sammlung Emil G. Bührle* (Zurich, 1958. Section of catalogue which includes Delacroix by E. Hüttinger), p. 86; Johnson 1963, pl. 53; L. Johnson, 'Delacroix et les Salons. Documents inédits au Louvre', 16 (1966), pp. 220, 229 n. 12.

Print: Lithograph in reverse by A. Mouilleron, for *Souvenirs d'artistes*, pl. 559, 1874/7 (repr. L. Johnson, op. cit., 1966, fig. 223).

The critic of the *Journal des Artistes* had this to say of the *Tam o'Shanter* that was exhibited at the Galerie Lebrun in 1829: 'Enfin, M. Delacroix [. . .] De loin, effet à la manière des décorations. De près, barbouillage informe. Voyez (n. 44) une Sorcière qui arrache la queue d'une jument' — words that could, like the description in the exhibition catalogue, apply equally well to the present version or to J109. A fortnight later the same journal reported: 'La Sorcière [. . .] vient d'en être relevée.'

Before discovering a drawing of a third, lost version that had belonged to Charles Blanc (Fig. 11) and evidence of the size of the Salon version, I (1963), followed by Sérullaz (*Mémorial*, no. 399), dated the present version '1849?', thinking that of the two versions then known this was the more likely to be the one Delacroix recorded working on at Champrosay in 1849. But since 1966 (op. cit.), the evidence, though still inconclusive, has seemed to me to favour identifying this version as the picture shown at the Salon of 1831 (for the arguments, see J109).

The Salon painting, listed in the Salon register as 'Tam O'Shanter et la Sorcière', was accepted by the Jury on 5 May (L. Johnson, op. cit., 1966, p. 220). It passed almost without comment from the critics, the only notice it did receive, in the *Gazette de France*, being both hostile and useless in helping to identify it today: 'Une vague passion d'énergie est venue tourmenter nos jeunes artistes de même qu'elle tourmente nos jeunes littérateurs; mais l'énergie doit avoir une grande et noble pensée comme celle qui animait Michel-Ange, autrement elle produit les folies révoltantes de M. Delacroix et de ses imitateurs. Voyez [. . .] les *Sorcières de Tam O'Shanter* de cet artiste.'

Overcleaning has rendered the post transparent and removed some detail from the spectral forms of the witches following Nannie, as well, no doubt, as from the masonry of the bridge.

---

[1] If not an error, this indication, without reference to an accompanying signature, apparently means that the painting was dated to 1825, not that it actually bore a date from Delacroix's hand.

140 THE BATTLE OF POITIERS,   Pl. 122
sketch

$20\frac{3}{4} \times 25\frac{1}{2}$ in. (52.8 × 64.8 cm) Relined
Inscribed bottom right: *ED*
Moreau pp. 189 n. 1, 311. R322 (1830)
1829
Walters Art Gallery, Baltimore

Provenance: Probably Delacroix's posthumous sale, Feb. 1864, lot 54 ('Le roi Jean à la bataille de Poitiers [. . .] Esquisse', 55 × 65 cm. Burty Ann ED: 'très montée de ton, vigoureuse, transparente paysage infini'),[1] to Baron de Laage, 4,700 fr.; N. V. Diaz, d. 1876; his sale 25 Jan. 1877, lot 323 ('Le roi Jean à la bataille de Poitiers. Esquisse terminée', 53 × 65 cm. Moreau-Nélaton annotated cat. *BN Estampes*: 'signé graté sur ? à droite E.D.'), to Baron de Beurnonville; his sale 29 Apr. 1880, lot 14 ('Le roi Jean à la bataille de Poitiers. Esquisse terminée', 54 × 65 cm), to Brame, 10,000 fr.; L. Tabourier, by 1885; his sale 20 June 1898, lot 19 (repr.), to Durand-Ruel, 18,500 fr.; they sold it to W. T. Walters of Baltimore, 29 June 1899 (Arch D-R).

Exhibitions: Probably *Bd Italiens*, Paris 1864, no. 6 ('Le roi Jean à la bataille de Poitiers [. . .] Esquisse', 54 × 66 cm, lent by Baron de Laage); *EBA*, Paris 1885, no. 214; *Centennale*, Paris 1889, no. 269; Baltimore 1951, no. 20; Toronto-Ottawa 1962-3, no. 2, repr.; Louvre 1963, no. 121, *M* no. 123, repr.; Baltimore 1968, no. 61.

Literature: Silvestre *Delacroix* (1855), p. 81; Silvestre *Documents nouveaux* (1864), pp. 4 f.; A. Cantaloube, *Eugène Delacroix, l'homme et l'artiste* (Dentu, Paris, 1864), pp. 39, 56; *The Walters Collection* (Friedenwald Press, Baltimore, 1901), no. 180; Moreau-Nélaton I. 102, repr. fig. 72; Meier-Graefe 1922, repr. p. 108; Escholier I, repr. opp. p. 238; Hourticq 1930, pl. 30; R. Huyghe, 'Le portrait de Jenny Le Guillou et la bataille de Nancy par Delacroix', *Bulletin des Musées de France*, III (1931), p. 6; E. King, 'Delacroix's Paintings in the Walters Art Gallery', *Journal of the Walters Art Gallery*, I (1938), pp. 87, 97 f., 108 n. 10, repr. fig. 19; *Journal* III. 373 and n. 3; *Kunsthaus Zürich, Sammlung Emil G. Bührle. Festschrift zu Ehren von Emil G. Bührle zur Eröffnung des Kunsthaus-Neubaus und Katalog der Sammlung Emil G. Bührle* (Zurich, 1958), under no. 154 (Degas copy); L. Eitner, 'Homage to Delacroix' (review of exhibition Toronto-Ottawa 1962-3), *Apollo*, LXXVII (1963), p. 32; T. Reff, 'Degas's Copies of Older Art', *Burl Mag*, CV (1963), p. 251 and n.; Huyghe, p. 192; G. Fries, 'Degas et les Maîtres', *Art de France*, IV (1964), pp. 353 and n., 355 f.; Maltese, p. 138; Trapp, p. 179, repr. fig. 103.

Copy: Canvas by Degas, 54.5 × 65 cm. Sale René de Gas, 10 Nov. 1927, lot 78; Collection Bührle, Zurich, from 1947; with Nathan, Zurich, 1973.

See J141

¹ Two reasons make it uncertain that this is the sketch which passed in the posthumous sale: it does not bear the wax seal of that sale and is not recorded as having passed in it in any of the catalogues of later sales. On the other hand, there is no evidence that another oil sketch of the subject ever existed, and the seal could have been removed when the picture was relined, some time before 1934.

Robaut, who believed the picture which passed in the Diaz sale of 1877 came from Delacroix's posthumous sale, listed the wrong dimensions and failed to record the inscribed initials in his *catalogue raisonné*, but noted the measurements as 54 × 65 cm in Tracings II and added: 'signé à dr. du revers de la brosse: ED'.

141 THE BATTLE OF POITIERS　　Pl. 123

$44\frac{7}{8} \times 57\frac{1}{2}$ in. (1.14 × 1.46 m)
Signed and dated bottom left: *E. Delacroix, 1830*
Moreau pp. 189, 258. R321.
Musée du Louvre

Provenance: Commissioned in 1829 by the Duchesse de Berry, who fled to England at the time of the July Revolution of 1830, leaving it unpaid for; her sale 8 Dec. 1830, lot 10 ('Le roi Jean à la bataille de Poitiers'); Delacroix regained possession of it in unknown circumstances, perhaps by obtaining an injunction to prevent its passing in the Berry sale, and in November 1831 arranged for its sale by M. Paillet, *commissaire-expert des Musées Royaux* (*Correspondance* I. 295 f.); Vicomte d'Osembray from 1831 (?), certainly by 1855, to at least 1864; Marmontel; his sale 7 March 1870, lot 4, to Aguado, 42,650 fr.; Eugène Pereire, by 1885; with Barbazanges, by Dec. 1921 (Dieterle R); with Hodebert, by 1925; with Matthiesen, Berlin, by 1926; bought from them by the Louvre (RF3153), decree of 11 March 1931.

Exhibitions: *Universelle*, Paris 1855, no. 2919; *Bd Italiens*, Paris 1864, no. 158; *EBA*, Paris 1885, no. 162; Paris 1922, no. 59; Petit Palais, Paris 1925, no. 79; Amsterdam 1926, no. 42, repr.; Louvre 1930, no. 51A, repr. *Album*, p. 30; R.A. London 1932, no. 435; Orangerie, Paris 1933B, no. 85; Buenos Aires 1939, no. 47; San Francisco 1940–2, no. 35, repr.; New York 1941, no. 42; Atelier Delacroix, Paris 1946B, G; id., Paris 1947, no. 7; id., Paris 1952, no. 15, detail repr.; Warsaw 1956, no. 39, repr.; Moscow Leningrad 1956, p. 44, repr.; Stockholm 1958, no. 122; Louvre 1963 no. 120, *M* no. 122, repr.; Berne 1963–4, no. 28; Bremen 1964, no. 26; Munich 1964–5, no. 93, repr.; Kyoto–Tokyo 1969, H-9, repr. in colour.

Literature: E. Loudun [A. Balleyguier], *Exposition universelle de 1855* (Ledoyen, Paris, 1855), p. 115; (mentioned by other reviewers of this exhibition but without discussion); Silvestre *Delacroix* (1855), p. 81; P. de Saint-Victor, 'Eugène Delacroix', *Le Moniteur universel*, 27 June 1881; H. Houssaye, 'L'Exposition des œuvres d'Eugène Delacroix à l'Ecole des Beaux-Arts', *Revue des Deux Mondes*, LXVIII (1885), p. 666; M. Vachon, 'Maîtres modernes. Eugène Delacroix à l'Ecole des Beaux-Arts

mars–avril 1885' (L. Baschet, Paris, 1885), p. 22, repr. (pl. unnumbered); Moreau-Nélaton I. 102, 163, repr. fig. 69, II. 156; W. G. Constable, 'French Painting in Amsterdam', *Burl Mag*, XLIX (1926), p. 227; Escholier I. 235, 239, repr. opp. p. 239; Hourticq 1930, pl. 30; R. Huyghe, 'Le Portrait de Jenny Le Guillou et la Bataille de Poitiers par Delacroix', *Bulletin des Musées*, III (1931), pp. 5 f., *Bataille de Nancy* repr. by error, p. 5; *Correspondance* I. 295 n. 2, 408, III. 254 and n.; E. King, 'Delacroix's Paintings in the Walters Art Gallery', *Journal of the Walters Art Gallery*, I (1938), pp. 97 f. and n., repr. fig. 20; Sterling-Adhémar, no. 673, pl. 237; Johnson 1963, pl. 20; Huyghe, pp. 187, 191, 192, 193, 198, 455; Maltese, pp. 37, 137 f., repr. pl. 25, colour detail King John group, pl. XI; Trapp, pp. 93, 178 ff., repr. fig. 102. (See also J140.)

The battle of Poitiers was engaged on 19 September 1356, between the armies of Edward, Prince of Wales, and King John of France. Fighting against great numerical odds, the English troops routed two French battle corps, then fell on King John, who in spite of a brave defence was taken prisoner. Delacroix has chosen this climactic moment in the battle, when the French king is encircled and about to be captured by the Black Prince's troops. His fourteen-year-old son, later known as Philip the Bold and who was to be awarded the duchy of Burgundy in recognition of his courage at Poitiers, stands beside him. Less belligerent than in the sketch (J140), Philip is shown as more apprehensive than bold: a more delicate perception of what his reactions must have been before he set about defending his father. The principal changes between the sketch and final version, however, are that in the latter the horizon is lowered, thus silhouetting the King's head, and his alone, against the sky, and the battle standards, also raised against the sky, are moved into positions where they stress centres of action; the Black Prince's standard is uppermost in the right foreground.

In December 1828, before leaving for Rome, Horace Vernet left a copy of Gros's sketch for the *Battle of Nazareth* with Delacroix for safekeeping (*Correspondance* v. 147). It was no doubt the copy by Montfort, formerly attributed to Géricault, now in the Musée Calvet, Avignon. Delacroix greatly admired the original sketch, now in the Museum at Nantes, and thought that it would not have gained by being finished on a larger scale (cf. his essay on Gros of 1848 in *Œuvres Litt*, I. 173 f.). He clearly owes much to Gros's conception, having had a replica before his eyes when he did this battle-piece. Though a finished picture, the *Poitiers* retains, by neo-classical standards, many of the qualities of a sketch. Above all, it owes to the Gros the vision of a battle which, while containing many graphic details of individual combat, subordinates them to a grand total impression of a furious mêlée—in contrast to David's *Sabines*, for example.

Beyond Gros, Delacroix seems to have drawn inspiration in a general way for vivid and naïvely observed details of medieval soldiers in combat from Spinello Aretino's fourteenth-century fresco in the Campo Santo, Pisa, *The Combat of St Efisio against the Pagans of Sardinia*. A number of apparently unidentified pen drawings of details from this and other frescoes in the Campo Santo are contained in the Louvre sketch-book RF23355 (see particularly fols. 21ᵛ–23ʳ). They were evidently copied from *Pitture a fresco del Campo Santo di Pisa intagliate dal Cav. Carlo Lasinio*, Florence 1822 (the Spinello is engraved on pl. IV). Though the sketch-book appears to have been used mainly in the period 1823–4, it contains notes dated as late as September 1829, and Delacroix's copies could therefore have been done after he received the commissions for his first medieval battle-pieces, *Nancy* and *Poitiers*.

Eight sheets of drawings and sketches described as for the *Battle of Poitiers* passed in Delacroix's posthumous sale (lot 320), to Jacques Leman and another buyer for 52 fr., according to Robaut (R1559), to Moufflard for 26 fr., according to Burty Ann ED. None of these has to my knowledge been positively identified.

The *Battle of Poitiers* has attracted very little attention from the critics since it was painted. Paul de Saint-Victor referred to it briefly in 1881 (op. cit.) as a 'tableau de jeunesse, d'une exécution encore un peu grêle, mais tout brillant de verve et d'ardeur.' In 1926 it was dismissed as 'melodramatic nonsense' by W. G. Constable (op. cit.), and received more thoughtful consideration in 1963 from Lorenz Eitner who, writing of the sketch (op. cit., under J140), observed:

[It] contains within its small format a compositional invention of sweeping power. Under rain-sodden clouds pierced by sun-glare (never did Delacroix come closer to Constable than in this passage), a wide landscape of freshest green spreads far into the blue distance. [...] The whole scene is conceived in one encompassing vision, rather than *composed*, in the ordinary sense, by the addition of part to part. There is no gap between the dramatic theme and its pictorial realisation: a single inventive act has engendered image and meaning.

It is usually assumed that a passage in a letter from Delacroix to Pierret, dated to December 1828 or January 1829 by Joubin, saying that he has 'quelqu'espoir d'arranger quelque chose avec la duchesse de Berry' refers to the commission for this picture (*Correspondance* I. 234 n. 2); but it could equally well refer to the *Quentin Durward and the Balafré* (J137), also painted for the Duchess, and is therefore not a certain proof of the date of the commission for *Poitiers*, which could have come considerably later in 1829. In writing to a supposed member of the Duchesse de Berry's entourage on 1 November 1830, Delacroix, claiming payment for the picture following the Duchess's flight to England, points out that he devoted six to eight months of his time to it and suggests that it had been ready for delivery

upon approval by the Duchess, who had been prevented from visiting his studio to see it by the arrival in Paris of her father, King of Naples (ibid. 259 and n.). The King visited Paris in May, therefore Delacroix presumably began work on the commission no earlier than September 1829. In the same letter Delacroix states: 'Le tableau n'a pas été livré, c'est-à-dire porté au château', but he would appear to have delivered it to one of the Duchess's agents by 8 December 1830, since it was listed in the catalogue of her sale on that date, together with the *Quentin Durward and the Balafré*, about which there seems never to have been a question of non-payment or non-delivery. By May 1831, he may have regained full possession of both pictures, for he wrote to Gustave Planche at the end of that month to say that he planned to send the *Quentin Durward* to the Salon, but thought he would not have time to submit 'ma *Bataille*' (ibid. 283 and n.), perhaps because there was insufficient time to varnish it (cf. ibid. 295 f.: '[*La Bataille de Poitiers*] n'est pas verni[e] et il serait bon de le faire avant de l'exposer.') He could, however, have been referring to the *Battle of Nancy* (see J143).

Frustrated both in his ambition to see his picture in a Royal collection and to exhibit it publicly at a Salon, Delacroix later in the decade considered the subject for the ceiling of the *Salle des Conférences* in the Palais Bourbon (*Bib AA*, MS. 250, fol. 117), but in this too he was disappointed, as the decoration of that room was not allocated to him.

142 THE BATTLE OF NANCY,   Pl. 124
sketch

18½ × 26¾ in. (47 × 68 cm) E.D.
Moreau pp. 174 n. 3 (1828), 189 n. 2, 312. R261 (1828)
1828/9
Ny Carlsberg Glyptotek, Copenhagen

Provenance: Delacroix's posthumous sale, Feb. 1864, lot 56, to Baron de Laage, 4,500 fr.; Victor Chocquet, d. 1891; Marie Chocquet, his widow; her sale, 1 July 1899, lot 46 (as 'Le roi Jean à la bataille de Poitiers' and with wrong dimensions, but with correct repr.), to Edgar Degas, 6,700 fr.; his sale, 26 March 1918, lot 26 (repr.), to Trotti, 31,000 fr.; Wilhelm Hansen, Copenhagen; bought for the Ny Carlsberg Glyptotek (I.N. 1905), Copenhagen, 1923.

Exhibitions: Bd Italiens, Paris 1864, no. 5; Copenhagen 1928, no. 53; Louvre 1930, no. 48; Copenhagen 1945, no. 69; Copenhagen 1957–8, no. 36.

Literature: A. Cantaloube, *Eugène Delacroix, l'homme et l'artiste* (E. Dentu, Paris, 1864), p. 39; J. Barbey d'Aurevilly, *Les Œuvres et les hommes* (Slatkine reprint, Geneva, 1968, from Paris 1886 ed.), VII (*Sensations d'art*), p. 52; Moreau-Nélaton I. 101, repr. fig. 75; Escholier I. 233 f.;

anon. [C. Petersen], *Franske malerier i Ny Carlsberg Glyptotek* (B. Lunos, Copenhagen, 1929), p. 12, repr.; Hourticq 1930, pl. 25; L. Swane, *Fransk Malerkunst fra David til Courbet* (Gad, Copenhagen, 1930), p. 31; H. Rostrup, 'Delacroix og hans Arbejder i Danske Samlinger', *Kunstmuseets Aarsskrift*, XVI-XVIII (1929-31. Copenhagen, 1931), pp. 157, 159, 161, repr. fig. 3, fig. 4, detail of Charles the Bold and Claude de Bauzemont; R. Huyghe, *Discovery of Art* (Thames and Hudson, London, 1959; translated from *Dialogue avec le visible*, 1955, same pagination), pp. 228, 231, 232, repr. fig. 213; H. Rostrup, *Ny Carlsberg Glyptotek, Danske og franske malerier og tegninger* (Copenhagen, 1961), no. 884, repr. p. 43; T. Charpentier, 'A propos de la *Bataille de Nancy* par Eugène Delacroix', *Revue du Louvre*, 13 (1963), *passim*, repr. fig. 5; Huyghe, pp. 193, 207, repr. fig. 166; L. Johnson, in Cat. Exh. Edinburgh-London 1964, under no. 111; Maltese, p. 139. (For references to this sketch in Delacroix's writings, see J143).

See J143.

143 THE BATTLE OF NANCY,   Pl. 125
DEATH OF CHARLES THE BOLD,
DUKE OF BURGUNDY

$94\frac{1}{8} \times 141\frac{3}{8}$ in. (2.39 × 3.59 m) Relined
Signed and dated bottom right: *EUG. DELACROIX.*
              F. 1831.
Moreau pp. 174, 189, 203 f. R355
Musée des Beaux-Arts, Nancy

Provenance: Commissioned by the Government on 28 Aug. 1828 for the municipal museum of Nancy; 4,000 fr. (Piron).

Exhibitions: Salon 1834, no. 494 ('Bataille de Nancy, mort du duc de Bourgogne, Charles-le-Téméraire, le 5 janvier 1477./Le duc, aigri par ses derniers désastres, livre cette bataille contre toute prudence, ayant la neige à la figure, et par un temps glacé qui fit la perte de sa cavalerie. Lui-même, embourbé dans un étang, fut tué par un chevalier lorrain au moment où ils s'efforçait d'en sortir.'); *Universelle*, Paris 1855, no. 2920; *Bd Italiens*, Paris 1864, no. 2; *EBA*, Paris 1885, no. 157; Geneva 1918, no. 72; Basle 1921, no. 66, repr.; Louvre 1930, no. 55, repr. *Album*, p. 31; Louvre 1963, no. 196, 2 repr.; Berne 1963-4, no. 33, repr.; (Edinburgh-London 1964, no. 25, repr. Not exhibited); Moscow 1969, no. 31, repr.

Literature: *Journal du Département de la Meurthe*, 21 Sept. 1828; *Correspondance* I. 408, III. 246; G. Planche, *Salon de 1831* (Pinard, Paris, 1831), reprint in *Études sur l'Ecole française (1831-1852)* (Michel Lévy, Paris, 2 vols., 1855), I, p. 67; *Précis des travaux de la Société Royale des Sciences, Lettres et Arts de Nancy, de 1829 à 1832* (Hissette, Nancy, 1833), p. 186; D. [Delécluze], 'Salon de 1834', *Journal des Débats*, 8 March 1834; B. H. [Hauréau], 'Salon de 1834', *La*

Tribune Politique et Littéraire, 15 March 1834; Ch. L. [Lenormant], 'Salon de 1834', *Le Temps*, 22 March 1834; A. T. [Tardieu], 'Salon de 1834', *Le Courrier Français*, 30 March 1834; G. Planche, 'De l'école française au Salon de 1834', *Revue des Deux-Mondes*, 3rd ser. II (1 Apr. 1834), pp. 56 f.; W., 'Salon de 1834', *Le Constitutionnel*, 11 Apr. 1834; T. Gautier, 'Salon de 1834', *La France Industrielle*, I, no. 1 (Apr. 1834), pp. 18 f.; H. Hd., review of Salon of 1834, *La Quotidienne* (quoted by G. Save, op. cit. *infra*, 1899, p. 131); Alexandre D. [Decamps], *Le Musée, Revue du Salon de 1834* (Ledoux, Paris, 1834), pp. 58 f.; G. Laviron, *Le Salon de 1834* (Libr. Louis Janet, Paris, 1834), pp. 89-93; H. Sazerac, *Lettres sur le Salon de 1834* (Delaunay, Paris, 1834), pp. 139 f.; A. Turpin, 'Exposition de peinture et de sculpture de 1834. Sujets militaires. Eugène Delacroix. *Bataille de Nancy*', *Journal de l'Armée*, II (1834), pp. 138 f.; A. Vergnaud, *Examen du Salon de 1834* (Delaunay et Roret, Paris, 1834), p. 15; T. Gautier, 'Exposition universelle de 1855', *Le Moniteur universel*, 19 July 1855; M. Du Camp, *Les Beaux-Arts à l'Exposition universelle de 1855* (Libr. nouvelle, Paris, 1855), p. 112; E. Gebauer, *Les Beaux-Arts à l'Exposition universelle de 1855* (Libr. Napoléonienne, Paris, 1855), p. 37; A. de la Forge, *La Peinture contemporaine en France* (Amyot, Paris, 1856), p. 72; L. de Pesquidoux, *Voyage artistique en France* (Michel Lévy, Paris, 1857), p. 176; L. Clément de Ris, *Les Musées de province* (Vve J. Renouard, Paris, 2 vols., 1859-61), I, p. 31 (chapter on Musée de Nancy dated 22 Oct. 1853); P. de Saint-Victor, 'Eugène Delacroix', *La Presse*, 4 Sept. 1863; A. Cantaloube, *Eugène Delacroix, l'homme et l'artiste* (E. Dentu, Paris, 1864), pp. 38 f.; Silvestre *Documents nouveaux* (1864), p. 4; Piron, p. 107; *Notice des tableaux . . . exposés au Musée de Nancy* (Imp. Collin, Nancy, 1875), p. 95, no. 177; R. Ménard, *L'Art en Alsace-Lorraine* (C. Delagrave, Paris, 1876), p. 492, repr. (Lançon etching) opp. p. 492; P. de Saint-Victor, 'Eugène Delacroix', *Le Moniteur universel*, 27 June 1881; A. Collignon, 'Souvenirs artistiques et littéraires de la Bataille de Nancy', *Mémoires de la Société d'Archéologie lorraine*, XLIV (1894), pp. 311-13; *Musée de Nancy . . . Catalogue descriptif et annoté* (Imp. Crépin-Leblond, Nancy, 1897), pp. iv, 117 f., no. 355 (repr. opp. p. 132 in 1909 ed.); G. Save, 'La mort du Téméraire, tableau de Delacroix au Musée de Nancy', *Bulletin des Sociétés artistiques de l'Est*, V (1899), pp. 127-32; C. Pfister, *Histoire de Nancy* (Berger-levrault, Paris and Nancy, 1902), I, pp. 538 and n., 541, repr. (Casse drawing after group of Charles the Bold and Claude de Bauzemont) p. 539, III, p. 645; Moreau-Nélaton I. 99, 101, 102, 145, 163, repr. fig. 114, II. 155 f.; Meier-Graefe 1922, p. 43, repr. p. 110; Escholier I. 233 f., repr. p. 236 (wrongly identified as the sketch) and p. 237, II. 190; H. Rostrup, 'Delacroix og hans Arbejder i Danske Samlinger', *Kunstmuseets Aarsskrift*, XVI-XVIII (1929-31. Copenhagen, 1931), pp. 156-62, repr. fig. 5;

Hourticq 1930, pls. 36, 37, detail of Charles the Bold and his horse, 38, detail from right with Duke of Lorraine; R. Huyghe, *Discovery of Art* (Thames and Hudson, London, 1959; translated from *Dialogue avec le visible*, 1955, same pagination), pp. 226–32, repr. fig. 214; T. Charpentier, 'A propos de la *Bataille de Nancy* par Eugène Delacroix', *Revue du Louvre*, 13 (1963), pp. 95–104, repr. fig. 8; L. Johnson, 'The Delacroix Centenary in France—I', *Burl Mag*, CV (1963), pp. 298, 301, repr. fig. 12; Huyghe, pp. 187, 191, 192, 193, 198, 207, 279, 331, 332, 455, repr. fig. 165; L. Johnson, 'The Delacroix Centenary in France—II', *Burl Mag*, CVI (1964), pp. 261 f., 264; Maltese, pp. 17, 37, 125, 139, 155, repr. fig. 33, pl. XIII, colour detail of Charles the Bold and his horse; L. Johnson, 'Eugène Delacroix et les Salons. Documents inédits au Louvre', *Revue du Louvre*, 16 (1966), pp. 219, 222, 230 n. 17; Trapp, pp. 139, 180 f., 180 n. 11, 181 nn. 12–15, 345, repr. fig. 104; Bortolatto, repr. in colour pl. XXXII.

Prints: Etching by A. Lançon for R. Ménard, *L'Art en Alsace-Lorraine*, 1876. Group of Charles the Bold and Claude de Bauzemont engraved after a drawing by R. Casse for C. Pfister, *Histoire de Nancy*, 1902.

Copies: Oil painting by Pierre Andrieu (his sale 6 May 1892, lot 147). Canvas by Victor de Bouillé (1790–1866), 35.6 × 54.9 cm (detail of right foreground repr. in T. Charpentier, op. cit., 1963, fig. 9).

The commission was granted by the Minister of the Interior on 28 August 1828,[1] in anticipation of an official visit to Nancy by Charles X on 15 and 16 September 1828. On the latter date, the Minister, accompanying the King on a visit to the Museum of Nancy, publicly announced that the picture had been commissioned for that institution (*Journal du Département de la Meurthe*, 21 Sept. 1828). The Société Royale des Sciences, Arts et Lettres de Nancy was consulted about which episode connected with the battle should be chosen. A choice of three scenes was put forward by three members of the Society and submitted to the artist with a full description of how each scene might be represented: the Duke of Lorraine ordering full funerary honours to be paid to Charles the Bold; the finding of Charles the Bold's body after the battle; and the incident finally chosen, proposed by M. de Caumont who, 'persuadé que le sentiment de la gloire nationale sera plus vivement flatté par le spectacle de l'événement qui termina la carrière aventureuse de l'intrépide et téméraire duc de Bourgogne, propose au peintre de reproduire sur la toile le combat [. . .] dans lequel Charles reçut le coup mortel' (*Précis . . . Soc. Roy. de Nancy*, 1833, p. 183). Representing the end of the Duke of Burgundy's formidable challenge to the French crown, the subject thus seems to have had, in official eyes, a certain propaganda value, both regional and national; as suggested by Charpentier (op. cit., 1963, p. 97), the Duke

of Lorraine can, like Charles X, be seen to stand for legitimacy, while Charles the Bold, like Napoleon, receives his just deserts for pride and ambition. It is doubtful, however, whether Delacroix himself thought of the scene in these terms.

Delacroix first mentions the commission in early October 1828: 'Le ministre de l'Intérieur, homme aimable sous tous les rapports, m'a commandé un tableau pour le musée de la ville de Nancy, représentant *la Mort de Charles le Hardi ou le Téméraire*, grand libertin de sa nature', he wrote to Soulier (*Correspondance* I. 223). And to Guillemardet, on 4 October: 'le ministère de l'Intérieur m'a commandé un tableau dont le sujet est tout-à-fait dans ce qui me plaît à faire, c'est la mort de Charles le Téméraire. Je compte mettre à contribution tes connaissances archéologiques à ce sujet' (*Lettres intimes*, pp. 151 f.). On 5 November, he wrote to Pierret: 'S'il en est temps encore, écris à Louis [Schwiter] qu'il me rapporte le plus de vues qu'il pourra de différents côtés de la chapelle et du local où a été tué Charles le Téméraire' (*Correspondance* I. 231). By 25 February 1829, the oil sketch was ready and on that day Delacroix wrote to Viscount de la Rochefoucauld, Superintendent of Fine Arts, to request an appointment to submit it for approval (ibid. 237 f.). The main difference between the sketch (J142) and final picture is the suppression of the building in the left background, a change which was perhaps made for a purely aesthetic reason, 'to stress the unrelieved horizontality of the plain', as suggested by Huyghe (op. cit., 1959, p. 231); but it may also have come about because Delacroix never received adequate views, of the sort that he requested from Nancy, of the chapel of the Commandery of St. John of Jerusalem, near which Charles the Bold's body was found and his encampment lay. Certainly the sketches of the edifice in Delacroix's known studies bear little resemblance in form or scale to the actual bell tower and chapel of St. John, though the oil sketch suggests some knowledge of the tower at least (for an illustration of the structure as it appeared in 1876, see Pfister, op. cit., 1902, I, p. 88).

The progress and date of completion of the final canvas have not been conclusively determined. Dated 1831 but left apparently unfinished in Delacroix's studio when he departed for Morocco in 1832, it was expected at Nancy shortly after 4 May 1833,[2] being presumably finished by then; but no record of the date of its arrival has yet been found. It was accepted for the Paris Salon on 19 February 1834 (L. Johnson, op. cit., 1966); which raises the question of whether its shipment to Nancy may not have been postponed until after the closure of the Salon. Joubin, followed with some reserve in *Mémorial*, believes that a passage in an undated letter from Delacroix to Royer-Collard, Chef de la division des sciences et arts au Ministère de l'Intérieur, evidently written shortly before the artist's departure for Morocco in January 1832, refers to the *Battle of Nancy* and to a request for an advance payment on it: 'Je m'occupe de confectionner quelque chose qui puisse à la rigueur passer pour un commencement d'esquisse. Cela sera en règle avant mon départ. Je crois avoir compris qu'il suffit que Bertin [Inspecteur des Beaux-Arts] le voie d'ici à deux jours. D'ailleurs, je ne toucherai qu'alors l'avance en question' (*Correspondance* I. 297 and n., 298 and n.); in which case the painting would hardly have been begun when Delacroix left for North Africa. On the other hand, Planche states in his review of the Salon of 1831: 'On parle d'une *bataille de Nancy*, fort avancée à ce qu'il paraît. L'aurons-nous avant la clôture du Salon? Nous le souhaitons bien sincèrement, mais nous n'en savons rien encore.' And in his review of the Salon of 1834, the same author writes of the painting as 'commencée il y a cinq ans'. Furthermore, Delacroix wrote to Planche on 28 May 1831, saying 'Je n'aurai pas le temps, je crois, de mettre ma *Bataille* [au Salon]' (*Correspondance* I. 283); which suggests that it was not impossible that the work would be ready before the closure of the Salon. Though the '*Bataille*' in question may well have been Poitiers (J141), as assumed by Joubin, it could also have been Nancy, especially since it is known from his Salon review that Planche was interested in its progress. In March 1832, Delacroix wrote to Pierret from Morocco asking him to reduce the tension of the spring on the easel holding the *Battle of Nancy* (ibid. 234), without mentioning what stage the picture had reached. If it was not ready to be dispatched to Nancy before the spring of 1833, a fair amount of work was presumably done on it after Delacroix returned from North Africa in July 1832, but as a whole it has much more in common with works done before the Moroccan journey than after.

Accepted by the Salon jury of 1834 by a majority of only three votes (L. Johnson, op. cit., 1966), the picture was severely criticized on both historical and artistic grounds at the Salon and later. Laviron (op. cit., 1834), the only Salon critic to cite a historical text in support of his criticism, quoted from Barante's account of the battle in *Histoire des ducs de Bourgogne*, recently published (1826) and no doubt consulted by Delacroix for his painting. Laviron concluded: 'Ces circonstances et d'autres encore tendent à prouver que le duc de Bourgogne a été assassiné à l'écart [. . .] M. Delacroix aime mieux le faire tuer par un cavalier lorrain, en présence de deux armées'. Save (op. cit., 1899, pp. 131 f.) was also to claim:

le duc vaincu s'était enfui *seul*, puisque personne ne fut témoin de sa fuite, ni de sa mort. [. . .] Vraisemblablement aucun témoin n'assista à cette scène, parce que ni les soldats lorrains, ni les prisonniers bourguignons, interrogés pendant les trois jours qui précédèrent la découverte du corps, ne savaient rien de cet épisode [. . .] Donc cette foule de combattants qui [. . .] entoure le Téméraire, et surtout le duc René que l'on voit à cinquante mètres de lui, escorté de toute sa chevalerie, sont abusivement en contradiction avec la vérité historique.

Save held further that there was no engagement of troops at the point where Charles was killed and that in any case the Duke of Lorraine and his cavalry were coming from the wrong direction, from the right instead of from the left.

The exact circumstances of Charles the Bold's death remain obscure, but, even if it is not allowed that for purposes of narrative clarity Delacroix could hardly have avoided representing both dukes, it is certain that in the earliest accounts of the battle he could have found sanction for showing the Duke of Burgundy among a crowd of combatants at the time of his death, and might reasonably, if perhaps wrongly, have concluded from the Duke of Lorraine's own account that he was within sight of the incident. Philippe de Commynes, for example, who was in the service of Charles the Bold, reported: 'entre autres, y mourut sur le champ ledit Duc de *Bourgogne*: & ne veus point parler de la maniere, pourtant que je n'y estois point: mais m'a esté conté de la mort dudit Duc par ceux qui le virent porter par terre, & ne le peurent secourir, parce qu'ils estoient prisonniers; mais à leur veuë ne fut point tué, mais par une grande foulle de gens, qui y survindrent, qui le tuerent, et le depoüillerent en la grande troupe sans le connoître.' (*Mémoires de Messire Philippe de Comines*, Godefroy ed. augmented by Lenglet du Fresnoy (Rollin, London and Paris, 1747, 4 vols.), II, p. 288). The Duke of Lorraine recounts how, spotting the position of the Duke of Burgundy's artillery, he sent his *avant-garde* to attack the Burgundian flank, throwing the enemy into confusion, then: 'abandonnerent les Bourguignons l'artillerie, & après quelque resistance se mirent en fuite, en laquelle Monsieur de Bourgoigne aussi sur un cheval noir fut abbatu & tombé en une fosse auprès de Saint Jean'. (*La vraye déclaration du fait et conduite de la bataille de Nancy*, ibid. IV, p. 493.)

The unhorsing of Charles the Bold by the lance of a knight of Lorraine, Claude de Bauzemont, while trying to spur his horse out of a pond, is not only described in detail in de Caumont's programme for the painting submitted to Delacroix (*Précis . . . Soc. Roy. de Nancy*, 1833, p. 183), but finds some historical support in a chronicle of Lorraine by a writer living under René II, quoted by Dom Calmet whose work was brought to Delacroix's attention by de Caumont (ibid. 184): 'tous lesdicts Suisses & ladicte Chevallerie à grands coups de lances, d'espées, de hallebardes & de picques, la chasse au Duc donnoient. [. . .] Ung nommé Claude de Bausemont vint joindre le Duc de Bourgongne, ung coup de lance sur la crepiere lui donna; incontinant d'autres sur lui tous chargerent subitement.

'[. . .] Ledit Duc fut arresté dedans ung prez, près dudict Sainct Jean, là fut tué'. (R. P. Dom Calmet, *Histoire de Lorraine* (Nancy, 1745–57, 7 vols., VII, p. cxxxiii.)

The armour, though sometimes vague in form or inaccurate in detail, is historically sound in general effect.

It must be conceded to Delacroix's critics, however, that if standards of strict historical accuracy are to be applied, such major dispositions of troops from both armies could hardly have been seen from the point of view chosen by Delacroix; for, assuming that point to be almost the same as in the oil sketch, the principal engagement and concentration of troops would have been behind the spectator (for a plan of the battle, see Pfister, op. cit., 1902, I, between pp. 484 and 485).

Having noted some of the historical texts which no doubt contributed to Delacroix's conception of the battle, it is now necessary to turn to certain criticisms of its artistic qualities. 'Une pochade d'atelier, confuse et sans vérité, où tout est faux' (Hauréau, op. cit., 1834); 'un véritable jeu de cartes aux figures bigarrées, sans caractère' (Turpin, op. cit., 1834); and 'ce sont des figures jetées au hasard et intitulées: *Bataille de Nancy*' (W., op. cit., 1834) are typical of the unfavourable opinions expressed by the Salon reviewers. But in fact the confusion of battle is masterfully controlled, as in Gros's oil sketch for the *Battle of Nazareth*, a copy of which Horace Vernet had left with Delacroix for safe-keeping at the beginning of December 1828 (*Correspondance* v. 147), and the psychological observation of single figures is superior to Gros's. The design consists essentially of wedges in depth, the principal one being formed on one side by the Duke of Lorraine's cavalry, and on the other by the more fragile line created by Charles the Bold and the lance that is about to bring him down, paralleled approximately by the ragged line of Burgundians and dead horse on the left. The hand that strikes the fatal blow is by the apex of the wedge, foiled against the snow roughly in the centre of the picture. By this arrangement, Delacroix draws the eye to the most crucial gesture in the narrative and also makes the overall situation immediately clear in visual terms: the lone, almost unobserved struggle of the Duke of Burgundy to save his life set against the compact mass of the Duke of Lorraine's triumphant cavalry; and made to balance it pictorially, even to dominate it in interest, by being placed closer to the eye in the pictorial space. The placing of Charles the Bold and his horse, trapped in the corner of the composition, is an inspired touch. Also, how steadily yet apprehensively, how accurately he takes the measure of the lance! By contrast, how gingerly yet covetously the enemy halberdier on the right stoops to grasp a sword that might have saved the life of the disarmed Charles.

Among the few favourable comments at the Salon, the appreciation of the figure of Charles the Bold by Planche (quoted in *Mémorial*) and Gautier may by mentioned. The latter wrote (op. cit., 1834): 'la figure de Charles-le-Téméraire [. . .] n'a pu être conçue et exécutée que par un homme de génie', and added, 'l'aspect morne et triste de cette bataille, dans la neige et le brouillard, est admirablement rendu; [. . .] Géricault seul eût fait des chevaux

supérieurs à ceux-là.' Robaut was to point out (under R 290) the similarity between Charles the Bold's mount and Delacroix's lithograph, *Wild Horse* (Delteil, no. 78), which is dated December 1828. Delacroix's own partiality to the picture is documented in two places. In an unpublished letter dated 4 March 1855 to the curator of the Museum of Nancy, requesting to borrow it for the Universal Exhibition of 1855, he says that he regards it as 'l'un des moins faibles que j'ai produits' (Municipal Archives, Nancy, misquoted by Charpentier, op. cit., 1963, p. 95); and on a visit to Nancy in 1857, he noted: 'Au Musée, où mon tableau est placé trop haut et privé de lumière. Toutefois, il ne m'a pas déplu' (*Journal* III. 118).

Gros's *Napoleon on the Battlefield of Eylau* (Louvre), a picture greatly admired by Delacroix for its blend of realistic detail and the ideal, has been noted as an obvious precedent for a battle-piece set in snow (e.g. Hourticq 1930); and more recently Trapp (p. 181) has remarked perceptively on the resemblance between the fallen soldier in the right foreground and David's *Death of Bara*. As an earlier influence, I have suggested (Cat. Exh. Edinburgh–London 1964, no. 111) that the line of cavalry engaging foot-soldiers on the right may owe something to a similar engagement on the left of one of Pierre Bontemps's reliefs of the Battle of Marignan for the base of the tomb of Francis I in the Abbey of St. Denis, Delacroix having noted on the study belonging to René Huyghe (see below): 'les batailles de François Ier sur son tombeau et de Maximilien'. The most direct debt to the Bontemps relief is perhaps to be found in the line of foot-soldiers seen from the back in the middle of the sheet of studies in the Ny Carlsberg Glyptotek (recto. See below). Escholier's (I. 233) comparison of the oil sketch with Uccello's battle-pieces seems irrelevant.

The picture has suffered considerable damage, partly owing to the use of bitumen. The canvas was patched in 1865, cleaned and restored between 1896 and 1903, and extensively restored in 1931 (cf. Charpentier, op. cit., 1963, p. 103 and n. 33). It was recleaned for the centennial exhibition of 1963, restored and relined at the Louvre in 1968.

Nine sheets described as drawings and sketches for the *Battle of Nancy* passed to Moureau for 23 fr. in Delacroix's posthumous sale (lot 326. R1544). Three of these have been identified: (1) A panoramic, scribbly exploration of the battle array, drawn in pencil, showing the chapel on the left and bearing some notes of things to be consulted (see above. Coll. R. Huyghe, Paris, 21.2 × 32.8 cm, repr. Huyghe, op. cit., 1959, fig. 210 and *Mémorial* no. 197; (2) a pencil drawing, with the chapel still on the left, but the receding line of cavalry and fallen horse now clearly taking form on the right; and the group of Charles the Bold and Claude de Bauzemont dominating the composition in the centre foreground (Louvre, RF9354, 30 × 45 cm, repr. *Mémorial* no. 198); and (3) a sheet of pencil drawings and slight water-colour studies, working out this group primarily in two pencil studies, recto and verso (Ny Carlsberg Glyptotek, Copenhagen, I.N. 2788, 28 × 24.5 cm, repr. Huyghe, op. cit., 1959, fig. 211 (recto), 212 (verso). For a sensitive analysis of the relation between oil sketch, drawings and final picture, see ibid. 226–32.

¹ The Minister of the Interior to the Mayor of Nancy, Paris, 28 August 1828: 'J'ai l'honneur de vous annoncer que par décision de ce jour, j'ai arrêté que Mr Eugène de la Croix, serait chargé de l'exécution d'un tableau pour le musée qui est placé dans l'hôtel de ville de Nancy.

Le sujet sera pris dans le récit de la bataille livrée le 5 janvier 1577 [*sic*] sous les murs de Nancy même vers les 5 ou 6 heures du matin.

[. . .] J'ai l'espoir que la mesure dont je vous donne la nouvelle sera agréable à vous et aux habitans de la ville que vous administrez'. (Municipal Archives, Nancy: Musée 1828).

² The Prefect of Meurthe to the Mayor of Nancy, Nancy, 4 May 1833: 'J'ai l'honneur de vous informer que M^r le Ministre du Commerce et des Travaux Publics me prévient que le tableau de la bataille de Nancy, peint par Mr Eugène de Lacroix [. . .] me parviendra prochainement par la voie du roulage.

Je vous autorise à faire payer sur le Fonds des Dépenses imprévues de 1833, les frais d'encadrement, d'emballage et de transport qui restent à la charge de la ville.' (Municipal Archives, Nancy: Musée 1833.)

A document dated 27 August 1833 in the same file, announcing the shipment of a case weighing 160 kg, does not refer to the *Battle of Nancy* as stated by Charpentier (op. cit., 1963, p. 95 n. 1), but to a portrait of the King by Mlle Blanchard.

144 LIBERTY LEADING THE PEOPLE   Pl. 126

102⅜ × 138 in. (2.60 × 3.50 m) Signed and dated on beams right, centre: *Eug Delacroix/1830*.

Moreau pp. 170, 205. R326

Musée du Louvre

Provenance: Bought by the State for 3,000 fr. in October 1831, following the Salon (cf. *La Caricature*, 13 Oct. 1831), and hung, apparently for a few months only, in the Musée du Luxembourg; returned to the artist for safekeeping about July 1839; re-entered the Luxembourg around the end of May 1849; given to the Louvre by the Direction des Beaux-Arts (Inv. RF129), Nov. 1874.¹

Exhibitions: Salon 1831, no. 511 ('Le 28 juillet./La liberté guidant le peuple.')²; *Universelle*, Paris 1855, no. 2926; *Bd Italiens*, Paris 1864, no. 37; *Centennale*, Paris 1889, no. 258; Louvre 1930, no. 53, repr. *Album*, p. 29; Louvre 1945B, no. 16; Paris 1948, no. 566; Warsaw 1956, no. 38, repr.; Moscow-Leningrad 1956, no. 42, repr.; Louvre 1963, no. 122, *M* no. 124, 2 repr.; Paris, Detroit, New York 1974–5, no. 41, repr.

Literature: Anon., 'Notes sur le Salon de 1831', *L'Artiste*, I (1831), p. 146 (*Liberty* passage quoted in full n. 2 below); V. Schoelcher, 'Salon de 1831', ibid. 227; ibid., II (1831), pp. 179 f.; anon., 'Ouverture du Salon de 1831', *Le Courrier français*, 2 May 1831; Ed. R., review of Salon, *Gazette*

Littéraire, II (1831), no. 23 (5 May), p. 364; D. [Delécluze], *Journal des Débats*, 7 May 1831; F., 'Salon de 1831', *Journal des Artistes*, I (1831), no. XIX (8 May), pp. 347 f.; anon., id., *La Quotidienne*, 8 May 1831; anon., id., *Moniteur des Arts*, 9 May 1831; anon., id., *Journal du Commerce*, 26 May 1831; L. P. [Peisse], 'M. Delacroix. — Romantisme' (5th article on Salon), *Le National*, 30 May 1831; anon., review of Salon, *Le Constitutionnel*, 4 June 1831; C. M., id., *L'Avenir*, 9 June 1831; Melchior F. S., id., *Le Voleur*, 31 July 1831; 'Nouvelle des Arts', *La Caricature*, 13 Oct. 1831; A. Jal, *Salon de 1831. Ebauches critiques* (Dénain, Paris, July 1831), pp. 44 f., 110; anon., *L'Observateur aux Salons* [*sic*] *de 1831* (Gauthier, Paris, n.d.), 3rd ed., pp. 3, 9 (*Liberty* listed first under Ière salle, then 3e. salle, grande galerie. No commentary); C. P. Landon, *Annales du Musée et de l'Ecole moderne des Beaux-Arts. Salon de 1831 . . . par Ambroise Tardieu* (Pillet, Paris, 1831), pp. 44–6; C. Lenormant, *Les Artistes Contemporains. Salon de 1831* (Mesnier, Paris, 1833 ed.), I, pp. 195–7; G. Planche, *Salon de 1831* (Pinard, Paris, 1831), pp. 107–13, repr. (Porret wood-engraving) p. 106; *Explication des ouvrages de peinture et de sculpture de l'école moderne de France, exposés dans le Musée royal du Luxembourg* (Vinchon, Paris, 1832), Supp., no. 160; H. Heine, 'Salon de 1831', *De la France*, 1857 ed. (*Œuvres complètes*, M. Lévy, Paris), pp. 339–41; T. Thoré, 'Artistes contemporains. M. Eugène Delacroix', *Le Siècle*, 25 Feb. 1837; P. Petroz, 'Exposition universelle des Beaux-Arts', *La Presse*, 5 June 1855; C. Perrier, id., *L'Artiste*, XV (1855), 6th livraison (10 June), p. 74; P. Mantz, 'Salon de 1855', *Revue française*, II (10 June–10 Oct. 1855), pp. 174 f.; T. Gautier, 'Exposition universelle de 1855', *Le Moniteur universel*, 19 July 1855; E. About, *Voyage à travers l'exposition des Beaux-Arts* (Hachette, Paris, 1855), p. 179; M. Du Camp, *Les Beaux-Arts à l'Exposition universelle de 1855* (Libr. nouvelle, Paris, 1855), pp. 95–7; E. Gebauer, same title (Libr. Napoléonienne, Paris, 1855), pp. 35 f.; E. Loudun [A. Balleyguier], *Exposition universelle de 1855* (Ledoyen, Paris, 1855), p. 115; G. Planche, *Etudes sur l'école française* (M. Lévy, Paris, 1855), pp. 62–5; T. Silvestre, *Histoire des artistes vivants. Etudes d'après nature. Delacroix* (Blanchard, Paris, n.d. [1855]), pp. 58, 65 and pl. from photo by Baldus (reprinted, excluding p. 65 ref. to official concealment of *Liberty* following Salon, in T. Silvestre, *Les Artistes français*, 1855 (1926 ed., I, pp. 25, 29)); A. de la Forge, *La Peinture contemporaine en France* (Paris, 1856), pp. 53–7; E. de Mirecourt, *Eugène Delacroix. Les contemporains* (Havard, Paris, 1856), p. 74; E. Chesneau, 'Le Mouvement moderne en peinture. Eugène Delacroix', *Revue Européenne*, XVIII (1861), p. 489 (reprinted in *La Peinture française au XIXe siècle. Les Chefs d'écoles* (Didier, Paris, 1862), p. 333); id., *L'Art et les Artistes Modernes . . .* (Didier, Paris, 1864; reprinted from *Le Constitutionnel*, 1863), pp. 347 f.; C. Blanc, 'Eugène Delacroix', *GBA*, XVI (1864), p. 23 (reprinted in *Les Artistes de mon temps* (Firmin-Didot, Paris, 1876), pp. 45 f.); L. Chardin, 'Retour à Eugène Delacroix', *L'Artiste*, 7th ser. II (1864), pp. 148 f.; A. Dumas, *Causerie sur Eugène Delacroix*, lecture of 10 Dec. 1864, pp. 70-3 of MS. in *BN Estampes* (see *Literature* for J112 and Tourneux p. 27 for further details. These pages are published in the final instalment of the lecture as printed in *La Presse*, 7 Jan. 1865. They are also partially quoted, from the MS., in Moreau-Nélaton I. 113 f.); A. Cantaloube, *Eugéne Delacroix . . .* (Dentu, Paris, 1864), pp. 25 f.; Piron, p. 106; P. Petroz, *L'Art et la critique en France* (Baillière, Paris, 1875), pp. 48-51; F. Villot, *Notice des tableaux exposés . . . [au] Louvre. 3ᵉ partie. Ecole française* (C. de Mourgues, Paris, 1878, 9th ed.), Supp. p. 18, no. 755; J. Claretie, *La Vie à Paris* (Havard, Paris, 1880), pp. 99 f., 149; E. Cardon, Obituary for Etienne Arago, *Moniteur des Arts*, 11 March 1892; G. Lafenestre and E. Richtenberger, *Le Musée national du Louvre* (Quantin, Paris, n.d. [1893]), p. 280, no. 209; A. Dayot, *Journées révolutionnaires 1830-1848, d'après des peintures, sculptures, dessins . . .* (Flammarion, Paris, 1897), repr. p. 65; Moreau-Nélaton I. 113, 118-20, repr. fig. 81; Meier-Graefe 1922, repr. p. 111; Brière 1924, p. 77, no. 209, repr. pl. LVIII; Escholier I. 264-76, repr. opp. p. 266, details, opp. p. 268 (man wearing top-hat), opp. p. 270 (Liberty); Hourticq 1930, repr. pl. 33, details, pl. 34 (man wearing top-hat), 35 (boy with pistol); A. Joubin, 'Modèles de Delacroix', *GBA*, XV (1936), pp. 353, 354, repr. fig. 2 (detail of man in top-hat and corpse below); L. Rudrauf, 'Une variation sur le thème du radeau de la Méduse', *Actes du deuxième congrès international d'Esthétique et des Sciences de l'Art*, Paris, 1937, II, pp. 500-5; A. Joubin, 'Logis de Delacroix', *BSHAF*, 1938, p. 64; Rudrauf, pp. 40, 41 f., 50, 243 f., 253, 340; Cassou 1947, pl. 10, full-page detail of Liberty and boy with pistols, opp. p., followed by full-page details of man brandishing sword on left, head of Liberty (actual size), figure with top-hat, head of boy with pistols (actual size); P. Ladoué, 'Le Musée français des artistes vivants', *GBA*, 6th per. XXXIV (1948), p. 196; A. Mongan (ed.), *One Hundred Master Drawings* (Harvard University Press, Cambridge, Mass., 1949), p. 148; H. Adhémar, 'La Liberté sur les barricades de Delacroix, étudiée d'après des documents inédits', *GBA*, 6th per. XLIII (1954), pp. 83-92, repr. fig. 1; G. Hamilton, 'The Iconographical Origins of Delacroix's *Liberty leading the People*', in *Studies in Art and Literature for Belle da Costa Greene* (ed. D. Miner, Princeton University Press, 1954), pp. 55-66 (+8 unnumbered plates), repr. opp. p. 66; Sterling-Adhémar, no. 669, pl. 235; G. Busch, *Eugène Delacroix: Die Freiheit auf den Barrikaden* (Reclam Werkmonographien No. 52, Stuttgart, 1960); C. de Tolnay, '"Michelange dans son atelier" par Delacroix', *GBA*, LIX (1962), p. 52 n. 14; P. Gaudibert, 'Eugène Delacroix et le Romantisme révolutionnaire: à propos de *la Liberté sur les barricades*', *Europe*, XLI (1963), no. 408 (April), pp. 4-21,

repr. between pp. 8 and 9; Johnson 1963, pp. 38 f., repr. pl. 19; Huyghe, pp. 199-201, repr. in colour pl. XIII, colour detail of buildings in background, pl. XIV; T. Reff, 'Copyists in the Louvre, 1850-1870', *AB*, XLVI (1964), p. 555 and n.; R. Houyoux and S. Sulzberger, 'Fernand Khnopff et Eugène Delacroix', *GBA*, 6th per. LXIV (1964), p. 183; A. Chastel, 'L'Année Delacroix', *Art de France*, IV (1964), p. 333; L. Johnson, 'The Delacroix Centenary in France—II', *Burl Mag*, CVI (1964), p. 261; H. Lüdecke, *Eugène Delacroix und die Pariser Julirevolution* (Deutsche Akademie der Kunst zu Berlin, Berlin, 1965), pp. 6-18, repr. p. 7; Maltese, pp. 13, 16, 35, 39, 41, 43, 50, 124, 138, 153, 154, repr. pl. 31, colour pl. XII (detail, man wearing top-hat, with figures to either side of him up to left edge of Liberty); L. Johnson, 'Eugène Delacroix et les Salons. Documents inédits au Louvre, *Revue du Louvre*, 16 (1966), p. 220; T. Prideaux *et al.*, *The World of Delacroix* (Time Inc., New York, 1966), full-page colour detail of Liberty and boy with pistols, p. 100; S. Ringbom, 'Guérin, Delacroix and "The Liberty"', *Burl Mag*, CX (1968), pp. 270-4; H. Bessis, 'Philippe Burty et Eugène Delacroix', *GBA*, 6th per. LXXII (1968), p. 196; id., 'L'Inventaire après décès d'Eugène Delacroix', *BSHAF*, année 1969 (published 1971), p. 213, no. 102; E. Kozhina, *Romanticheskaya bitva, ocherki frantsuzskoi romanticheskoi zhivopisi 1820-kh gg.* (Iskusstvo, Leningrad, 1969); J. Vergnet-Ruiz, 'Une Inspiration de Delacroix? La Jeanne Hachette de Labarbier', *Revue du Louvre*, XXI (1971), pp. 81-5, repr. fig. 4; Trapp, pp. 98-104, repr. in colour pl. IX; M. and A. Sérullaz, 'Dessins inédits de Delacroix pour "La Liberté Guidant le Peuple"', *Revue de l'Art*, no. 14 (1971), pp. 57-62, repr. fig. 1; L. Johnson, 'Pierre Andrieu, un "polisson"?', ibid., no. 21 (1973), pp. 68, 69 nn. 20 and 21; D. Pinkney, *The Revolution of 1830* (Princeton University Press, 1972), p. 256; T. Clark, *The Absolute Bourgeois: Artists and Politics in France 1848-1851* (Thames and Hudson, London, 1973), pp. 17-19, 20, 22, 29, 59, 126-9, 140, 141, repr. pl. 6; R. Herbert, 'Baron Gros's Napoleon and Voltaire's Henri IV', in *The Artist and Writer in France: Essays in Honour of Jean Seznec*, ed. F. Haskell *et al.* (Clarendon Press, Oxford, 1974), p. 67 n. 59.

Prints: Schematic wood-engraving by Porret for G. Planche, *Salon de 1831* (Moreau, p. 142, no. 18); second state used as a heading for a contemporary pamphlet, *Un fait inconnu de Juillet 1830*. Wood-engravings for poster and frontispiece for Louis Blanc, *Histoire de dix ans* (1840). Lithograph by A. Mouilleron, *c.* 1848. Etching by Salmon. Colour poster for Exhibition Louvre 1945. Id. (Liberty and boy with pistols) for Detroit part of Exhibition Paris, Detroit, New York 1974-5.

Copies: P. Andrieu, oil sketch with variations, canvas, 63 × 80 cm. Private collection, Basle. (Sometimes attributed to

Delacroix. Discussed in L. Johnson, op. cit. *supra*, 1973, repr. fig. 6. See also under STUDIES below.)

Unidentified artist, oil sketch, 61 × 50 cm. L. Benatov, Paris (repr. Cat. Exh. Cézanne, Gemeentemuseum, The Hague, 1956, no. 7, and wrongly attributed to Cézanne).

Unidentified artist, French nineteenth century. (Noted in *Liberty* file, Service de documentation, Louvre, as in Coll. Gobin, Paris, 1950s.)

Unidentified artist, canvas, signed 'Eug. Delacroix 1830' in same place as on the original. Coll. Louis Frat, Grenoble, 1956. With Sedelmeyer, Paris, 1907. (See same file in Louvre for photograph and some further details.)

The July Revolution, which this painting commemorates, broke out right after the publication of Polignac's four notorious Ordinances, signed on 25 July 1830 and published in *Le Moniteur* the next day. They abolished the freedom of the press, dissolved the newly elected Chamber, reorganized the electoral system so as to increase the power of the aristocracy and raised the property-taxes required to qualify the industrial and commercial bourgeoisie for the franchise. These provocations, which mainly affected the middle classes, joined to existing grievances of the workers over unemployment, low wages and bad housing, brought matters to a head. In three days, the 'Trois Glorieuses', Charles X's Ultra Monarchy was overthrown by a spontaneous uprising of the Paris workers led by former soldiers of the Empire, national guardsmen, students of the Ecole polytechnique and—by the ideal of Liberty. Beginning on Tuesday 27 July, the insurrection gained full momentum that night, and on 28 July the Hôtel de Ville, fiercely defended by the royal troops, fell, was retaken and fell again to the insurgents. This was the crucial episode of the Revolution, ensuring its success. On the twenty-ninth, those troops which remained loyal to the King withdrew from the capital. Hopes of creating a Second Republic were soon frustrated and the Duke of Orleans, from the younger branch of the Bourbon dynasty, acceded to the throne as Louis-Philippe, King of the French. Under his régime, the republican ideals for which the Revolution had been fought were cynically flouted. Daumier, thought to have been wounded by a sabre during the July Revolution, was to continue the battle by means of his cartoons.[3]

Though Delacroix here painted the most enduring image of the July Revolution, one that has continued to be adopted as an emblem by those rebelling against entrenched authority from the Revolution of February 1848 to the uprisings of May 1968, his own political and physical position during the 'Trois Glorieuses' has been the subject of much debate. Alexandre Dumas (loc. cit., 1864) provides the sole allegedly eyewitness account of his presence in the streets at the time, commenting also on his political attitude. Having said that the (wrong) supposition that the man wearing a top-hat in the picture was Delacroix led to the belief that he fought in the Revolution and was an ardent republican, Dumas claims to establish the facts and dispel legends:

Lorsque, le 27 juillet, je rencontrai Delacroix du côté du pont d'Arcole et qu'il me montra quelques-uns de ces hommes que l'on ne voit que les jours de révolution, et qui aiguisaient sur le pavé l'un un sabre, l'autre un fleuret, Delacroix [. . .] me témoigna sa peur de la façon la plus énergique. Mais, quand Delacroix eut vu flotter sur Notre-Dame le drapeau aux trois couleurs, quand il reconnut, lui fanatique de l'Empire, [. . .] l'étendard de l'Empire, ah! ma foi, il n'y tint plus; l'enthousiasme prit la place de la peur, et il glorifia ce peuple qui, d'abord, l'avait effrayé.

While Dumas's account has often been viewed with scepticism and is no doubt embroidered, Delacroix's lack of participation in the fighting, his apprehension and his mistrust of republican insurgents at the time of the July Revolution are all confirmed in essence by letters which have recently come to light: Delacroix supplies his own account of the events in a letter of 17 August 1830 written to his nephew in Malta: 'Nous avons été pendant trois jours au milieu de la mitraille et des coups de fusil; car on se battait partout. Le simple promeneur comme moi avait la chance d'attraper une balle ni plus ni moins que les héros improvisés qui marchaient à l'ennemi avec des morceaux de fer emmanchés dans des manches à balai. Jusqu'ici tout va le mieux du monde. Tout ce qu'il y a de gens de bon sens espère que les feseurs [*sic*] de république consentiront à se tenir au repos.'[4] In a letter of 12 October 1830, addressed to his brother, a former general of the Empire, and providing the first sure sign of his decision to paint the picture, Delacroix writes, a little defensively perhaps, of his lack of involvement in the actual fighting: 'J'ai entrepris un sujet moderne, *Une barricade* . . . et si je n'ai pas vaincu pour la patrie, au moins peindrai-je pour elle' (*Lettres intimes* [1954], p. 191). In an excellent study of Delacroix and revolutionary romanticism, Gaudibert (op. cit., 1963) has shown how in 1830 Bonapartism and republican sentiments were confused and compatible, but by the time of the 1848 Revolution and Second Empire the distinction between Bonapartism in its imperialist aspects and purely republican ideals had become more clear-cut. Thus it was quite possible for Delacroix, an admirer of Napoleon, in whose service one of his brothers had been killed in action, the other severely wounded, to have been impassioned by the spectacle of the tricolour flying on Notre-Dame, as related by Dumas, yet not to have felt any urge to fight to bring it about, nor to have held much brotherly love for the militant proletarians who did. That, indeed, is probably an accurate summary of Delacroix's attitude to the July Revolution. In any case, the tricolour that, hoisted on the north tower of Notre-Dame on the morning of 28 July, galvanized a populace which for fifteen years had seen only the royal white flag, is depicted on a minute scale in Delacroix's painting and, its triad of hues magnified in the standard borne by the imaginary Liberty, relieves the sombre harmony of the composition as a whole (see Gaudibert too for a good analysis of the colour scheme, ibid. 10).

A large pen-and-ink drawing of the assault on the pont d'Arcole, signed 'E Delacroix', in the Fogg Museum, was long believed to lend weight to that part of Dumas's account which placed Delacroix close to the bridge on 27 July (A. Mongan, loc. cit., 1949, repr. p. 149; Hamilton, op. cit., 1954, repr. pl. 18), but, having been more recently ascribed to Raffet by the Museum (cf. Trapp, p. 94 n. 12; Johnson, op. cit., 1973, p. 69 n. 20), cannot be said to support Dumas's story. The pont d'Arcole was a suspension bridge which connected the Ile de la Cité to the place de Grève (now the place de l'Hôtel de Ville). The seizure of the bridge by the insurgents, under heavy fire, on 28 July was a vital step in taking the Hôtel de Ville. Though the position of the towers of Notre Dame in Delacroix's painting cannot be said literally to localize the action at a precise point in the capital, it could be meant to suggest that Liberty is leading the assault on the Hôtel de Ville from the south.[5] It is conceivable that Delacroix chose to convey this impression because he was, if Dumas is right, in the area on the first day of the Revolution, but more likely that he did so merely because the decisive victories were won on the Right Bank, in large part by assaults from the opposite bank.

By far the most convincing and important contemporary evidence of an actual episode in the Revolution having a direct influence on Delacroix's picture is contained in an anonymous pamphlet headed 'Un fait inconnu de juillet 1830' and datable to 1831. The author states that Delacroix took inspiration from the heroic action of Anne-Charlotte D., a poor laundry-girl who, dressed in only a petticoat ('jupon'), went in search of her young brother Antoine, an apprentice gilder who was fighting in the streets on 27 July. At length, she fell on Antoine's naked corpse; found carrying arms, he had just been shot by a platoon of Swiss troops. Counting ten bullet wounds in his chest, she swore to kill as many Swiss. She shot nine, but as she tore her tenth cartridge a Captain of lancers killed her with a blow of his sabre. In this incident, whether it be rumour or fact or, most likely, a mixture of both, would seem to lie the seed of Delacroix's conception of the half-nude corpse in the left foreground and a scantily clad Liberty armed with a musket, before pictorial influences began to play their part.

It has sometimes been held that a colour order placed by Delacroix on 20 September 1830 indicates that he had begun the *Liberty* by then (*Correspondance* I. 258 and n.),[6] but, as pointed out in *Mémorial* (no. 124), this is by no means certain and it is not until 12 October, in the letter to his brother first published by Dupont and cited above, that we learn Delacroix has decided to do the picture. On 6 December he writes to Guillemardet 'j'ai fini, ou peu s'en

manque, mon tableau' (*Correspondance* I. 262). On 13 April 1831 it was accepted by the Salon jury (L. Johnson, loc. cit., 1966). The Salon opened on 1 May, at which time the *Liberty* was apparently badly placed, to be moved later to a better spot (Planche, op. cit., 1831, p. 64), probably above the entrance to the grande galerie (Jal, op. cit., July 1831, p. 110. Cf. also *L'Observateur aux Salons de 1831*).

Delacroix's only major painting on a subject from contemporary French history, the *Liberty* also owes more to Géricault than do any of his large Salon paintings since the *Barque de Dante* of 1822 (J100). In theme—a significant contemporary event treated on a monumental scale—it coincides more exactly than the *Dante* with Géricault's central aim as realized in the *Raft of the Medusa*; in style—an energetic realism tempered by classical ideals—and in the earthy palette relieved by a celestial radiance, Delacroix, faced with the task of depicting the immediate hopes and suffering of his countrymen in a dramatic episode, reverts to the example of Géricault. There is a certain affinity with the *Raft* in the way the composition is arranged in a pyramid mounting to a peak of aspiration, though Delacroix does not combine his pyramid with a diagonal in depth, but rather with a planar disposition of the figures. In this, he develops the design of his own *Barque de Dante* with its recumbent figures spread across the foreground in front of and below a line of standing figures: now the two rows are more subtly and more fully interrelated—for example, in the way that the foreshortened thigh of the striding urchin forms a visual continuity with the left thigh of the corpse he is about to advance over.

In detail, the debt to Géricault can be seen in the half-draped corpse, which, as often remarked since 1855 (M. Du Camp, op. cit., 1855, p. 95), is an adaptation of the figure in the right foreground of the *Raft of the Medusa*, a figure from which Delacroix had done a powerful drawing (repr. Escholier I. 53). Géricault is to be found too in the bust-length figure of the dead carabinier on the far right, which complements in painting the tribute Delacroix had paid verbally in his *Journal* on 30 December 1823 (I. 41), after a visit to the dying artist: 'je suis revenu tout enthousiasmé de sa peinture: *surtout une étude de tête du carabinier. S'en souvenir.*' It may be compared, for example, to the half-length *Carabinier* by Géricault which entered the Louvre in 1851.

Jullian (op. cit., 1963, p. 102) has drawn attention to the influence of a lithograph, *L'Allocution* (*28 Juillet 1830*), by Charlet, another specialist in military subjects greatly admired by Delacroix, in the boy wearing a helmet on the far left (repr. F. Lhomme, *Charlet*, Paris, 1892, p. 27). Hamilton (op. cit., 1954) has studied the possible influences of other popular prints issued immediately after the July Revolution. Ringbom points to several more or less convincing analogies between the *Liberty* and the *Aurora and*

Cephalus and *Morpheus and Iris* painted by Delacroix's master Guérin (op. cit., 1968, both Guérin repr.). The possibility of a livelier if less likely influence is suggested by Vergnet-Ruiz (op. cit., 1971), who believes Delacroix may have found the model for the figure of Liberty in the heroine of Lebarbier's painting, *Jeanne Hachette au siège de Beauvais par le duc de Bourgogne en 1472*, shown at the Salon of 1784 and hung at Beauvais from 1826.

Among earlier influences that have been proposed are Rembrandt's *Night Watch* (Tolnay, op. cit., 1962), and battle scenes done by Eisen and Moreau-le-Jeune to illustrate Voltaire's *Henriade* (Herbert, loc. cit., 1975, without repr. or specific examples but stating that Delacroix 'must have looked at them' for the *Liberty*. If he did, Moreau-le-Jeune's engraving of Henri IV storming the ramparts of Paris (Bocher no. 1606-7) seems the only likely influence). Of special interest is Delécluze's comment (op. cit., 1831), contemporary with the first showing of the picture: 'Ce tableau peint avec verve, coloré dans plusieurs de ses parties avec un rare talent rappelle tout à fait la manière de Jouvenet'; for, though the critic refers to no specific work by Jouvenet and Delacroix scarcely mentions him in his writings, there is undoubtedly a marked resemblance between the dramatic conjunction of vitality, inspired by a supernatural ideal, and death in the *Liberty* and in Jouvenet's *St. Peter healing the Sick with his Shadow* (now Chapel of Hôpital Laënnec, Paris; Saint-Etienne-du-Mont, Paris, in 1830; repr. A. Schnapper, *Jean Jouvenet*, Paris, 1974, pl. 6). There are also similarities of lighting and arrangement. A few years later Gros was to be compared to Jouvenet in terms which apply equally well to Delacroix and indicate what Delécluze may have had in mind: 'plus guidé par l'imagination que par la science et la réflexion, Gros, remarquable par la franchise, la savante liberté de son pinceau, le jet hardi de ses lignes et la merveilleuse animation de ses figures, me paraît surtout pouvoir être comparé à Jouvenet' (quoted ibid. 160, from *Précis . . . des travaux de l'Académie de Rouen*, 1836).

Whatever minor debts Delacroix may owe to ephemeral popular imagery and to the cool example of his master, it is clear that his *Liberty* belongs in a grander, more vital stream of French painting which stems, in his own century, from Gros and most of all from Géricault. To this is added a dimension of psychological awareness—a depiction of scales of anxiety balanced against the invincible energy of the Liberty—which is particular to Delacroix, as in the end is the spirit of the whole picture, a spirit which, in spite of Delacroix's apparently lukewarm attitude towards the 'feseurs de république', conveys better than any other visual image of the 'Trois Glorieuses' the kind of exaltation caught by Heine in these words (op. cit., 1831, p. 341): 'Les dieux, qui du haut du ciel contemplaient ce sublime combat, jetaient des cris d'admiration; ils auraient volontiers quitté

leurs sièges d'or et seraient descendus sur la terre pour se faire citoyens de Paris!' More than in Gros's *Aboukir* or *Eylau*, more even than in Géricault's *Raft of the Medusa*, a historic moment is made universal because Delacroix introduces an allegorical figure which motivates the entire action and can stand for the spirit of liberty in all ages. Containing perhaps a trace of Guérin's influence, also perhaps embodying the idea of an Antique Victory (Hamilton, op. cit., 1954, p. 66, fig. 25), the figure of Liberty has always seemed to me (Johnson 1963, p. 38) essentially a free adaptation of the Aphrodite of Melos, which, discovered in 1820, was first shown in the Louvre in 1821 and according to the critic Vitet, in a passage copied by Delacroix, contributed with the Elgin marbles to upsetting French artists' previous notions of the Antique: 'Ce type de beauté contrariait toutes nos traditions: ce n'était ni la raideur de David, ni la noble ampleur de Lebrun; un accord imprévu des dons les plus contraires, un insupportable mélange d'idéal et de réalité, d'élégance et de force, de noblesse et de naturel confondaient notre jugement' (1860, quoted *Journal* III. 262). It is precisely the mixture of real and ideal in the Liberty which some critics found intolerable at the Salon of 1831, but which, harmonizing seemingly contradictory qualities, lends her the vitality to challenge preconceived ideals that Guérin's Iris lacks.

Of the other figures, the man in the foreground wearing a top-hat has been the subject of most controversy. Thought within Delacroix's lifetime, as Dumas relates, to be a self-portrait (a case of mistaken identity that has persisted well into the present century) and later held to be a 'transposition' of Delacroix's friend Frédéric Villot (Joubin, op. cit., 1936, p. 364), it in fact represents Etienne Arago, a zealous republican. Appointed director of the Théâtre du Vaudeville, then in the rue de Chartres, in 1829, he took an active part in the July Revolution and is said to have supplied arms to the insurgents from the properties room of his theatre. He is identified as the man in the top-hat by Cardon, in an obituary (loc. cit., 1892), and during Arago's lifetime by Claretie (op. cit., 1880, p. 149. For a lithograph portrait of Etienne Arago in 1848, see Dayot, op. cit., 1897, p. 127; and for a summary of his chequered career, which ranged from collaborating with Balzac to being Mayor of Paris, Ladoué, op. cit., 1948). On the basis of a study of official records of casualties in the July Revolution, Pinkney believes (op. cit., 1972, p. 256) that this figure does not deserve so conspicuous a place as a symbol of the bourgeoisie's role in the actual fighting. He also finds that the urchin brandishing pistols gives a misleading impression, because only four boys of comparable age are recorded to have lost their lives. Yet, as he acknowledges, a prefect of police reported in 1832 that the urchins of Paris were always in the forefront of resistance in revolutionary movements; to which may be added, in support of Delacroix *versus* statistics, the eyewitness evidence contained in Planche's criticism of the painting (op. cit., 1831): 'le gamin [. . .] pris sur le fait [. . .] rappelle à tout le monde ce qu'ils ont vu en juillet dernier.' The artisan brandishing a sabre on the far left stands, rightfully without doubt, for the prominent part played by artisans, especially masons, in the 'Trois Glorieuses': the dead and wounded masons and cabinet-makers alone outnumbered the casualties from the middle and upper bourgeoisie (Pinkney, op. cit., pp. 255 f.). The figure with cocked hat in the background epitomizes the role of the students from the Ecole polytechnique in helping to direct the uprising.

The reaction of the general public to the *Liberty* at the Salon of 1831 is not well documented. Heine records (op. cit., 1831) that he always saw a throng of visitors in front of it and therefore concluded that it was one of the paintings which attracted the most attention. Planche (op. cit., 1831), on the other hand, got the impression it was not enjoying the public success he thought it deserved. The picture was received with mixed feelings by the professional critics, who, though not on the whole absolute in their praise or blame, divided roughly into those who judged the realism ignoble, the colouring drab or distastefully livid and the allegorical Liberty a contradiction within itself or within the context of the whole (e.g. Jal, Peisse, Tardieu); and those who by contrast admired the combination of truth to nature and artistic licence, and recognized that the subject demanded a wide use of earthy colours (e.g. Planche, Schoelcher, Lenormant). Thoré, a few years after the Salon, resolves most concisely the argument about anomalies in the central figure (op. cit., 1837): 'Est-ce une jeune fille du peuple? est-ce le génie de la liberté? C'est l'un et l'autre; c'est, si l'on veut, la liberté incarnée dans une jeune fille. L'allégorie véritable doit avoir ce caractère, d'être à la fois un type vivant et un symbole [. . .] Ici encore, M. Delacroix est le premier qui ait employé un nouveau langage allégorique.' At the Salon itself Planche typified the attitude of like-minded critics, saying (op. cit., 1831) the allegory raised the harsh reality to a higher plane: 'en l'élevant, elle l'éloigne; elle ajoute à nos souvenirs d'hier la majesté que l'histoire seule, et la plus lointaine, possède et semble se réserver comme un privilège exclusif.' Planche went on to declare the corpses in the foreground to be 'd'une exécution irréprochable'; then, turning to what he saw as faults, criticized the perspective for leaving the position of the background in doubt and, also unsure what stage the combat had reached, considered that the point reached in time as well as space by the insurgents ought to have been made clearer; but concluded that it was the most beautiful picture in the Salon, to understand it fully as much time and study were needed, he declared, as to appreciate the operas *Don Giovanni* or *Sémiramide*.

Lenormant shared Planche's enthusiasm while also re-pudiating his objections to the treatment of space and time: 'Une scène ouverte, un nuage de fumée à travers lequel les tours de Notre-Dame [. . .] désignent, dans un sens général, la ville où la grande révolution s'est passée, le dispensent de toute explication topographique [. . .] Le combat touche à sa fin' (Lenormant's thoughtful review is quoted at greater length in the Cat. Exh. Paris, Detroit, New York 1975, no. 41).

Criticism at the Universal Exhibition of 1855 again revolved largely around the question of the mixture of allegory and realism, adding nothing to the earlier debate. Only in 1861-2, when Chesneau stresses the dichotomy, does the old question assume some fresh relevance; for Manet, committed to the painting of modern life, was to cause a scandal in 1863 with his *Déjeuner sur l'herbe* by placing a man fully clothed in modern dress alongside a contemporary woman stripped of clothing and of allegory. With reference to the placing of the man with top-hat next to the Liberty, Chesneau writes (op. cit., 1861, reprinted 1862): 'Le paletot de la réalité produit un effet discordant lorsqu'il mêle ses plis aux draperies symboliques de l'allégorie.' And concludes: 'j'affirme l'incapacité constitutionnelle de M. Delacroix à rendre la vie contemporaine.'

STUDIES: Thirty-one sheets of studies listed as for the *Liberty* passed in Delacroix's posthumous sale under lot 319, twenty-one probably going to Arosa and later to pass in his sale as part of an album (27 Feb. 1884, lot 165bis, to Dr. Suchet), the rest to Moufflard.[7] About twenty-three of these are known today. A further study is reproduced from a sketch-book in Robaut Tracings II. In addition, an oil sketch was listed as by Delacroix in Inv. Delacroix, no. 102, but cannot be identified with any lot in the posthumous sale, and may have been a sketch by Andrieu, wrongly ascribed to the master in the inventory, but nevertheless reflecting an early stage in the development of the composition (see *Copies* above). Of the known drawings, only one is a composition study proper; a large portion of the others are devoted to working out the figure of Liberty:

Composition

1. Black lead, 19.2 × 30.2 cm, E.D., private collection, Paris (repr. M. and A. Sérullaz, op. cit., 1971, fig. 5). Varies from the final composition mainly on the right: figure adoring Liberty on that side as well as a seated figure propped up by a kneeling one. No definition of background. (Andrieu's oil sketch reflects this design.)

Liberty (2-8, full-length figures arranged in a tentative sequence of development)

2. Brush and brown wash (verso, black lead), 20.8 × 23.5 cm, E.D., private collection, Paris (repr. ibid., figs. 6 and 7). Flag raised in left hand on recto, in right hand on verso; other figures lightly indicated around Liberty on both sides of sheet.

3. Black lead, 23 × 34.5 cm, E.D., private collection, Paris (repr. ibid., fig. 8). Sheet includes schematic studies for the boy with pistols and a fallen figure, also an unrelated composition (copy ?) of figures with *putti*.

4. Black lead, 22.5 × 35 cm, E.D., private collection, Paris (repr. ibid., fig. 9). Liberty bare-breasted without head or whole arms, some details of folds of her drapery. Study of hand with sabre for figure behind Liberty to left in the painting. Schematic studies for the man to the right of him holding a gun and biting off the end of a cartridge (this part of sheet, slightly rearranged, repr. upside down R1558).

5. Black lead with touches of white chalk, 32.4 × 22.8 cm, E.D., Louvre, RF4522 (ex-Degas coll. Repr. *Mémorial*, no. 125). Nude study in pose close to final figure; traces of drapery below waist.

6. Black lead heightened with white chalk on brown paper, 29.1 × 19.6 cm, E.D., Louvre, RF4523 (ex-Degas coll. Repr. *Mémorial*, no. 126). Similar figure with drapery, roughly indicated, approaching final arrangement.

7. Black lead heightened with white chalk on brown paper, 28.4 × 20.5 cm, E.D., Louvre, RF4524 (ex-Degas coll. Repr. *Mémorial*, no. 127). More detailed studies of drapery.

8. Black lead, 16.5 × 10.5 cm, page in sketch-book of 66 leaves, sale Champfleury 26 Jan. 1891, lot 552. R Ann 325bis. Whereabouts unknown (traced in pencil Robaut Tracings II). With gun and tricolour, closer to the figure as painted than any published study, but loose ends of sash round waist falling, bunch of folds in dress, running from waist to bottom left, not so marked, especially at bottom. This key motif, like a gushing spring at once tumbling towards the adoring youth and stressing the fluent and effortless advance of Liberty, thus appears, like the full profile view of the head, to have been developed at a late stage. Colour notes transcribed in Tracings II are the only ones certainly connected with the painting (apart from the documentary notes on Study no. 20 here) and show that Delacroix first planned a green dress for Liberty, but a green already combined with much of the ochreish yellow chosen for the drapery as painted: 'Drap bleu: bleu de prusse et terre d'ombre brûlée/robe verte sur un fond sale jaune verdâtre: clairs: jaune naples, ocre jaune, terre verte. demi-teinte: Vert émeraude, jaune naples./Terrains: terre de Cassel et blanc. Ocre de ru et blanc — Massicot et blanc. Par dessus un peu de massicot et terre verte, pour rendre moins roux.'

9. Black lead, 16.4 × 11.2 cm, E.D., private collection, Paris (repr. M. and A. Sérullaz, 1971, fig. 10). The head, without Phrygian cap, three-quarter profile to left.

10. Black lead, 16.5 × 14 cm, E.D., Detroit Institute of Arts, 65.151 (repr. ibid., fig. 11). The same, the planes more accented and showing more of the neck and throat.

11. Black lead, 23 × 18.3 cm, E.D., private collection, Paris (repr. ibid., fig. 12). Study for a right arm in foreshortening holding a gun.

12. Black lead, 22 × 12.1 cm, E.D., private collection, Paris (repr. ibid., fig. 13). Very similar study, but now the left arm as in the painting.

Man with Sabre, far left

13. Pencil, 29.8 × 20.8 cm, E.D., private collection, Paris (repr. ibid., fig. 14). A full-length study, sketchy but establishing the pose of the painted figure.

Man with top-hat behind Liberty

14. Pencil, 17 × 27.5 cm, E.D., private collection, Paris (repr. ibid., fig. 4). An early idea, with three other summarily drawn figures of uncertain relation to the painting.
See also 4.

Boy with Pistols

15. Pencil, 22.5 × 34.3 cm, E.D., private collection, Paris (repr. ibid., fig. 16). Studies for the lower half of the figure.

16. Black lead, 22 × 30 cm, E.D., private collection, Paris (verso only repr. ibid., fig. 15, slight brush and brown wash study, possibly for figure of Liberty).
See also 3 and Pre-publication Note, p. viii.

Full-length corpse, right foreground

17. Black lead, 21.2 × 32.5 cm, E.D., private collection, Paris (repr. ibid., fig. 17). Summary early sketch for the two corpses in the foreground, clothing barely indicated.

18. Black lead, 21.8 × 31.6 cm, E.D., private collection, Paris (repr. ibid., fig. 18). More detailed study of the full-length corpse alone, clothed. Summary sketch for youth adoring Liberty.

19. Black lead, 14.8 × 21.9 cm, E.D., private collection, Paris (repr. ibid., fig. 19). Detailed study of the trousers, with legs in different position from the figure as painted.

20. Black lead, 20 × 13 cm, E.D., Louvre, RF9237 (repr. *Mémorial*, no. 128, and notes transcribed, but read 'buffleteries' for 'buffletoires'). Documentary studies for the uniform, and the Royal device on the pouch carried by the urchin, with notes of colours and materials.

Carabinier

21. Black lead, 17.6 × 22.6 cm, E.D., private collection, Paris (repr. M. and A. Sérullaz, 1971, fig. 20). The gloved right hand, whole. Profile of youth adoring Liberty.

Setting

22. Black lead, 16.8 × 14 cm, E.D., Louvre, RF9236 (repr. *Mémorial*, no. 129). Studies of buildings. Though the blocks of houses are architecturally similar to those in the painting, the arrangement is quite different. The complex of buildings at the lower left of the sheet includes in the background what may be a summary indication of the top of the north tower of Notre-Dame, with the spire of the Sainte-Chapelle to the right of it, consistent with a view from the place de Grève (now de l'Hôtel de Ville). Further research is needed, however, into the identity of the monuments sketched elsewhere on the sheet. Though from the posthumous sale, it is not certain that this sheet was included in the lot sold as studies for the *Liberty*.

Miscellaneous

23. Black lead, 18.8 × 21.8 cm, E.D., private collection, Paris (repr. M. and A. Sérullaz, 1971, fig. 2). Wounded man, full-length seated frontally, carried on a litter. An early idea, abandoned.

24. Black lead, 19.9 × 28.8 cm, E.D., private collection, Paris (repr. ibid., fig. 3). Various sketches of heads and figures of uncertain relation to the painting.

CONDITION: The seams where the canvas is joined are visible across the full width of the paint surface, at the level of the urchin's left knee and the top of his beret. Some bitumen damage in shadows.

¹ The detailed history of the removals of the *Liberty*, which were related to politics, is as follows: it was evidently shown at the Musée du Luxembourg during at least part of the year 1832, as it is listed in the 1832 edition of their catalogue of exhibited pictures, but soon put in store lest it encourage insurrection under the July Monarchy (according to Dumas, cited in Moreau-Nélaton I. 119. See also *Charivari*, 5 July 1839, on early concealment of paintings of the July Revolution). There was a democratic revolt in early June 1832, for example. However, no document has come to light showing precisely when the *Liberty* was taken down. By February 1837, Thoré (op. cit. *infra*) was asking: 'Mais où est-elle aujourd'hui ? [. . .] Donnez-nous du moins la liberté en peinture.' It was returned to Delacroix by his friend François Cavé, Directeur des Beaux-Arts (Dumas: Moreau-Nélaton I. 119), probably in July 1839, when orders were given to remove from their stretchers and store all pictures inspired by the Revolution (*Charivari*, 5 July 1839, cited by H. Adhémar, op. cit. *infra*, 1954, pp. 89 f. and n.); kept at Frépillon, in the house of Delacroix's aunt, Mme Riesener, for the remainder of Louis-Philippe's reign, according to Dumas (cited Moreau-Nélaton I. 119). Immediately after the Revolution of February 1848, Delacroix took steps to restore it to the nation; as a result a proposal to reclaim it and hang it in the Luxembourg or elsewhere was approved by the Minister of the Interior on 11 March 1848 (*Correspondance* II. 345 and n., with full text of letter to the Minister from the Directeur des Musées nationaux containing the proposal). In April 1848 Delacroix wrote to his friend Frédéric Villot, now Keeper of Paintings at the Louvre, pressing for the placement of his picture (*Correspondance* II. 360 and n.; Joubin's date revised by Adhémar, op. cit. *infra*, 1954, p. 90 n. 17). Nothing came of this, and in May, with the consent of Charles Blanc, Directeur des Beaux-Arts, Delacroix lent it to Alphonse Jame, a painter and art dealer, who intended to exhibit it at Lyon for gain and evidently shipped it there, but the plan to show it seems to have fallen through; at the beginning of January 1849 Delacroix wrote to Jame at Lyon demanding that the canvas be dispatched to the 'directeur du Musée du Louvre' (*Journal* I. 252 f. and n.). On 21 May 1849, Jeanron, Directeur des Musées, wrote to Villot instructing him to go

to the Luxembourg and find a place to hang the *Liberty*, 'que depuis longtemps déjà nous avons ici' (Archives du Louvre, P 30, published in full by G. Lacambre in Cat. Exh. Paris, Detroit, New York 1974-5, p. 379). Villot replied by a letter of 28 May proposing to hang it in the place of a Blondel and below an Aligny (ibid., cited without reference by Adhémar, op. cit. *infra*, 1954, p. 91 and n.). Jeanron wrote again to Villot on 30 May, saying 'J'ai pris rendez-vous avec Mr Naigeon [Curator of Musée du Luxembourg] pour demain à 4 heures pour en finir avec le placement de la Liberté.' (Archives du Louvre, P30, published in full by G. Lacambre, loc. cit.). It is thus presumed to have hung in the Luxembourg for some months from the end of May 1849 until Jeanron ceased to be Directeur des Musées in 1850. Put in store again, it was released for the Exposition universelle of 1855 at Delacroix's request and with Napoleon III's permission (Dumas, quoted in Moreau-Nélaton I. 119 f.; and letter of 11 April 1855 from Count de Nieuwerkerke instructing that it be taken to the Tuileries for the Emperor's approval—Archives du Louvre, P30, cited by Lacambre, loc. cit.); returned to storage after the exhibition; shown at the Luxembourg 1861-74 (Lacambre, loc. cit., p. 380) before entering the Louvre.

² The 5th supplement of the Cat. Exh. Luxembourg, Paris 1830, lists 'Une barricade' by Delacroix under no. 508, a title which could, it seems, refer only to the *Liberty*, which is called exactly that in a letter of 12 October 1830 from Delacroix to his brother (see main entry). The exhibition, organized for the benefit of those wounded in the July Revolution, opened on 14 October (Adhémar, op. cit. *infra*, 1954, p. 87), and the *Liberty* was all but finished on 6 December 1830 (*Correspondance* I. 262). Therefore it may be assumed that Delacroix intended to show his picture there at a late stage. But in the event he must have withheld it from the public until the Salon, otherwise *L'Artiste* (I. 146) would not have announced a week before the Salon: 'M. Delacroix nous montrera une *Scène de barricades de juillet*, qui jouit parmi les artistes d'une réputation à laquelle la sanction du public ne manquera sans doute pas.'

³ For a brief and witty summary of the activities of other artists and writers during the July Revolution, see H. Adhémar (op. cit., 1954), p. 86.

⁴ L. Johnson, 'Eugène Delacroix and Charles de Verninac: an Unpublished Portrait and New Letters', *Burl Mag*, CX (1968), p. 517.

⁵ From no point of view could the towers of Notre-Dame be seen in reality as they are in the painting. Disregarding height, the relationship between the two towers corresponds with a viewpoint taken slightly to the west of the place de l'Hôtel de Ville, but from that point part of the west face of the north tower is visible, as it is not in the painting. Thus Delacroix shows the north tower from a position approximately in line with the façade of the present Hôtel de Ville. At that point the real south tower is hidden by the north tower. (See also Hamilton, op. cit. *supra*, 1954, for a discussion of the view of Notre Dame in relation to the action; and Study no. 22 below.)

⁶ The colours ordered were: '4 vessies de bitume, 4 de terre de Cassel, 2 de jaune de Naples, 1 de laque jaune, 2 de Cobalt.' Of these five, only two correspond to the eight noted on Study 8 below.

⁷ According to Robaut (No. 1558), twenty-one were bought by Moufflard and ten by Arosa. Burty Ann ED notes, however, that Arosa bought twenty-one at the posthumous sale. This is probably right: the group of seventeen studies listed below, in a French private collection, all from the posthumous sale, come from Arosa through Dr. Suchet, from whom they were acquired by M. de Launay in 1896 (cf. M. and A. Sérullaz, op. cit., 1971, p. 60); Arosa is likely therefore to have bought more than ten studies at the posthumous sale.

145 MIRABEAU CONFRONTS   Pl. 128
THE MARQUIS DE DREUX-BRÉZÉ,
preliminary sketch

$26\frac{7}{8} \times 32\frac{3}{16}$ in. (68.2 × 81.7 cm)* E.D.

R359 (1831. No repr.)

1830/1

Musée du Louvre

Provenance: Delacroix's posthumous sale, Feb. 1864, lot 141 (without dimensions), to Jadin, 200 fr.; Denys-Cochin, after

1885 to 1915; Dr. G. Viau, March 1916, d. c. 1942; Société des Amis de Delacroix (by his bequest ?); acquired by the Louvre (RF1953-41), 1953.

Exhibitions: *EBA*, Paris 1885, no. 120 (with the dimensions listed by Robaut for the Copenhagen sketch (J146): 78 × 92 cm. Lent by Emmanuel Jadin and provenance from the posthumous sale noted); Louvre 1930, no. 58, repr. *Album*, p. 32; Petit Palais, Paris 1936, no. 235; Atelier Delacroix, Paris 1938, no. 14; id., Paris 1939, no. 62; id., Paris 1946A and B, no. 50; id., Paris 1947, no. 8; id., Paris 1948, no. 101; id., Paris 1949, no. 123; id., Paris 1950, no. 102; id., Paris 1951, no. 120; id., Paris 1952, no. 73; Louvre 1963, no. 144, *M* no. 145, repr.; Kyoto-Tokyo 1969, H-10, repr.; Atelier Delacroix, Paris 1969-70 (no cat.); id., Paris 1971 (no cat.); id., Paris 1973 (no cat.).

Literature: *Journal* III. 216 and n.; Meier-Graefe 1922, p. 44 n. 1; Hourticq 1930, pl. 35; L. Venturi, 'Delacroix', *L'Arte*, N.S. II (1931), p. 59, repr. fig. 3; H. Rostrup, op. cit. 1931 under J146, p. 163, repr. fig. 6; *Correspondance* I. 265 n. 2; Rudrauf, p. 39; Sterling-Adhémar, no. 676, pl. 239.

A rapid sketch which establishes the basic design of the more finished competition sketch (J146). The most significant difference in content from the final version is the inclusion of soldiers clearing the tribunes in the right background, a detail noted on the first sheet of studies for the *Mirabeau* in the Louvre sketch-book RF9148, fol. 1ʳ: 'Soldats fesant evacuer les tribunes'.

Venturi (op. cit., 1931) found the final sketch pedantic and inexpressive by contrast with the vitality of this first version, but it is hard to see how such spontaneity could have been preserved in a picture where, given its subject and purpose, details of costume and architecture had to be elaborated and heads of historical figures made clearly recognizable. Indeed, Delacroix may well have employed an expert perspectivist to draw the precisely delineated architecture, as he is known to have done in some other pictures. Rostrup (op. cit., 1931) and Rudrauf (p. 39) have already commented on the superficiality of Venturi's judgement.

146 MIRABEAU CONFRONTS   Pl. 129
THE MARQUIS DE DREUX-BRÉZÉ,
final sketch

Wood panel, 30⅝₁₆ × 39¾ in. (0.77 × 1.01 m)
Signed and dated bottom right: *Eug. Delacroix 1831*
R360 and correction p. 484
Ny Carlsberg Glyptotek, Copenhagen

Provenance: Bouruet-Aubertot, by 1860; his posthumous sale (anon.) 22 Feb. 1869, lot 6, to a member of the family, 22,100 fr.; M. Bouruet-Aubertot, his son, d. 1882; with Georges Petit, 1884 (R Ann); Mme H. Bouruet-Aubertot, previous owner's widow ?, by 1885 to at least 1889; Hector

Brame, by 1910; bought for the Ny Carlsberg Glyptotek (I.N. 1751), Copenhagen, 1914.

Exhibitions: Shown with the other sketches entered for the competition, Ecole des Beaux-Arts, Paris, Feb. 1831; *Bd Italiens*, Paris 1860, no. 164; *Bd Italiens*, Paris 1864, no. 128; Society of French Artists 1, London 1870-1, no. 60, rearranged Feb. 1871, no. 144; London 1871, no. 1196; Durand-Ruel, Paris 1878, *h.c.*; *EBA*, Paris 1885, no. 160; *Centennale*, Paris 1889, no. 252; exhibited at the Durand-Ruel Gallery, Paris, May 1893 (R Ann), for sale ?; Cassirer, Berlin 1907, no. 13 (in the trade); Petit, Paris 1910, no. 79; Copenhagen 1914, no. 75, repr.; Copenhagen 1928, no. 173; *Louvre* 1930, no. 59, repr. *Album*, p. 33; Copenhagen 1945, no. 70.

Literature: Anon., 'Les Trente-Deux Mirabeau', *Figaro*, 9 Feb. 1831; anon., 'Mirabeau à l'Ecole des Beaux-Arts', *L'Artiste*, I (1831), p. 5; *Correspondance* I. 265 and n., 270 n. 1; Silvestre *Delacroix* (1855), p. 81; Z. Astruc, *Beaux-Arts. Le Salon intime. Exposition au boulevard des Italiens* (Poulet-Malassis, Paris, 1860), pp. 39 f.; P. de Saint-Victor, 'Eugène Delacroix', *La Presse*, 4 Sept. 1863; A. Cantaloube, *Eugène Delacroix, l'homme et l'artiste* (Dentu, Paris, 1864), pp. 54 f.; Piron, p. 107; Moreau-Nélaton I. 116, repr. fig. 86, II. 194; Escholier I. 277, repr. opp. p. 280; C. Mauclair, 'Delacroix', *L'Art et les Artistes*, N.S. XVIII (1929), repr. p. 152; anon. [C. Petersen], *Franske malerier i Ny Carlsberg Glyptotek* (Lunos, Copenhagen, 1929), p. 13, repr.; Hourticq 1930, pl. 35; L. Swane, *Fransk malerkunst fra David til Courbet* (Gad, Copenhagen, 1930), p. 33; L. Venturi, 'Delacroix', *L'Arte*, N.S. II (1931), p. 59, repr. fig. 4; H. Rostrup, 'Delacroix og hans Arbejder i Danske Samlinger', *Kunstmuseets Aarsskrift*, XVI-XVIII (1929-31). Copenhagen, 1931), pp. 163-7, repr. fig. 7; Rudrauf, pp. 39, 43; *Journal* II. 283 n. 1, III. 264 n. 1; H. Rostrup, *Ny Carlsberg Glyptotek, Danske og franske malerier og tegninger* (Copenhagen, 1961), p. 36, no. 885; J. Sloane, *Paul Marc Joseph Chenavard* (University of North Carolina Press, Chapel Hill, 1962), p. 184; Huyghe, pp. 201 f., 254, 256, 293, repr. pl. 183; Trapp, pp. 55, 104, 107-10, repr. fig. 56.

In the *Moniteur universel* of 30 September 1830, Guizot, Minister of the Interior, announced a competition for three paintings to decorate the wall behind the rostrum in the new Chamber of Deputies, then under construction in the Palais Bourbon, and stated the conditions: the first and largest picture, to fill the central place on the wall, was to represent *la séance royale du 9 août 1830, où le Roi Louis-Philippe Iᵉʳ prête serment à la Charte constitutionnelle*; the second, to be placed on the left, *la séance de l'Assemblée constituante du 23 juin 1789, au moment où Mirabeau répond au maître des cérémonies qui presse l'assemblée de se séparer*: 'Allez dire à votre maître que nous sommes ici par l'ordre du peuple, et que nous n'en sortirons que par la puissance des bayonnettes'; and

Fig. 18. *The Chamber of Deputies, Paris.*

the third, to go on the right as a pendant to the *Mirabeau*, *Boissy d'Anglas, président de la Convention nationale, saluant la tête du député Féraud, que les révoltés du Ier prairial an 4, lui présentent en le menaçant* (see Fig. 18). The size of the final side paintings was to be 4.71 × 6.17 m and the payment 20,000 fr. each. The oil sketches submitted to the competition were required to be at least one sixth of the size of the final paintings. Delacroix chose to compete only for the *Mirabeau* and the *Boissy d'Anglas*. The closing date of the competition for the former, as stated in Guizot's decree, was 1 February 1831, and for the latter 1 April 1831. Delacroix's name headed a list of some twenty artists who signed an unsuccessful appeal to the Minister for an extension of the

second deadline because they had to finish work for the Salon (Archives nationales, F²¹ 584, no. 139). The final judgement of the *Mirabeau* sketches was made on 6 March 1831, by a jury which included Delacroix's master Guérin, Gros and Ingres; Hesse won the commission (*Moniteur universel*, 15 February and 7 March 1831). In the preliminary selection of sketches for the *Boissy d'Anglas*, Vinchon and Court headed a list of thirteen, Delacroix came eleventh; on 22 April 1831, the final choice was made and Vinchon won (*Journal des Débats*, 26 April 1831). Coutan won the competition for the *Oath of Louis-Philippe*. He died in 1837, leaving it unfinished, and Court was commissioned to complete it, receiving the final payment in September

1838 (Archives nationales, F²¹ 584, no. 285). In spite of the impression created by Joly's cross-section of the Chamber (Fig. 18), it was the only one of the three paintings to be hung in the position it was intended for (cf. Archives nationales, F²¹ 584, no. 394 and 401). It was probably removed in 1848 and is now on deposit at Versailles. Hesse received the final payment for his *Mirabeau* in April 1838 (Archives nationales, F²¹ 584, no. 173); his painting is now in the Musée de Picardie, Amiens. Vinchon's *Boissy d'Anglas* was finished by December 1834 (Archives nationales, F²¹ 584, no. 308); it is apparently the picture which now hangs in the Town Hall of Annonay (Ardèche), the town which in 1789 had elected Boissy d'Anglas as deputy to the States-General. Thus, in terms of winning a permanent place in the Palais Bourbon, Delacroix did better to get commissions later to decorate the Salon du Roi and Library than to win the competitions.

It was the policy of Louis-Philippe, following the downfall of Charles X's Ultra royalist régime in July 1830, to promote belief in his desire to respect the constitutional ideals of the French revolution, and it is within this context that the choice of subjects for the competition must be seen. Guizot, in presenting his programme, dated 25 September 1830, to the King for approval, elucidates the political significance of the choice of Mirabeau and Boissy d'Anglas as subjects: 'La résistance au despotisme et la résistance à la sédition déterminent les limites des devoirs d'un député' (Archives nationales, F²¹ 584, no. 166). By the time the final paintings were completed, however, it was clear that Louis-Philippe's régime was much less liberal than had been hoped and insurrections of workers had been suppressed with a ruthlessness that brought discredit to the government. It may well be that in the circumstances it was judged impolitic to install these examples of despotism challenged and insurrection defied in the French legislature.

Though the competitions were democratically organized, there was widespread dissatisfaction with the outcome in progressive artistic circles and it was generally felt that the best artists had not won. Gustave Planche, for example, protested that the three winning compositions would result in three final paintings that were 'décrépites et chétives, irréprochables sous tous les rapports, mais détestables' (*Salon de 1831*, p. 200). Delacroix, at the invitation of the editor, wrote a long letter, dated 1 March 1831, to *L'Artiste*, deploring the system of public competitions as favouring mediocrity, and pleading the case for direct commissions (*L'Artiste*, 1, pp. 49 ff.; *Correspondance* 1. 268 ff.). Edouard Bertin made an official report in April 1831 and arrived at similar conclusions (quoted in Rosenthal, op. cit., 1914 (under J147 *Literature*), p. 7 n. 2).

Mirabeau's protest to Dreux-Brézé occurred on the morning of 23 June 1789 in the Salle des Menus Plaisirs at Versailles, where the States-General assembled. The King had retired, and most of the nobles and some of the clergy withdrawn, when the Grand Master of the Ceremonies came forward and asked the assembly to disperse, thus provoking the defiance of the deputies of the Third Estate expressed in the words attributed to Mirabeau.

Delacroix's treatment of the subject attracted little comment in France in the nineteenth century, and scarcely more in the first half of the twentieth. The fullest analysis during the artist's lifetime was written by Astruc (op. cit., 1860), who admired the conception of Dreux-Brézé, 'Pauvre marquis! pauvre gazelle! que vient-elle faire dans cet antre des lions?', and saw the red pattern of the carpet as a portent of the blood that was to be shed during the Revolution. Characterizing the picture as a 'chef d'œuvre de couleur, de simplicité, de vie dramatique', he concluded: 'Je désire attirer votre attention sur la lumière générale, la galerie couverte à colonnes grises, le tapis, les velours, les tentures bleues du fond. Le dessin est d'un style, d'une pureté rare [. . .] Voyez le naturel des gestes, la vivacité des groupes — dans ce sentiment historique qui les ordonne.'

In the present century, Escholier has appreciated Delacroix's skill in characterizing the conflict between two totally different worlds, through the contrast and gap between the energetic Mirabeau and his exquisite antagonist—an arrangement most deliberately selected by the artist for reasons elucidated in his acute criticism of his friend Chenavard's sketch for the same competition (repr. Sloane, op. cit., 1962, fig. 30): 'la venue de M. de Brézé n'a peut-être pas été annoncée de manière à trouver l'Assemblée réunie en un seul groupe pour le recevoir et en quelque sorte pour lui faire tête; mais le peintre ne peut exprimer autrement cette idée de résistance: l'isolement du personnage de Brézé est indispensable' (*Journal* II. 284).

The most serious twentieth-century study of the picture is by Rostrup (op. cit., 1931), who establishes Helman's engraving after Charles Monet's drawing, *Ouverture des Etats Généraux à Versailles le 5 mai 1789*, as the most probable source for Delacroix's setting; identifies the figure with the long face just behind Mirabeau as Bailly, who administers the oath in David's *Serment du Jeu de Paume*; and suggests that Vachez's *Tableaux historiques de la Révolution française* may have been consulted for Mirabeau's features. It may be added that the forceful gesture of Mirabeau appears to derive from that of Cromwell, another famous anti-monarchist, in Hall's engraving of 1789 after Benjamin West's *Cromwell dissolving the Long Parliament* (Fig. 19). The pose of the figure leaning steeply to the left in the background of Delacroix's picture seems also to have been suggested by the Speaker in the print. It is known from notes on the sheet of studies in the Sérullaz collection that Delacroix wished to consult engravings of West in connection with the *Mirabeau* (see below).

Huyghe's attempt (pp. 201 f.) to see an inherent conflict between Delacroix's classical education and romantic temperament in the contrast between his *Mirabeau* and *Boissy d'Anglas* would be more convincing if the subjects—the controlled defiance of rational men in contrast to mob violence—did not in themselves impose quite different treatment, and if they had been freely chosen by Delacroix instead of being set by the government.

Though Delacroix did not win the competition and the winning design was never installed in the Chamber, the subject was not to be excluded forever from the Palais Bourbon; for the same scene was treated by Dalou in a bronze bas-relief, the plaster model of which was shown at the Salon of 1883, and set into a wall in the Salle Casimir-Périer where it remains to this day. Robaut records that he and a number of artists thought that the Dalou had been influenced by Delacroix's picture.

Fourteen sheets of studies identified as for the *Mirabeau* passed to Boissier for 19 fr. in Delacroix's posthumous sale (lot 322. R1562). Most of these have not been traced. One of

them, in the Sérullaz collection, Paris, is of particular interest in revealing the kind of sources Delacroix turned to in preparing his picture, as he notes on it: 'emprunter des gravures de Trumbull et de West / Moreau le jeune / portraits de Reynolds chez Dittmer / demander à Mlle Sophie des caricatures anglaises — id. à la bibliothèque / lithographies de Traviès à Feuillet / Moreau le jeune' (*Mémorial*, no. 146, repr.). Delacroix may have looked at Moreau le jeune's *Réception de Mirabeau aux Champs-Elysées* and his prints of the *National Assembly* and *Opening of the States-General*, both showing the interior of the Salle des Menus Plaisirs, and with smooth columns instead of the fluted ones in the Helman engraving to which Delacroix was primarily indebted for the setting.

In addition, there are six sheets of pencil drawings of figures from the period of the Revolution, including studies for the heads of Mirabeau and Bailly, contained in the Louvre sketch-book RF9148, fols. 1^r, 2^r, 3^r, 4^v, 5^r, 6^r (Mirabeau, repr. *Mémorial*, no. 147, Huyghe, fig. 184).

Fig. 19. *Cromwell*, J. Hall after Benjamin West.

147 BOISSY D'ANGLAS AT THE   Pl. 130
NATIONAL CONVENTION, sketch

$31\frac{1}{8} \times 40\frac{15}{16}$ in. (0.79 × 1.04 m)
Signed and dated bottom left: *Eug. Delacroix 1831*
Moreau p. 190. R353 and Additions p. 484
Musée des Beaux-Arts, Bordeaux

Provenance: Bouruet-Aubertot, probably after spring 1855
(cf. *Correspondance* III. 255) and certainly by 1860, d. 1869;
Amédée Larrieu, Bordeaux, had bought it for 35,000 fr. by
May 1869[1] (asking 50,000 fr. for it in 1878—R Ann); John
Saulnier, Bordeaux, by 1885; his sale 5 June 1886, lot 34
(repr., heliograph of Sirouy's lithograph), to the city of
Bordeaux for the Musée des Beaux-Arts, 40,000 fr.

Exhibitions: Shown with the other sketches entered for the
competition, Ecole des Beaux-Arts, Paris, Apr. 1831;
Universelle, Paris 1855, no. 2925; *Bd Italiens*, Paris 1860,
Supp., no. 344; *Bd Italiens*, Paris 1864, no. 126; *Soc. Amis
des Arts*, Bordeaux 1869, no. 642; Durand-Ruel, Paris 1878,
no. 149; *EBA*, Paris 1885, no. 196; Paris 1886, no. 75;
Centennale, Paris 1889, no. 260; Louvre 1930, no. 57 (Smith
College version (J(R)42) repr. by error, *Album*, p. 34); Petit
Palais, Paris 1936, no. 236; Paris 1937, no. 317; London
1959, no. 116; Louvre 1963, no. 141, *M* no. 142, repr.;
Berne 1963-4, no. 32; Bremen 1964, no. 30; Edinburgh-
London 1964, no. 24 (Edinburgh only); Kyoto–Tokyo 1969,
H-11, repr. in colour; Atelier Delacroix, Paris 1971 (no cat.).

Literature: *Journal* I. 424 and n.; *Correspondance* I. 270 n. 1,
408, III. 255 and n.; anon., 'Boissy d'Anglas. Concours',
L'Artiste, I (1831), p. 122; L. Boulanger, 'Un des cinquante
Boissy d'Anglas', ibid. 123; D. [Delécluze], 'Concours pour
le troisième tableau destiné à orner la Chambre des
Députés', *Journal des Débats*, 19 Apr. 1831; G. Planche,
Salon de 1831 (Imp. Pinard, Paris, 1831), p. 200; P. Petroz,
'Exposition universelle des Beaux-Arts', *La Presse*, 5 June
1855; P. Mantz, review of id., *Revue française*, II (1855),
p. 174; M. Du Camp, *Les Beaux-Arts à l'Exposition
universelle de 1855* (Libr. nouvelle, Paris, 1855), pp. 110 f.; E.
Gebauer, same title (Libr. Napoléonienne, Paris, 1855),
p. 35; E. Loudun [Alph. Balleyguier], *Exposition universelle
de 1855* (Ledoyen, Paris, 1855), p. 115; Silvestre *Delacroix*
(1855), p. 81; T. Silvestre, *Les Artistes français* (Paris, 1855),
Crès ed. (Paris, 1926), I, pp. 26 f.; C. Vignon, *Exposition
universelle de 1855* (Fontaine, Paris, 1855), p. 204; A. de la
Forge, *La Peinture contemporaine en France* (Amyot, Paris,
1856, p. 51); T. Gautier, review of replenished exhibition
Bd Italiens, Paris 1860, *Moniteur universel*, 5 May 1860; Z.
Astruc, *Beaux-Arts. Le Salon intime. Exposition au boulevard
des Italiens* (Poulet-Malassis, Paris, 1860), pp. 43, 45 f.; P.
de Saint-Victor, 'Eugène Delacroix', *La Presse*, 4 Sept.
1863; A. Cantaloube, *Eugène Delacroix, l'homme et l'artiste*
(Dentu, Paris, 1864), p. 54; L. Chardin, 'Retour à Eugène
Delacroix', *L'Artiste*, 7th ser. II (1864), p. 149; Piron,

p. 107; P. Proudhon, *Du principe de l'art et de sa destination
sociale* (Garnier, Paris, 1865), pp. 128 f.; P. Burty,
'Exposition de la Société des Amis des Arts de Bordeaux',
GBA, 2nd per., 5th livraison (May 1869), pp. 421 f. and n.;
L. Ulbach, *Misères et grandeurs littéraires* (Calmann Lévy,
Paris, 1885), p. 269, E. Vallet, *Catalogue des tableaux . . . du
Musée de Bordeaux* (Imp. Gounouilhou, Bordeaux, 1894),
pp. 151 f., no. 499; L. Rosenthal, *Du romantisme au réalisme*
(Laurens, Paris, 1914), p. 7; Moreau-Nélaton I. 116, 163,
repr. fig. 87, II. 156, 194; Meier-Graefe 1922, p. 44 and n.;
Escholier I. 277-80, repr. p. 278; Cassou 1947, pl. 11, full-
page detail of right half opp. p.; Johnson 1963, p. 49, repr.
pl. 22; Huyghe, pp. 187, 188, 192, 198, 201, 202, 254, 256,
269, 293, 455, repr. in colour pl. XVI; Maltese, pp. 17, 37,
153, 154, repr. pl. 28; Trapp, pp. 55, 104-7, 109, 173, 346,
repr. fig. 54.

Prints: Etching by Bracquemond (Salon 1881. Repr.
Escholier I. 279). Lithograph by Sirouy, 1883.

Copy: Canvas by Pierre Andrieu (?), 40.7 × 54.2 cm. Smith
College Museum of Art (J(R)42).

For details of the competition for which this sketch was
entered, see J146.

About four o'clock in the afternoon of 20 May 1795, a mob
broke into the National Convention in the Tuileries and
began to threaten Boissy d'Anglas (1756-1826), who was in
the chair. A young deputy, Jean Féraud, who intervened to
protect him, was shot, then decapitated and his head thrust
on a pike before Boissy d'Anglas, who bowed to it and
refused to be intimidated. For several hours the crowd
continued to shout for 'bread and the Constitution', while
many of the Moderate deputies made good their escape.
About nine o'clock, Boissy d'Anglas resigned the chair to
Vernier, and by midnight, with the arrival of reinforce-
ments, the rabble had been driven from the hall. In addition
to being a famous episode of the French Revolution, the
incident may have held a particular personal interest for
Delacroix, since he had been a schoolfriend of the son of
J. B. Louvet de Couvrai, who delivered the oration at
Féraud's funeral (*Correspondance* I. 7).

A more violent scene than the *Mirabeau* and in a style
regarded as more characteristic of Delacroix's genius, the
Boissy d'Anglas has always excited greater attention from the
critics than its pendant. Before the competition sketches
were judged, Louis Boulanger (op. cit., 1831) rushed
impetuously to its support: 'Mon peintre, c'est Delacroix
[. . .]. Tout cela vit, tout cela se meut, se tord et accélère le
mouvement du sang dans vos artères. [. . .] C'est l'accent de
la nature saisi dans ce qu'il a de plus inattendu'. In 1855,
Petroz (op. cit.) proclaimed: 'Le Boissy d'Anglas [. . .] est
une esquisse qui par sa verve, peut être mise à côté de ses
meilleurs petits tableaux. [. . .] Les figures sont largement
indiquées, groupées avec adresse, les touches confuses de

près, prennent, vues à distance, une forme appréciable et deviennent des corps noyés dans une atmosphère chaude et poudreuse.' And in a climax of romantic appreciation Silvestre wrote in the same year (op. cit.):

Le peuple s'engouffre comme un fleuve colère dans l'enceinte de la Convention nationale. Murailles, escaliers, galeries, craquent et chancellent; ouvriers, clubistes, guenillards, montent les uns sur les autres en se cassant les membres; les représentants restent immobiles; [. . .] les tricoteuses penchées du haut des tribunes éclatent en tonnerres d'applaudissements. Un jour rare glisse péniblement dans la salle par-dessus les têtes qui foisonnent; la poussière soulevée par les trépignements vole en tourbillons dans cette atmosphère orageuse, traversée par l'éclair livide des baïonnettes.

The romantic encomiums may seem unduly effusive, but, on considering the unity and power of Delacroix's conception of one man standing firm against a wave of violence in contrast to Vinchon's crude insistence on a multiplicity of genre details in his large canvas at Annonay, one can only echo Gautier's regret that it was never realized on a larger scale and feel with him (op. cit.): 'Quel magnifique tableau eût fait cette esquisse.'

A reaction came with Proudhon (op. cit., 1865), the social reformer and champion of Courbet's realism, who, while admiring the energy of Delacroix's sketch, criticized it for failing to show any sympathy for the insurgents. '[C'est] que si, dans cette déplorable journée, la légalité fut pour la Convention, on ne peut pas dire que le droit était contre le peuple; que les députés qui appuyaient l'émeute étaient d'aussi honnêtes gens, pour le moins, que le député conservateur Féraud; et que les quatre têtes que fit tomber, à quelques jours de là, la guillotine des modérés, payèrent au quadruple celle qu'avait tranchée l'aveugle colère de la masse. Voilà ce qu'il était du devoir de l'artiste de comprendre et de faire sentir.'

Sixteen sheets of drawings identified as for the *Boissy d'Anglas* passed to Moufflard for 11 fr. in Delacroix's posthumous sale (lot 323. R1563). One of these may have been the drawing of the empty Convention Hall preserved in the Musée Carnavalet (*Mémorial*, no. 144, repr.). The view is reversed in the oil sketch, in order no doubt to direct the main lines of the composition from right to left, towards the centre of the wall for which it was designed.

The picture has suffered severe damage from bitumen, particularly in the left background, and much detail has been lost which appears in Bracquemond's etching. Robaut noted that it already seemed to him more 'craquelé' when he saw it at Bordeaux in 1887 than in the Saulnier sale of the previous year. It has been restored at least twice in the past fifty years.

¹ P. Burty (op. cit. *infra*, 1869, p. 421 n. 1): 'Elle a été récemment payée 35.000 francs par M. Amédée Larrieu. Elle appartenait à M. Bouruet-Aubertot.'

148 INTERIOR OF A DOMINICAN CONVENT IN MADRID   Pl. 131

$51\frac{1}{4} \times 64\frac{1}{8}$ in. (1.30×1.63 m)
Signed and dated bottom centre: *EUG. DELACROIX 1831*
Moreau pp. 174, 255. R351 and Additions p. 484
Philadelphia Museum of Art (W. P. Wilstach Collection)

Provenance: Duc d'Orléans, by Jan. 1836 (*Correspondance* I. 408);¹ sale Duchesse d'Orléans, 18 Jan. 1853, lot 18 ('Intérieur d'un couvent. L'amende honorable.'), 3,105 fr.; Van Isacker; his sale, 24 Apr. 1857, lot 14 (same title), to A. Bouruet-Aubertot, 5,450 fr.; in his possession to at least 1864 and possibly to his death in 1869;² bought by Brame (R Ann) for 10,000 fr. (*Mémorial*); Edwards; his sale, 7 March 1870, lot 3 ('L'Amende honorable.' Photo repr.), apparently bought in or sold to a member of the family,³ 47,000 fr.; with Durand-Ruel, Paris, by 1872; James Duncan of Benmore, by 1885; his sale (Duncan, de Londres), 15 Apr. 1889 (Paris), lot 10 ('Intérieur d'un couvent de dominicains à Madrid ou: L'Amende honorable.' Photo repr.), to Durand-Ruel (Arch D-R, no. 2331), 35,000 fr. (R Ann); purchased for the Wilstach Collection, Philadelphia, in June 1894, after the deaths of Mr. (1870) and Mrs. W. P. Wilstach (*c.* 1893), founders of the collection, from funds bequeathed by Mrs. Wilstach for further acquisitions.

Exhibitions: Salon 1834, no. 495 ('Intérieur d'un couvent de Dominicains, à Madrid. Un jeune homme d'une grande famille, forcé de faire des voeux, est conduit devant l'évêque, qui visite le couvent, et accablé de mauvais traitements en sa présence. (Sujet tiré de *Melmoth*, roman anglais)'.); Gal. Beaux-Arts, Paris 1846B, no. 20 ('Prise d'habit chez les Dominicains.'); Bd Italiens, Paris 1860, Supp., no. 343 ('L'Amende honorable.'); Bd Italiens, Paris 1864, no. 132 (same title); London 1871, no. 1194 (same title); EBA, Paris 1885, no. 74 (same title); Durand-Ruel, New York 1887; included in special exhibition, Philadelphia Museum of Art, March–Apr. 1937 (no cat.); Louvre 1963, no. 199, repr.; Edinburgh–London 1964, no. 23, repr.

Literature: D. [E. J. Delécluze], 'Salon de 1834', *Journal des Débats*, 8 March 1834; B. H. [Hauréau], 'Salon de 1834', *La Tribune politique et littéraire*, 15 March 1834; A. T. [Tardieu], 'Salon de 1834', *Le Courrier français*, 30 March 1834; G. Planche, 'Histoire et philosophie de l'art. IV. De l'école française au Salon de 1834', *Revue des Deux Mondes*, 3rd ser. II (1 Apr. 1834), pp. 57 f.; Ch. L. [Lenormant], 'Salon de 1834', *Le Temps*, 11 April 1834; W., 'Salon de 1834', *Le Constitutionnel*, 11 Apr. 1834; T. Gautier, 'Salon de 1834', *La France industrielle*, I, no. 1 (Apr. 1834), p. 19; Alexandre D. [Decamps], *Le Musée, Revue du Salon de 1834* (Ledoux, Paris, 1834), pp. 59 f.; H. Sazerac, *Lettres sur le Salon de 1834* (Delaunay, Paris, 1834), p. 141; A. D. Vergnaud, *Examen du Salon de 1834* (Delaunay et Roret,

Paris, 1834), p. 15; Clément de Ris, 'Exposition de la Société des Artistes', *L'Artiste*, 4th ser. VIII (1847), p. 173; A. de Montaiglon, 'Exposition annuelle de l'Association des Artistes Peintres', *Le Moniteur des Arts*, 24 Jan. 1847, p. 201 (reprinted in *Articles publiés dans le Moniteur des Arts du 13 décembre 1846 au 31 janvier 1847* (Imp. Dondey-Dupré, Paris, 1847), p. 68); Silvestre *Delacroix* (1855), p. 81; T. Silvestre, *Les Artistes français*, 1855 (1926 ed. I, p. 29); T. Gautier, review of replenished exhibition *Bd Italiens*, Paris 1860, *Moniteur universel*, 5 May 1860; Z. Astruc, *Beaux-Arts. Le Salon intime. Exposition au boulevard des Italiens* (Poulet-Malassis, Paris, 1860), pp. 43, 44; A. Cantaloube, *Eugène Delacroix, l'homme et l'artiste* (Dentu, Paris, 1864), p. 26; Piron, p. 107; H. Houssaye, 'L'Exposition des œuvres d'Eugène Delacroix à l'Ecole des Beaux-Arts', *Revue des Deux Mondes*, LXVIII (1885), p. 668; G. Dubosc, 'Le Palais de Justice de Rouen dans l'œuvre d'Eugène Delacroix', *Journal de Rouen*, 7 Sept. 1902; A. Robaut, *L'Œuvre de Corot, catalogue raisonné et illustré, précédé de l'histoire de Corot et ses œuvres par Etienne Moreau-Nélaton* (Floury, Paris, 1905; reprint Laget, Paris, 1965), I. 266 f.; Moreau-Nélaton I. 125, 145 f., 149, 163, repr. fig. 115, II. 58, 114, 194; *Catalogue of the W. P. Wilstach Collection, Memorial Hall* (Commissioners of Fairmount Park, Philadelphia, 1922), pp. 37 f., no. 90; Meier-Graefe 1922, p. 44 n. 1; Escholier I. 262 f., 262 n. 2, II. 190, 192; *Correspondance* I. 294 n. 1 (Burty ed. 1880, I. 165 n. 1), II. 289 f., 290 n. 1, IV. 174 n. 2; *Philadelphia Museum of Art Bulletin*, XXXIII, no. 176 (Jan. 1938), repr. (no pagination); P. Durand-Ruel, 'Mémoires', in L. Venturi, *Les Archives de l'impressionnisme* (Durand-Ruel, Paris, New York, 1939), II, p. 218; *Journal* I. 68 n. 2, 193 nn. 3 and 4, III. 286 and n. 4, 375 and n. 8; E. Lambert, 'Delacroix et l'Espagne', *Revue des Arts*, I (1951), pp. 160 f.; L. Johnson, in Cat. Exh. Toronto-Ottawa 1962–3, under no. 5; Johnson 1963, pp. 39 ff., 121, repr. pl. 21; Huyghe, pp. 190, 279, 369, 378, repr. in colour pl. XXIII; Cat. Exh. Bremen 1964, p. 282; Maltese, pp. 37, 125, 153 f., repr. pl. 29; L. Johnson, 'Eugène Delacroix et les Salons. Documents inédits au Louvre', *Revue du Louvre*, 16 (1966), p. 222; Trapp, p. 115 and n. 27.

Print: Etching by Boilvin for the *Galerie Durand-Ruel*, 1873, pl. 37.

The scene is inspired by a passage in Charles Robert Maturin's *Melmoth the Wanderer* (I, pp. 281 ff., 1892 ed.), which was first published in London in 1820. A French translation appeared in 1821. The hero of this 'Gothic' tale, set in the late eighteenth and early nineteenth centuries, is the illegitimate son of the Duchess of Moncada, who when not yet thirteen years old is forced against his will to enter a convent in order to expiate his mother's sin, in spite of the fact that she has by now married the Duke who begat him. Of a rebellious spirit, he is savagely persecuted by the

brethren and at length, in the incident chosen by Delacroix, dragged, 'half driven mad, half-murdered', before the visiting Bishop and mistreated in his presence.

Delacroix departs from Maturin's text in several particulars. In the novel, the scene occurs in the church of a convent in Madrid. Delacroix makes no attempt to reconstruct an authentic Spanish setting, but instead bases his interior on the Gothic Hall of the Palais de Justice at Rouen. Maturin also refers to the religious as Jesuits, whereas Delacroix clothes his figures in Dominican habits, possibly because he felt that their contrasting tones offered richer pictorial effects than Jesuit robes. Finally, Delacroix shows the Bishop seated on a throne beneath a canopy; in the book, he stands at an altar with the Father Superior, and the hero is led to him up the steps of the altar.

On 30 September 1831, Delacroix wrote to Pierret from Valmont, saying: 'J'ai trouvé à Rouen de quoi faire un tableau qui m'inspire assez. Nous verrons cela cet hiver.' (*Correspondance* I. 294.) As first pointed out by Burty, in a footnote to this letter in his 1880 edition of the *Correspondance*, Delacroix was presumably referring to this picture, which was beginning to take shape in his mind as a result of seeing the Palais de Justice at Rouen. An unpublished drawing of the Hall by Delacroix must have been done at that time and have served as a study for the painting (private collection, Mehun-sur-Yevre, France). Delacroix had considered doing a series of drawings or prints from *Melmoth the Wanderer* as early as April 1824 (*Journal* I. 68), but this appears to be his first, and last, painting inspired by Maturin. He notes the subject, among several other religious themes, in a sketch-book used mainly, perhaps wholly, in 1831: 'l'espagnol condamné par l'eveque dans Melmoth' (Louvre RF9148, fol. 31ᵛ).

Some critics were puzzled at the Salon of 1834, and to a man they seem to have had no knowledge of the novel which had inspired the picture; nor did they recognize the source of the architectural setting. Vergnaud (op. cit., 1834) confessed: 'Je ne sais de quelle espèce de convention [classique ou romantique] peut être le no. 495, *Intérieur d'un couvent de Dominicains*.' Théophile Gautier (op. cit., 1834), more perceptive, recognized the affinity with Granet's dark interiors: '*Le couvent de Dominicains* à Madrid nous introduit dans un intérieur d'une telle beauté, que nous le mettons au-dessus de tout ce qu'a fait M. Granet, pour la gravité et la mélancolie de la couleur; puis ces figures sont autrement vivantes, autrement animées que les maquettes d'ébène et d'ivoire que M. Granet plante au milieu des murs, couleur d'encre, de ses souterrains et de ses églises.'

Gustave Planche (op. cit., 1834) found: 'Le ton des pierres et le détail des croisées sont d'une grande finesse. Les figures sont bien disposées, mais ne sont pas d'une exécution aussi avancée que l'église elle-même, ce qui est fâcheux; en outre elles sont placées trop bas sur la toile et disparaissent presque entièrement dans l'immense vaisseau de l'église'; and concluded astutely: 'très probablement les figures ont été ajoutées long-temps après l'achèvement de l'architecture.' Though the picture is dated 1831, it was not exhibited before 1834 and it is therefore quite possible that there was a considerable time-lag between the completion of the setting and the insertion of the figures. Criticism by Planche of the scale of the figures and, by others, of their distribution seems ill-considered, however. While the setting was obviously a major interest of the artist's for its own sake, the use of broad, empty intervals between the figures are as effective, in a different context, as in some ballet scenes by Degas; and the awesome height of the dimly lit vault in proportion to the figures aptly enhances the mood of the scene that is being acted out below.

It was not until 1964 that the painting in the centre background was shown to derive from Titian's *Assumption of the Virgin* in the Cathedral of Verona, through a copy in oils by Géricault owned by Delacroix (Cat. Exh. Bremen 1964, p. 282, with repr. of Géricault's copy, now in the Kunsthalle, Bremen).

Despite his enthusiasm in 1834, Gautier acknowledged his ignorance of the subject when he wrote of the picture again in 1860 (op. cit.), and at that time Delacroix wrote to him to say that it was 'bêtement, mais légendairement baptisé *l'Amende honorable*', and it was only necessary to open the Salon catalogue of 1834 to discover the proper title and source (*Correspondance* IV. 174 f.). The misnomer seems to have first occurred in print in 1853, in the catalogue of the Orléans sale, and has proved tenacious ever since.

Robaut (under R351 and op. cit., 1905) has recorded how on a visit with Corot to the Palais de Justice at Rouen in July 1872, the landscape painter was moved to recollect this picture:

Nous étions assis sur un des bancs qui font le tour de la salle des Pas-Perdus; [Corot] était là silencieux depuis un moment, les yeux levés sur les hautes voûtes en bois sculpté, quand tout à coup il s'écria: "Quel homme! quel homme!" Il revoyait dans sa pensée le tableau de l'Amende honorable que nous avions admiré ensemble quelques jours auparavant dans les galeries Durand-Ruel. Pour lui, la salle n'était rien, Delacroix était tout, quoique celui-ci n'eût fait que s'en inspirer comme fond à des personnages de Melmoth.

A small version (60.65 × 73.7 cm), with slight variations, is preserved in the Krannert Art Museum, University of Illinois, Urbana. It is apparently the 'répétition' of the Philadelphia version that Amédée Cantaloube (op. cit., 1864) mentions as being in Alfred Bruyas's 'cabinet' at Montpellier, but now seems to me to be a copy by a pupil, probably Pierre Andrieu who was in close touch with Bruyas after Delacroix's death. (For a reproduction and fuller account of the provenance of this copy, see Cat. Exh. Toronto-Ottawa, 1962-3, no. 5.).

[1] Moreau states (p. 174): 'Peint pour S.A.R. Mgr le Duc d'Orléans', but if that is correct it is curious that the Duke is not listed as the owner in the

catalogue of the Salon of 1834, as he is for the *Prisoner of Chillon* (no. 555). According to Piron, who does not name the first owner, the original purchase price was 1,200 fr.

[2] He lent it to the exhibition *Bd Italiens*, Paris 1864, and according to an annotation in a catalogue of the Edwards sale of 1870, which belonged to Moreau-Nélaton, it was in the Bouruet-Aubertot collection till 1869 (*BN Estampes*). It was not listed in the catalogue of Bouruet-Aubertot's posthumous sale of 22 Feb. 1869, and therefore appears to have been sold privately to Brame before the collector's death or shortly thereafter.

[3] It was listed as lent by 'Mr. C. Edwards' in the catalogue of the exhibition London 1871.

149 CHARLES V AT THE MONASTERY OF YUSTE   Pl. 132

$34\frac{5}{8} \times 45\frac{1}{4}$ in. (0.88 × 1.15 m)[1]
Signed and dated 1831, top right
Moreau p. 173. R354
Whereabouts unknown

Provenance: Count de Mornay, probably by 1833;[2] anon. sale (by Defer), including seven paintings by Delacroix in the Mornay collection, 18 Jan. 1850, lot 115 ('Charles-Quint sous l'habit de moine retiré au monastère de Saint-Juste', without dimensions), apparently withdrawn; his sale (M. le comte de M.), 29 March 1877, lot 1 ('*Charles-Quint au couvent de Saint-Just*. Il est de grandeur naturelle, vu à mi-corps, jouant de l'orgue; un jeune moine debout, à sa droite, l'écoute avec recueillement. Signé et daté 1831') to the Marquis de la Valette, 9,600 fr.

Exhibitions: Salon 1833, 1st Supp., no. 3003 ('L'empereur Charles Quint au monastère de St.-Just. Il essaie en touchant de l'orgue de se distraire de sa mélancolie et des souvenirs qui le rejettent malgré lui dans le passé.'); *Gal. Beaux-Arts*, Paris 1848, no. 25 (lent by Count de Mornay); Alsace-Lorraine, Paris 1874, no. 120 (lent anonymously. Dimensions listed as 0.87 × 1.15 m).

Literature: Anon., 'Salon de 1833', *Le Constitutionnel*, 15 Apr. 1833; Ch. L. [Lenormant], review of Salon of 1833, *Le Temps*, 23 Apr. 1833; E. Delécluze, id., *Journal des Débats*, 26 Apr. 1833; H. de Vielcastel, 'Salon de 1833. Charles-Quint, par Delacroix', *Bagatelle, Journal de France*, 2 May 1833, p. 313, pl. 31 (Delacroix's lithograph); A. Annet and H. Trianon, *Examen critique du Salon de 1833* (Delaunay, Paris, 1833), p. 98; T. Gautier, 'Salon de 1833', *France littéraire*, VI (1833), p. 159; A. Jal, *Les Causeries du Louvre* (Ch. Gosselin, Paris, 1833), pp. 76-80; P. de Saint-Victor, 'Exposition de tableaux au profit de la Caisse de secours de la Société des Artistes', *La Semaine*, 30 Jan. 1848, p. 407; Silvestre *Delacroix* (1855), p. 81; A. Dumas, *Causerie sur Eugène Delacroix*, lecture of 10 Dec. 1864, p. 98 of MS. in *BN Estampes* (see *Literature* for J112 and Tourneux p. 27 for further details); Moreau-Nélaton I. 140, 143, 163, Delacroix's lithograph repr. fig. 99; Escholier I, Delacroix's lithograph repr. p. 283, II. 186; *Correspondance* I. 408, II. 290 n. 1; *Journal* I. 49 n. 1, 306 n. 1, 332 n. 1; L. Johnson,

'Eugène Delacroix et les Salons. Documents inédits au Louvre', *Revue du Louvre*, 16 (1966), pp. 221, 229 n. 13.

Print: Lithograph, possibly reversed,[3] by Eugène Delacroix, 1833 (Moreau p. 48. R453. Delteil no. 92), reproduced here.

Delacroix sent few paintings to the Salon of 1833, in the year following his North African journey, and this was his only canvas that was not a portrait to be shown. Though rejected by 11 votes to 10 by the Salon jury at their meeting of 18 February (L. Johnson, op. cit., 1966), it was accepted later and received qualified praise from the critics. Théophile Gautier's comments, being his first published reference to Delacroix, are of particular interest: 'Quoiqu'il y ait de la mollesse dans l'exécution, et un certain affadissement dans la couleur, il règne dans cette toile une mélancolie admirable. La tête de Charles-Quint est d'une philosophie et d'une satiété étonnamment exprimée et sentie. Le jeune religieux est tout un poème.' The anonymous critic of *Le Constitutionnel*, attributing the picture's lack of success with the public to its 'harmonie modeste', its lack of warm and sparkling colour, found the conception admirable and thought Delacroix should have developed it on a 10 ft. canvas. He concluded: 'S'il avait donné à la tête fort expressive de Charles-Quint un peu plus de force de dessin, et à l'ensemble une plus grande chaleur de ton, l'ouvrage aurait eu un succès immense.'

Paul de Saint-Victor, impressed by the antithesis between this painting and the 1835 version of the *Combat of the Giaour and Hassan* (Petit Palais, Paris) when they were exhibited together in 1848, remarked: 'Le pinceau qui, tout à l'heure, montait dans le bruit et dans la flamme jusqu'à la plus haute note de la gamme, descend sans saccades, sans brusquerie, sans effort dans le pâle demi-jour de Lesueur.'

Writing towards the end of 1846 of the prospect of exhibiting it at a later date, Delacroix observed in a letter to Dauzats '[le *Charles-Quint*] est dans un état pitoyable et a besoin comme je vous ai dit d'une grande réparation.' (*Correspondance* II. 290.)

Delacroix is known to have painted two smaller versions of this subject: one, said by Moreau (p. 173 n. 1) to have been painted for Mme Boulanger in 1837, showed the young religious listening from outside at an open window (R654, 17 × 25 cm); the other, signed and dated 1839 and painted on paper laid down on panel according to Moreau (p. 173 n. 1), was a small replica of the Salon version and measured 12 × 17 cm (R695). In addition to these, Delacroix planned

in 1855 a '*Charles Quint faisant ses adieux à ses serviteurs en entrant au monastère de Saint-Juste*' (*Journal* II. 306), which seems never to have been realized.

In 1557, the year before his death at the age of fifty-eight, Charles V, having abdicated his thrones, retired to a little house attached to the monastery of Yuste in Estremadura. Though he did not lead the life of an ascetic or restrict his social life to contacts with the monks, the contrast between his life as the greatest potentate in Europe and his retirement was bound to capture the Romantic imagination. Delacroix does not record his attitude to the Emperor's retirement at Yuste in writing, but in 1853, long after this picture and its variants were painted, he did reflect on Charles V's qualities and take consolation from some of his human weaknesses after reading an article on this period of his life (*Journal* II. 48 f.). The first indication of his desire to paint this subject seems to be a note in a sketch-book used mainly, perhaps wholly, in 1831: 'Charles quint allant se faire moine' (Louvre RF9148, fol. 31ᵛ).

One of Alfred de Musset's earliest poems, 'Charles-Quint au monastère de Saint-Just', was published posthumously in 1859, thirty years after it was written, and may not have been known to Delacroix as early as 1831, but is worth citing as evidence of Romantic interest in Charles V's last days about the time when Delacroix painted his first picture on the theme.

[1] Moreau, followed by Robaut, gives the vertical dimension as 75 cm; but these dimensions, taken from the catalogue of the Mornay sale of 1877, are more consistent with those, including frame, listed in the Salon register of 1833 (1.20 × 1.46 m), and with the proportions of Delacroix's lithograph of the painting.

[2] The picture is said by Moreau, followed by Robaut, to have originally belonged to Mlle Mars and to have been bought at her sale, at an unspecified date, by Count de Mornay for 2,000 fr. Probably speculating on the basis of this information, Moreau-Nélaton (I. 140) claims Delacroix gave it to Mlle Mars on his return from North Africa in 1832. If so, she evidently owned it no longer in 1833 because it is listed in the Salon catalogue of that year as belonging to 'M. H . . . M . . .'. This was presumably Count de Mornay whose second name was Henri and who is recorded as the owner in January 1848. The actress Mlle Mars was Count de Mornay's mistress, and may at some time have had the picture in her possession, but the Count would appear to have been the original owner, unless Mlle Mars had a sale between 1831 and 1833. The only sale of a Mlle Mars listed in Lugt in the relevant period was held at Versailles on 7 May 1838, had no connection with the famous actress's property and included no pictures by Delacroix. According to Alexandre Dumas père (op. cit. *infra*, 1864), Mornay bought the picture and gave it to Mlle Mars.

[3] Robaut expressed uncertainty in R Ann about the correct way round for the composition of the painting, which, being unknown to him, he illustrated with this lithograph. The description in the catalogue of the Mornay sale of 1877, saying that Charles V plays while a young monk stands 'à sa droite', suggests that in the painting the monk may have been by the Emperor's right hand, not by his left as in the print.

Religious Paintings

150 CHRIST BROUGHT BEFORE CAIAPHAS

Pl. 133

11 × 13 in. (28 × 33 cm)
R16 (1818); probably also R1461
1818?
Whereabouts unknown

Provenance: Delacroix's posthumous sale, Feb. 1864, probably part of lot 150 ('Trois compositions datant de la jeunesse du maître', without dimensions), to Carvalho, 130 fr. (Burty Ann ED); sale Vicomte de Carvalhido (pseudonym of Carvalho?), 14 March 1870, lot 43, to Laisnez, 112 fr.; anon. sale, 21 March 1891, lot 16, to Bernheim-Jeune, 800 fr.; sold by them to Lippmann, Apr. 1893 (Arch B-J); bought back from him by Bernheim-Jeune, 4 Dec. 1895, and sold by them to Bessonneau of Angers, 14 Jan. 1897 (ibid.); repurchased from him, 19 Sept. 1901 and sold to Cognacq, 24 Apr. 1902 (ibid.); sale succession de M. B..., 30 May 1913, lot 56, 440 fr.; Henry Dewez, Geneva; mixed sale (including his pictures, listed as 'Property of a gentleman'), Sotheby's London, 11 Dec. 1957, lot 134, bought in at £280 and apparently sold privately before the owner's death in 1964.

Exhibitions: None.

Literature: Escholier I. 41 f.

Robaut dates this work to 1818 and lists it as an entry for a 'Concours d'esquisse' at the Ecole des Beaux-Arts, but the subject set for the annual oil sketch competition was not a biblical one in 1818, nor in any other year from 1816 to 1823 inclusive. So if this picture was painted for a competition, it could only have been for one arranged informally by a professor at the Ecole and no record exists of the subjects set by individual teachers. Nor is there other external evidence known that would help to date it firmly. In style, it is clearly a very immature work and plausibly listed in Robaut as the first religious subject treated by Delacroix.

The moment chosen is Peter's denial of Christ on the porch of the palace of the high priest Caiaphas. In 1849, Delacroix contemplated treating this subject again, but the project apparently came to naught (*Journal* I. 295).

Though conventional and cluttered in composition and weak in detail, this early attempt to integrate multiple figures into a dramatic group contains devices found later in some of Delacroix's most famous canvases, notably in the *Entry of the Crusaders into Constantinople* (Louvre. Salon 1841), with its main action set on a terrace above a landscape, its kneeling and gesticulating figures in the foreground directed towards a central group farther back, its spears rising against the sky and figures on one side ascending from the city.

151 THE VIRGIN OF THE HARVEST

Pl. 134

$49\frac{1}{4} \times 29\frac{1}{8}$ in. (1.25 × 0.74 m) Sight: * $48\frac{7}{16} \times 29$ in.
Signed and dated lower right: *EUG. DE LA CROIX./*
ANN ~ 1819 ~ /AET ~ 21 ~
Moreau p. 219. R25.
Church of Orcemont (Seine-et-Oise)

Provenance: Commissioned by an unknown patron for the village church of Orcemont at a price of 15 fr.

Exhibitions: EBA, Paris 1885, no. 180bis (h.c., R Ann and *Bib AA* MS. 298ter, no. 180bis); Louvre 1930, no. 3, repr. *Album*, p. 9; Louvre 1963, no. 3, repr.; Edinburgh-London 1964, no. 3.

Literature: Piron, pp. 55 f.; Moreau-Nélaton I. 32 f., repr. fig. 9, II. 245; Escholier I. 42, repr. opp. p. 32; *Journal* I. 474 n. 5; Huyghe, pp. 106, 109, 132, full-page repr. pl. 71; Maltese, pp. 20, 21, 22, 124, 143, repr. pl. 1; Trapp, pp. 16, 226, 233, 234, repr. fig. 10, p. 15.

This is Delacroix's first known commission. Piron reports the artist as saying: 'trompé dans mes prévisions, j'étais tenté de désespérer, lorsqu'un Mécène tombé du ciel vint me commander, pour l'église de son village près de Paris, une Vierge tenant l'enfant Jésus, sans compter saint Jean-Baptiste, et m'offrir 15 francs pour le tout. Vous jugez qu'ils furent acceptés.' Piron goes on: 'Delacroix, depuis, ne savait pas bien ce qu'était devenu ce tableau. Mais l'esquisse existait, et il ne nous la montrait pas sans une certaine émotion.' Moreau (p. 219 n. 1) adds: 'Ce Tableau fut exécuté par Delacroix spécialement pour l'église d'Orcemont, sur la demande d'un ami, chez lequel il se trouvait en villégiature pendant l'été de 1819, aux environs de Rambouillet, et donné par lui, la même année, à la Fabrique de cette modeste commune.' An unpublished letter to Moreau from the Curé of Orcemont, dated 30 January 1879, adds that the friend was an architect, who approached Delacroix after a former Mayor of Orcemont and Entrepreneur des bâtiments de la couronne complained that there was not even a picture of the Virgin in his church (Moreau N). The architect was perhaps Duponchel, who helped Delacroix to get the commission for the Lottin decorations (J(L)87) a few months later.

The picture stands on a plain wooden altar on the north wall of the village church of Orcemont, near Rambouillet, one bay below the main altar. It is painted in the brittle and mannered Raphaelesque style favoured by Guérin and other neo-classicists at the period. Though clearly in the tradition of Raphael's Florentine Madonnas, its similarity to the *Belle Jardinière* in the Louvre, of which Delacroix copied a detail (J11), has been exaggerated at the expense of its marked

Mannerist qualities. While accepting that the *Belle Jardinière* was the main inspiration, Maltese also sees the influence of Michelangelo, and a departure from Raphael, in the contrapposto and in the Christ-child's gesture of blessing.

The catalogue of Delacroix's posthumous sale lists four sheets of studies for this painting under lot 302, but Burty Ann ED indicates that in fact this lot consisted of seven sheets, six of which went to Robaut for 25 fr. and one to Grzymala for 35 fr. The following studies known today bear the stamp of the sale: 1. A sheet of four composition studies, pencil, pen and brown wash on tracing paper, 18.7 × 24.8 cm (Louvre, RF9198, repr. Sérullaz *Dessins*, pl. VII, fig. 10 and Huyghe, pl. 69); 2. A full-scale drawing in pencil on tracing paper of the upper half of the Virgin and the head of the Christ-child, 50.8 × 34.3 cm (Louvre, RF9910, repr. *Mémorial*, no. 4); 3. A detailed drawing in Conté crayon heightened with white chalk for the Christ-child, done from an infant girl model, 43.7 × 27.4 cm (R29, Louvre RF9162, repr. *Mémorial*, no. 5). Robaut also lists, as R Ann 25bis, a study for the Virgin's head in black crayon heightened with white, 20 × 12 cm, which he bought at Delacroix's posthumous sale (repr. Tracings 1). In addition to these drawings stamped with the seal of the posthumous sale, there are: a charcoal study of the Virgin half-length with the head and raised arm of the Christ-child, the Virgin's hair hanging loose down to her shoulders (Louvre sketch-book RF23356, fol. 25^v, repr. Sérullaz *Dessins* pl. VIII, fig. 11); two drawings for the head of the Virgin in the Louvre sketch-book RF9141, fol. 6^v and 18^r; and Robaut records (under R27), with neither description nor illustration, a water-colour study, 34 × 28 cm, which belonged to Chocquet.

Several oil sketches are also recorded. Moreau states there were two, one of which measured 41 × 37 cm and was 'presque conforme au Tableau'. This is listed by Robaut under no. 26 without an illustration or record of ownership, and it has never come to light; it is likely that it was in fact the sketch for the *Virgin of the Sacred Heart*, which appears to have been misleadingly described in the Cat. Exh. *Bd Italiens*, Paris 1864, as a sketch for Delacroix's first painting (see J152, n. 2), a description which may have led Moreau into error. Moreau (pp. 219 f.) describes the second sketch thus: 'H. 32^c, L. 12^c [*sic*], très-différente. Dans cette dernière, la Vierge, vêtue d'une robe bleue, à corsage rouge, porte un long voile descendant sur ses épaules. Les bras de l'enfant Jésus retombent tous les deux le long de son corps. Sur le terrain du premier plan, ni fleurs, ni gerbes de blé'; and lists Riesener as the owner. This is evidently Robaut's no. 27, described, though not illustrated, as a slight variant painted on paper, 32 × 22 cm, Chocquet being given as the owner. It passed in the Chocquet sale 1 July 1899, lot 56 (support and dimensions now listed as canvas, 31 × 15.5

cm, and the provenance from Riesener mentioned), to Baron Saint Joachim (R Ann) for 600 fr. and has not, to my knowledge, been heard of since (J(L)106).

Robaut lists, under no. 28, a third painting of the subject, which was described as a sketch for the *Virgin of the Harvest* in the catalogue of the exhibition *EBA*, Paris 1885, no. 180. Robaut, who was himself the owner, describes it as painted on paper, 86 × 58 cm, and illustrates it with one of his small engravings. He sold it to Cheramy for 300 fr. (R Ann). It appears, however, to have been merely a copy after Delacroix and was sold as such in the sale of Cheramy's estate, 15 April 1913, lot 40. According to Dieterle R, it was with Schoeller in 1948, who was asking 2000,000 fr. for it.

The original paint surface of the picture at Orcemont had suffered considerable damage from damp, particularly in the foreground and the shadows of the Virgin's drapery, when it was restored for the centenary exhibition of 1963. The plate in Huyghe reveals its condition before restoration.

152 THE VIRGIN OF THE   Pl. 134
SACRED HEART, sketch

16$\frac{1}{8}$ × 10$\frac{5}{8}$ in. (41 × 27 cm) E.D.
Moreau p. 318. R36 (repr. under R35)
1821
Private collection, France

Provenance: Delacroix's posthumous sale, Feb. 1864, lot 133, to Dr. Isambert, 420 fr.; his sale, 9 March 1877, lot 22, 250 fr.; Haro, by 1885; sale Haro & fils, 30 May 1892, lot 89 ('Notre-Dame des Douleurs', 32 × 26 cm[1]), 620 fr., perhaps bought in; with Haro in Feb. 1894 (R Ann); his sale, 2 Apr. 1897, lot 135 (as by Delacroix and Géricault), 205 fr.; Rigaud; bought from him by Bernheim-Jeune, May 1921, and sold by them to Kuaq, Oct. 1923 (Arch B-J).

Exhibitions: *Bd Italiens*, Paris 1864, no. 79 (as 'Esquisse terminée de son premier tableau, la Vierge', 41 × 27 cm);[2] *EBA*, Paris 1885, no. 101; Kyoto-Tokyo 1969, H-2, repr. in colour; Atelier Delacroix, Paris 1973 (no cat.)

Literature: Escholier I, repr. opp. p. 56.

Though Delacroix wrote to his sister on 28 July 1820, saying that he might be delayed in joining her for the summer holidays because he had to do some 'esquisses peintes et des ébauches' and submit them to the Bishop of Nantes for approval (*Correspondance* v. 63), there are good reasons for believing that this and other oil studies for the *Virgin of the Sacred Heart* (J63 and J(L)108) were completed only after the holidays, most probably not before the beginning of 1821, and perhaps never submitted to the Bishop. In a letter to his sister a fortnight later, Delacroix was already less certain that the Bishop would require to see a sketch: 'à moins [. . .] que mon bon évêque ne veuille voir une esquisse colorée du tableau' (*Correspondance* v. 70); and since Géricault, who was officially supposed to be painting the picture, was in England, it is indeed difficult to see how Delacroix could have presented sketches for approval in his stead. Furthermore, it is clear from letters which Delacroix wrote during his holidays and early in 1821 that he was having difficulties with the composition (see J153), and this would not have been the case had he already painted this oil sketch, which differs in no significant way, except size, from the final painting.

¹ Though these dimensions differ from those listed by Robaut, there is no doubt that this lot was R36, for it is so identified in R Ann.

² In his annotated copy of the second edition of the catalogue of this exhibition (*Bib AA*, MS. 297ᵇⁱˢ), Robaut writes: 'On croirait qu'il est question de la Vierge des Moissons [J151]. Au contraire, c'était la Vierge du Sacré Cœur, Nantes.' Haro is listed as the owner in the catalogue, but that too appears to be an error, since Isambert had bought this sketch at Delacroix's posthumous sale and it was to pass in his own sale in 1877.

153 THE VIRGIN OF THE SACRED HEART

Pl. 135

101⅝ × 59⅞ in. (2.58 × 1.52 m)*
Moreau p. 220. R35 (no repr.)
1821
Cathedral of Ajaccio

Provenance: Commissioned by the Minister of the Interior from Géricault for the Cathedral of Nantes, *c*. Jan. 1820, at 2,400 fr.; Géricault had passed the commission on to Delacroix by July; ready for delivery by May 1822; sent to Corsica by the Minister of the Interior, and installed in the Cathedral of Ajaccio on 17 Feb. 1827.

Exhibitions: Louvre 1930, no. 6; Louvre 1963, no. 6, repr.

Literature: *Journal du Département de la Corse*, 24 Feb. 1827; *Journal des Artistes*, 25 March 1827, p. 191; L. Batissier, 'Géricault', *Revue du dix-neuvième Siècle*, 1842 (reprint in P. Courthion (ed.), *Géricault raconté par lui-même et par ses amis* (Cailler, Geneva, 1957), p. 56); 'Théodore Géricault. Lettres du comte de Forbin relatives à l'acquisition du Naufrage de la Méduse de Géricault', *Archives de l'art français*, I (1851-2), issue of Jan. 1851, pp. 72 f., 73 n. 1; 'Géricault. Billet communiqué par M. Labouchère', ibid., III (1853-5), issue of 15 Jan. 1855, pp. 315 f.; F. Villot, *Notice des tableaux exposés dans les galeries du Musée impérial du Louvre, 3ᵉ partie, Ecole française* (Paris, 1855), p. 151; Baron de Girardot, 'Théodore Géricault. Correspondance officielle relative au tableau qui lui avait été commandé pour Nantes', *Archives de l'art français*, 2nd series, II (1862), pp. 72-80; Piron, p. 105; Clément, pp. 175 f., 194 and n.; C. Bosc, *Les Ephémérides ajacciennes (1790-1869)* (Impr. Fabiani, Bastia, 1897), p. 49; 'Allocution de M. Maurice Tourneux', *Réunion des Sociétés des Beaux-Arts des Départements ... du 2 au 5 Juin 1903—27ᵉ Session* (Typographie Plon-Nourrit, Paris, 1903), pp. 13 f.; M. Tourneux, 'Particularités intimes sur la vie et l'œuvre de Géricault',

BSHAF, 1912, pp. 60 f. and n. 1; J. Campi, 'Edifices religieux d'Ajaccio XVᵉ–XVIIIᵉ siècle' (Librairie M. Paoli, Ajaccio, 1913), p. 13 and n.; Moreau-Nélaton I. 39-41; Escholier I. 52 f., 55, 56, 58; *Correspondance* I. 70 n. 1, 87 n. 1, 110 n. 1, 116 n. 2, 147 n. 1, v. 63 n. 1, 70 and n., 79 n. 2, 99 n. 3, 105 and n., 137 and n.; *Lettres intimes*, p. 115 and n.; Escholier 1963, p. 14; Huyghe, pp. 106, 109, 132, repr. pl. 72; Maltese, pp. 21, 22, 23, 39, 124, 144, 154, repr. pl. 3; P. Pool, *Delacroix* (Paul Hamlyn, London, 1969), p. 30, repr. in colour pl. 5; Trapp, pp. 16, 226, 234, repr. fig. 12, p. 17; L. Eitner, *Géricault's Raft of the Medusa* (Phaidon, London, 1972), p. 61 n. 24.

There has been much confusion over the history, subject, cost and intended destination of this painting. By reference to one unpublished file in the Archives nationales, but drawing mainly on documents already published in a variety of places, all the essential facts can be accurately determined. On 31 December 1819, Count Auguste de Forbin, directeur des Musées, wrote to Géricault offering him on behalf of the *Maison du roi* a commission for a painting at a price of 6,000 fr., half to be paid in 1820, half in 1821 (*Archives de l'art français*, 1851). The subject was not specified in the letter. However, on 12 January 1820 a royal ordinance granted 60,000 fr. to buy paintings or statues for the churches of the kingdom, and consequently an undated list of forty-one paintings ordered or to be commissioned was drawn up, including: 'Gericault. Prix du tableau commandé pʳ la Cath.ˡᵉ de Nantes 2400 [fr.]' (Archives nationales F¹⁹ 4538). The price of the commission originally offered by Forbin is thus seen to be reduced by more than half, the subject to be a religious one, which would predictably be of little interest to Géricault, and the commission to be part of a general programme for embellishing the churches of France during the Restoration. On 21 April 1820, the architect of the Department of the Loire-Inférieure wrote to his Prefect informing him of the Bishop of Nantes's intention that 'le tableau soit placé dans une des chapelles du bas-côté septentrional [de la cathédrale], à la suite de celle du baptistère, et qu'il fait partie du retable de l'autel, qui n'est que provisoire et qu'il m'a invité de projeter à cet effet'; further, the Bishop 'doit proposer pour sujet de tableau, *la Dévotion au sacré cœur de Jésus et de Marie*'; for Géricault's use, the architect joined a sketch of the chapel, now lost, showing his design for an altar in the Gothic style and including the shape and dimensions (12 pieds 5 pouces by 8 pieds 1 pouce, i.e. 4.03 m × 2.62 m) of the painting required (de Girardot, op. cit., 1862, pp. 72-4, 78). In a letter to his sister dated 28 July 1820, Delacroix gives the first indication that Géricault has handed the commission over to him: 'Il vient de m'arriver une commande. [. . .] C'est un tableau pour un évêque de Nantes' (*Correspondance* v. 63). Delacroix made only limited progress that year, in spite of efforts to draw during bouts of fever while staying with his sister in the Forest of Boixe in September and early October: on 20 October 1820, he wrote to Pierret: 'L'idée de ce tableau que j'ai à faire me poursuit comme un spectre. [. . .] J'ai plus d'une fois essayé de dessiner pendant ma fièvre, et ce qui m'a le plus affligé, c'est que tout ce que j'ai voulu chercher pour mon tableau n'a été que misérable' (ibid. 1. 87). And on 6 December 1820, he complains in a letter to his sister: 'la personne [Géricault] qui m'a commandé mon tableau est partie étourdiment sans m'en laisser les mesures' (ibid. 1. 106). On 12 February 1821 comes the first indication in the writings of Géricault, who had gone to England, that he had abandoned the commission: 'j'envoie au diable tous les Sacré Cœur de Jésus' (Clément, pp. 193 f.). Meanwhile, Delacroix had been struggling on, and wrote to Soulier on 26 January: 'le tableau dont je suis chargé me [prend] beaucoup de moments. [. . .] Je ne vois presque dans le monde que [Pierret] et mon tableau devant lequel je sèche' (Correspondance 1. 110, 112). He confided to the same correspondent in a letter of 21 February that although he had been working on his painting since the beginning of January, 'Je fais, je défais, je recommence, et tout cela n'est point ce que je cherche encore' (ibid. 1. 116 f.). It was still unfinished at the end of March (ibid. 1. 123). In the middle of April, he wrote to his sister: 'T'ai-je parlé de l'argent que j'ai dépensé en modèles pour mon tableau ? Je dois encore la toile depuis quatre mois et je voudrais bien la payer' (ibid. v. 79); then nothing till 8 December, when he told her: 'je ne puis parvenir à toucher l'argent de mon tableau' (ibid. v. 99), by which date the picture had presumably been finished for some time, as far as Delacroix was concerned. Géricault was not to return to Paris from London until later in the month and, according to Théodore Lebrun, when he did: 'peu content du Sacré-Cœur qu'on lui avait fabriqué, il se décida à traiter le sujet lui-même. [. . .] Je ne doute pas que s'il avait eu le temps d'achever ce tableau, nous aurions de lui un autre chef-d'œuvre' (letter dated 6 April 1836, in M. Tourneux, op. cit., 1912). But Lebrun admits his recollection of this period is incomplete, and there is no other evidence of Géricault's dissatisfaction with Delacroix's painting, nor is there any sign that Géricault repainted it. There is admittedly a gap of some five months between Géricault's return from England and his letter to the Minister of the Interior quoted below, informing him that the painting is ready to be collected. The most probable explanation of this delay, however, is not that Géricault, or Delacroix under his supervision, was reworking the picture during that period, but that, having been abroad for twenty months, he had to leave a decent interval after his return in which he might be assumed by the authorities, who cannot have been ignorant of his absence, to have painted the canvas himself. Géricault to the Minister of the Interior, 14

May 1822: 'J'ai l'honneur de vous donner avis que le tableau dont j'ai été chargé pour la cathédrale de Nantes est terminé.

'Je prie Votre Excellence de vouloir bien le faire enlever après l'examen préalable, et d'en ordonnancer le payement sur lequel je n'ai demandé aucun à compte' (Archives de l'art français, 1855). Forbin signed an order dated 8 July 1822 for payment of 2,400 fr. to Géricault, 'comme prix intégral du tableau qui lui a été commandé par le Ministère pour la Cathédrale de Nantes' (Archives nationales F¹⁹ 4538). On 30 August, Delacroix was still inquiring, from the country and by now impatiently, whether Géricault had paid him (Correspondance 1. 147).

For reasons that remain obscure, but possibly because the dimensions were nowhere near those requested, the painting was apparently never delivered to Nantes and no more is heard of it till 17 February 1827, the date of an article published a week later in the Journal du Département de la Corse, reporting that it had just arrived ('vient d'arriver') at Ajaccio on board the corvette l'Emulation. According to this report, the picture had been sent by the Minister of the Interior at the request of the Prefect of Corsica (Count Lantivy) and had been destined for the high altar in the Cathedral of Ajaccio, but, a preliminary trial having shown that position to be unsuitable, it was placed on the first altar to the left on entering by the main door of the Cathedral. It remains there to this day, well illuminated by a window in the entrance wall, but in danger of further deterioration from the proximity of four large candles, which are regularly lighted on the altar. The same newspaper report gives the subject of the painting as Triomphe de la Religion and specifies: 'on désigne comme en étant l'auteur, un artiste nommé Géricault.' It seems not to have been known officially, in France any more than in Corsica, that Géricault was not the author, and this information was not made public before 1842, when Batissier published his article on Géricault in the Revue du dix-neuvième Siècle, stating that Delacroix had painted the picture, but did not know what had become of it. Delacroix was not alone: Moreau, Robaut and every other student of Delacroix remained ignorant of its whereabouts until 1930, when it was rediscovered in Ajaccio and brought to Paris for the exhibition at the Louvre in that year.

The painting has often been thought, even by the most recent authorities, to have been commissioned for the Convent of the Sacred Heart at Nantes, instead of for the Cathedral. The origin of this confusion lies no doubt in Villot's statement in a Louvre catalogue (op. cit., 1855) that it was 'destiné à la maison du Sacré-Cœur de Nantes', and in the description of the oil sketch (J152) in Delacroix's posthumous sale catalogue as 'Esquisse d'un tableau [. . .] pour la chapelle des dames du Sacré-Cœur, à Nantes'. One of the northern side chapels of the Cathedral of Nantes is, however, called the 'Chapelle du Sacré Cœur', and it was almost certainly with a view to placing the picture in that chapel that the Bishop of Nantes proposed the subject. There was thus never any question of its being commissioned for the Ladies of the Sacred Heart. The local architect had instructed that the picture was to receive daylight from the left (de Girardot, op. cit., 1862, p. 78), and it is from that side that the light is arranged in the oil studies (J63, J152 and J(L)108) and final painting. It must therefore have been intended to stand at the east end of the chapel.

The numerous preliminary drawings fall into two main categories: (1) those, no doubt the earliest, where the Virgin hovers, both arms outstretched and in various states of instability, above a group of devotional figures including a mother with several naked infants (Louvre sketch-book RF9141, fol. 44ᵛ, repr. Huyghe pl. 73; Louvre, RF9196, repr. Sérullaz *Dessins* 1952, pl. XII; *Bib AA* MS. 243, unpublished; and (2) those where the Virgin, with or without suppliants below, assumes approximately the same stable, central, statuesque pose employed in the final painting (Louvre, RF9195, repr. *Mémorial* no. 12; RF9161, repr. ibid. no. 13; Louvre, ex-Atelier Delacroix, repr. ibid. no. 10; Louvre, RF9197, repr. Sérullaz *Dessins* 1952, pl. XIII, fig. 20; Louvre sketch-books, RF23357, fol. 25ᵛ, RF23359, fol. 37ʳ; a pair of water-colour studies, each 10.8 × 6.7 cm (sight), showing the Virgin alone, one with a brown skirt against a blue sky, the other with a blue skirt against a colourless sky, Coll. the late Roger Leybold, Sceaux). The complexity of the suppliant figures and of their spacing in depth is progressively reduced, but none of the known drawings (and some are certainly missing) shows the simplified solution for the lower half found in the oil-sketch (J152) and finished work: three half-length figures placed in the foreground and acting as the stable base of a pyramidal composition crowned by the Virgin's head.

The general development is thus away from a Baroque solution towards one more classic and hieratic; also, the onus of devotion to the Sacred Heart, which it will be recalled was the subject set by the Bishop, is finally placed less on the figures within the composition than on the spectator without. The picture is more monumental, more robust and more *tenebroso*, in short more like a Géricault, than Delacroix's first religious commission, the *Virgin of the Harvest* (J151); and the principal reason for this is undoubtedly that Delacroix had no choice but to emulate Géricault, who was thought by the Ministry to be executing the commission he had been given. The colouring, too, is that of the Géricault of the *Raft of the Medusa*: ochres, browns, dark blue and dark red.

Maltese (p. 144) sees an influence of Michelangelo's Bruges Madonna in the pose of the Virgin and notes (p. 39), perceptively, an adumbration of the *Liberty* of 1830 (J144) in her exhortatory, triumphal attitude.

154 THE AGONY IN THE GARDEN

Pl. 136

115¾ × 142½ in. (2.94 × 3.62 m)
Moreau pp. 168, 220 f. R176 (1826)
1824/7
Saint-Paul-Saint-Louis, Paris

Provenance: Commissioned by 1824 for the City of Paris, at a price of 2,400 fr.[1]

Exhibitions: Salon 1827–8, no. 293 ('Le Christ au jardin des Oliviers'); *Universelle*, Paris 1855, no. 2908; *Bd Italiens*, Paris 1864, no. 13; *Universelle*, Paris 1878 ('Catalogue Général de l'Exposition spéciale de la ville de Paris et du Département de la Seine'), no. 151; *EBA*, Paris 1885, no. 25; Louvre 1930, no. 30, repr. *Album*, p. 17; Musée Galliera, Paris 1946, no. 17; Louvre 1963, no. 86, *M* no. 89, 2 repr.; Paris, Detroit, New York 1974–5, no. 40, repr.

Literature: *Journal* I. 45 n. 1, 61 n. 2, 89 n. 2, 91 n. 4, II. 321 and n.; *Correspondance* I. 407, 426, II. 411, III. 248 and n., 252 and n.; anon. Salon review, *La Pandore*, 6 Nov. 1827; id., *Le Figaro*, 7 Nov., 21 Dec. 1827; ed., *Le Mentor*, 7 Nov. 1827; P., 'Salon de 1827', *Journal de Paris*, 8 and 24 Nov. 1827; L. V. [Vitet], Salon review, *Le Globe*, V, no. 95 (10 Nov. 1827), p. 505; anon. Salon review, *Journal du Commerce*, 11 Nov. 1827; id., *Courrier des Théâtres*, 25 Nov. 1827; A.N., Salon review, *L'Observateur*, II, no. 95, 8 Dec. 1827, p. 467; D. [E. Delécluze], Salon review, *Journal des Débats*, 20 Dec. 1827, 21 March 1828; A. Bérard *et al.*, *Annales de l'Ecole française des Beaux-Arts* (C. P. Landon, Paris, 1827), p. 73, engraved repr. by Normand pl. 30, opp. p. 70; anon. Salon review, *La France Chrétienne*, 13 Jan. 1828; A. Jal, *Esquisses, croquis, pochades, ou tout ce qu'on voudra, sur le Salon de 1827* (Ambr. Dupont et Cⁱᵉ, Paris, 1828), pp. 113–15, lithographic repr. by Poterlet opp. p. 113; [A. D. Vergnaud], *Examen du Salon de 1827. Novembre. Première partie* (chez Roret, Paris, 1828), pp. 9 f.; *Visite au Musée du Louvre, ou guide de l'amateur à l'Exposition . . . (Année 1827–1828) . . . par une société de gens de lettres et d'artistes* (Leroi, Paris, 1828), pp. 15 f.; T. Thoré, 'Artistes contemporains; Eugène Delacroix', *Le Siècle*, 24 Feb. 1837 (reprinted by M. Du Seigneur, 'Eugène Delacroix et Théophile Thoré', *Journal des Arts*, 24 Oct. 1890); P. Mantz, 'Artistes contemporains. Eugène Delacroix', *L'Artiste*, 5th ser. IV (issue of 15 Jan. 1850), p. 82; C. Baudelaire, 'Exposition universelle', *Le Pays*, 3 June 1855, reprinted in *Curiosités esthétiques*, 1868 (*Œuvres*, Pléiade ed. Paris 1932, II, p. 160); P. Petroz, review of 'Exposition universelle', 5 June 1855; T. Gautier, 'Exposition universelle', *Le Moniteur universel*, 19 July 1855; M. Du Camp, *Les Beaux-Arts à l'Exposition universelle de 1855* (Libr. Nouvelle, Paris, 1855), p. 115; E. Gebauer, *Les Beaux-Arts à l'Exposition universelle de 1855* (Libr. Napoléonienne, Paris, 1855), p. 33; E. Chesneau, 'Le

Mouvement moderne en peinture', *Revue Européenne*, XVIII (1861), p. 499; id., *La Peinture française au XIXᵉ siècle. Les Chefs d'école* (Didier, Paris, 1862), p. 353; A. Dumas, *Causerie sur Eugène Delacroix*, lecture of 10 Dec. 1864, pp. 64 f. of MS. in *BN Estampes* (see *Literature* for J112 and Tourneux p. 27 for further details); Silvestre *Documents nouveaux* (1864), p. 29; A. Cantaloube, *Eugène Delacroix* . . . (E. Dentu, Paris, 1864), p. 39; Piron, p. 106; P. de Saint-Victor, *Le Moniteur universel*, 27 June 1881; Tourneux, pp. 47, 49, 50, 52, 53, 54; Moreau-Nélaton I. 77 f., 84, 89, 163, 185, repr. fig. 51, II. 88, 156, 244 f.; Escholier I. 170, 172, repr. p. 171, II. 307, III. 219; Hourticq 1930, pl. 17; M. Florisoone, 'El Hispanismo de Delacroix', *Revista española de Arte*, II (1933), p. 392, repr. p. 393; L. Johnson, 'The Early Drawings of Delacroix', *Burl Mag*, XCVIII (1956), pp. 23 f.; M. Florisoone, 'La Genèse espagnole des "Massacres de Scio" de Delacroix', *Revue du Louvre*, 13 (1963), pp. 199 and n., 202 and n.; L. Johnson, 'The Delacroix Centenary in France—I', *Burl Mag*, CV (1963), p. 302; Huyghe, pp. 173, 176, 178, 183, 249, 256; Maltese, pp. 34, 35, 36, 44, 75, 77, 81, 124, 139, repr. in colour pl. IX; L. Johnson, 'Eugène Delacroix et les Salons. Documents inédits au Louvre', *Revue du Louvre*, 16 (1966), p. 220; P. Georgel, 'Delacroix et Auguste Vacquerie', *BSHAF* for 1968 (1970), pp. 181, 188; Trapp, pp. 77, 78–81, 82, 226, 233, 234, 242, 345, repr. fig. 41. (Several further references and quotations from nineteenth-century critics will be found under no. 40 in Cat. Exh. Paris, Detroit, London 1974–5.)

Prints: Line engraving by Normand fils from a drawing by Fremy, in A. Béraud, op. cit., 1827. Lithograph by Hippolyte Poterlet, in A. Jal, op. cit., 1828.

Copy: R Ann records (p. 53) that a M. Bruyas of Lyon (unconnected with Alfred Bruyas of Montpellier, according to Robaut) asked Delacroix for a reduced copy of this canvas and it was painted by Chenavard. It has never been discovered.

Though no official documents concerning this commission have come to light, it has generally been assumed on the basis of references in the *Journal* to work for 'le préfet' that it was commissioned in 1824 by the Prefect of the Seine, Count de Chabrol, for the church in which it hangs. On 12 January 1824 Delacroix notes: 'Fait, cette semaine passée, l'esquisse du préfet' (*Journal* I. 44 f.), which was presumably an oil sketch for this commission to be submitted to the Prefect for approval and may well have been the lost sketch recorded and copied by Robaut (J(L)109). If so, the composition of the final painting had been established, except for very minor alterations, by January 1824. A canvas primed and stretched for Delacroix on a 'chassis de 11 pieds sur 8' on 9 January 1824 was most probably for this painting (unpublished bill from the colour merchant Leroy, M-

Nélaton Doc., bound in *Lettres à Pierret*, II). Further references in the *Journal* in 1824 thus seem to apply to work on the final canvas: 30 April: 'Pour mon tableau du *Christ*, les anges de la mort tristes et sévères portent sur lui leurs regards mélancoliques.'; 1 May: 'J'ai eu un délire de composition ce matin à mon atelier, et j'ai retrouvé des entrailles pour ce tableau du *Christ*, qui ne me disait rien.'; and finally, 3 May: 'Penser, en faisant mes anges pour le préfet, à ces belles et mystiques figures de femmes [in the Soult collection, see the *Copy of a St. Catherine* (J22)], une, entre autres, qui porte ses tétons dans un plat [*St. Agatha*, by Zurbarán, Musée de Montpellier, as first noted by Joubin]' (*Journal* I. 89 f., 90, 91 and Joubin's note). There is no further record of the picture before 8 October 1827, when it was accepted for exhibition at the Salon (Johnson, op. cit., 1966). Thus the actual date of completion of Delacroix's first official commission for a religious painting (the *Virgin of the Sacred Heart* (J153), though a state commission, was passed on unofficially by Géricault) is unknown; but the conception in detail and much of the execution seem to date from 1824, at a time when the artist was deeply interested in Spanish painting. That interest may account in some measure for the lack of idealization and the ochreish flesh modelling of the Christ, which was generally found disagreeable by critics of the Salon of 1827; but the type of Christ, as well perhaps as the diagonal arrangement of the composition, seems also to owe something to Rubens (see the print, *Agony in the Garden*, by Petrus de Bajllieu after Rubens reproduced in Trapp, fig. 42).

While there is a relatively slight increase of colour since the *Virgin of the Sacred Heart* of 1821, the composition is notably more dynamic and unified, with its dramatic and luminous funnel-like arrangement broadening from lower left to upper right to culminate in the triad of troubled angels, which were as widely admired by the Salon critics as the Christ was found displeasing. Though Delacroix writes only of the 'belles et mystiques figures de femmes' of the Soult gallery in connection with the angels, they were likened to 'jolies demoiselles anglaises' by Delécluze in 1827 (loc. cit.) and Gautier, writing in 1855 (loc. cit.), found in them 'un volontaire souvenir de Lawrence', a view that is hard to share since the central angel is hardly more 'English' than the blonde, classical figure of Spring in the *Four Seasons* of 1821 (J97), and the drapery of the foremost angel is at least as classicizing as in the *Spring*, which it resembles from the waist down. Even if it is difficult to establish precise analogies with paintings from the Soult collection, Thoré was perhaps closer to the mark than his colleagues when he wrote in 1837 (op. cit.): 'Quand il faut faire *Jésus-Christ au jardin des oliviers* et de beaux anges qui entrouvrent les nuages c'est Murillo qui domine.'

According to Moreau (p. 221), part of the landscape was painted by Paul Huet. This author was also the first to publish the same information about the landscape in the *Portrait of Schwiter* (J82), which was also submitted to the Salon jury of 1827, and it seems unlikely that he would have published such statements on these two major paintings had they not come from a source that he trusted.

According to Huyghe (p. 249), the hanging of the picture in the church of Saint-Paul-Saint-Louis after the Salon 'made a considerable stir', but he cites no evidence in support of this statement. It is not known exactly where the painting was hung in the church, but in a letter to the curé dated 5 April 1855, Delacroix, having borrowed it for his retrospective show at the Exposition universelle in that year, complained of the state it had fallen into by being placed against a wall and too high up to be properly looked after:

grâce à la restauration dont il avait un si grand besoin, par suite de la place fâcheuse qu'il occupe, appliqué à une muraille, le tableau vous reviendra, je le crois, dans un état bien préférable à celui où il se trouvait. Peut-être la vue de ce que les soins ont pu faire pour le rendre véritablement visible, ce qu'il était à peine, sous les couches de la moisissure et des vernis, vous suggéra-t-elle, comme à moi, la pensée qu'il y aurait peut-être lieu à le placer de manière à ce que des soins bien entendus lui conservent de la durée. A la hauteur où il est placé et dans la difficulté que présente son entretien, il doit périr dans peu d'années. (*Correspondance* v. 194f. See also Dumas, op. cit., 1864.)

Thoré had noticed as early as 1837 that the humidity was beginning to tarnish it. It was cleaned, revarnished and put on view for a while at the Petit Palais after being taken from storage at the end of World War I (Escholier I. 170, 172).

Escholier (I. 172) reproduces a brown wash study (R1522 and R Ann, margin to R176) which establishes the essentials of the final composition, except that the Christ is younger, unbearded and in a more vertical, kneeling position. A wash drawing which, if by Delacroix, probably reflects an earlier thought for the composition and shows Christ seated rigidly on the ground with a single angel present (as in Luke 22: 43, the only one of the Gospels to mention an angel at all) is reproduced in Huyghe (pl. 182). A pencil drawing of two angels published by P. Georgel (op. cit., 1970, p. 188, repr. fig. 5) as a study by Delacroix for the group of angels does not appear from the reproduction to be by the master. A signed water-colour with two angels on the left and the Christ facing in that direction (R177. Coll. late Mme D. David-Weill) is less likely to be a study for this painting (as it is listed in *Mémorial*, no. 90, repr.) than a self-sufficient variant. The relationship to the final painting of an elaborate though freely executed water-colour composition of vertical format, showing the Christ seated facing out of the picture with no angels present, is unclear (R182; Louvre, RF23325; repr. in colour, Sérullaz *Dessins* 1952, pl. XLVII; *Mémorial*, no. 91, repr.), but it seems to me likely now, as in 1956 (op. cit.), to be an early alternative composition for the final work.

Moreau (p. 221), followed by Robaut (R357), states that in 1831 Delacroix painted a reduced version of this canvas for the singer Adolphe Nourrit (1802–39. See J(L)110).

Of the two oil paintings of this subject listed by Robaut under the same year as the picture in Saint-Paul-Saint-Louis, 1826, R183 is probably almost entirely by Poterlet (J(D)18); and R181, which had been mistakenly identified by Moreau (p. 221) as the oil sketch for the final painting, has generally been thought since Moreau-Nélaton (II. 48, repr. fig. 262; repr. also in P. Georgel, op. cit., 1970, fig. 4) to be a much later work, related to the pastel datable to 1847 (R999; repr. Moreau-Nélaton II, fig. 261) and to the painting dated 1851 in the Rijksmuseum, Amsterdam (*Mémorial*, no. 427, repr.): all three differ from the church painting in showing Christ unattended by angels and stretched full-length on the ground, in keeping with Matthew 26: 39: 'And he went a little farther, and fell on his face, and prayed.'

¹ According to Robaut, p. 481; 3,000 fr. according to Piron, p. 106, who is generally less reliable for prices.

155 MARY MAGDALEN AT THE   Pl. 137 FOOT OF THE CROSS

$13\frac{3}{8} \times 10\frac{1}{4}$ in. (34 × 26 cm)
Signed and dated bottom right: *Eug. Delacroix 27 mai/1829*
R296
Private collection, Switzerland

Provenance: Painted for the stockbroker Alfred Saucède (?);[1] sale M.S. [Schwabacher] of Vienna and M. L.R. 23 March 1875, lot 21, 1,220 fr.; anon. sale (by Bloche), Hôtel Drouot, 26 Jan. 1876, lot 16, bought in at 1,650 fr. (reserve 3,000 fr.); anon. sale (by Pillet), Hôtel Drouot, 29 Jan. 1877, lot 21; Georges Viau; with Winkel & Magnussen, Copenhagen, 1918; Hodebert, by 1926; Dr. Hans Graber, Zurich, by 1939; with Galerie Paul Vallotton, Lausanne, 1976; sold by them to the present owner, 1976.

Exhibitions: Exhibition of French art organized by Winkel & Magnussen, dealers of Copenhagen, Charlottenberg, Sweden, Oct. 1918, no. 83 (asking 35,000 Kr.); Zurich 1939, no. 317.

Literature: Escholier I. 256, repr. p. 257.

Print: Etching by Charles Courtry, 1869 according to Béraldi, no. 230. (There is no example of this print among the classified works of Courtry in *BN Estampes*, but one is contained in M-Nélaton Port. IV.)

Delacroix's exceptional, and perhaps for an oil painting unique, inclusion of the month and day when signing and dating this picture suggests that the date had some special significance, now lost, for the artist or the person for whom it was painted.

¹ According to Escholier (I. 256), who cites no supporting evidence and misspells the name as 'Saussède'. Whether Escholier is right or not, Robaut (Corrections and Additions, p. 483) is surely wrong in identifying this picture as lot 132 in Delacroix's posthumous sale.

156 PIETÀ   Pl. 137

$9\frac{7}{16} \times 12\frac{5}{8}$ in. (24 × 32 cm)
Moreau pp. 96, 264. R297
1829
Whereabouts unknown

Provenance: Frédéric Villot, by 1850; his sale (M. F.V.) 11 Feb. 1865, lot 3 ('La Vierge et le Christ mort', 24 × 33 cm), 435 fr.; Van Praet of Brussels, by 1873 (?); bought with his entire collection by Henri Garnier, Jan. 1893 (R Ann); Mme A. Cohen of Antwerp; her sale (Mme A. C. d'A.), 14 May 1920, lot 4 (repr.), 17,200 fr.¹

Exhibitions: None.

Literature: *Journal* I. 337, III. 373—Supp.; C. Mauclair, 'Delacroix', *L'Art et les Artistes*, XVIII N.S. (1929), repr. p. 157.

Print: Etching in reverse by Frédéric Villot, signed and dated 1837.

In the catalogue of the Villot sale this picture is said to have been painted in 1829 and is described as 'pas entièrement terminée dans toutes ses parties'. Since Villot helped to compile the catalogue and was a personal friend of Delacroix's by 1829, the dating is almost certainly reliable.

¹ This list of owners follows Robaut down to 1893. According to Moreau (p. 264), the picture was bought by Diaz at the Villot sale, though he also records that it belongs 'Aujourd'hui [1873] à M. Van-Praët'. A pencil note on the Villot etching in M-Nélaton Port. IV states further that it passed in the Baron de Beurnonville sale, 29 Apr. 1880.
A painting described in the catalogue as 'Le Christ descendu de la croix', 25 × 31 cm, did pass in the Diaz sale, 25 Jan. 1877, lot 324, to de Beurnonville for 2,200 fr., and then passed in his sale in 1880 with the same description, to an unknown buyer for 1,750 fr., lot 17. The *Christ descended from the Cross* which passed in these two sales is unaccounted for by Robaut, and may well have been another, lost version. If it is our version and was bought by Diaz at the Villot sale, as recorded by Moreau, it is most unlikely to have belonged to Van Praet by 1873, as also recorded by Moreau. The most satisfactory way of resolving the difficulty, apart from assuming the existence of two versions, would be to suppose that Van Praet acquired the painting at or after the de Beurnonville sale of 1880.

157 ECCE HOMO   Pl. 138

Oil on panel, cradled: $12\frac{5}{8} \times 9\frac{7}{16}$ in. (32 × 24 cm)
Signed bottom right: *Eug. Delacroix*
R1554 (1830. No repr.)
c. 1850?
Private collection, Switzerland

Provenance: Mme Herbelin, by 1853; Madeleine Lemaire (Joubin, loc. cit. *infra*); with Tedesco, Apr. 1928 (Dieterle R); M. X . . ., 1936 (Joubin, loc. cit. *infra*); the present owner, by 1963.

Exhibitions: *Bd Italiens*, Paris 1864, no. 31 ('Le Christ au roseau', 33 × 25 cm, listed as lent by Mme Herbelin); Berne 1963–4, no. 27; Bremen 1964, no. 25.

Literature: *Correspondance* III. 154 n. 3.

Joubin convincingly identified R1554 with a picture offered as a gift to Mme Herbelin and mentioned in a letter datable to 1853 where the artist gallantly explains to her: 'Il faut que je me sois bien mal expliqué pour que vous ayez pu comprendre que je vous prêtais seulement la petite et très imparfaite esquisse que j'ai pris la liberté de vous offrir. C'est précisément son peu d'importance qui m'a donné la confiance que vous voudriez bien la considérer comme un souvenir du plaisir que j'ai éprouvé à savoir dans vos mains mon autre tableau [*The Supper at Emmaus*, dated 1853, the Brooklyn Museum].' (*Correspondance* III. 154).

Robaut had never seen the original, which he knew only from the description in the catalogue of the exhibition *Bd Italiens*, Paris 1864, and evidently dated it to 1830 because he guessed that it was closely related to a water-colour of the same subject shown at the Salon of 1831 (R339, no repr.) and to the etching dated 1833 (Delteil no. 14). The figure of Christ is in fact very similar in pose to that of the etching, which depicts Christ alone, but the painting appears for stylistic reasons to be a much later elaboration of the print and to fit more convincingly in the years around 1850—in the period, that is, when Delacroix apparently offered it to Mme Herbelin. It has nevertheless seemed useful to include it in this volume for purposes of documentation, since Robaut placed it in 1830 together with a lost, unfinished version of the same subject (J(L)111) and it has not, to my knowledge, been previously reproduced.

Landscape, Still Life, Genre

158 THE CHURCH OF VALMONT ABBEY   Pl. 139

$18\frac{1}{8} \times 15$ in. $(46 \times 38$ cm)*
Signed and dated bottom left: *Eug. Delacroix/1831*
R352
Private collection, Paris

Provenance: Probably Alexandre Bataille, owner of Valmont Abbey, d. 1841, and by his bequest to Delacroix, who bequeathed it in 1863 to Louis Auguste Bornot,[1] owner of the Abbey since 1841, d. 1888; by descent to the present owner through the successive owners of the Abbey: Camille Bornot, d. 1921, his son; Jacques Béraldi, d. 1963, his great-nephew.

Exhibitions: Louvre 1930, no. 55A; Atelier Delacroix, Paris 1937B, no. 4; id., Paris 1963, no. 8 (transferred to Louvre in May); Louvre 1963, no. 147, M no. 148, repr.

Literature: Probably Inv. Delacroix, no. 319 or 320; Moreau-Nélaton I. 125, repr. fig. 90; Escholier I. 256, repr. p. 258; R. Huyghe, 'L' Exposition Delacroix au Musée du Louvre', *Bulletin des Musées de France*, II (1930), repr. p. 122; A. Conan, 'Delacroix à l'Abbaye de Valmont', *Art de France*, III (1963), p. 274 and n. 17; Huyghe, p. 207, repr. fig. 153; T. Prideaux *et al.*, *The World of Delacroix* (Time Inc., New York, 1966), repr. p. 43 (alongside a photograph of the Abbey).

Valmont Abbey, near Fécamp, belonged successively during Delacroix's maturity to two of his cousins. On his occasional visits, the remains of this ancient Benedictine abbey and the tombs it contained were a source of intense pleasure and curiosity to the artist. During his early years, he stayed at Valmont first as a boy, in 1813, returned in the autumn of 1829, and again in September 1831, when this picture was apparently painted. It depicts the ruins of the church, which had been rebuilt in the sixteenth century. The figure seated on the left sketching is usually said to represent Delacroix, but this can only be speculation as the features are unrecognizable. The subject and its treatment are typical of many a picture of ruins painted in the Romantic period and may be compared, for example, to the earlier painting of the ruined Abbey of Saint Omer by Delacroix's friend Bonington, where a human figure is also introduced among the ruins as an indication of scale.

Lot 597 in Delacroix's posthumous sale (R1809) comprised fifty sheets of studies described in the catalogue as 'Ruines de l'Abbaye de Valmont, vues extérieures et intérieures. Détails d'architecture, tombeaux, etc. Aquarelles, sépias et croquis.' Of these, a detailed water-colour, also in the possession of M. Bornot's descendants, is remarkably similar to this painting and could have served as a study for it, as suggested by Robaut (R Ann, marginal note to R352). It is reproduced in colour by Annie Conan (op. cit., 1963, p. 275) whose article contains excellent reproductions of other water-colours done at Valmont, as well as some useful details of the history of the Abbey. A less developed water-colour of the same part of the ruins seen from a less oblique angle is preserved in the Louvre (RF9250, repr. *Mémorial*, no. 149). Another water-colour from the posthumous sale, a finished view taken from the chapel and including the colonnade shown here, was with Nathan, Zurich, in 1964 (Cat. Exh. Edinburgh–London 1964, no. 116, repr.).

[1] According to Robaut (Additions, p. 484), followed in Cat. Exh. Louvre 1930, this picture was part of lot 219 in Delacroix's posthumous sale; he adds in R Ann that it was knocked down to M. Bornot. It does not, however, bear the seal of the posthumous sale and Bornot bought only one picture from that lot at the sale (Burty Ann ED), which was unquestionably R554 (J159). Our picture appears therefore to have been either no. 319 or 320 in Inv. Delacroix, probably the latter, which are described respectively as: '1 tableau représentant un intérieur d'église provenant de la succession Bataille légué à M. Borno [*sic*]' and '1 autre tableau représentant un intérieur de cloître provenant de la succession Bataille légué à M. Borno'. It may well be that one of these pictures, whose present location is unknown to me, corresponded closely to a water-colour of another part of the church, which passed in Delacroix's posthumous sale and also belongs to M. Bornot's descendants (R1092. Repr. in colour, A. Conan, op. cit. *infra*, p. 273)—just as our painting is intimately related to the water-colour, which seems to be a pendant to the other, in the same collection and illustrated in the same article, p. 275 (see below).

159 LANDSCAPE WITH CHÂTEAU, PROBABLY VALMONT   Pl. 140

Cardboard, $6\frac{11}{16} \times 10\frac{7}{16}$ in. $(17 \times 26.5$ cm)* E.D.
R544 (1834)
Private collection, Paris

Provenance: Delacroix's posthumous sale, Feb. 1864, part of lot 219 ('Quinze études diverses de paysages', without dimensions or further description. Lot no. still attached to surface), to Bornot (Burty Ann ED), 270 fr.; by descent to the present owner, as J158.

Exhibitions: Louvre 1930, no. 211A; 'Le Second Empire', Musée Jacquemart-André, Paris 1957, no. 101; Atelier Delacroix, Paris 1963, *h.c.*

Literature: Escholier I, repr. p. 260.

Though catalogued by Robaut under the title *Vue prise à Champrosay*, the view itself, combined with the fact that the painting was bought by the owner of Valmont Abbey at Delacroix's posthumous sale, leaves little room for doubt that the location is in fact Valmont. Mme Méra, one of the owners of the Abbey today, believes it is a view of the Château of Valmont, taken from a point close to the present cemetery.

Robaut's date of 1834 also seems to be purely arbitrary, and the picture is included here because it is impossible to be sure, in the present state of knowledge of Delacroix's landscape paintings, that it could not as well have been painted during his visit to Valmont in 1829 or 1831, as during one of his stays there in 1834 and later. A further reason for placing it in this volume is that its early provenance has sometimes been confused with J158's.

160 LANDSCAPE WITH SNOW   Pl. 141

Wood panel, cradled, 9 × 14 in. (22.8 × 35.5 cm)*
Damaged, possibly false E.D.[1]
R543 (1834)
Knoedler & Co., Paris

Provenance: Delacroix's posthumous sale, Feb. 1864, lot 216 ('Effet de neige', without dimensions or further description. Burty Ann ED: 'très-juste'), to Filhs, 260 fr.; sale M. C., 13 Apr. 1865, lot 30 ('Paysage. Effet de neige', 22 × 35 cm, with mention of provenance from Delacroix sale), 125 fr.; Victor Chocquet, by 1877, d. 1891; Marie Chocquet, his widow; her sale, 1 July 1899, lot 51 ('La neige', with full description corresponding to this view, 'panneau, 21 × 33½ cm'), to Haro, 760 fr.; sale Henri Haro, 12 Dec. 1911, lot 211, to Bernheim-Jeune, 600 fr.; Dr. Hans Graber, Zurich, by 1939; acquired from a Swiss source by Knoedler, New York, 25 Sept. 1957; they sold it to Mrs. Bernard Combermale, New York, 7 March 1958; and bought it back from her, 7 Dec. 1961; with Knoedler, Paris, 1968.

Exhibition: Zurich 1939, no. 323.

Literature: J. Rewald, 'Chocquet and Cézanne', *GBA*, LXXIV (1969), p. 76.

Robaut specified the location as Champrosay, but questioned whether this could be right in R Ann. He seems to have had no firmer grounds for dating this landscape study to 1834. It is included in this volume because it seems that it could well have been painted within a time-span marked by two other snow scenes, the *Winter* of 1821 (J94) and the *Battle of Nancy* dated 1831 (J143).

[1] Though painted on a wood panel instead of on canvas, the support listed by Robaut, this seems without doubt to be R543, which Robaut lists as lot 216 in Delacroix's posthumous sale and as belonging to Chocquet in 1877. The 'E.D.' seal of Delacroix's posthumous sale is not, however, mentioned in the catalogue of the Chocquet sale of 1899, which does record it in the case of some other works by Delacroix. An original seal may have been removed when the cradle was fitted and a false one added after the Chocquet sale.

161 STILL LIFE WITH LOBSTERS   Pl. 142

31$\frac{11}{16}$ × 41$\frac{15}{16}$ in. (0.805 × 1.065 m)
Signed bottom left: *Eug. Delacroix*.
Moreau p. 169. R174 (1826)
1826–7
Musée du Louvre

Provenance: Painted for General Charles Cyr, Comte de Coëtlosquet, d. 1836; Philippe Rousseau, painter; acquired from him by Adolphe Moreau, June 1843, d. 1859; by descent to his grandson, Etienne Moreau-Nélaton; he donated it to the Louvre in 1906 (RF 1661). At Musée des arts décoratifs 1907–34; transferred to Louvre 1934.

Exhibitions: Salon 1827–8, no. 300 ('Tableau de nature morte'); *Soc. Amis des Arts*, Bordeaux 1855, no. 171; Alsace-Lorraine, Paris 1874, no. 118; *EBA*, Paris 1885, no. 154; *Centennale*, Paris 1900, no. 219; Louvre 1930, no. 28; Atelier Delacroix, Paris 1945, no. 3; Petit Palais, Paris 1946, no. 155; Atelier Delacroix, Paris 1948, no. 19; Orangerie, Paris 1952, no. 87; Louvre 1963, no. 95, *M* no. 98, repr.; Atelier Delacroix, Paris 1973 (no cat.).

Literature: Anon., review of Salon 1827–8, *Le Mentor*, 15 Nov. 1827; anon., id., *Journal du Commerce*, 14 Jan. 1828; Silvestre *Delacroix* (1855), p. 80; E. Feydeau, 'Collection de M. Adolphe Moreau', *L'Artiste*, 7th ser. III (1858), p. 294; *Catalogue de la Collection Moreau . . .* (Frazier-Soye, Paris, 1907 and 1923), no. 53, repr.; Moreau-Nélaton I. 81, 85, 163, repr. fig. 52, II. 246; Brière 1924, p. 82; Escholier I. 182–4, repr. opp. p. 184; Hourticq 1930, pl. 15; *Correspondance* I. 183 n. 1, 196 n. 2, III. 11 n. 2; *Journal* I. 90 n. 3; Sterling-Adhémar, no. 663, pl. 232 and colour frontispiece; C. Sterling, *Still Life Painting from Antiquity to the Present Time* (new revised ed. in English, Pierre Tisné, Paris, 1959), pp. 94, 97, repr. in colour pl. 80 (1st French ed., also 1959, p. 89, pl. 80); E. Gombrich, *Meditations on a Hobby Horse* (Phaidon, London, 1963), pp. 100 f., repr. fig. 49 ('Tradition and Expression in Western Still Life', reprint of review of Sterling's book *Still Life Painting . . .* first published in *Burl Mag*, CIII (1961)); Huyghe, pp. 167, 173, 517 n. 14, repr. in colour pl. VII; Maltese, pp. 33, 124, 149, repr. pl. 17; L. Johnson, 'Eugène Delacroix et les Salons. Documents inédits au Louvre', *Revue du Louvre*, 16 (1966), p. 220; Trapp, pp. 59, 77, repr. fig. 23; Bortolatto, double-page repr. in colour, pls. XX–XXI, full-page repr. in colour of left background with huntsmen, pl. XXII.

Moreau was the first to record, in 1873, that this picture was painted for 'M. le général de Coëtlosquet' at Beffes (Cher) in 1826. His information was possibly based on a then unpublished letter from Delacroix to Soulier dated 23 March 1850, in which the artist writes: 'Il y a un mois ou deux on m'a fait voir le tableau d'animaux que j'ai fait à

Beffes, il y a quelque vingt-quatre ans! Le pauvre marquis [*sic*] est mort à son tour et le tableau était à vendre.' (*Correspondance* III. 11). But, as Escholier (I. 182) was to point out, if the painting was perhaps begun in 1826, it was certainly not finished before 1827, since Delacroix wrote to Soulier in a letter from Paris dated 28 September 1827: 'J'ai achevé le tableau d'animaux du général et je lui ai déterré un cadre rococo que je fais redorer et qui fera merveille. Il a déjà donné dans l'œil à une provision d'amateurs et je crois que cela sera drôle au Salon.' (*Correspondance* I. 197.) While there is no proof that Delacroix was at Beffes in 1827, he was evidently staying at the General's country house in June 1826, as shown by Joubin (cf. *Correspondance* I. 182 ff., 184 n. 4, 185 and n. 1). It therefore seems from Delacroix's letters, in only two of which the picture is actually mentioned, that it must have been begun and well advanced at Beffes in 1826, but finished in Paris in 1827. It was accepted for the Salon on 12 October 1827 (Johnson, op. cit., 1966). According to Moreau-Nélaton (I. 85), it was still in the 'rococo frame' chosen by Delacroix when he donated it to the Louvre in 1906.

Despite its exceptional quality and fresh conception, this masterful fusion of still life and panoramic landscape was scarcely noticed at the Salon, receiving only grudging praise in *Le Mentor* and a facile jibe in the *Journal du Commerce*. The critic of the former wrote condescendingly: 'La nature morte sourit au pinceau de M. Delacroix. Ce peintre devrait encore s'amender et montrer plus de correction dans certains endroits; il a du génie mais le génie a souvent besoin d'être dirigé pour ne pas s'égarer.' The critic of the latter: 'Le tableau de nature morte de M. Delacroix est vraiment un tour de force: il est impossible de faire un plus grand abus d'un beau talent.' Notwithstanding an unfortunate reference to the 'sonorous pathos of Delacroix's lobsters', Charles Sterling's comments on the picture in his book *Still Life Painting* (1959) and earlier in the catalogue of the exhibition Orangerie, Paris 1952, are the most thoughtful and instructive that have been written. Noting, in his catalogue, a combination of the Flemish Baroque still-life tradition, continued in France by Oudry and Desportes, and of the modern English landscape tradition, notably of Constable in his opinion, Sterling concludes in his book (op. cit., 1959, p. 94): 'Delacroix took his cue from Rubensian Baroque and its derivative, English Romanticism, and these helped him to express the concord of still life and landscape with freshness and originality.'

Though crustaceans are found in still-life painting as early as the first century A.D., the unusual idea of placing a pair of cooked lobsters on open ground in the countryside of England or northern France may have been most immediately inspired by the presence of a red lobster in the foreground of Wilkie's *Chelsea Pensioners reading the Gazette of the Battle of Waterloo* (Wellington Museum, London), a painting much admired by Géricault and which Delacroix would have seen at the British Institution in 1825. The still more surprising appearance of a live green lizard in this habitat may best be explained as a wish to introduce the colour complement of the lobsters, as well as an animate creature to stir the dead.

As for the Scottish tartan, which has often been noted as an 'English' touch, it is interesting that Delacroix had noted his intention of asking Dr. Meyrick, the famous collector of arms and armour, how he made tracings of tartans; in an unpublished sketch-book from his English journey of 1825, he wrote: 'au dr. Meyrick sa manière de tracer les rayures des clans ecossais'.

This highly accomplished still life, the only one known in the period up to 1832, may not have sprung into being entirely without precedent in Delacroix's work, for Silvestre *Delacroix* (1855) records, together with this picture, a 'Nature morte, poissons, grives, etc. (en Angelterre)' (J(L)114), which may have been a work painted by Delacroix in England in 1825 and left there, to disappear without a trace.

A still-life painting on a wooden door from an outhouse at the Abbey of Valmont, near Fécamp, mentioned as a genuine early Delacroix by Sterling in his catalogue of the exhibition Orangerie, Paris 1952, and later in *Mémorial*, is a most dubious precedent. The work in question still hangs in the former abbey and represents a duck, hare and cock hanging above a pile of vegetables. Mme Méra, present owner of the property and of the painting, gave me an account of the oral tradition concerning its origins. According to this story, M. Bornot, her great-grandfather, removed the painted door from a shed used for storing game, in order to preserve it from the weather. When Delacroix subsequently visited Valmont, he is said to have protested that he had intended it to remain on the outhouse, and he painted another picture in the same place, to stay there. About 1928, Mme Méra and her father scrubbed the old shed door and found faint traces of painted hounds and of a large horn.

Dismissing the possibility that Delacroix could have painted the detached door on his visit to Valmont at the age of fifteen, in 1813, he could not have done it before his next visit in 1829, that is to say three years after he began the *Still Life with Lobsters*. It seems to me in any case not to be from his hand, and possibly to be by his cousin Léon Riesener.

162 A MORTALLY WOUNDED   Pl. 143
BRIGAND QUENCHES HIS THIRST

$12\frac{13}{16} \times 16$ in. (32.5 × 40.7 cm) Relined (dimensions of existing original canvas, 32.1 × 40 cm)
Signed lower right: *Eug. Delacroix*
Moreau pp. 169, 266. R126 (1825)

c. 1825

Öffentliche Kunstsammlung, Kunstmuseum, Basle

Provenance: Painted for M. Du Sommerard in 1825, according to Moreau; his sale 11 Dec. 1843, lot 22, 330 fr.; M. A. Dugléré, by 1848; his sale 1 Feb. 1853, lot 43, 985 fr.; M. Bruissin ?, by 1864; M. Dupont, rue des Gourdes, Orleans, by 1884; anon. sale (by Féral), 29 March 1893, lot 14 (mention of Du Sommerard provenance and Salon of 1827. 'Signé à droite. Bois', 33 × 40 cm), bought in at 18,000 fr. (R Ann); M. Beurdeley, by 1900; A. Beurdeley sale 6 May 1920, lot 33, repr., to J. B. Stang, 46,200 fr.; his collection, Oslo, to at least 1930; with Eugène Blot, Paris, by 1937; acquired by the Kunstmuseum, Basle (Inv. no. 1726), 1939.

Exhibitions: Salon 1827, no. 297 (listed as lent by M. Du Sommerard); ? *Bd Italiens*, Paris 1864, Supp. to 2nd ed., no. 310 ('Le Brigand', 33 × 43 cm, lent by M. Bruissin); Exposition des Beaux-Arts, Orleans May 1884, no. 68; *EBA*, Paris 1885, no. 75; *Centennale*, Paris 1900, no. 227; St. Petersburg 1912, no. 199; Copenhagen 1914, no. 73, repr.; Oslo 1928, no. 46, repr.; Louvre 1930, no. 25, repr. *Album*, p. 14; Louvre 1963, no. 94, *M* no. 97, repr.; Berne 1963-4, no. 6.

Literature: Anon. Salon review, *Journal du Commerce*, 11 Nov. 1827; anon. Salon review, *La Pandore*, no. 1649, 24 Nov. 1827; P., 'Salon de 1827', *Journal de Paris*, 24 Nov. 1827; anon. Salon review, *Le Figaro*, 21 Dec. 1827; *Visite au Musée du Louvre, ou guide de l'amateur à l'exposition . . . (année 1827-28) . . . par une société de gens de lettres et d'artistes* (Leroi, Paris, 1928), p. 201; A. Jal, *Esquisses, croquis, pochades ou tout ce qu'on voudra sur le Salon de 1827* (Ambr. Dupont et Cie, Paris, 1828), p. 110; Silvestre *Delacroix* (1855), p. 80; Piron, p. 106; Robaut, p. 480 (Additions and Corrections); P. Burty, 'Eugène Delacroix à l'Ecole des Beaux-Arts', *L'Illustration*, no. 2195 (21 March 1885), p. 199; G. Dampt, *Eugène Delacroix. A propos de la dernière exposition de ses œuvres* (Tresse, Paris, 1885), p. 14; F. Monod, 'L'Exposition centennale de l'art français à Saint-Pétersbourg', *GBA*, 4th period VII (1912), p. 308; Moreau-Nélaton I. 86, repr. fig. 53; Escholier I. 216; P. Jamot, 'L'Art français en Norvège', *La Renaissance*, XII (1929), p. 94, repr. p. 106; *Öffentliche Kunstsammlung Basel, Katalog 1946* (Basle, 1946), p. 131, repr.; L. Johnson, 'The Delacroix Centenary in France—I', *Burl Mag*, CV (1963), repr. p. 299, fig. 5; Maltese, pp. 33, 135, 146, repr. pl. 11; L. Johnson, 'Eugène Delacroix et les Salons. Documents inédits au Louvre', *Revue du Louvre*, 16 (1966), pp. 220, 228 n. 10.

Prints: Lithograph in reverse by Mouilleron, with title *Brigand blessé*; another state with title *La Mort du Brigand*, and inscribed below left: 'Cabinet de Mr A. Dugléré, *Les Artistes Anciens et Modernes* (Impr. lith. Bertauts, Paris, 1848-62), vol. 1, 1st year, no. 14.

This painting was listed in the catalogue of the Salon of 1827 (for which exhibition it was accepted on 8 October) under the title *Un pâtre de la campagne de Rome, blessé mortellement, se traîne au bord d'un marais pour se désaltérer*. But it was entered in the register of works submitted to the Salon jury as *Brigand se traînant près d'un ruisseau* (see L. Johnson 1966, p. 220), which, in conjunction with the titles *Brigand blessé* and *La Mort du Brigand* on the Mouilleron lithograph published during Delacroix's lifetime, suggests that the artist intended to represent an outlaw and not merely an innocent shepherd wounded in unexplained circumstances. Italian brigands as well as *contadini* were popular subjects with Romantic artists; Léopold Robert, for example, a leading specialist in the type, had shown a *Brigand en prière* and *La mort d'un brigand* at the Salon of 1824. But this appears to be Delacroix's only essay of the sort, and it is entirely free from the picturesque sentimentality that often characterizes the genre.

The qualities of observation in the painting were widely recognized by the critics, but Delacroix was taxed with a taste for ugliness, which was a common reproach directed at artists of the new school by reactionaries. The comments of the anonymous reviewer for the *Visite au Musée du Louvre* are typical. Having evoked the elegantly clad shepherds and shepherdesses set in idyllic landscapes of the Arcadian tradition, which he calls the 'beautiful', the author continues: 'voici le laid: M. Delacroix, qui semble avoir pris à tâche de peindre la nature sous ses aspects hideux, nous représente un berger se désaltérant dans l'eau croupissante d'un marais. Et quel berger! sa figure annonce un brigand, son costume un vagabond sans asile. Un ciel épais, une terre stérile, un marais noir et boubeux, tels sont les accessoires de cet ouvrage, plein de vérité et de talent, mais à qui on ne reprochera pas d'embellir la nature.'

The critic of *Le Figaro*, on the other hand, argued: 'cette figure n'a pas besoin d'être belle. [. . .] On voit tous les efforts qu'a faits ce malheureux pour arriver à son but: l'expression de sa figure est magnifique, le mouvement bien saisi, la pensée profonde. Nous reconnaissons les défauts de M. Delacroix; qu'on ne lui conteste pas ses deux qualités: la beauté de la couleur et la justesse de la pantomime.'

It is probable on grounds of technique that the picture was painted after the English journey of 1825: the attempt to simulate the texture of the sheepskin jacket by the actual roughness of the impasto finds a close parallel in the tablecloth in the *Mephistopheles appears before Faust* (J116), which was certainly painted after the journey. Both passages reflect the kind of technical experiments that seem to have resulted from Delacroix's contact with Bonington on their return from England.

Copies: 1. A version in reverse on wood, 20.3 × 31.7 cm, from the collection of Steven Juvelis, Lynn, Mass., was sold as the original for 800 gns. in a mixed sale at Christie's on 7 July 1961, lot 36. It was probably copied from Mouilleron's lithograph, possibly by Delacroix's pupil Emile Knoepfler. It was with Tooth, London, in 1963.

2. A copy on canvas laid down on cardboard, bearing the seal of Delacroix's posthumous sale on the back and measuring 21.9 × 16.2 cm, in the Reinhart collection, Winterthur, has been con-

sidered a preliminary sketch for the original. It is probably by Pierre Andrieu.

3. A version measuring 58 × 70 cm, signed 'en toutes lettres', is recorded in Dieterle R as being sold from the collection of a M. Lemaire, Director of the 'Etoile Belge', after his death in 1906; it was proposed to Dieterle by a M. Dumont of Brussels in February 1922.

LOST WORKS

Academy Figures, Nudes, Studies of Limbs

L1 NUDE GIRL RECLINING IN   Pl. 144
A LANDSCAPE

$25\frac{3}{16} \times 31\frac{1}{2}$ in. (64×80 cm)
R18 (1818)
Present whereabouts unknown

Provenance: Gift from the artist to his housekeeper Jeanne Marie Le Guillou, who later gave it to Constant Dutilleux (R Ann); his sale, 26 March 1874, lot 2 (lith. repr.), 2,000 fr.; Kleinberger, by 1885 (R Ann); anonymous sale [Maurice Sand], 31 March 1890, lot 34, bought in at 400 fr. (R Ann); Dr. Viau? (Dieterle R).

Exhibitions: None.

Literature: Probably Inv. Delacroix, no. 57.

Print: Lithograph by Alfred Robaut, in catalogue of Dutilleux sale 1874.

Fig. 20. *Nude Girl in a Landscape*, Delacroix.

This work is known to me only from Robaut's lithograph, reproduced here, and from the smaller print in his *catalogue raisonné*. A clause in Delacroix's will refers to 'plusieurs croquis ou peintures' on the back of which he has designated that they are to belong to Jenny Le Guillou (*Correspondance* (Burty 1878), p. iv). In view of the provenance from Jenny Le Guillou that is claimed by Robaut (who was Dutilleux's son-in-law), it seems likely that this was one of those paintings and probably the picture listed in Inv. Delacroix under no. 57 as '1 tableau représentant un *Enfant endormi*, par M. Delacroix'.

A very closely related composition drawing, with slight variations in the landscape, is contained in a sketch-book that Delacroix was using in the period 1818/19, the date which is given for the painting in the catalogue of the Dutilleux sale (Louvre, RF23356, fol. 39^r. Fig. 20 here).

Robaut notes in R Ann: 'Delacroix qui garda toute sa vie cette ancienne étude s'en est servi pour le petit génie en dessous du groupe d'Homère (Coupole du Luxembourg).' There is, however, very little similarity between the pose in this study and the figure to which Robaut refers on the dome in the Senate Library, painted in the 1840s (repr. in Sérullaz *Peintures murales*, pl. 76).

It was decided not to include this picture in the exhibition *EBA*, Paris 1885, apparently because Georges Petit did not like it (R Ann); it had been brought to Petit by Kleinberger with a letter from Baron de Beurnonville, according to an annotation by Robaut in his copy of the second edition of the catalogue of the exhibition *EBA*, Paris 1885 (*Bib AA*, MS. 298ter, no. 239^G).

L2 MALE ACADEMY FIGURE:
STANDING

Dimensions unknown
Part of R1470? (1820. No repr.)
Whereabouts unknown

Provenance: ?Delacroix's posthumous sale, Feb. 1864, part of lot 200 ('Dix-sept études et académies', without dimensions), to P. Andrieu, 230 fr.; P. Andrieu; his sale, 6 May 1892, lot 181 ('Académie d'homme debout').

Exhibitions: None.

Literature: None.

Delacroix's assistant Pierre Andrieu is recorded in Burty Ann ED as buying two items from lot 200 at the master's posthumous sale, one of which was an academy figure that went for 230 fr. It is possible that it was the same figure which passed as a Delacroix in the Andrieu sale in 1892, and they are therefore not recorded in separate entries here.

L3 MALE ACADEMY FIGURE: Pl. 144
STANDING, SIDE VIEW, FACING RIGHT

$32\frac{11}{16} \times 96\frac{1}{2}$ in. (83×38 cm. Cut down from 1.03×0.59 m ?)
Part of R1470 (1820. No repr.)
Whereabouts unknown

Provenance: Delacroix's posthumous sale, Feb. 1864, part of lot 200 ('Dix-sept études et académies', without dimensions), to Geoffroy Dechaume, 200 fr. (R Ann, Robaut Tracings, Burty Ann ED); his sale, 14 Apr. 1893, lot 28 ('Etude de nu', 83×38 cm, and stated to be from Delacroix's posthumous sale), 210 fr.

Exhibition: *EBA*, Paris 1885, no. 91 (dimensions listed as 1.03×0.59 m).

Literature: None.

This work is known only from Robaut's drawing of it in Tracings v (Supp.), reproduced here. It has not come to light since it passed to an unknown buyer at the Dechaume sale in 1893.

L4 A SMALL ACADEMY FIGURE AND OTHER STUDIES

Dimensions unknown
Part of R1470 (1820. No repr.)
Whereabouts unknown

Provenance: Delacroix's posthumous sale, Feb. 1864, part of lot 200 ('Dix-sept études et académies', without dimensions), to Paul Huet, 170 fr. (Burty Ann ED),[1] d. 1869.

Exhibitions: None.

Literature: R. P. Huet, *Paul Huet . . .* (H. Laurens, Paris, 1911), p. 381.

In a letter to Sollier dated 17 April 1864, Paul Huet described this canvas, among other works that he bought at Delacroix's posthumous sale, as 'une toile sur laquelle sont divers fragments tels que des chevaux, une tête et une petite figure académique' (R. P. Huet, op. cit.). Its subsequent history is unknown to me.

[1] See J5, n. 1.

L5 ODALISQUE LYING ON A DIVAN

$14\frac{3}{16} \times 18\frac{1}{8}$ in. (36×46 cm)
Whereabouts unknown

Provenance: Haro in 1864.

Exhibition: *Bd Italiens*, Paris 1864, no. 44 ('Odalisque étendue sur un divan', 36×46 cm).

Literature: None.

This picture is known to me only from the description in the catalogue of the exhibition *Bd Italiens*, Paris 1864, where it is listed as lent by Haro, Delacroix's colour merchant. Of the known paintings of a woman lying on a bed, the dimensions in the catalogue correspond most closely with those of the Fitzwilliam *Odalisque* (J10), but this cannot be the same picture unless it was owned by Barroilhet in 1864 and lent to the exhibition in Haro's name.

L6 WOMAN LYING ON A SOPHA   Pl. 144

Approximately $8\frac{1}{4} \times 10\frac{5}{8}$ in. (21×27 cm)
R Ann 323bis (1830)
Whereabouts unknown

Provenance: Pierre Andrieu; his sale, 6 May 1892, lot 173 ('Femme étendue sur un sofa', without dimensions), to Saverdey, 75 fr.

Exhibitions: None.

Literature: None.

R Ann amplifies the description given in the Andrieu sale, as follows: 'Ebauche. Toile de 3 environ (21×27). Tout le torse est nu, le reste est recouvert d'étoffe; elle est tournée à gauche, accoudée sur le bras droit, le gauche étendu.' There is also a rough drawing of the picture in Robaut Tracings II, reproduced here.

The fact that this picture passed in Andrieu's sale as a Delacroix and is listed in R Ann is no guarantee of its authenticity, but so long as it remains untraced the possibility of its being by Delacroix cannot be ruled out.

L7 STUDY OF A WOMAN IN BED

$9\frac{7}{8} \times 13$ in. (25×33 cm)
R55 (1822)
Whereabouts unknown

See J(R)2.

L8 STUDY OF A LEFT LEG

Life-size, dimensions of surface unknown
R Ann 53bis (*c.* 1822)
Whereabouts unknown

Provenance: ?Delacroix's posthumous sale, Feb. 1864, part of lot 200 ('Dix-sept études et académies', without dimensions), to P. Andrieu ?, 70 fr.;[1] P. Andrieu; his sale, 6 May 1892, lot 176, 85 fr.

Exhibitions: None.

Literature: Inv. Delacroix, no. 110? ('un tableau représentant *une étude de jambes* par [Delacroix]'.)

This study is known to me only from the catalogue of the Andrieu sale and from the slightly more detailed description in R Ann, where it is listed as 'une étude de jambe gauche gr. [grandeur] nature' together with a full reference to the sale. Many of the works attributed to Delacroix in the sale of his assistant Pierre Andrieu were of doubtful authenticity, but it is possible that this study was one of the several paintings that Andrieu is known to have bought at the master's posthumous sale and which remain unaccounted for.

¹ Andrieu is recorded in Burty Ann ED as buying two pictures from this lot, one for 230 fr. (see J(L)2) and the other for 70 fr.

L9 A MAN'S FOOT

$8\frac{5}{8} \times 13$ in. (22×33 cm)
Whereabouts unknown

Provenance: Unknown.

Exhibitions: Atelier Delacroix, Paris 1945, no. 52; id. 1946 A & B, no. 46; id. 1952, Supp., no. 86.

Literature: None.

This work is known to me only from the summary descriptions in the catalogues of the Atelier Delacroix exhibitions listed above, and I can therefore only record it without comment on its authenticity and date.

L10 ASSORTED STUDIES AND ACADEMY FIGURES

(Lot 200, Delacroix's posthumous sale, Feb. 1864)
R1470 (1820)

Lot 200 was described in the catalogue of the posthumous sale merely as: 'Dix-sept études et académies'. Robaut could account for only three of these in his published *catalogue*

raisonné, and for a further two or three in R Ann. There were in fact more than seventeen pictures in the lot, for a total of nineteen items are listed in Burty Ann ED, with the names of the buyers and the prices. These annotations are transcribed in full below; where they have been definitely or tentatively identified with pictures catalogued elsewhere in this volume, references are added in square brackets.

130 fr.	- étude homme	- Chassaux
420	- id femme nue	- Thoré [J4]
340	- id	- Minoret
210	- id	- Arosa

peinture
manre.
Rubens

420	- femme étude nue	- Cadart [J(O)2 ?]
200	- Académie	- Dechaume [J(L)3]
155	- id	- Berryer
140	- id homme	- Hervez
230	- id	- Andrieux [P. Andrieu. J(L)2 ?]
165	- id	- P. Huet [J5]
100	- id	- de Blanzay
70	- id	- Andrieux [P. Andrieu. J(L)8 ?]
200	- Etude	- Dieterle [J2]
235	- Academie	- Belly [J(M)1]
170	- id	- P. Huet [J(L)4]
55	- id	- P. Huet [J(O)1 ?]
26	- id	- Lejeune
32	- id	- Marchal de Calvi
13	- Guerrier [buyer]	- 2 études nos. 200-1 [this is the first note on the list of items in lot 201.]

Works which may have been included in this lot but which I am unable to identify with individual annotations are: J1, J3, J(L)9, J(O)3, J(M)2, J(D)1.

Copies after the Masters

Lost copies for which there is no external evidence of date are included in this volume, as are doubtful and rejected copies unless there is evidence that Delacroix did an authentic version after 1831.

L11 AN ALLEGORICAL FIGURE, after RAPHAEL

$11\frac{13}{16} \times 8\frac{11}{16}$ in. (30×22 cm)
R1926 (No repr.)
Whereabouts unknown

Provenance: Delacroix's posthumous sale, Feb. 1864, lot 153 ('Figure allégorique [d'après Raphael]'), to M. Detrimont, 355 fr.

Exhibitions: None.

Literature: S. Lichtenstein, 'Delacroix's Copies after Raphael', *Burl Mag*, CXIII (1971), p. 599, no. 3.

This copy is known only from the summary description in the posthumous sale catalogue which repeats that in Inv. Delacroix (no. 339), and to which Robaut added nothing except the name of the purchaser and the price.

L12 TRITON, after **RAPHAEL**, detail from the **TRIUMPH OF GALATEA**

$6\frac{11}{16} \times 8\frac{11}{16}$ in. (17 × 22 cm)
R1927 (No repr.)
Whereabouts unknown

Provenance: Delacroix's posthumous sale, Feb. 1864, lot 154 ('Fragment d'une figure de Triton dans le Triomphe de Galathée'), to Francis Petit, 65 fr.; anon. sale (Expert: Petit), Paris 14 May 1866, lot 21 ('Fragment du Triomphe de Galathée, d'après Raphael').

Exhibitions: None.

Literature: Probably Inv. Delacroix, no. 148 (as 'figures d'Eoles d'après Raphael'); S. Lichtenstein, 'Delacroix's Copies after Raphael', *Burl Mag*, CXIII (1971), pp. 530, 599, no. 4.

This copy is known only from the descriptions in the catalogues of the two sales listed above and in Inv. Delacroix.

Since Delacroix never went to Italy, he could not have seen the original fresco in the Farnesina and must have made his copy from a reproduction, possibly from a photograph as suggested by Robaut, but more probably from an engraved or painted copy by another artist.

L13 THE THEOLOGICAL VIRTUES, after **RAPHAEL**

$12\frac{3}{16} \times 9\frac{1}{16}$ in. (31 × 23 cm)
R Ann, margin to R1464 & 1465 (*c.* 1818/9)
Whereabouts unknown

Provenance: Baronne de Ruble, by 1885.

Exhibition: Alsace-Lorraine, Paris 1885, no. 115 ('Les Vertus théologales (Copie d'après Raphael)').

Literature: S. Lichtenstein, 'Delacroix's Copies after Raphael', *Burl Mag*, CXIII (1971), p. 599.

This copy is known only from the description in the catalogue of the exhibition Alsace-Lorraine, Paris 1885, to which it was lent by the Baronne de Ruble, and from the note in R Ann, which merely adds the opinion that it dated from *c.* 1818/19. It was presumably done from a reproduction of the group personifying Faith, Hope and Charity in the Stanza della Segnatura.

L14 PORTRAIT OF A YOUTH, after **PARMIGIANINO**

(Louvre, RF1506. Attr. to Raphael when copied)
$24\frac{13}{16} \times 18\frac{7}{8}$ in. (63 × 48 cm)
Moreau p. 319. R1925 (No repr.)
Whereabouts unknown

Provenance: Delacroix's posthumous sale, Feb. 1864, lot 151, to Thoré for Emile Pereire, 3,250 fr.; Pereire sale, 6 March 1872, lot 13, to M. Febvre (Moreau & Robaut) or Tabourier (Moreau-Nélaton annotated copy of Delacroix sale catalogue, 1864, *BN Estampes*), 3,750 fr.; Comtesse de Paris, by 1874.

Exhibition: Presumably Alsace-Lorraine, Paris 1874, no. 111 (as 'Copie du portrait du Louvre, dit l'Homme noir, attribué à Francia', without dimensions, lent by 'S.A.R. Mme la comtesse de Paris').

Literature: Silvestre *Delacroix* (1855), p. 83; Silvestre *Documents nouveaux* (1864), p. 20; *Journal* I. 474 n. 5, III. 168; S. Lichtenstein, 'Delacroix's Copies after Raphael', *Burl Mag*, CXIII (1971), pp. 533, 599.

Neither Moreau nor Robaut attempted to date this copy, but it is likely to have been early, since Silvestre (op. cit., 1864) couples it with the study after Raphael's *Belle Jardinière* (J11), as an example of those copies by Delacroix which were no more than 'tours de patience et de subtilité'. It is mentioned only once by Delacroix, late in life, simply to note a loan: 'Prêté à Mme Halévy, en partant pour Champrosay, les deux copies de Raphaël, *l'Enfant* [J11] et le *Portrait à la main*.' (*Journal* I. 474, entry for 6 July 1852.) It has never been reproduced, nor come to light since the

Fig. 21. *Portrait of a Youth*, Parmigianino.

exhibition Alsace-Lorraine, Paris 1874 where it is presumed to have been shown under no. 111, lent by the Comtesse de Paris. The Surintendant des bâtiments du Comte de Paris has been unable to find any trace of it in the residences of the present head of the French Royal Family.

The original (Fig. 21) was attributed to Raphael throughout Delacroix's lifetime. It was at one time thought to be a self-portrait, but is not so listed in the Louvre catalogues that were published during the first half of the nineteenth century.

L15 PASTORAL CONCERT, after GIORGIONE (Louvre, RF1136)

$15\frac{3}{8} \times 17\frac{3}{4}$ in. (39 × 45 cm)[1]
R1936 (No repr.)
Before 11 April 1824
Whereabouts unknown

Provenance: Delacroix's posthumous sale, Feb. 1864, lot 158, to Paul Van Cuyck, 1,200 fr.; his sale, Paris 7 Feb. 1866, lot 11, 490 fr.

Exhibitions: None.

Literature: Planet *Souvenirs*, p. 63 (?); D. Farr, *William Etty* (Routledge & Kegan Paul, London, 1958), p. 60; L. Johnson, review of ibid., *Burl Mag*, CI (1959), p. 298; Huyghe, p. 115; Maltese, p. 52; F. Haskell, 'Giorgione's *Concert Champêtre* and its Admirers', *Journal of the Royal Society of Arts*, CXIX (1971), p. 551.

All trace of this copy, which was about one third the size of the original, has been lost since the Van Cuyck sale in 1866. Though stated by some writers to have been painted in 1824, Delacroix's only reference to it, on 11 April 1824, is in a context which suggests that it might have been as early as the presumed portrait of Elisabeth Salter (J61) and the first portrait of Charles de Verninac (J62), i.e. before 1820. After enumerating some artists whose works possess the qualities of modelling that he is currently seeking, and mentioning these two early portraits of his own as having those qualities, he continues: 'Je l'aurais atteint plut tôt, si j'avais vu que cela ne pouvait aller qu'avec des contours bien fermes. Cela est éminemment dans la femme debout de ma copie du Giorgione, *des femmes nues dans une campagne*.' (*Journal* I. 75.)

Louis de Planet records that in 1843, when he was working as an assistant for the ceiling paintings in the Library of the Chamber of Deputies, Delacroix, in criticizing one of de Planet's own pictures, advised him to make use of the 'petit *Concert champêtre* de Giorgione pour les nuages, les copier juste et voir pour les arbres comment dans le tableau de Giorgione les arbres se détachent avec netteté sur le nuage blanc et avec plus de douceur sur le ciel bleu'. (Planet *Souvenirs*, p. 63.) In a footnote to this passage,

Joubin thought that the reference was to a copy after the Giorgione by de Planet, but it could equally well be to Delacroix's copy, just as there are references elsewhere in the *Souvenirs* to de Planet's being advised to consult Delacroix's copies after Rubens.

The *Pastoral Concert* may have had an influence on the grouping of the figures in the *Femmes d'Alger* of 1834 and on their relaxed monumentality, as I suggested in a series of lectures on Delacroix given at Cambridge University in the Lent term of 1968.

[1] According to the catalogue of Delacroix's posthumous sale; H. 43 × W. 33, according to that of the Van Cuyck sale, 1866.

L16 HEAD OF CARDINAL IPPOLITO DE' MEDICI, after TITIAN

No. 25-30 canvas: $31\frac{7}{8} \times 25\frac{5}{8} - 36\frac{1}{4} \times 28\frac{3}{4}$ in.
   (81 × 65-92 × 73 cm)
R786 (1843)
Whereabouts unknown (Never existed?)

Provenance: Unknown.

Exhibitions: None.

Literature: See Moreau p. 76.

It is probable that, through misinterpreting Moreau, Robaut wrongly inferred that a copy of this description by Delacroix existed. For illustration, he reproduces only a wood engraving by Frédéric Villot depicting the head from Titian's three-quarter length portrait of Cardinal Ippolito de' Medici in the Palazzo Pitti, Florence. This engraving was printed on the second state of a sheet of woodcuts by Villot, two of which—*Head of a Turk* and *Head of an Old Woman* (J87)—were done after a pen drawing and painting by Delacroix; but unlike these two, the head of the Cardinal is not stated by Moreau (p. 76) to have been done after Delacroix. In fact, his description of the second state of the print leaves almost no room for doubt that it was Villot's own study after Titian: 'Tiré sur une grande feuille *avec* le portrait de vieille femme [*peint par Delacroix*] *et* deux croquis de M. Villot représentant, l'un *la tête du cardinal Hippolyte de Médicis*, d'après Titien, et l'autre *un Joueur de mandoline assis*, fragment d'un tableau peint par M. Villot.'

The strongest reason for believing that a copy by Delacroix existed is that Robaut claimed to know its size, recording that it was on a 'Toile de vingt-cinq à trente'; but since he had evidently not seen it and listed no owners, this may have been sheer guesswork. If it was a copy of only the head covering the whole canvas, it would indeed be surprising had it been as large as even a No. 25 canvas, for in that case it would have been on a much greater scale than the original Titian, and Delacroix generally reduced the scale of his models.

L17 STUDY after VERONESE

Dimensions unknown
R1953 (No repr.)
Whereabouts unknown

Provenance: Delacroix's posthumous sale, Feb. 1864, part of lot 176 ('Six toiles contenant des fragments d'études d'après Rubens, Véronèse, Murillo, etc.', without dimensions), to Gaultron, 18 fr.

Burty Ann ED makes it possible to identify five of the six studies which made up lot 176 in the posthumous sale as by artists other than Veronese. By process of elimination, the sixth study must therefore have been after Veronese if the printed designation in the sale catalogue is accurate. It was presumably either one of the three pictures listed as copies after details in the *Marriage at Cana* in Inv. Delacroix (see J14) or the painting described in the same inventory under no. 75 as '1 tableau représentant *St Georges, St Benoît, et Ste Catherine*, d'après Veronese, par M. Delacroix'.

L18 LAMENTATION OVER THE DEAD CHRIST, after SÉBASTIEN BOURDON (Louvre, RF2807)

$16\frac{1}{8} \times 9\frac{7}{8}$ in. (41×25 cm)
Whereabouts unknown

Provenance: Delacroix's posthumous sale, Feb. 1864, lot 236 (as a copy by Géricault), to Dejean, 650 fr.

Exhibitions: None.

Literature: Silvestre *Delacroix* (1855), p. 83; Inv. Delacroix, no. 62; Silvestre *Documents nouveaux* (1864), p. 20; Clément, p. 321, no. 175.

Though this greatly reduced copy was catalogued in Delacroix's posthumous sale as a Géricault, Silvestre (op. cit., 1864) states firmly that this was an error on the part of Burty and the copy was really by Delacroix, to whom it is also attributed in Inv. Delacroix. The original (Fig. 22) was painted for the altar of the collegiate church of Saint-Benoît in Paris. Mariette found the colouring exceptionally good. Delacroix probably saw it for the first time when it was hung in the Musée Napoléon. All trace of his copy has been lost since 1864. It was probably a very early study, for it is apparently to this copy that Delacroix refers in a sketch-book used between 1825 and 1830, when noting a loan to Scheffer of a 'Christ Mort esquisse d'après Bourdon au Musée très ancienne' (Louvre, RF9144, fol. 22ᵛ).

L19 A BLACKSMITH'S FORGE, after LOUIS LE NAIN (Louvre, RF540)

Dimensions unknown
Whereabouts unknown

Fig. 22. *Lamentation over the Dead Christ*, Sébastien Bourdon.

Provenance: Probably Delacroix's posthumous sale, Feb. 1864, lot ?

Exhibitions: None.

Literature: Champfleury, *Essai sur la vie et l'œuvre des Lenain, peintres Laonnais* (Impr. Ed. Fleury et Ad. Chevergny, Laon, 1850), p. 40; Inv. Delacroix, no. 48.

No. 48 in Inv. Delacroix is described as '1 tableau représentant l'intérieur d'une forge, d'après Lenain, auteur inconnu'. No picture answering this description is listed in the catalogue of Delacroix's posthumous sale or has come to light since; but it seems very possible, from a passage written by Champfleury (op. cit., 1850), that it was an early copy done by Delacroix himself in the Louvre: '[. . .] si M. Viardot était jamais entré dans l'atelier d'Eugène Delacroix, il y aurait vu une copie de Lenain faite au Louvre par l'illustre peintre dans sa jeunesse.' (I am indebted to Professor Francis Haskell for this reference.) The *Maréchal dans sa forge* is the Le Nain that is most likely to have been accessible to Delacroix at the Louvre in his youth.

An unfinished painting, *A Blacksmith*, also lost (J(L)115), may have been an independent work by Delacroix related to this copy.

L20 FOUR SKETCHES after MURILLO

Dimensions unknown
R1951 (No repr.)
Whereabouts unknown

Provenance: Delacroix's posthumous sale, Feb. 1864, part of lot 176 ('Six toiles contenant des fragments d'études d'après Rubens, Véronèse, Murillo, etc.', without dimensions), to M. X . . ., 67 fr.

Exhibitions: None.

Literature: None, except Robaut.

Robaut does not list the title of this, or of any of the other five items which made up lot 176 in the posthumous sale; but he records that his no. 1951 (part of that lot, which he misleadingly lists under the general heading of copies after Rubens) was knocked down to a M. X . . . for 67 fr., and the only item which went for that price is identified in Burty Ann ED as: '4 Pochades d'après Murillo'. It has not come to light since 1864.

No copy by Delacroix after Murillo seems to be definitely recorded anywhere but in the description of lot 176 in the catalogue of the posthumous sale and the annotation to it. Théophile Silvestre states, however, in the context of a discussion of Delacroix's copies: 'Une *Madeleine* de Murillo l'avait enchanté et retenu dans la galerie du maréchal Soult' (Silvestre *Documents nouveaux* (1864), p. 21), which may mean that Delacroix copied the Murillo. In that case, these four sketches may have been done in the Soult collection and have included a *Magdalen*, if they were not all painted after the same picture. For references to the Soult collection in Delacroix's own writings, see J22.

L21 THE ARCADIAN SHEPHERDS, after POUSSIN?

Dimensions unknown
Whereabouts unknown

Provenance: Delacroix's posthumous sale, Feb. 1864, part of lot ?; Philippe Burty; his sale 2 March 1891, lot 8 ('Les

Bergers d'Arcadie. Esquisse provenant de la vente après le décès de l'artiste. Toile.'), 100 fr.

Exhibitions: None.

Literature: None.

This work is known only from the description in the catalogue of the Burty sale, quoted in full above. It may have been a study after the version of Poussin's *Arcadian Shepherds* in the Louvre.

L22 JACOB HAVING PEELED THE   Pl. 145 RODS IN ORDER THAT THE FLOCKS OF LABAN SHALL CONCEIVE, after a seventeenth-century painting of the Genoese School?

24 × 39⅜ in. (0.61 × 1.00 m)
R1928 (No repr.)
Whereabouts unknown

Provenance: Delacroix's posthumous sale, Feb. 1864, lot 159 ('La Vierge aux Bergers [d'après l'Ecole italienne]', 0.61 × 1.00 m), to M. Carlier, 170 fr.; Burckhardt, by 1930.

Exhibitions: None.

Literature: None, other than Robaut.

This copy is known to me only from the photograph reproduced here, which clearly shows a lot no. 159 in the lower left corner on a label of the type used for Delacroix's posthumous sale. In a list of Delacroix photographs compiled by the Archives photographiques in Paris c. 1930, Domenico Tiepolo was given as the source, Burckhardt as the owner and Delacroix's posthumous sale, lot 159, as the provenance. There seems to be no reason to doubt the provenance, but to judge from the photograph this copy is not indisputably from Delacroix's hand, the central figure seeming especially scratchy and weak. A firmer opinion must be deferred until the actual painting is found.

The subject is from Genesis 30: 37–8, and the model appears to have been a work not by Tiepolo, but of the Genoese School. (I am indebted to Michael Levey for identifying the subject and suggesting the School.)

If this copy is by Delacroix and he knew the subject, it is interesting to reflect that the story is related in Genesis only shortly before the struggle of Jacob with the Angel (32: 24–32), which is the subject of one of Delacroix's last and most famous mural paintings, in Saint-Sulpice.

L23 JACOB HAVING PEELED THE RODS . . ., after a seventeenth-century painting of the Genoese School?

Dimensions unknown
R1929 (No repr.)
Whereabouts unknown

Provenance: Delacroix's posthumous sale, Feb. 1864, lot 160 ('Fragment de la même composition' [as lot 159; J(L)22], without dimensions), to M. Fabius Brest, 46 fr. (Burty Ann ED and Moreau-Nélaton annotated copy of Delacroix sale catalogue, 1864, *BN Estampes*).

Exhibitions: None.

Literature: None, except Robaut.

This copy is known only from the summary description in the posthumous sale catalogue, to which Robaut added nothing except the name of the purchaser and a price.

L24 ADORATION OF THE MAGI, after RUBENS

$25\frac{5}{8} \times 20\frac{7}{8}$ in. (65 × 53 cm)
R1940 (No repr.)
Whereabouts unknown

Provenance: Delacroix's posthumous sale, Feb. 1864, lot 164 ('Adoration des Mages [d'après Rubens]', 65 × 53 cm), to M. de Carcenac, 655 fr.

Exhibitions: None.

Literature: As for J(R)6.

This copy is known only from the description in the catalogue of Delacroix's posthumous sale, in spite of attempts to identify it with J(R)6. That description gives no indication from which of the several versions of the subject by Rubens the copy was made. The Louvre version is given as the model in Robaut, but this may be incorrect as Robaut does not appear to have seen Delacroix's copy.

L25 FLYING FIGURES, after RUBENS, detail from a painting in the MEDICI CYCLE (Louvre)

Dimensions unknown
Whereabouts unknown

Literature: *Journal* I. 330 n. 1; B. White, 'Delacroix's Painted Copies after Rubens', *AB*, XLIX (1967), p. 43.

This study, which was probably not painted before 1849, is known only from the following entry of 7 January 1850 in the *Journal* (I. 331): 'Lui [à Haro] redemander aussi l'*Arabe accroupi*, qui devait être sur la grande toile où était la *Suzanne* [R1246; collection late Vicomtesse de Noailles], que j'ai achevée pour Villot. — Sur la toile ci-dessus, il devait y avoir des petites figures volantes d'un des tableaux de *Marie de Médicis* faits de mémoire.' Since the majority of the paintings in the Medici cycle contain flying figures, it is impossible to know to which of them Delacroix refers.

L26 SKETCHES OF THE HOLY TRINITY, after RUBENS (Royal Museum of Fine Arts, Antwerp)

Dimensions unknown
R1952 (No repr.)
Whereabouts unknown

Provenance: Delacroix's posthumous sale, Feb. 1864, part of lot 176 ('Six toiles contenant des fragments d'études d'après Rubens, Véronèse, Murillo, etc.', without dimensions), to M. X . . ., 30 fr.

Exhibitions: None.

Literature: None, except Robaut.

Robaut does not list the title of this, or of any of the other five items which made up lot 176 in the posthumous sale; but he records that his no. 1952, part of that lot, was knocked down to a M. X . . . for 30 fr., and the only item which went for that price is identified in Burty Ann ED as: 'Pochades d'après Rubens — la Trinité d'Anvers'. It has not come to light since 1864.

It is possible that these sketches were not done before 1839 or 1850, years when Delacroix visited Antwerp, noting on the latter occasion: 'Je ne pouvais me détacher du tableau de la *Trinité*' (*Journal* I. 405). But he does not record copying from it, and as long as his sketches are lost there is no means of judging whether they were done from an engraving before he saw the original. They are therefore included in this volume.

L27 HEADS OF WOMEN, after RUBENS, details from the MEDICI CYCLE (Louvre)

$31\frac{1}{2} \times 25\frac{5}{8}$ in. (80 × 65 cm)
R1944 (No repr.)
Whereabouts unknown

Provenance: Delacroix's posthumous sale, Feb. 1864, lot 173 ('Têtes de Femmes. Musée du Louvre, Histoire de Marie de Médicis', 80 × 65 cm), to M. Filhston, 110 fr.

Exhibitions: None.

Literature: B. White, 'Delacroix's Painted Copies after Rubens', *AB*, XLIX (1967), p. 49.

No trace of this copy has been found since 1864. It is possible that it is the canvas hanging closest to the ceiling on the lefthand wall in Renard's wood engraving of Delacroix's studio in the rue Notre-Dame de Lorette, published in *L'Illustration* in September 1852 (repr. in T. Prideaux *et al.*, *The World of Delacroix* (Time Inc., New York, 1966), p. 130).

L28 APOLLO, after RUBENS, detail from GOVERNMENT OF THE QUEEN (Louvre, RF2096)

$21\frac{5}{8} \times 15\frac{3}{4}$ in. (55 × 40 cm)
Whereabouts unknown

Provenance: M. Félix Gérard, by 1885.

Exhibition: *EBA*, Paris 1885, no. 158 (as 'Copie d'après Rubens, au Louvre', 55 × 40 cm).

This copy after a painting in the Medici cycle is known to me only from the description in the catalogue of the exhibition *EBA*, Paris 1885, to which Robaut adds the following details in his annotations to the second edition of that catalogue (*Bib AA*, MS. 298*ter*): '(Apollon vu de face) non signé.'

A copy after the same figure in the Rubens is recorded in the collection of M. Eugène Spiro, Paris, in 1938, and described as 'copy by Delacroix (?) of the figures of Athena and Apollo', by Edward King in 'Delacroix's Paintings in the Walters Art Gallery', *Journal of the Walters Art Gallery*, I (1938), p. 109 n. 15. That might have been the copy now in the Fogg Art Museum (Acc. no. 1946.59; 76.2 × 62.2 cm), which was formerly attributed to Delacroix and cannot be identified with the lost work shown in 1885.

L28a CHRIST AT THE TOMB, after RUBENS

$9\frac{1}{16} \times 12\frac{5}{8}$ in. (23 × 32 cm)
Whereabouts unknown

Provenance: Carvalho, by 1864.

Exhibition: *Bd Italiens*, Paris 1864, no. 170 ('Le Christ au tombeau. (Copie d'après Rubens.)', 23 × 32 cm, lent by M. Carvalho).

This work is known to me only from the description in the catalogue of the 1864 exhibition.

L29 ST. GEORGE, after RUBENS, detail from VIRGIN AND CHILD WITH SAINTS (Church of St. Jacques, Antwerp)

Dimensions unknown
Whereabouts unknown

Provenance: Dr. C. Hofstede de Groot?

Exhibitions: None.

Literature: B. White, 'Delacroix's Painted Copies after Rubens', *AB*, XLIX (1967), pp. 37, 38, 43, 46, repr. fig. 10.

I would not attribute this copy to Delacroix in the absence of a further history and on the basis of reproductions only, and therefore reserve judgement.

L30 A STUDY AFTER RUBENS

Dimensions unknown
R1949 or 1954 (No repr.)
Whereabouts unknown

Provenance: Delacroix's posthumous sale, Feb. 1864, part of lot 176 ('Six toiles contenant des fragments d'études d'après

Rubens, Véronèse, Murillo, etc.', without dimensions), to Gaultron, 100 fr. or 11 fr.

Two studies after Rubens are noted without titles in Burty Ann ED as part of lot 176 in the posthumous sale; they were knocked down to Gaultron for 100 fr. and 11 fr. One was probably the *Job Tormented by Demons* (J15); the other may have been either Inv. Delacroix, no. 124: '1 *fragment de tête d'après Rubens par M. Delacroix*'; or no. 240: '1 *ébauche, tête d'étude d'après Rubens par Delacroix*'.

L31 TOMYRIS, after RUBENS (*Tomyris with the Head of Cyrus*, Louvre RF2084)

$15\frac{3}{4} \times 12\frac{5}{8}$ in. (40 × 32 cm)
R1938 (No repr.)
Whereabouts unknown

Provenance: Delacroix's posthumous sale, Feb. 1864, lot 168 ('Thomiris [d'après Rubens]. Musée du Louvre', 40 × 32 cm), to M. Thoré, 305 fr.

Exhibitions: None.

Literature: B. White, 'Delacroix's Painted Copies after Rubens', *AB*, XLIX (1967), pp. 37, 48.

This copy is known only from the description in the catalogue of Delacroix's posthumous sale.

L32 PORTRAIT OF A WOMAN, after VELAZQUEZ?

$25\frac{5}{8} \times 21\frac{1}{4}$ in. (65 × 54 cm)
R1933 (No repr.)
Whereabouts unknown

Provenance: Delacroix's posthumous sale, Feb. 1864, lot 175 (as 'Portrait de femme [d'après une peinture ancienne]'), to Piron, 550 fr.; his sale (feu M***), 21 Apr. 1865, lot 11 (as 'Portrait d'une Dame espagnole, représentée en buste. D'après un tableau de Velasquez'), 155 fr.

Exhibitions: None.

Literature: Probably Inv. Delacroix, no. 64.

This picture has not come to light since the Piron sale of 1865, the catalogue of which describes it as a copy after Velazquez. Though it was not so described in the catalogue of Delacroix's posthumous sale, and the identification may therefore be inaccurate, it is probably the picture listed earlier as '1 *portrait de femme*, d'après Velasquez par M. Delacroix' under no. 64 in Inv. Delacroix.

L33 'RUEGA POR ELLA' ('She prays for her'), after GOYA (*Caprichos* Pl. 31)

$9\frac{7}{8} \times 7\frac{7}{8}$ in. (25 × 20 cm)
R Ann p. 423 (1832)
Whereabouts unkown

Provenance: Alfred Sensier; his sale, 10 Dec. 1877, lot 4 ('Figures. Etude', 25 × 20 cm).

Exhibitions: None.

Literature: None.

This picture is known only from a small sketch in R Ann (between pp. 422 and 423), on which it is impossible to base an opinion of its authenticity, but from which it is at least clear that the model was Plate 31 of Goya's *Caprichos*. Robaut recognized, in the notes on his sketch, that it was done after Goya, but failed to specify the source, describing the copy as 'Jeune fille assise à sa toilette. Une autre la coiffe. Une autre vieille à genoux regarde en face. Soupçon d'ébauche par ED^x [Eugène Delacroix].'

It is well known that Delacroix drew numerous studies after the *Caprichos*, including at least one after Plate 31, probably for the most part in the first half of the 1820s, but this and the following number are the only evidence that he may have painted oil studies from them. Six etchings from the series passed in his posthumous sale (lot 826), but the titles are not known, nor is the date when he acquired them. Robaut apparently placed this study in 1832 merely because Delacroix visited Spain in that year. The most complete account of Delacroix's interest in the *Caprichos* is in M. Florisoone, 'Comment Delacroix a-t-il connu les "Caprices" de Goya?', *BSHAF*, 1957, pp. 131–44.

L34 'QUIEN MAS RENDIDO?', after   Pl. 145
GOYA (with studies of missal covers and a Turkish jacket)

19$\frac{11}{16}$ × 24 in. (50 × 61 cm)[1]
R Ann, margin to no. 1919 (No repr.)
c. 1824/5
Whereabouts unknown

Provenance: Delacroix's posthumous sale, Feb. 1864, part of lot 189? ('Deux études d'après des armures, des casques et des cottes de mailles. Deux toiles', without dimensions),[2] which was sold to Count Duchâtel, 520 fr., and M. Aubry, 60 fr.; Philippe Burty; his sale, 2 March 1891, lot 7 ('Etude de deux personnages. D'après Goya, et sur la même toile une selle arabe et un antiphonaire. Provenant de la vente après le décès de l'artiste.'), 400 fr.; P. A. Cheramy; his sale, 5 May 1908, lot 188 ('Etude de selle arabe et de personnages, d'après Goya. A droite et au fond, des broderies d'or sur velours rouge. A gauche, deux figures esquissées. Une jeune femme debout, qui semble repousser les assiduités d'un galant portant une épée.'), to Mme Langweil, 1,800 fr.

Exhibitions: None.

Literature: None.

This canvas is known to me only from Robaut's copy in coloured chalks contained in Tracings V (Supp.) and reproduced here. This shows the dominant colours of the Turkish jacket and missal covers to have been red and gold. The sketch after Goya was taken from Plate 27 of the *Caprichos*, 'Quien Mas Rendido?' ('Which of them is the more overcome?'). The animated, black silhouette of the gallant seems to adumbrate Delacroix's own portrait of Paganini (J93).

For references to Delacroix's interest in the *Caprichos*, see the preceding number.

[1] According to the catalogue of the Cheramy sale 1908; 40 × 60 cm according to R Ann.
[2] In the margin to his no. 1919, under which he catalogues this lot, Robaut notes in R Ann: 'L'une de ces toiles 40 × 60 à Mr Cheramy représente deux couvertures d'anciens missels, une veste turque et en bas à g. [gauche] une copie d'après Goya: Scène galante.' Since this description does not correspond in any detail with that given for lot 189 in the catalogue of the posthumous sale, it may be wondered whether the picture did not pass as part of another lot—possibly of lot 221: 'Diverses toiles: études, esquisses et ébauches.'

L35 THE NIGHT WATCH, after ?

Dimensions unknown
R1950 (No repr.)
Whereabouts unknown

Provenance: Delacroix's posthumous sale, Feb. 1864, part of lot 176 ('Six toiles contenant des fragments d'études d'après Rubens, Véronèse, Murillo, etc.', without dimensions), to M. Carvalho, 60 fr.

Exhibitions: None.

Literature: None, except Robaut.

Robaut does not list the title of this, or of any of the other five items which made up lot 176 in the posthumous sale; but he records that his no. 1950, part of that lot, was knocked down to M. Carvalho for 60 fr., and the only item which went for that price is identified in Burty Ann ED as: 'La garde de nuit de   trois personnages les autres à peine ébauchés.' It has not come to light since 1864.

It is possible that this was a study after Rembrandt's *Night Watch* (Delacroix was in Amsterdam in 1839—*Correspondance* II. 40) or after an engraving of it, but it seems unlikely that the annotation of Burty Ann ED would have left a blank for the name of the author of so famous a picture, and it is therefore more probable that it was copied from a painting by a lesser artist.

L36 COPIES AFTER VARIOUS MASTERS
(Fragonard, Rembrandt, Valentin, Van Dyck)

The following copies after masters who are not mentioned in the section devoted to Delacroix's copies in the catalogue of his posthumous sale are attributed to him in Inv. Delacroix. The attributions to Delacroix as well as the identification of the masters from whom the copies were made may well be incorrect.

No. 194. '2 esquisses d'après Fragonard'.
No. 140. '1 tableau représentant *les pèlerins d'Emmaüs* d'après Rembrandt'.

No. 143. '1 tableau représentant la *Sainte Famille* d'après Rembrandt'.
No. 144. '1 tableau représentant *St Mathieu* d'après Rembrandt'.
No. 88. '1 tableau représentant la *Figure de St Jean*, d'après Valentin'.
No. 98. '1 copie d'un portrait d'homme, d'après Van Dyck'.

Costume, Accessories, Arms and Armour

L37 A TURKISH JACKET   Pl. 145
See J(L)34

L38 A FIGURE IN GREEK   Pl. 146
COSTUME
(Front view, dancing)
15¾ × 13 in. (40 × 33 cm)
R85 (1823)
c. 1824/5?
Whereabouts unknown

Provenance: Delacroix's posthumous sale, Feb. 1864, lot 178 ('Le même [personnage en costume souliote (lot 177; J28)], vu de face et dansant', 40 × 33 cm), to M. Delisle, 460 fr.; Mme Delisle, by 1885.

Exhibition: EBA, Paris 1885, no. 27 ('Souliote dansant')[1]

Literature: See P. Guigou ref. for 1885, under J29 (*Literature* and n. 2).

This picture is known to me only from the engraving in R, reproduced here, and from a larger drawing by Robaut, on which his engraving was based, in Tracings I.

For illustrations and discussion of the series of Greek costume studies of which this was apparently a part, see J28–J31.

[1] Robaut notes in his annotated copy of the second edition of the catalogue of this exhibition (*Bib AA*, MS. 298*ter*), that the painting shown under this number belonged to Mme Delille (apparently a misspelling of Delisle), who did not wish her name to appear in the catalogue, and not to M. Boulanger-Cavé who was listed as the owner in her place. He notes further that it was no. 84 in his *catalogue raisonné* (i.e. lot 177 from the posthumous sale), but it is clear that it was in fact no. 85 (lot 178): (*a*) from the description of it in the exhibition catalogue as a dancing figure, and (*b*) from a reproduction in Tracings I which is inscribed as lot 178 from the posthumous sale bought by 'Mr Delille' and corresponds to the reproduction of that lot which illustrates No. 85 in the *catalogue raisonné*.

L39 MAN IN GREEK COSTUME   Pl. 146
STANDING IN A LANDSCAPE
9⅞ × 7⅛ in. (25 × 18 cm)
R79 (1823)
c. 1823/4

Whereabouts unknown

Provenance: Baron Louis Schwiter; his sale, 26 March 1890, lot 5 ('Albanais debout, dans un paysage et tenant des pistolets', canvas 24 × 19 cm), 720 fr.

Exhibitions: None.

Literature: None, except Robaut.

No trace of this picture has been found since it passed in the Schwiter sale in 1890. The best illustration of it known to me is an old photograph, reproduced here, from the collection of Charles Cournault, a close friend of Louis Schwiter. An inscription on the back of the photograph says that the picture was painted by Delacroix in the course of an afternoon at Schwiter's home.

L40 A GREEK
13 × 9⅝ in. (33 × 24.5 cm)
Whereabouts unknown

Provenance: M. Collot; his sale, 29 May 1852, lot 13 ('Un Grec, canvas 33 × 24.5 cm), to 'Scheder',[1] 86 fr.

Exhibitions: None.

Literature: None, other than T. Silvestre, cited in n. 1.

This work is known to me only from the description in the catalogue of the Collot sale. I am unable to identify it with any work catalogued by Moreau and Robaut.

[1] According to T. Silvestre, *Decamps* (*Histoire des Artistes Vivants*, Blanchard, Paris, 1856), p. 187. Possibly a misspelling of [Eugène] Schneider, 1805-75, industrialist, politician and collector.

L41 'GREEK OFFICER' STANDING IN A LANDSCAPE
15¾ × 11¹³⁄₁₆ in. (40 × 30 cm)
Moreau pp. 269 f. R80 (1823. No repr.)
Whereabouts unknown

Provenance: Richard Wallace sale, 2 March 1857, lot 18 ('Un Albanais', without further description), 280 fr.; ?Achille Piron sale, 21 Apr. 1865, lot 3 ('Officier grec debout dans un paysage. (N'ayant pas fait partie de la vente d'Eugène Delacroix.)', 40 × 30 cm), 1,700 fr.

Exhibitions: None.

Literature: *Correspondance* III. 235 n. 1.

This picture was unknown to Robaut, who merely recorded the dimensions listed by Moreau and its provenance from the Richard Wallace sale, which he wrongly dated 1877. Moreau, in addition to listing the dimensions, supplemented the bare title given in the catalogue of the Wallace sale with this description: 'Officier Grec. Il est debout, vêtu d'un riche costume, la main passée dans une ceinture où pendent des pistolets et un sabre; derrière lui, un fond de paysage à l'état d'esquisse.' The measurements and description accord well with the particulars listed for lot 3 in the catalogue of the Piron sale of 1865 (a lot unaccounted for by Moreau and Robaut), making it likely that this painting also passed in that sale.

Joubin suggests that it is perhaps to this picture, which was unknown to him also, that Delacroix refers in a certificate dated 29 December 1854 authenticating 'deux petits tableaux appartenant à M. Weyl, représenatant: l'un un *Grec en costume*'. (*Correspondance* III. 234 f.) I am unable to confirm or deny this identification, but see no reason why Weyl's picture should have been this one rather than, e.g. J(L)42.

L42 STUDY OF A GREEK

$16\frac{1}{2} \times 12\frac{1}{4}$ in. (42 × 31 cm)
Whereabouts unknown

Provenance: Haro, by 1864.

Exhibition: *Bd Italiens*, Paris 1864, no. 64 ('Etude de Grec', 42 × 31 cm).

Literature: None.

I am unable certainly to identify this study, which was lent by Haro to the 1864 exhibition, with any known work or any lost work mentioned in sources other than the catalogue of this exhibition. To judge by the dimensions listed there, it is just possible that it was the Gothenburg *Study of a Figure in Greek Costume* (J29) or the lost *'Greek Officer' Standing in a Landscape* (J(L)41). But, among other possibilities, it could also have been bought by Haro at Delacroix's posthumous sale out of one of the lots which included groups of studies that cannot all be individually identified.

L43 THREE STUDIES OF GREEK COSTUME

$16\frac{15}{16} \times 25\frac{3}{16}$ in. (43 × 64 cm), before separation.
R1482 (1822. No repr.)
Whereabouts unknown

Provenance: Delacroix's posthumous sale, Feb. 1864, lot 187 ('Costume de Grec. Trois études sur la même toile', 43 × 64 cm), apparently cut into three separate studies before the sale and, according to Burty Ann ED, sold to: Dauzats, 100 fr.; Ph. Rousseau, 75 fr.; Muret, 180 fr.

Exhibitions: None certain.

Literature: None, except Robaut.

These studies are known only from the description in the catalogue of the posthumous sale. A study on cardboard that has been claimed to be one of them will be found under J(R)23.

For illustrations and discussion of the series of costume studies of which these may have been a part, see J28–J31.

L44 THREE FIGURES PRESUMED IN GREEK COSTUME

$13\frac{3}{8} \times 23\frac{5}{8}$ in. (34 × 60 cm)
R1487 (1823. No repr.)
Whereabouts unknown

Provenance: Delacroix's posthumous sale, Feb. 1864, lot 180 ('Trois figures sur la même toile',[1] 34 × 60 cm), 300 fr.[2]

Exhibitions: None.

Literature: None, except Robaut.

This picture is known only from the description in the catalogue of the posthumous sale. Robaut apparently never saw it.

For illustrations of known studies of Greek costume, see J28–J31.

[1] Since the three lots before this and the two after it were of figures in Greek ('Souliote') costume, it is presumed that the figures on this canvas were in similar dress.
[2] This price, but no buyer, is noted in M-Nélaton Ann ED; Robaut lists neither price nor buyer. According to Burty Ann ED, Ph. Rousseau bought this lot for 250 fr.; but see J31, n. 2.

L45 STUDY OF A MAN IN 'ORIENTAL' (PROBABLY ARAB) COSTUME   Pl. 146

$13 \times 9\frac{7}{16}$ in. (33 × 24 cm)
R77 (1823) and part of R1485
Whereabouts unknown

Provenance: Delacroix's posthumous sale, Feb. 1864, part of lot 188 ('Trois études de costumes d'hommes de l'Orient', without dimensions), probably to Prévost, 255 or 155 fr.; M. Mercier, by Dec. 1875.

Exhibitions: None.

Literature: None, except Robaut.

Under R1485, Robaut catalogued lot 188 from the posthumous sale as consisting of three canvases of unknown size, two of which were knocked down to M. Prévost for 255 fr. and 155 fr.; the third went for 215 fr., to Busquet according to Burty Ann ED (not to Muret, as recorded by Robaut who seems to have got confused with one of the buyers of the previous lot). But Robaut had already listed two of them under R77 and 78, giving the dimensions of both as 33 × 24 cm and the owner of both as M. Mercier. Mercier had evidently acquired them by 1875, as Robaut notes on his tracings of them in Tracings 1: 'calqué chez M. Mercier X^bre 1875.' Since he owned the pair, it seems likely that he had acquired the two bought by Prévost at the posthumous sale and that the picture from the lot which is not reproduced or described by Robaut was the one bought by Busquet (J(L)47).

This picture and the following number are known to me only from the small illustrations in Robaut and from the full-scale tracings in Tracings 1, reproduced here. The costumes appear to be North African and may therefore not have been painted before Delacroix's Moroccan journey of 1832.

L46 STUDY OF A MAN IN 'ORIENTAL' (PROBABLY ARAB) COSTUME, WITH SPEAR   Pl. 146

13 × 9$\frac{7}{16}$ in. (33 × 24 cm)
R78 (1823) and part of R1485
Whereabouts unknown

Provenance: Delacroix's posthumous sale, Feb. 1864, part of lot 188 ('Trois études de costumes d'hommes de l'Orient', without dimensions), probably to Prévost, 255 or 155 fr.; M. Mercier, by Dec. 1875.

Exhibition: None.

Literature: None, except Robaut.

A picture that was claimed to be R78 passed in a sale at the Hôtel Drouot on 23 June 1958, lot 112 ('Costume d'Orient. Carton parqueté', 33 × 23 cm)

See the preceding number for discussion of the early history of this study.

L47 STUDY OF MALE 'ORIENTAL' COSTUME

Dimensions unknown
Part of R1485 (1823. No repr.)
Whereabouts unknown

Provenance: Delacroix's posthumous sale, Feb. 1864, part of lot 188 ('Trois études de costumes de l'Orient', without dimensions), probably to Busquet (see J(L)45), 215 fr.

Exhibitions: None.

Literature: See J(D)7.

Part of the lot in Delacroix's posthumous sale which comprised the two previous numbers and the only one of the three not reproduced by Robaut. A study at Cleveland (J(D)7) and a study of a bearded Arab (J(D)6) have in recent years both been advanced, from the same commercial source, as this lost picture. Whatever their individual qualities may be, they cannot both be the missing study, and in my opinion there is a strong possibility that neither is.

L47a STUDIES OF ARMOUR

Dimensions unknown
Part of R1919 (No repr.)
Whereabouts unknown

Provenance: Delacroix's posthumous sale, Feb. 1864, part of lot 189 ('Deux études d'après des armures, des casques et des cottes de mailles. Deux toiles', without dimensions), to Count Duchâtel, 520 fr., or M. Aubry, 60 fr.

Exhibitions: None.

Literature: None, except Robaut.

See also J(O)4.

L48 A HORSE AND THREE MEN-AT-ARMS, sketch

6$\frac{5}{16}$ × 9$\frac{7}{16}$ in. (16 × 24 cm)
R1508 (1825. No repr.)
Whereabouts unknown

Provenance: Delacroix's posthumous sale, Feb. 1864, lot 145 ('[Esquisse.] Un cheval et trois hommes d'armes', without dimensions), to Charlet, 150 fr.; anon. sale (by Petit), 14 May 1866, lot 22 ('Un cheval et trois hommes d'armes', without dimensions or further description); sale L . . ., 14 May 1873, lot 21 ('Hommes d'armes et cheval; étude', 16 × 24 cm, with mention of provenance from the posthumous sale), 105 fr.; Duc de Trévise?

Exhibited: ?Paris 1927, no. 275 ('Hommes d'armes', lent by the Duc de Trévise).

Literature: None, except Robaut.

This work is known to me only from the descriptions in the catalogues of the sales listed above.

Miscellaneous Orientalia

L49 A WOUNDED MAMELUKE AND HIS HORSE AMONG RUINS

Dimensions unknown
1823
Whereabouts unknown

This painting, which is not recorded by Robaut, is known to me only from the description contained in the following letter from Delacroix to the Mayor of Douai, a document[1] which has not to my knowledge been previously published:

PARIS, le 24 Juin 1823.

Monsieur le Maire,
J'ai adressé aujourd'hui chez M. DUBOIS et GRILLON, une caisse contenant un tableau, que je vous prie de vouloir bien admettre à l'exposition de la Ville de Douai. Voici la notice explicative du sujet:
Un Mameluck blessé s'est réfugié dans des ruines avec son cheval. Il prête l'oreille et s'effraye au bruit d'une escarmouche qui se rapproche du lieu de sa retraite.
Je désirerais en avoir la somme de *deux cent francs*.
J'ai l'honneur d'être avec respect, Monsieur le Maire, votre très humble et très obéissant serviteur.
E. DELACROIX
Rue de Grenelle St Germain
n° 118
Pour le cas où le tableau ne serait point acheté, je vous prie de vouloir bien le renvoyer à cette adresse.

[1] Archives municipales de Douai 2 R39.

L50 TURKS SMOKING

Dimensions unknown
Whereabouts unknown

Provenance: Anonymous sale, 7 Dec. 1855, lot 33 ('Turcs fumant', without dimensions or further description), 421 fr.

Exhibitions: None.

Literature: None.

This painting is known to me only from the catalogue of the above sale which, occurring in Paris during the lifetime of Delacroix, is unlikely to have contained a work falsely attributed to him.

L51 INDIAN ARMED WITH A KUKRI

$16 \times 12\frac{5}{8}$ in. (40.7 × 32 cm)
Signed bottom left
Moreau p. 171 n. 2. R362 (1831. No repr.)
c. 1831
Whereabouts unknown

Provenance: Alexandre Dumas, *c.* 1831; M. Janot (Dieterle R); with Feral, June 1924 (Dieterle R).

Exhibitions: None.

Literature: Silvestre *Delacroix* (1855), p. 80.

According to Moreau, Delacroix painted a copy of the picture of this subject that he exhibited at the Salon of 1831 (J39), for Alexandre Dumas 'à la suite de l'Exposition'. Neither he nor Robaut, who evidently knew of the copy only from Moreau, gives any further description of it.

Jean Dieterle, however, who saw what appears to have been that copy in June 1924, recorded in Dieterle R that it was of the same dimensions as the Salon version, but 'moins bon — plus terne', and signed bottom left.

According to Silvestre *Delacroix* (1855), which, it must be stressed, was published during the artist's lifetime, there were two 'répétitions' by Delacroix of the original version, 'dont l'une avec variantes'. None with variations is, to my knowledge, recorded elsewhere or has come to light since 1855.

Horses and Other Animals

L52 A NORMAN HORSE

Dimensions unknown
Moreau p. 321. R1868 (No repr.)
Whereabouts unknown

Provenance: Delacroix's posthumous sale, Feb. 1864, lot 208 ('Cheval normand', without dimensions), to Lambert, 1,200 fr.

Exhibitions: None.

Literature: None, other than Moreau and Robaut.

This picture has not to my knowledge come to light since the posthumous sale of 1864. A painting which is claimed to be it is catalogued under J(R)26.

L53 WHITE HORSE, 'LE FLORIDO'

$17\frac{3}{4} \times 21\frac{1}{4}$ in. (45 × 54 cm: dimensions listed by Robaut for R75)
Probably Moreau p. 321 and R75 (1823)
1824
Whereabouts unknown

Provenance (of R75): Delacroix's posthumous sale, Feb. 1864, lot 202 ('Cheval blanc attaché dans une écurie', without dimensions), to Paul Verdé Delisle, 1,080 fr.

Exhibition: *EBA*, Paris 1885, no. 28.

Literature: *Journal* I. 61 n. 4.

Among a list of loans made in 1829, Delacroix noted 'à qui ai-je prêté le cheval blanc le Florido fait au manège avec Scheffer en 1824 [?]' (Louvre sketch-book, RF23355, fol. 42ᵛ.). This unpublished note may refer to a study of a white horse that Delacroix mentioned in 1824 and which Joubin plausibly identifies as R75: on 16 March of that year the artist wrote in his *Journal* (I. 61): 'Vu Scheffer et le sauteur de son manège'; and on the following day, 'Rencontré Henri Scheffer au Palais-Royal. Chez Leblond. J'ai fait un cheval à l'écurie.' On the other hand, the note about the loan could also refer to a study which Delacroix did a few days later, definitely in the company of Scheffer (whether with Ary or his younger brother, Henry, is never clear): '*Hier, dimanche 21 mars* [1824]. — Fait une étude au manège avec Scheffer.' Joubin makes no attempt to identify that study.

If the picture of 'le Florido' is identical with R75, then it is known, not only from the print in Robaut, but from the copy in oils attributed to Alexis Pérignon, in the Burrell Collection, Glasgow (J(R)31). According to Robaut, Delacroix was very attached to R75 and hung it in his dining-room.

L54 WHITE HORSE, AT REST

11 × 12⅝ in. (28 × 32 cm)
1824
Whereabouts unknown

Provenance: Probably sale Renié, Champmartin, 27 Jan. 1888, lot 115 ('Cheval blanc au repos', *attributed* to Delacroix, without dimensions); G. Moreau-Chaslon; his sale, 8 June 1889, lot 49 ('Cheval blanc, au repos. Etude faite chez Marochetti, à Vaux, en 1824', 28 × 32 cm), 200 fr.

Exhibitions: None.

Literature: None.

This is known to me only from the description in the catalogue of the Moreau-Chaslon sale of 1889, and its authenticity may not be certain, particularly if it is the work of the same title which was merely attributed to Delacroix in the Renié, Champmartin sale the previous year. It is however certain that Delacroix did do some horse studies in the company of Champmartin in 1824 (*Journal* I. 30) and that in April of the same year this painter introduced him to the sculptor Charles Marochetti whose horse Delacroix mounted (and fell off) a little later (ibid. 83, 93). It is therefore perfectly possible that Delacroix painted a horse study at Marochetti's in 1824, and also that Champmartin owned horse studies by Delacroix that were unknown to

Robaut. But it is also possible that Champmartin did studies of his own at the same time, some of which might have become firmly, and wrongly, attributed to Delacroix by the time they passed in the Moreau-Chaslon sale of 1889.

This and the following two numbers are listed here, less in the conviction that they were genuine works by Delacroix than to draw attention to a possible source of confusion following the death of Champmartin and the dispersal of the contents of his studio in 1884.

L55 A SADDLED CHESTNUT, AT REST

10¼ × 15 in. (26 × 38 cm)
Whereabouts unknown

Provenance: G. Moreau-Chaslon; his sale, 8 June 1889, lot 50 ('Alezan sellé et au repos. Etude provenant de l'atelier du peintre Champmartin', 26 × 38 cm), 200 fr.

Exhibitions: None.

Literature: None.

This is known to me only from the description in the catalogue of the Moreau-Chaslon sale of 1889, and its authenticity has yet to be proved. Could it perhaps be identical with lot 270 ('Cheval à l'écurie', without dimensions) or part of lot 272 ('Quatre études de chevaux', without dimensions) which were both listed as by Champmartin in his studio sale of 28 January 1884? And did lot 270 in that sale become lot 114 ('Cheval à l'écurie', without dimensions), which was listed as attributed to Delacroix in the Renié, Champmartin sale of 27 January 1888?

L56 HORSE AT REST

9⅞ × 13 in. (25 × 33 cm)
Whereabouts unknown

Provenance: G. Moreau-Chaslon; his sale, 8 June 1889, lot 51 ('Cheval au repos. Etude provenant de l'atelier du peintre Champmartin', 25 × 33 cm), 250 fr.

Exhibitions: None.

Literature: None.

Same commentary as for J(L)55.

L57 STUDY OF A DAPPLE-GREY HORSE   Pl. 147

11¹³⁄₁₆ × 16⁹⁄₁₆ in. (30 × 42 cm). Enlarged from about 20 × 30 cm when Chocquet had the original study stuck on a larger canvas, by Aug. 1877.[1]
Part of R1860 (No repr.)
1824?
Whereabouts unknown

Provenance: Delacroix's posthumous sale, Feb. 1864, part of lot 210 ('Quatorze études diverses de chevaux'), to Detrimont, 420 fr. (Burty Ann ED);[2] acquired from him by Victor Chocquet, by Aug. 1877, d. 1891; Marie Chocquet, his widow; her sale 1 July 1899, lot 60, to Bernheim-Jeune (Arch B-J, no. 9,635), 500 fr.

Exhibition: Possibly *Soc. Amis des Arts*, Bordeaux 1864, no. 173 ('Etude de cheval gris', dimensions and owner unlisted, but stated to be from the posthumous sale).

Literature: J. Rewald, 'Chocquet and Cézanne', *GBA*, LXXIV (1969), p. 76.

This study is known only from Robaut's copy in chalk of 1877, reproduced here. It is possibly the picture which Delacroix refers to in his *Journal* (I. 64) on 28 March 1824: 'Au manège. Peint le cheval gris'.

  [1] Robaut Tracings V (Supp.), inscription on the back of his drawing of this study.
  [2] The inscription referred to in the previous note, and which dates from August 1877, states that Chocquet acquired our picture from Detrimont. Since Chocquet's painting was later said, in the catalogue of his widow's sale of 1899, to bear the seal of Delacroix's posthumous sale and Detrimont is recorded as having bought only one study at this sale, I have assumed that the picture which Detrimont brought at Delacroix's sale and that which Chocquet acquired from him are one and the same; but it is of course possibly that Detrimont came into possession of other horse studies from the posthumous sale without having bought them personally at the sale. See J(L)61 for another lost study of a horse which belonged to Detrimont.

L58 TWO ENGLISH FARM HORSES

Wood panel, $15\frac{3}{4} \times 24\frac{13}{16}$ in. (40 × 63 cm)
Moreau pp. 169 (1825) and 278. R128 (1825) and 1014 (No repr.)
Probably 1825
Whereabouts unknown

Provenance: Paul Barroilhet, by 1852; his sale, 12 March 1855, lot 16 ('Chevaux de ferme. Panneau', 40 × 63 cm. MS. note in *Bib AA* copy of sale cat.: 'bonne couleur. Jambes de devant courtes.'), 1,015 fr.; Loysel, by 1885.

Exhibitions: Probably Douai 1827, no. 95 ('Chevaux de ferme anglais (étude d'après nature)'); Salon 1827–8, no. 295 ('Deux chevaux de ferme anglais'); Musée Colbert, Paris 1830A, no. 188 ('Deux chevaux de ferme anglais'); probably id., Paris 1830B, no. 75 ('Etude de chevaux de ferme anglais'); *Gal. Beaux-Arts*, Paris 1852, no. 130 ('Chevaux de ferme. b. [bois]').

Literature: MM. Chenoux, *Notice sur l'exposition des produits de l'industrie et des arts qui a eu lieu à Douai en 1827* (Impr. Wagrez, Douai, 1827), p. 28; *Visite au Musée du Louvre, ou guide de l'amateur à l'exposition . . . (année 1827–1828) . . . par une société de gens de lettres et d'artistes* (Leroi, Paris, 1828), p. 219; C. Blanc, in Introduction to catalogue of the Barroilhet sale, Paris, 12 March 1855;

Moreau-Nélaton I. 86; Escholier I. 216; L. Johnson, 'Eugène Delacroix et les Salons. Documents inédits au Louvre', *Revue du Louvre*, 16 (1966), p. 220.

Robaut catalogued the 'Deux chevaux de ferme anglais' that was shown at the Salon of 1827–8 under 1825, the year in which Moreau said it had been painted, but he had evidently never seen it as he neither reproduced it nor listed the dimensions. He catalogued separately, under 1847 and also without a reproduction, the 'Chevaux de ferme' that passed in the Barroilhet sale in 1855. Escholier was the first to suggest, convincingly, that they were one and the same painting; he justly thought that Robaut ought to have deduced the correct period of Barroilhet's picture from Charles Blanc's appreciation of it (loc. cit., 1855) as a work with 'la finesse et le charme d'un Bonington, en même temps qu'on y retrouve le mâle souvenir de Géricault.' Further, though not in itself conclusive, support of the view that Barroilhet's painting was also the Salon painting may be found in the fact that the dimensions of the latter, undoubtedly with frame, are listed in the Salon register in the Louvre as 60 × 83 cm (L. Johnson, 1966), and if the dimensions of the former are subtracted from these, exactly the same figure of 10 cm is arrived at for the width of the vertical and horizontal sides of the frame.

The appearance of the painting can be reconstructed only from verbal descriptions, no reproduction of any sort being known. After it had passed in the Barroilhet sale, Moreau (p. 278) described it thus: 'Deux chevaux, qui viennent de quitter la charrue, sont attachés à la porte d'une habitation.' Further details, the principal being that one of the horses was white, are given in the only reference to the picture in the Salon reviews of 1827–8 (op. cit., 1828): 'M. Delacroix n'a pas été très-heureux dans la composition de ce petit tableau; des deux chevaux qu'il a représentés, l'un a la tête mal posée, et l'autre est à peine aperçu des spectateurs. Toutefois, il y a, dans le corps du cheval blanc, une imitation parfaite de la nature. Quant aux détails, ils sont ['peu' omitted by printer?] soignés, comme dans toutes les compositions grandes ou petites du même auteur; toujours le même système: c'est pourtant à M. Delacroix à changer.'

The picture may well have been done in England, for Moreau (p. 169) affirms, perhaps on the strength of sound verbal information, that it was painted in 1825, and if, as is to be presumed, it is in addition the picture of English farm horses that was described as a study after nature in the catalogue of the exhibition Douai 1827, it would seem to belong firmly within the period of the English visit, in the summer of 1825. Local comment at Douai was more enthusiastic than informative, but interesting nevertheless in comparing the work to Géricault—like Blanc nearly thirty years later: '*Etude de chevaux de ferme.*—Voilà une belle étude, digne en tout de Géricault, il y a long-temps que je n'avais vu de chevaux peints avec cette vérité, cette chaleur, cette vigueur de coloris.' (Chenoux, 1827.)

This picture was accepted by the jury of the Paris Salon on 12 October 1827 (L. Johnson, 1966).

L59 STUDY OF A CART HORSE

$7\frac{7}{8} \times 9\frac{7}{8}$ in. (20 × 25 cm)
Part of R1860 (No repr.)?
Whereabouts unknown

Provenance: Delacroix's posthumous sale, Feb. 1864, part of lot 210? ('Quatorze études diverses de chevaux', without dimensions); Alfred Saucède; his sale, 14 Feb. 1879, lot 12 ('Cheval de roulage. Etude provenant de la vente après décès de l'artiste', 20 × 25 cm), 150 fr.; M. Moreau-Chaslon; his sale, 6 Feb. 1882, lot 30 ('Cheval de trait harnaché. Jolie étude provenant de la vente Delacroix. Collection Saucède').

Exhibitions: None.

Literature: None.

This study is known to me only from the descriptions in the catalogues of the Saucède and Moreau-Chaslon sales. Though it was probably part of lot 210 of Delacroix's posthumous sale, I am unable to identify the buyer. For a list of the buyers and prices of pictures in this lot that are not identified, see J(L)64.

L60 STUDIES OF HORSES

Dimensions unknown
Part of R1871 (No repr.)
Whereabouts unknown

Provenance: Delacroix's posthumous sale, Feb. 1864, part of lot 211 ('Dix études ébauchées'), to [Edouard] Frère, 175 fr. (Burty Ann ED); probably his studio sale, 29 Nov. 1889, lot 217 ('Etudes de chevaux', without dimensions or further description).

Exhibitions: None.

Literature: None, other than Robaut no. 1871.

I am unable to identify this work with any of the known paintings of horses from the posthumous sale or with any lost work reproduced by Robaut.

L61 STUDY OF A HORSE'S HEAD   Pl. 147

Dimensions unknown
Whereabouts unknown

Provenance: Eugène Detrimont; his sale 14 Apr. 1876, lot 26 ('Tête de cheval', with no further details).

Exhibitions: None.

Literature: None.

This study is known to me only from Robaut's drawing in Tracings V (Supp.), reproduced here and from which it is impossible to form an opinion of its authenticity. Neither in Robaut Tracings nor in the catalogue of the Detrimont sale is it stated whether the study came from Delacroix's posthumous sale, where Detrimont is known to have bought one study of a horse (see J(L)57).

L62 THREE BURNT CHESTNUT HORSES

Dimensions unknown
Whereabouts unknown

Provenance: Delacroix's posthumous sale, Feb. 1864, *h.c.*, 450 fr.

Exhibitions: None.

Literature: None.

An annotation between lots 209 and 210 in Thoré ED runs: 'S. [sans] Nº — 3 Chevaux alezan brûlé'. The price but no buyer is listed.

L63 STUDIES OF SEVEN HORSES   Pl. 147

Dimensions unknown
Part of R1871 (No repr.)
Whereabouts unknown

Provenance: Delacroix's posthumous sale, Feb. 1864, part of lot 211 ('Dix études ébauchées'), to Edouard Frère, 100 fr. (R Ann and Burty Ann ED); his studio sale 29 Nov. 1889, lot 216, to Cheramy, 400 fr. (R Ann); he disposed of it shortly after the sale (R Ann).

Exhibitions: None.

Literature: None, other than Robaut no. 1871.

This painting is known only from Robaut's copy in chalk in Tracings V, reproduced here. Robaut notes the colour of each horse on his drawing as follows, from top left: 'blanchâtre reflets jaunes; Isabelle foncé; gris bleuté; bai brun; Isabelle clair; bai-clair; cheval de selle bai clair.'

L64 ASSORTED STUDIES OF HORSES

Dimensions unknown
Part of R1860 (No reprs.)
Whereabouts unknown

Provenance: Delacroix's posthumous sale, Feb. 1864, part of lot 210 ('Quatorze études diverses de chevaux', without dimensions), to various buyers, listed below.

Nine studies that have been catalogued here were, or in two or three instances may have been, among the fourteen that made up lot 210 of the posthumous sale. They are: J42, J43, J44, J47, J50, J52, J(L)57, J(L)59, J(L)61. A list follows of the buyers and prices as noted in Burty Ann ED for the items in lot 210 which I am unable to identify singly: Scott, 425 fr.; Barroilhet, 135 fr.; Lehmann, 210 fr.; Lambert, 105 fr.; Delaage, 250 fr.; de Calonne, 260 fr.; Lehmann, 200 fr.; Delille [for Delisle], 170 and 360 fr. [one of these studies was J52]; Ph. Rousseau, 440 fr.

L65 ASSORTED SKETCH-STUDIES OF HORSES

Dimensions unknown
Part of R1871 (No reprs.)
Whereabouts unknown

Provenance: Delacroix's posthumous sale, Feb. 1864, part of lot 211 ('Dix études ébauchées [de chevaux]', without dimensions), to various buyers, listed below.

Of the ten sketch-studies which made up lot 211 at the posthumous sale, four have been accounted for (J51, J(L)60, J(L)63, J(M)4, the provenance of the last being uncertain). A list follows of the buyers and prices as noted in Burty Ann ED for the items in lot 211 which I am unable to identify singly: Belly, 100 fr.; Lejeune, 13 fr.; id., 20 fr. (2 studies); Brest, 31 fr.; Lejeune, 19 fr. (2 studies).

L66 STUDY OF A LION'S HEAD

$9\frac{7}{16} \times 7\frac{1}{2}$ in. (24 × 19 cm)
Part of R1879 (No repr.)
1830 ?
Whereabouts unknown

Provenance: Delacroix's posthumous sale, Feb. 1864, part of lot 214 ('Trois autres études d'animaux', without dimensions), to Paul Verdé Delisle, 400 fr.; Soultzener, by 1885.

Exhibition: EBA, Paris 1885, no. 26.

Literature: None, except Robaut.

Described in Robaut as 'vue de profil, au regard fixé vers l'horizon', this study was dated to 1830 in the catalogue of the exhibition *EBA*, Paris 1885, where it was also listed as belonging to M. Boulanger-Cavé. Robaut noted, however, in his copy of the second edition of the catalogue (*Bib AA*, MS. 298ter) that the true lender was Mme Delille (i.e. Mme Verdé Delisle), who had wished to be unnamed, and that the study was about the same as the water-colour R774, which he had catalogued under the year 1843 (Louvre M.I. 893, repr. in colour, C. Roger-Marx and S. Cotté, *Delacroix* (Pall Mall Press, London, 1970), p. 53).

L67 STUDY OF A CAT

Canvas laid down on wood panel, $5\frac{1}{2} \times 6\frac{5}{16}$ in. (14 × 16 cm)
Part of R1879 (No repr.) ?
Whereabouts unknown

Provenance: Delacroix's posthumous sale, Feb. 1864, ? part of lot 214 ('Trois autres études d'animaux', without dimensions), to Prévost, 180 fr., or Moureau, 150 fr.; sale Alfred Saucède, 14 Feb. 1879, lot 13 ('Un Chat. Etude', with dimensions and support, and claim of provenance from the posthumous sale).

Exhibitions: None.

Literature: None.

This work is known to me only from the description in the catalogue of the Saucède sale.

Portraits and Studies of Heads

L68 PORTRAIT OF ELISABETH

$19\frac{11}{16} \times 15\frac{3}{4}$ in. (50 × 40 cm)
Moreau p. 227 (1817–18). R13 (1817. No repr.)
Whereabouts unknown

Provenance: Mme Leblond, widow of the artist's friend Frédéric Leblond, by 1873.

Exhibitions: None.

This portrait, which has never been reproduced, is described thus by Moreau: 'Coiffée en cheveux avec de grosses coques avançant sur le front, elle soutient sa tête de la main droite.

'De face, les vêtements et la main légèrement indiqués, la tête et la poitrine seules achevées.

'Non signé.'
Under his next entry, for a portrait of Rose (J(L)69), he adds: 'Ces deux femmes, bien chères au cœur du grand Artiste, sont représentées grandeur nature et en buste.'

If Moreau's identification and dating are correct, the sitter was doubtless Elisabeth Salter (see J61).

This portrait was apparently unknown to Robaut, except from Moreau's description, and was no longer owned by Mme Leblond when his catalogue was published in 1885, his sole comment on its history being: 'Appartenait à madame veuve Leblond'. It is not listed in the catalogue of the Gebauer Sale at Cléry in 1904, where other early works by Delacroix that had belonged to Leblond were sold.

L69 PORTRAIT OF ROSE

$22\frac{7}{8} \times 16\frac{15}{16}$ in. (58 × 43 cm)
Moreau p. 228 (1817–18). R14 (1817. No repr.)
Whereabouts unknown

Provenance: Unrecorded.

Exhibitions: None.

This portrait has never been reproduced, unless it be identical with the *Head of a Woman in Bed* (J(O)8). It is known only from Moreau's description which, in addition to the dimensions, contains the following details: 'La tête repose sur un oreiller; elle semble dormir. Non signé, ni daté [. . .] grandeur nature et en buste.' Robaut was evidently unable to trace or identify the picture and added nothing to Moreau's information.

For further information about Rose, see J4.

L70 A GENIUS: STUDY OF A WOMAN'S HEAD

$17\frac{5}{16} \times 13$ in. (44 × 33 cm)
R1902 (No repr.)
Whereabouts unknown

Provenance: Delacroix's posthumous sale, Feb. 1864, lot 195 ('Un Génie. Etude de tête de femme'), to M. Lambert, 310 fr.

Exhibitions: None.

This work is not reproduced by Robaut, who had apparently never seen the original and took his description of it from the catalogue of Delacroix's posthumous sale. It has never come to light since. It is possibly the same study as that listed under the following number.

L71 STUDY OF A HEAD, WITH STAR

Dimensions unknown
Before 1820?
Whereabouts unknown

This study is described in a list of works that Delacroix compiled in later life as '*Tête d'étude*, fort ancienne, avec une étoile sur la tête.' (*Journal* III. 374—Supp.). It is listed immediately under the *Head of Actaeon* (J60), which is also described as 'fort ancienne', and may have been of about the same date.

It is perhaps more than a coincidence that the *Genius* listed under the preceding number was catalogued next to the *Head of Actaeon* in Delacroix's posthumous sale: it could be identical with the present study, the descriptions simply varying slightly.

L72 HEAD OF A MAN, STUDY FOR A HISTORY PAINTING

$21\frac{5}{8} \times 18\frac{1}{8}$ in. (55 × 46 cm)
R1903 (No repr.)
Whereabouts unknown

Provenance: Delacroix's posthumous sale, Feb. 1864, no. 194 ('Etude de tête d'homme, destinée à un tableau de genre historique.'), to M. Bernier, 200 fr.

Exhibitions: None.

This work is not reproduced by Robaut, who had apparently never seen the original and took his description of it from the catalogue of Delacroix's posthumous sale. It has never come to light since.

L72a HEAD OF AN ORIENTAL WOMAN

Cardboard, $7\frac{1}{2} \times 6\frac{5}{16}$ in. (19 × 16 cm)
R Ann 47*bis* (1821)
Whereabouts unknown

Provenance: J. Paton; his sale 24 Apr. 1883, lot 61, 510 fr., to M. Bernheim jeune, who still had it in 1889 (R Ann); Albert Millaud; his sale 25 Nov. 1889, lot 222, 300 fr.

Exhibitions: None.

Literature: None.

Robaut describes this picture in R Ann as 'Femme d'Orient (ou) Orientale—Buste' and, in addition to listing the two sales in which it passed, comments: 'Léon Riesener a donné (au dos) la garantie écrite—Sinon, on hésiterait beaucoup faute de touche maîtresse.'

See also J79 (final paragraph).

L73 PORTRAIT OF CHARLES SOULIER   Pl. 148

$55\frac{7}{8} \times 43\frac{5}{16}$ in. (1.42 × 1.10 m)
R105 (1824)
c. 1820
Whereabouts unknown

Provenance: Delivered to the sitter on the artist's death in 1863 (R); Paul Soulier, his son, by Sept. 1878.

Exhibitions: None.

Literature: None, other than Robaut and *Correspondance* ref. below.

This full-length, unfinished portrait of one of Delacroix's closest friends is unfortunately known only from the small print in Robaut, and from the better copy, reproduced here, in Tracings I, where it is noted by Robaut as taken on 1 September 1878 at Avon, near Fontainebleau, where the sitter's son lived.

Though Robaut dates this picture to 1824, it was probably, as held by Joubin, the portrait referred to in a letter of 22 October 1820 from Delacroix to Soulier at Florence: 'Je vois vos yeux dans ce portrait que vous ne m'avez pas laissé finir' (*Correspondance* I. 110 and n. 2). Soulier had left for Italy for a period of two years, arriving in Florence by August 1820, the date of his first letter to Delacroix from Italy (see ibid. 83, 92 f.). His Christian name is given as Raymond in most of the Delacroix literature and sometimes as Edouard (*Journal* II. 370 n. 1; index to Huyghe), but Alfred Dupont has pointed out that Delacroix letters he published are addressed to Charles Soulier (*Lettres intimes*, p. 165 n. 1). According to his own account, Soulier met Delacroix in 1816 and the young pupil of Guérin was curious to learn the technique of water-colour which Soulier, an amateur artist who had spent part of his childhood in England, had been taught by Copley Fielding (for Soulier's account of the early stages of his relationship with Delacroix, see *Correspondance* I. 37 n. 2). He began his career as secretary to the Marquis de la Maisonfort, went on to serve at the French Legations in Florence and Naples, and was later employed in the administration of canals at Saint-Mammès.

Some colours are noted in the entry for this portrait in Robaut: 'le teint pâle, les cheveux châtain foncé, vêtu de drap bleu sombre [. . .] Le fauteuil et le canapé [. . .] sont en bois d'acajou et recouverts d'étoffe verte. Dans le fond, une draperie rouge'.

Robaut catalogues another portrait in oils of Soulier (see following number); a bust-portrait in water-colour (R62. Private collection, Paris) and a sepia study of Soulier full-length seated playing a guitar (R63), both of which he places in 1823 without argument; and a lithographic three-quarter profile study of Soulier, whom he calls Frédéric (amended to Eudore in R Ann), and, following Moreau (p. 29), dates to 1826 (R192. Delteil no. 53).

L74 PORTRAIT OF CHARLES SOULIER

$17\frac{3}{4} \times 15$ in. (45 × 38 cm)
Moreau p. 230. R125 (1825. No repr.)
Whereabouts unknown

Provenance: Unrecorded.

Exhibitions: None.

Literature: None, other than Moreau and Robaut.

This portrait is first recorded by Moreau (1873), who places it in 1825, calling the sitter 'M. Soulier de Saint-Mamès' [*sic*] and stating: 'Il est debout, une main dans le gilet, l'autre cachée derrière le dos.' He lists no owner. Robaut, who had apparently never seen the portrait, gives the same description, adding no information as to ownership and no reproduction.

L75 PORTRAIT OF A CHILD (ADRIEN ?)   Pl. 148

$7\frac{7}{8} \times 6\frac{5}{16}$ in. (20 × 16 cm)
R61 (1823)
1822 ?
Whereabouts unknown

Provenance: Charles Soulier; Paul Soulier, his son, by 1878.

Exhibitions: None.

Literature: See below.

This portrait is known only from the small print in Robaut, reproduced here, and from the tracing in Robaut Tracings I. The latter is inscribed: 'Calqué à Avon près Fontainebleau le 1er 7bre [Septembre] 1878 [. . .] La tête seule est à peu près faite; le reste n'est que tracé.'

'Mr. Soulier à qui appartient ce joli échantillon croit se rappeler que son père pensait que c'était un fils de Fielding.' This identification was rejected in the published Robaut, where the picture is listed merely as 'Portrait d'enfant'. Joubin (*Journal* I. 69 n. 3 and correction to this, III. 525) connects it wholly unconvincingly with the portrait of Delacroix's nephew, Charles de Verninac, mentioned in the *Journal* on 6 April 1824 (J62).

The sitter seems most likely to be a schoolboy by the name of Adrien, whose portrait Delacroix promised to paint for Soulier in 1820–1, and who, Joubin reasonably conjectures (*Correspondance* I. 98 n. 1, 123 n. 2, 141 n. 2), was the son of Soulier's mistress, referred to by Delacroix as 'la *Cara*' or 'J'. Delacroix wrote to Soulier at Florence on 24 November 1820, saying: 'Je n'ai pas oublié la commission dont tu m'as chargé pour le portrait du petit garçon' (ibid. 98). Evidently referring to the same matter, he stated in a letter of 30 March 1821: 'Je n'ai pas encore entendu parler d'Adrien. Je ne sais si on pourra obtenir facilement qu'il sorte de son lycée pour poser. Dans tous les cas, je suis toujours à ta disposition pour cela' (ibid. 123). Writing again to Soulier, at Naples, a month later, he informs him: 'Je n'entends parler en aucune façon du petit bonhomme et du portrait à faire. Je suis prêt. Je n'attends plus que l'homme' (ibid. 127). He writes on 30 July of the same year: 'C'est M. Viéton, précepteur de ton petit bonhomme, qui avait à me remettre une lettre de toi, par laquelle tu me l'adressais pour le portrait. Mais il se trouve que le petit ne peut en aucune façon sortir de son collège à cette intention. Je suis donc forcé malgré ma bonne volonté d'attendre un peu plus tard' (ibid. 129). Finally, a passage in a letter of 15 April 1822 to Soulier at Rome may refer to the portrait of Adrien, but could also mean that Delacroix had promised to paint a portrait of Soulier's mistress as well (see J(L)76): 'J'ai vu la *Cara*. Elle s'est donnée la peine de venir chez moi; j'étais dans ce moment enfoncé dans le travail dont je sors. [. . .] Au premier jour je m'acquitterai avec un vif plaisir de la promesse que je t'ai faite' (ibid. 141–2).

L76 THE MISTRESS OF CHARLES (DE VERNINAC? SOULIER?)

Panel. Dimensions unrecorded.
Whereabouts unknown

The only record of this portrait, which was presumably by Delacroix, is an inscription in the artist's hand on a sheet of horse studies in the Louvre (RF9719): 'Prêté à Decaisne la maîtresse de Charles sur panneau'. (Henri Decaisne (1799–1852), a history painter, is first mentioned by Delacroix in the *Journal* on 17 April 1824.) There is no other evidence of Delacroix painting a mistress either of his nephew Charles de Verninac or of his friend Charles Soulier, unless the final quotation from the *Correspondance* in the preceding entry be interpreted to mean that he was planning to portray the latter's mistress in 1822. The inscription seems, however, more likely to refer to the artist's nephew than to Soulier, to whom Delacroix usually refers by his surname. In that case, the picture would have been painted before Charles de Verninac's death in 1834, and most probably before his departure for South America in 1831 (see J62 and J92).

L77 PORTRAIT OF MADEMOISELLE LA... (probably LAURE)

$23\frac{5}{8} \times 15\frac{3}{4}$ in. (60 × 40 cm. Moreau: H. 40, W. 60 cm)
Moreau p. 229 (1824). R97 (1824. No repr.)
Whereabouts unknown

Provenance: Unrecorded.

Exhibitions: None.

Literature: *Journal* I. 79 n. 4.

This portrait is known only from the description published by Moreau: 'Représentée en buste, vêtue d'une robe de couleur foncée, serrée à la taille par une large ceinture que coupe une boucle très-haute. Non signé, ni daté.' Robaut, who evidently had no first-hand knowledge of the picture, followed Moreau's description, except for transposing his dimensions on the assumption that the height must have exceeded the width. He added that he thought the sitter was a model by the name of Laure. This persuasive opinion was no doubt based on knowledge of the following entry of 18 April 1824 in the then unpublished *Journal* (I. 79–80): 'A l'atelier à neuf heures. Laure venue. Avancé le portrait. C'est une chose singulière que l'ayant désirée tout le temps de la séance, au moment de son départ, assez précipité à la vérité, ce n'était plus tout à fait de même.' Delacroix mentions Laure on several other occasions between April and June 1824 (ibid. 78, 87, 105, 111–14). She may have served as a model for the *Massacres de Scio* (J105) and, according to André Joubin ('Les Modèles de Delacroix', *GBA*, xv (1936), p. 355), she posed for the *Greece on the Ruins*

of Missolonghi (J98) and the *Woman with Parrot* (J9), but there is in fact no secure evidence of which figures she posed for and hence of what she looked like.

L78 PORTRAIT OF ANNE CLAIRE PIERRET (?)   Pl. 148

$8\frac{11}{16} \times 7\frac{7}{8}$ in. (22 × 20 cm)
R70 (1823)
Whereabouts unknown

Provenance: Mme J. B. Pierret, mother of the sitter.

Exhibitions: None.

Literature: None, except Robaut.

This portrait is known only from the small print in Robaut, reproduced here, and from the tracing in Robaut Tracings I. Though identified as 'Juliette Pierret enfant' in the former, it is noted as 'Anne Claire Pierret malade' on the tracing. The latter identification is more likely to be correct if Robaut's date of 1823 is accurate, because Juliette was not born till November 1822, whereas Claire was born in August 1821 (see J85 and J86).

L79 PORTRAIT OF ANNE CLAIRE PIERRET (?)   Pl. 149

$17\frac{3}{4} \times 14\frac{3}{16}$ in. (45 × 36 cm)
R Ann 121bis (1825) and part of R1904
Whereabouts unknown

Provenance: Delacroix's posthumous sale, Feb. 1864, part of lot 201 ('Onze études de têtes et portraits'), to Count de Calonne, 90 fr.

Exhibitions: None.

Literature: None published.

This study is known only from Robaut's drawing of it in Tracings I, reproduced here. The following notes appear under R121^{bis}, in the margin of R121 (*Portrait of Anne Claire Pierret*—J85): 'Le même enfant a encore été peint ailleurs par Eug. Delacroix.

'Je revois en janvier 1892, chez M. le Cte de Calonne, une tête d'étude et buste grandeur nature vue de trois quarts où se trouve encore l'étiquette 201, de la Vente posthume. Voir *croquis additions*. Il y avait dans le lot 201 onze articles. Celui-ci 90 francs à Mr de C. 45^c × 36^c.'

Neither Robaut's identification nor his dating can be considered reliable in this case.

L80 PORTRAIT OF COUNT DEMETRIUS DE PALATIANO IN SULIOT COSTUME

$16\frac{1}{8} \times 13$ in. (41 × 33 cm, according to Robaut[1]) Moreau p. 99, 168, 231 (1826). R 170 (1826. Repr. from Villot etching) 1826
Whereabouts unknown

Provenance: Apparently remained in Delacroix's possession as late as 1857, but not until his death;[2] belonged to 'M. P. . .' in 1865, according to Piron.[3]

Exhibition: Salon 1827, no. 292 ('Portrait de M. le comte de P. en costume souliote').

Literature: ? *Correspondance* II. 239 and n.; *Journal* I. 89 n. 1; Piron, p. 106; G. Opresco, 'Identification du "Palicar" de Delacroix', *GBA*, LXVII (1966), p. 128; L. Johnson, 'Delacroix et les Salons. Documents inédits au Louvre', *Revue du Louvre*, 16 (1966), p. 220.

Print: Etching in reverse by Frédéric Villot, d. 1833 (Moreau p. 99; Fig. 23 here).

Copies: Copied in 'small dimensions' by Frédéric Villot, according to robaut (under R170): possibly J(R)33 or J(R)34.

This portrait presents two major problems in that the wrong version has been taken for the original for nearly a century and it has never been established exactly who the model is.

Fig. 23. *Count Palatiano*, F. Villot after Delacroix.

The objections to accepting the general opinion that the Cleveland portrait is the version shown at the Salon of 1827 are set out under the entry for that picture (J(R)33) and for J(R)34; here the question of the model's identity will be discussed.

The identification of the anonymous 'comte de P.' of the Salon catalogue as 'Comte Palatiano' was established no later than 1873, by Moreau (p. 99) in his description of Villot's etching from the portrait. No subsequent literature has gone beyond stating the obvious, that the Count was a Greek aristocrat whose costume, associated with the freedom fighters in the War of Independence, must have intrigued Delacroix at a time when he was an ardent Philhellene. (Opresco's opinion (1966) that he was a Romanian by the name of Balaciano is unconvincing in view of Delacroix's own references in the *Journal* to Palatiano's being a Greek—quoted n. 2 here).

Count Demetrius de Palatiano, whom the portrait in fact represented, was born of an ancient and noble Greek family at Corfu on 5 December 1794. The fourth of seven children of Senator Nicholas and Santa Palatiano, *née* Countess Sordina, he was, according to family tradition, an 'enfant terrible'. He left home at the age of nineteen and travelled widely, first in Albania, Epirus and the Ionian islands, then in Italy and Germany, before coming to England, where he married. He claimed in a letter to his sister Nina, Lady Adam, wife of the Lord High Commissioner of the Ionian Islands, then under British administration, that the King of Bavaria, with whom he is said to have been on friendly terms, invested him with the title of Count and it was recognized by Lord Bathurst or Lord Goderich (Colonial Secretaries). While the Commonwealth Office and Bavarian State Archives have been unable to confirm his right to the title, he certainly used it for official documents in England. Styling himself the 'Honorable Count Demetrius de Palatiano' in a sworn affidavit in support of his application for denizenship, dated 6 October 1834, he declares that he 'has been resident in England for near nine years last past' and goes on to give particulars of his two English marriages, the first to Catherine Elizabeth Marrie, in St. George's, Hanover Square, on 22 September 1826; the second, following her death and that of their two children, to Elizabeth Ann Hartley, in the same church on 14 July 1834. Having stated that his reason for applying to become a 'Denizen of this Realm' is to remove any doubts as to his entitlement to his wife's large fortune should he survive her, he concludes by proclaiming his 'deep predilection for the habits of Englishmen and a deep reverence for [their] Laws', and his intention of making this country his future residence.

Letters Patent for Denization once granted, on 23 December 1834, the attractions of life in England seem to have quickly palled, for the Count returned to Greece with his bride, travelling in grand style and at a leisurely pace via Paris, Munich and Venice, to arrive at Corfu on 28 April 1835. Two children were born in Athens, a further four in other European cities. The family eventually settled in Naples, where Demetrius died at the age of fifty-six on 2 February 1849.

He is characterized in family recollections as unstable and flighty. Said to have narrowly escaped being beheaded while in the service of the tyrant Ali Pasha, he developed a preference for frequenting Christian court circles. Always the *grand seigneur*, he ran through vast sums in travelling and in distributing largesse. Having no practical sense of the value of money, he remained improvident to the end and died in financial straits. His investment in such abortive projects as a secret mechanical device for propelling ships without sail or steam had evidently done little to check the depletion of his wealth.

In England, he moved in high society. Countess Bathurst, for example, attended his first wedding in 1826, and he spent his honeymoon at Waldershare Park, near Dover, the seat of the Earl of Guilford, a famous Philhellene portrayed in a lithograph by Ingres.[4]

His connections with France are more obscure. According to the family's biographical note (see n. 4), he was in Paris in 1825; according to his own sworn affidavit quoted above, he must have come to reside in England after October 1825, but not long after. He may well, therefore, have stopped in Paris on his way to London, around the end of 1825 or early in 1826, and met Delacroix there. A meeting about that time accords well with the presence on the latter pages of a sketch-book bought by Delacroix in England of studies which he himself refers to as drawings of Palatiano's costume.[5] Other evidence points to a date in the first quarter of 1826 for the portrait: studies of the same sort of dress, apparently also modelled by Palatiano, are to be found on a sheet with a very early idea for the *Marino Faliero* (J112), which was being finished in April 1826. Bonington, too, did drawings and at least one painted portrait of Palatiano in Suliot costume, it is believed at the same time as Delacroix. He is known to have been working in Delacroix's studio for part of the winter of 1825-6 and to have left Paris for Venice on 4 April 1826. Finally, Moreau states, though without giving his reasons for thinking so, that the Delacroix portrait was painted in 1826. It was accepted by the Salon jury on 8 October 1827 (L. Johnson, op. cit., 1966).

If, from a pictorial point of view, it may have been the costume that most attracted Delacroix and other artists to Count de Palatiano, his colourful and extravagant personality must also have had a strong appeal at a period when the memory of Byron and his Philhellenism deeply influenced French Romantic art. The romantic appeal of the Palatiano family has survived into the twentieth century, Dr. Palatiano, a latter-day kinsman of Demetrius, having

supplied the model for Count D., a man of 'distinctly Byronic cast', in Lawrence Durrell's *Prospero's Cell*.[6]

In addition to the studies already enumerated in note 5, there is a group of drawings of Greek costume in the Louvre which are listed as preliminary studies for the portrait of Count de Palatiano in *Mémorial* (nos. 81-7 inclusive, RF9225-31, all repr.), together with a very fine drawing of a back view of a full-length figure, from Delacroix's posthumous sale, lent to the exhibition Louvre 1963 by Claude Roger-Marx (*Mémorial* no. 88, repr.). Though Count de Palatiano may well have posed for all these studies, none shows him standing full-length facing the viewer, as in the final painting, and four show him from the back. They can therefore be interpreted as studies for the Salon painting only in the very broadest sense, if at all. The only studies in the Louvre that represent the final design are on a sheet with multiple, unrelated studies. Scratchily drawn with pen and brown ink, one shows the final pose on a small scale, the other the weapons, belt and skirt on a larger scale. The sheet (RF10330) is, however, contained in one of the Pierret albums and cannot be securely attributed to Delacroix, but may, rather, be by any one of several lesser artists working close to him at the time.

A sheet from Delacroix's posthumous sale in the Baltimore Museum of Art has three full-length, pencil studies of a standing man with moustache wearing Suliot costume and seen from the front, which, though differing in stance from the final version and not including the weapons, seem to be more immediately connected with it than do any of the studies reproduced in *Mémorial*.

For further painted studies of Greek costume, see J28-J31 and J(L)38-J(L)44.

[1] These dimensions are doubtless based on the wrong assumption that the version exhibited at *EBA*, Paris 1885, no. 31, was the original portrait shown at the Salon of 1827 (see J(R)33). The measurements listed in the Salon register for 1827, almost certainly including the frame, and width preceding height, are 38 × 43 cm (L. Johnson, op. cit. *infra*, 1966).

[2] Discussing the striking effects obtained by earlier masters in naïvely rendering an effect of nature from the model, Delacroix writes on 3 Feb. 1847: 'Mon petit Grec (le *Comte Palatiano*) a le même accent' (*Journal* I. 176). On 5 Aug. 1854, reflecting on how artists of talent follow the same evolution from timidity and dryness at the beginning, to breadth and neglect of detail at the end of their careers, he concludes: 'Le *comte Palatiano* comparé à mes récentes peintures' (ibid. II. 226).

Both entries suggest that Delacroix had the portrait at hand on those dates. On 1 April 1857, he includes '*Le Grec Palatiano*' in a list of works that all seem to have belonged to him at the time (ibid. III. 90). Nothing of that description passed in his posthumous sale, nor was mentioned in his will.

[3] The identity of Monsieur P. has never been established, but it appears to have been neither Piron himself nor the dealer Petit (who owned at least one of the copies J(R)33 and J(R)34), since Piron lists both their names in full as owners of other Salon paintings by Delacroix.

[4] Apart from the information taken from Palatiano's affidavit of 1834, and the date of his Denization (both Public Record Office, H.O. 1/11), all biographical details come from family papers, either in Corfu or in England, especially from a typewritten biography of a few pages compiled at Corfu in 1930 by Mr. Constantine Beauclerk Palatiano, great-nephew of Demetrius. On the occasion of the Delacroix exhibition at the Louvre in 1930, Constantine and his son Anthony travelled to Paris, where they

bought a photograph of the portrait, then proceeded to England and visited Demetrius's daughter Mrs. White, who was over ninety. It was for the instruction of the English branch of the family, which survived through the female line only, that the biographical note was written. The dates of birth and death are taken from that, without independent confirmation from official sources.

⁵ List of loans dated 9 September 1829: 'Un livre de croquis acheté en Angleterre où sont des dessins du Costume Palatiano' (Louvre sketch-book RF23355, fol. 43ʳ). The sketch-book referred to can only be Louvre RF9143 which was bought from a London supplier and contains studies done in England on the first six sheets, drawings apparently all done in France on the other pages. The studies of Palatiano's costume most closely related to the portrait, but worn by a figure not recognizable as Demetrius, are on fol. 11ᵛ (black lead, full-length, from the back), 12ʳ (black lead, full-length, standing three-quarters to the left). There are further pencil and water-colour studies of Greek costume on fol. 12ᵛ (repr. Sérullaz *Dessins*, fig. 71), 13ʳ, 17ʳ (repr. ibid., fig. 72).

⁶ See *Lawrence Durrell and Henry Miller: a Private Correspondence* (G. Wicks, ed.; Faber & Faber, London, 1963), p. 210. I am much indebted to Miss Sybille Pantazzi for bringing this letter to my attention. It was the essential clue that enabled me, with the further help of Mr. Durrell, Dr. Theodore Stephanides (the 'arcane professor of broken bones' in *Prospero's Cell*), Mr. Anthony Palatiano, and Mr. D. A. Hartley Russell, great-grandson of Demetrius, to establish the identity of Delacroix's model. It is unique in my experience to have met or corresponded with such a variety of kind and interesting people when working on a single picture by Delacroix. I wish therefore, exceptionally, to thank them all warmly at this point rather than in the general list of acknowledgements at the beginning of this volume.

L81 PORTRAIT OF MADAME DALTON   Pl. 149

21¼ × 17¾ in. (54 × 45 cm)
Moreau p. 233 (1831). R363 (1831)
Whereabouts unknown

Provenance: M. de Courval, by 1873; in his possession at Rugles, Eure, Aug. 1878 (Robaut Tracings II).

Exhibitions: None.

Literature: Escholier I. 154.

The artist's friendship with Eugénie Dalton is believed to have dated from about 1825 when Delacroix is said (Moreau p. 172) to have given her his *Tam o'Shanter* (J109), and effectively ended in 1839 when she settled in Algeria. The years 1827 to *c.* 1831 seem to have been the period of their most intimate relationship, as inconstant lovers. Moreau-Nélaton (I. 104), drawing on a note in Philippe Burty's files which was in turn based on information from Count de Mornay, informs us that Mme Dalton had been a dancer at the Opéra and was married to an Englishman. She was reputed to have been Horace Vernet's mistress. It is known further that she was a painter who exhibited at the Salons between 1827 and 1840. According to Robaut (p. 100), several of her landscapes were corrected or retouched by Delacroix and could pass for works of the master. Some, he says, passed under his name in his posthumous sale. She died of cancer at Algiers in 1859 (see C. Bernard, 'Une Liaison orageuse', *Nouvelles Littéraires*, 9 May 1963, p. 8, which is the most complete account, based on new material,

of the relationship between Delacroix and Mme Dalton. Another account is contained in R. Escholier, *Delacroix et les femmes* (Fayard, Paris, 1963), pp. 71-6, 227-30. Fragmentary references to the friendship are to be found also in the *Journal*, *Correspondance* and *Lettres intimes* (pp. 169-71, on Soulier's involvement). The most explicit record of Delacroix's attempt to seduce Mme de Forget, who eventually supplanted Mme Dalton in his affections, while continuing his liaison with Mme Dalton is contained in a letter to his nephew dated 1 May 1830 (in L. Johnson, 'Eugène Delacroix and Charles de Verninac: an Unpublished Portrait and New Letters', *Burl Mag*, CX (1968), p. 516).

All trace of this portrait has been lost since it was catalogued by Robaut in 1885, and listed as still belonging to M. de Courval. Though in his published catalogue Robaut repeated Moreau's dimensions, 65 × 54 cm, he listed them as 54 × 45 cm in Robaut Tracings II, and these measurements are followed here as being the more likely to have been taken from the original by Robaut himself.

A portrait drawing of the sitter (R364) has survived (Coll. Mrs. Walter Feilchenfeldt, Zurich. Repr. Huyghe, fig. 22 and *Mémorial*, no. 66).

L82 SIX STUDIES OF HEADS OR PORTRAITS

Dimensions unknown
Part of R1904 (No repr.)
Whereabouts unknown

Provenance: Delacroix's posthumous sale, Feb. 1864, part of lot 201 ('Onze études de têtes et portraits', without dimensions).

Exhibitions: None certain.

Literature: None known, except Robaut.

Of the total of eleven paintings in lot 201 of Delacroix's posthumous sale, five have been accounted for: J61, J63, J89, J90 and J(L)79. The buyers and prices of the first and last of these five are also known. The individual buyers and prices fetched by the other nine are itemized in Burty Ann ED, where it is also noted, rather unhelpfully, whether each picture was a head or a study. The annotations for these nine are as follows: 1. Guerrier — 2 études nᵒˢ 200-1 [i.e., one from lot 200: 'Dix-sept études et académies'], 13 fr.; 2. Tissot — Etude, 150 fr.; 3. P. Meurice — ditto, 180 fr.; 4. Michel — tête, 255 fr.; 5. Guerrier — ditto, 115 fr.; 6. Belly — ditto, 49 fr.; 7. Lejeune — ditto, 50 fr.; 8. Lejeune — étude, 95 fr.; [Saint-] Maurice — ditto, 38 fr.

Some of the six missing studies may have been painted after 1831, but they are catalogued here as a group for the sake of convenience. An unidentified study that was listed in the catalogue of the Exh. *Bd Italiens*, Paris 1864, as lent by a M. Bucquet and described as 'Tête d'étude', 38 × 33 cm (Supp. to 3rd ed., no. 313), may have come from this lot.

L83 HEAD OF A YOUNG WOMAN   Pl. 149

$7\frac{7}{8} \times 5\frac{7}{8}$ in. (20 × 15 cm)
R Ann p. 423 (1832)
Whereabouts unknown

Provenance: Alfred Sensier; his sale, 10 Dec. 1877, lot 7 ('Tête de Femme. Esquisse', 20 × 15 cm).

Exhibitions: None.

Literature: None.

This study in oils is known only from the slight sketch in R Ann (between pp. 422 and 423) reproduced here, to which Robaut joined this colour note: 'Cheveux roux, teint frais'. There is insufficient evidence on which to base an opinion of its authenticity.

Robaut's listing of the picture under the year 1832 seems to have been arbitrary, the chance result of his pairing it with a copy after Goya's *Caprichos* (J(L)33) which passed in the same sale.

L84 PORTRAIT OF A WOMAN

Dimensions unknown
Date unknown
Whereabouts unknown

Provenance: Achille Piron; his sale, 21 April 1865, lot 10 ('Portrait de Femme. (Ebauche.)').

Exhibitions: None known.

Literature: None known.

This portrait is known to me only from the summary description, quoted above, in the catalogue of the Piron sale. I have been unable to identify it with any of the portraits catalogued by Robaut.

L85 PORTRAIT STUDY OF A YOUNG WOMAN

Approx. $10\frac{5}{8} \times 8\frac{5}{8}$ in. (27 × 22 cm)
R Ann 192ter (1826)
Whereabouts unknown

Provenance: P. Andrieu; his sale, 6 May 1892, lot 172 ('Etude de femme'), 100 fr.

Exhibitions: None.

Literature: None.

This work is known to me only from the summary title listed in the Andrieu sale catalogue and from the fuller description in R Ann, entered after Robaut had seen it at the time of the sale and which runs thus: 'Portrait de Jeune Femme (Etude) — t. [toile] de 3 en hauteur. Simple esquisse, mais qui, à la hauteur où elle se trouvait, m'a paru d'une extrême suavité. La tête est vue de face, yeux bruns et doux; cheveux noirs, peignoir blanc, poitrine découverte. N° 172 Vente posth: Pierre Andrieu. 100 fr.' Many of the works which passed under Delacroix's name in the sale of his assistant Andrieu were of doubtful authenticity, and it seems clear that Robaut was unable to inspect this study closely. Until the picture comes to light, the attribution to Delacroix must therefore be viewed with some scepticism.

Allegory, Mythology and Decorations

L86 NEMESIS   Pl. 150

$9\frac{7}{8} \times 13$ in. (25 × 33 cm)
R12 (1817)
Whereabouts unknown

Provenance: Delacroix's posthumous sale, Feb. 1864, lot 143 ('Némésis [Esquisse]', without dimensions), to Count Grzymala, 200 fr.

Exhibitions: None.

Literature: None, except Robaut.

This sketch has not come to light since 1885 and is known only from the small print in Robaut, reproduced here, and from a tracing, taken in December 1875, in Tracings 1.

L87 DECORATIONS FOR LOTTIN DE SAINT-GERMAIN'S DINING-ROOM

Bases of the lunettes: $46\frac{7}{8}$ in. (1.19 m)?[1]
1820
Probably destroyed *c.* 1855

Literature: Silvestre *Delacroix* (1855), p. 80; L. Clément de Ris, *Critiques d'art et de littérature* (Didier, Paris, 1862. Chapter on Delacroix dated April 1857), pp. 381 f.; L. Johnson, 'Some Early Murals by Delacroix', *Burl Mag*, CXVII (1975), pp. 650-8.

Among Delacroix's works listed by L. de Virmond at the end of Silvestre (1855) is a scheme of decorations unmentioned in later catalogues and described as 'Six ou sept dessus-de-portes demi-circulaires chez M. Lottin-Saint-Germain, dans les environs de la Sainte-Chapelle.' Clément de Ris, writing in 1857, also mentions decorations for the house of a M. Lottin de Saint-Germain on the Île de la Cité, describing them as 'quelques trumeaux' and specifying that they were done before 1821 on the recommendation of Duponchel, who was to play so important a part in getting Delacroix included in Count de Mornay's mission to Morocco in 1832. I connected these references with a passage in a letter dated 1 March 1820 where Delacroix wrote to his sister of paintings 'que tu te rappelles que j'ai faites près du palais et dont j'attends encore le payement' (*Correspondance* V. 34); and showed that a M. Lottin de Saint-Germain, 'imprimeur du Roi' by 1822, was living very close to the Palais de Justice on the Île de la Cité as early as 1818, at 1 rue de Nazareth, a street that was destroyed by 1855, to make way for extensions to the Law Courts.

On the basis of the scant literary evidence set out above and of studies in the Louvre, I tentatively concluded that the decorations for Lottin, for which the commission may have been received and studies begun by the summer of 1819, were painted in the winter of 1819–20 for the dining-room of his house in the rue de Nazareth and comprised five paintings, distributed on three walls and perhaps executed directly on to them. A note in Moreau N, which came to light after my findings were in proof, specifically assigned the decorations, described as 'Dessus de Porte', to 1820, but added nothing else to the earlier sources. The most likely subjects were: a man roasting meat on a spit and, probably on the same wall to the left of it, a woman with a child holding a rabbit (two advanced water-colour studies for lunettes, Louvre, RF23356, fol. 12ᵛ, repr. Johnson, op. cit., fig. 32); a sleeping Bacchic figure and a woman milking a goat to feed a child, on the right and left respectively of the side wall opposite (Louvre, RF9146, fol. 36ᵛ and RF9243, repr. ibid., figs. 30 and 39); a nymph and satyr on the end wall, facing the windows in the opposite wall (Louvre, RF9146, fol. 36ᵛ, repr. ibid., fig. 30). All the paintings, with the possible exception of the *Nymph and Satyr* on the end wall, appear to have been lunettes.

The studies, like the lunettes painted for Talma's dining-room in 1821 (J94–J97), show the influence of Graeco-Roman wall paintings from Herculaneum and its environs, of classical statuary and Raphael. Baroque influence in the development of the scheme is also suggested by a pencil copy of *putti* from the surrounds of two medallions on the ceiling of the Farnese Gallery (repr. L. Johnson, op. cit., fig. 33. Professor J. D. Stewart brought my attention to the source of Delacroix's copy).

The commission appears to have brought Delacroix too little to buy a suit (*Correspondance*, loc. cit.).

[1] This measurement is taken from a diagram of a lunette marked '3 pieds 8 pouces' on a sheet of studies which appear to be connected with the Lottin commission (Louvre, RF23356, fol. 21ᵛ). The note is assumed to refer to the old French foot of 32.5 cm, not the contemporary English one.

L88 COMBAT BETWEEN TWO KNIGHTS

Chimney-piece. Medium, support and dimensions
  unknown.
1824

Literature: L. Johnson, *Some Early Murals by Delacroix*, *Burl Mag*, CXVII (1975), p. 658 n. 18.

This work is known only from the following description contained in a note made by Moreau of decorations done by Delacroix in private houses:

> '1824 Pour *Lui-même*
>   Un devant de cheminée
>   représentant un combat de
>   2 chevaliers' (Moreau N).

It was presumably painted at 118, rue de Grenelle, Delacroix's Paris address in 1824, as given in the Salon catalogue of that year.

L89 LANDSCAPE WITH TORRENT

Chimney-piece. Medium, support and dimensions
  unknown.
1827

Literature: L. Johnson, *Some Early Murals by Delacroix*, *Burl Mag*, CXVII (1975), p. 658 n. 18.

This work is known only from the following description contained in a note made by Moreau of decorations done by Delacroix in private houses:

> '1827 Pour Mʳ Pierret
>   Un devant de cheminée
>   représentant un Torrent
>   au milieu d'un paysage'
>   (Moreau N).

It was probably painted at 17 rue du Bac, the Paris address in October 1827 of Delacroix's close friend, Jean-Baptiste Pierret.

L90 LEDA

$9\frac{7}{8} \times 7\frac{1}{2}$ in. (25 × 19 cm)
R384 (1832. No repr.)
1827?
Whereabouts unknown

Provenance: Frédéric Leblond, by 1832 to at least 1864, d. 1872.

Exhibitions: Musée Colbert, Paris 1832, no. 143; *Bd Italiens*, Paris 1864, no. 105.

Literature: Anonymous, 'Exposition du Musée Colbert au profit des familles des indigens cholériques', *L'Artiste*, III (1832), 18ᵉ livraison, p. 198; anonymous review of the same exhibition, *Journal des Artistes et des Amateurs*, I, no. 21 (20 May 1832), p. 370; Silvestre *Delacroix* (1855), p. 80; Moreau-Nélaton I. 141.

This picture was known to Robaut only from the scant description, 'Une Léda', in the catalogue of the exhibition at the Musée Colbert in 1832, and he supposed, no doubt wrongly, that it might be a sketch for the fresco *Leda and the Swan* which Delacroix painted at Valmont in 1834 (repr. Sérullaz *Peintures murales*, pl. 2). It was described as a 'Léda couchée' in the review of the exhibition in the *Journal des Artistes*; as a 'petite Léda au bain' in Silvestre; the catalogue of the exhibition *Bd Italiens*, Paris 1864, supplies the dimensions; and according to an annotation in the copy of the catalogue in *BN Estampes* (gift of B-Prost) it was: 'Absolument primitif; au point d'en douter'.

Fig. 24. *Leda*, Delacroix.

A group of pen-and-ink studies of a Leda with the swan, on a sheet in the Louvre (RF5276. Fig. 24 here), is probably connected with this lost painting. The verso of the sheet contains studies for the *Death of Sardanapalus* (J125), painted in 1827, thus the Leda could have been painted about that time, though the comment 'absolutely primitive' in the 1864 exhibition catalogue does not accord well with the refinement of style that one would expect in a small-scale nude

study painted in the same year as the *Woman with Parrot* (J9), and indeed finds in the Leda drawings. Nor do the comments of the reviewer for *L'Artiste* in 1832 seem, on the face of it, to support a date as advanced as 1827; describing it as a sketch, he writes that it 'semble ne lui [à Delacroix] appartenir ni par le choix du sujet ni par le style classique dont on y trouve la trace. C'est sans doute une ébauche d'élève; mais elle acquiert quelque prix en la considérant comme opposition complète à la manière actuelle du jeune peintre.' These comments may, however, simply indicate, not that the picture was painted before 1827, but that it was done quickly for the artist's friend Leblond with no intention of bringing it to a high degree of finish.

The programme for a Leda, the opening sentence of which corresponds well with the studies reproduced here, is contained in one of Delacroix's sketch-books in the Louvre (RF9145, fol. 2ᵛ):

Leda. Son étonnement naïf en voyant le cygne se jouer dans son sein autour de ses belles épaules [not 'jambes', as transcribed by Sérullaz] nues et de ses cuisses éclatantes de blancheur. Un sentiment nouveau s'éveille dans son esprit troublé. Elle cache à ses compagnons son mystérieux amour: je ne sais quoi de divin rayonne dans la blancheur de l'oiseau divin dont le col entoure mollement les membres délicats [et dont] le bec amoureux et téméraire ose effleurer les charmes les plus secrets. La jeune beauté troublée d'abord et cherchant à se rassurer en pensant que ce n'est qu'un oiseau. Ses transports n'ont pas eu de témoin, elle en vient à désirer qu'il fût plus qu'une brute [this clause incompletely deciphered by Sérullaz]. Couchée sous un ombrage frais au bord des ruisseaux qui réfléchissent ses beaux membres nus et dont le crystal [*sic*] effleure le bout de ses pieds, elle demande aux vents cet objet de son ardeur qu'elle n'ose appeler.

The dating of the sketch-book is problematic. Sérullaz (*Peintures murales*, p. 23) dates it 1820-6, but since the only reason given for the earlier date is that it contains studies for the *Barque de Dante* (J100) and those studies are actually copies of Italian paintings, it may not have been in use that early. Much of the sketch-book does, however, seem to have been used in the period 1824-6, and the note on Leda and the swan could therefore be close in date to the drawings of the subject on the Louvre sheet.

The picture is mentioned only once by Delacroix, when he merely includes its title ('Une Léda') in a list of pictures that he compiled in the 1840s (*Journal* III. 371—Supp.). It has not come to light since 1864.

Historical and Literary Subjects

L91 ROMAN WOMEN DONATING THEIR JEWELLERY   Pl. 150

$12\frac{5}{8} \times 15\frac{3}{4}$ in. (32×40 cm)

R19 (1818)

Probably 1818

Whereabouts unknown

Provenance: Paul Chenavard, by 1885 (presumably a gift from the artist, before 1863), d. 1895.

Exhibitions: None.

Literature: Silvestre *Documents nouveaux* (1864), pp. 21 f.; Moreau-Nélaton I. 29; Escholier I. 41; Sérullaz *Dessins* 1952, p. 15; *Mémorial*, mentioned under no. 1.

Without giving a date, Silvestre (op. cit.) wrote of this sketch: 'Je connais aussi une esquisse juvénile de Delacroix, laquelle eut, au concours de l'Ecole des Beaux-Arts (professeur Le Thière), le numéro 38: *Les Femmes romaines offrant leurs bijoux à la patrie*. On y voit percer la personnalité de l'auteur de *Sardanapale* et du *Massacre de Scio* à certains airs de tête, à la souplesse des chairs, à l'inflexion des bras et des mains. L'intelligence de l'élève échappe aux canons de l'Ecole.' Robaut dated it to 1818, adding that the subject was that treated by the students at the Ecole des Beaux-Arts 'au concours d'esquisse de cette année'. This is not the subject of either of the painted sketches crowned in 1818 and preserved at the Ecole, which are Etienne Dubois's *Despair of Alexander after Slaying Clitus*, judged 7 March 1818,[1] and Monvoisin's *Death of Cleopatra*, dated October 1818; nor is the subject represented in any other oil sketch from the years 1816–23 preserved at the Ecole. However, on 10 March 1818, forty-three 'esquisses' of an unspecified subject were judged at the Ecole as the 'Premier Essay [*sic*] de l'Admission au Grand Concours de Peinture et de Sculpture', and only twenty students were admitted to the second trial.[2] It is quite possible that this sketch by Delacroix was placed thirty-eighth in that first trial for the Prix de Rome. A dating of 1818 is made the more acceptable by the presence in a Louvre sketch-book, which was certainly in use in 1817–18, of two advanced composition studies of the same subject though differing in design (RF9146, fol. 9ᵛ and 10ʳ; repr. Sérullaz *Dessins* 1952, pl. III, figs. 4 and 5, and, both on a smaller scale, in *Mémorial*, no. 1). This oil sketch is known only from the small print in Robaut and the copy in Tracings I, reproduced here; it has not come to light since 1885.

As related by Plutarch (*Camillus*, x), the women of Rome donated their gold and jewellery to the Republic as a contribution towards a golden bowl offered to Apollo by Camillus to commemorate his victory over Veii. As an *exemplum virtutis*, the subject had found favour with French painters in the late eighteenth century, a *Piété et générosité des dames romaines* by Nicolas Brenet having been shown at the Salon of 1785, a *Générosité des dames romaines* by Louis Gauffier, at the Salon of 1791 (now respectively, Château de Fontainebleau, Musée des Beaux-Arts, Poitiers. Repr. in R. Rosenblum, *Transformations in Late Eighteenth Century Art* (Princeton, 1967), figs. 86 and 88. Ibid. 86 f., for further discussion of the literary sources of the subject and its treatment by French artists).

If this sketch may have shown marks of an original talent in the points mentioned by Silvestre, it would not appear to have departed significantly from the neo-classical canons of the Ecole in composition.

[1] *Assemblées des professeurs et jugements*, IV, MS., Ecole des Beaux-Arts, Paris.
[2] Ibid.

L92 DEATH OF A ROMAN GENERAL?   Pl. 151

$12\frac{13}{16} \times 15\frac{15}{16}$ in. (32.5×40.5 cm)

R1464 (1818)

Probably 1820

Whereabouts unknown

Provenance: Exchanged by the artist for the project of a fellow student, from whom M. Mimard-Roussel had acquired it by 1871 (Robaut).

Exhibitions: None.

Literature: None, except Robaut.

According to Robaut, this sketch, which he entitled '*Mort d'un général romain*', was painted for a competition at the Ecole des Beaux-Arts in 1818. Both the top competition sketches for 1818 preserved at the Ecole are of classical death scenes: Etienne Dubois's *Despair of Alexander after Slaying Clitus* (at a banquet) and Monvoisin's *Death of Cleopatra*; but neither of these episodes is represented in Delacroix's sketch, which seems indeed to show a fallen warrior brought into a tent from the battlefield, his gear having been removed and left at the entrance. The subject does not correspond, either, to any of the other competition sketches preserved at the Ecole from the years 1817 to 1823. The dimensions listed by Robaut, however, tally within a millimetre with the regulation size for competition sketches (12 by 15 *pouces*) agreed at a meeting of professors at the Ecole on 7 March 1818 and announced only after the competition of that semester.[1] This fact, in addition to the character of the subject and to the information about provenance recorded by Robaut, leaves little doubt that this sketch was an official assignment connected with Delacroix's training at the Ecole des Beaux-Arts, designed to prepare him to compete for the Prix de Rome. A composition drawing for it is contained in a Louvre sketch-book (RF9153, fol. 50ᵛ), which is inscribed with the date '13 juillet 1820' on fol. 16ᵛ. Robaut's dating of 1818 thus appears to be too early by two years. The picture's close ties with the French neo-classical tradition seem to be stressed by the presence in the same sketch-book (fol. 43ᵛ) of a finished drawing after the figure of a young Greek fastening his sandal in the foreground of David's *Leonidas at Thermopylae* of 1814 (Louvre).

This oil sketch has not come to light since Robaut catalogued it and is known only from his small print and his larger coloured drawing of it in Tracings I, reproduced here.

¹ *Assemblées des professeurs et jugements*, IV, MS., Ecole des Beaux-Arts, Paris.

L93 STUDY FOR ONE OF THE DAMNED IN THE BARQUE OF DANTE

$9\frac{7}{16} \times 12\frac{5}{8}$ in. (24 × 32 cm)
R1475 (1822)
Whereabouts unknown

Provenance: Delacroix's posthumous sale Feb. 1864, lot 197 ('Fragment d'étude pour un des damnés dans le tableau de Dante et Virgile', 21 × 32 cm), to M. Aubry, 280 fr.

Exhibitions: None.

Literature: None, except Robaut.

Study 3i under J100 may be an early studio copy of this.

L94 REBECCA AND THE WOUNDED IVANHOE

Dimensions unknown
1823
Whereabouts unknown

Provenance: Bought from the artist by Amable Paul Coutan in Dec. 1823; his sale (anon.) 9 March 1829, lot 49 ('Sujet tiré d'Ivanhoë, roman de Walter Scott. Ivanhoë blessé et malade se fait rendre compte par la jeune Juive de l'attaque que l'on fait du château où il est renfermé,' without dimensions), 150 fr.

Exhibitions: None.

Literature: Silvestre *Delacroix* (1855), p. 80; Tourneux, p. 140; L. Johnson, Cat. Exh. Edinburgh–London 1964, mentioned under no. 68.

On 30 December 1823, Delacroix noted in his *Journal* (I. 40): 'J'ai vendu ces jours-ci à M. Coutan, l'amateur de Scheffer, mon tableau exécrable d'*Ivanhoë*. Le pauvre homme! et il dit qu'il m'en prendra quelques-uns encore; je serais d'autant plus tenté de croire qu'il n'est pas émerveillé de

celui-ci.' There is no reason to doubt that this was the picture inspired by *Ivanhoe* which passed six years later in the Coutan sale and seems never to have come to light since. The description in the sale catalogue makes it clear that it represented a scene from chapter xxx in Scott's novel, when Rebecca describes to Ivanhoe the assault that is being made by the Black Knight and Locksley's men on the castle in which he is imprisoned. It is the earliest recorded painting by Delacroix of a subject from *Ivanhoe*, which was first published in a French translation in Paris in 1820. He treated the same scene much later in a painting dated to 1847 by Robaut (No. 1000; Archives photographiques, BAP 11818), but which seems more likely to be the '*Petit Ivanhoë et Rebecca*' that Delacroix was working on in 1858 (*Journal* III. 213).

L95 MASSACRES OF CHIOS, detail

$27\frac{9}{16} \times 34\frac{5}{8}$ in. (70 × 88 cm)
Whereabouts unknown

Provenance: Sale Alexandre Dumas, 12 May 1892, lot 38 ('Le Massacre de Chio [*sic*]. Fragment. H. 70 × L. 88 cm.')

Exhibitions: None known.

Literature: None known.

This work is known to me only from the description in the Dumas sale catalogue, where it is listed as a Delacroix. But it was conceivably a copy by another artist from the Salon painting (J105).

L96 LEICESTER

Dimensions unknown
1824
Whereabouts unknown

There is no record of this picture other than an entry in the *Journal* (I. 71) on 9 April 1824: 'Achevé le *Leicester*', which presumably refers to an oil painting now lost, but could also perhaps refer to a finished water-colour or drawing.

The subject was possibly inspired by Walter Scott's *Kenilworth* (1821), in which the Earl of Leicester, Queen Elizabeth's favourite, was a leading character. A small *Amy Robsart and Leicester* was painted two or three years later by Bonington (Ashmolean Museum, Oxford).

L97 THE WITCHES' SABBATH,   Pl. 151
sketch

$12\frac{3}{16} \times 15\frac{3}{8}$ in. (31 × 39 cm)
R103 (1824)
Whereabouts unknown

Provenance: Delacroix's posthumous sale, Feb. 1864, lot 142 ('[Esquisse.] Le Sabbat de Faust', without dimensions to

Haro, 410 fr.; Dr. Isambert; his posthumous sale, 9 March 1877, lot 24 (description specifies that it is lot 142 from Delacroix's posthumous sale and lists the dimensions as 33 × 40 cm), 250 fr.; Baron de Beurnonville; his sale, 21 May 1883, lot 160 ('Départ pour le Sabbat. Etude', 32 × 41 cm), 250 fr.; sale D. [Dussol de Cette], 17 March 1884 ('Le départ pour le sabbat. Etude', 30 × 40 cm), 190 fr.

Exhibition: *Bd Italiens*, Paris 1864, no. 63 ('Le Sabbat de Faust. Esquisse', 33 × 41 cm, lent by Haro).

Literature: ? *Journal* III. 374—Supp.[1]

This sketch, of a subject which appears never to have been realized as a finished painting, is known to me only from the small print in Robaut and from the larger drawing in Robaut Tracings I, reproduced here. The picturesque description contained in Robaut further supplements the print: 'C'est une simple ébauche, intéressante surtout par la belle disposition de la ligne diagonale qui, des masses de rochers placés à gauche, s'élève vers les hautes ruines en forme de falaises qui dressent leurs cimes dans le vaste ciel et vers lesquelles s'élance, comme à l'assaut, la bande des sorciers, larves, lémures, afrites, goules, lamies, psylles, brucolaques et autres esprits nocturnes.'

See also J(O)9.

[1] Delacroix here includes in a list of pictures compiled in the 1840s: '[*Le Sabbat*], petite [esquisse] en grisaille, à Mgr. D.' Unless this sketch was returned to Delacroix before his death, having perhaps been lent to Mgr. D., it cannot have been the version that passed in his posthumous sale. There may therefore be two untraced sketches, one of which would be known only from this reference in the *Journal*.

L98 DESDEMONA AND EMILIA   Pl. 152

$9\frac{7}{16} \times 6\frac{11}{16}$ in. (24 × 17 cm)
R116 (1825) and Addition p. 480
Whereabouts unknown

Provenance: Given by the artist to his friend Charles Soulier, lived at Saint-Mammès s/Loing, 1839 to at least 1860, d. between 1864 and 1877; Paul Soulier, his son, at Avon near Fontainebleau, by Jan. 1877 to at least 1885.

Exhibition: *EBA*, Paris 1885, no. 203.

Literature: H. Rostrup, 'Delacroix og hans Arbejder i Danske Samlinger', *Kunstmuseets Aarsskrift*, XVI–XVIII (1929–31. Copenhagen 1931), pp. 180, 184; C. Merchant, 'Delacroix's Tragedy of Desdemona', *Shakespeare Survey*, 21 (1968), p. 84.

This work has not come to light since 1885 and is known only from the print in Robaut and the drawing in Tracings I reproduced here, which is inscribed: 'Très ancien tableau de Delacroix—vers 1824—Il est affreusement craquelé dans presque tout le fond, quand je le dessine, le 9 janvier 1877 chez Mᵣ Paul Soulier, fils [de] l'ancien ami auquel Eugène

Delacroix l'avait donné. Ce tableau n'est pas signé, à moins que la signature ne se dissimule sous la craq[uelure].'

The subject derives from the scene of the Willow Song in Shakespeare's *Othello* (IV. iii), of which Delacroix saw a production with Kean in the leading role in London in the summer of 1825; but the presence of a harp, for which there is no authority in Shakespeare, suggests that the picture owes at least as much to Rossini's opera *Otello*, of which Delacroix apparently saw the first performance at the Théâtre des Italiens in Paris in 1821 (see letter of 4 June 1821 to Piron—*Lettres intimes*, p. 133). As Rostrup was the first to point out, in establishing Delacroix's debt to Rossini, Desdemona accompanies herself on the harp as she sings the Willow Song (the aria 'Assisa al pié d'un salice') in the third and final act of the opera (op. cit., 1929–31, p. 184. For further discussion of the joint influence of Shakespeare and Rossini on Delacroix's treatment of subjects from *Othello*, see L. Johnson, Cat. Exh. Toronto-Ottawa 1962–3, no. 14, and especially C. Merchant, op. cit., 1968).

The following note written in English inside the front cover of a sketch-book that Delacroix was certainly using in 1825 (studies of the Elgin marbles) and 1826 (studies for *Greece on the Ruins of Missolonghi*—J98) suggests that Robaut's dating of this picture to 1825 may be exactly right: 'Othello and Desdemona—Desdemona tearing on his [*sic*] harp.—' (Louvre, RF9145). Despite the influence of Rossini, indicated also by this note, it may well be that Kean's performance in London, which prompted Delacroix to write at the time 'Les expressions d'admiration manquent pour le génie de Shakespeare qui a inventé Othello et Iago' (*Correspondance* I. 162), provided him with the stimulus he needed to attempt this, his first of several paintings on the subject of Othello.

Delacroix painted the same subject, twice as large and with minor variations in the design, in 1849–50. In that picture, also untraced, the harp was placed on the far side of Desdemona, and Othello was shown approaching in the distance on the right (R1172, repr. in reverse. It is known not only from this print in Robaut and from Laurens's lithograph, but more directly from a photolithograph in an album of reproductions of works in the Arosa collection at the time of his sale of 25 February 1878—see *Bib AA*, Album containing MS. copy of Arosa sale catalogue, pl. 29). A preliminary pencil drawing for the late version is in the Louvre (RF9221, repr. *Mémorial* no. 398).

L99 HAMLET SEES THE GHOST OF HIS FATHER

Dimensions unknown
R1731 (1845. No repr.)
1825/6
Whereabouts unknown*

Provenance: Alexander Dumas père, d. 1870.

Exhibition: Odéon, Paris, from Nov. 1845 (no cat. known)

Literature: T. Gautier, account of reopening of the Odéon and of the exhibition of paintings in the foyer, *La Presse*, 17 Nov. 1845 (reprinted in T. Gautier, *Histoire de l'art dramatique en France depuis vingt-cinq ans (4ᵉ série)* (Hetzel, Paris, 1859), p. 139); Lord Pilgrim [P. Mantz], 'Exposition de l'Odéon', *L'Artiste*, 4th ser. v (1845), 4th livraison (23 Nov.), p. 62; 'Courrier de Paris', *L'Illustration*, 6 Dec. 1845, p. 213, on same page caricatured as a composition of purely abstract scribbles in a frame; A. Dumas père, 'Eugène Delacroix', *Le Monde illustré*, XIII (July–Dec. 1863), p. 124.

Robaut appears to have known this picture only from the caricature in *L'Illustration* (Dec. 1845), which gives no idea of the composition except that it was of vertical format; and from a manuscript note, which he does not publish, found among Delacroix's papers. His date of 1845 is apparently based on the year of the exhibition at the Odéon, rather than on firm knowledge of when it was painted. More helpfully, however, he adds that it once belonged to Alexandre Dumas père; for by referring to Dumas's own writings, the date can be revised to the mid-1820s, even in the absence of the original. Recollecting the period of comparative prosperity when Delacroix was paid for the *Massacres de Scio* (J105) and able to visit England with the proceeds in 1825, Dumas (loc. cit., 1863) writes: 'Ce fut dans cette période de prospérité [. . .] que Delacroix fit son premier *Hamlet*, son *Giaour* [1826. J114], son *Tasse dans la prison des fous* [1824. J106] et *Marino Faliero* [1826. J112].

'J'ai acheté les trois premiers tableaux; ils sont encore aujourd'hui des plus beaux qu'ait faits Delacroix.'

If Dumas provides the date, others describe the lost painting. Théophile Gautier (loc. cit., 1845) writes: 'Le tableau représente *Hamlet* rencontrant l'ombre armée de son père sur les glacis de la citadelle d'Elseneur, par un de ces froids clairs de lune du Nord, temps de promenade des spectres. La lithographie a rendu célèbre cette composition, une des plus belles et des plus terrifiantes d'Eugène Delacroix.' Paul Mantz (loc. cit., 1845) confirms its similarity to the lithograph and observes: 'son tableau ajoute au mérite de la composition la splendeur sourde d'une couleur harmonieuse.' The note published in *L'Illustration* at the same period, though satirical, gives an idea of how atmospherically it must have been treated: 'sa main habile a judicieusement noyé l'exécution et les détails dans des flots de brume, de manière à en épargner entièrement la vue aux spectateurs.'

The lithograph (Delteil no. 105. Fig. 25 here) is dated 1843 and no doubt closely reflects the composition of the painting, as the reviewers quoted above say. The subject, taken from *Hamlet* I. v, refers to the lines, printed in French

Fig. 25. *Hamlet*, Delacroix.

translation on the lithograph: 'I am thy father's spirit [. . .] Revenge his foul and most unnatural murther.'

It would be of special interest to find this, Delacroix's first painting from *Hamlet*, perhaps even his first from Shakespeare. It has never been recorded as an early work since Dumas wrote about it. Judging from Dumas's recollection of the date, it may well have been inspired by some performance of *Hamlet* seen by Delacroix in London in the summer of 1825. Though he was bitterly disappointed to miss Young as Hamlet, he may have attended a performance by another actor (see *Correspondance* I. 163, 166 and Trapp p. 159 n. 54). It passed in none of the Dumas sales listed by Lugt.

L99a KING LEAR

11 × 7⅞ in. (28 × 20 cm)
Whereabouts unknown
Provenance: Anon. sale (by Petit) Paris 21 Apr. 1859, lot 15 ('le roi Léar [*sic*]', 28 × 20 cm), 485 fr.; Paul Meurice, by 1864.

Exhibition: Bd Italiens, Paris 1864, no. 137 ('Le roi Lear', 28 × 20 cm, lent by Paul Meurice).

Literature: P. Burty, 'Vente de tableaux modernes', *GBA*, II 3rd livraison (1 May 1859), p. 182.

This picture is known to me only from the sources cited above, which give no indication of its date. Philippe Burty specifies that the king is 'assis devant une table, dans une salle aux murs de laquelle sont appendues des panoplies étincelantes.'

The subject of Lear was noted down by Delacroix in a list of ideas for pictures as early as the first years of the 1820s (Louvre sketch-book RF 23357, inside front cover: transcribed *Journal* III. 342—Supp.).

L100 RICHARD I IN PALESTINE

15¾ × 12⅝ in. (40 × 32 cm)
R1555 (1830. No repr.)
Whereabouts unknown

Provenance: Haro, by 1864.

Exhibited: *Bd Italiens*, Paris 1864, no. 65 ('Richard en Palestine', 40 × 32 cm).

Literature: None, except Robaut.

This work was evidently known to Robaut only from the description in the catalogue of the 1864 exhibition, and does not seem to have come to light since. The title listed in the catalogue suggests that it may have depicted a scene from Scott's novel *The Talisman*, published in 1825 and issued in a French translation the same year. A detailed pencil drawing in the Musée des Beaux-Arts, Besançon, datable *c.* 1825 on style and apparently intended as a composition study, seems to represent an episode from chapter 1 of the novel, when the crusader Sir Kenneth encounters a Saracen emir, who later turns out to be Saladin, and engages him in combat (repr. Cat. Exh. Edinburgh-London 1964, pl. 42). It is possible that this lost painting was developed from that drawing and that the figure of Sir Kenneth came to be wrongly identified as Richard I, Saladin's chief antagonist in *The Talisman*.

L101 THE FINALE OF   Pl. 153
DON GIOVANNI

21¼ × 17⁵⁄₁₆ in. (54 × 44 cm)
Signed bottom right: *Eug. Delacroix*
Moreau p. 177. R100 (1824)
1826?
Whereabouts unknown

Provenance: Bought from the artist by Mme Louise Rang-Babut of La Rochelle, a former pupil, 400 fr., about 1846 (*Journal* I. 250); M. A. Marmontel, by 1885; his sale 28 March 1898, lot 86, 2,500 fr.

Exhibitions: *Gal. Lebrun*, Paris 1826, no. 46; Salon 1838, no.

460; *Bd Italiens*, Paris 1864, Supp. to 2nd ed., no. 291 ('Don Juan et le Commandeur', without dimensions or date; lent by Mme Louise Babut); *EBA*, Paris 1885, no. 142 ('Don Juan. — Dernière scène (1824). Salon 1838', 54 × 44 cm; lent by M. Marmontel).

Literature: L. V. [Vitet], 'Exposition des tableaux au bénéfice des Grecs', *Le Globe*, 3 June 1826; Silvestre *Delacroix* (1855), p. 80; Tourneux, p. 67; Moreau-Nélaton I. 192; Escholier II. 242; *Journal* I. 250 and n.; L. Johnson, 'Eugène Delacroix et les Salons. Documents inédits au Louvre', *Revue du Louvre*, 16 (1966), p. 223.

This picture, which is now known only from the small print in Robaut and the drawing in Tracings I reproduced here, is stated by Moreau to have been painted in 1824, and Delacroix did in fact attend a performance of *Don Giovanni* on 17 January 1824 (*Journal* I. 45), which could have provided the initial inspiration. The painting is, however, first recorded in the catalogue of the exhibition which opened for the benefit of the Greeks at the Galerie Lebrun in Paris on 15 May 1826, where it is described as follows: '*Don Juan*. C'est la dernière scène de la pièce, au moment où le valet aperçoit la statue du Commandeur, qui est encore hors de la porte. La femme de Don Juan s'enfuit, et lui-même, plein d'étonnement, se lève de table pour recevoir cet hôte étrange.' And it could be one of the works which Delacroix refers to in a letter of May 1826 as about to be finished: 'J'irai bientôt remettre *aux Grecs* ce que je finis en ce moment.' (*Correspondance* I. 181.)

It has generally been assumed that the painting which Moreau, followed by Robaut, dates to 1824 is the same as that exhibited at the Salon of 1838, and, for lack of evidence to prove the contrary, the same assumption has been made here; but, in view of the exceptionally long period between the date of execution and submission to a Salon, the possibility that there were two versions painted some fourteen years apart, one of which was bought by Mme Babut about 1846 and the other acquired independently by M. Marmontel by 1885, cannot be ruled out. The Salon picture was accepted on 19 February and was marked in the catalogue as belonging to the artist. The description in the catalogue leaves no doubt that, if not the same picture, it represented exactly the same subject as that shown in 1826: '*Dernière scène de Don Juan*. Le valet voit en dehors la statue du commandeur, et dans son effroi laisse échapper sa lumière. Dona Elvire s'enfuit, et don Juan surpris se lève de table.'

Delacroix greatly admired Mozart's *Don Giovanni*, as a masterpiece of Romanticism, and singled out the finale for comment in 1847: 'Quel chef-d'œuvre de romantisme! Et cela en 1785! [. . .] Le combat avec le Père, l'entrée du Spectre frapperont toujours un homme d'imagination' (*Journal* I. 185).

L102 CHARLES VII AND AGNÈS SOREL

Dimensions unknown
R Ann, margin to R137
Whereabouts unknown

Provenance: Duval Le Camus, painter and dealer; his sale (anon.), 17 Apr. 1827, lot 39 ('Charles VII et Agnès Sorel'), 159 fr.

Exhibition: Douai 1827, no. 93 ('Charles VII et Agnès Sorel').

Literature: None.

This painting was known to Robaut only from the description in the catalogue of the exhibition Douai 1827. He questioned in R Ann whether it might not have been the *Charles VI and Odette* (R137; J110) exhibited under the wrong title, but this is very unlikely because it was listed with R137, as a separate picture, in the catalogue of the Duval Le Camus sale held in the same year. It has not come to light since 1827.

L103 CARDINAL RICHELIEU SAYING MASS, sketch

Support unknown. $13\frac{3}{4} \times 9\frac{5}{8}$ in. $(35 \times 24.5$ cm)?
R256 (1828. No repr.)
Whereabouts unknown

Provenance: Charles Nuitter, archivist of the Opéra, by 1885.

Exhibitions: None.

Literature: ? Silvestre *Delacroix* (1855), p. 81 ('Deux esquisses avancées du *Richelieu* exposé en 1831 et détruit en 1848 au Palais-Royal.'); *Mémorial*, mentioned under no. 130.

This work is known to me only from Robaut, who simply records that it was an oil sketch of *Cardinal Richelieu saying Mass in the Palais-Royal* (see J130–J132), belonging to Charles Nuitter. A pencil tracing in Robaut Tracings I, inscribed with the dimensions '$35 \times 24\frac{1}{2}$', may have been done from it (see J132).

L104 MAZEPPA   Pl. 153

$10\frac{7}{16} \times 13\frac{3}{4}$ in. $(26.5 \times 35$ cm)[1]
R262 (1828)
Whereabouts unknown

Provenance: David d'Angers, d. 1856; his son;[2] anon. sale, 6 May 1896, lot 31 ('*Mazeppa*. Il est attaché, nu, sur un cheval lancé au galop, à travers la plaine, sous un ciel qui s'éclaire d'un irradiement d'incendie. A droite, dans la vallée, des chevaux affolés s'enfuient', 30×40 cm).

Exhibitions: None.

Literature: *Journal* I. 60 n. 4; *Mémorial*, mentioned under no. 119; Huyghe, p. 488; H. Bock, in Cat. Exh. Bremen 1964, p. 266; L. Johnson, in Cat. Exh. Edinburgh–London 1964, mentioned under no. 90; Trapp, p. 64 and n.

This painting has not come to light since 1896 and is known only from the small print in Robaut, reproduced here, and from the drawing by Robaut in Tracings I.

Mazeppa became a popular theme with French Romantic artists soon after the publication of Byron's poem of that title in 1816. Géricault did a lithograph of the subject, dated 1823, in collaboration with Eugène Lami (Delteil, no. 94) and Clément lists a painting by him in the period 1820-4. Horace Vernet painted a large *Mort du cheval de Mazeppa* in 1825 (destroyed by fire in the Palais Bourbon, 1961) and exhibited it, together with a smaller *Mazeppa aux loups* (Musée Calvet, Avignon), at the Salon of 1827-8 (part of no. 1031). Louis Boulanger also exhibited a painting of Mazeppa being tied to the horse at the same Salon (1st Supp., no. 1435), as well as designing several lithographs of the theme. A painting by Eugène Lami of the same size and subject as Delacroix's passed in the same sale on 6 May 1896. In poetry, Victor Hugo in *Les Orientales* (1829) conceived Mazeppa as a symbol of genius carried away by inspiration.

Byron's poem is based on a passage in Voltaire's *Histoire de Charles XII*. Ivan Mazeppa (1644-1709) was born of a noble Polish family in Podolia and became a page at the court of the King of Poland. According to Voltaire, he was involved in an intrigue with the wife of a Polish count, who had him lashed naked to a wild horse, which was let loose and eventually dropped dead from exhaustion in the plains of the Ukraine. Mazeppa was released by Cossacks and in time became their hetman and a prince of the Ukraine under Peter the Great.

Delacroix has chosen a moment when Mazeppa is nearing the end of his journey (canto xvii), and the Cossacks who rescued him are apparently arriving in the distance on the right, it being noted in R Ann: 'Signaler l'énorme bande de chevaux qui arrive de loin à droite.'

While it seems clear that Delacroix was influenced very strongly by the design of Géricault's lithograph, the commentary in Robaut goes too far in stating that this canvas 'a été peinte d'après la composition lithographiée par Géricault'. Also, Robaut's date of 1828 is followed by a question mark in Tracings I and cannot be regarded as secure. Delacroix was certainly considering the subject of Mazeppa much earlier, as early as 1824, but in what form, if any, it was realized at that time is not clear. On 14 March 1824, he noted: 'M. Coutan m'a donné envie de faire *Mazeppa*' (*Journal* I. 60); and on 17 March: 'Penser, en faisant mon *Mazeppa*, à ce que je dis dans ma note du 20 *février*, dans ce cahier, c'est-à-dire calquer en quelque sorte la nature dans le genre du *Faust*' (ibid. 62); which suggests that he had a painting, perhaps this one, in mind, since the note to which he refers runs: 'Toutes les fois que je revois les gravures du *Faust*, je me sens saisi de l'envie de faire une toute nouvelle peinture, qui consisterait à calquer pour ainsi dire la nature' (ibid. 52). By 11 April, there is some doubt whether he has begun at all: 'Je suis, depuis une heure, à balancer entre *Mazeppa, Don Juan, le Tasse*, et cent autres' (ibid. 73). Finally, on 11 May, he noted among subjects from Byron that appealed to him: '*Les imprécations de Mazeppa* contre ceux qui l'ont attaché à son coursier, avec le château du Palatin renversé dans ses fondements' (ibid. 100).

Two pencil drawings, which if not contemporary with these *Journal* entries can hardly be more than two or three years later, are preserved in the Musée Magnin, Dijon (Inv. no. 253) and the Louvre (RF9218). The former represents Mazeppa being tied to the horse, with the palace as a background; the latter shows the horse swimming across a river with Mazeppa tied on its back. They passed in Delacroix's posthumous sale with a lot (316) of eight sheets of drawings of the subject. From the same lot, Robaut illustrated (R1493) another drawing of Mazeppa being lashed to the horse, without an architectural setting. A signed water-colour of *c.* 1824, which represents Mazeppa at approximately the same moment in the narrative as in this painting, is preserved in the Ateneumin Taidemuseo, Helsinki (repr. Huyghe, pl. 329; Cat. Exh. Edinburgh–London 1964, pl. 38).

¹ According to Robaut. 30 × 40 cm, according to catalogue of sale 6 May 1896.
² Robaut adds in Tracings I: 'qui le tient de son père, lequel a écrit derrière la toile Eugène Lacroix.'

L105 THE YOUNG RAPHAEL MEDITATING IN HIS STUDIO

$17\frac{3}{4} \times 14\frac{3}{16}$ in. (45 × 36 cm), probably with frame¹
Moreau p. 171. R356 (1831. No repr.)
Whereabouts unknown

Provenance: Painted for Count de Mornay, according to Moreau; anon. sale (by Defer), including seven paintings by Delacroix in the Mornay collection, 18 Jan. 1850, lot 121 ('Raphaël', without dimensions or further description), 80 fr.

Exhibition: Salon 1831, no. 515 ('Le jeune Raphaël méditant dans son atelier.').

Literature: Silvestre *Delacroix* (1855), p. 80; Moreau-Nélaton I. 118; Escholier I. 276; *Journal* I. 332 n. 1, III. 372 n. 6; L. Johnson, 'Eugène Delacroix et les Salons. Documents inédits au Louvre', *Revue du Louvre*, 16 (1966), pp. 219, 220.

This small picture passed unnoticed by the critics at the Salon of 1831, for which it was accepted on 17 April (Johnson, 1966). Since Mornay is not listed as the owner in the Salon catalogue, it may be wondered if Moreau was correct in stating that it was painted for him. Never reproduced, it is described by Moreau as showing Raphael seated on a stool, his elbow leaning on a table. It has not come to light since it passed in the sale of 19 January 1850. Delacroix refers to it without comment in a list of pictures that he compiled in the 1840s: '*Le jeune Raphaël* (Mornay).' (*Journal* III. 372—Supp.)

Fig. 26. *Studies of Heads*, Delacroix.

A pencil drawing listed as a preliminary study for this painting passed in the Villot sale of 11 February 1865 for 50 fr., lot 34 (Moreau p. 296; R369). Moreau's and Robaut's descriptions of the lost painting may well have been based not on knowledge of the original canvas, but on the description of the drawing given in the Villot sale catalogue, which is: 'Raphaël jeune dans son atelier. Il est assis sur un escabeau, le coude appuyé sur une table, la tête reposant sur sa main, et dans l'attitude de la méditation.' The two brush and brown wash studies of the head of a clean-shaven young man, evidently Raphael, illustrated here (Fig. 26) are also most probably connected with the lost Salon painting, since

they are on the same sheet (Louvre, RF9640) as a study for a painting shown in the same Salon, the *Indian armed with a Kukri* (J39), and correspond with certain details in the description of the Villot drawing.

> [1] Listed in the Salon register for 1831 (cf. L. Johnson, op. cit. *infra*, p. 220).

Religious Paintings

L106 SKETCH FOR THE VIRGIN OF THE HARVEST

Paper, $12\frac{5}{8} \times ? \ 8\frac{11}{16}$ in. ($32 \times ? \ 22$ cm)

Moreau pp. 219 f. R27 (No repr.)

1819

Whereabouts unknown

Provenance: See under J151.

Exhibitions: None.

Literature: Piron, p. 56; J. Rewald, 'Chocquet and Cézanne', *GBA*, LXXIV (1969), p. 77.

For discussion of this sketch, see J151

L107 CHRIST BEFORE PILATE   Pl. 154

$9\frac{7}{16} \times 14$ in. (24×35.5 cm) Relined[1]

Signed bottom left: *E. Delacroix*

R22 (1819)

1819?

Whereabouts unknown

Provenance: ? Delacroix's posthumous sale, Feb. 1864, part of lot 221 ('Diverses toiles: études, esquisses et ébauches', without dimensions); Alfred Robaut; acquired from him by P. A. Cheramy after 1885 (R Ann).

Exhibition: *EBA*, Paris 1885, no. 181.

Literature: J. Meier-Graefe and E. Klossowski, *La Collection Cheramy . . .* (R. Piper, Munich, 1908), p. 86, no. 140; Huyghe, p. 109.

This picture is known to me only from the small print in Robaut and from the larger drawing with some colour, showing Christ's robe to be red, in Tracings I, reproduced here. Though not listed in Robaut as an entry for the oil sketch competition at the Ecole des Beaux-Arts in 1819, it is so designated in the catalogue of the exhibition *EBA*, Paris 1885, when it still belonged to Robaut. But, as already pointed out in discussing the *Christ brought before Caiaphas* (J150), no biblical subjects were set for the annual sketch competition at the Ecole between 1816 and 1823, and therefore if this was painted for a competition, it could only have

been for one set informally by a professor. Also, it was not customary to sign sketches for competitions at the Ecole.

Robaut does not state where he acquired the work, nor mention a provenance from the posthumous sale, but it may well be identical with a picture listed in Inv. Delacroix under no. 206 as '1 tableau représentant *le Christ devant Ponce Pilate* par Delacroix, 5F.', which is otherwise unaccounted for.

The composition is of a seventeenth-century classical type, as pointed out by Huyghe, and, perhaps more significantly, of a kind used later by Delacroix in a painting of Romantic literary inspiration. The pattern of a figure of authority seated on a tribune in the foreground to one side with the accused held farther back on the other side, a kneeling figure before him, is found in *The Two Foscari*, dated 1855 (Musée Condé, Chantilly) and, with an arrangement still closer to the *Christ before Pilate*, in a preliminary drawing for it of 1847 (Fitzwilliam Museum, Cambridge; repr. Cat. Exh. Edinburgh-London 1964, fig. 82).

> [1] In July 1877, according to R Ann.

L108 TWO ANGELS: STUDY   Pl. 154
FOR THE VIRGIN OF THE
SACRED HEART

$9\frac{1}{2} \times 7\frac{7}{8}$ in. ? (24×20 cm ?)

R37

1821

Whereabouts unknown

Provenance: According to Robaut (addition to R37, p. 479), Delacroix's posthumous sale, Feb. 1864, part of lot 221 ('Diverses toiles: études, esquisses et ébauches', without dimensions); Dr. Verdier, by June 1874 (Robaut Tracings I).

Exhibitions: None.

Literature: See J152 and J153.

This study for the two angels on the right of the *Virgin of the Sacred Heart* (J153) is known only from the engraving in Robaut, reproduced here. Though width exceeds height in the dimensions listed by Robaut and in his engraving, this may not reflect the true proportions of the lost canvas, for he notes on his tracing of it: 'sur une toile en hauteur' (Tracings I).

L109 THE AGONY IN THE GARDEN   Pl. 155
(Sketch for the painting in Saint-Paul-Saint-Louis)
$9\frac{5}{8} \times 12\frac{13}{16}$ in. (24.5 × 32.5 cm)
R Ann 176bis
1824?
Whereabouts unknown
Provenance: M. Bruyas, Lyon, by 1892.
Exhibitions: None.
Literature: None.

This oil sketch is known only from the drawing in Tracings I, reproduced here, and from Robaut's description of it in R Ann, as follows: 'En avril 1892, je vois à Lyon chez M. Dusserre M^d [marchand] de tableaux, qui vient de la restaurer, une esquisse de ce même sujet T $24\frac{1}{2} \times 32\frac{1}{2}$. On remarque comme différences principales avec le grand tableau [the *Agony in the Garden* in Saint-Paul-Saint-Louis]: d'abord moins d'inclinaison à la tête du Christ — ensuite plus de simplicité dans la masse des anges et enfin la figure de gauche, disciple endormi, est tout à la fin dans l'angle inférieur — c.-à-d. beaucoup plus bas que le Christ. Superbe de couleur, appartient à M. Bruyas de Lyon (Rien du Bruyas de Montpellier).' For discussion of the painting to which it relates, see J154.

L110 THE AGONY IN THE GARDEN
$19\frac{11}{16} \times 43\frac{5}{16}$ in. (0.50 × 1.10 m)
Moreau p. 221. R357 (No repr.)
1831
Whereabouts unknown
Provenance: Painted for the singer Adolphe Nourrit in 1831, according to Moreau.
Exhibitions: None.
Literature: None, other than Moreau and Robaut.

Described as a 'Reduction' of the painting in Saint-Paul-Saint-Louis (J154) by Moreau, who also supplied the dimensions, this picture was unknown to Robaut, who merely transcribed the particulars given by Moreau, while expressing doubts about the accuracy of the dimensions. It has never come to light, and it is possible that the picture which belonged to Nourrit should be identified as R183 (J(D)18).

L111 ECCE HOMO, unfinished
$15\frac{3}{4} \times 12\frac{5}{8}$ in. (40 × 32 cm)
R1553 (1830. No repr.)
Whereabouts unknown

Provenance: Delacroix's posthumous sale, Feb. 1864, lot 116 (under 'tableaux inachevés': 'Ecce Homo', 40 × 32 cm), to Lejeune, 100 fr.
Exhibitions: None.
Literature: *Journal* III. 89 n. 1.

This picture was not seen by Robaut, who presumably dated it to 1830 solely because a water-colour of the same subject was exhibited at the Salon of 1831, and it has not come to light since the posthumous sale. As indicated by Joubin, it is probably one of the pictures described by Delacroix in a list drawn up on 1 April 1857 as: '*Christ au roseau, tête* (deux tableaux)' (*Journal* III. 90). But Joubin was evidently wrong in thinking that the second picture was R1554 (J157), since that does not depict a head only and in any case already belonged to Mme Herbelin in 1857, while the list seems to consist exclusively of works still in the artist's possession.

L112 JESUS AND THE PARALYTIC   Pl. 155
$9\frac{7}{16} \times 11$ in. (24 × 28 cm)
R324 (1830)
Whereabouts unknown

Provenance: Victor Chocquet, by Aug. 1877 (Robaut Tracings II), d. 1891; Mme Chocquet, Yvetot, his widow, d. 1899; her sale, 1 July 1899, lot 53, 330 fr.
Exhibitions: None.
Literature: J. Rewald, 'Chocquet and Cézanne', *GBA*, LXXIV (1969), p. 76.

Described in Robaut as a sketch 'd'un ton vineux très doux', this picture has not come to light since the Chocquet sale and is known only from the small print in Robaut and the drawing in Tracings II, reproduced here. It appears to represent the moment when Jesus said: 'Rise, take up thy bed, and walk' (John 5: 8).

L113 INTERIOR OF A CHURCH WITH A RELIGIOUS PRAYING
$13\frac{3}{4} \times 12\frac{5}{8}$ in. (35 × 32 cm)
R1798 (No repr.)
Whereabouts unknown

Provenance: Delacroix's posthumous sale, Feb. 1864, lot 93 ('Intérieur d'église', 35 × 32 cm. Burty Ann ED: 'gris lumineux, religieux en prière'), to Lavorez, 900 fr.
Exhibitions: None.
Literature: None, except Robaut.

This work is included in this volume as its date is unknown and publication of extra details of its appearance from Burty Ann ED may help to identify it if it comes to light.

Still Life, Genre, Interiors without Figures

L114 STILL LIFE WITH FISHES, THRUSHES, ETC.

Dimensions unknown

1825?

Whereabouts unknown

Provenance: In England by 1855.

Exhibitions: None.

Literature: Silvestre *Delacroix* (1855), p. 80.

This picture is not listed by Moreau or Robaut and is known to me only from the description in Silvestre *Delacroix* (1855): 'Nature morte, poissons, grives, etc. (en Angleterre)'; which, being so specific and occurring during the artist's lifetime, seems without doubt to refer to a genuine work that has not come to light. See also J161.

L115 A BLACKSMITH

$12\frac{1}{4} \times 9\frac{1}{2}$ in. (31×24 cm)

R1653 (No repr. 1833)

Whereabouts unknown

Provenance: Delacroix's posthumous sale, Feb. 1864, lot 129 ('Un Forgeron', 31×24 cm), to Piron, 280 fr.

Exhibitions: None.

Literature: Inv. Delacroix, no. 255.

This picture, listed as unfinished in the posthumous sale, may well have been painted earlier than 1833, where Robaut placed it, apparently without having seen it and assuming that it was done in the same year as an aquatint engraving of the same title, which Moreau (pp. 23–4) had dated to 1833. It was noted as being 'très ancien' in Burty Ann ED, and may be related to a copy of Louis Le Nain's *Maréchal dans sa forge* owned, and perhaps painted, by Delacroix (J(L)19).

L116 INTERIOR OF A CHAPEL

16×12 in. (40.6×30.5 cm)

R1799 (No repr.)

Whereabouts unknown

Provenance: Delacroix's posthumous sale, Feb. 1864, lot 94 ('Intérieur de chapelle', 35×26 cm), to Baron Dejean, 1,105 fr.; Diot; he disposed of it to an American dealer in 1880[1]; Dr. Angell, Boston, by 1887; Erwin Davis; his sale, New York 19 March 1889, lot 65 ('Interior of a Church', 12 [w.] × 16 [in.]), $325.

Exhibition: *Bd Italiens*, Paris 1864, no. 165 ('Vue d'une chapelle. Esquisse,' 36×28 cm).

Literature: E. Durand-Gréville, 'La peinture aux Etats-Unis. Les galeries privées', *GBA*, XXXVI (1887), p. 70.

This work is included in this volume as its date is unknown. It was seen by Durand-Gréville in 1887 in the collection of Dr. Angell in Boston.

---

[1] R. Ann: '(février 1888) Mr Diot me dit avoir cédé cette pièce à un M^d d'Amérique, en 1880.'

DOUBTFUL WORKS

Under this heading are listed paintings which give rise to various shades of doubt, ranging from judgement reserved to outright rejection. Within the divisions of subject, which are the same as those used for the accepted and lost works, the pictures in this section are arranged in the following sequence, each letter before a catalogue number denoting the category to which the painting has been assigned.

O = Open.

Judgement reserved, owing to inconclusive evidence.

M = Mutilated.

Damage or overpainting is so extensive as to make it either impossible to judge if the picture was originally from Delacroix's hand or, if it was, pointless to list it among his surviving works, owing to its condition.

D = Doubtful.

Works which in my opinion are not authentic, but where I acknowledge that there could be room for disagreement or that new evidence might lead me to revise my opinion.

R = Rejected.

This category is reserved for paintings which I cannot conceive could in any circumstances be rightly attributed to Delacroix.

Only those works are listed here which seem to risk being accepted as certainly authentic for such reasons as their having been shown in major exhibitions, acquired for public collections, mentioned in significant literature or widely publicized.

Academy Figures, Nudes or Single Reclining Figures

O1 MALE ACADEMY FIGURE: Pl. 156
STANDING, FRONT VIEW

$21\frac{5}{8} \times 11\frac{15}{16}$ in. (55×30.3 cm.[1])* Relined. E.D.
Part of R1470 (1820. No repr.)?
1817/18?
Maurice Perret-Carnot, Neuilly-sur-Seine

Provenance: ? Delacroix's posthumous sale, Feb. 1864, part of lot 200 ('Dix-sept études et académies', without dimensions), to Paul Huet, 55 fr. (Burty Ann ED); by descent (?) to the present owner.

Exhibitions: Bordeaux 1963, no. 2.

Literature: None certain.

It is difficult to accept this weak study as by Delacroix. On the other hand, Paul Huet is recorded as buying an academy study very cheaply at Delacroix's posthumous sale (see J5, n. 1)—a study that is otherwise unaccounted for—and this picture bears the seal of that sale (though it has apparently been transferred on to a new stretcher) and is in the family of Paul Huet's granddaughter. These considerations lead me to reserve judgement and to try rather to think how such a stylistically feeble work might be fitted into Delacroix's authentic *œuvre*. It could, for example, be one of the very first studies in oils that Delacroix painted of a nude: we cannot be sure how inept some of them might have been. In favour of its authenticity, it may also be said that a close

counterpart to the texture, and even the form, of the modelling is to be found in a drawing of an academy figure from *c.* 1818 contained in one of Delacroix's sketch-books in the Louvre (RF9141. fol. 26^r) and reproduced here (Fig. 27).

[1] The original canvas is a fragment unevenly cut along the left edge. It measures, approximately, 50×27 cm (maximum, at top) to 19 cm (minimum, at bottom).

O2 FEMALE ACADEMY FIGURE: Pl. 158
SEATED

$31\frac{7}{8} \times 25\frac{5}{8}$ in. (81×65 cm) Relined
R Ann 83bis (1823. No repr.); Part of R1470? (1820).
1817/20?
Musée du Louvre

Provenance: ? Delacroix's posthumous sale, Feb. 1864, part of lot 200 ('Dix-sept études et académies', without dimensions); bought by F. Vieussa in 1895 for 5 fr. (R Ann and Tracings 1); P. Dubaut, by 1926, to at least 1930 (green wax monogram of his collection on back); Dr. Georges Viau; sale his estate, 11 Dec. 1942, lot 99 (repr.), to the Louvre (RF1942-14), aided by the Société des Amis du Louvre, 1,500,00 fr.

Exhibitions: Paris 1927, no. 267; Louvre 1930, no. 4, repr. *Album*, p. 9; Louvre 1945A, no. 81; Petit Palais, Paris 1946,

The model who posed for this picture was claimed to be Mlle Rose in the catalogue of the Viau sale of 1942, and this identification has since been universally accepted in the Delacroix literature. It was further claimed in the same catalogue, and earlier in the exhibition Louvre 1930, that the painting passed in Delacroix's posthumous sale in 1864, and this provenance has also been accepted without demur. But both claims are open to question. In my view, it is by no means certain that this is the same model who posed for studies which unquestionably represent Rose (see J4); the nose particularly seems quite different. As far as coiffure and features are concerned, she could as well be the model Mlle Victoire, who is represented in the same sketch-book that contains drawings by an unknown artist of Mlle Rose and other Parisian models around 1820 (Fig. 28).

Fig. 27. *Academy Figure*, Delacroix.

no. 153; Orangerie, Paris 1947, no. 65; Venice 1956, no. 1; Louvre 1963, no. 25, repr.; Bordeaux 1964, no. 114, repr.; Munich 1964-5, no. 91, repr.; Kyoto–Tokyo 1969, H-4, repr. in colour; Atelier Delacroix, Paris 1970 (no cat.).

Literature: Escholier I, repr. p. 31; C. Mauclair, 'Delacroix', *L'Art et les Artistes*, XVIII N.S. (1929), repr. p. 166; Cassou 1947, no. 2, repr. of whole and a full page detail head to knees; H. Wellington (ed.), *The Journal of Eugène Delacroix* (Phaidon, London, 1951), p. 483, repr. pl. 1; R. Huyghe, *Dialogue avec le visible* (Flammarion, Paris, 1955), p. 95, repr. fig. 87; G. Bazin, *Trésors de la peinture au Louvre* (Somogy, Paris, n.d. (1957)), p. 258; Sterling–Adhémar, no. 659, pl. 230; Maltese, pp. 23, 144 f., repr. pl. 4; G. Mras, *Eugène Delacroix's Theory of Art* (Princeton University Press, Princeton, 1966), p. 52, repr. fig. 11 (showing condition in 1927); T. Prideaux *et al.*, *The World of Delacroix* (Time Inc., New York, 1966), full page colour repr. p. 30.

Fig. 28. *Mlle Victoire*, anonymous.

As for the provenance, Robaut records in R Ann that the engineer M. F. Vieussa found ('retrouve') this study for 5 fr. in 1895, adding 'Cette étude ne porte pas la marque de la Vente [posthume Delacroix] (Peut être par omission.).' He reproduces it in black chalk heightened with white in Tracings I, and adds 'tiré du N° 200 Vp ED^x [Vente posthume Delacroix]'; as an afterthought, he noted below 'quoiqu'on ne voie pas la *marque* de la V.p.' This picture, then, was bought from an unknown source for the suspiciously low price of 5 fr. some thirty years after Delacroix's posthumous sale, in which Robaut assumed it had passed, though he evidently had some misgivings since he noted twice that it did not bear the stamp of the sale. Most of the academy studies which comprised lot 200 in the posthumous sale are, however, lost and the possibility that this picture was part of the lot cannot be entirely excluded; it is about the same size as the female academy figure now in Mexico, which was knocked down to Thoré from that lot for 420 fr. (J4), and might be a painting, otherwise un-accounted for, which is described under the same lot in Burty Ann ED, as a study of a female nude, 'peinture manière Rubens', and noted as sold to the dealer Cadart for 420 fr.

In approaching the problem of attribution by way of style, one is hampered by the loss of so many early works that might serve as a basis for comparison, academy studies in particular. While not denying the very high quality of this study, I cannot see any true analogy for its style in the more certainly authentic works of Delacroix. Maltese alone has remarked, very aptly, on the Davidian characteristics of the style, noting especially the type of summary brushwork of the background; to which it may be added that the olive tonalities of the setting are also very Davidian. Though Delacroix was not free of debts to David, there seems at least a possibility that this painting is by one of the many highly competent artists who were more closely bound to the Davidian manner than he.

Dates ranging from 1817–24 have been proposed for this picture, c. 1821–2 being the favourite guess. In the opinion of Bazin (1957), 'l'ascendant de Géricault, encore très sensible dans cette toile, nous reporte à la période 1820–1822.' The hair-style of the model is of a type that can be found as late as 1822 in French portrait drawings, but seems more characteristic of a period before 1820.

O3 THREE LIFE STUDIES OF A   Pl. 159
FEMALE NUDE

19⅜ × 23¹³⁄₁₆ in. (49.2 × 60.5 cm)* Relined
R Ann 97bis (1824) and part of R1470 (No repr.)
Claude Aubry, Paris

Provenance: ? Delacroix's posthumous sale, Feb. 1864, part

of lot 200 ('Dix-sept études et académies', without dimen-sions); Maurice Duseigneur (R Ann); M. Vieussa, engineer, by 1893 (R Ann); Duc de Trévise (Aubry); inherited from him by M. de Cossé Brissac (Aubry); with Claude Aubry, 1975.

Exhibitions: None.

Literature: None.

Though Robaut lists this canvas in R Ann as part of lot 200 from Delacroix's posthumous sale, it does not bear the seal of that sale, nor is Maurice Duseigneur, the first owner of the picture listed by Robaut, recorded as a buyer at the sale (for a list of prices and buyers that cannot be attached to known works from lot 200, see J(L)10). I personally find it difficult to reconcile its style with works of indisputable authenticity, but, recognizing the uncertainty surrounding attributions of Delacroix's academy figures and the experi-mental nature of his style at the period of the *Massacres de Scio* (J105), when these studies for captive women would most likely have been painted, would not categorically exclude it in face of Robaut's acceptance.

Robaut Tracings I contains a copy in coloured chalks taken in June 1894, when the canvas belonged to Vieussa. Robaut gives the measurements at the time as 47 × 59.5 cm.

M1 NEGRO ACADEMY FIGURE: Pl. 157
STANDING, BACK VIEW

Paper laid down on canvas: 17⅛ × 12⅝ in. (43.5 × 32 cm)*
Worn E.D.
R15 (1817. No repr.)
c. 1818?
Mme Léonardo Bénatov, Paris

Provenance: Delacroix's posthumous sale, Feb. 1864, part of lot 200 ('Dix-sept études et académies', without dimen-sions), to Léon Belly, painter, 235 fr. (Burty Ann ED and R); his sale, 11 Feb. 1878, lot 210 ('Diable', 43 × 32 cm), to Brame, 200 fr.; Dr. Sabourod; bought from him by M. Léonardo Bénatov *c.* 1936.

Exhibitions: Berne 1963–64, no. 11; Bremen 1964, no. 11.

Literature: None, except Robaut.

It is here assumed that this is the academy study which Belly is known to have bought at the posthumous sale and which in turn passed in his own sale, where it was described as a 'Devil' and listed with dimensions that tally within 0.5 cm. Our picture also seems to correspond with the sup-plementary description of R15 which Robaut includes (p. 479) in his 'Additions et Corrections': 'Le modèle est nu debout, vu de dos, le bras droit reposant sur une fourche.' On the other hand, this is such a mutilated patchwork (e.g. a whole section, which includes the lower part of the legs, appears to have been added by a second hand after the rest of the figure was painted) and the brushwork on the whole so inept, that I find it impossible to attribute it securely to Delacroix in its present state. It may be pointed out, however, that the curved parallel hatchings used to model the back of the thighs find a counterpart in a drawing of a Negro model from behind, which is part of a series of sketches done from the same model *c.* 1818, contained in one of Delacroix's sketch-books in the Louvre (RF9141, fol. 37ʳ. Fig. 29 here).

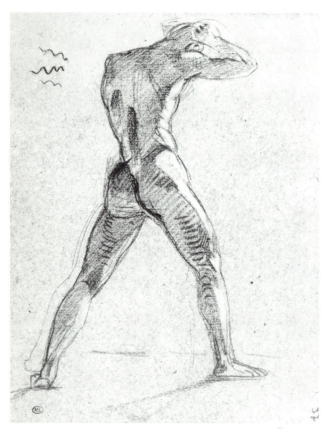

Fig. 29. *Academy Figure*, Delacroix.

M2 MALE ACADEMY FIGURE,   Pl. 160
PROBABLY POLONAIS: SEATED

Original size, as reproduced: $31\frac{7}{8} \times 26$ in. $(81 \times 66$ cm), including replacement of canvas cut from lower right quarter.

Present size of upper half (marked with black lines in reproduction): $17\frac{5}{16} \times 22\frac{1}{16}$ in. $(44 \times 56$ cm) E.D. Present size of lower section unknown.

Part of R1470 (1820. No repr.) ?

Unknown private collection, U.S.A. (torso)
Unknown private collection, Paris (leg)

Provenance: ? Delacroix's posthumous sale, Feb. 1864, part of lot 200 ('Dix-sept études et académies', without dimensions); Georges Clairin, painter; his sale 5 Feb. 1920, lot 220, 400 fr.; anon. sale, Hôtel Drouot, Salle 10 (by Bellier & Cailac), 24 Dec. 1948, lot 105; mixed sale of modern pictures, Versailles (by P. Martin), 2 May 1965 (upper half only), lot 113 (repr. of canvas before cutting), to Galerie Philadelphie, Paris.

The original painting is stated in the catalogue of the 1965 sale at Versailles to have been reduced to its present dimensions 'pour des raisons d'esthétisme'. I have seen neither part and cannot therefore properly judge the authenticity of either the painting or the seal of Delacroix's posthumous sale that is said to be on the stretcher. In addition to being dissected, the picture appears in reproduction to have suffered some repainting, particularly in the part of the leg that has been cut off.

Though it is claimed in the 1948 and 1965 sale catalogues that Clairin acquired this work at Delacroix's posthumous sale and that on the back it bears a statement to that effect signed by Clairin, it may be noted that there appears to be no contemporary record of Clairin's having purchased any lots at that sale or been present (for a list of buyers and prices that cannot be attached to known works in lot 200, see J(L)10. On the other hand, the picture seems to represent the same model as J5, who is thought to be Polonais, and the history claimed for it may well be genuine, Clairin (a friend of Paul Huet's son) having perhaps acquired it at the time of the sale from someone who bid on his behalf or resold it to him immediately.

D1 STUDY OF A MULATRESS   Pl. 162

$22\frac{1}{4} \times 9\frac{7}{8}$ in. $(56.5 \times 25$ cm)* Relined. E.D.
Part of R1470 ? (1820. No repr.)
Fitzwilliam Museum, Cambridge

Provenance: ? Delacroix's posthumous sale, Feb. 1864, part of lot 200 ('Dix-sept études et académies', without dimensions); P. A. Cheramy; his sale, 5 May 1908, lot 189, to Coteau, 240 fr.; Cautin; Georges Renand ?; with Alex Reid & Lefevre, London; bought from them by the Fitzwilliam Museum (PD. 3—1954), with a contribution from the National Art-Collections Fund, 1954.

Exhibitions: Charpentier, Paris 1953, no. 51, repr.; Lefevre, London 1954, no. 6, repr.

Literature: *The Connoisseur*, CXXXIII (1954), repr. p. 260; *Art News*, 53 (1954), repr. p. 47; *Fifty-First Annual Report of the National Art-Collections Fund: 1954* (Hertford House, London, 1955), p. 28; *Fitzwilliam Museum Cambridge Annual Report 1954* (University Press, Cambridge, 1955), pp. 5 f., repr. pl. IV; J. W. Goodison *et al.*, *Fitzwilliam Museum Cambridge. Catalogue of Paintings* (Printed for the Syndics of the Fitzwilliam Museum, Cambridge, 1960), I, pp. 172–4; E. Haverkamp-Begemann *et al.*, *Drawings from the Clark Art Institute, A Catalogue Raisonné of the Robert Sterling Clark Collection . . .*, *Williamstown* (Yale University Press, New Haven and London, 1964), I, p. 90; Huyghe, p. 521 n. 17; L. Johnson, in Cat. Exh. Edinburgh–London 1964, mentioned under no. 9.

Though this picture was exhibited in Paris as by Delacroix in 1953, with two more paintings falsely attributed to him (J(R)1 and J(R)38), and was bought as genuine by the Fitzwilliam Museum in the following year, the attribution appears to have been tacitly doubted at least as early as 1908, since it was not included in the catalogue of the Cheramy collection published by Meier-Graefe and Klossowski in that year. After 1954, Huyghe suggested that it was by Delacroix's friend, the dilettante painter Jules-Robert Auguste (see J. W. Goodison *et al.*, 1960, pp. 173, 174 n. 8; Huyghe). While this alternative attribution failed to convince, there was no longer confidence in the ascription to Delacroix, and the painting was listed merely as 'French School, *c.* 1820–25' in the Fitzwilliam Museum's Catalogue of Paintings (1960). I suggested in the catalogue of the exhibition Edinburgh–London 1964 that it be ascribed to Decamps, on the grounds of its stylistic affinities with two paintings of Indians (J23 and J25) which I then thought to be by Decamps. I have revised not only my opinion of the paintings of Indians, on the strength of new evidence (see J23), but also my belief that they are necessarily by the same hand as this study, which is of such crudity in, for example, the hands and head-dress, that I cannot believe it to be by Delacroix. For several reasons, however, I classify it as a doubtful picture rather than rejecting it outright: (1) our knowledge of Delacroix's academy figures is far from complete, and it is therefore necessary to be cautious in excluding works which may be very early and whose defects could be due to inexperience; (2) the presence of the seal of Delacroix's posthumous sale on the stretcher of this study suggests that it was part of lot 200 in the sale, in which case it would in its original state most probably, though not certainly, have been by Delacroix (for a list of buyers and prices that cannot be attached to known works in lot 200, see J(L)10); (3) the picture is in poor condition, with a considerable amount of over-painting, which accounts for some of the crudities—but not all in my opinion.

A similar full-length nude study in pen and brown ink (16.9 × 10.6 cm), which appears to represent the same model, is preserved in the Clark Art Institute, Williamstown, Mass. It also bears the monogram of Delacroix's posthumous sale, and passed more recently in the Degas sale

in 1918, but its authenticity does not seem to me beyond question either (repr. in facsimile in E. Haverkamp-Begemann *et al.*, op. cit., II, pl. 21).

R1 MALE ACADEMY FIGURE: Pl. 160
STANDING, FRONT VIEW, HANDS BEHIND BACK

$31\frac{7}{8} \times 25\frac{5}{8}$ in. (81 × 65 cm)
Whereabouts unknown

Provenance: Pierre Dubaut.[1]

Exhibitions: Atelier Delacroix, Paris 1946 A & B, no. 49; id., Paris 1952, Supp. no. 85; Charpentier, Paris 1953, no. 50; Bordeaux 1963, no. 3.

Literature: None.

[1] An earlier provenance from the Rouart collection is claimed in the Cat. Exh. Bordeaux 1963, where the picture is also said to have been shown under no. 37 in the Exh. Atelier Delacroix, Paris 1945. No. 37 was in fact the male academy figure J5, which was lent by M. Perret-Carnot. No. 38, a lithograph, was however lent by Louis Rouart, whose name is listed directly beneath the entry for the preceding number. This double misinterpretation of the Atelier Delacroix catalogue appears to be the only basis for the provenance given at Bordeaux.

R2 STUDY OF A WOMAN IN BED   Pl. 161

Oil on paper laid down on canvas, $10\frac{3}{4} \times 13\frac{3}{4}$ in.
   (27.3 × 35 cm)
R55 (1822)?
Artemis Fine Arts U.S., New York

Provenance: (If R55: Pierret (Robaut Tracings 1); anon. sale (by Pillet & Féral), Hôtel Drouot 24 May 1879, part of lot 56,[1] to Alfred Robaut, 10 fr. (R Ann); he sold it immediately to Léon Charly, 25 fr. (R Ann)); Mrs. Greely S. Curtis, Boston (label on back); with Sotheby's Jan. 1965; with Artemis Fine Arts.

Exhibitions: None.

Literature: None, except Robaut.

This study corresponds to Robaut's illustration of R55, but cannot be authentic. Therefore either it is R55 and Robaut wrongly attributed it to Delacroix, or it is a copy of a lost original—possibly a forgery based on Robaut's illustration. If it is in fact R55, the provenance from Pierret suggests that it might be by Pierret himself, an amateur painter. Robaut describes R55 as an 'esquisse' (R Ann) on canvas, 25 × 33 cm, and identifies the model as Lisette. This identification is based solely on the implausible assumption that she is a peasant by the name of Lisette whom Delacroix admired during a visit to his brother in the country and mentioned at the time in a letter to Pierret dated 18 August 1822—without however saying that he painted her (*Correspondance* I. 144;

Burty ed. 1878, p. 66; 1880, I. 89). Robaut's date of 1822 for the study is also evidently based on the date of the letter.

If there was indeed an autograph version of which our study is a reflection, it could have been the early picture referred to by Delacroix in 1850 as 'une étude couchée d'après *Caroline*'. (*Journal* I. 383.) But see also J6 and J(O)8.

¹ It is stated in the sale catalogue: 'Sous ce numéro qui sera divisé, seront vendus environ 37 tableaux ou aquarelles, par Delacroix, Dejobert et autres.'

[1] It is stated in the sale catalogue: 'Sous ce numéro qui sera divisé, seront vendus environ 37 tableaux ou aquarelles, par Delacroix, Dejobert et autres.'

R3 NUDE WOMAN RECLINING ON A DIVAN Pl. 161

$8\frac{11}{16} \times 11\frac{1}{4}$ in. (22 × 28.5 cm)
Whereabouts unknown

Provenance: Georges Aubry, by 1926; anon. sale, 23 Nov. 1938, lot 58 ('Odalisque', as attributed to Delacroix), 5,800 fr.

Exhibitions: Paris 1927, no. 263; Louvre 1930, no. 43.

Literature: Escholier I, repr. in colour opp. p. 220.

Copies after the Masters

Doubtful and rejected copies are included in this volume unless there is evidence that Delacroix
did an authentic version after 1831.

D2 COPY, after VERONESE, detail from THE MARRIAGE AT CANA Pl. 163
(Louvre, RF1192)

$25\frac{1}{2} \times 32\frac{1}{8}$ in. (64.8 × 81.6 cm)
Whereabouts unknown

Provenance: Presumably the painting described in Goupil's books as 'Etude d'après Véronèse', which the firm bought from a M. Vaïsse of Marseille [presumably Edouard, a stockbroker] in May 1873, and sold to Haseltine of Philadelphia on 4 August 1881 (Arch Goupil/Boussod, vol. 6, p. 202; vol. 11, p. 1); John G. Johnson, Philadelphia; he gave it to the Wilstach Collection, Philadelphia Museum of Art, 1912; sold at public auction by Samuel T. Freeman & Co., Philadelphia, 30 October 1954, lot 218 (repr.) as R 1931, to Herman V. Baker of Philadelphia.

Exhibitions: None.

Literature: E. Durand-Gréville, 'La peinture aux Etats-Unis. Les galeries privées', *GBA*, XXXVI (1887), p. 71; *Catalogue of the W. P. Wilstach Collection, Memorial Hall* (The Commissioners of Fairmount Park, Philadelphia, 1922), no. 91.

This copy, representing the heads of the bride and groom, on the extreme left of the Veronese, and four heads in their vicinity, does not appear from photographs to be stylistically compatible with the one known copy in oils by Delacroix from the *Marriage at Cana* (J14); nor has its provenance from Delacroix's atelier been established beyond reasonable doubt.

D3 ANGEL, after RUBENS, detail from THE VIRGIN WITH ANGELS Pl. 165
(Louvre, RF2078)

Oils on paper, $9\frac{7}{16} \times 7\frac{1}{2}$ in. (23.9 × 19 cm)*
Musée du Louvre (Cabinet des Dessins)

Provenance: Etienne Moreau-Nélaton; his gift to the Louvre (RF 10173), 1927.

Exhibition: Louvre 1930, no. 227A.

Literature: P. Fierens, 'Eugène Delacroix, admirateur et copiste de Rubens', *Pictura*, II (1946), p. 5; Escholier 1963, repr. in colour p. 115; B. White, 'Delacroix's Painted Copies after Rubens', *AB*, XLIX (1967), pp. 37, 47, fig. 26.

It is not known where Moreau-Nélaton acquired this copy of the angel directly beneath the Virgin in Rubens's painting, and there is no indication in the form of a stamp that it passed in Delacroix's posthumous sale in 1864, nor can it be positively identified with any lot described in the catalogue of that sale. I find it impossible to attribute it firmly to Delacroix on stylistic grounds alone and, though it could conceivably be an early study from his hand, it must in the absence of more definite information about its history be considered a doubtful attribution.

D4 THE ENTOMBMENT, after RUBENS (Church of Saint-Géry, Cambrai) Pl. 164

28 × 21 in. (71.1 × 53.3 cm) E.D.
R1946 (No repr.)
Joslyn Art Museum, Omaha, Nebraska

Provenance: Delacroix's posthumous sale, Feb. 1864, lot 166 ('Le Christ mis au tombeau [d'après Rubens]', 71 × 52 cm), to M. Lecoq, 630 fr.; Marcel Bernheim, by 1927; Dr. H. Graber, Zurich, by 1939; with Knoedler & Co., New York; purchased from them by Joslyn Art Museum, 1958.

Exhibitions: Zurich 1939, no. 377; Providence 1975, no. 83, repr.

Literature: Silvestre *Delacroix* (1855), p. 83; Escholier II, repr. p. 277; B. White, 'Delacroix's Painted Copies after Rubens', *AB*, XLIX (1967), pp. 38, 41, 47, repr. fig. 31.

This copy, which I have never seen, appears to be the picture which passed under Delacroix's name as lot 166 in his posthumous sale, but it does not seem from reproductions to be an autograph work. It is possibly a study from the latter half of the 1820s by Delacroix's friend Hippolyte Poterlet, with whose copy after Rubens's *Last Communion of St. Francis* at Antwerp (Collection Perret-Carnot, Paris) it shares some characteristics of handling. Delacroix is known to have possessed a fairly large quantity of oil sketches by Poterlet, including most probably the copy just mentioned, and though the provisions of his will were that 'toutes les esquisses de Poterlet' be shared by four of his artist friends, one or more of these sketches might easily have been mistaken for his own work by his executors and innocently included in the posthumous sale under his name. (On the bequest of the Poterlet sketches, see Delacroix's will, in *Correspondance* (Burty 1878), p. viii; and R. P. Huet, *Paul Huet* (H. Laurens, Paris, 1911), p. 362.)

The model of this copy was identified in the catalogue of the exhibition Zurich 1939 as the oil sketch of the subject in the Alte Pinakothek, Munich, but Barbara White (1967) showed that the true model was the altarpiece at Cambrai for which the Munich picture was a preliminary sketch.

D5 SUSANNA AND THE ELDERS,   Pl. 165
after RUBENS
$10\frac{5}{8} \times 13\frac{3}{4}$ in. (27 × 35 cm)
R737 (1841)
Museum of Fine Arts, Lille

Provenance: Constant Dutilleux; his posthumous sale, 26 March 1874, lot 9 (repr.), to Michel Cerf, 400 fr.; M. Binart; bought by the City of Lille, 1878.

Exhibitions: Louvre 1963, no. 312, *M* no. 309, repr.; Kyoto-Tokyo 1969, H-17, repr.

Literature: A. Herlin, *Supplément au catalogue [des tableaux, bas-reliefs et statues exposés dans les galeries du Musée des tableaux de la ville de Lille*, 5th ed. 1875] *de M. Ed. Reynart, Juin 1881* (Impr. Lefebvre-Ducrocq, Lille, 1881), p. 263, no. 784; *Catalogue des tableaux du Musée de Lille précédé d'une notice historique par Jules Lenglart* (Impr. Lefebvre-Ducrocq, Lille, 1893) p. 83, no. 234; B. White, 'Delacroix's Painted Copies after Rubens', *AB*, XLIX (1967), pp. 37, 39, 46, repr. fig. 29.

Print: Lithograph by Alfred Robaut, 8.5 × 11.3 cm, repr. in catalogue of Dutilleux sale, 1874.

This is one of several pictures in the Dutilleux sale of 1874 that are claimed in the catalogue to have come into Dutilleux's possession directly from Delacroix's easel, and not all of which are of certain authenticity (see e.g. J(R)35). The same source describes it as a 'souvenir d'une des plus belles œuvres de Rubens, exécuté de mémoire par

Delacroix au retour d'un voyage qu'il fit en Belgique vers 1850.' It does not, however, seem possible that Delacroix could have painted it from memory of a work by Rubens that he had seen in Belgium, for the composition, which was apparently never executed as a painting by Rubens, is known only from an engraving by Christopher Jegher which was based on a drawing by Rubens. Though presumably based on the Jegher print, as suggested by Robaut, the composition is reversed in this copy (juxtaposed reproductions are in B. White, op. cit., figs. 29 and 30). Robaut, while repeating his view expressed in the catalogue of the Dutilleux sale that the copy was done after seeing an original model in Belgium, dates it to 1841 in his *catalogue raisonné*, that is to say, after Delacroix's first journey to Belgium in 1839 instead of his second in 1850. The catalogues of the Museum of Lille follow the later date.

The timid brushwork and unsure definition of form make it unlikely, in my opinion, that it is by Delacroix at all.

R4 THE MYSTIC MARRIAGE OF ST. CATHERINE, after CORREGGIO (Louvre, RF1117)
$10\frac{13}{16} \times 11\frac{1}{4}$ in. (27.5 × 28.5 cm)*
Musée des Beaux-Arts, Lyon

Provenance: Léon Riesener; his sale, 10 Apr. 1879, lot 225 (as 'Sainte famille (d'après Corrège)', 27 × 28 cm), 350 fr.; P. A. Cheramy, by 1907; his sale, 5 May 1908, lot 186, to Musée des Beaux-Arts, Lyon (B-827).

Exhibition: Bordeaux, 1963, no. 6.

Literature: L. Rouart, 'La Collection de M. Cheramy', *Les Arts*, no. 64 (Apr. 1907), p. 24; P. Dissard, *Le Musée de Lyon. Les Peintures* (Laurens, Paris, 1912), p. 19; H. Focillon, *La peinture au XIXᵉ siècle* (Laurens, Paris, 1927), p. 175; C. Mauclair, *Le Palais Saint-Pierre* (Paris, n.d. [1929], Coll. 'Les Musées d'Europe'), p. 70; M. Vincent, *Catalogue du Musée de Lyon*, VII, *La Peinture des XIXᵉ et XXᵉ Siècles* (IAC Les Editions de Lyon, Lyon, 1956), pp. 53 f., repr. pl. xv, fig. 3; K. E. Maison, *Themes and Variations* (Thames and Hudson, London, 1960. German ed., *Bild und Abbild*, published Munich and Zurich, 1960), fig. 157.

Though this copy was included in Riesener's posthumous sale as a Delacroix, the attribution is unconvincing and the picture may be by Riesener himself, whose work was much influenced by Correggio.

R5 SIX STUDIES OF HEADS   Pl. 163
(said to be after VERONESE)
13 × $16\frac{1}{8}$ in. (33 × 41 cm) E.D. (false ?)
Léonardo Bénatov, Paris

Provenance: Unknown.

Exhibitions: ?Atelier Delacroix, Paris 1963, *h.c.*; Bremen 1964, no. 23.

Literature: None.

In spite of the red wax monogram 'E.D.' on the stretcher and the designation of the subject as 'The Concert (Studies of Heads), after Veronese' in the Bremen exhibition, these crude studies appear to have no connection with either Delacroix or Veronese.

R6 ADORATION OF THE MAGI, after RUBENS

$25\frac{3}{8} \times 21\frac{1}{16}$ in. (64.5 × 53.5 cm)* Relined
Kunstmuseum, St. Gallen, Switzerland

Provenance: Vautier (?), 1926; Dr. Carl Werner, Lugano-Castagnola, by 1963; bought by the Kunstmuseum, St. Gallen, 1974.

Exhibitions: Berne 1963–64, no. 25; Bremen 1964, no. 21, repr.

Literature: B. White, 'Delacroix's Painted Copies after Rubens', *AB*, XLIX (1967), pp. 37, 38, 39, 46, repr. fig. 7.

The identification of this copy with lot 164 in Delacroix's posthumous sale (see J(L)24), proposed in the Berne and Bremen exhibition catalogues and by B. White, is in my opinion unacceptable: this painting bears neither the seal of the posthumous sale nor the stylistic attributes of a genuine Delacroix. It appears to have been done from Jean Witdoeck's engraving in reverse (repr. B. White, fig. 8) of the altar-piece by Rubens commissioned for the Convent Church of the White Sisters of Louvain, later in the collection of the Dukes of Westminster (1805–1959), and now in the Chapel of King's College, Cambridge.

R7 ADORATION OF THE MAGI, after RUBENS (Musée des Beaux-Arts, Lyon)

$6\frac{7}{8} \times 10\frac{1}{4}$ in. (17.5 × 26 cm)
Musée des Beaux-Arts, Lyon

This very inferior study, which belonged to Paul Jamot when it was shown in the Delacroix exhibition Louvre 1930, no. 228, is no longer attributed to Delacroix. Archives photographiques negative BAP 11889.

R8 APOTHEOSIS OF THE DUKE OF BUCKINGHAM, after RUBENS (National Gallery, London)

$25\frac{1}{4} \times 25\frac{1}{4}$ in. (64.2 × 64.2 cm)
Diameter of circular painted subject: $24\frac{1}{2}$ in. (62.2 cm)
Akron Art Institute, Ohio*

Provenance: With French & Co., New York; purchased from them by the Akron Art Institute, 1957.

Exhibition: Providence 1975, no. 81, repr.

Literature: *Burl Mag*, XCVIII, no. 642 (Sept. 1956), repr. p. vii (advertisement); B. White, 'Delacroix's Painted Copies after Rubens', *AB*, XLIX (1967), pp. 37, 38, 39, 43, 49, repr. fig. 6; G. Martin, *National Gallery Catalogues. The Flemish School* (London, 1970), p. 150 n. 41, 152.

Though this copy is known to me in reproduction only, I can neither see nor find any justification for attributing it to Delacroix. The original oil sketch by Rubens was not in the collection of David Wilkie in 1825, where Barbara White supposed that Delacroix might have seen it during his English journey, and its exact location in England at the time is unknown (see G. Martin, p. 152 and n. 45).

R9 ASSUMPTION OF THE VIRGIN, after RUBENS (Royal Museum of Fine Arts, Brussels)

Dimensions unknown
Whereabouts unknown

Provenance: Redon.

Exhibition: Paris 1926, no. 41.

Literature: B. White, 'Delacroix's Painted Copies after Rubens', *AB*, XLIX (1967), pp. 38, 43, 44, 47, repr. fig. 16.

Archives photographiques negative BAP 5394.

R10 BOAR HUNT, after RUBENS   Pl. 168

Oils on paper laid on canvas
$21\frac{5}{16} \times 28\frac{1}{8}$ in. (54.2 × 71.5 cm)
Signed with false monogram *ED* bottom left
Neue Pinakothek, Munich

Provenance: Bessonneau, Angers;[1] with Paul Cassirer, Berlin; purchased by the Neue Pinakothek (Inv. no. 8717), 1913.

Exhibitions: Winterthur 1947, no. 126; Hanover 1949, no. 2, repr.; Orangerie, Paris 1951, no. 29 (as *attributed* to Delacroix); Munich 1964–5, no. 95, repr.

Literature: J. Meier-Graefe, *Eugène Delacroix, Beiträge zu einer Analyse* (R. Piper, Munich, n.d. [1913]), p. 53 n. 1; J. Meier-Graefe 1922, p. 34 n. 1; *Katalog der Neuen Pinakothek zu München* (Munich, 1922), p. 14; H. Tietze, 'Les Peintres français du XIXe siècle dans les musées allemands', *GBA*, XVII (1928), p. 109; K. Martin, *Die Tschudi-Spende* (Munich, 1962), p. 32; *Französische Meister des 19. Jahrhunderts. Kunst des 20. Jahrhunderts. Ausgestellte Werke I. Neue Pinakothek und Staatsgalerie München* (Hirmer, Munich, 1966), pp. 31 f., repr. fig. 1; B. White, 'Delacroix's Painted Copies after Rubens', *AB*, XLIX (1967), p. 50, repr. fig. 28.

The original Rubens of this subject has been in the Dresden Gallery since 1749, but a number of early copies or studio versions exist, and it has been suggested in the 1966 Neue Pinakothek Catalogue that, during his visit to the Netherlands in 1839, Delacroix could have seen one of these which was in Royal collections in Brussels and The Hague between 1825 and 1850. That version is now in the Glasgow Art Gallery and Museum (their Catalogue, *Dutch and Flemish, Netherlandish and German Paintings* (Glasgow, 1961), I, p. 120, no. 715; II, repr. p. 23).

On stylistic grounds, I find it impossible to accept this copy as by Delacroix. The uncertainty of its early provenance and the false monogram reinforce this opinion.

---

[1] 'Bessaneau, Angers', according to the Neue Pinakothek Catalogue, 1966, but this is evidently a misspelling of the well-known Angevin collector's name. It has not been possible to confirm this provenance, which was apparently supplied by a dealer (letter to the author from the Direktion der Bayerischen Staatsgemäldesammlungen, 16 December 1969); the misspelling does not inspire confidence that it was not based on hearsay.

R11 'CHRIST À LA PAILLE', triptych after RUBENS (Royal Museum of Fine Arts, Antwerp)

Wood panels. Centre (*Christ at the Tomb*), $10\frac{5}{8} \times 7\frac{1}{4}$ in. (27 × 18.5 cm); wings (*St. John the Evangelist, Virgin and Child*), each $10\frac{5}{8} \times 3\frac{3}{8}$ in. (27 × 8.5 cm)
Whereabouts unknown

Provenance: Most probably Victor Mottez, by 1863; Georges Aubry; his sale, 11 March 1933, lot 74.

Exhibitions: *Virgin and Child* panel, ? Basle 1937, no. 17; ? Zurich 1939, no. 379.

Literature: Most probably Inv. Delacroix no. 276; B. White, 'Delacroix's Painted Copies after Rubens', *AB*, XLIX (1967), pp. 38, 39, 43, 44, 47, repr. fig. 18.

This copy passed as a Delacroix in the Aubry sale of 1933 and does not appear to have been doubted since, though the attribution to Delacroix appears from reproductions to be highly dubious on stylistic grounds. In view of its triptych form and wooden support, it seems most probable that this is the painting described under no. 276 in Inv. Delacroix as '1 panneau triptyque d'après Rubens par M. Mottez (il est reconnu que ce tableau appartient à M. Mottez et avait été déposé chez Delacroix).' Victor Mottez (1809-97) was a pupil of Ingres's.

A copy of the wing representing the Virgin and Child was lent as a Delacroix from a private collection in Zurich to the exhibitions Basle 1937 and Zurich 1939, but dimensions, support and provenance were listed in neither of the catalogues and I am unable to determine whether it was one of the panels from the Aubry sale.

R12 CHRIST ON THE CROSS, after RUBENS (*Le Coup de Lance*, Royal Museum of Fine Arts, Antwerp)

$19\frac{1}{4} \times 14\frac{1}{2}$ in. (49 × 37 cm)
Whereabouts unknown

Provenance (according to B. White, op. cit. *infra*): M. Heuscher, Wuppertal; his sale, 30 Jan. 1963, lot 82.

Exhibitions: None.

Literature: B. White, 'Delacroix's Painted Copies after Rubens', *AB*, XLIX (1967), pp. 38, 43, 44, 46, repr. fig. 17.

Though this copy is unknown to me except from photographs, I can see no justification either in its history or in its appearance in reproduction for attributing it to Delacroix.

R13 EDUCATION OF THE VIRGIN, after RUBENS (Royal Museum of Fine Arts, Antwerp)

$18\frac{1}{4} \times 15\frac{1}{16}$ in. (46.3 × 38.3 cm)*
Mme Robert Siohan, Paris

Provenance: Said to have been given by Delacroix to Ary Scheffer (in Cat. Exh. Atelier Delacroix, Paris 1932); Mme Noémi Renan, by 1932; by descent to the present owner, who also inherited the former studio of Ary and Henry Scheffer.

Exhibition: Atelier Delacroix, Paris 1932, no. 42.

Literature: K. E. Maison, *Themes and Variations* (Thames and Hudson, London, 1960), p. 119, fig. 152; B. White, 'Delacroix's Painted Copies after Rubens', *AB*, XLIX (1967), pp. 38, 43, 46, repr. fig. 9.

This copy is perhaps by Delacroix's friend Alexandre Colin (1798-1875), since the name 'Mr Colin' is written in ink on two labels on the back—one on the stretcher, the other on the frame. The attribution to Delacroix himself is unconvincing.

R14 A TOURNEY, after RUBENS (Louvre, RF2116)

Pl. 168

$15 \times 21\frac{5}{8}$ in. (38 × 55 cm)
Whereabouts unknown

Provenance: ? Sale P. A. Cheramy, 5 May 1908, lot 184 ('*Le Tournoi*, d'après Rubens. Copie', 41 × 55 cm), to Javal, 900 fr.; with Geneviève Aymonier, Paris, *c.* 1965-7; sold at public auction by Rheims, Paris 16 Feb. 1967.

Exhibitions: None.

Literature: None.

R15 THE VIRGIN WITH ANGELS, after RUBENS (Louvre, RF2078)

$45\frac{11}{16} \times 35\frac{1}{4}$ in. (1.16 × 0.895 m)
St. James Episcopal Church, Del Rio, Texas

Provenance: Private collection, Charleroi, Belgium, by 1946; then (according to B. White, op. cit. *infra*), Rev. Dr. John Torok; with Spencer A. Samuels, New York; Mrs. Sarah C. Blaffer; her gift to present Owner.

Exhibitions: None.

Literature: P. Fierens, 'Eugène Delacroix, admirateur et copiste de Rubens', *Pictura*, II (1946), pp. 5 f., full-page repr. p. 8, detail p. 9; B. White, 'Delacroix's Painted Copies after Rubens', *AB*, XLIX (1967), pp. 37, 47, repr. fig. 25.

As Fierens, who published this copy in 1946, states (op. cit.): 'Aucun signe extérieur n'autorise peut-être à l'attribuer à Delacroix.' Neither do there appear to be any stylistic grounds for supporting this author's intuition that it is by Delacroix.

R16 LANDING OF MARIA   Pl. 166
DE' MEDICI AT MARSEILLE, after RUBENS (Louvre, RF 2090)

$15\frac{3}{4} \times 12\frac{13}{16}$ in. (40×32.5 cm)*
R260 (1828. No repr.)
Madame Gans, Paris

Provenance: Delacroix's posthumous sale ?, Feb. 1864, lot 171 (as 'L'Embarquement de Marie de Médicis [d'après Rubens]. Musée du Louvre', 40×32 cm), to Arosa (Burty Ann ED, where described as a 'pochade', and Moreau-Nélaton annotated copy of Delacroix sale catalogue, 1864, *BN Estampes*), 105 fr.; his sale, 25 Feb. 1878, lot 44 (as 'L'Embarquement de Marie de Médicis'), to Barbedienne, 310 fr.; purchased by J. Dieterle, dealer, May 1957 (Dieterle R); with Alfred Daber; present owner, by 1966.

Exhibitions: None.

Literature: Album of photolithographs of pictures in the Arosa collection (privately printed by 1878, never distributed commercially. Annotated copy in *Bib AA*, bound together with Arosa sale catalogue), repr. no. 20; *Journal* I. 294 n. 1; B. White, 'Delacroix's Painted Copies after Rubens', *AB*, XLIX (1967), pp. 37, 44, 48 (confused with J(R)17); J. Thuillier and J. Foucart, *Le Storie di Maria de'Medici di Rubens al Lussemburgo* (Rizzoli, Milan, 1967; ed. in French, Paris 1969), p. 77.

This canvas, which has not been relined but could have been placed on a new stretcher since 1864, does not bear the wax seal of Delacroix's posthumous sale. Comparison with the reproduction in the album of the Arosa collection leaves no doubt, however, that it is the picture of this subject which passed in the Arosa sale in 1878, and that picture was, according to Robaut, in the posthumous sale of 1864. The dimensions, too, correspond almost exactly with those of lot 171 in the posthumous sale, as do the (erroneous) titles given in the catalogues of both sales. Thus it seems likely that this copy was the one catalogued as a Delacroix under lot 171 in the posthumous sale. Nevertheless, though a lively sketch and richly coloured, it does not appear to be from Delacroix's hand. In contrast with the copy of the single *Nereid* (J16), the foreshortening of the head of the same

figure here is misunderstood, as is the anatomy of the triton on the extreme left, to mention only two infelicities. It may well be that this study is, as noted in the *Bib AA* copy of the Arosa sale catalogue (probably at the time of the sale), 'de Poterlet ou de quelqu'un des amis de jeunesse de Delacroix'. As evidence of Delacroix's superior understanding of the Rubens, there is not only his copy of the *Nereid* but his pencil drawing with colour notes taken from the same area of the original as the study under discussion (Louvre, A.D. 5. Best repr., nearly full-size, in T. Prideaux *et al.*, *The World of Delacroix* (Time Inc., New York, 1966), p. 46. Also repr. in Escholier I, p. 63).

R17 LANDING OF MARIA DE'   Pl. 166
MEDICI AT MARSEILLE, after RUBENS (Louvre, RF2090)

$15\frac{3}{8} \times 12\frac{1}{4}$ in. (39×31 cm)
Private collection, Paris

Provenance: Granoff Gallery, Paris, 1948; bought from them by Claude Bréart de Boisanger, Dec. 1948 (Dieterle R); with J. P. Durand-Matthiesen, Geneva, 1967.

Exhibitions: Bordeaux 1963, no. 45; Atelier Delacroix, Paris 1973 (no cat.)

Literature: B. White, 'Delacroix's Painted Copies after Rubens', *AB*, XLIX (1967), p. 48 (confused with J(R)16; M. Sérullaz, 'A propos de l'Exposition Delacroix et la peinture libérée' *Revue du Louvre*, XXIII, no. 6 (Nov.-Dec. 1973), p. 365 and n., repr. fig. 3.

This is definitely not the copy of this subject which passed in the Arosa sale in 1878 (see J(R)16), as claimed in the catalogue of the exhibition Bordeaux 1963, followed by B. White and M. Sérullaz, and there is thus no reason to agree with these sources that it also passed in Delacroix's posthumous sale, particularly since it does not bear the wax monogram of that sale and is unlikely to have been mistaken for a Delacroix by the organizers of the sale.

R18 THE ARRIVAL OF MARIA DE'
MEDICI AT LYON, after RUBENS (Louvre, RF2091)

Wood panel, $7\frac{11}{16} \times 6\frac{1}{8}$ in. (19.5×15.5 cm)
Private collection, Switzerland

Provenance: Vicomte de Gaillard, Paris; with Claude Aubry, Paris, by 1963; with J. P. Durand-Matthiesen, Geneva; private collection, Switzerland, by 1967.

Exhibition: Bordeaux 1963, no. 59.

Literature: Repr. in *Burl Mag*, CV, no. 720 (March 1963), p. lx (advertisement); B. White, 'Delacroix's Painted Copies after Rubens', *AB*, XLIX (1967), p. 48, no. 20; J. Thuillier and J. Foucart, *Le Storie di Maria de' Medici di Rubens al Lussemburgo* (Rizzoli, Milan, 1967; ed. in French, Paris 1969), p. 78.

Another version of the same subject, measuring 66 × 50 cm, with an unknown earlier and subsequent history passed in an anonymous sale, Paris, 5 March 1895, lot 5,600 fr.

R19 BIRTH OF THE DAUPHIN, after RUBENS (Louvre, RF2092)

Cardboard, $18\frac{1}{8} \times 13$ in. (46 × 33 cm)
Prince Paul of Yugoslavia, Paris

Provenance: Unknown.

Exhibition: Bordeaux 1963, no. 61.

Literature: B. Brown, 'Delacroix's Painted Copies after Rubens', *AB*, XLIX (1967), p. 48; J. Thuillier and J. Foucart, *Le Storie di Maria de' Medici di Rubens al Lussemburgo* (Rizzoli, Milan, 1967; ed. in French, Paris 1969), p. 80.

Though claimed in the catalogue of the exhibition Bordeaux 1963 to be part of Robaut 1949–54 ('Fragments de copies d'après Rubens'), this sketch does not bear the seal of Delacroix's posthumous sale, whereas all the copies listed by Robaut under those numbers passed in that sale. Nor does the quality of this copy justify the supposition that it could have passed in the sale without being stamped, or had the seal destroyed since 1864.

R20 MARIA DE' MEDICI ON HORSEBACK, after RUBENS, detail from THE TRIUMPH OF JÜLICH (Louvre, RF2097)

$13 \times 9\frac{1}{2}$ in. (33 × 24.2 cm)*
Private collection, U.S.A.

Provenance: Rudolf Beckers Gallery, Düsseldorf, by 1965; Synco Industries, New York, by 1970.

Exhibitions: None.

Literature: *Apollo*, LXXXI, no. 39 (May 1965), repr. p. cxii (advertisement); B. White, 'Delacroix's Painted Copies after Rubens', *AB*, XLIX (1967), pp. 37, 49, repr. fig. 24.

Another copy of this detail was sold as a Delacroix, for 380 fr., in the Ary Scheffer sale of 15 March 1859, in the catalogue of which it is described as 'Marie de Médicis à cheval', canvas 45 × 37 cm (lot 14); but in a review of the sale published during Delacroix's lifetime, Charles Blanc pointed out that it was in fact a copy by Géricault, who had given it to Delacroix, who in turn lent it to Scheffer and later allowed him to keep it (*GBA*, II (1859), p. 47). Lorenz Eitner has asked ('Géricault at Winterthur', *Burl Mag*, XCVI (1954), p. 257) whether that copy might not be a picture in Switzerland that is attributed to Géricault; it is reproduced

in colour in *Sammlung Hans E. Bühler: Géricault . . .*, with Foreword by P. Dubaut (Verlag Buchdruckerei, Winterthur, 1956), no. 10.

R21 THE FULL RECONCILIATION Pl. 167 OF MARIA DE' MEDICI AND HER SON, after RUBENS (Louvre, RF2104)

$24\frac{3}{8} \times 20\frac{1}{16}$ in. (61.8 × 51 cm)* Relined
Dubious *E.D.* on new stretcher.
Wallraf-Richartz Museum, Cologne

Provenance: Wildenstein & Co., New York, by 1960; Wallraf-Richartz Museum, 1964.

Exhibitions: None.

Literature: *Wallraf-Richartz-Museum der Stadt Köln. Verzeichnis der Gemälde* (Cologne, 1965), p. 211, no. 3182; H. Keller, 'Delacroix vor Rubens (ein Farbvergleich)', *Wallraf-Richartz-Jahrbuch*, XXVII (1965), pp. 423–5, full-page repr. p. 424; B. White, 'Delacroix's Painted Copies after Rubens', *AB*, XLIX (1967), pp. 37, 43, 49 (no. 25), repr. fig. 14; J. Thuillier and J. Foucart, *Le Storie di Maria de' Medici di Rubens al Lussemburgo* (Rizzoli, Milan, 1967; ed. in French, Paris 1969), p. 91.

This copy cannot be considered authentic either on stylistic grounds or on the strength of the indistinct red wax seal on the stretcher, which has passed for a genuine seal of Delacroix's posthumous sale. No copy that can be identified with this subject is listed in the catalogue of the posthumous sale, and it is most unlikely that a canvas of this size and degree of finish would have been included in the mixed lot (176) of 'fragments d'études d'après Rubens [*et al.*]' (see J(L)26). Foucart (op. cit.) suggests that it is perhaps by Louis Mettling (active *c.* 1870–90).

R22 THE FULL RECONCILIATION Pl. 167 OF MARIA DE' MEDICI AND HER SON, after RUBENS (Louvre, RF2104)

$11\frac{5}{8} \times 8\frac{7}{8}$ in. (29.5 × 22.5 cm)
Private collection, Switzerland

Provenance: Galerie du Bac, Paris, 1947; Schaeffer Gallery, New York; with J. P. Durand-Matthiesen, Geneva; private collection, Switzerland, by 1967.

Exhibition: Galerie du Bac, Paris, 1947 (no cat.)

Literature: B. White, 'Delacroix's Painted Copies after Rubens', *AB*, XLIX (1967), pp. 37, 49 (no. 26), repr. fig. 15; J. Thuillier and J. Foucart, *Le Storie di Maria de' Medici di Rubens al Lussemburgo* (Rizzoli, Milan, 1967; ed. in French, Paris 1969), pp. 90 f.

I agree with the opinion already expressed by Foucart (op. cit.), that this copy is not from Delacroix's hand.

Costume, Accessories, Arms and Armour

O4 STUDIES OF ARMOUR

Pl. 169

$18\frac{1}{8} \times 21\frac{5}{8}$ in. (46×55 cm)* Relined. E.D.[1]
Part of R1919 (No repr.)
c. 1823/4
Dr. Konrad Feilchenfeldt, Zurich

Provenance: Presumably Delacroix's posthumous sale, Feb. 1864, part of lot 189 ('Deux études d'après des armures, des casques et des cottes de mailles. Deux toiles', without dimensions), which was sold to Count Duchâtel, 520 fr., and M. Aubry, 60 fr.; Duc de Trévise, by 1924; his sale, 19 May 1938, lot 22 (repr.), to Walter Feilchenfeldt, Amsterdam, 41,000 fr. (removed to Zurich 1939); by descent to the present owner, his son.

Exhibitions: Géricault, Paris 1924, no. 323; Paris 1927, no. 274;[2] Petit Palais, Paris 1936, no. 831 (Supp.); Zurich 1939, no. 319; Venice 1956, no. 11; Schaffhausen 1963, *h.c.*; Berne 1963-4, no. 7; Bremen 1964, no. 7.

Literature: Escholier I, repr. p. 159; *Journal* I. 90 n. 3.; L. Johnson, 'Delacroix at the Biennale', *Burl Mag*, XCVIII (1956), p. 327.

These studies were dated to c. 1830 in the catalogues of the exhibitions Zurich 1939 and Venice 1956; I suggested (1956) that it was not impossible they had been painted in 1825, when Delacroix is known to have made studies in the Meyrick collection in London, or shortly thereafter.

All the pieces of armour can now be identified as belonging to the Musée de l'Armée in Paris, and from the collection that in the 1820s was in the Musée d'Artillerie, place Saint Thomas d'Aquin, Paris. Top, left to right: 1. Tonlet armour with mark of Kunz Lochner, Nuremberg, probably made for Emperor Maximilian II, c. 1550 (Musée de l'Armée, G 182); 2. Tonlet armour for foot-combat in the lists, of Italian make, c. 1550 (G 181); 3. Helmet of Henri Ier, duc de Montmorency, Constable of France, of French make, c. 1565-70 (G 145). I have been unable to identify the mail shirt represented at the bottom of the canvas together with a detail of the links, but at least one object of this sort was in the Musée d'Artillerie and can be seen in a print of 1860 illustrating the interior (*BN Estampes*, Va 270i).

A water-colour study of the piece of armour depicted in the top left is to be found, with studies of other pieces now in the Musée de l'Armée, on fol. 26 of the sketch-book in the Kunsthalle, Bremen, which has been thought to be entirely from Delacroix's hand c. 1823/4 (Cat. Exh. Bremen 1964, no. 105-30). Though I originally followed the compilers of the Bremen catalogue in accepting Delacroix's authorship, suggesting, however, at the same time the possibility of a strong influence of the Fieldings on some of the weaker composition studies ('Delacroix Drawings at Bremen', *Master Drawings*, II (1965), pp. 415 ff.), I now believe that a large proportion of the studies contained in the sketch-book, including the studies of armour on fol. 26, is from another hand—apparently from the hand of a British artist working in close association with Delacroix at the period of the *Massacres de Scio*; one indication of this is the inscription in English on a sheet of studies of a mace and hammer: 'The Length of the Hammer head' (fol. 54). The most likely artist would seem to be Thales Fielding, but too little is known about his work to allow of a more than tentative attribution.

In the absence of other canvases corresponding to the description of lot 189 in the catalogue of Delacroix's posthumous sale, there is little reason to doubt that this painting was part of that lot; and it may very well be also the canvas referred to by Delacroix in a note c. 1849: 'Prêté à Lehmann, le 22 mars [. . .] une [toile] d'*Armures*, faite au Musée d'artillerie.' (*Journal* I. 251.) But even if these references were sure, they would not be proofs that it is by Delacroix himself, and certain timidities of handling, particularly in the plinth and the bottom of the armour which rests on it so insecurely, suggest that it could be from a less distinguished hand, quite possibly the same as drew the study of the identical piece of armour in the Bremen sketchbook. I therefore believe the attribution should be left open until more is known about the minor artists working around Delacroix in the 1820s.

[1] The seal is on a piece of wood, presumed to have been cut from the original stretcher, inlaid into the present stretcher.
[2] This picture does not appear to have been included in the exhibition Louvre 1930, as claimed in the catalogue of the Duc de Trévise sale.

O5 A PERSIAN HELMET, EIGHTEENTH CENTURY

Pl. 169

$19\frac{3}{16} \times 10\frac{11}{16}$ in. (48.7×27.2 cm)* E.D.
Moreau p. 321. R1918 (No repr.)
c. 1823/4
Musée du Louvre

Provenance: Delacroix's posthumous sale, Feb. 1864, lot 190 ('Etude de casque circassien', 48×27 cm), to Alfred Stevens for Van Praet, Brussels, 1,200 fr.; bought by Boussod, Valadon & Cie from Henri Garnier (who had bought the Van Praet collection *en bloc* in Jan. 1893—R Ann 297), 11 Jan. 1893, and sold by them to P. A. Cheramy, 6 Feb. 1893 (Arch Goupil/Boussod); his sale, 5 May 1908, lot 183, to Haro, 650 fr.; Alfred Baillehache, by 1921; his sale, 23 May 1922, lot 19, to Guerlain, 620 fr.; Société des Amis de Delacroix, by 1937; acquired by the Louvre (RF1953-39), 1953.

Exhibitions: Art Musulman, Paris 1893, no. 112; Cassirer, Berlin 1907, no. 22; Basle 1921, no. 85; Atelier Delacroix, Paris 1937B, no. 20; id., Paris 1938, no. 20; id., Paris 1939, no. 72; id., Paris 1947, no. 5; id., Paris 1948, no. 102; id., Paris 1949, no. 124; id., Paris 1950, no. 103; id., Paris 1951, no. 10; id., Paris 1952, no. 74; id., Paris 1963, no. 142; id., Paris 1969–70 (no cat.); Munich 1972, no. 344, repr.

Literature: J. Meier-Graefe and E. Klossowski, *La Collection Cheramy . . .* (R. Piper, Munich, 1908), p. 113, no. 267 (repr.); *Journal* I. 90 n. 3; Sterling–Adhémar, no. 665, pl. 233; C. von Heusinger, in Cat. Exh. Bremen 1964, under no. 117; L. Johnson, 'Delacroix Drawings at Bremen', *Master Drawings*, II (1965), pp. 417 f., 419 n. 3.

Various dates have been assigned to this study, with no evidence being adduced in support of them: Meier-Graefe and Klossowski placed it *c.* 1833; it has been habitually assigned to the English journey of 1825 in exhibitions at the Atelier Delacroix since 1937; Joubin thought the helmet might have been among the 'armes de Mameluk' that Delacroix was expecting to receive from General Coëtlosquet at the beginning of May 1824—at a period when he was making studies of arms with one of the Fielding brothers (*Journal* I. 90 and n. 3); the picture is dated to 1826 in Sterling–Adhémar. I suggested (1965) a date of 1823, on the strength of pencil and water-colour studies in the Bremen sketch-book which had correctly been identified by Heusinger as from the same helmet (fols. 25, 28; latter sheet repr. in L. Johnson, op. cit., fig. 5); but these are some of the studies in the sketch-book that I am no longer able to accept as by Delacroix, and there seems to be a strong possibility that this study in oils is from the same hand—perhaps that of Thales Fielding (see the preceding number).

D6 STUDY OF A BEARDED ARAB,   Pl. 170
THREE-QUARTER LENGTH, FACING LEFT

Paper laid down on canvas, $9\frac{3}{4} \times 8\frac{1}{16}$ in. (24.8 × 20.5 cm)*
E.D.

Albert Loeb, Paris

Provenance: Claimed to be from Delacroix's posthumous sale, Feb. 1864, part of lot 188 ('Trois études de costumes d'hommes de l'Orient', without dimensions: J(L)45-47); Vieussa, 1893 (ink inscription on binding paper); with Claude Aubry; with Albert Loeb.

Exhibitions: None.

Literature: None.

In the absence of any proof that this study formerly belonged to Prévost or Busquet, the claim that it was part of lot 188 in Delacroix's posthumous sale should, in my opinion, be viewed with caution (see J(L)45-47 and J(D)7). The seal of the posthumous sale, on the cross-bar

of the stretcher, though not a perfect imprint, appears to be genuine. Therefore this work, if not part of lot 188, was probably included with a larger lot of studies of unspecified subjects; but it seems that, at best, it could have been no more than a very summary sketch by Delacroix, which has been extensively repainted since his death.

D7 STUDY OF A KNEELING   Pl. 171
FIGURE IN TURKISH COSTUME

Paper laid down on canvas, $17 \times 12\frac{3}{4}$ in. (43.2 × 32.4 cm)*
E.D.

Cleveland Museum of Art

Provenance: Claimed to be from Delacroix's posthumous sale, Feb. 1864, part of lot 188 ('Trois études de costumes d'hommes de l'Orient', without dimensions; J(L)45-47); anonymous sale, Hôtel Drouot, Salle 10, 6 March 1967, lot 7, to Claude Aubry; he sold it to Paul and Odette Wurzburger; they donated it to the Cleveland Museum of Art (70.159), 1970.

Exhibitions: None.

Literature: C. Bernard and A. T. Lurie, 'Some Aspects of Delacroix's Orientalism', *Bulletin of the Cleveland Museum of Art*, LVIII (1971), pp. 123-7, repr. fig. 1;[1] ibid. 168, 170.

On grounds of style and conflicting accounts of its recent history provided by the same owner, this work should in my opinion be regarded as a doubtful attribution. It is claimed to be a study from Delacroix's posthumous sale of which no description survives except that it depicted male oriental costume. While the handling approximates Delacroix's manner of the 1820s (Robaut—R1485—dated the relevant study from the posthumous sale to 1823, sight unseen), the pose and costume anomalously match the figure of the Turk surrendering in the late variant of the *Combat of the Giaour and Hassan*, dated 1856 (R1293. Fogg Art Museum; repr. Escholier III, opp. p. 230; Trapp, fig. 62). Though it bears a wax monogram 'ED' on the stretcher and, on the front, a printed label of the appropriate lot number in Delacroix's posthumous sale, so long as the history cannot be securely documented farther back than 1967 or the authenticity of the materials established by scientific tests, this study should not be admitted into Delacroix's *œuvre*.

[1] It is stated in n. 4 of this article that I suggested in a letter to the Museum, dated 9 June 1969, 'Delacroix had painted the figure on paper.' In fact, I merely inquired whether the study was painted on paper and, not yet having seen it, deliberately avoided suggesting that I thought Delacroix had painted it.

D8 A MAN IN GREEK COSTUME   Pl. 173
SEATED BY THE SEA

$13\frac{3}{8} \times 11$ in. (34 × 28 cm)
Moreau p. 273. R1048 (1848. No repr.)
Whereabouts unknown

Provenance: M. Albert, dancing master at the Paris Opéra; his sale, 15 March 1866, lot 4 ('Officier grec, assis sur un tertre dominant la mer', 34 × 28 cm), 1,240 fr.

Exhibitions: None.

Literature: None, other than Moreau and Robaut.

When Robaut catalogued this picture, it was unknown to him and he merely copied the details from Moreau—inaccurately, for the date of the Albert sale. Later he came to know it from a Lecadre photograph and revised the date of execution to 1827-38 (R Ann, margin to R1048). He also reproduced it in Tracings III, there dating it 1825-7. It is known to me only from this drawing by Robaut and from an old photograph, reproduced here, in M-Nélaton Port. II. From the latter, it appears most unlikely to have been by Delacroix.

For authentic studies of this type of costume, see J28–J31 and J(L)39.

D9 TWO STUDIES OF A MAN   Pl. 172
IN GREEK COSTUME

(Back and side views)
$17\frac{7}{8} \times 15\frac{3}{4}$ in. (45.4 × 40 cm)* E.D.
R1480 (1822. No repr.) ?
Arthur Cohen, New York

Provenance: Possibly Delacroix's posthumous sale, Feb. 1864, lot 182bis, to Dauzats, 205 fr.;[1] ? his posthumous sale, 1 Feb. 1869, lot 411 (as 'Deux Arabes' *after* Delacroix, without dimensions), 40 fr.;[2] with Georges Aubry, by 1930; D. David-Weill; Mme D. David-Weill, his widow, d. 1970; with Marianne Feilchenfeldt, Zurich, 1973; with Messrs. P. & D. Colnaghi, London, 1973; sold by them to the present owner.

Exhibitions: Louvre 1930, no. 13A; Atelier Delacroix, Paris 1947, no. 13.

Literature: None.

While both this picture and the following number may well have passed in Delacroix's posthumous sale as his own work, the style and proportions are in my opinion uncharacteristic of his work in general and are, particularly, distinct from his authentic studies of Greek costume (J28–J31, J(L)39). The following number, which appears to be by the same hand, could even be a study by a painter friend depicting Delacroix himself dressed in Greek costume.

[1] These are the particulars which Robaut gives for R1480 and to which he adds nothing except the subject. Though the printed sale catalogue does not list a lot 182bis, Burty Ann ED adds to lot 182, which is described in the catalogue as 'Deux autres études séparées' and was knocked down to Paul Huet (J30), a 182bis and a 182ter which went to Dauzats for 205 fr. and 105 fr.

respectively. No more details are noted; and Robaut does not mention a lot 182ter, which should possibly be identified with J(D)10.

[2] The Cohen studies of Greek costume bear the more recent inscription, 'Maures (Esq.)', on the back (see J31, n. 3), which suggests that they might well have been mistaken for Arabs at an earlier date.

D10 STUDY OF A SEATED MAN   Pl. 173
IN GREEK COSTUME

$13\frac{9}{16} \times 9\frac{1}{4}$ in. (34.5 × 23.5 cm)* E.D.
Private collection, Paris

Provenance: Possibly Delacroix's posthumous sale, Feb. 1864, lot 182ter, to Dauzats, 105 fr. (Burty Ann ED).

Exhibitions: None.

Literature: None.

See the preceding number.

R23 'SULIOT SOLDIER' (Back view)

Cardboard, $13 \times 8\frac{1}{4}$ in. (33 × 21 cm)
Whereabouts unknown

Provenance: Anonymous sale, Hôtel Drouot, Paris 11 Dec. 1957, lot 70 (as 'Soldat Souliote', repr.); anonymous sale, Galerie Charpentier, Paris 13 June 1958, lot 67 (repr.).

Exhibition: Wildenstein, London 1952, no. 6.

Though identified in the catalogue of the 1952 exhibition with R1482 and lot 187 of Delacroix's posthumous sale (see J(L)43), and claimed in the two sale catalogues of the 1950s to bear the ED seal of that sale, the association of this crude study with Delacroix is extremely dubious.

R24 STUDY OF ARMOUR

Oils on paper, $10\frac{3}{4} \times 6\frac{3}{4}$ in. (27. 3 × 17.2 cm, sight)*
Raymond Escholier, Paris

Provenance: Léon Riesener; Mme Léouzon-le-Duc, his granddaughter; by descent to the wife of the present owner.

Exhibitions: Wildenstein, London 1952, no. 9; Atelier Delacroix, Paris 1969; id., 1969-70 (no cat.)

Literature: Escholier I, repr. opp. p. 152.

This is stated in the catalogue of the exhibition Wildenstein, London 1952, to have been painted by Delacroix in the Meyrick collection in England in 1825, but the armour cannot be identified with any piece from that collection, nor is the study attributable to Delacroix on stylistic grounds. I must add that Madame Escholier told me in May 1967, in a conversation of which I took notes at the time, that Léon Riesener's daughter thought that it was not by Delacroix.

Miscellaneous Orientalia

R25 TURKISH (?) HORSEMAN AIMING A PISTOL
Pl. 174

Wood Panel, $11\frac{13}{16} \times 8\frac{11}{16}$ in. (30 × 22 cm)*
R46 (1821)
Whereabouts unknown

Provenance: Prince Galitzine (Robaut Tracings 1); obtained from him by Dr. Horteloup, by 26 Nov. 1875 (ibid.); acquired from his heirs by Schoeller, 1950 (Dieterle R); anon. sale (by Schoeller and Ader), Hôtel Drouot, Salle 9, 6 July 1950, h.c., to Katia Granoff, 240,000 fr.; anon. sale (by Ader), Palais Galliera, 16 June 1966, lot 80 ('Le coup de fusil.' Repr.), to M. Morin (?), 16,000 fr.

Exhibition: 'Plaisirs de la Campagne', Galerie Charpentier, Paris 1954, no. 41 ('Le coup de fusil').

Literature: Escholier I. 110.

Robaut identified this painting with lot 79 in Delacroix's posthumous sale, but the dimensions of that lot are listed as 14 × 33 cm in the catalogue of the sale. It seems, therefore, that the true lot 79 was the *Cavalier turc au galop* that was to belong to Louis Bazille (J40); not catalogued by Robaut, it is recorded elsewhere as bearing the seal of the posthumous sale and having the dimensions listed for lot 79 in the sale catalogue. The present painting bears a blob of red wax on the back which, devoid of initials, appears to be a singularly inept attempt to forge the seal of Delacroix's posthumous sale that would be expected to be found on the picture if Robaut's record of its provenance were correct.

Horses

O6 AN ARAB HORSE WITH BLUE BLANKET
Pl. 175

Paper laid down on canvas, $7\frac{1}{2} \times 9\frac{5}{8}$ in. (19 × 24.5 cm)* E.D. Moreau p. 321. R1863 (No repr.)
1823
The late Jean Dieterle, Paris

Provenance: Delacroix's posthumous sale, Feb. 1864, lot 206 ('Cheval arabe avec une couverture bleue', without dimensions), to Scott, 720 fr.; thence by inheritance to C. Bourdil, Monte Carlo; his posthumous sale, Hôtel Drouot, Salle 12, 18 Nov. 1942, to Jean Dieterle, 20,700 fr., d. 1972.

Exhibitions: Soc. Amis des Arts, Bordeaux 1864, no. 174 ('Etude de cheval arabe', dimensions and owner unlisted, but stated to be from the posthumous sale); Charpentier, Paris 1948, h.c. ?[1]; Paris 1972, no. 256, repr.

The early history and catalogue references above are given on the tentative assumption that, as claimed by the late owner, this is lot 206 from Delacroix's posthumous sale, but the identification cannot be considered certain. I have not been able to confirm the provenance from Scott, the purchaser of lot 206 at the posthumous sale, and if this relatively minor study was that lot, it is hard to understand why it should have fetched one of the highest prices paid for any of the horse studies at the sale. In favour of the identification, though not entirely reliable as evidence, is a plate on the front of the frame, inscribed: 'Société des Amis des Arts de Bordeaux Exposition de 1864'; and a pencil inscription on binding paper on the back: 'M. Scott Monte Carlo'. T. B. G. Scott became President of the Société des Amis des Arts de Bordeaux in 1864 and was doubtless the anonymous lender of the 'Etude de cheval arabe' to their exhibition of 1864.

Independently of its provenance, a reason for thinking this study is authentic, despite its general weakness and some overpainting, is that it is clearly related to a pencil study on the same sheet of the Bremen sketch-book (fol. 56) as the drawings for J46, and seems to have been developed from that study. But until the provenance can be more firmly established, it seems prudent to leave the attribution open.

The paper this study is painted on is irregularly cut at a diagonal running from nearly halfway up the left edge to about 1″ from the top of the right edge.

[1] There is a printed label on the back for this exhibition, but if listed in the catalogue it is incorrectly identified.

O7 A ROAN
Pl. 175

$14\frac{3}{8} \times 16\frac{15}{16}$ in. (16.5 × 43 cm) E.D.[1] Relined
R71 (1823) ?
Private collection, Scandinavia

Provenance: ? Delacroix's posthumous sale, Feb. 1864, lot 209 ('Cheval rouan', without dimensions), to Lambert, 620 fr.; Richard Goetz; sale of his sequestered property, 23 Feb. 1922, lot 5 ('Cheval rouan (1823)', 37 × 44 cm, stated to be lot 209 from the posthumous sale and to bear the seal of that sale on the back), to Grünwald, 400 fr.; W. Loewenstein, New York (label on stretcher); private collection, Norway, by 1946; with Tore Gerschman, Stockholm.

Exhibition: Oslo 1946, no. 2.

Literature: None known, except Robaut.

This work, which is known to me only from photographs, resembles Robaut's small print illustrating his no. 71, but the dimensions are slightly larger than those listed by Robaut (30 × 40 cm), and its history between 1864 and 1922 is uncertain. It cannot therefore be identified as R71 with complete confidence. Even if it were proved to be R71, there would in my opinion, and judging from photographs, be some doubt that it was correctly attributed to Delacroix at the time of his sale.

¹ The seal is on an old piece of wood inset into a new stretcher. An old label to the left of the seal is inscribed with the inventory number 18648, and 'Delacroix/Cheval Marron'. The title 'Cheval marron' is also printed on an early Druet photograph (no. 56968) of this painting, preserved in the archives of the Wildenstein Gallery in New York.

M3 A BAY ATTACHED TO A POST IN A FIELD   Pl. 176

$7\frac{1}{2} \times 8\frac{3}{8}$ in. (19 × 21.3 cm)* E.D.
R1866 (No. repr.)
Mr. and Mrs. Paul Mellon, Washington, D.C.

Provenance: Delacroix's posthumous sale, Feb. 1864, lot 84 ('Cheval bai attaché à un poteau dans la campagne', 18 × 20 cm), to Haro, 300 fr.; remained in the Haro family till 1934, when it was placed in a mixed sale (*experts*, E. and R. Haro) held at Neuilly-sur-Seine on 22 Feb., lot 13; with Wildenstein & Co., New York; acquired from them by the present owners, Dec. 1960.

Exhibitions: *Bd Italiens*, Paris 1864, no. 43; Atelier Delacroix, Paris 1932, no. 40.

Literature: None.

Although there appears to be no reason to doubt that this is the picture which passed as lot 84 to Delacroix's colour merchant, Haro, at the posthumous sale, it has evidently suffered since from such extensive and crude overpainting as to deprive the attribution to Delacroix of any real meaning. Haro is reported by two contemporary sources, Philippe Burty and Léon Riesener, to have 'finished' works left incomplete by Delacroix—in the manner of an apothecary acting like a doctor, as Riesener put it (both sources are quoted in H. Bessis, 'Trois albums de dessins de Pierre Andrieu au Cabinet des Dessins', *Revue du Louvre*, 18 (1968), p. 148 n. 5).

M4 RUMP OF A CHESTNUT HORSE   Pl. 176

$12\frac{5}{8} \times 9\frac{5}{8}$ in. (32 × 24.5 cm)* E.D.
Part of R1871?
Claude Aubry, Paris

Provenance: ? Delacroix's posthumous sale, Feb. 1864, part of lot 211 ('Dix études [de chevaux] ébauchées'); with J. P. Durand-Matthiesen, Geneva, by 1963; mixed sale, Sotheby's, London 2 July 1969, lot 114 (repr.), to Aubry, £1,000.

Exhibitions: Berne 1963–4, no. 8; Bremen 1964, no. 8.

Literature: None certain.

This study has been so heavily overpainted as to leave Delacroix's hand unrecognizable, if it was ever present. The canvas bears the trade-mark of Haro, Delacroix's colour merchant, and the new stretcher bears an apparently authentic seal of Delacroix's posthumous sale, cut however from an old stretcher. It is therefore possible that this was originally one of the more sketchy studies in lot 211 of Delacroix's posthumous sale, a later hand having attempted to 'finish' it. For a list of buyers and prices of studies in lot 211 that cannot be identified with specific pictures, see J(L)65.

D11 BROWN DAPPLED HORSE WITH BLACK MANE AND TAIL, FACING RIGHT   Pl. 177

$10\frac{1}{4} \times 17\frac{3}{4}$ in. (26 × 45 cm)* False E.D. on stretcher.
Mme Léonardo Bénatov, Paris

Provenance: Durand-Ruel (Dieterle R, margin to R1860)¹; Georges Hue (ibid.); anon. sale, Hôtel Drouot, Salle 14, 9 Feb. 1941, to Léonardo Bénatov, 28,500 fr. (ibid.).

Exhibitions: Berne 1963–4, no. 10; Bremen 1964, no. 9.

Literature: None certain.

The seal of Delacroix's posthumous sale does not seem to me genuine; nor does the style, when seen in relation to the comparable study in the Méra collection (J49), convince me that the attribution to Delacroix is correct.

¹ An ink inscription on the back of the frame, 'Delacroix N° 3494', may refer to a Durand-Ruel inventory number.

D12 STUDY OF A HORSE GALLOPING

$10\frac{5}{8} \times 13\frac{3}{4}$ in. (27 × 35 cm, according to Robaut Tracings.)
Signed bottom right: *E.D.*
Whereabouts unknown

Provenance: Victor Chocquet, by Aug. 1877 (Robaut Tracings v—Supp.), d. 1891; Marie Chocquet, his widow; her sale 1 July 1899, lot 59 ('Etude de cheval. De ¾ à droite et de dos, lancé au galop. Signé à droite, en bas: E.D.', 28 × 36 cm), 1,100 fr.; Henri Haro sale, 12 Dec. 1911, lot 212, to Letellier, 920 fr.

Exhibitions: None.

Literature: J. Rewald, 'Chocquet and Cézanne', *GBA*, LXXIV (1969), p. 76.

This picture is known to me only from the drawing in Robaut Tracings V, where the attribution to Delacroix is, however, questioned.

R26 A BAY, FACING RIGHT   Pl. 177

12 × 17½ in. (30.5 × 44.5 cm)
Wildenstein & Co., London (1967)

Provenance: With de Bayser, Paris; sale at Sotheby's, London 13 July 1960, lot 82, to Wildenstein, £500.

Exhibition: Kunstmuseum, St. Gallen (Switzerland), 1954, no. 15.

Literature: None.

This study is claimed to be lot 208 from Delacroix's posthumous sale (see J(L)52), but neither its quality nor the fragment of red sealing wax on the stretcher, held to be a piece of the seal of the posthumous sale, inspires confidence in this claim.

R27 STUDIES OF HORSES

13¾ × 35 in. (35 × 89 cm)
Private collection, Paris

Provenance: Claude Roger-Marx, by 1937; Dr. Simon; his sale (anon.), Galerie Charpentier, 10 June 1955, 400,000 fr.; with Alfred Daber; sold by him to the mother of the present owner.

Exhibition: Gobin, Paris 1937, no. 23.

Literature: None.

This canvas contains about seven studies of horses and is claimed in the catalogue of the Simon sale to bear the seal of Delacroix's posthumous sale on the stretcher, but the seal is badly cracked and of doubtful authenticity.

R28 STUDY OF A HORSE,   Pl. 178
FACING RIGHT

10⅝ × 8¼ in. (27 × 21 cm) Damaged and doubtful E.D.
Private collection, Paris

Provenance: Uncertain.

Exhibition: Bordeaux 1963, no. 69.

Literature: None.

This study was claimed in the catalogue of the exhibition Bordeaux 1963 to be lot 209 from Delacroix's posthumous sale, the *Roan* discussed here under J(O)7. The style, the broken wax 'ED' seal of doubtful authenticity on the

stretcher, and the highly inaccurate entry in the exhibition catalogue combine to destroy any confidence in the attribution to Delacroix.

R29 STUDY OF A WHITE HORSE   Pl. 178

Canvas on millboard, 7¹¹⁄₁₆ × 9⅞ in. (19.5 × 25 cm)
Musée Bonnat, Bayonne

Provenance: Léon Bonnat, d. 8 Sept. 1922; by his bequest to the town of Bayonne, Musée Bonnat (Inv. no. 1031).

Exhibition: *Exposition d'Œuvres originales d'Eugène Delacroix*, Musée Bonnat, Bayonne, 1963, no. 3.

Literature: *Ville de Bayonne. Musée Bonnat. Catalogue Sommaire* (Musées nationaux, Paris, 1930), p. 116, no. 769.

There appears to be no justification in either its history or its style for attributing this study to Delacroix. It does not bear the seal of the artist's posthumous sale.

R30 TWO HORSES AT A STABLE   Pl. 179

9⅝ × 7½ in. (24.5 × 19 cm)* False signature bottom right: *Eug. Delacroix*.
R Ann, margin to R1860
Dr. Peter Nathan, Zurich

Provenance: Champfleury, by 1885; his sale 28 Apr. 1890, lot 6 ('Intérieur d'écurie', 23 × 18 cm), 105 fr.; Dr. Georges Viau; his sale 11 Dec. 1942, lot 96, 225,000 fr.; Dr. Fritz Nathan, Zurich, by 1963, d. 1972; the present owner, his son.

Exhibitions: EBA, Paris 1885, no. 43; ? Charpentier, Paris 1948, no. 49 ('Chevaux à l'écurie', without dimensions or owner); Berne 1963–4, no. 9, repr.; Bremen 1964, no. 10.

Literature: None.

Although this picture is listed in R Ann alongside the printed entry for R1860, under which number the fourteen studies of horses in lot 210 of Delacroix's posthumous sale are grouped without individual descriptions, it is not mentioned as bearing the seal of the posthumous sale, nor is the signature noted by Robaut or reproduced on his drawing of this painting in Tracings V (Supp.). The signature is first recorded in the catalogue of the Viau sale in 1942. The doubts that must arise from the uncertainty of the provenance before the picture belonged to Champfleury and from the false signature are fully confirmed by the style.

R31 WHITE HORSE, PROBABLY   Pl. 179
'LE FLORIDO'

18¹⁄₁₆ × 21⅝ in. (45.9 × 55 cm)*
R Ann, marginal note to R75 (1823)
Glasgow Art Gallery and Museum (Burrell Collection, Inv. 251.35/250)

Provenance: Copy, thought to be by Alexis Pérignon, after a painting by Delacroix which Paul Verdé Delisle, Pérignon's nephew, bought at the master's posthumous sale in Feb. 1864 (J(L)53); with Bernheim-Jeune, March 1885; Pierre Verdé Delisle (grandson of Paul); bought from him by Jean Dieterle for 10,000 fr., 19 March 1929; sold by him, in association with Tedesco frères, to Sir William Burrell, Aug. or Sept. 1931,[1] 18,500 fr.

Exhibitions: Louvre 1930, no. 13 (as R75); London 1975, no. 21 (as R75)

Literature: C. Thompson, 'Delacroix's Chess Players', *The Scottish Art Review*, VI, no. 3 (1957), p. 12.

This picture has passed as R75 (J(L)53) since 1930, but the combined absence of the seal of Delacroix's posthumous sale on the back and of firm accent in much of the brushwork lead me to conclude that it is the copy of which the following details are noted in R Ann, as a MS. annotation to R75: 'Ce Nᵒ 75 a été copié à même dimension et très servilement (par M. Pérignon je crois). Je vois cette copie en mars 85 chez M. Bernheim jeune. Elle est beaucoup moins ferme que

l'original dans les jambes surtout. De plus le D qui est dans le cartouche du haut manque du pittoresque et du lazzi à la manière EDˣ.'

The painter Alexis Pérignon, to whom Robaut presumably refers here, was, M. R. Verdé Delisle told me, the brother of the mother of Paul Verdé Delisle, who bought the original Delacroix at the posthumous sale. His name occurs several times in the *Journal* and *Correspondance* during Delacroix's later years, when the two artists were on friendly terms.

The connection between Pérignon and the Verdé Delisle family makes it very possible that the latter, in addition to owning the original, came into possession of the copy during the nineteenth century, in circumstances which are not clear (perhaps on the death of Pérignon in 1882, or perhaps when it was with Bernheim-Jeune in 1885—if it was not they who placed it with Bernheim-Jeune and failed to sell it), leading eventually to the confusion between copy and original.

[1] In a letter of 3 June 1957 to Mr. Colin Thompson at the National Gallery of Scotland, M. Jean Dieterle says the picture was sold 'par nous' to Burrell on 25 Sept. 1931. According to the relevant entry in Burrell's purchase book for 1931, he bought it on 18 August from Tedesco frères.

Portraits and Studies of Heads

O8 HEAD OF A WOMAN IN BED   Pl. 181

$13\frac{11}{16} \times 21\frac{1}{4}$ in. (34.7 × 54 cm)* Relined
Moreau p. 228? R1311 (1857)
1823/4?
Claude Aubry, Paris

Provenance: Sale M.H.L., 13 March 1873, lot 22 ('La Morte', 34 × 51 cm), 530 fr.; ? anonymous sale, Hôtel Drouot 5 Oct. 1876, to M. Charly, 125 fr.;[1] anonymous sale, Hôtel Drouot, Salle 11, 1 Dec. 1943, to Georges Aubry.

Exhibitions: Atelier Delacroix, Paris 1963, no. 24 (as 'La Dormeuse (Mme Dalton)'); Kyoto-Tokyo 1969, H-38, repr.

Literature: Huyghe, pp. 30, 549, pl. 7.

Robaut listed this painting as 'La morte. — Etude d'après nature' and dated it to 1857 on the strength of an inscription on the back in an unknown hand, recording this title and date.

The identification of the model as Mme Dalton, given in the catalogue of the exhibition Atelier Delacroix, Paris 1963, seems entirely fanciful. Huyghe's suggestion (p. 30) that the study represents Delacroix's sister on her deathbed in 1827 seems to be belied by the features of the subject and by her apparent youth: Henriette de Verninac died at the age of forty-seven. His opinion that the technique is consistent with a period some thirty years earlier than Robaut's date is,

on the other hand, entirely convincing; but if the picture is by Delacroix at all, the technique and the tonal modelling in a range of ochres, browns and black fit better to my mind in the period of the *Massacres of Chios* (J105) than of the *Death of Sardanapalus* (J125). This study may in these respects, if not in quality, be compared to the head of the dead mother in the right foreground of the *Massacres of Chios*. It also recalls Géricault's studies of severed heads, though the impasto is less thickly applied here.

Even assuming that the picture is from Delacroix's hand, the identity of the model is bound to remain conjectural unless new evidence comes to light. It is conceivable that this is an early study of Caroline referred to by Delacroix on 9 July 1850 (though R55 (see J(R)2) or R106 (J6) could also be that study). In discussing the simple technique of a figure of St. Francis by Rubens, he writes: 'Le gris de l'ébauche paraît partout. Un très léger ton local sur les chairs et quelques touches un peu plus empâtées pour les clairs.

'Se rappeler souvent l'étude de *Femme au lit*, commencé il y a un mois environ; le modelé déjà arrêté dans le ton local, sans rehauts d'ombres et de clairs. J'avais trouvé cela, il y a bien longtemps, dans une étude couchée d'après *Caroline*. L'instinct m'avait guidé de bonne heure' (*Journal* 1. 383). In an unpublished letter from Malta dated 12 November 1829, Charles de Verninac wrote to Delacroix referring to 'l'époque de la maladie de Caroline', but without specifying when the illness occurred (Coll. late M. Roger Leybold); it was perhaps on that occasion that this study was painted. If it does indeed represent Caroline, and the same Caroline with whom Delacroix evidently had an affair in 1819, then the possibility of its portraying Jenny Le Guillou in her youth would also have to be considered when assessing arguments for and against identifying Jenny with Caroline (see J84). It is difficult, in my opinion, to accept that this is the same woman as in Delacroix's portrait of Jenny Le Guillou of *c.* 1840 (Louvre. Repr. Huyghe, pl. 32); which could mean either that this is not Caroline or that Jenny and Caroline were not one and the same person.

Finally, it is possible that this is a portrait listed, perhaps wrongly, as 'Rose' by Moreau (p. 228), which has never been identified (see J(L)69); for Moreau states: 'La tête repose sur un oreiller; elle semble dormir', and of the known early works this study fits his description. The dimensions diverge considerably from those given by Moreau, whose measurements of portraits are not, however, always reliable (see e.g. *Madame Dalton,* J(L)81).

¹ According to Robaut. I have been unable to confirm that the picture passed in a sale on that date. The only sale at the Hôtel Drouot on this day listed by Lugt was a mixed sale held in Room 5 on 4 and 5 October, but this painting is not in the catalogue. It could, however, have passed under no. 150, which was reserved for pictures that had not been catalogued.

M5 SELF-PORTRAIT   Pl. 180

13¾ × 10⅝ in. (35 × 27 cm)
R69 (1823)
Foundation Emil Bührle, Zurich

Provenance: Given to Constant Dutilleux by Jenny Le Guillou, Delacroix's housekeeper (R Ann); his sale 26 March 1874, lot 1 (repr.), 2,750 fr.; Baron de Beurnonville; his sale 24 March 1883, lot 157 (apparently bought in or withdrawn); his sale (baron de B.) 21 May 1883, lot 157, 800 fr.; Henri Rouart, by 1885; his sale 9 Dec. 1912, lot 182 (repr.), to Ernest Rouart, his son, 11,000 fr., to at least 1930; W. Walter, Paris; purchased from a Swiss dealer in 1951 by Emil Bührle, Zurich.

Exhibitions: EBA, Paris 1885, no. 195; Copenhagen 1914, no. 72; Rosenberg, Paris 1928, no. 8; Louvre 1930, no. 66; Atelier Delacroix, Paris 1932, no. 2; Zurich 1939, no. 301, repr.; Basle 1939, no. 213, repr.; Venice 1956, no. 12; Zurich 1958, no. 110.

Literature: Escholier II. 223, repr. opp. p. 216; Hourticq 1930, pl. 29; A. Joubin, 'Delacroix vu par lui-même', *GBA*, 6th per., XXI (1939), p. 306 n. 1; L. Johnson, 'Delacroix at the Biennale', *Burl Mag*, XCVIII (1956), pp. 327 and n. 2; *Sammlung Emil G. Bührle, Festschrift zu Ehren von Emil G. Bührle zur Eröffnung des Kunsthaus-Neubaus und Katalog der Sammlung Emil G. Bührle* (Kunsthaus, Zurich, 1958),

p. 85; R. Huyghe *et al.*, *Delacroix* (Hachette, Coll. Génie et Réalités, Paris, 1963), frontispiece in colour.

Print: Lithograph by Alfred Robaut, in catalogue of Dutilleux sale 1874.

Robaut states in R Ann that the lower part of the face, from the nose down, was painted by Constant Dutilleux, his father-in-law: 'Cᵗ Dutilleux montrant cette étude inachevée me témoigne tous ses regrets de la voir en cet état et il ajoute, quelques mois après: "Si j'osais, pourtant!" Devinant alors sa pensée, je vais au devant de ses explications et je reprends vivement: "Oui, oui, même pour la mémoire du Maître, il *faut* sauver l'œuvre que personne ne regarderait à cause de cette ablation et que le reste finirait même par être supprimé!" C'est alors que Dutilleux s'armant de courage remplit, du mieux qu'il put, le bas de la figure.' In a further annotation to his no. 69, Robaut added, alongside a note that this picture had since been acquired by Henri Rouart: 'qui ignore que *tout le bas de la figure à partir du nez* a été peint *complètement par C. Dutilleux* à qui Jenny avait offert cette œuvre *sacrifiée* par Delacroix lui-même.' Robaut, surprisingly, did not mention these facts in the published version of his catalogue, where the portrait is reproduced as it appeared after Dutilleux's interference. Joubin (op. cit., 1939), without referring to Robaut's notes, drew attention for the first time in print to the fact that the picture had suffered much from repainting and enlargement. In 1956, I published Robaut's annotations and stated that in addition to painting all parts below the level of the tip of the nose, Dutilleux had evidently added the painted strips of canvas (approximately 4.5 cm wide) that are attached to the top and left edges of the original fragment. In spite of the evidence, which might be thought to be conclusive, this portrait is ascribed to Delacroix without reserve in the 1958 catalogue of the Bührle collection, and reproduced as the frontispiece to a book that was published in 1963 to commemorate the centenary of the artist's death.

Dates ranging from 1824 to 1838, which have been proposed in ignorance of the facts known to Robaut, require no comment. The fragment by Delacroix seems consistent with Robaut's date of 1823, but could be as early as 1819.

D13 PORTRAIT OF PAUL   Pl. 182
BARROILHET (?) IN TURKISH
COSTUME

18¼ × 14¹⁵⁄₁₆ in. (46.3 × 38 cm)*
R173 (1826)
1826?
Musée du Louvre

Provenance: Gérard, in Nov. 1879;¹ M. P. Tesse (R); Gérard fils; bought from him by Bernheim-Jeune, Feb. 1892, who sold it to Cheramy, Feb. 1893 (Archives B-J, no. 6.089); P. A. Cheramy sale 5 May 1908, lot 163 (as 'Le

Chanteur Baroilhet en Turc'), to Baron Vitta, 3,600 fr.; his gift to the Atelier Delacroix, *c.* 1934; acquired by the Louvre (RF1953-37), 1953.

Exhibitions: Art Musulman, Paris 1893, no. 110; Nice 1930, no. 6; Louvre 1930, no. 45, repr. *Album*, p. 25; Atelier Delacroix, Paris 1934, no. 1 (then regularly included in the exhibitions at the Atelier until acquired by the Louvre in 1953—repr. as frontispiece for Cat. Exh. Atelier Delacroix, Paris 1937A); Zurich 1939, no. 309; Venice 1956, no. 10; Bordeaux 1960, no. 115, repr.; Atelier Delacroix, Paris 1963, no. 144; id., Paris 1967, no. 3; id., Paris 1969-70 (no cat.); id., Paris 1973 (no cat.)

Literature: *Journal* (1893-5 ed.) I. 301 n. 1; J. Meier-Graefe and E. Klossowski, *La Collection Cheramy . . .* (R. Piper, Munich, 1908), no. 206; Escholier I. 212, repr. in colour opp. p. 210, III. 128; *Journal* I. 217 n. 2; Sterling-Adhémar, no. 664, pl. 233; Johnson 1963, p. 51, repr. pl. 10; Escholier 1963, p. 39, repr. in colour p. 40; Huyghe, p. 205, repr. pl. 131.

This portrait poses a problem that can be simply stated: either it represents the French baritone Paul Barroilhet[2] and is not by Delacroix or it does not portray Barroilhet and could be by Delacroix. The former alternative is the more acceptable. Robaut was the first to record that the sitter was believed to be the singer, stating in the entry for this picture: 'on croit que le maître a fait ici le libre portrait du chanteur Baroilhet', and the identification has not been contested by subsequent writers. Also Robaut's dating of 1826 has been accepted, within a year either way, by everyone except Meier-Graefe-Klossowski (1908) who, while accepting that the sitter was Barroilhet, rightly held that in that case Robaut's date must be wrong. Certainly, comparison of this portrait with a photograph of Barroilhet (Fig. 30) seems to bear out Robaut's identification, but since the presumed sitter was born only in 1810,[3] this study could hardly be earlier than the mid-1840s, by which time Delacroix's style was quite unlike this. Stylistically and in its rich colouring it would make more sense as a Delacroix of *c.* 1826, but many infelicities of handling and drawing, the right leg and foot for instance, render his authorship doubtful at least.

---

[1] Inscription on copy in coloured crayons in Robaut Tracings I: 'Etude très riche de tons que me prête Gérard en 9bre 1879'.

[2] The name is almost invariably spelt with a single r in the Delacroix literature, but it contains two in the signatures on the autograph letters preserved in the Bibliothèque de l'Opéra, Paris, and in biographical notices compiled during his lifetime (see n. 3).

[3] Not 1805, as stated in the Delacroix literature. He was born at Bayonne on 22 September 1810, according to F. Roch, 'Notice biographique sur M. Barroilhet, artiste de l'Académie Royale de Musique', in M. E. Pascallet (ed.), *Revue générale biographique et nécrologique* (2nd ed., Paris, 1845), p. 6; see also F. J. Fétis, *Biographie universelle des musiciens* (2nd ed., Paris, 1860), I, under P. Barroilhet. He retired from the Opéra in 1847 and became a collector, of Delacroix among others. He died suddenly in Paris, in April 1871, while playing dominoes (see F. J. Fétis, op. cit., *Supplément et complément* (Paris, 1878), I).

Fig. 30. *Paul Barroilhet*, photograph.

D14 HEAD OF A WOMEN IN A RED TURBAN   Pl. 181

$16\frac{1}{4} \times 13\frac{7}{8}$ in. (41.3 × 35.2 cm)

False signature and date lower left: *EugDelacroix/1831*[1]

Moreau p. 283. R358 and 450 (catalogued twice by error, as Robaut admitted in the *Additions et Corrections* p. 484, where the picture is reproduced).

1831?

City Art Gallery, Bristol

Provenance: Frédéric Villot; his sale (M.F.V.) 11 Feb. 1865, lot 6, 145 fr.; Luquet; his sale 30 March 1868, lot 34; Giroux; his sale ('Liquidation de l'ancienne Maison Giroux') 7 March 1884, lot 26, 495 fr.; Comte Armand Doria, by 1885; his sale 4 May 1899, lot 140, 830 fr.; Dr. Sabouraud; with Benezit, Paris, Dec. 1946 (Dieterle R358); with Alfred Daber, by Jan. 1962; purchased from him by the Bristol City Art Gallery for £9,800 with the aid of a grant of £3,320 from the Victoria and Albert Museum, and a contribution of £500 from the National Art-Collections Fund, 1962.

Exhibitions: *EBA*, Paris 1885, no. 64; Cassirer, Berlin 1907, no. 12; Daber, Paris 1962, no. 3 (2 repr., pl. III in colour); Bordeaux 1963, no. 17; Edinburgh–London 1964, no. 26; Liverpool 1968, no. 26.

Literature: *Fifty-Ninth Annual Report of the National Art-Collections Fund: 1962* (Hertford House, London, 1963), p. 21, repr. pl. VIII; Escholier 1963, repr. in colour p. 101; R. Escholier, *Delacroix et les femmes* (Fayard, Paris, 1963), p. 73.

According to information in the catalogue of the Villot sale of 1865, which was no doubt supplied by Villot himself, this picture was painted by lamplight in 1831. In spite of a provenance that might normally be considered reliable, from the collection of a once intimate friend of the artist, the ascription to Delacroix is far from convincing. The addition of a false signature and date between 1868 and 1873 (see n. 1) suggests that some doubts were felt about its authenticity in the years immediately following Delacroix's death. The suspicions that must be aroused by the spurious signature appear to be confirmed by a heaviness in the modelling, especially in the neck, hair and turban, and by other crudities of handling, such as the ear and the wide brushstrokes across the bottom of the canvas.

The model has never been identified, though Escholier (*Delacroix et les femmes*) has suggested without much conviction that it may represent Mme Dalton. It was also said to be a study 'pour une figure du "Sardanapale"' (J125) in the catalogue of the Doria sale of 1899; this in spite of the fact that it was stated in the same catalogue to be dated 1835.

¹ The picture is stated in the catalogue of the Villot sale of Feb. 1865, which Villot himself helped to compile, to have been painted in 1831, but there is no mention of a signature or date on the canvas, whereas these are scrupulously recorded in entries for other paintings in the catalogue; nor is there mention of a signature and date in the catalogue of the Luquet sale of 1868. Moreau (1873), however, states: 'Signé à gauche. Daté 1833.' The rather primitive signature and date, untypically applied to a *tête d'étude*, were thus evidently added between 1868 and 1873. It is the discrepancy between the dates given in the sale catalogue and in Moreau which caused Robaut to catalogue this picture twice, once under 1831 (R358) and again under 1833 (R450). When he was able to see and reproduce the picture himself, at the time of the Giroux sale in 1884 (see R p. 484), he was unable to decide if it was dated 1831 or 1833 and doubted the authenticity of both signature and date, which he noted as 'faux?' on his drawing in Tracings II.

R32 PORTRAIT OF   Pl. 183
M. WASHINGTON IN GREEK COSTUME
Panel. 18⅛ × 13¾ in. (46 × 35 cm) E.D.
Moreau p. 230. R124 (No repr.)
1825?
Private collection, Paris

Provenance: Delacroix's posthumous sale Feb. 1864, lot 76 (as 'Grec debout, tenant un fusil'. Burty Ann ED: 'vers

1827.'), to Pastré, 800 fr.; Mme Pastré de Régny; with Lorenceau, Paris, May 1948 (Dieterle R124).

Exhibition: Bordeaux 1963, no. 8.

Literature: None, other than Moreau and Robaut.

Moreau (1873) was the first to date this portrait to 1825 and to identify the model as a M. Washington, stating that he was a friend of the artist's. It is not known on what evidence he based these conclusions, which were all followed by Robaut, who had clearly never seen the picture. No one by the name of Washington (except George, the first President of the United States) is mentioned in Delacroix's published writings, but Moreau presumably had verbal information from a source he trusted. The painting does not, in any case, appear to be from Delacroix's hand and must have been falsely classified with his works in the catalogue of his posthumous sale. A painter of oriental subjects by the name of Georges Washington, born at Marseille in 1827, may be both the subject and the executant.

R33 PORTRAIT OF COUNT   Pl. 184
DEMETRIUS DE PALATIANO IN
SULIOT COSTUME

16⅛ × 13 in. (41 × 33 cm)* Traces of false signature bottom left.¹
Cleveland Museum of Art

Provenance: Entered in Arch Goupil/Boussod as *Figure turque*, under nos. 15099, 15136, 15138, 15510:² (1) acquired on 26 Jan. 1881 from de Laage for an unspecified sum and sold to Daupias on 1 Feb. 1881 for 6,700 fr.; (2) repurchased from Daupias on 7 Feb. 1881 at an unspecified price and sold to Hattat on the same date for 7,500 fr.; (3) bought back from Hattat on 8 Feb. 1881 for 4,200 fr., sold to Goldschmidt of Frankfurt on 4 Apr. 1881 for 7,500 fr.; (4) bought back from Goldschmidt on 22 June 1881 at 2,430 fr. and received 4,200 fr. from Escribe on 25 May 1887.³ On this last date it passed in the sale liquidation Goupil & Cⁱᵉ (auctioneer, Escribe), lot 43 ('Figure turque', 39 × 31 cm), to Brame, 2,550 fr. [6,105 fr. without name of buyer: ann. cat. Knoedler's, London]; P. A. Cheramy, by 1907; his sale, 5 May 1908, lot 159, repr. (as by Delacroix, Salon 1827), to Schoeller (for Count Pastré: Dieterle R), 18,100 fr.; Count Pastré, to at least 1930; D. David-Weill; Mme D. David-Weill, his widow, d. 1970; with Robert Schmit, Paris; with Eugene Thaw, New York; Cleveland Museum of Art (73.33), 1973.

Exhibitions: (In every catalogue as by Delacroix, and generally Salon 1827) *EBA*, Paris 1885, no. 31 ('Le comte Palatiano, en costume de Palikare. Salon 1827', 41 × 33 cm.

Lent by Boussod, Valadon & Cie); Petit, Paris 1910, no. 74; Paris 1922, no. 64; Louvre 1930, no. 27, repr. *Album*, p. 15; Louvre 1963, no. 77, *M* no. 80, repr.; Berne 1963-4, no. 17; Paris 1966-7, no. 102; Schmit, Paris 1972, no. 15, repr. in colour.

Literature: (Earliest evidence of ownership and major monographs only.) Probably Georges Seurat, notes of 11 November 1881 taken at Goupil's, published by F. Fénéon, in *Bulletin de la vie artistique*, 1 April 1922, and reprinted in J. de Laprade, *Seurat*, 2nd ed., Paris 1951, p. 91;[4] L. Rouart, 'La Collection de M. Chéramy' [*sic*], *Les Arts*, no. 64 (Apr. 1907), p. 22, repr. p. 26; J. Meier-Graefe and E. Klossowski, *La Collection Cheramy* (Piper, Munich, 1908), no. 157, repr.; L. Roger-Milès, *Vingt peintres du XIXe siècle. Chefs-d'œuvre de l'école française* (Imp. Geo. Petit, Paris, 1911), p. 150, repr. (Borrel etching) p. 137; Moreau-Nélaton I. 86, repr. fig. 60; Escholier I. 214, repr. opp. p. 214; Hourticq 1930, repr. p. 14; Huyghe, pp. 166, 173; Trapp, pp. 59 and n., 77, 120.

Print: Etching by F. M. Borrel, for L. Roger-Milès, *Vingt peintres du XIXe siècle*, 1911.

In spite of the unanimity of opinion published since 1885, that this is the portrait of Count Palatiano exhibited at the Salon of 1827, documentary and stylistic considerations make it impossible to maintain this view or to retain the attribution to Delacroix. Its early history as recorded in Arch Goupil/Boussod (see *Provenance*) shows that it was sold back to these dealers three times within five months, at a very substantial loss on the two occasions when the return price is listed. Then it remained unsold for six years, until it was put up for auction in 1887. Such a history suggests that from an early date few had faith in its authenticity. The fact that Goupil/Boussod, Valadon repeatedly entered it in their books, and sold it at public auction, under the title *Figure turque*, in spite of its bearing on the stretcher the inscription, recently uncovered, 'Ebauche du Portrait du Cte Palatiano peint par E. Delacroix dans l'atelier de Villot gravé par Villot en 1833',[5] suggests further that they had no confidence in its being an autograph version of the portrait of Count Palatiano shown at the Salon. It is inconceivable that this picture, which is at once too highly finished to be a preliminary sketch and too little finished in parts to be a Salon portrait, could have been painted as a sketch for the lost Salon painting, which must have been roughly the same size (see J(L)80). Unfortunately, in the course of those years when it was lying on Boussod, Valadon's hands, it found its way into the crucially important exhibition *EBA*, Paris 1885, and hence into the basic literature, as the original portrait of Count Palatiano.[6] Very crudely painted in parts, particularly the right foot and left hand, it must in fact be considered a copy after the lost original. If Robaut was right in listing Villot as the first owner (see n. 3), it might well be

the copy by Frédéric Villot, who also engraved the original, described in Robaut (under R170) as 'une copie de petites dimensions qui appartient à son [Villot] fils.' For a more finished copy of the lost original, see J(R)34. For biographical details of Count Palatiano, a discussion of dating and of the studies connected with his portrait and reproduction of Villot's etching of it, see J(L)80.

[1] The signature, *Eug. Delacroix*, which had all but disappeared when the picture was acquired for Cleveland, was already faint and partially obliterated when I inspected it in the David-Weill collection in 1960. It is just visible in the reproduction in Escholier (1926). It first appears, scarcely discernible, in the reproduction in Louis Rouart's article of April 1907 and a little later in Meier-Graefe and Klossowski's catalogue of the Cheramy collection, 1908, though it is not mentioned in their text. It was presumably added after 1885, since Robaut noted then that it was not signed (in annotation to 2nd ed. of cat. exh. *EBA*, Paris 1885: *Bib AA*, MS. 298ter, no. 31).

[2] When labels and binding paper were removed at my request from the back of the picture by the Cleveland Museum of Art in 1975, this last number was revealed in three places on the stretcher, in each case preceded by the letters 'G & C', undoubtedly standing for 'Goupil et Compagnie'. It is the stock number used in the last entry for the *Figure turque* in Arch Goupil/Boussod, with a cross-reference to the earlier stock numbers 15138 and 15099. No. 15136 is used for the second entry, which has a cross-reference to no. 15099.

[3] Robaut (R Ann, margin to R170) notes the following owners before the picture was acquired by Goupil, for 4,000 fr. according to him: Villot, Heymann, Verdier, Petit; but Robaut may have partially confused its history with that of J(R)34.

[4] Seurat describes the picture as an '*Oriental*' by Delacroix and analyses it in some detail, writing of the 'tête très fine, merveilleuse. [. . .] le manteau empâté dans les ornements brodés d'or [. . .] Les ombres et tout le reste, hachés et vibrants, — la pommette, les ombres du turban. C'est l'application la plus stricte des principes scientifiques vus à travers une personnalité.' It seems that Seurat could only be referring to our picture, which was with Goupil/Boussod, Valadon from June 1881 to May 1887.

[5] One of the Goupil stock numbers mentioned in n. 2 is heavily marked over this inscription, which may therefore be assumed to have existed when the picture was with Goupil's.

[6] That the Cleveland picture is the painting which Boussod, Valadon & Cie are known from several sources to have lent to the exhibition *EBA* 1885, where it was shown as the Salon portrait of Count Palatiano and accepted as such by Robaut, is firmly established by the fact that between 1 January 1861 and 5 November 1918 the books of Goupil/Boussod, Valadon list no work by Delacroix other than the *Figure turque*, which is now known to be the Cleveland picture (see *Provenance* and n. 2), that could be thought to represent Count Palatiano.

R34 PORTRAIT OF COUNT DEMETRIUS DE PALATIANO IN SULIOT COSTUME
Pl. 185

$15\frac{13}{16} \times 12\frac{7}{16}$ in. (40.2 × 31.6 cm)* Relined. Signature scratched into the paint surface bottom right: *Eug. Delacroix*

Private collection, New York

Provenance: Francis Petit, d. *c.* 1879 (for possible previous owners, see preceding number, n. 3); with Charles Haseltine, Philadelphia; A. J. Antelo, Philadelphia, by 1893, d. Jan. 1903; his sale, Philadelphia, 24 March 1903, lot 90, repr. (as by Delacroix, 'An Albanian Officer', stated in cat.

to have been the 'admiration of Mr. Wm. H. Stewart in Paris, and would have been bought for his collection' had it not already been sold), $2,400; sale Charles Cramp and other owners, Philadelphia, 9 Nov. 1903, lot 474, repr. (same description, but adding that, when admired by Stewart, it was in the possession of Francois [*sic*] Petit, who owned it 'until his death'); Alfred Devereux, grandson of A. J. Antelo; he sold it to Knoedler's, New York, Jan. 1914 (their stock no. C4221 on stretcher); they sold it to James J. Hill of St. Paul, Minnesota, at a New York address, 1914, d. 1916; with French & Co., New York; with Nathan, Zurich, 1960; with Adolphe Stein, Paris, by 1964 to *c.* 1969; with Claude Aubry, Paris.

Exhibition: Philadelphia 1893, no. 38 (as 'An Albanian Officer', lent by A. J. Antelo).

Literature: None known.

Cleaner in outline, particularly in the right foot, and crisper in detail than the Cleveland version (preceding number), this may well reflect the lost Salon painting more accurately.

Examination under the microscope shows the signature to have been scratched into the surface at the same time or a few months after the paint was applied. There is no known instance of Delacroix's having incised a full signature into a painting. This method of signing may have been adopted by one of his pupils or friends as a means of indicating that the picture was a replica,[1] done perhaps under Delacroix's supervision. It was possibly painted by Frédéric Villot, who may have been its first owner (see J(R)33, n. 3 and end of main entry).

[1] Students competing at the Ecole des Beaux-Arts sometimes scratched the names of their professors into the surface of their paintings, albeit less delicately than here. Dassy, for example, a pupil of Meynier, did this with his prize-winning *Torso* of 1821 preserved at the Ecole des Beaux-Arts.

Allegory

R35 GREECE ON THE RUINS   Pl. 186
OF MISSOLONGHI, sketch

$16\frac{1}{2} \times 10\frac{13}{16}$ in. (42 × 27.5 cm)*
R206 (1827. No repr.)
c. 1850?
Oskar Reinhart Collection, Winterthur

Provenance: Constant Dutilleux; his posthumous sale, 26 March 1874, lot 6 ('N'a jamais passé en vente.' Lithographic repr.), 580 fr.; Alfred Robaut, his son-in-law, 1874?–1885; he sold it to P. A. Cheramy for 1,000 fr. in 1885 (R Ann); his sale, 5 May 1908, no. 152, not sold; sale his estate, 15 Apr. 1913, lot 17, to the dealer Cassirer, 5,000 fr.; Oscar Schmitz, Dresden, d. Zurich 1933; his collection bought by Messrs. Wildenstein; Oskar Reinhart, 1936.

Exhibitions: *EBA*, Paris 1885, no. 178; Art Musulman, Paris 1893, no. 109; Cassirer, Berlin 1907, no. 8; Rosenberg, Paris 1928, no. 7; Louvre 1930, no. 37; Wildenstein, Paris 1936, no. 27, repr.; Zurich 1939, no. 316.

Literature: In addition to the catalogues of the exhibitions listed above, the following selected references may be found useful: Meier-Graefe 1922, p. 20 n. 1, repr. p. 100; P. Courthion, *Le Romantisme* (Editions d'Art Albert Skira, Geneva, 1961), repr. in colour p. 31; L. Johnson, 'Pierre Andrieu, un "polisson"?', *Revue de l'Art*, no. 21 (1973), p. 68 and n., repr. fig. 5; R. Koella, *Collection Oskar Reinhart* (Bibliothèque des Arts, Paris, 1975), pp. 134, 334, repr. pl. 52.

The authenticity of this 'sketch', thought to be a preliminary study for the painting of 1826 (J98), was not challenged in the Delacroix literature before 1973, when I attributed it to Pierre Andrieu (op. cit.) and published the following note about it from R Ann (margin to R 206): 'Cédé à M. Cheramy 1000 fr. 1885, avec extrait de lettre d'Andrieu laquelle dit que c'est de Delacroix tandis que lui s'est vanté de l'avoir peinte.' The attribution depends on whether one believes Andrieu's boast of having painted it himself or his letter certifying that it was painted by Delacroix. In my opinion, the style leaves no doubt that it is a copy by Andrieu after J98.

Historical and Literary Subjects

O9 THE WITCHES' SABBATH   Pl. 189

$31\frac{7}{8} \times 39\frac{3}{8}$ in. (0.81 × 1.00 m)*

Private collection, Paris

Provenance: ? Bequeathed by the artist to George Sand in 1863, d. 1876; Mme Lauth-Sand, by 1930; Mme Alexandrine de Rothschild, d. 1965; by her bequest to Edmond de Rothschild, her nephew.

Exhibition: (Louvre 1930, provisional cat., no. 76, not exhibited.)

Literature: ? Silvestre *Delacroix* (1855), p. 82; ? Delacroix's will, 3 Aug. 1863, transcribed in *Correspondance* (Burty 1878), p. vi; ? Inv. Delacroix, no. 137; Escholier II. 164, repr. opp. p. 166; *Journal* III. 374 n. 5—Supp.

This picture is omitted from Robaut either by accident or design. It is stated in Escholier and in the provisional catalogue of the exhibition Louvre 1930 to be the sketch of this subject which Delacroix left to George Sand. The bequest is described in his will as 'une grande esquisse représentant le *Sabbat de Faust* (effet de nuit)'. Though he does not specify in the will that the work is from his hand, it is attributed to him in Inv. Delacroix, where it is described under no. 137 as '1 tableau représentant le *Sabbat de Faust* par [M. Delacroix] légué à Mme Sand'. And the sketch he left to George Sand is likely to have been a work which appears in a list compiled by Delacroix in the 1840s and restricted apparently to pictures from his own hand, as '*Le Sabbat*, grande esquisse, clair de lune.' (*Journal* III. 374 —Supp.) It should, moreover, probably be identified with the work listed during his lifetime in Silvestre *Delacroix* (1855), as '*Le Sabbat*, grande esquisse destinée à un diorama (1833).'

The problem is that for stylistic reasons it is difficult to attribute the present picture to Delacroix without reserve; which raises the question of whether it is certainly the sketch left to George Sand and, if so, whether it might not even then be the work of a pupil (George Sand's son Maurice?) influenced by Delacroix's ideas for compositions on this subject that were never realized as finished paintings. A water-colour of the subject passed in his posthumous sale (lot 309. R269 (1828)) and was sold to Cheramy by Robaut in 1887 (R Ann). An oil sketch, placed in 1824 by Robaut, also passed in the posthumous sale (J(L)97).

O10 COMBAT BETWEEN TWO   Pl. 190
HORSEMEN IN ARMOUR

$31\frac{3}{4} \times 39\frac{3}{8}$ in. (0.807 × 1.00 m)*

Apparently false signature bottom right: *Eug. Delacroix*

Moreau p. 318. R1512 (1825)

Musée du Louvre

Provenance: Probably Delacroix's posthumous sale, Feb. 1864, lot 144 ('[Esquisse.] Deux chevaliers combattant dans la campagne', without dimensions or further description), to Isambert (Burty Ann ED) or Haro (Moreau and Robaut), 820 fr.; Haro, by Aug. 1864; Comte de Lambertye; his sale (Comte . . .), 17 Dec. 1868, lot 21 ('Combat de chevaliers. Vente Delacroix', 0.80 × 1.00 m), 2,020 fr.; anon. sale, 3 June 1884, lot 12 ('Combat de Cavaliers', 78.5 × 31 [*sic*] cm),[1] to Diot, 1,350 fr.; Étienne Moreau-Nélaton, by 1906; he donated it to the Louvre in 1906 (RF 1655). At Musée des arts décoratifs 1907–34; transferred to Louvre 1934.

Exhibitions: Bd Italiens, Paris 1864, no. 49 ('Deux chevaliers combattant dans la campagne. Esquisse', 0.80 × 1.00 m, lent by Haro); Louvre 1930, no. 54 (as 'Etude pour la bataille de Nancy'); Atelier Delacroix, Paris 1946A and B, no. 2; id., Paris 1963, no. 140; id., Paris 1974 (no cat.)

Literature: *Catalogue de la Collection Moreau . . .* (Frazier-Soye, Paris, 1907 and 1923), no. 56; Moreau-Nélaton I. 100 f., repr. fig. 76, II. 246; Brière 1924, p. 82; Hourticq 1930, pl. 18; Sterling-Adhémar, no. 670, pl. 236; Huyghe, pp. 279, 301, repr. fig. 203; Bortolatto, repr. in colour pl. XIII, full-page colour detail of horseman on right, pl. XIV.

Though unconfirmed by the presence of a seal of Delacroix's posthumous sale on the back, the identification of this painting with lot 144 in that sale, proposed by Moreau, Robaut and later cataloguers, appears to be corroborated by the description, which adds dimensions, of the picture of this subject in the catalogue of the exhibition *Bd Italiens*, Paris 1864.

The difficulty lies in determining whether it was rightly or wrongly attributed to Delacroix at the time of the sale, and, if rightly, whether it was not extensively tampered with after the sale. Robaut was of the opinion that the signature had been added after the sale, and while it is difficult to disagree with him on that point, it must also be asked if the additions were limited to the signature. Some areas of the picture, particularly the horses' legs and the ground about them, seem consistent with a genuine work by Delacroix such as *Two Horses Fighting in the Open* of c. 1828 (J54), but it is hard to reconcile the appearance of the surface as a whole with early paintings of comparable scenes, with the *Combat of the Giaour and Hassan* (J114), for example, or the *Battle of Nancy* (J143), for which Moreau-Nélaton (I. 100) considered this to be a preliminary study. A possible, and to my mind likely, explanation for this inconsistency of style is that, described as an 'esquisse' in the catalogue of the posthumous sale, the picture was in a very much sketchier state at the time of Delacroix's death than now, and that Haro had it 'finished' and signed before disposing of it. That Haro was capable of such an act is recorded by Léon Riesener, as well as by Philippe Burty who wrote in 1885: 'Les esquisses, les ébauches, les frottis, acquis à la vente posthume par M. Haro, avaient été déplorablement terminés.' (Note published by H. Bessis, 'Trois albums de dessins de Pierre Andrieu au Cabinet des Dessins', *Revue du Louvre*, 18 (1968), p. 148 n. 5. See also J(M)3).

This may in its original state have been the sketch Delacroix refers to in a list of his works compiled in the 1840s, as 'L'esquisse commencée pour Leblond, 2 chevaliers.' (*Journal* III. 371 —Supp.) Dated to 1825 by Robaut, followed by Huyghe (1963), it is placed 'probably contemporary with the *Battle of Nancy*' in the Catalogue of the Moreau Collection, about 1830 by Brière and Sterling–Adhémar, and in 1826 by Hourticq.

¹ The width given in the catalogue is evidently an error, and Robaut's listing of this sale in the provenance is no doubt reliable since the auction was held in Paris only shortly before his *catalogue raisonné* was published.

D15 THE BARQUE OF DANTE, sketch   Pl. 188

Cardboard, sight size $5\frac{7}{16} \times 8\frac{1}{4}$ in. (13.8×21 cm)*
Raymond Escholier, Paris

Provenance: Apparently given by the artist to his cousin Léon Riesener; by descent to the wife of the present owner.

Exhibition: Atelier Delacroix, Paris 1963, no. 135.

Literature: None.

Stylistically, this sketch does not seem to be from Delacroix's hand and it is listed here as a doubtful rather than a rejected work only because it bears this pen inscription on a label on the back:

Une des premières idées d'un Dante, par
Eugène Delacroix.
M'a été donné par lui
[signed] L Riesener

D16 THE EXECUTION OF MARINO FALIERO, sketch   Pl. 191

Cardboard, $13\frac{3}{4} \times 10\frac{5}{8}$ in. (35×27 cm)
Presumably Moreau p. 257 and R161 (1826. No repr. R Ann adds 'Peint sur' to the printed description 'Papier'.)
Whereabouts unknown

Provenance: Presumably Frédéric Villot; presumably his sale (M.F.V.) 11 Feb. 1865, lot 4 ('Marino Faliero [. . .] Esquisse peinte sur carton du tableau exécuté en 1826 et exposé en 1827', 35 × 27 cm. Moreau-Nélaton annotated

catalogue of the sale, *BN Estampes*: 'à peine fait'), 420 fr.; Point and Le Senna (Dieterle R); anon. sale, 17 May 1929, lot 48 (as R161 and out of Villot sale), to MM. Léon Helft, fils, 19,600 fr.; with them to at least 1930; Baron Cassel van Doorn, Englewood, N.J., U.S.A.; sale his estate, Parke Bernet, New York 9 Dec. 1955, lot 295, repr., to Bernard Reis, $1,700.

Exhibition: Louvre 1930, no. 32.

Literature: *Mémorial*, mentioned under no. 92; *Wallace Collection Catalogues. Pictures and Drawings . . .* , 16th ed. (London, 1968), p. 86.

Though this sketch appears to have an excellent provenance and I have not seen the original, I find it impossible to accept its authenticity on the evidence of a photograph. With the pointed arch in the lower right, it reflects however an early stage in the development of the final painting of this subject (see J112 and Fig. 12), and such infelicities as the head of the executioner could be the result of retouching by a later hand. But these various characteristics seem best explained by attributing it to an artist such as Poterlet, who is known to have been working in close touch with Delacroix in the latter half of the 1820s and to have painted analogous versions of his pictures of that period (see J114 and J125).

D17 RENAISSANCE SCENE   Pl. 191

$19\frac{5}{16} \times 29\frac{1}{2}$ in. (49×75 cm)¹
Signed bottom right: *Eug. Delacroix.*
Whereabouts unknown

Provenance: Said to have been given by George Sand to Gustave Chaix d'Est Ange, d. 1876; Gustave Chaix d'Est Ange, his son; Mlle Sipière, his stepdaughter, by 1907; E. du Bourg, Comte de Bozas, her husband (?), by 1930; sale Chaix d'Est Ange, 11 Dec. 1934, lot 2 (repr.); Pearl White, in U.S.A. (?)

Exhibitions: Louvre 1930, no. 205, repr. *Album*, p. 26.

Literature: J. du Teil, 'La Collection Chaix d'Est-Ange', *Les Arts*, no. 67 (July 1907), p. 20; Hourticq 1930, repr. p. 75; Huyghe, p. 206, repr. pl. 151.

The history of this picture down to 1907 is taken from Baron Joseph du Teil (op. cit.). Chaix d'Est Ange was a famous lawyer and acquaintance of Delacroix's.

Though there is a drawing for the setting and, possibly, for the head of the principal figure on a sheet that has been attributed to Delacroix in an album in the Louvre (RF10418. Exh. Louvre 1930, no. 772b; Louvre 1963, *Cat. de Visite*, no. 149, withdrawn), neither the painting nor the signature seems to me authentic from photographs.

¹ According to the catalogue of the sale Chaix d'Est Ange, 1934; 57 × 77 cm, according to that of the exhibition Louvre 1930 and Hourticq 1930.

R36 THE BARQUE OF DANTE   Pl. 188

$10\frac{3}{4} \times 14$ in. (27.3 × 35.5 cm)*

R50 (1822. No repr.)

Peter Nathan, Zurich

Provenance: Received from the artist by Alphonse Royer (R), d. 1875; by his bequest to Charles Narrey (R); by his bequest to Mme Jane Nicollet; she sold it to Jean Dieterle, 3 March 1937; he sold it to Rosenberg; he sold it to D. David-Weill (history after Narrey from Dieterle R); Mme D. David-Weill, his widow, d. 1970; with Peter Nathan, Zurich, by 1973.

Exhibitions: *EBA*, Paris 1885, no. 158 ('Dante et Virgile dans la barque (Réduction.)', 25 × 34 cm, lent by M. Ch. Narrey. Removed between 1st and 2nd editions of the catalogue); Louvre 1963, no. 27, M no. 28, repr.; Petit Palais, Paris 1968–9, no. 266.

Literature: L. Johnson, 'The Delacroix Centenary in France—I', *Burl Mag*, CV (1963), p. 305, repr. fig. 4; Trapp, p. 24 and n.

Robaut described his No. 50 as follows:

Toile. — H. O^m 25, L. O^m 34. — Réduction du précédent [the Salon painting, J100] avec une légère suppression.

Appartient à M. Charles Narrey, à qui il a été légué par M. Alphonse Royer, qui l'avait lui-même reçu de Eugène Delacroix.

His drawing of it in Tracings I is inscribed in the lower right corner: 'il n'y a pas dans ce coin les 2 bustes d'hommes qui se mordent.' The 'légère suppression', unspecified in Robaut's published catalogue, is thus defined and corresponds with the present picture, which also bears an old pen inscription on the stretcher:

> J'ai promis à notre ami Delacroix de ne pas laisser toucher à cette esquisse; — j'ai tenu ma promesse — bien que tu n'aies rien promis fais comme moi.
>
> [signed] Baude. (Pour Alphonse Royer)[1]

These facts, combined with the details of later provenance recorded in Dieterle R, establish this picture as R50, and on Robaut's authority it was accepted as a genuine work in 1963, being shown as a sketch for the Salon painting in the centennial exhibition at the Louvre, rather than as the 'réduction' Robaut supposed it to be.

On stylistic grounds alone the attribution to Delacroix now seems to me unacceptable, and there is good reason to suppose that Robaut also revised his opinion in spite of the ostensibly excellent provenance, since he noted alongside the entry for this picture in the first edition of the catalogue of the exhibition *EBA*, Paris 1885: 'à supprimer' (*Bib AA*, MS. 298), and it was deleted from the second edition. It is probably a pupil's copy, as the inscription on the stretcher leaves little doubt that it came from Delacroix's studio.

[1] Sérullaz (*Mémorial*, no. 28), altering 'Pour' to 'A', interprets the parenthesis as meaning that the inscription was written by Baude to Royer

and therefore concludes that the former was the first owner. In view of Robaut's statement that the latter personally received the picture from Delacroix and of the fact that Baude was Royer's doctor (Dieterle R), it seems more likely that Baude wrote and signed the note on behalf of his patient, who was perhaps too ill to write it himself and wished to leave these instructions to his heir.

R37 DEATH OF CATO   Pl. 187

$23\frac{5}{8} \times 17\frac{5}{16}$ in. (60 × 44 cm)

R113 (1824)

Musée Fabre, Montpellier

Provenance: Alfred Bruyas, Montpellier, by Jan. 1869; by his bequest to the town of Montpellier, Nov. 1876.

Exhibitions: Paris and Berne 1939, no. 37 and 31.

Literature: A. Bruyas *et al.*, *La Galerie Bruyas* (Quantin, Paris, 1876), pp. 270 f. (catalogue entry by A. Bruyas); G. Lafenestre and E. Michel, *Musée de Montpellier*, in *Inventaire général des richesses d'art de la France. Province. Monuments civils* (Plon, Paris, 1878), I, p. 204; *Catalogue des peintures et sculptures exposées dans les galeries du Musée Fabre . . .* (Imp. Serre et Roumégous, Montpellier, 1904), no. 149; Meier-Graefe 1922, repr. p. 94; A. Joubin, *Catalogue des peintures et sculptures exposées dans les galeries du Musée Fabre de la ville de Montpellier* (Blondel La Rougery, Paris, 1926), no. 460; Escholier I, p. 132, repr. p. 129; Hourticq 1930, pl. 12; Huyghe, pp. 176, 206, 522 n. 20, repr. pl. 144 and fig. 9; Bortolatto, repr. in colour pl. III.

Print: Lithograph by J. Laurens, pl. 4 in his series entitled 'Galerie Bruyas'.

In a letter from Paris dated 13 January 1869, Théophile Silvestre wrote to Alfred Bruyas, acknowledging receipt of a photograph of this painting: 'J'ai bien tardé à vous remercier de la photographie du *Caton*, d'après votre tableau d'Eugène Delacroix. Elle me semble donner une bonne idée de la peinture. L'épreuve, douce et bien fondue, rend le mieux possible l'original, particulièrement remarquable par l'exécution; car la chûte assez étrange du personnage est plutôt une Académie très bien peinte qu'un *Caton*, même en dégringolade. La tête est d'un caractère ample et magnifique de statue antique; et le modelé des chairs d'une palpitante souplesse. L'influence de Géricault s'y fait un peu sentir.'[1] This is the first record, to my knowledge, of the picture's being in the possession of Alfred Bruyas and attributed to Delacroix. It is not known from what source he acquired it. The attribution was rightly questioned by Lafenestre and Michel in their 1878 catalogue of the Montpellier Museum, in which it was also stated that the picture was first attributed to Géricault. Doubts about Delacroix's authorship were reiterated in the Museum's catalogues of 1904 and 1926. In view of these doubts, expressed from as early as 1878 in the official catalogues of the institution which owns the painting, it is remarkable that it should have been reproduced and commented on by Robaut (1885), Escholier (1926) and Huyghe (1964) without any indication of its being a controversial attribution, the last author even making it serve to illustrate a development in Delacroix's style. In my opinion the painting is wholly uncharacteristic of Delacroix and I feel no hesitation in rejecting it.

Robaut assigned the picture to the year 1824 (a date which has been generally followed ever since), evidently because he thought it showed the influence of an academy figure known as *Hector* which David had painted in Rome in 1778 and, according to Robaut, exhibited at the Salon of 1824. While there is an undeniable similarity between the diagonal disposition of the figure here and in David's *Hector* (also in the Musée Fabre, since 1851; there is a copy in the Louvre—RF3697), a similarity illustrated by Huyghe (pls. 144 and 145), it should be remarked that no paintings by David are listed in the catalogue of the Salon of 1824 and its supplements. The basis of Robaut's dating therefore appears to be as insecure as the attribution.

¹ *Bib AA*, MS. 215 Correspondance de Th. Silvestre avec A. Bruyas 1854-1875, I, doc. 10.

R38 DEATH OF CATO, sketch

Wood panel, $9\frac{1}{2} \times 7\frac{3}{16}$ in. (24.2 × 18.3 cm)* False E.D.
Private collection, Paris

Provenance: With Gairac; he sold it to Léon Suzor, by 1958, d. 1962; anon. sale (by Ph. Engelmann), Hôtel Drouot, 19 March 1965, lot 79; the present owner, by June 1966.

Exhibition: Charpentier, Paris 1953, no. 52.

Literature: None.

This picture, claimed in the catalogue of the 1965 sale to be a study for the painting of the same subject at Montpellier (J(R)37), is equally wrongly attributed to Delacroix.

R39 FAUST, WAGNER AND THE POODLE, sketch

Pl. 192

Oil on cardboard, $14\frac{3}{4} \times 11\frac{1}{4}$ in. (37.5 × 28.5 cm) Andrieu sale stamp bottom right
R Ann 238ter (1827)
Musée des Beaux-Arts, Le Havre

Provenance: Pierre Andrieu; his sale 6 May 1892, lot 180 ('Faust, Méphisto et le barbet', without dimensions or further description), 205 fr.; anon. sale, Hôtel Drouot, 11 March 1909, lot 27, 810 fr.; Charles Auguste Marande; by his bequest to the Musée des Beaux-Arts (A 444), Le Havre, 1936.

Exhibitions: None.

Literature: Bortolatto, no. 900.

Though listed in the catalogue of the Andrieu sale as by Delacroix (an attribution that has not been contested since 1892), this picture, justly described in R Ann as an 'esquisse indécise', is clearly by Andrieu rather than by his master.

R40 FAUST, WAGNER AND THE POODLE

Pl. 193

$16\frac{1}{8} \times 13$ in. (41 × 33 cm)
False signature and date bottom left: *Eug. Delacroix/1825*.
R Ann 238bis (1827).
Whereabouts unknown

Provenance: Alexandre Dumas fils; his sale 12 May 1892, lot 36 ('*Faust et le docteur Wagner*. Faust et Wagner devisant dans la campagne sont poursuivis par le barbet. La nuit va bientôt paraître et le paysage est déjà enveloppé des vapeurs du soir; le ciel est encore enflammé par les reflets du soleil qui a disparu à l'horizon. Signé à gauche: Eug. Delacroix. Toile, 40 × 31 cm.'), to Brame (?), 3,655 fr.; Jules Ferry (?); A. Ferry, by 1912 (Dieterle R); Mme Abel Ferry, to 1965; bought from her by Walter Goetz, who sold it to Eugene Thaw, New York, who in turn sold it to Krugier, a Swiss dealer; mixed sale, Christie's, London 28 June 1968, lot 35 (repr.), £5,500 (bought in ?).

Exhibitions: None.

Literature: None.

Robaut listed lot 36 in the Dumas sale as R Ann 238bis, perhaps without having seen it, and the present painting is presumed to be that lot. Though it is, in my opinion, by Pierre Andrieu, it may, with the previous number, reflect a lost painting by Delacroix; for during the artist's lifetime Silvestre *Delacroix* (1855) listed (p. 80) immediately after the *Mephistopheles Appears before Faust* (J116) a *Faust et Méphistophélès dans les champs*, referring probably to the subject of this painting which, treated with the same design in the *Faust* series of lithographs (Delteil, no. 61), has been consistently misnamed by the French cataloguers, including Robaut, as *Faust, Mephistopheles and the Poodle*.

R41 THE MURDER OF THE BISHOP OF LIÈGE, sketch

Pl. 194

$23\frac{5}{8} \times 28\frac{15}{16}$ in. (60 × 73.5 cm)
Moreau p. 246 n. 1 ?
Destroyed during World War II

Provenance: ? the 'esquisse de l'Evêque de Liège' sold by Petit to P. Durand-Ruel, Feb. 1872, 18,000 fr., who returned it 16 June 1877 (Toupet, op. cit. *infra*, 1963, p. 90 n. 28); Georges d'Espagnat, by 1930, to at least 1939.

Exhibitions: Louvre 1930, no. 41 (as 'une première pensée pour le tableau de 1829'), repr. *Album*, p. 26; Zurich 1939, no. 311 (as R. 196 [J133]).

Literature: M. Toupet, 'L'Assassinat de l'évêque de Liège par Eugène Delacroix', *Revue du Louvre*, 13 (1963), pp. 89-91, 90 n. 28, repr. fig. 8; Maltese, p. 151, under no. 24.

This work has no established history before 1930, and the 'Réduction' referred to in Moreau p. 246 n. 1 is more likely to be J133 than this sketch, as is the sketch bought from Petit by Durand-Ruel in 1872. From photographs it appears in any case to have been a pupil's copy based on the Lyon sketch (J133).

R42 BOISSY D'ANGLAS AT THE NATIONAL CONVENTION, sketch   Pl. 195

$16 \times 21\frac{5}{16}$ in. (40.7×54.2 cm)*
Signed lower left: *E.D.*
Smith College Museum of Art, Northampton, Mass.

Provenance: Durand-Ruel, Paris, by 1896; with Durand-Ruel, New York, May 1896 to Feb. 1919; Paul Sachs, U.S.A., Feb. 1919 to May 1921; with Durand-Ruel, New York, May 1921 to Nov. 1928; purchased from them by the Smith College Museum of Art, Nov. 1928. (Whole provenance from Arch D-R.)

Exhibitions: Chicago 1930, no. 4, repr.; Louvre 1930, no. 56; Knoedler, New York and Chicago 1938-9, no. 42, repr.; Hartford 1942, no. 42; Wildenstein, New York 1942-3, no. 421, repr.; Wildenstein, New York 1944, no. 6, repr.; Detroit 1950, no. 30; Hartford 110, 1952; Knoedler, New York 1953, no. 13; Winnipeg 1954, no. 18; Fogg 1955, no. 3; Toronto-Ottawa 1962-3, no. 3, repr.; Louvre 1963, no. 142,

M no. 143, repr. (As by Delacroix in every case, though with some reserve about the authenticity of the monogram expressed in the first catalogue of Louvre 1963, and the attribution to him rejected in *M*, following opinions expressed elsewhere.)

Literature: A. Churchill, 'Three Unpublished Paintings by Eugène Delacroix', *Bulletin of Smith College Museum of Art*, no. 11 (Apr. 1930), pp. 2, 6 f., repr. on cover, 2 details actual size, pp. 4 and 5; ibid., no. 13 (May 1932), p. 17, repr.; L. Eitner, 'Homage to Delacroix' (review of exhibition Toronto-Ottawa 1962-3), *Apollo*, LXXVII, no. 1 (Jan. 1963), p. 33; L. Johnson, 'The Delacroix Centenary in France—I', *Burl Mag*, CV, no. 724 (July 1963), pp. 301-2; Trapp, p. 104 n. 27.

This work was long thought to be a preliminary sketch for the final competition sketch, signed and dated 1831, in the Musée des Beaux-Arts, Bordeaux (J147), having been so identified in the catalogue of the exhibition Louvre 1930. In January 1963, Lorenz Eitner (op. cit.), in a review of the exhibition Toronto-Ottawa 1962-3, cast doubts on its authenticity by drawing attention to the 'hardness and dryness of its brushstrokes'. Later in the same year, Sérullaz (first catalogue exhibition Louvre 1963, no. 142), while not denying Delacroix's authorship, expressed some reserve about the authenticity of the monogram and thought the work might be a 'replica' rather than a preliminary sketch; and I (op. cit., July 1963), after seeing it exhibited alongside the Bordeaux version in the Louvre, revised my earlier opinion that it was an autograph sketch and suggested it was a competent copy of J147, possibly painted by Andrieu under Delacroix's supervision. Finally (Nov. 1963), the attribution to Delacroix was abandoned by Sérullaz in *Mémorial*, no. 143. To Trapp 'the rejection of the work as a copy seems unduly severe'.

Religious Paintings

D18 THE AGONY IN THE GARDEN   Pl. 196

$10\frac{5}{8} \times 13\frac{3}{4}$ in. (27×35 cm)
False (?) signature bottom right: *Eug. Delacroix*
R183 (1826)
1826?
Whereabouts unknown

Provenance: M. Paravey; his sale 13 Apr. 1878, lot 21, bought in at 910 fr.; with Georges Petit, 1885; Paul Périer; his sale, 7 Apr. 1908, lot 4, to Bonjean, 2,400 fr.; M. J. Homberg; his sale (M.J.H.), 11 May 1923, lot 5 (repr.), to Moch, 17,200 fr.

Exhibition: *EBA*, Paris 1885, no. 238.

Literature: See below.

This picture, which is attributed to Delacroix without reservation by Robaut, is known to me only from the photograph in M-Nélaton Port. III, reproduced here, and the reproduction in the catalogue of the Homberg sale. It nevertheless seems most probably to be from the hand of Hippolyte Poterlet, with perhaps some retouching by Delacroix. It should probably be identified as a work described by Delacroix, in a list of pictures that he compiled in the 1840s, as: 'Esquisse du *Christ aux Oliviers* commencée par Poterlet, finie par moi.' (*Journal* III. 372—Supp.)

According to Théophile Silvestre (*Documents nouveaux* (1864), p. 29), 'Sitôt que Delacroix avait esquissé un tableau important, *Sardanapale* ou *Le Christ au Jardin des Oliviers*, il courait avec un croquis de son œuvre et une toile blanche chez son ami [Poterlet], qui, en deux heures, lui avait donné son avis en lui faisant une esquisse à sa manière. Delacroix tenait infiniment à voir comment, à sa place, Poterlet eût peint le tableau.' This may well be Poterlet's idea for the *Agony in the Garden*, as the sketch referred to under J125 (n. 10) is his conception of the *Death of Sardanapalus*.

On his drawing of this painting in Tracings I, Robaut notes: 'On dit que M. Paravey l'avait acheté à la vente de Nourrit à qui Delacroix l'aurait donné autrefois—tableau en mauvais état.' This raises the question of whether this might not be the painting which Moreau says Delacroix painted for the singer Nourrit in 1831 (see J(L)110); in which case Moreau would, as Robaut suspected, have listed the wrong dimensions. It is possible that in 1831 Delacroix added some finishing touches to this sketch by Poterlet and presented it

to Nourrit. A Nourrit sale is not, however, listed in Lugt and the dimensions of his picture cannot, therefore, be checked.

R42a BISHOP AND CHOIRBOY

Wood panel, $11\frac{9}{16} \times 9\frac{1}{2}$ in. (29.4 × 24.1 cm)
R1702 (1831–1840)
Whereabouts unknown

Provenance: Zacharie Astruc, by 1885; mixed sale (by Chayette), Palais d'Orsay, 24 Oct. 1979, 100,000 fr.

Exhibitions: None.

Literature: *Gazette de l'Hôtel Drouot*, 88th year, no. 32 (21 Sept. 1979), p. 1, repr. This weak picture is described in glowing terms in the commentary in Robaut, written no doubt by Chesneau, but R Ann contains the more apposite, unpublished note: 'Œuvre fort indécise—aucune garantie.'

Landscape, Genre, Interiors without Figures

D19 MOUNTAINOUS LANDSCAPE WITH TOWER   Pl. 197

$10 \times 13\frac{1}{8}$ in. (25.3 × 33.3 cm)*
R1472 (1821)
Messrs. Wildenstein, New York

Provenance: M. P. de Laage; Alfred Robaut; Count Armand Doria, by 1885; his sale, 4 May 1899, lot 141, 620 fr.; Le Marchand of Rouen; his sale, Paris 13 May 1932 (Dieterle R); P. Landowski, Boulogne-sur-Seine, by 1947; with Wildenstein, New York, by 1966.

Exhibited: EBA, Paris 1885, no. 65 (as 'Paysage romantique').

Literature: None, except Robaut.

Robaut described this as a 'paysage composé', to distinguish it from a naturalistic landscape of an actual site seen by the artist, and dated it to 1821 without giving his reasons. Though further research into Delacroix's landscape paintings might vindicate Robaut's attribution, the grainy texture, bland brushwork, heavy colouring and facile composition, as well as an uncertain early history, all seem to argue against this being a genuine work by Delacroix of any period.

D20 INTERIOR WITH OWL   Pl. 200

$9\frac{1}{16} \times 12\frac{3}{16}$ in. (23 × 31 cm)
Initialled on bottom panes of window: *ED*
R252 (1828)
Whereabouts unknown

Provenance: ? Given by the artist to Dr. A. Warnier, d. 1875; in 1863 left with, and later bequeathed to, his brother C. Warnier who, retired from the army at Arras, owned it in 1876.[1]

Exhibitions: None.

Literature: Huyghe, p. 191.

This work had apparently not been seen by Robaut when he catalogued it, as 'Intérieur d'alchimiste', and he may have had some doubts about its authenticity; for he did not make his own tracing of it and, with a query, relied on a photograph and tracing by Charles Desavary. The latter is preserved in Tracings I with this note: 'calqué par Ch. Desavary qui a fait la photog[raphie] — à voir?' It is known to me only from the photograph reproduced here, which is probably by Desavary and contained in M-Nélaton Port., no. 4. It seems to me from the photograph and from the suspicious form of signature to be almost certainly a false attribution and I refrain from rejecting it outright only because the original has not come to light.

[1] A note signed by C. Warnier and dated Arras 17 Aug. 1876, giving the history of the picture, is contained in M-Nélaton Port. ('Doubles'). It claims that, 'selon une certitude presqu' entière', the picture was given by Delacroix to Dr. Warnier, who played a diplomatic and military role in Morocco from 1844. But, even if certain, that would not of course mean that it was necessarily by Delacroix.

D21 THE POACHER   Pl. 200

$27\frac{9}{16} \times 21\frac{11}{16}$ in. (70×55 cm)
R1551 (1820/30)
Whereabouts unknown

Provenance: Zacharie Astruc, by 1885.

Exhibitions: None.

Literature: None, except Robaut.

This picture is known to me only from the description and print in Robaut reproduced here. It was most probably not an authentic work, since Robaut added the marginal comment in R Ann: 'œuvre bien douteuse? et décrite ici malgré moi.'

R43 AN ATTIC   Pl. 198

$15\frac{3}{8} \times 12\frac{3}{16}$ in. (39×31 cm). Very worn E.D.
R1800 (No repr.)
M. E. Labeyrie, Versailles

Provenance: Delacroix's posthumous sale, Feb. 1864, lot 96 ('Intérieur d'un cellier de paysan', 40×32 cm), to Gibert, 1,225 fr.; M. H. Labeyrie, by 1930; the present owner, by 1963.

Exhibitions: *Cercle des Arts*, Paris 1866; Louvre 1930, no. 208B; Bordeaux 1963, no. 14.

While it is here assumed, on the grounds of the dimensions and the 'ED' seal on the stretcher, that this is the picture which passed as lot 96 in the posthumous sale, I find it impossible to believe that the irrational construction, mediocre brushwork and puny accessories are from Delacroix's hand. It is apparently the work of another artist (the author of *Interior with Stove* (J(R)44)?), mistakenly classified as a Delacroix at the time of his death.

R44 INTERIOR WITH STOVE   Pl. 199

$20\frac{1}{16} \times 17\frac{5}{16}$ in. (51×44 cm)
False signature bottom left: *Eug. Delacroix*
Musée du Louvre

Provenance: Probably M. Moreau-Chaslon, by 1885 (see *Exhibitions* below); Henri Rouart, by 1900; his sale 9 Dec. 1912, lot 189 (repr.), to the Société des Amis du Louvre, 30,000 fr.; they donated it to the Louvre (RF2058) in 1913.

Exhibitions: Probably the 'Intérieur d'atelier d'artiste', 50×40 cm, lent by M. Moreau-Chaslon to *EBA*, Paris 1885, and suppressed between the 1st and 2nd edition of the catalogue (see Robaut's annotated copy of the 1st edition (no. 155), *Bib AA*, MS. 298); *Centennale*, Paris 1900, no. 222 ('Coin d'atelier: le Poêle'); Louvre 1930, no. 52; Petit Palais, Paris 1936, no. 234; id., Paris 1946, no. 156; Orangerie, Paris 1947, no. 64; Agen–Grenoble–Nancy 1958, no. 16, repr.; Atelier Delacroix, Paris 1963, no. 143; Berne 1963–4, no. 31, repr.; Bremen 1964, no. 29, repr.; Atelier Delacroix, Paris 1969 (no cat.).

Literature (selected): Brière 1924, p. 79; Escholier I, repr. p. 255; L. Venturi, 'Delacroix', *L'Arte*, N.S. II (1931), fig. 5; Sterling–Adhémar, no. 673, pl. 237; Escholier 1963, full-page colour repr. p. 97; Maltese, pp. 100, 136, repr. in colour pl. VIII.

Though this picture has been listed as an authentic Delacroix in all Louvre catalogues since Brière 1924 and is usually dated about 1830, there is no doubt that Robaut considered the attribution wrong. Not only did he apparently reject it from the exhibition *EBA*, Paris 1885, but in a letter to M. Brière dated 8 May 1922, Etienne Moreau-Nélaton stated: 'Pour le poêle, je n'ose me prononcer! Je vous montrerai une photo annotée par Robaut, qui se refusait à l'admettre comme un Delacroix authentique.' (When I consulted this letter in the 1950s it was preserved in the file for *Liberty leading the People* in the Service de documentation at the Louvre.)

In my opinion, Robaut was unquestionably right in excluding the work from Delacroix's œuvre. It may be by Champmartin, a friend of Delacroix's youth, since it apparently belonged to Moreau-Chaslon, who owned some paintings from Champmartin's studio.

CONCORDANCE

R = Robaut (except before a number in the J column); R Ann = Annotated Robaut; B = Bortolatto; J = Johnson.

Numbers in parentheses under B indicate pictures that are illustrated by photographs here but not in Bortolatto. A stroke before a number under R indicates that the corresponding number under J, R Ann or B is only one of several pictures listed under the single number in Robaut. 'v.' before a Robaut or Bortolatto number means the picture is referred to, but not actually listed, under that number. An asterisk after a Bortolatto number in parentheses indicates that a picture not illustrated by a photograph in the Italian edition of 1972 is so illustrated in the French edition of 1975.

Costume, Accessories, Arms and Armour

J	R	R Ann	B
23	1488		65
23a	82		(64)
24	1489		(66)
25	1483		63
26	424		237
27	1917		(858)
28	84		(71)
29	1486	85bis	(70)
30	1479	85ter	43 (repr. under 46, as R1482)
31	1481		45
32	382		228

Academy Figures, Nudes

J	R	R Ann	B
1	/1470		
2	/1470		
3	171		33
4	83		49
5	/1470, v.15		21
6	106		93
7	v.383, 384		184
8	175		146
9	383		171
10	140		128

Miscellaneous Orientalia

J	R	R Ann	B
33	123		116
34	265		326
35	977		111
36			
37	610		(272)
38	172		139
39	325		196
40			

Copies

J	R	R Ann	B
11	24		(866)
12		32bis	896
13	1932		(893)
14	1930		(897)
15	prob. 1949 or 1954		
16	1943		873
17	1948		(870)
18	1945		(882)
19	259		(871)
20	1947	39bis	874
21		204ter	861
22			(860)

Horses and Other Animals

J	R	R Ann	B
41	30		16
42	/1860		
43	/1860		(v.829–41)
44	/1860		
45	73		(79)
46	1867		(854)
47	/1860		(v.829–41)
48	74		(82)
49	72		81
50	76		(84)
51	/1871		(842–51)
52	/1860		(v.829–41)

Horses and Other Animals (*cont.*)

J	R	R Ann	B
53	130		(119)
54	131		(120)
55	1304		721
56	264		(178)
57	/1879		(826 or 827)
58	379		(225)*
59	323		194

Portraits and Studies of Heads

J	R	R Ann	B
60	1509		(124)*
61	/1904		3
61a			
62	448 ?	361 (margin)	
63	prob. /1904		25
64	40		35
65	1460		10
66	51		41
67	64		77
68			
69	361		(221)
70	60		(74)
71	115		103
72	120		114
73	258		(182)
74	293		188
75	257		181
76	328		197
77	95		91
78	66		88
79	47		106
80	162		108
81	99		(109)
82	190		133
83			165
84	716		151
85	121		115
86	215		164
87	788		37
88	98 and ?184		107 and (?147)
89	207 and /1904		155
90	prob. /1904		(v.814–23)
91	294		(189)*
92			252 (as R448)
93	386		209

Allegory and Decorations

J	R	R Ann	B
94	1451		32
95	1453		31
96	1452		30
97	1454		29
98	205		131

Historical and Literary Subjects

J	R	R Ann	B
99	prob. 1462		(v.13)
100	49		38
101	108		98
102	138		126
103		211bis	
104	166		145
105	91		92
106	88		97
107	118		(113)
108		118bis	
109	v.136 and 197		129 and v.167
110	137		(125)
111	139		127
112	160		144
113	201		95
114	202		130
115	200		168
116	226		170
117	1492		99
118	67		87
119	158		143
120	157		141
121	156		142
122			
123	153		(140)
124	168		
125	198		158
126			
127	1515		(135)
128	87		172
129	320		198
130	255		175
131	253		174
132		254	
133	196		152
134	prob. 1474	291bis	153
135	292		185
136	195		154
137	1714	760bis	(367)*
138		201bis	94

Historical and Literary Subjects (*cont.*)

J	R	R Ann	B
139	v.136 and 197		542
140	322		193
141	321		192
142	261		183
143	355		207
144	326		195
145	359		213
146	360		212
147	353		210
148	351		208
149	354		215

Religious Paintings

J	R	R Ann	B
150	16 and prob. 1461		(7)
151	25		17
152	36		23
153	35		22
154	176		136
155	296		187
156	297		(190)
157	1554		(201)

Landscape, Still Life, Genre

J	R	R Ann	B
158	352		214
159	544		420
160	543		(260)
161	174		157
162	126		96

LOST WORKS

Academy Figures, Nudes, Studies of Limbs

J	R	R Ann	B
L1	18		8
L2	/1470?		
L3	/1470		
L4	/1470		
L5			
L6		323bis	
L7	55		
L8		53bis	
L9			
L10	1470 (see also all /1470s)		50–62

Copies

J	R	R Ann	B
L11	1926		865
L12	1927		863
L13		p. 392	864
L14	1925		867
L15	1936		894
L16	786		895
L17	1953		887
L18			
L19			
L20	1951		885
L21			
L22	1928		(891)
L23	1929		892
L24	1940		880
L25			
L26	1952		886
L27	1944		869
L28			
L28a			
L29			
L30	1949 or 1954		888 (R1954)
L31	1938		881
L32	1933		859
L33		p. 423	
L34/37		1919 (margin)	
L35	1950		884
L36			

Costume, Accessories, Arms and Armour

J	R	R Ann	B
L38	85		72
L39	79		(85)
L40			
L41	80		86
L42			
L43	1482		47 and 48
L44	1487		73
L45	77 and /1485		67
L46	78 and /1485		68
L47	/1485		69
L47a	/1919		205
L48	1508		122

Miscellaneous Orientalia

J	R	R Ann	B
L49			
L50			
L51	362		218

Horses and Other Animals

J	R	R Ann	B
L52	1868		853
L53	75		
L54			
L55			
L56			
L57	/1860		v.829–41
L58	128 and 1014		121
L59	/1860		v.829–41
L60	/1871		842–51
L61			
L62			
L63	/1871		v.842–51
L64	/1860		v.829–41
L65	/1871		v.842–51
L66	/1879		828
L67	/1879 ?		826 or 827 ?

Portraits and Studies of Heads

J	R	R Ann	B
L68	13		2
L69	14		4
L70	1902		825
L71			
L72	1903		824
L72a		47bis	
L73	105		104
L74	125		118
L75	61		75
L76			
L77	97		100
L78	70		76
L79		121bis	
L80	170		
L81	363		220
L82	/1904		v.814–23
L83		p. 423	
L84			
L85		192ter	

Allegory, Mythology, and Decorations

J	R	R Ann	B
L86	12		1
L87			
L88			
L89			
L90	384		230

Historical and Literary Subjects

J	R	R Ann	B
L91	19		9
L92	1464		11
L93	1475		40
L94			
L95			
L96			
L97	103		102
L98	116		112
L99	1731		422
L99a			
L100	1555		202
L101	100		101
L102		137 (margin)	
L103	256		
L104	262		176 (wrong repr.)
L105	356		216

Religious Paintings

J	R	R Ann	B
L106	27		19
L107	22		15
L108	37		24
L109		176bis	
L110	357		217
L111	1553		199
L112	324		200
L113	1798		857

Still Life, Genre, Interiors without Figures

J	R	R Ann	B
L114			
L115	1653		250
L116	1799		856

DOUBTFUL WORKS

Academy Figures, Nudes or Single Reclining Figures

J	R	R Ann	B
O1	/1470?		(v.50–62)
O2	/1470?	83*bis*	36
O3	/1470	97*bis*	(v.50–62)
M1	15		(5)
M2	/1470?		(v.50–62)
D1	/1470?		(v.50–62)
R1			
R2	55?		42?
R3			

Copies

J	R	R Ann	B
D2			
D3			875 (as R1949)
D4	1946		(883)
D5	737		876
R4			862
R5			
R6			
R7			
R8			
R9			
R10			
R11			
R12			
R13			
R14			
R15			
R16	260		872
R17			
R18			
R19			v.884–8
R20			
R21			
R22			

Costume, Accessories, Arms and Armour

J	R	R Ann	B
O4	/1919		204
O5	1918		148
D6			v.69
D7			v.69
D8	1048		(520)

J	R	R Ann	B
D9	1480		(44)
D10			
R23			
R24			229

Miscellaneous Orientalia

J	R	R Ann	B
R25	46		(34)

Horses

J	R	R Ann	B
O6	1863		(855)
O7	71		(80)
M3	1866		(852)
M4	/1871?		(v.842–51)
D11			
D12			
R26			
R27			
R28			
R29			(901)
R30		1860 (margin)	
R31		75 (margin)	83 (as R75)

Portraits and Studies of Heads

J	R	R Ann	B
O8	1311		166
M5	69		78
D13	173		156
D14	358 and 450		219
R32	124		(117)
R33			134 (as R170)
R34			

Allegory

J	R	R Ann	B
R35	206		132

Historical and Literary Subjects

J	R	R Ann	B
O9			180 (as R269 ?)
O10	1512		123
D15			
D16	161		
D17			243
R36	50		39
R37	113		105
R38			
R39		238ter	(900)
R40		238bis	
R41			
R42			211

Religious Paintings

J	R	R Ann	B
D18	183		(138)
R42a	1702		(284)

Landscape, Genre, Interiors without Figures

J	R	R Ann	B
D19	1472		(26)
D20	252		(179)
D21	1551		191
R43	1800		(206, as R1800 ?)
R44			110

Index of Locations

Excluding Doubtful Works

General Index

Catalogue numbers are in bold type. The *Exhibitions* and *Literature* sections in the catalogue entries are not indexed

253

N.S. COLLEGE OF ART & DESIGN

3 9360 01200 4068